International Investment Management

International Investment Management synthesizes investment principles, Asian financial practice, and ethics reflecting the realities of modern international finance. These topics are studied within the Asian context, first through the medium of case studies and then via the particular conditions common in those markets including issues of religion and philosophy.

This book has a five-part structure beginning with the core principles behind the business of investments including securities analysis, asset allocation and a comprehensive analysis of modern finance theory. This gives students a comprehensive understanding of investment management by going through the theories, ethics and practice of investment management. This text provides a detailed overview of International Banking Law and International Securities Regulation.

This book is an essential text for business and law school students who wish to have a thorough understanding of investment management. It is also perfect as a core text for undergraduate finance majors and graduate business students pursuing a finance, and/or business ethics concentration, with a particular focus on Asia.

Kara Tan Bhala is the President and Founder of Seven Pillars Institute for Global Finance and Ethics and a Visiting Research Fellow at Queen Mary University of London, UK.

Warren Yeh is currently a Managing Partner with Adapa Partners, LLC, a long/short Asian equity hedge fund. Prior to co-founding Adapa in 2000, he was Managing Director of Vickers Ballas (USA) Inc., the US subsidiary of Singapore's largest brokerage.

Raj Bhala is the Associate Dean for International and Comparative Law, and holds the Rice Distinguished Professorship, at the University of Kansas School of Law, USA.

International Investment Management

Theory, ethics and practice

Kara Tan Bhala, Warren Yeh and Raj Bhala

LONDON AND NEW YORK

First published 2016
by Routledge
2 Park Square, Milton Park, Abingdon, Oxon OX14 4RN

and by Routledge
711 Third Avenue, New York, NY 10017

Routledge is an imprint of the Taylor & Francis Group, an informa business

© 2016 Kara Tan Bhala, Warren Yeh and Raj Bhala

The right of Kara Tan Bhala, Warren Yeh and Raj Bhala to be identified as the authors of this work has been asserted by them in accordance with Sections 77 and 78 of the Copyright, Designs and Patent Act 1988.

All rights reserved. No part of this book may be reprinted or reproduced or utilised in any form or by any electronic, mechanical, or other means, now known or hereafter invented, including photocopying and recording, or in any information storage or retrieval system, without permission in writing from the publishers.

Trademark notice: Product or corporate names may be trademarks or registered trademarks, and are used only for identification and explanation without intent to infringe.

Even where gender-neutral formulations are not explicitly used in the text, all gender-specific terms are to be considered to refer to both the feminine and the masculine form.

British Library Cataloguing in Publication Data
A catalogue record for this book is available from the British Library

Library of Congress Cataloging in Publication Data
A catalog record for this book has been requested

ISBN: 978-0-415-69752-1 (hbk)
ISBN: 978-0-415-69814-6 (pbk)
ISBN: 978-1-315-64006-8 (ebk)

Typeset in Bembo
by RefineCatch Limited, Bungay, Suffolk

Printed and bound in the United States of America by Publishers Graphics, LLC on sustainably sourced paper.

For my mother, Betty Yuen, one of the strongest women I know.
Dr Kara Tan Bhala

To all the friends and family who have shaped my life and career.
Warren Yeh

For our friend, Father Michael ('Mick') Mulvany, Pastor, Corpus Christi Catholic Church, Lawrence, Kansas, who inspired me to do better through his world-class homilies and spiritual direction on social justice and our obligations to the marginalized, which he gave freely with courage and passion amidst rising global inequality.
Associate Dean and Professor Raj Bhala

Contents

List of figures	xi
List of tables	xii
Preface	xiv
Acknowledgements	xvii

PART I
Three finance paradigms — 1

1 Modern finance theory — 3
    1.1 Introduction 3
    1.2 The time value of money 3
    1.3 Risk and returns 7
    1.4 Portfolio allocation between risky and risk-free assets 13
    1.5 Capital asset pricing model 23
    1.6 Arbitrage pricing theory 31
    1.7 Efficient Market Hypothesis (EMH) 33

2 Behavioural finance — 41
    2.1 A critique of modern finance theory 41
    2.2 Behavioural finance 51
    2.3 Behavioural finance and ethics 66
    2.4 Limitations of behavioural finance and further work 69

3 Islamic finance — 74
    3.1 Introduction 74
    3.2 Shari'a 76
    3.3 Principles and ethics of Islamic finance 79
    3.4 Determination of compliance with Shari'a 87
    3.5 Forms of Islamic finance I: profit- and loss-sharing-based transactions 90
    3.6 Forms of Islamic finance II: non-profit and loss-sharing-based transactions 95
    3.7 Islamic insurance: takaful 101
    3.8 Sukuk and securitization 104
    3.9 Issues in Islamic finance 109

viii   Contents

PART II
Practice of investment management   113

4   International financial instruments   115
    4.1   Equity 115
    4.2   Debt: sovereign, corporate, municipal 117
    4.3   ETFs, mutual funds, open-end, closed-end 119
    4.4   Foreign exchange spots and derivatives 121

5   International financial markets   134
    5.1   Introduction 134
    5.2   Exchanges: global and emerging markets 134
    5.3   OTC markets 143
    5.4   High-frequency trading 146
    5.5   Dark pools 151
    5.6   Bond markets 156
    5.7   Clearing and settlement systems 166

6   International financial players   178
    6.1   Introduction 178
    6.2   Commercial banks 179
    6.3   Commercial bank activities 180
    6.4   Investment banks 186
    6.5   Investment banking activities 187
    6.6   Asian investment banks 192
    6.7   Broker-dealers 194
    6.8   Investment managers 196
    6.9   Central banks 200
    6.10 International organizations 208

7   Security analysis   215
    7.1   Introduction 215
    7.2   Financial statements 215
    7.3   Financial ratios 218
    7.4   Valuations 222
    7.5   Stock analysis 231
    7.6   Industry analysis 263
    7.7   Economic analysis 265
    7.8   Tying the different analyses together 268

PART III
Ethical issues in Asian investing   269

8   Overview of ethical theories – philosophy   271
    8.1   Introduction 271
    8.2   Utilitarianism 271
    8.3   Duty-based (deontological) theories 278

        8.4   *Justice theories 284*
        8.5   *Virtue ethics 290*

9   **Overview of ethical theories – religion**   298
        9.1   *Introduction 298*
        9.2   *Buddhism 298*
        9.3   *Christianity 305*
        9.4   *Hinduism 310*
        9.5   *Judaism 314*
        9.6   *Summary and conclusion 318*

10   **Ethical issues in investment management**   322
        10.1   *Introduction 322*
        10.2   *Insider trading 322*
        10.3   *Market manipulation 329*
        10.4   *Market timing 333*
        10.5   *Fees 335*
        10.6   *Managing Shari'a compliant assets 343*

PART IV
Legal issues in Asian investing   347

11   **Overview of international securities regulation**   349
        11.1   *Introduction 349*
        11.2   *International securities transactions 349*
        11.3   *International regulation of securities 350*
        11.4   *Inbound transactions 355*
        11.5   *Outbound transactions 367*
        11.6   *The Volcker Rule 368*

12   **Overview of international banking law**   383
        12.1   *Defining 'international banking' activities 383*
        12.2   *International bank supervision and Basel Committee 388*
        12.3   *Inbound bank supervisors 391*
        12.4   *Inbound regulations 393*
        12.5   *Outbound regulation 402*
        12.6   *Capital adequacy 403*

13   **Investment, trade, and 13 financial sanctions:**
     Iran case study (1979–2012)   412
        13.1   *Why sanctions matter in international investment*
               management 412
        13.2   *Four issues and responses 413*
        13.3   *Tragedy 415*
        13.4   *Metrics 416*
        13.5   *First three of ten phases to 1996 419*
        13.6   *Phase 4: 1996 ILSA emphasis on petroleum 420*

13.7 Phases 5 and 6: 2001 ILSA extension, 2006 IFSA, and
extraterritoriality 427
13.8 Phase 7: 2010 CISADA emphases on trade embargo, refined
gasoline, asset freezes, and human rights 431

14 More investment, trade, and financial sanctions: Iran case study, continued (2012–16) — 451
14.1 Phase 8: 2012 Defense Act tightening financial sanctions 451
14.2 Phase 9: 2012 Iran–Syria Act *new expansive constrictions* 459
14.3 Phase 10: 2013 Defense Act tightening energy, shipping, and financial sanctions, plus shipbuilding, port, and precious metal sanctions 473
14.4 Necessary, but not sufficient? 477

PART V
Case studies in Asian financial markets — 515

15 Disclosure and market manipulation: the case of CITIC Pacific — 517
15.1 CITIC Pacific 517
15.2 Ethical analysis 520

16 Insider trading: the case of Huiyuan Juice — 524
16.1 Huiyuan Juice Group 524
16.2 Ethical analysis 526

17 Market manipulation, price rigging, and false trading: the case of Sino Katalytics — 529
17.1 Sino Katalytics 529
17.2 Ethical analysis 532

18 Insider dealing: the case of Water Oasis — 535
18.1 Water Oasis Group 535
18.2 Ethical analysis 537

Bibliography — 539
Index — 559

Figures

1.1	The risk return trade-offs	13
1.2	Distribution of returns of various portfolios from 1926 to 2013	13
1.3	Capital allocation line	15
1.4	Capital market line	16
1.5	The efficient frontier	21
1.6	Utility curves for investors J and K	22
1.7	Utility curves for investor J	22
1.8	Utility curves and efficient frontier	23
1.9	Capital market line and efficient frontier	24
1.10	Security market line	27
1.11	Valuing securities using the security market line	28
1.12	Capital market line with lending and borrowing at risk-free rate	29
1.13	Head and Shoulders Formation	35
2.1	The Kahneman-Tversky value function	56
2.2	The expected utility function	56
2.3	A typical probability weighting function	58
3.1	Islamic banking model	92
3.2	Types of Islamic finance	97
3.3	The Retakaful process	104
4.1	Hypothetical spot FX transaction	123
4.2	Hypothetical forward FX transaction	124
4.3	Hypothetical forward FX transaction	124
4.4	Hypothetical currency swap FX transaction	131
5.1	Asian local currency (LCY) bond market (in US$ billions)	160
5.2	Federal Reserve payment system	167
6.1	Seesaw history of bank activity regulation in the US	184
6.2	Narrow and universal banking country spectrum	185
6.3	Pre-tax profits of 1,000 largest banks in world	193
6.4	Basic wire transfer	205
7.1	Top-down and bottom-up investment analysis	267
10.1	Categorization of market manipulation techniques	332
12.1	General organizational chart of financial holding company	397
12.2	Organizational chart of HSBC North America	397
12.3	Basic organizational chart of Bank of America Corporation	398

Tables

1.1	Returns of mutual fund	8
1.2	Cash flows	9
1.3	Probability distribution of stock A	11
1.4	Expected value of stock A	11
1.5	Correlation coefficient and portfolio standard deviation	17
1.6	Calculation of covariance for stock S	19
1.7	Calculation of covariance for bond B	19
1.8	Portfolio with different weightings of two assets	20
2.1	Average beta for the 30 stocks in the DJIA for alternative time periods using different indexes as proxies for the market	46
3.1	Summary table of forms of Islamic finance	102
5.1	Stock market capitalization, total GDP, and GDP growth in BRICS and selected other developing countries	139
5.2	Explaining relationships between growth in stock market capitalization and GDP	140
5.3	Domestic equity market capitalization (in US dollars, millions) for exchanges in BRICS and selected other developing countries	141
5.4	International expansion of developed country exchanges	142
5.5	Types of offshore bonds	163
5.6	Major regional clearing houses	170
6.1	Top 10 global merger and acquisition advisers	191
6.2	Best Asian investment banks	192
7.1	Tencent Holdings: income statement	234
7.2	Tencent Holdings: balance sheet	241
7.3	Tencent Holdings: cashflow statement	252
7.4	Simple earnings model for Tencent Holdings	260
7.5	Financial and valuation metrics for Tencent Holdings	261
7.6	Sum of the parts valuation for Tencent Holdings	263
7.7	Peer group valuation comparison	265
8.1	Steps in utilitarian analysis	276
9.1	Ethical stands of major religions on key aspects of finance	319
10.1	Percentage of funds that outperformed their benchmarks after adjusting for survivorship bias, 1997–2011	340
11.1	Regulation D	363
11.2	Types of issuing companies	366

11.3	Activities exempt from proprietary trading definition	371
12.1	US capital standards pre-31 December 2014	406
12.2	US capital standards post-31 December 2014	406
12.3	Basel II and Basel III capital requirements	406
14.1	Synopsis of November 2013 *Joint Plan of Action*	478
14.2	Synopsis of April 2015 *Framework Agreement* (Lausanne Accord)	486
14.3	Key details of July 2015 *Joint Comprehensive Plan of Action*	492
15.1	Specified persons	517
15.2	Mark-to-market loss	518
15.3	Amount of deliverable AUD	519
15.4	Mark-to-market loss	519
15.5	Amount of deliverable AUD	519
17.1	Purchases by Mr Yau (volume and price per share)	530
17.2	Purchases by Mr Chui (volume and price per share)	530
17.3	Sales by Mr Yau (volume and price per share)	531
17.4	Percentage of sales and purchases of total trade in shares	531
17.5	Price and turnover of Sino Katalytic shares	531

Preface

Synthesizing three extant theories

This book is a first of its kind and unique in three ways.

First, unlike other textbooks on investments, this one gives as much space to other finance theories as it does to the predominant, mainstream theory known as modern finance theory (MFT). The text is, of course, about finance, specifically investment management, with details, descriptions, and instructions on financial markets, players, instruments, and security analysis. But the text speaks of behavioural finance and Islamic finance in addition to MFT.

As an offspring of neoliberal economics, the latter has been useful in modelling financial markets and guiding investment decisions. MFT gives one view but not the full 360-degree perspective of markets and instruments. After five decades or so of habitual use, MFT has hardened into an orthodox ideology only lately questioned, and only by some in the higher rankings of financial academia. This book gives an objective critique of MFT and the reasons that logically follow from the critique, why students of investments should be wary and aware of the shortcomings of MFT. Fortunately, other finance paradigms are establishing themselves that counter these deficiencies.

The two other increasingly influential finance theories are behavioural finance and Islamic finance. This book provides the student with details of both approaches. Behavioural finance has to do with the psychology of individuals and groups and how this affects behaviour in financial markets. The behavioural finance approach complements, not supplants, MFT, which completely disregards human psychology and behaviour and their consequences on investment decisions. Together, behavioural finance and MFT provide a fuller perspective of financial markets, but still not the 360-degree view. For a more comprehensive view of markets, Islamic finance, the third theory we discuss in this book, is required.

Islamic law, or *Sharī'a* (transliterated simply as Shari'a) is the foundation of Islamic finance. One key principle of this approach is the requirement to be ethical. MFT does not propound any deliberate purpose to finance. Through rational self-interest and profit maximization, the financial system achieves economic efficiency. In contrast, Islamic finance states unequivocally that the purpose of finance is to help people and the community to flourish. Islamic finance must contribute to the development and good of the Islamic community. Therefore, the fundamental feature of Islamic finance is socio-economic justice. Being based on Islamic law, Islamic finance contains a comprehensive system of ethics and moral values. The ethical element is missing in both MFT and behavioural finance. Synthesized, the three theories together provide the most complete insight into markets. The synthesis of theories still does not provide the full 360-degree view, because there are likely to be other finance theories waiting to be discovered. However, they do present a more extensive view than can be obtained from the aspect of a single one of the theories. We know of no other attempt to synthesize the three extant finance theories.

Incorporating financial ethics

Second, this book is not just about investment management, but also about ethics, specifically financial ethics. We intend for the student to understand ethical theories and apply these theories as working, viable frameworks in everyday financial practice. Too often, ethics is treated as a laundry list of dos and don'ts, a dry, unexplained catalogue for behaving in the right way. The ethics section of this book instructs the student, who will be a future or is currently, a finance professional, on the method of 'doing' ethics. This method requires the use of human reason, applying appropriate ethics theories, and coming to the right action through internal and external discourse.

The text first presents and explains philosophical ethical theories. A chapter discussing religious-based ethics follows the chapter on secular ethical theories. The former cannot be ignored. After all, the vast majority of the world receives ethical instruction based on religious upbringing. Throughout the chapters on ethics, examples are given to help the student apply each theory to a situation. Application of theory is just as important as knowledge of theory because ethics is ultimately defined by action driven by reason. Indeed, the last section of the book gives case studies with detailed explanations of why a particular act in a real financial case was unethical. Thus, the book incorporates practical ethics into investment practice.

Introducing pertinent legal concepts

For non-lawyers, it is not possible to practise international investment management without knowing something of the law. For lawyers, law is their 'bread and butter'. Investment professionals need to know at least enough about the law to stay out of trouble, and lawyers have to guide them as to how to do so efficiently and with integrity. Moreover, investment professionals need to know at least the outlines of how their discipline is regulated (or not). Again, lawyers have to provide wide counsel on this matter.

Accordingly, the third unique contribution of this book is its synthesis of legal concepts pertinent to the practice of international investment management with the theory and ethics of that management. The text provides a reasonably detailed overview of International Banking Law and International Securities Regulation. Those topics affect the everyday work environment, as they are the rule-oriented paradigms in which managers operate, and with which they must comply. The book also provides careful case studies of international sanctions. They raise ethical and practical, and detailed and policy, questions that managers confront. As many high-profile investigations and prosecutions demonstrate, failure to comply with sanctions has grave consequences.

To be sure, this book is not a legal treatise. Its legal coverage is suitable for use in a business class setting without supplementary legal materials, and in a law school with supplementation. We are confident the coverage of legal matters essential for investment professionals will highlight the uncomfortable reality that law and ethics do not always coincide: behaviours and transactions that are legal may not be ethical. When there is a disparity, we think it arises in part because of a long-term secular trend in law away from Natural Law (which holds law and morality are intimately related), and towards Positivism (which claims there is no necessary connection between law and morality). That very debate may be of interest to some readers. But, in any event, we hope the coverage of relevant legal matters will help improve the dialogue between investment managers and lawyers, by 'starting early'; that is, in school.

The journey to this edition

We are grateful this book materialized despite a couple of distressing setbacks. *International Investment Management* was inspired by the financial ethics course, which Kara taught at a conventional US business school. It was one of a tiny handful of such courses taught in the US business academy. The course was cancelled, thanks (at least in part) to opposition to the teaching of financial ethics.

Coinciding with the abrupt withdrawal of an agreed-upon co-author, the course cancellation ostensibly was a blow to scholarship and teaching in the subject of financial ethics. The two events – which seemed, perhaps, to be somehow linked – did more than slow progress on this book. These events were an emotional blow. Authors – especially women seeking a new paradigm in a conventional, male-dominated field – must be resilient against such blows if their project ever is to see the light of day.

God does indeed work in mysterious ways. Unexpectedly, another co-author filled in with enthusiasm. And, who could have foreseen the coincidence of the (1) post-2008 global economic slump and subsequent outcry in civil society against Wall Street; that is, the 1 versus 99 per cent movement, and (2) 2013 naming of Francis as the 266th Pope followed by his statements about modern financial capitalism? These events, splashed out almost daily across global media, called attention to the importance of financial ethics to a degree that no business school professor, nor any book promotion tour, ever could.

Not just happily, but vitally, financial ethics continues to grow in its reach and influence. There is a higher level of interest and a realization of its significance by regulators, senior management of financial institutions, clergy – a realization occurring to even educators, but for the most quantitatively trapped and ideologically rigid.

To that quest, namely, the flourishing of research, promotion, and education about financial ethics, Seven Pillars Institute for Global Finance and Ethics, and its many supporters around the world will remain faithful. Ultimately, possibly in the not too distant future, the teaching and practice of finance will be enhanced by ethics becoming an integral part of financial theory.

Acknowledgements

We owe a considerable debt to Professor Costanza Russo of the Queen Mary University of London (QMUL), along with the QMUL faculty and staff, and our collective mentor, Professor Joseph J. Norton, the James L. Walsh Distinguished Faculty Fellow and Professor in Financial Institutions Law at Southern Methodist University (SMU), Dedman School of Law. Thanks to all of them, earlier versions of this book were used in Dr. Kara Tan Bhala's course in Global Finance and Ethics at QMUL. It is a joy to work with and learn from them, and we look forward to using the complete published text in that course.

We wish to thank our Research Assistants, Matthew Cooper, Madeline Heeren, Aqmar Rahman, Spencer Toubia, and Steven Wu. They are outstanding graduates of the University of Kansas School of Law (2015). Their contributions were invaluable and their dedication exceptional.

Thank you to Angela Raimondo for her calm and collected help in formatting and proofreading the manuscript.

Finally, our gratitude also goes to Shera Bhala, a most patient, understanding and generous teenage daughter and niece.

Dr Kara Tan Bhala
Mr Warren Yeh
Associate Dean and Professor Raj Bhala

Part I
Three finance paradigms

1 Modern finance theory

1.1 Introduction

This chapter describes in detail the four fundamental concepts of modern finance theory:

1 The time value of money
2 Risk and return
3 The capital asset pricing model (CAPM)
4 The efficient market hypothesis.

Modern finance theory began, arguably, with the development of portfolio theory in 1952 by Harry Markowitz.[1] Before modern finance theory, the field consisted of rules and recommendations used primarily by practitioners. Finance was descriptive and not mathematical. Investors and financiers observed the world and used a few rules they thought applied. Practitioners did not work from a comprehensive and universally applicable framework. Indeed, investors believed rules changed with changing market conditions. The financial environment and practice evolved with the development of modern finance theory.

Modern finance theory is mathematical and claims to be positivistic, or value neutral. The theory derives from neoclassical economic theory and has a strong emphasis on quantitative models. The theory assumes the following:

1 Agents are rational
2 Agents are utility maximizing
3 Financial markets are efficient
4 Expected returns and risks determine asset prices.

There are six generally accepted, founding thinkers of modern finance theory. Markowitz developed portfolio theory. Sharpe and Lintner put forward the CAPM.[2] Modigliani and Miller gave the world arbitrage principles. Black, Fisher, and Scholes, established option pricing theory.[3] Fama posited efficient markets.[4]

1.2 The time value of money

The foundational concept on which all of finance rests is the time value of money. This idea refers to the fact that a dollar (or whatever currency applies, be it yuan or yen) received today is worth more than a dollar received at some time in the future. The dollar

4   *Three finance paradigms*

today has a value called the present value. This dollar can be invested and earn interest thereby growing to a larger number of dollars in the future. This larger amount is called the future value. Implicit in every modern, non-Islamic, financial concept and model is the assumption that money has time value.

> PV is the present value of money.
> FV is the future value of money.
> The rate of interest per period is r.

The number of time periods between the present and the future, in years, months, quarters, or whatever, is chosen, is t.

Thus, the relationship of FV to PV given r, over a number of time periods t is:

$$FV = PV(1 + r)^t$$

Future value in a single period investment

If you invest 100 renminbi in a savings account that pays 10 per cent per year, how much will you have in the account after one year? In other words, what is the future value, FV, if present value, PV is 100, t is 1 and r is 10 per cent or 0.1?

$$F = 100(1+.01)$$
$$= 100(1.1)$$
$$= 110$$

Thus, the 100 renminbi in this case grows to 110 renminbi after one year at an interest rate of 10 per cent.

Future value in a multi-period investment

If the 100 renminbi is left in the savings account for five years, how much will there be at the end of the period, if the interest rate remains at 10 per cent per year?

In this case:

$$t = 5$$
$$r = 10$$
$$PV = 100$$

Thus, $FV = 100(1+0.1)5$
$$= 100(1.1)5$$
$$= 100(1.61051)$$
$$= 161.051$$

After five years in the savings account, the future value of 100 renminbi compounding at 10 per cent per year will be 161.051 renminbi.

How did we arrive at the formula for future value: $FV = PV(1 + r)^t$?

Let's go through a series of steps compounding interest over a period of time.

Compounding

In the above example, the interest amount earned each year is reinvested and interest is earned on that interest. The earning of interest on interest is called compounding and the resultant interest is compound interest.

Simple interest is not reinvested and is the amount earned on interest for one period only on the original principal.

The calculation for FV in the previous example can be broken down into five steps that calculate interest earned at each period.

Step 1, Period 1:

Principal amount	=	$100
Interest rate, r	=	10% or 0.1
Amount accumulated at the end of period 1	=	Principal $(1+r)$
	=	$100(1+0.1)$
	=	$100(1.1)$
	=	110

Step 2, Period 2:

Amount at the end of period 1	=	110
Amount accumulated at the end of period 2	=	$110(1.1)$
	=	121
But 110 is obtained through $100(1.1)$		
Thus, amount accumulated at the end of period 2 can also be written as:	=	$100(1.1)(1.1)$
	=	$100(1.1)^2$
	=	121

Step 3, Period 3:

Amount at the end of period 2	=	121
Amount accumulated at the end of period 3	=	$121(1.1)$
	=	133.1
Or it can be written as	=	$100(1.1)(1.1)(1.1)$
	=	$100(1.1)^3$
	=	133.1

Step 4, Period 4:

Amount at the end of period 3	=	133.1
Amount accumulated at the end of period 4	=	$133.1(1.1)$
	=	146.41
Or	=	$100(1.1)(1.1)(1.1)(1.1)$
	=	$100(1.1)^4$
	=	146.41

Step 5, Period 5:

Amount at the end of period 4	=	146.41
Amount accumulated at the end of period 5	=	$146.41(1.1)$
	=	161.051

Three finance paradigms

Or
$$= 100(1.1)(1.1)(1.1)(1.1)(1.1)$$
$$= 100(1.1)^5$$
$$= 161.051$$

It may have now become obvious that compounding interest over a number of time periods has a formulaic pattern, such that:

Amount at the end of period = Principal amount $\times (1 + r)^t$

Where:

Amount at the end of period is the future value or FV and
Principal amount is the present value or PV.

Thus we arrive at the formula given for FV as:

$$FV = PV \times (1 + r)^t$$

The formula $(1 + r)^t$, where r is percentage of interest and t is periods, is sometimes known as the future value of interest factor, future value factor, or $FVIF(r,t)$.

There are relatively painless and quick ways to calculate future values without working out $(1+r)$ to the power of large numbers. One way is to refer to tables that contain future value factors for some common interest rates and time periods. However, tables are now less used to calculate future values because sophisticated calculators have the ability to work out future values even more quickly and with greater accuracy.

Discounting

Calculating the future value answers the question, 'how much will I have after t years, at r rate of interest, if I start out with x amount of money?' There will be times when we need to know the converse. How much do we need to start out with if we want to end up with y amount on money after t years at r rate of interest? In other words, how do we find present values given knowledge of future values, time periods, and rate of interest?

As we saw, the formula for future value calculation is:

$$FV = PV \times (1+r)^t$$

Solving for PV we get:

$$PV = FV/(1+r)^t$$

Example:

How many renminbi will you have to invest today to receive 10,000 renminbi in five years, at an interest rate of 10 per cent?

$$PV = FV/(1+r)^t$$
$$= 10,000/(1+0.1)^5$$

$$= 10{,}000/(1.1)^5$$
$$= 10{,}000/1.61$$
$$= 6{,}209$$

Therefore, you have to invest 6,209 renminbi today to earn 10,000 renminbi in five years at an interest rate of 10 per cent.

Clearly, future value is compounding money forward, while present value is discounting money back to the present. Therefore, present value is the reverse of future value.

1.3 Risk and returns

Risk

The risk of an investment is the uncertainty associated with its future return. Any investment involves some degree of risk and its rate of return is related to the amount of risk to which the investment is exposed.

The higher the risk of an investment, the higher the expected return. This relationship is known as the risk return trade-off. To explain this inverse relationship, imagine an investor who wants little risk and is satisfied with the return that comes with the level of risk. If the investor is offered another investment that has higher risk, it seems reasonable that she would want a higher return for taking on the extra risk. Otherwise, she sticks with her original low risk, lower return investment.

Measurement of risk

The standard deviation is a measure of the risk of an investment. The definition of standard deviation is the dispersion of outcomes around the expected value.

Two factors are required to measure risk. The first is the possible **rates of return** on an investment and the second is the **expected value**.

1. *Rates of return*

    Single period rate of return.
    The rate of return from an investment is measured in the following way:

    $$\text{Rate of return} = \frac{(\text{End value} - \text{Beginning value}) + \text{Income}}{\text{Beginning value}}$$

Example:

A Malaysian stock starts the year at a price of MYR 10. At the end of one year, the stock price is MYR 12. It pays a dividend of MYR 0.5. The total rate of return is:

$$\frac{(12-10)+0.5}{12}$$
$$= 20.8\%$$

8 *Three finance paradigms*

Table 1.1 Returns of mutual fund

	Year 1	Year 2	Year 3
Assets under management (MYR million)	100	120	109
Return over year (%)	10	(5)	20
Total assets before inflow	110	114	130.8
Net inflow	10	(5)	10
Assets under management at the end of year	120	109	140.8

Multi-period rate of return

A single period rate of return is simple to calculate but is far less common an occurrence than a multi-period rate of return. In this case, consider an investor who is choosing between mutual funds. She wishes to calculate one fund's rate of return over the past three years.

Arithmetic average return

To calculate the arithmetic average return of the mutual fund over the three years:

$$\text{Arithmetic Average} = (10 - 5 + 20)/3$$
$$= 8.33\%$$

The arithmetic average tends to result in a higher average if negative figures are in the series. A geometric average gives more weight to negative returns.

Geometric average return

Unlike the arithmetic average, the geometric average return takes into account compounding. The formula to calculate geometric average return is:

$$r_g = [(1+r_1)(1+r_2)(1+r_3) \ldots (1+r_n)]^{1/n} - 1$$

To calculate the geometric average of the example given above using the formula:

$$r_g = [(1.10)(0.95)(1.20)]^{1/3} - 1$$
$$= 0.0784 \text{ or } 7.84\%$$

Note the average return is higher – 8.33 per cent – a higher average than the geometric average return −7.84 per cent. The geometric average is also called the time-weighted average return because it ignores the period-to-period variation in funds under management.

Mutual funds in the US are required to report their past returns using a time-weighted average. The rationale for this requirement is the inability of fund managers to control the flow of funds into the mutual funds they manage.

Table 1.2 Cash flows

Time	0	1	2	3	4
Net cash flow (MYR million)	−100	−10	5	−10	140.8

Dollar-weighted average

The dollar-weighted average return calculation is used when we want to take into account the flow of money into a mutual fund. This calculation is not unlike the one undertaken in corporate finance to determine the capital budgeting of a project. The dollar-weighted average return of a mutual fund is akin to the internal rate of return (IRR) of the project.

If the fund is a 'project' then the initial MYR 100 million and subsequent cash inflows are investments into the project and are negative cash flows because they are not returns that come from the project. The final value of the fund in the ultimate time period is the liquidation value of the 'project' and therefore constitutes the total that may be taken out of the project.

The formula to calculate the IRR of a project is:

$$NPV = \frac{CF_1}{1+IRR} + \frac{CF_2}{(1+IRR)^2} + \frac{CF_n}{1+IRR^n} = 0$$

Using the formula for our example above we get:

$$140.8 = \frac{100}{1+RR} + \frac{-5}{(1-IRR)^2} + \frac{10}{(1+IRR)^3}$$
$$= -35.5\%$$

Real rates of returns

Inflation

Inflation is the rise in the price of goods and services in an economy. The rate of inflation is the rate at which prices are rising. In the US the Consumer Price Index or CPI is the measure of the rate of inflation. Generally, a country's CPI measures the changes in prices paid by urban consumers for a representative basket of goods and services. Increases in the prices paid indicate a rise in inflation.

The rates of returns we calculated in the previous sections did not take into consideration inflation. If an investment has a rate of return of 10 per cent over a year, unless inflation was 0 per cent over the same period, the real rate of return for the investment is likely to be lower. Inflation erodes the rate of return of an investment because it reduces the purchasing power of a currency.

Consider a return of $100 in one year. Over the same year inflation was 3 per cent. This means that the price of goods and services increased by 3 per cent. This in turn means that more dollars are necessary to buy the same basket of goods and services. Conversely, a dollar is now worth 3 per cent less and the $100 return is worth $97.

10 Three finance paradigms

If the interest rate is 10 per cent and inflation rate is 3 per cent, the nominal interest rate is equal to 10 per cent but the real interest rate is 7 per cent. Real interest rates are therefore the combination of nominal interest rates and inflation rates.

An approximate way of calculating real interest rates is to subtract the inflation rate from the nominal rate, such that:

$$R = r - i$$

Where: R is the real rate
r is the nominal rate
i is the inflation rate

The exact relationship of real and nominal interest rates is:

$$1 + R = \frac{1+r}{1+i}$$

In other words:

$$R = \frac{r-i}{1+i}$$

Example:

A five-year Treasury bill returns 3 per cent in one year. The rate of inflation during the year is 2 per cent. What is the real rate of return over the year for the Treasury bill?

$$R = \frac{0.03 - 0.02}{1 + 0.02}$$
$$R = 0.98\%$$

The real rate of return is much lower than the nominal rate. Inflation reduces the purchasing power money and is therefore a destroyer of the value of money. For this reason, most central banks, including the Federal Reserve Bank in the US, are charged with the responsibility of keeping inflation rates low and typically below a certain rate such as 2 per cent.

Expected value

The expected value is the average return of various possible economic scenarios. Each scenario has a probability attached to it as well as an expected return in that scenario. The list of possible returns and their corresponding probabilities is called the probability distribution.

An example of a probability distribution is illustrated in Table 1.3

Given the probability distribution tabled below, the expected value of the stock A is calculated by using the formula:

$$EV = \Sigma R_s P_s$$

Table 1.3 Probability distribution of stock A

Scenario for economy	Stock A's return for each scenario (%)	Probability of each scenario
Strong growth	20	0.25
Moderate growth	10	0.5
Negative growth	−10	0.25

Table 1.4 Expected value of stock A

Scenario for economy	Stock A's return for each scenario R_s	Probability of each scenario P_s	$R_s \times P_s$	Deviation from EV $R_s - EV$
Strong growth	20%	0.25	5.0	12.5
Moderate growth	10	0.50	5.0	2.5
Negative growth	−10	0.25	−2.5	−17.5
		SUM:	7.5 (EV)	

Where:
R_s is the return in each scenario
P_s is the probability of the scenario occurring
The EV of Stock A for the probability distribution in Table 1.3 is

$$\begin{aligned} EV &= (20 \times 0.25) + (10 \times 0.5) + (-10 \times 0.25) \\ &= 5 + 5 - 2.5 \\ &= 7.5 \end{aligned}$$

Variance

Let's say the scenario of strong growth occurs. The difference between actual return of stock A in this scenario and its expected value is 20 − 7.5 per cent or 12.5 per cent. If we take the probability of each scenario and multiply it with the square of the difference, we get the variance, or the value of the squared deviation from the mean.
Thus:

$$\begin{aligned} \text{Variance} &= \Sigma P_s (R_s - EV)^2 \\ &= 0.25(12.5)^2 + 0.5(2.5)^2 + 0.25(-17.5)^2 \\ &= 0.25(156.25) + 0.5(6.25) + 0.25(306.25) \\ &= 39.06 + 3.13 + 76.56 \\ &= 118.75 \end{aligned}$$

The **standard deviation**, σ, measures the spread of outcomes around the expected value, EV.
σ is also the square root of variance:

12 Three finance paradigms

$$\sigma = \sqrt{\text{Variance}}$$
$$= \sqrt{\Sigma P_s(R_s - EV)^2}$$

Thus, the σ of stock A = $\sqrt{118.75}$
= 10.9

Risk premium

We have discussed nominal rates, inflation rates, rates of returns, and how to calculate the standard deviation, σ, or risk of an investment.

In the best-case scenario of investing, we want an investment that carries no risk, in a zero inflation environment. You will then be assured of receiving the expected rate of return of the investment without concern for a decline in the purchasing power of your investment return. Alas, this scenario is an ideal. Zero interest rate environments are rare. However, there are in existence, so far, risk-free assets.

Treasury bills, money market funds, and bank deposits are risk-free assets that have a risk-free rate of interest. These assets are called risk-free because their returns are certain and the assets are safe. For instance, Treasury bills are risk-free because first, they are backed by the guarantee of the US government and second, their short duration makes them less affected by interest rate fluctuations. After the financial crisis of 2008 and the subsequent downgrading of long-term US debt by Standard & Poor's (S&P), some now argue that Treasury bills are no longer risk-free. Indeed, a few argue that there is no such thing as a risk-free asset. This statement may be true in practice. However, for the purpose of calculating risk premium, modelling efficient diversification and ultimately, for the CAPM asset pricing model, the risk-free asset and rate are necessary and to a large and relative extent, extant.

Money market funds comprise in the main of three forms of securities: Treasury bills, bank certificates of deposit (CDs), and commercial paper issued by top-rated institutions. These instruments have short durations – from a few weeks to two years, thus making them in large measure immune to interest rate risk. There is also little risk of default or credit risk attached to these investments. Thus, compared to the risk and volatility of long-term bonds and common stock, money market funds are essentially risk-free.

In contrast to risk-free assets, risky assets are associated with some level of risk. The risk may be economic, industry-based, firm-specific, politically driven, or even weather related. As mentioned in the first part of this section, the higher the perceived risk of an investment the higher returns are demanded. After all the investor may as well leave her money in risk-free assets if the return of a risky asset is the same or lower than the risk-free rate.

This difference in return between the risk-free rate and the rate of return of a risky asset is called the risk premium.

Risk premium = rate of return of risky asset − risk-free rate

The risk premium is different for each investment. An AAA rated bond of a corporation will have a lower risk premium than the stock of the same corporation.[5] The risk premium of a stock is called the **equity risk premium**.

It has been the case over almost the past hundred years in the US that bonds have a lower risk premium and lower return than equities. This relationship of risk to reward is shown in the two figures:

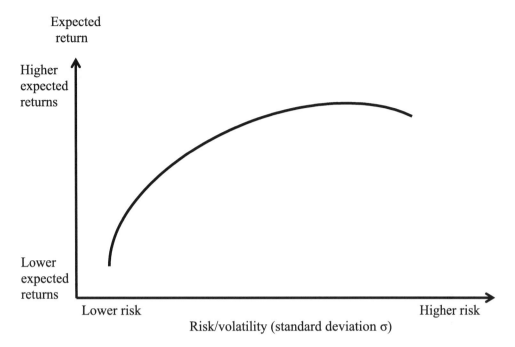

Figure 1.1 The risk return trade-offs.

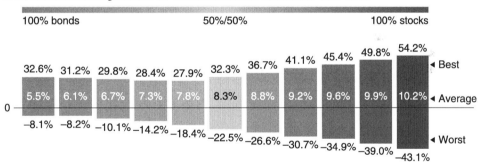

Figure 1.2 Distribution of returns of various portfolios from 1926 to 2013.

Source: Vanguard (https://personal.vanguard.com/us/insights/investingtruths/investing-truth-about-risk).

1.4 Portfolio allocation between risky and risk-free assets

We have discussed and analysed the characteristics of a risky asset, learning about rates of return and calculating the risk associated with the asset. We have also described risk-free assets and risk premiums. We now examine the risk-return combinations when we make different allocations in a portfolio between risky and risk-free assets. The risky asset is

14   Three finance paradigms

either a single risky asset or it can be a portfolio of two or more risky assets. If the risky asset is a portfolio of multiple risky investments, for the purpose of determining the capital allocation line, consider the risky portfolio as a single risky asset.

The capital allocation line

Let's take a portfolio that consists of a risk-free asset and a risky asset. The most direct and simplest way of reducing risk in such a portfolio is to adjust the weight of the risk-free asset in the portfolio. If y is the weight of the risky asset, then $(1-y)$ is the weight of the risk-free asset.

Risk-free assets, by definition, have a standard deviation of 0 or $\sigma_{rf} = 0$. Thus, the larger $(1-y)$ is in the portfolio, the lower the risk of the portfolio.

The actual rate of return of the portfolio of risky assets is R_{ra}
The expected return of the portfolio of risky assets is $E(R_{ra})$
The standard deviation of the portfolio of risky assets is σ_{ra}
The rate of return on the risk-free asset is R_{rf}, which is the same as the risk-free rate.
The standard deviation of the combined portfolio of risky asset and risk-free asset is σ_{cp}
We use the following example to derive the capital allocation line.

$$R_{ra} = 15\%$$
$$\sigma_{ra} = 25\%$$
$$R_{rf} = 5\%$$

The risk premium on the risky asset is $E(R_{ra}) - R_{rf} = 10\%$

To derive the two end points of the capital allocation line we find out what the standard deviation and expected returns on the combined portfolio are when $y = 1$ and $(1-y) = 1$.

When the entire portfolio is made up of the risky asset, the weighting of the risky asset is 100 per cent. Thus, $y = 1$.

When $y = 1$
$\sigma_{cp} = 25\%$
$E(R_{cp}) = 15\%$

This combination of risk and return is plotted as point T in Figure 1.3.

When the entire portfolio is made up of the risk-free asset, the weighting of the risk-free asset is 100 per cent. Thus, $(1-y) = 1$

When $(1-y) = 1$
$\sigma_{cp} = 0\%$
$R_{rf} = 5\%$

This risk reward combination is plotted as F on the capital allocation line.

If $y = 0.5$, that is, half the portfolio of risky and risk-free assets is in risky assets. This implies that the other half of the portfolio is in a risk-free asset.

The return of the entire portfolio is therefore: $E(R_{cp}) = 0.5 \times 5\% + 0.5 \times 15\% = 10\%$
The standard deviation of the entire portfolio is: $\sigma_{cp} = 0.5 \times \sigma_{ra} = 0.5 \times 25\% = 12.5\%$
This risk reward combination is plotted as G in Figure 1.3.

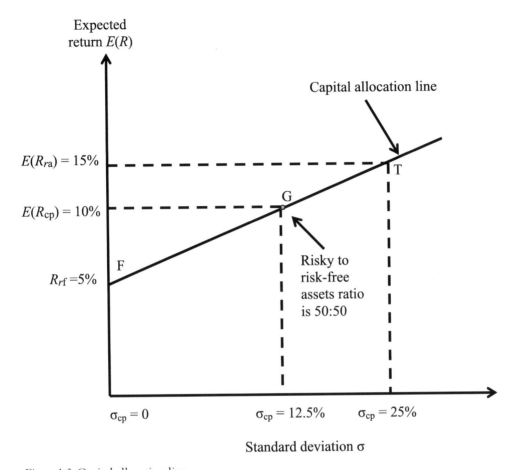

Figure 1.3 Capital allocation line.

The capital allocation line has a slope S, that is the increase in expected return of the portfolio of risky and risk-free assets for each unit of additional risk. The slope is often called the reward-to-variability ratio.

In the example given above:

$$S = \text{the slope of the line} = \frac{E(R_{ra}) - R_{rf}}{\sigma_{cp}} = \frac{15 - 5}{25} = 0.4$$

The reward-to-variability ratio is therefore 0.4.

Capital market line

When the risk-free asset is one-month T-bills and the risky portfolio of assets is the broad index of common stocks, the capital allocation line is called the **capital market line** (CML). We examine the CML in the context of the CAPM in a later section.

16 Three finance paradigms

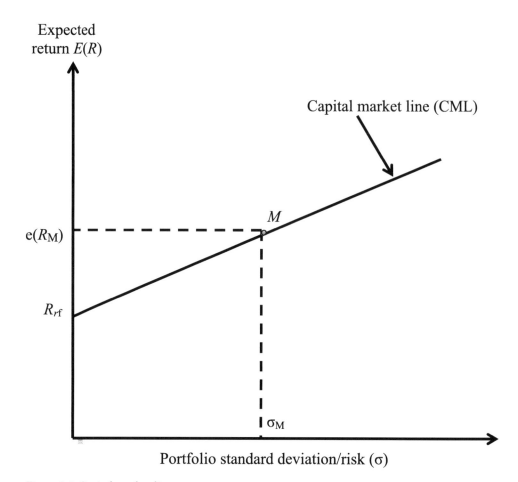

Figure 1.4 Capital market line.

The formula for the CML may be written as:

$$E(R_p) = R_{rf} + \frac{[E(R_M) - R_{rf}]\sigma_p}{\sigma_M}$$

Where: $E(R_p)$ is the expected return on any portfolio
         R_{rf} is the risk-free rate
         $E(R_M)$ is the expected rate of return of the market
         σ_M is the standard deviation of the market
         σ_p is the standard deviation of the portfolio

The CML formula derives from the basic equation for a straight line:

$$Y = a + bX$$

Standard deviation for a two-asset portfolio

Earlier, we calculated the standard deviation for a single risky asset. We now calculate the standard deviation for a two-asset portfolio that contains risky assets.

The goal in this exercise is to learn how we establish a portfolio of assets that will produce the optimum returns at the lowest possible level of risk.

Theoretically, the primary task of portfolio management is asset allocation first and stock selection next. The manager must decide on the mix of assets within the risky asset portfolio. Then that manager must determine the mix between risky assets and risk-free assets.

The first step is to calculate the standard deviation of a portfolio with two risky assets to determine optimum allocation between these two assets. In the example, we assume the two assets are a stock s, and a bond, b. To calculate the standard deviation of a two-asset portfolio we need to determine the **correlation coefficient**, which is the measure of how the two assets move with each other. The value of the correlation coefficient can be from -1 to $+1$.

For most variables, the correlation coefficient usually falls between the two values. Correlations can be of the following type:

> When one variable moves in line with the other so that if returns on an investment A are in exact proportion to the returns on another investment B, then the two investments are perfectly correlated.
>
> When returns on A increase when returns on B increase then the two variables are positively correlated.
>
> When the returns on A increases when returns on B decreases, then the variables A and B are negatively correlated.
>
> When the returns on A have no relationship to returns to B then the two variables are uncorrelated.

The important point to note is: two assets with a zero, low, or negative correlation of returns reduce the overall risk of the combined portfolio.

Thus, in the example, if the stock, s, performs poorly in a recession but the bond, b, performs well then the two assets are negatively correlated.

The correlation coefficient of two assets is calculated using the formula:

$$\text{Correlation coefficient, } \rho = \frac{Covariance_{sb}}{\sigma_s \times \sigma_b}$$

Table 1.5 Correlation coefficient and portfolio standard deviation

Correlation coefficient (ρ_{sb})	Portfolio standard deviation (σ_p)
+1.0	7.49
+0.5	6.70
0.0	5.81
−0.5	4.77
−1.0	3.41

18 Three finance paradigms

The covariance is a measure of how returns of two elements, in this case asset returns, vary with each other, or co-vary, over time. The formula to calculate covariance is:

$$\text{Covariance} = \Sigma(\text{return}_s - \text{expected value}_s)(\text{return}_b - \text{expected value}_b)\text{probability}$$

We can calculate the covariance of S and B using the figures from Tables 1.6 and 1.7.

$$\begin{aligned}\text{Covariance} &= (12.5)(-6.75)(0.25) + (2.5)(1.25)(0.5) + (-17.5)(4.25)(0.25) \\ &= (-21.09) + (1.56) + (-18.59) \\ &= -38.13\end{aligned}$$

Correlation

$$\begin{aligned}\text{Coefficient}, \rho &= \frac{\text{Covariance}_{sb}}{\sigma_s \times \sigma_b} \\ &= \frac{-38.13}{10.89 \times 4.08} \\ &= -.086\end{aligned}$$

The standard deviation of the two risky asset portfolio is then calculated using the formula:

$$\sigma p = \sqrt{W_s^2 \sigma_s^2 + W_b^2 \sigma_b^2 + 2W_s W_b \rho_{sb} \sigma_s \sigma_b}$$

Where W is the weight of the assets, s and b, in the portfolio.

In this example, we assign a weighting of 50 per cent for s and for b in the portfolio.

Using Formula I and the figures in Table 1.6, we calculate the standard deviation of the portfolio with risky assets, s and b, as:

$$\begin{aligned}\sigma_p &= \sqrt{(0.5)^2(10.9)^2 + (0.5)^2(4.08)^2 + 2(0.5)(0.5)(-0.86)(10.9)(4.08)} \\ &= \sqrt{29.69 + 4.17 + (-19.06)} \\ &= \sqrt{14.8} \\ &= 3.85\end{aligned}$$

The standard deviation of 3.85 for the portfolio of two risky assets is less than the standard deviation of either asset. When the correlation between two assets in a portfolio is less than +1, the risk of the whole portfolio tends to be reduced.

The point to note in this entire exercise of risk reduction through diversification is that in portfolio management the risk of the portfolio is less dependent on the risk of one asset in the portfolio than on how the asset affects the standard deviation of the portfolio through correlation with other assets in the portfolio.

Compare the return of the two-asset portfolio in the example above with the return on the bond portfolio. A portfolio that is 100 per cent invested in bond B produces an expected return of 3.75 per cent and a standard deviation of 4.08. In the case of a two-asset portfolio, p, with a weighting of 50 per cent stock s and 50 per cent bond b, the risk is reduced to σ_p or 3.85 without a decrease in portfolio returns. Indeed the return R_p of the portfolio increases to the weighted average of the returns of s and b such that:

[(0.5)(7.5) + (0.5)(3.75)]
= 5.63

Although our example is of a two-asset portfolio, it is possible to derive the standard deviations and portfolio returns of multiple asset portfolios. Of course, the computations grow substantially. The formula to calculate the standard deviation for a multiple asset portfolio with N assets is:

$$\sigma_p = \sqrt{\sum_{s=1}^{N} W_s^2 \sigma_s^2 + 2\sum_{s=1}^{N-1}\sum_{b=s+1}^{N} 2 W_s W_b \rho_{sb} \sigma_s \sigma_b}$$

Table 1.6 Calculation of covariance for stock S

Scenario for economy	Probability	Rate of return (%)	Probability x rate of return	Deviation from expected value	Squared deviation	Probability x squared deviation
Strong growth	0.25	20	5	12.5	156.25	39.0625
Moderate growth	0.5	10	5	2.5	6.25	3.125
Negative growth	0.25	−10	−2.5	−17.5	306.25	76.5625
		SUM (EV)	7.5		Variance (sum)	118.75
					Standard deviation of S (SQRT variance)	10.89724736

Table 1.7 Calculation of covariance for bond B

Scenario for economy	Probability	Rate of return	Probability x rate of return	Deviation from expected value	Squared deviation	Probability x squared deviation
Strong growth	0.25	−3	−0.75	−6.75	45.5625	11.390625
Moderate growth	0.5	5	2.5	1.25	1.5625	0.78125
Negative growth	0.25	8	2	4.25	18.0625	4.515625
		SUM (EV)	3.75		Variance (sum)	16.6875
					Standard deviation of B (SQRT variance)	4.08503366

Three finance paradigms

The efficient frontier

Harry Markowitz designed the portfolio model that is described in the preceding sections. Markowitz demonstrated that the dispersion (called the variance) of the rate of return is a meaningful measure of portfolio risk. He derived a formula for measuring this risk or the standard deviation of a portfolio of assets. *The main idea that emerges from Markowitz's portfolio theory is that diversifying the assets in a portfolio reduces the total risk of the portfolio.* In addition, Markowitz's model shows how to diversify risk in a portfolio.

In the section describing the correlation coefficient, we noted that the overall risk of a portfolio is lowered when the correlations between the assets in the portfolio are low, zero, or negative. The other crucial factor that affects diversification is the weighting of the assets in the portfolio. If we produce several two-asset portfolios with different weightings of each asset and different standard deviations (but with constant correlation coefficient), we generate a table of values shown in Table 1.8.

If we plot the expected returns R_p against the standard deviations for each portfolio, a graph like the one shown in Figure 1.5 emerges.

If we graphed the returns of the seven different portfolios with different possible weights, we see an efficient set of portfolios lies along the curved line in Figure 1.5. *This line is called the **efficient frontier** because it represents the portfolios with the best rate of return for a given level of risk or the minimum risk for a given level of return.* In other words, every point on the efficient frontier has either: (A) a higher return for equal risk than any other portfolio below the frontier or (B) a lower risk for equal rate of return than any other portfolio below the frontier. Note: portfolios do not exist above the efficient frontier.

Example:

Take portfolios A and C on the efficient frontier graph. Portfolio A has a lower risk than portfolio C and yet both portfolios have the same rate of return. Clearly, one chooses portfolio A to minimize risk for the same return.

Similarly, take portfolios B and C on the efficient frontier graph. Portfolio B has a higher return for the same level of risk than portfolio C. Clearly, one chooses portfolio B to maximize returns for the same level of risk.

Although Figure 1.5 shows 12 points such as portfolios, a fully developed efficient frontier may be based essentially on an unlimited number of portfolios.

The portfolio on the efficient frontier an investor chooses depends on the investor's risk-return trade-off preferences. A risk-averse investor will choose portfolio A, while a risk-oriented investor will choose portfolio B.

Table 1.8 Portfolio with different weightings of two assets

Portfolio	Weight W_s	Weight W_b	Return R_p	Standard deviation σ_p
A	0.0	1.0	3.75	4.08
B	0.2	0.8	4.50	1.80
C	0.4	0.6	5.25	2.59
D	0.6	0.4	6.00	5.21
E	0.8	0.2	6.75	8.01
F	1.0	1.0	7.50	10.89

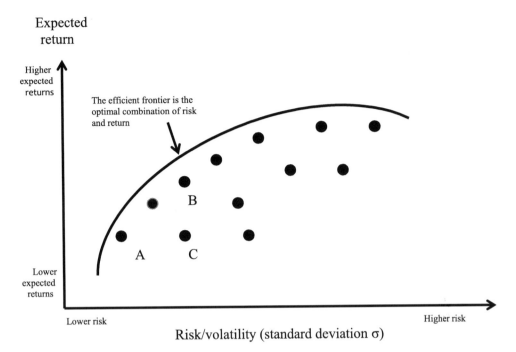

Figure 1.5 The efficient frontier.

Note: Each dot represents a portfolio. The closer the portfolio to the efficient frontier, the better return with lowest risk.

The optimal portfolio

Investor utility

An investor's utility curve or indifference curve characterizes the risk–return trade-off preferences of that investor. The more risk-averse the investor is, the steeper will be the curve. In Figure 1.6, investor J is more risk averse than investor K. In the case of the latter, she demands more incremental return for every unit of risk.

An investor J will have a set of utility curves as shown in Figure 1.7. This set represents the possible utility curves for investor J. Although investor J has a distinct risk–return profile, she still wishes to obtain the highest return for the same level of risk. She therefore wants a utility curve to be the highest curve possible. Thus, she would choose curve J1 over J3.

If used with the efficient frontier, the utility curve determines the portfolio on the efficient frontier that best fits the risk–return preference of the investor. Figure 1.8 shows three sets of utility curves for investor J.

Investors must theoretically match their utility curves with the efficient frontier to obtain their own optimal portfolio. This is the portfolio that best matches their risk–return preferences with the best investments available in the market as represented by points on the efficient frontier.

22 *Three finance paradigms*

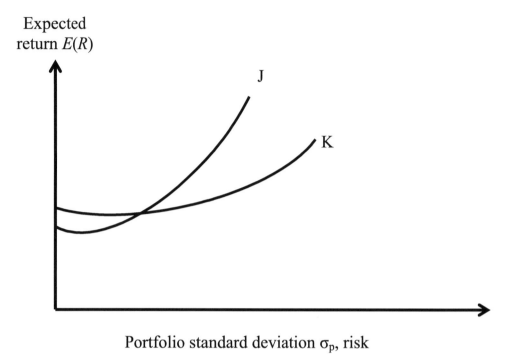

Figure 1.6 Utility curves for investors J and K.

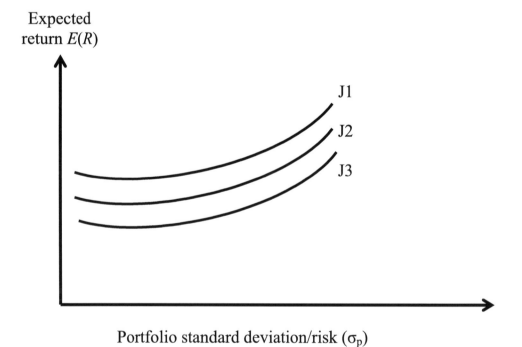

Figure 1.7 Utility curves for investor J.

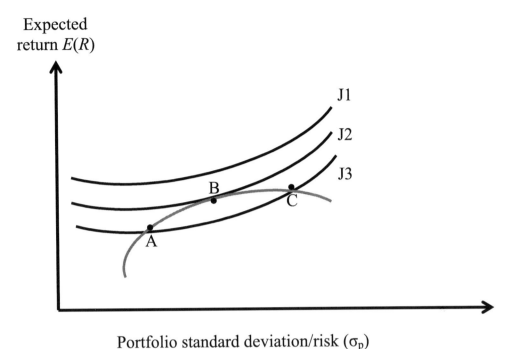

Figure 1.8 Utility curves and efficient frontier.

In Figure 1.8, investor J's optimum portfolio is at point B along the efficient frontier shown as the blue curved line. At points A and C on the efficient frontier that cross utility curve J3, the level of returns are less for a given level of risk than J2. Investors impose their own risk-return utility curves to the efficient frontier to determine the point of tangency for maximum utility.

1.5 Capital asset pricing model

Markowitz's portfolio theory is the basis of the CAPM. The major factor that allows the progression of portfolio theory to capital market theory is the concept of the risk-free asset. The risk-free asset has a risk-free rate of return and a standard deviation of zero. These two characteristics mean that a risk-free asset lies on the y-axis of a portfolio graph. In addition, a risk-free asset has zero correlation with all risky assets. From this assumption, William Sharpe originated the generalized theory of capital asset pricing under conditions of uncertainty from the Markowitz portfolio theory in the early 1960s.[6] He received the Nobel Prize for this achievement. Lintner and Mossin derived similar theories independently.[7] Hence, we often refer to the Sharpe–Lintner–Mossin (SLM) CAPM.

Under the CAPM, we combine the capital allocation line with the efficient frontier, as shown in Figure 1.9.

24 *Three finance paradigms*

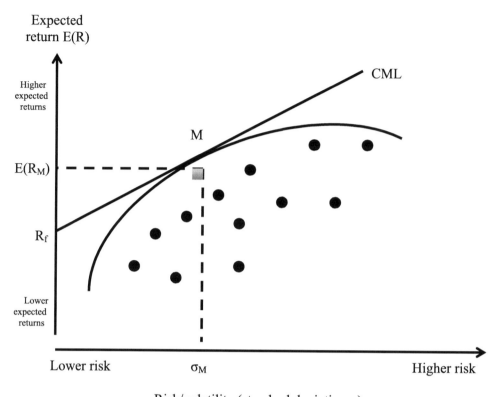

Figure 1.9 Capital market line and efficient frontier.

Note: Each dot represents a portfolio. The closer the portfolio to the efficient frontier, the better return with lowest risk.

To recap:

1 The efficient frontier represents portfolios, with different weightings of a multitude of risky assets, which offer the best rate of return for a given level of risk or the minimum risk for a given level of return.
2 The capital allocation line or CAL shows the combination of risk and reward for a portfolio comprising of a risk-free and risky asset.

In Figure 1.9 the CAL is tangent to the efficient frontier at point M. This point is the optimal risky portfolio of investments every investor wishes to hold. While the weighting of risk-free assets versus risky portfolio may differ for each investor, the risky portfolio will be the same portfolio of risky assets for every investor because M is the optimal risky portfolio.

When all investors choose to hold the same proportion of stocks in portfolio M, the proportion of stocks in the aggregate risky portfolio will be the same as the proportion of stocks in portfolio M. For example if China Telecom is 1 per cent in portfolio M, then China Telecom is also 1 per cent in the aggregate risky portfolio. As the market is the aggregate of all individual portfolios, portfolio M thus becomes the market portfolio. The line from the risk-free rate through point M is the best attainable CAL. The CAL in this case is the CML.

If a stock, say News Corporation, is not in the market portfolio, no investor will want to hold the stock. The price of News Corp's share will fall because demand is zero. However, as the News Corp's share price gets cheaper, it begins to look more attractive relative to other stocks. Ultimately, News Corp's price will reach a level that it becomes a buy and investors will then include the stock in the optimal risky portfolio. The upshot is that all stocks will be included in the optimal risky portfolio. The sole consideration for inclusion is the price of the stock. When a stock is considered cheap, investors will buy the stocks but if it is considered expensive, investors will sell it.

The market portfolio contains all risky assets and includes US common stocks, non-US common stocks, US and non-US bonds, options, real estate, commodities, art, stamps, or antiques. The portfolio is completely diversified which means risks unique to any particular investment in the portfolio is diversified away. This unique risk of a risky asset is also known as **unsystematic risk**.

As this risk is eliminated through diversification in a market portfolio, only **systematic risk** remains. Systematic risk is measured by the standard deviation of returns of the market portfolio. Factors that affect systematic risk are macroeconomic variables (interest rate volatility, money supply) and industry variables.

Uses of CAPM

1. To determine the risk of an individual security versus the market

The systematic risk or beta is the only relevant risk in CAPM. The risk of any investment is measured against the beta of the market to determine if the returns should be higher or lower. If we plot the expected return of an individual stock versus the return of the market over a number of periods, we get a straight line represented by the formula:

$$R_i = \alpha_i + \beta R_M + c$$

Where R_i = Expected return of the individual stock i
α_i = the point at which the line crosses the y-axis
β = the slope of the line
R_M = market return
c = the random error term

The formula indicates how volatile the individual stock is relative to the market through the beta coefficient. When β is 1.5 say, if the market moves up by certain percentage points, the individual stock is calculated to move 1.5 times that amount. In other words, *beta measures the correlation of an individual stock's total return to the market portfolio.*

The beta of the market will always be 1.0 as it is the correlation of the return of the market portfolio to itself.

Expected returns are lower if a security has a beta less than the market, and higher returns if the security has a beta greater than the market. In the former case, the security is less risky than the market while in the latter case, it is one in which the risk of the security is greater than the market. Thus, the risk premium, such as the difference between market return and risk-free return $(R_i - R_f)$ of a security, is proportional to its beta and to risk premium of the market portfolio $(R_M - R_f)$. If we double the beta of a security, the risk premium for investors willing to hold the security is also doubled. We can formulate the relationship of the risk premium of a security to its beta such that:

$$\text{Risk premium of security} = \beta(R_M - R_f)$$

Clearly, the beta is important in analysing risk and return. In investment management, the beta of a security must therefore be identified. This service is provided by an assortment of financial data providers, such as Bloomberg, Value Line, Standard & Poor's, and some brokerage houses.

Sometimes there is a wide range of beta values for a particular stock. The differences are attributable to the index against which the beta is calculated, the time period used for the calculation, and the adjustments made to raw betas to reflect the fact that beta is used as a future expected value.

2. To determine the expected returns of individual securities

The discussion in (1) above described how we calculate a stock's beta, given its return and the market return. Conversely, we can calculate the expected or required return of an individual security given its beta. The security market line (SML) shows the risk and return for an individual security. (Recall the CML shows the risk and return for portfolios of risky and risk-free assets.)

The equation for the SML is given by:

$$R_i = R_f + \beta(R_M - R_f)$$

Where R_i = expected return for the individual security i
R_f = risk-free rate of return
β = beta or systematic risk
R_M = expected market return

The slope of the SML is the risk premium of the individual security or $\beta(R_M - R_f)$.

The SML plots the return of an individual security against its beta, which is the relevant measure of risk for individual securities held in market portfolio. In CAPM we are only interested in systematic risk or beta. Hence, in the SML we use beta as the measurement of risk and not the standard deviation of the individual security.

From the SML, we can determine the required rate of return of a security if we know its beta. The required rate of return is one that will compensate investors for the risk of that security, as well as for the time value of money. Indeed, obtaining expected returns of a security is a primary utility of CAPM. In market equilibrium, the SML is the line on which all fairly priced assets lie.

The CAPM may also be used in determining the necessary rate of return for projects, such as building a high-speed rail from Shanghai to Beijing, to attract investors. In corporate financing decisions, management can use the CAPM to obtain the minimum internal rate of return (IRR) or 'hurdle rate' of the project.

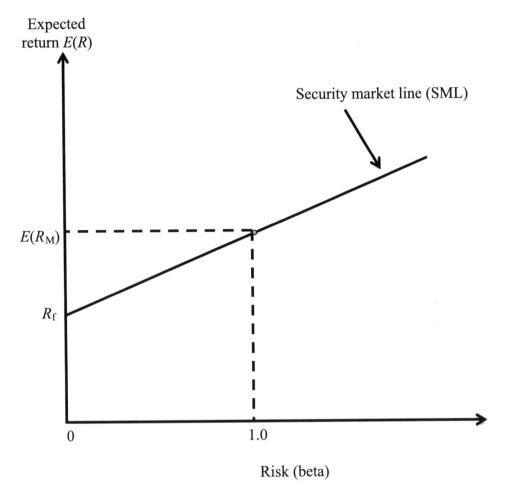

Figure 1.10 Security market line.

3. To identify undervalued and overvalued assets

Using the SML, we can compare the required rate of return of a security against its estimated rate of return over a specific time period to determine if the security is an appropriate investment. The difference between a security's estimated return and its required return is often called its alpha or its excess return. If the alpha is positive, the security is undervalued, if the alpha is negative the security is overvalued. If the alpha is zero, the security is on the SML and is fairly valued. Thus, overvalued securities plot below the SML while undervalued securities plot above the SML.

In Figure 1.11, securities A and B are above the SML and we therefore would buy A and B as we want to own them in our portfolios. Securities C and D are below the SML and we would not buy them for our portfolios, and we would sell them out of our portfolios if they are in our portfolios at the current time.

28 *Three finance paradigms*

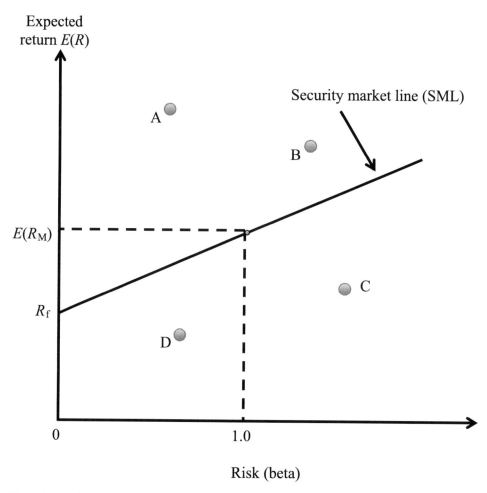

Figure 1.11 Valuing securities using the security market line.

Lending and borrowing

In Figure 1.12, an investor may want to increase returns than is available at M, the market portfolio, and is willing to take increased risk. To do this, the investor can invest in one of the risky portfolios on the efficient frontier at a higher point than M such as risky portfolio, Z at point Z. Alternatively, our investor can borrow money at the risk-free rate and invest the borrowed money in the risky asset portfolio at point M.

If the investor borrows 50 per cent of his original worth at the risk-free rate, the weighting of the risk-free portfolio will be negative 50 per cent or −0.50. The expected return of the portfolio of risk-free and risky asset will then be:

$$
\begin{aligned}
E(Rp) &= \gamma(R_f) + (1-\gamma)E(R_M) \\
&= -0.50(R_f) + (1-(-0.5))E(R_M) \\
&= -0.50(R_f) + 1.50E(R_M)
\end{aligned}
$$

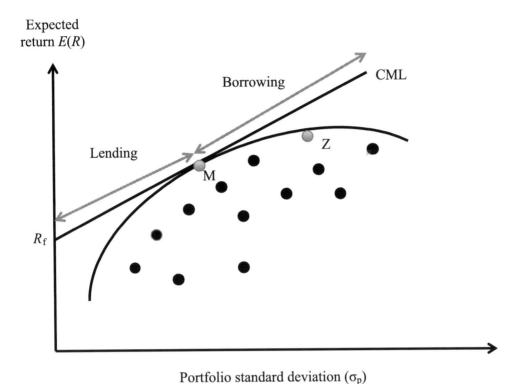

Figure 1.12 Capital market line with lending and borrowing at risk-free rate.

Where γ is the weight of the risk-free portfolio and $(1-\gamma)$ is the weight of the risky portfolio.

To be at a point between M and Z, we buy portfolio M and borrow money at the risk-free rate to increase the weighting of M in our overall portfolio.

Passive strategy using the CML

Pursuing a passive strategy of stock investing, such as holding a basket of stocks that is the market portfolio, is an efficient way of investing. Passive investors use the CML as the optimal CAL. The market portfolio is assumed to be in equilibrium implying the prices of stocks on the CML reflect all information. Investors have traded on the information and have either bought up or sold down the prices of stocks. Consequently, there is no more profit to be made. Active investors do the work of analysing securities, buy and sell stocks based on their work, and thereby drive the price of stocks to their equilibrium level as expressed in the CML. Passive investors take a 'free ride' on the security analysis of active investors. Notably, the active investor will end up on the CML as any other portfolio will be less efficient than the CML.

Clearly, the cost of investing passively is far less than the cost of investing in an actively managed mutual fund. Over the long term, this cost savings accumulate to such an extent that long-term performance of the average passive index fund is generally better than that of the average actively managed fund of the same type.

The following CAPM paradox exists: Passive investing is costless and efficient. Active investing is costly and ends up with the same market portfolio. Why follow an active investment strategy? Yet, if no investor does security analysis how are stocks going to achieve equilibrium prices?

Assumptions of CAPM

It is important to understand that CAPM is a model embedded in a simplified version of the world. We therefore, need to know the assumptions made by the model:

1. All investors are rational and wish to maximize their expected utility, measuring the performance of investments with the use of means and standard deviations of portfolio returns.
2. The market is made up of investors with homogenous expectations such as all investors have identical estimates of probability distributions for future rates of returns. They use the same expected returns, standard deviations, and correlations to generate the efficient frontier and optimal market portfolio.
3. Investors cannot affect prices because the market is a perfectly competitive one.
4. The market is efficient and self-adjusts to maintain equilibrium.
5. All investments are infinitely divisible. It is possible to buy or sell fractional shares of any asset or portfolio.
6. All investors have the same one-period time horizon.
7. All investors have access to unlimited borrowing or lending opportunities at risk-free rates.
8. All investors do not pay taxes or transaction costs on securities traded.

CAPM and how it fits the data

On a broad view, CAPM provides a useful framework for thinking about risk and returns of portfolios. Higher returns are associated with higher beta portfolios. However, when we look with greater granularity at the model versus real-world data, the fit is imprecise.

When the model first appeared, Black, Jensen, and Scholes tested the veracity of CAPM.[8] Fama and MacBeth also did tests on CAPM.[9] The results of both studies supported CAPM in that average returns were higher for higher beta portfolios. The results did not support CAPM in that the reward for beta was less than the predictions made by the model. Thus, empirical testing did not give incontrovertible evidence of the predictive value of the model.

The theory took another body blow when Roll published a paper forwarding the thesis that CAPM is necessarily untestable because the true market portfolio can never be observed.[10] However, CAPM supporters responded by pointing out that a broad market index can be used as a proxy for the market portfolio and the error is within acceptable limits.

In 1992 Fama and French further damaged the standing of CAPM in a widely discussed study.[11] The academics controlled for a broad range of firm characteristics, such as size of the firm, and market to book value. The results, after controlling for these factors, showed that the firm's beta did not contribute anything to the prediction of future returns. Subsequent studies have further shown that beta is not the sole measure of risk. Other risk factors such as liquidity and risk premiums come into play in determining the returns of a portfolio.

As a portfolio manager of a two billion dollar fund investing in Asia ex-Japan, CAPM barely made an impression on me (Kara Tan Bhala, a co-author of this book). The investment community acknowledges CAPM and portfolio theory but the use of the models is limited. There is a nod to the concepts of systematic and unsystematic risk and diversification. Beta is even commonly used as a measure of systematic risk, yet CAPM in its full measure is not well established among practitioners.

1.6 Arbitrage pricing theory

As we saw earlier, CAPM makes quite a few assumptions including assumptions about investor preferences. The simplified world of CAPM is a common target of critiques of the model.

The arbitrage pricing theory (APT) is burdened with fewer assumptions and is an alternative model for explaining stock prices and stock returns. The theory has three major assumptions:

1. Capital markets are perfectly competitive.
2. Given a choice between more wealth and less wealth that is certain, investors always prefer more wealth.
3. The stochastic process generating asset returns can be represented as a multiple factor model.

APT, developed by Stephen Ross[12] in the 1970s, moves away from mean-variance efficient portfolios. Instead, the return of an investment is dependent on more than one factor.

Arbitrage is the exploitation of price discrepancies of assets to earn risk-free profits. For example, KEPCO, or Korea Electric Power, is traded on the Korean Stock Exchange as well as on the New York Stock Exchange (NYSE). In theory, the prices of KEPCO on both exchanges should be exactly the same, after consideration of trading costs. Yet, mispricings do occur. If the stock trades higher in Korea than in New York, arbitrageurs will simultaneously sell short the stock in Korea and use the money from the short sale to buy the stock on the NYSE. The net price differential between the two markets will produce a sure profit, without any net investment. Hence, the arbitrageur earns risk-free profits, theoretically. The increased selling of KEPCO in Korea brings down the price, while the increase buying of KEPCO in New York increases the price. Eventually the price difference between the two locations is arbitraged away and the arbitrage opportunity disappears. Thus, arbitrage requires market participants to act on price discrepancies so that prices will move back to equilibrium.

High Frequency Traders (HFT) make use of these mispricings to make risk-free profits. The mispricing of assets may occur for only a couple of seconds. However, all HFTs are computerized and most HFT computer systems are located, literally, next to Exchange computers, to decrease detection times of any asset mispricing and to make super-fast trade execution. HFT computers issue buy and sell orders in a split second and therefore are able to take advantage of price differentials to make arbitrage profits.

The arbitrage pricing model describes the expected return on a stock as a function of multiple factors.

32 Three finance paradigms

Research shows that a few major factors affect stock returns.[13] These include: interest rate risk, business cycle risk, inflation, and changing risk premium risk. However, the return of an asset may be dependent on one factor or on many factors up to n. The formula for return in the arbitrage pricing model is given as:

$$R_{s,t} = E(R_s) + b_{s,1}F_{1,t} + b_{s,2}F_{2,t} + \ldots + b_{s,n}F_{n,t}$$

Where:
- $R_{s,t}$ = Return on stock s at time t
- $E(R_s)$ = Expected return on stock s
- $b_{s,n}$ = Sensitivity of stock s to factor n
- $F_{n,t}$ = Value of factor n at time t
- $e_{i,t}$ = Error term specific to stock s at time t

The return of a stock is affected by unexpected changes in factors, F_n. For instance, let's say factor 1 or F_1 represents changing interest rates. If interest rates go up more than expected then a stock that is sensitive to a change in interest rates, such as a bank stock, will decline while stocks that are not sensitive to interest rate changes, such as the stock of, say, a cookie company, will barely be affected.

The measure of the sensitivity of the stock's return to factor F_1 is given by b_1. The b is often called the beta. The factor sensitivity of a portfolio is calculated by adding the weighted beta for each factor. The weight is the proportion of market value each stock contributes to the portfolio.

The error term e is the unexpected portion of the return of the stock s that is not explained by the factors. This error term represents the unexpected events unique to firm s. In the case of KEPCO it may be the change in regularity regimes for the utility or a takeover that affects only KEPCO but is not taken into account in expected return, $E(R_s)$. This random variable e drops out of the equation because we assume that in a diversified portfolio, e, approaches zero as all systematic risk is eliminated.

Example:

Suppose we have two stocks, KEPCO, k, and Kookmin Bank, b. Assume two factors affect the returns of both stocks but in different amounts such that:

$$R_k = 10\% - 2F_{1,t} + 4F_{2,t}$$
$$R_b = 20\% - 4F_{1,t} + 3F_{2,t}$$

In KEPCO's case, the stock is less sensitive to factor F_1 than Kookmin Bank. If F_1 is the change in interest rate, it seems reasonable that Kookmin Bank is more sensitive to changes in rates than the electric utility. The stock declines more if there is an unexpected interest rate increase. Note the negative sign before the factor sensitivity indicates an inverse relationship between expected return and the factor in question.

In contrast, KEPCO is more sensitive to F_2 than Kookmin Bank. F_2 may be the change in economic growth rates (GDP). If GDP increases more than expected, investors will infer that electric usage will increase as manufacturing activity rises, thus leading to higher revenues for KEPCO. Higher economic growth rates also impact on Kookmin Bank's returns but less so than for KEPCO.

Modern finance theory

The two stocks are weighted evenly in a portfolio such that the weight of KEPCO is 50 per cent and that of Kookmin Bank is 50 per cent. Thus the portfolio risk is dependent on the weight of each stock in the portfolio and the stock's sensitivity to the two factors, F_1 and F_2.

Multiplying both sides of the equations by the respective weights, we get:

$$(0.5)R_k = (0.5)(10\%) - (0.5)(2)F_{1,t} + (0.5)(4)F_{2,t}$$
$$= 5\% - F_{1,t} + 2.5F_{2,t}$$

In other words, a 50 per cent weighting of KEPCO will have a 5 per cent expected portfolio return, a negative sensitivity of 1 to interest rate risk, and a sensitivity of 2 to economic growth risk.

For Korean Bank the APT equation fills out as follows:

$$(0.5)R_b = (0.5)(20\%) - (0.5)(4)F_{1,t} + (0.5)(3)F_{2,t}$$
$$= 10\% - 2F_{1,t} + 1.5F_{2,t}$$

A 50 per cent weighting of Kookmin Bank will have a 10 per cent expected portfolio return, a negative sensitivity of 2 to interest rate risk, and a sensitivity of 1.5 to economic growth risk.

The overall portfolio return and factor risk sensitivity is obtained by combining the results of the above two equations to get:

$$\text{Portfolio Return } R_p = (5\%+10\%) - (1+2)F_{1,t} + (2.5+1.5)F_{2,t}$$
$$= 15\% - 3F_{1,t} + 4F_{2,t}$$

The expected return of the portfolio is 15 per cent with a negative sensitivity of 3 to interest rate risk, and a sensitivity of 4 to economic growth risk. The portfolio is highly sensitive to unexpected changes in interest and growth rates.

The relevance of APT

Clearly, APT in theory helps determine how important various factors are to the returns of a stock or a portfolio. The model enables a portfolio manager to construct portfolios that are either sensitive or insensitive to particular factors. If interest rates are expected to remain low for an extended period of time, as in the era of the Great Recession, but a portfolio manager believes from her analysis that interest rates are likely to rise, she will construct a portfolio that is sensitive to unexpected changes in interest rates. Conversely, if the manager is bearish on growth rates in a market that has not factored in slowing economic growth, she will construct a portfolio that is less sensitive or even inversely sensitive to falling growth rates.

1.7 Efficient Market Hypothesis (EMH)

The hypothesis

The efficient market hypothesis states that stock prices already reflect all available information. This means the market has information on the economy, the industry, and the firm. Consequently, stock prices have moved as a result of this knowledge. According to the theory, if new information with a positive impact on the earnings of a particular company emerges, investors will purchase the stock of that company, push up its stock price, thereby resulting in the price reaching equilibrium and fair value again. Similarly, if the news is bad for a company's share price (loss of a major client, for instance) then investors will sell the shares until once again the price reaches fair value.

New information comes out at random and is unpredictable. Stock prices move on new information. Therefore, stock price movements are also random and unpredictable. We say that stock prices follow a random walk.

Thus, EMH postulates markets as efficient because they have already absorbed all available information and prices have adjusted quickly and accordingly. But some markets are less efficient than others. For example, some emerging markets, like the African markets, are less efficient because they are less well covered by research analysts. Data in markets such as these are not as easily obtained as data in the US market.

How do we interpret the term 'all available information'? There are three different forms of the hypothesis depending on our interpretations.

Weak form of EMH

This version of the EMH postulates that stock prices already reflect information from all market trading data, such as historical prices, volumes, interest rates, or growth rates. The implication of this version is that there is no relationship between the past and future prices of securities. If there is a relationship between some past price movement and future prices, this relationship would already have been spotted, used, and rendered ineffective.

Consequently, if weak form EMH is true then technical analysis is useless because past trends in stock prices do not predict future prices. Technical analysis is the study of past trends in stock prices to discern recurring patterns that may be the basis of prediction of future prices. Technical analysts study charts of prices and volumes of stocks or markets going back in time.

One common basic chart is the 'head and shoulder' formation as shown in Figure 1.13. The price rises to a peak and then falls, rises to a higher peak and then falls, and finally rises to a peak lower than the previous peak and then falls. The two lower peaks are the shoulders and the highest peak in the middle is the head. This type of chart formation of a market or a stock presages a further decline in prices. A sell signal comes when the decline breaks through the neckline of the chart.

Semi-strong form of EMH

This version of the EMH states that all publicly available information on a firm is already reflected in the firm's stock price. This publicly available information includes fundamental information on revenues, profit margins, clients, products, competitors, quality of management, business strategy, etc. The implication of this version of EMH is that investors cannot use fundamental analysis to find undervalued or overvalued stocks because all fundamental information is already in the share price.

While technical analysis does not work for weak form EMH, both technical analysis and fundamental analysis does not work for semi-weak form EMH.

A majority of investment professionals carry out fundamental research to discover the true fair value of a firm's stock price. Analysts drill down on a firm's financial statements.

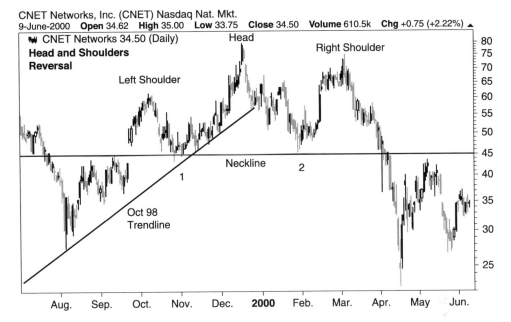

Figure 1.13 Head and Shoulders Formation.

Source: StockCharts.com

Research focuses on earnings, expected dividends, industry information, interest rate forecasts, and other related data relevant to determining the firm's value. This single piece of data is the Holy Grail of investment analysis. If the price of the stock trades below its fair value the stock is undervalued and should be purchased. If the stock price trades above its fair value, the stock is overvalued and should be sold. Investment professionals believe they can be the first or one of the first to know the true fair value of a stock and profit from the knowledge, before that information is known in the market and reflected in the price. The underlying presumption of active portfolio management is that semi-strong EMH is false.

Strong form of EMH

This version of EMH proposes that stock prices reflect all information available about a firm including the information privy only to insiders. Strong form EMH holds that no one has access to privileged information that enables superior risk-adjusted returns. Information about mergers, acquisitions, earnings, and other company announcements, prior to being made public, is already in the share price of a company. This is the extreme form of EMH as it admits to no information that is not already in the market.

This position clearly is not in agreement with insider trading laws, specifically rule 10b-5 of the Securities Exchange Act of 1944. This rule limits trading by company insiders, directors, consultants, accountants, and owners. Trading on information obtained from insiders is a violation of the law. The law and strong form EMH are clearly discordant. If the latter were true, the rule 10b-5 would be unnecessary – insiders cannot profit from information that is already priced into the market. Even insiders cannot get better than normal returns from trading on insider information.

Empirical results of studies on EMH

(A) Tests on weak form EMH are inconclusive and debatable on interpretation grounds.

Weak form EMH states that stock prices are random and unpredictable. Past prices cannot predict future prices.

1. Early empirical studies indicate that there is little correlation between stock prices over time and the low correlation is not statistically significant.[14]
2. Later empirical studies suggest there may be some serial correlations (such as the tendency for stock returns to be related to past returns) over a short period of time.[15]
3. Later studies seem to demonstrate over a longer time frame, short-term positive serial correlations are followed by negative serial correlations and vice versa.[16] One interpretation of this result is that prices overreact to good or bad news. The overreaction is then followed by a correction in prices.
4. Other later studies also suggest that over longer time frames, extreme stock market movements tend to reverse themselves. Best performing stocks in a time period become worst performing stocks over the proceeding time period and vice versa.[17]
5. Yet other later studies imply stock market returns are predictable. For instance:
    a. Dividend yields can predict stock market returns.[18]
    b. Earnings yield also predict market returns.[19]
    c. The spread of yields between high- and low-grade bonds help predict market returns.[20]

(B) Tests on semi-strong EMH find several exceptions to the hypothesis.

Semi-strong EMH posits that all fundamental information is already reflected in stock prices. Research finds there are violations to this proposition.

1. Portfolios of low-price/earnings ratio stocks have higher average returns than high-price/earnings portfolios on a risk-adjusted basis.[21]
2. Portfolios consisting of small firms outperform large-firm portfolios on a risk-adjusted return basis by 4.3 per cent annually.[22] Subsequent studies show that most of the outperformance occurs almost exclusively in the first two weeks of January.[23] Tax-loss selling at the end of the year is the common but largely unsatisfying reason given for the small-firm effect. Investors sell loss-making stocks at the end of the year to get the benefit of tax losses. Proceeds from these sales are not reinvested into the market until the start of the New Year. Small stocks are less liquid and their prices are more likely to move up when large amounts of buy orders are initiated. The question is why this anomaly is still extant.
3. A study by Fama and French finds the ratio of the book value of a firm to the market value of its equity appears to be a predictor of returns.[24] Subsequent tests question the strength of this finding but does not refute its conclusion.[25]
4. After controlling for the size of the firm and the book value to market value effects, Fama and French further find that beta does not appear to be a predictor for returns.[26]

This empirical result is damaging to the primary assumption of modern finance theory, that is, markets are rational. According to modern finance theory, because markets are rational, returns are correlated with risk. Yet, Fama and French's results demonstrate markets are indifferent to systematic risk but are affected by book value to market value ratios – the latter in violation of strong form EMH.

5   If semi-strong form EMH is correct, new information on a firm should be absorbed relatively quickly as price adjusts to the information accordingly. Thus, better-than-expected earnings announcements should result in a jump in share price while worse-than-expected earnings announcement should result in a fall in share price. In theory prices should be affected immediately, the earnings news should then be discounted and will have no further effect on stock prices. Research finds that earnings announcement surprises do have the expected directional impact on share prices.[27] However, the effect of earnings announcement surprises on share price lingers for a much longer time than EMH predict. Cumulative abnormal returns continue for both positive and negative earnings surprise for a sustained period of time. Investors can therefore make abnormal profits by waiting for any earnings surprise, and then buy the stock of a company that announces better-than-expected earnings. This type of trade should not be possible under an efficient market paradigm.

Another study on the longevity of price effects from earnings announcement deals a further blow to semi-strong form EMH.[28] This study finds that companies with positive earnings surprises in one quarter also have higher than normal share price increases in the following quarter. This result implies the market did not adjust future earnings taking into account current earnings announcements – not an occurrence one associates with market efficiency.

(C) There is no significant empirical evidence supporting strong form EMH.

Strong form EMH states all public information including insider information is already reflected in stock prices. This version of EMH implies not just efficient markets but perfectly efficient markets.

1   Studies support the superior performance of insiders who buy and sell shares based on inside information.[29]
2   Rozeff and Zaman show that even investors who follow the direction of insider trades after information on the trades are public may enjoy superior returns.[30]

A possible problem with studies on EMH

Studies that show anomalies running counter to EMH may suffer from incorrect measurement of risk or beta. Outperformance of stock returns due to a trading strategy must be due to the strategy and not to normal beta-driven returns. Researchers must therefore determine the beta to ascertain normal returns. Any returns above the normal returns are attributed to trading strategy. Superior returns as a result of trading strategy imply inefficient markets.

If, however, beta is incorrectly measured, risk-adjusted superior returns are also incorrect. Markets may be efficient after all. While there is general agreement that some beta mis-measurement may be attributed to studies using risk-adjusted returns, many also concede the existence of anomalies that reflect market inefficiencies. In other words, there are situations that provide opportunities for abnormally high risk-adjusted returns.

Implications for EMH

The idea that markets are highly efficient no longer holds sway in numerous quarters of finance. It never persuaded a swathe of practitioners in the first place. Warren Buffet is one of the more prominent sceptics. Too much evidence has built up against EMH since the theory was first postulated. We can reasonably say markets are efficient to a certain extent — markets certainly are not perfectly efficient but they are also not wholly inefficient.

If finance were a science, the efficient market hypothesis would have been discarded in its original form and replaced with another, more robust theory, if there is one to be discovered. However, finance is not a science despite the desire of some that the discipline be so. Finance is a social science. As such financial theory is subject to the changing, equivocal, and unpredictable psychology of human groups and human individuals.

Indeed, should we even give the title of a hypothesis, such as theory, to the efficient market hypothesis? Derman prefers to categorize the idea as a model[31]. He gives a devastating critique of the efficient markets model, as he prefers to call it, and of CAPM. In the next chapter, we discuss Derman's and other critiques of EMH, CAPM, and the assumptions of modern finance theory. Chapters 5 and 6 look at alternative frameworks of finance theories.

Notes

1 Harry Markowitz, "Portfolio Selection," *Journal of Finance* 7 (1952): 77–91.
2 William F. Sharpe, "Capital Asset Prices: A Theory of Market Equilibrium Under Conditions of Risk," *Journal of Finance* 19 (1964): 425–42; John Lintner, "The Valuation of Risk Assets and the Selection of Risky Investments in S": 13–37; J. Mossin, "Equilibrium in a Capital Asset Market," *Econometrica* 34 (1966): 768–83.
3 Fischer Black and Myron Scholes, "The Pricing of Options and Corporate Liabilities," *Journal of Political Economy* 81 (1973): 637–54.
4 Eugene F. Fama, "Efficient Capital Markets: A Review of Theory and Empirical Work," *Journal of Finance* 25 (1970): 383–417.
5 Rating agencies, such as S&P, Moody, and Fitch, rate the creditworthiness of bonds.
6 Sharpe, 768–83.
7 John Lintner, "Security Prices, Risk and Maximal Gains from Diversification," *Journal of Finance* 20, No. 4 (December 1965): 587–615; J. Mossin, "Equilibrium in a Capital Asset Market," *Econometrica* 34, No. 4 (October 1966): 768–83.
8 Fischer Black, Michael C. Jensen, and Myron Scholes, "The Capital Asset Pricing Model: Some Empirical Tests," *Studies in the Theory of Capital Markets*, ed. Michael C. Jensen (New York, NY: Praeger, 1972).
9 Eugene F. Fama and James MacBeth, "Risk, Return and Equilibrium: Empirical Tests," *Journal of Political Economy* 81 (March 1973): 607–36.
10 Richard Roll, "A Critique of the Capital Asset Theory Tests: Part I: On Past and Potential Testability of the Theory," *Journal of Financial Economics* 4 (1977): 129–76.
11 Eugene F. Fama and Kenneth R. French, "The Cross Section of Expected Stock Returns," *Journal of Finance* 47 (June 1992): 427–65.
12 Stephen A. Ross, "Return, Risk and Arbitrage," *Risk and Return in Finance*, eds. I. Friend and J. Bicksler (Cambridge, MA: Ballinger, 1976).

13 Nai-fu Chen, "Some Empirical Tests of the Theory of Arbitrage Pricing," *Journal of Finance* 38 (December 1983): 1393–414; Richard Roll and Stephen A. Ross, "An Empirical Investigation of the Arbitrage Pricing Theory," *Journal of Finance* 35 (December 1980): 1073–103.
14 Harry Roberts, "Stock Market 'Patterns' and Financial Analysis: Methodological Suggestions," *Journal of Finance* 1 (March 1959): 11–25; Sidney S. Alexander, "Price Movements in Speculative Markets: Trends or Random Walks" *Industrial Management Review* (May 1961): 26; Eugene F. Fama, "The Behavior of Stock Market Prices," *Journal of Business* 38, No. 1 (January 1965): 34–105.
15 Jennifer Conrad and Gautam Kaul, "Time-Variation in Expected Returns," *Journal of Business* 61 (October 1988): 409–25; Andrew W. Lo and Craig MacKinlay, "Stock Market Prices Do Not Follow Random Walks: Evidence from a Simple Specification Test," *Review of Financial Studies* 1 (Spring 1988): 41–66.
16 Eugene F.Fama and Kenneth R. French, "Permanent and Temporary Components of Stock Prices," *Journal of Political Economy* 96 (April 1988): 246–73; James Poterba and Lawrence Summers, "Mean Reversion in Stock Prices: Evidence and Implications," *Journal of Financial Economics* 22 (October 1988): 22–59.
17 W. F. M. De Bondt and R. H. Thaler, "Does the Stock Market Overreact?" *Journal of Finance* 40 (1985): 793–805; W. F. M. De Bondt and R. H. Thaler, "Further Evidence of Investor Overreaction and Stock Market Seasonality," *Journal of Finance* 42 (1987): 557–81; Navin Chopra, Joseph Lakonishok, and Jay R. Ritter, "Measuring Abnormal Performance: Do Stocks Overreact?" *Journal of Financial Economics* 31 (1992): 235–68.
18 Eugene F. Fama and Kenneth R. French, "Dividend Yields and Expected Stock Returns," *Journal of Financial Economics* 22 (October 1988): 3–25.
19 John Y. Campbell and Robert Shiller, "Stock Prices, Earnings and Expected Dividends," *Journal of Finance* 43 (July 1988): 661–76.
20 Donald B. Keim and Robert F. Stambaugh, "Predicting Returns in the Stock and Bond Markets," *Journal of Financial Economics* 17 (1986): 357–90.
21 Sanjoy Basu, "The Investment Performance of Common Stocks in Relation to Their Price Earnings Rations: A Test of the Efficient Market Hypothesis," *Journal of Finance* 32 (June 1977): 663–82; Sanjoy Basu, "The Relationship between Earnings Yield, Market Value, and Return for NYSE Common Stocks: Further Evidence," *Journal of Financial Economics* 12 (June 1983): 129–56.
22 Rolf Banz, "The Relationship between Return and Market Value of Common Stocks," *Journal of Financial Economics* 9 (March 1981): 3–18.
23 Marshall E. Blume, and Robert F. Stambaugh, "Biases in Computed Returns: An Application to the Size Effect," *Journal of Finance Economics* (1983); 387–404; Ronald B. Keim, "Size Related Anomalies and Stock Return Seasonality: Further Empirical Evidence," *Journal of Financial Economics* 12 (June 1983): 13–32; Marc R. Reinganum, "The Anomalous Stock Market Behavior of Small Firms in January: Empirical Tests for Tax-Loss Effects," *Journal of Financial Economics* 12 (June 1983): 89–104.
24 Eugene F. Fama and Kenneth R. French, "The Cross Section of Expected Stock Returns," *Journal of Finance* 47 (June 1992): 427–65; Marc R. Reingamum, "The Anatomy of a Stock Market Winner," *Financial Analysts Journal* (March–April 1988): 272–84.
25 S. P. Kothari, Jay Shanken, and Richard G. Sloan, "Another Look at the Cross Section of Expected Stock Returns," *Journal of Finance* 50, No. 2 (March 1995): 185–224.
26 Fama and French, 430–45.
27 George Foster, Chris Olsen, and Terry Shevlin, "Earnings Releases, Anomalies, and the Behavior of Security Returns," *The Accounting Review* 59, No. 4 (October 1984): 574–603.
28 Victor L. Bernard and Jacob K. Thomas, "Post-Earnings-Announcement Drift: Delayed Price Response or Risk Premium?" *Journal of Accounting Research* 27 (1989): 1–36.
29 Jeffrey F. Jaffe, "Special Information and Insider Trading," *Journal of Business* 47 (July 1974): 410–28; Dan Givoly and Dan Palmon, "Insider Trading and Exploitation of Inside Information: Some Empirical Evidence," *Journal of Business* 58 (1985): 69–87; H. Nejat

Seyhun, "Insiders' Profits, Costs of Trading and Market Efficiency," *Journal of Financial Economics* 16 (1986): 189–212.
30 Michael S. Rozeff and Mir A. Zaman, "Market Efficiency and Insider Trading: New Evidence," *Journal of Business* (January 1988): 24–5.
31 Emanuel Derman, *Models.Behaving.Badly.: Why Confusing Illusion with Reality can Lead to Disaster, on Wall Street and in Life* (New York, NY: Free Press, 2011).

References

Bodie, Zvi, Alex Kane, and Alan Marcus, *Essentials of Investments*, 5th ed. (New York, NY: McGraw-Hill/Irwin, 2003).

Hirt, Geoffrey and Stanley Block, *Fundamentals of Investment Management*. (New York: NY: Mcgraw-Hill/Irwin, 2003).

Reilly, Frank K. and Keith C. Brown, *Investment Analysis Portfolio Management*, 7th ed. (Mason, OH: Thomson South Western, 2003).

2 Behavioural finance

2.1 A critique of modern finance theory

In Chapter 1, we described the individual theories – the time value of money, risk, and return, capital asset pricing model (CAPM), arbitrage pricing model (APT), and the efficient market hypothesis (EMH) that together make up what we call modern finance theory (MFT). In the first part of this chapter we offer a detailed critique of MFT. It is wise to comprehend the limitations of financial theories that have become important in practice and, consequently, affect the lives of billions. We follow this critique with an account of the benefits of MFT, which are many, if we use MFT with an understanding of its shortcomings.

Theory versus model

The initial critique of MFT is definitional. The word 'theory' is not aptly applied to the groups of suppositions and ideas posited in the field of finance. If finance puts itself forward as a science, then its theories must, therefore, meet the standards applied to scientific theories. Thus, financial theories must have predictive value. The theories should also be verifiable and, according to Karl Popper, falsifiable. Once falsified, the existing theory should be modified or, if modification is impossible, completely scrapped.

Financial theories do not meet any of these criteria. They have little predictive value; otherwise we would be able to forecast future stock prices with greater accuracy than we currently do, and financial crashes would not occur. Indeed, humans have been attempting to predict the prices of financial assets for centuries but with little success. 'It is a fact that no one is very good at predicting stock prices.'[1] Thus, one fact EMH retells is this: we cannot predict future stock prices based on the information we have today. As this proposition is a truism, it is not controversial. Other propositions of EMH are more debatable, and we shall discuss them later.

In terms of falsifiability, if we take the example of EMH, we observe empirical evidence has disproved the theory time and again (see Chapter 1). If EMH were a scientific theory, it would have been discarded or improved 20 years ago. Yet, EMH continues to be somewhat blithely used, at least in the finance academy.

In contrast, scientific theories describe how the world works. For instance, the laws of thermodynamics have predictive value and have not been falsified. We can go on with examples: the law of gravity, Boyle's law of ideal gases, laws of motion, electromagnetic theory, and so on. We find the laws of science are not contingent but unconditional. In science, we have a level of certainty that is not even closely reached in finance. For example, the speed of light in a vacuum – 299,792,458 metres per second – is a physical constant; but what really is the fair value of a financial asset?

In truth, finance is not a science; it is a social science. The subjects of social science are humans. The subject of finance is essentially human behaviour as reflected in the markets and prices. As writers have noted, the human heart is inconstant and does not lend itself to capture by hard theories.

Perhaps a better term to use instead of theory is the one Emanuel Derman finds more appropriate. He refers to the system of ideas in finance not as theories but as models. Hence, the efficient market hypothesis becomes the efficient market model.[2] Theories describe the actual world; how it works, why it works the way it does, and how it will work. In contrast, according to Derman, models are analogies. MFT takes the approach where a world, not the one we live in, is postulated. An elegant mathematical framework is then built based upon this postulated world. This framework becomes the financial analogy of the real world. Thus, the efficient market hypothesis is a model of a hypothetical world instead of a correct hypothesis about the actual world.

Analogical reasoning is by no means disreputable. However, philosophers generally regard this type of reasoning as the weakest because there is no perfect analogy. For example we can analogize the Great Recession of 2008 with the Depression of 1932. The solution for getting out of the 1932 Depression was through Keynesian motivated government spending. The reasoning is that if these two dire economic problems are analogous, then the solution that worked for one problem should also work for the other. Thus, the solution to emerging from the Great Recession is also government spending. The weakness in this argument is, of course, that while the two economic events are similar, they are not identical. The solution, therefore, may not work. So when MFT uses the results obtained from its models and infers these results also should be happening in the actual world, the inference may be wrong because we derive the inference through analogical reasoning.

We can now see how the use of the terms 'model' versus 'theory' does have underlying implications because of what these terms actually signify. This critique of the definitional significance is a critique of the *methodology* of MFT. Another important criticism of MFT points at the *assumptions* of this system of ideas.

Assumptions and simplifications

Both EMH and CAPM create a world based on a number of assumptions. In this assumed world, the models begin with current views about the future. These views are plugged into the model, which then moves us back into the present to estimate current values.[3] The two weaknesses in this approach are first that the derived values are only as good as the perceived views of the future, and second, the perceptions are those of humans and are subjective.

Efficient market hypothesis

EMH assumes new information arrives uniformly, in small, steady increments. The new information causes stock prices to either fall or rise depending if the news is good or bad. However, this assumption does not accord with reality. Sometimes the news is so big and important that the stock price surges or plunges. In a market panic, selling pressure is intense and positive feedback loops start operating, so a fall in price leads to a bigger fall in price, and so on. Instead of rationality driving the price, fear decides price movements.

These types of events are not rare but do not fit into the efficient markets model of the smooth random walk.

The assumed behaviour of stock prices in the EMH is called a random walk or diffusion. The model expects stock prices to appreciate through time at an average rate of μ per year. This appreciation is called the stock price drift. As we already know from previous discussions, the movement up and down from the stock price trend, or drift, is called the volatility, represented by σ. According to EMH, the net volatility increases slowly, proportional to the square root of time, while the average rate of return increases faster over the same period because it is a product of time (μt). The higher the volatility, the larger the σ. In EMH, volatility is the measure of the uncertainty of returns of a stock. It is the measure of risk. A questionable assumption in EMH is the one it makes on how risk grows over time, summarized here by Derman:

> If you think of risk as the quantifiable uncertainty of imagined returns, then a key result of the EMM is that risk grows comparatively slowly, as the square root of time. Suppose you expect a stock to earn 30% in one year with a volatility of 10 percentage points. All circumstances being equal during the second year, you will correctly expect to earn double the return, 60% over two years. Counter intuitively, at least until you get used to the EMM [Efficient Market Model], you should not expect the uncertainty of the returns to double to 20%. After two years the uncertainty in returns is only its square root, about 14 percentage points. Risk grows more slowly in the model, though not necessarily in life itself.[4]

The model of how stock prices move as a random walk in the EMH is simply how we impose a framework on stock price movements, not necessarily what actually happens.

Surely it is too simplistic to conceptualize the risk of all stocks in the market being condensed into a single number. The other questionable assumption about risk EMH makes is that there is one risk such as the risk of volatility, σ. The risk of every stock in the market is condensed into this quantity. As we all know, there are more risks in the world than just mere volatility. EMH assumes one risk over the universe of financial assets. Yet, can we safely assume that stock risk, bond risk, currency risk, and commodity risk are one and the same? Similarly, risk may differ across sectors and industries so that the risk of the technology sector may not be the same risk as that of the utility sector. In addition, EMH ignores the risks that arise from the extreme greed and the irrational fear of crowds. As we experienced during the financial crash of 2008, liquidity dries up as fear overwhelms the market and counterparties fail together. EMH, therefore, simplifies complexity at a significant measure of loss to accuracy.

In choosing to model stock price movements as a random walk, EMH produces a result that shows stock prices moving too smoothly compared to observed movements of actual stock prices. Actual stock prices are more wildly random than those of the model. We see that happening in stock market crashes. We should note at this point that we obtain the value of sigma, mu, and lambda of stocks through the use of historical data. These values are calculated historically, looking backwards rather than forwards in time. This is another weakness of MFT.

EMH tells us what amount of return we demand for a certain amount of risk. Yet, a financial theory cannot dictate what return an investor should expect in exchange for taking on risk. The expectation depends on appetite and varies over time. We discuss the problem of assuming risk to be the same as uncertainty later in this section.

Capital asset pricing model (CAPM)

We criticize EMH for assuming only one risk that embodies all risks, arguing that this assumption is unrealistic. CAPM is an attempt to counter this criticism because it posits not one but two types of risk. CAPM is an extension of EMH but handles the issue of risk more realistically because it considers the risk of individual stocks and the risk of the entire stock market. Each stock has two kinds of risk embedded in it: (1) systematic, or market risk, which is the overall risk that affects everything in the market and (2) unsystematic risk, or risk that is independent of the market but specific to that particular stock. As we have seen in our discussion of CAPM in Chapter 1, systematic risk or its beta is unavoidable and is therefore the risk we should be rewarded for taking. Unsystematic risk can be diversified away by buying a portfolio of stocks whose specific risks cancel each other out. Therefore, in a diversified portfolio, a stock is theoretically affected by only the market risk.

Before proceeding, a further recap on what we learnt about CAPM in Chapter 1 may be useful. The beta of each stock describes its tendency to follow market price movements. The greater the beta of a stock, the more it responds to a market move. According to CAPM, the risk of any investment is measured against the beta of the market to determine if the returns should be higher or lower. If we plot the expected return of an individual stock versus the return of the market over a number of periods, we get a straight line represented by the formula:

$$R_i = R_f + \beta R_M + c$$

Where

R_i = Expected return of the individual stock i
R_f = the expected risk-free return
β = the slope of the line
R_M = market return
c = the random error term

The formula indicates how volatile the individual stock is relative to the market through the beta coefficient. When β is 1.5 say, if the market moves up by certain percentage points, the individual stock is calculated to move 1.5 times that amount. In other words, *beta measures the correlation of an individual stock's total return to the return of the market portfolio.*

The beta of the market will always be 1.0, as it is the correlation of the return of the market portfolio to itself.

Another way of stating the relationship of a stock's expected return to the beta of the stock is:

$$\text{Risk premium of security} = \beta(R_M - R_f)$$

or

$$R_i - R_f = \beta(R_M - R_f)$$

We can test the validity of this equation easily. Use a stock to demonstrate if this equation works out in reality. For example, we can use China Mobile, traded in Hong Kong.

China Mobile

Ri from 13 April 2013 to 13 April 2014 = (10.07)%R_M (Hang Seng Index returns) over the same period = 4.14%

$\beta = 0.984$

R_f(HIBOR) = 0.842%

Substituting into the CAPM formula $R_i - R_f = \beta (R_M - R_f)$ we get:

0.1007 − 0.00842 = 0.984(0.0414 − 0.00842)

(0.10912) = 0.984(0.03298) *or* 0.03245

But clearly, 10.91 per cent is not equal to 3.25 per cent.

In numerous examples, the two sides of the equation do not match up. Why? We may argue that the time period of one year is too short. On average, CAPM holds over long periods of time. The period under consideration may be a statistical fluctuation.

Another reason for the outcome of the testing is that we should be considering other risks, such as industry-specific risks, or risks associated with the group into which our stock belongs. If this argument is true, it already shows an inadequacy of CAPM, as the model does not consider other risks outside the market risk. Industry risk, small-cap risk, and growth-stock risk are supposedly subsumed into market risk. In any case, we see that CAPM is not constantly reliable.

Research on the reliability of the risk and return relationship put forward by CAPM shows mixed results. Douglas found the intercepts on the y-axis to be higher than the prevailing risk-free rates.[5] Sharpe and Cooper found a positive relationship between return and risk, although the relationship was not completely linear.[6] Fama and MacBeth found the risk and return relationship appeared to hold over time but not on a monthly basis.[7] A 1992 study by Fama and French was more detrimental to CAPM especially because Fama was a supporter of CAPM.[8] This study found the relationship between beta and the average rate of return did not hold from 1963–90. Their tests did show, however, that average returns seemed to be related to size and book-to-market equity – a positive relationship exists between return and book-to-market ratio and a negative relationship between return and size. Fama and French conclude that between 1963–90, beta was not related to average returns on stocks when other variables are considered, and also when considered alone. They suggest using a three-factor model of CAPM. A couple of subsequent studies show contrary results to Fama and French's study.[9] Perhaps the most damaging conclusion to the series of CAPM tests was made by Fama and French in 2004 – that the power of variables other than beta to explain average returns invalidates most of CAPM applications. They specifically reject using the CAPM to estimate the cost of equity capital and to evaluate performance of mutual fund managers.[10] Thus, in the end, we are left with no consistent, incontrovertible evidence that the risk and return relationship dictated by CAPM is enduringly true.

The market portfolio

One reason given why expected returns do not seem to be linearly related to betas as CAPM predicts is that studies do not use the true, universal market portfolio. We need

46   *Three finance paradigms*

to measure returns on a cap-weighted world portfolio that includes all assets. This task of creating a true market portfolio may be herculean.

Indeed, a significant critique of CAPM is the tricky question of what constitutes a market portfolio in practice, which in turn determines beta values. Should we, as commonly done in US textbooks on investment management, take the Standard & Poor's (S&P) Index of stocks to be the default market portfolio? Why should we not use instead the Morgan Stanley World Stock Index? If we are measuring the beta of a stock in Malaysia, should we not use a market portfolio that makes up the latter index rather than the stocks that go to make up Bursa Malaysia, the main index of the Kuala Lumpur stock exchange?

In theory the market portfolio includes all the risky assets in the economy. In addition, the assets are weighted in the portfolio according to their market value. Theoretically, therefore, the market portfolio should contain US stocks and bonds, non-US stocks and bonds, real estate, options, art, stamps, gold, and so on, with weights equal to their market value.

The idea of a market portfolio works fine in theory but is difficult if not impossible to implement when using the CAPM.[11] If we use the wrong market portfolio, we will derive an inappropriate beta against which to measure any alternative portfolio. The majority of studies involving CAPM choose the S&P 500 Index as their proxy market portfolio. The assumption is that the S&P 500 Index is highly correlated with the market portfolio.

A study by Reilly and Akhtar show the substantial difference in average betas for the 30 stocks in the Dow Jones Industrial Average during three different periods, with the use of three different indices to represent the market portfolio.[12] Reilly and Akhtar used the S&P 500 Index, the Morgan Stanley World Index, and the Brinson Partners Global Security Market Index (GSMI). The results show the security market line based off the proxy market portfolios to be completely different from the theoretical or 'true' market portfolio line. Average betas over all three periods were different for all three proxy market portfolios, as were mean index returns, and the standard deviation of index returns.

Table 2.1 Average beta for the 30 stocks in the DJIA for alternative time periods using different indexes as proxies for the market

Time period	S&P 500	MS World	Brinson GSMI
1983–1988			
Average beta	0.820	0.565	1.215
Mean index return	0.014	0.017	0.014
Standard deviation of index returns	0.049	0.043	0.031
1989–1994			
Average beta	0.991	0.581	1.264
Mean index return	0.010	0.004	0.008
Standard deviation of index returns	0.036	0.043	0.026
1983–1994			
Average beta	0.880	0.606	1.223
Mean index return	0.012	0.011	0.011
Standard deviation of index returns	0.043	0.043	0.029

Source: Frank K. Reilly and Keith C. Brown.[13]

Market proxies obviously affect the calculation of betas as well as standard deviation. The question of which is the best proxy for a particular security is debatable. Portfolio managers can select the market proxy that shows their performance in the best light.

Research on beta

We can test the stability of betas derived from the CAPM model. For example, Levy found beta for the 500 NYSE stocks to be unstable for individual stocks over 52 weeks, a short period. However, the stability of the beta for portfolios of stocks was higher than for a single stock.[14] In general, if the portfolio of stocks is large with 25 or 50 stocks, the beta is more stable. Other studies on portfolio size also tend to confirm the stability of beta increases substantially as portfolio size increases.[15]

Periods over 26 weeks also tend to produce more stable beta. Other studies by Baesel[16] and Altman, Jacquillat, and Levasseur[17] appear to support Levy's results with regard to the stability of beta increasing with length of the period being studied. Theobald states the optimal length of time for improved stability could be over 120 months, assuming the beta did not shift during the period.

Studies on beta stability have generally reached the same conclusion: individual betas are generally volatile over time while betas for portfolios tend to be stable. In the case of time periods, at least 36 months of data are needed to attain some level of stability.[18]

Published data of beta

There is little agreement in published estimates of beta. For example, Statman found little agreement in the value of beta published by various sources.[19] He used the Value Line Investment Survey and Merrill Lynch's Security Risk Evaluation Report. Both services use the same market model equation to calculate beta:

$$R_i = R_f + \beta R_M + c$$

Merrill Lynch estimates the beta using 60 monthly observations and the S&P 500 Index as the market proxy, while the Value Line estimates beta using 260 weekly observations and uses the NYSE composite series as the market proxy. Statman found the betas of the two sources showed no equality. Similarly, Reilly and Wright confirmed the dissimilarity of beta using a sample of over 1,100 securities for three non-overlapping periods.[20]

Other empirical tests that refute MFT

Thompson *et al.* carried out a data analysis to some of the portfolio selection of Markowitz and demonstrated the Markowitzian assumption of positive correlation of expected return and volatility is not supported by the data.[21] The study plots risk versus returns for 75 years (1926–2000) of one of the oldest large capitalization indices, the Ibbotson. The correlation is –0.317, negative rather than positive. The authors note, 'Clearly, the investors, operating rationally in the aggregate as the EMH supposes, see factors in the market beyond μ and σ'.[22]

According to Markowitz portfolio theory, all investors should hold the market portfolio because it should not be possible to create a portfolio lying above the capital market line (CML). According to the theory, one should simply invest in a passive basket of stocks that mimic the relevant index. Wojciechowski and Thompson did a long-term analysis of every year starting from 1970 to 2002. The survey has 50,000 portfolios consisting of random selections of stocks from the 1,000 highest market cap securities.[23] The research found 63 per cent of the portfolios selected randomly from the 1,000 largest market cap stocks lies above the CML. They conclude that index funds do not outperform managed funds because they represent the market portfolio, thus validating Markowitz's portfolio theory, as the theory's advocates advertise. Instead, index funds have outperformed managed funds because the latter have generally been poorly managed.

The Black–Scholes options pricing model also has been subject to empirical tests. Looking at historical data, Thompson *et al.* observe the Black–Scholes price for an option seldom agrees with the actual price quoted on the ticker.[24] The 'out' given by Black–Scholes proponents is not to use the actual market price of the option but to use the actual price in the Black–Scholes equation and solve for the 'implied volatility'. This move creates a strong circularity of argument and protects the Black–Scholes result from criticisms based on empirical results. Yet, according to Thompson *et al.*, 'For two different strike prices with the same date of execution, we typically get two different values of implied volatility'.[25] Once again, as with other models in MFT, empirical evidence seems to show a disturbing lack of accuracy in the options pricing model.

The lending and borrowing assumption

Before we embark on the task of determining a cap-weighted universal portfolio, we should note other assumptions of CAPM might make the effort unnecessary. According to Markowitz, CAPM has two related assumptions that (1) investors can lend all they have or can borrow all they want at the risk-free rate, and (2) investors can sell short without limit and use the proceeds of the sale to buy long positions are not realistic.[26]

Yet, in the real world, when investors borrow, they will pay more than the risk-free rate of interest and the amount of credit extend is limited to what lenders believe borrowers can repay. With regard to selling short, investors are not allowed an unlimited amount of shorting. Assumptions (1) and (2) are, therefore, unrealistic.

Markowitz contends if assumptions (1) and (2) do not hold in the real world, then the conclusion CAPM makes about the market portfolio being a mean-variance efficient portfolio no longer holds.[27] Indeed, the departure from efficiency can be 'quite substantial', so much so that 'the market portfolio can be about as inefficient as a feasible portfolio can get'.[28] When borrowing is limited, and short sales are prohibited or subject to real-world constraints, the composition of the portfolio of risky securities at one end of the efficient frontier is different from the composition at the other end. At the top end, the efficient frontier generally contains few securities, with more of the securities having higher expected returns. At the low end, the frontier has more diversified, low volatility securities.

In addition, when we do assume (1) and (2), the relationship of return to risk is linear. When the assumption is replaced by a more realistic description of the investor's investment constraints, the linear relationship between risk and return no longer follows. If this linear relationship is questionable, the reliability of its use in risk adjustment must also be questioned.

Further critiques of MFT's assumptions

During the 50-year history of MFT, CAPM's equilibrium pricing model was conjoined with EMH, which together are sometimes called the 'joint hypothesis'. As described earlier, tests done on EMH studying market efficiency over time showed anomalies, indicating little support for the theory. However, with the joint hypothesis, it was important that EMH be right. Consequently, when tests on the joint hypothesis repeatedly showed empirical failure, the blame is placed on CAPM but not the EMH.[29] Yet, 'there are so many holes in the [EMH] research that only the most dogmatic professors still accept what was commonly taken as absolute "truth" 20 years ago'.[30]

Risk assumptions

Risk in MFT has become equated with uncertainty. According to MFT, we can determine risk and therefore uncertainty. This assumption is a big one and unsupported by logic. According to Findlay *et al.*, in statistics, we have certainty, where the outcome of all future events are known and the probability of a known outcome is equal to one.[31] We can also have a situation of risk, where future events can have multiple outcomes, but we are able to assign probabilities to the outcomes. In a scenario of uncertainty, neither events nor outcomes are known. We cannot assign probabilities under scenarios of uncertainty. It would be a meaningless exercise.[32] These distinctions were already made by Frank Knight[33] and John Keynes[34] long before the 1950s.

Most reasonable people will agree we live in an uncertain world, which includes financial markets and their participants. MFT models the world as if it were a world of risk and not one of uncertainty. In other words, the models assume that probabilities can be assigned to outcomes. Risk is assumed to be uncertainty. Under this assumption, we are then able to make 'true' probability distributions in an uncertain (= risky) world.

With the assignation of probabilities we are able to arrive at expected returns, which we then use to calculate risk, or σ. By knowing sigma we can then derive risk premiums. In MFT, expected returns are equated with ex-ante returns. In turn, ex-ante returns are used to derive current values. We can see that the edifice of risk and return in MFT is built on the questionable assumption that risk is the same as uncertainty.

But uncertainty is not the same as risk. Under uncertainty, we do not know all future events or all their possible outcomes. We do not know the probabilities of all the unknowable outcomes and that these probabilities sum to one. It is, therefore, unrealistic to assume the correct probability distributions of everything until the world ends.[35]

Without knowledge of future events, outcomes and their probabilities, true future probability distributions cannot be obtained. Expected returns cannot, therefore, be computed. Deviations about risk cannot be derived.

> Equilibrium (beyond the simple market clearing at a point in time, temporary equilibrium, which has none of the other attributes of equilibrium) is simply an undefined concept in a world of true uncertainty. If it is granted that correct future probability distributions do not exist nor can their expectations be computed, it must also be granted that the future returns for stocks (or portfolios) may not be expressed in μ, σ space ... Such statistics may surely be computed historically; but lacking the neoclassical assumptions of both risk and stationarity (e.g., the return generating process), no necessary link (no less ex ante = ex post, at least stochastically) exists.[36]

Neoclassical assumptions of MFT

Overlying these specific assumptions are the larger ones MFT takes from neoclassical economics. The primary assumption is: economic agents are rational. Human rationality in the neoclassical view pursues a single goal – maximizing utility.

MFT makes five major assumptions:

1. Economic agents are always rational.
    Interestingly, ethics went through this phase with Kant's theory, which holds human reason as the final arbiter of moral values. Kant sought to refute David Hume – a Scottish philosopher and contemporary of Adam Smith, who proposes human emotions as the final arbiter of moral values. Contrast this situation with the one finance finds itself in at the moment. MFT assumes economic agents are always rational. However, Behavioural Finance Theory now tries to refute this assumption by taking greater account of emotions.
2. Rational agents are self-interested.
3. Rational agents only aim to maximize utility.
4. Utility or preference can be distilled to just one thing, economic utility or profits.
5. Thus, rational agents aim to maximize profits

These assumptions are accepted credo in free market capitalist systems. Yet, these assumptions were made to simplify a complex world to help finance researchers develop predictive models of a small portion of the world they were studying.

Are they correct assumptions? Yes, in a limited, qualified, view of the world and of humanity. Humans are rational, except when they are not. Have you ever 'cut off your nose to spite your face'? Experiments show people are not only motivated solely by profit but also by values such as fairness. Individuals are willing to punish unfair behaviour, even at some cost to their self-interest. Are we always and only economic agents? Or are we also parents, artists, teachers, friends, etc.?

Of course, applying MFT and its assumptions has resulted in much good for humanity. But like any theory, in science, or philosophy, theories must change when empirical evidence shows them to be flawed or inadequate.

Consequences of MFT on ethics

What have been the consequences of these assumptions? With the passage of time and constant use, ironically the assumptions have evolved into an ethic.

Thus:

1. Assume we are rational agents.
2. As rational agents, assume we maximize profits.
3. From the second point it is a short intellectual leap to, we *do* maximize profits, to
4. We *should* maximize profits.[37]

Consequently, *the assumption has become the ethic*. Hence, we arrive at the current state of knowledge in finance where, despite protestations by MFT proponents of the value neutral stance of the theory, the MFT ethic is to maximize profits.

Indeed, the assumptions of profit maximization behaviour and an all-knowing, providential market have replaced our need for ethics in finance. This 50-year or so process has led to the current conventional wisdom, ideology, and culture that ethics is inconsequential to Finance.

The upshot

What do we make of these studies on EMH and CAPM? First, these theories do not have empirical backing and as such are unreliable. They help us frame complex and uncertain market behaviour but they are not predictive. They are not scientific theories. Die-hard proponents of MFT maintain we should refine the models, not discard them. The rational pricing interpretation of these studies argues that a more sophisticated asset pricing model is needed. The three-factor model that incorporates company size and book-to-market equity values mentioned earlier captures variations in asset returns that CAPM misses.

In contrast, behaviourists maintain the results of tests of CAPM are evidence of irrational pricing caused by overreaction. Even with the three-factor model, it is impossible to tell whether the problem in explaining returns is because of irrational pricing or rational pricing in an incomplete model.

2.2 Behavioural finance

Introduction and description

Behavioural finance is the study of individual and group behaviour, with a basis in psychology and in financial decision-making. The goal is a better understanding of security returns. By implication, the subject rejects the key assumption of modern finance theory that (1) decision-makers are rational and (2) the only definition of rationality is utility maximization. For the sake of simplicity and quantification, modern finance theory takes no account of human psychology. This neglect, argues behavioural finance proponents, leads to the many anomalies in security pricing still not explained by the models of conventional finance.

One of the main tasks that behavioural finance has taken on is to explain these pricing anomalies using theories of human behaviour. In contrast to modern finance theory, behavioural finance has as its underlying assumption the characteristics of market participants that systematically influence individuals' decisions as well as market outcomes. It is important to stress the systematic influence of investor behaviour. EMH assumes that a large number of irrational investors with uncorrelated trading strategies cancel each other out. In such a market, trading volume is significant but because irrational investors trade with each other, prices in the market still remain close to fundamental values. In sum, unsystematic behavioural biases average out to zero across people. The behavioural finance approach to asset pricing postulates, however, that rules of thumb or heuristics and psychological biases are systematic and they do move prices away from fundamental values.

Remember, the efficient market hypothesis rests on three arguments. First, investors are rational and value securities rationally. Second, even if some investors are not rational, their trades are random and consequently cancel each other out without affecting prices. Third, even if the trades are irrational in a systematic way, rational arbitrageurs counter these trades and eliminate the influence of irrational investors on prices.

This chapter describes the behavioural finance theories, research, and empirical evidence that refute the first two arguments supporting EMH. The two major theories in behavioural finance are prospect theory and heuristics and biases theory. Both theories argue that people in general, and investors in particular, are not fully rational. The chapter describes the main arguments given by these theories and the experimental evidence supporting the arguments. The evidence from behavioural finance demonstrates that the deviation of investor behaviour from the rational is highly pervasive and systematic. Thus, the psychological evidence shows that investors not only behave irrationally but the irrationality is systematic rather than random. Following the descriptions of the theories and their corroborating evidence, the chapter goes into the theories' implications for financial markets and investors. The last section of the chapter gives a brief summary of the mounting evidence countering the third argument supporting EMH. In contrast to the EMH, behavioural finance argues that real-world arbitrage is risky and therefore limited. Finally, the chapter ends with suggestions for further work behavioural finance needs to do to strengthen and broaden the field.

History

Scholars generally recognize Daniel Kahneman and Amos Tversky's article on prospect theory in 1979 as the seminal work on behavioural finance. Both men are psychologists by training. Prospect theory is an alternative to expected utility theory, which describes decision-making under risk. Their work on prospect theory eventually earned Kahneman the Nobel Prize in Economics in 2002. Tversky was not eligible for the Nobel Prize as its rules prohibit posthumous awards (he died in 1996 at the age of 59.) The message in awarding the prize in economics to a psychologist is probably not lost to financial economists. Indeed, the Royal Swedish Academy stated that Kahneman was awarded the prize, 'for having integrated insights from psychological research into economic science, especially concerning human judgement and decision-making under uncertainty'.[38] The award certainly gave needed authority and respectability to behavioural finance.

This perspective was not always the case. Behavioural research in finance began with accounting. The research went through a cycle of rising, declining, and then rising again in the 1990s. Behavioural research in financial accounting started in the late 1960s. Ray Ball and Phil Brown showed that the market responded sharply to earnings announcement and the response lasted for many months.[39] The post-earnings announcement drift (Chapter 1) contradicts the efficient market hypothesis. While finance researchers at that time, who were still captured by modern finance theories, paid little attention to the results, behavioural researchers continued to conduct research on how auditors were affected by the order in which information is presented or whether the information includes irrelevant details.

As the research on behavioural financial accounting began to grow, traditional finance researchers began pointing to the deficiencies of the research. Gonedes and Dopuch argued behavioural research focused on the behaviour of the individual, whereas in an efficient market, equilibrium is attained by the system as whole and aggregate market behaviour, not by the actions of a single individual. Lab and field studies could not simulate the whole market with the competition among sources of information. Behavioural research of individuals was, therefore, irrelevant.[40] It became clear that academic research in behavioural finance would not advance the career of researchers. Instead these researchers worked on studying the behaviour of individual managers and auditors while receiving funding by public accounting firms.

Top journals in accounting were averse to publishing behavioural papers in financial reporting until the mid-1990s. The reason for the change was first, the growing evidence that markets were not efficient and second, technological advances allowed experimental researchers to address the criticism of Gonedes and Dopuch. Behaviourists who had been conducting research in other areas were able to shift their focus to financial reporting when the top journals were more amenable to publishing behavioural-centred work.

Especially since the award of the Nobel Prize to Kahneman, behavioural finance research has become acceptable and commonplace. There are specialist journals devoted to behavioural finance such as the *Journal of Behavioral Finance*. Indeed, the founding of the Academy of Behavioral Finance and Economics in 2008 brings the discipline into the mainstream of academic finance.

Prospect theory

Daniel Kahneman and Amos Tversky developed prospect theory, and their paper on the topic was published in *Econometrica* in 1979.[41] The paper is frequently cited as it is the seminal work on prospect theory and, indeed, behavioural finance. Kahneman and Tversky propose prospect theory as an alternative to subjective expected utility theory (EUT). The name of the theory comes from decision-making under risk as a choice between prospects or gambles.

Prospect theory distinguishes two phases when an individual goes through the process of making a choice.[42] The first phase is an early phase of editing. The second phase is that of evaluation. In the editing phase, a decision-maker analyses the prospects or choices on offer, and edits, or simplifies the representation of these choices. In the evaluation phase, the edited prospects are evaluated and the one with the highest value is chosen.

Before prospect theory the unquestioned theory on decision-making under risk and uncertainty was EUT. Even today, EUT is the dominant theory on decision-making and widely used for describing and predicting rational choice behaviour. Yet, the assumptions of human behaviour made in EUT are the same as the ones made in neoclassical economics, that is, human behaviour is rational and rationality is narrowly defined as being utility maximizing. Consequently, these assumptions hobble the predictive power of EUT and its failure in predictions is well proven. EUT is the basis of mean variance theory in finance, which in turn underlies Markowitz's modern portfolio theory. A critique of EUT is, therefore, a critique of modern portfolio theory.

Kahneman and Tversky's paper critiques EUT, arguing it is not an adequate descriptive model because according to the result of their studies on decision-making, the tenets of EUT are violated. The tenets of EUT are:

1 Individuals choose among alternatives based on the expected utility of outcomes or final states. The outcome is the final levels of their wealth and not gains or losses. EUT assumes individuals do not have a reference point because the initial state of wealth does not enter into the decision-making process.
2 Individuals are risk-averse in all their choices. They are risk-averse when facing either losses or gains. Risk aversion is equivalent to the concavity of the utility function.
3 Individuals treat risk objectively and weigh the outcomes by using the probability of each outcome.
4 Framing of alternatives does not affect choices of individuals.

54   *Three finance paradigms*

In contrast, prospect theory makes the following claims:

1   Individuals choose based on the changes in their wealth relative to a reference point. Thus, they do not choose based on the outcome in their final level of wealth but on losses or gains.
2   Individuals are risk-averse when all changes in wealth are perceived as gains, and are risk seeking when all changes in wealth are perceived as losses. Individuals put a greater weight on losses than they do on gains of equal amounts. The term Kahneman and Tversky use for this asymmetry between perceptions of gains and losses is 'loss aversion'.[43]
3   Individuals overweight small probabilities. The probability weighting function $\pi(p)$ is not the same as probability p.
4   Framing of alternatives affects the choices made by individuals.

(1) Gains and losses

People normally perceive outcomes as gains or losses, rather than as final states of wealth. Kahneman and Tversky argue that this feature of prospect theory is compatible with basic principles of perception and judgement, 'Our perceptual apparatus is attuned to the evaluation of changes or differences rather than to the evaluation of absolute magnitudes ... The same level of wealth, for example, may imply abject poverty for one person and great riches for another – depending on their current assets'.[44] People view gains and losses relative to a reference point. The reference point is generally the current asset position. (In experimental situations, respondents who are volunteer subjects start with a current asset position of zero. Therefore, the gains and losses coincide with actual amounts received or paid.)

Kahneman and Tversky's methodology was to ask volunteer test subjects to choose between various alternatives. For instance, imagine you have a concurrent choice within two pairs (A vs. B and C vs. D), where:

A: 4,000 with a probability of 80%   B: 3,000 for sure

C: –4,000 with a probability of 80%   D: –3,000 for sure

Kahneman and Tversky used the Israeli currency as the unit of measure. A significantly greater number of people chose B than A, and a significantly greater number of people chose C than D. This result violates EUT and mean-variance theory that assumes investors are always risk-averse and never risk-seeking.

According to the results, the preference between the negative prospects is the mirror image of the preference between positive prospects. The reflection of prospects around zero reverses the preference order. Kahneman and Tversky call this pattern the reflection effect.

The results imply risk aversion in situations where there is gain and risk-seeking in situations where there is loss. More people chose C over D, even though C had a lower expected value and meant a loss of 3,200, whereas D was a loss of 3,000. Conversely, in the scenario where the prospects were positive gains, a significant majority of people was risk-averse, preferring the choice of a certain 3,000 to a larger gain that is merely probable. These results are inconsistent with EUT and mean-variance models, according to which people are always risk-averse, never risk-seeking, and will choose to maximize utility. However, in the experiment above, outcomes that are certain are overweighted relative to uncertain outcomes. In situations of positive gain, there is a risk-averse preference for a sure gain over a larger, probable gain. When losses are involved, outcomes that are certain are also overweighted relative to uncertain outcomes. However, behaviour becomes risk-seeking as there is a preference for a loss that is probable over a smaller loss that is certain. In brief, 'The same psychological principle – the overweighting of certainty – favours risk aversion in the domain of gains and risk seeking in the domain of losses'.[45]

(2) The value function

The aversion to risk in the realm of positive gains and the seeking of risk in the realm of negative losses is represented in a value function that reflects changes in states of wealth from a given (subjective) reference point. A kink occurs in the value function. In addition, the slope of the value function is steeper for losses than for gains by a factor of 2 to 2.5 times (Figure 2.1: the Kahneman–Tversky value function). In prospect theory, losses are weighted more than gains. The value function has an S shape, being concave in the positive domain and convex in the negative domain, indicating risk aversion in the positive domain and risk-seeking in the negative domain. The slopes of the two sections of the S curve reflect the assumption (based on experimental evidence) that on average the disutility from losing a given value is always greater than the utility from gaining an identical value.[46] Thus, according to the Kahneman–Tversky value function, an individual will reject a prospect where the monetary gain exceeds a monetary loss because of a net loss in utility. This outcome is not predicted in EUT.

In addition, the concavity of the value function in the positive domain and the convexity in the negative domain reflects the principle that the psychological response is a concave function of the magnitude of physical or monetary change. Thus, in human psychology, the difference between a gain of 1,000 to a gain of 2,000 appears to be greater than the difference between a gain of 101,000 and a gain of 102,000. Similarly, the difference between a loss of 1,000 and a loss of 2,000 appears greater than the difference between a loss of 101,000 and a loss of 102,000, unless the larger loss is intolerable.

Comparing the Kahneman–Tversky value function to EUT, the latter's utility function is in the positive domain only. Gains and losses are assumed to be equal with regard to utility. The concavity of the EUT function represents the assumption that utility is estimated in terms of states of wealth where marginal increases in wealth are subject to diminishing returns. The reference point of EUT is the objective origin where the state of wealth is zero (Figure 2.2: the expected utility function). Note that the S-shaped value function for prospect theory is steepest at the reference point, in contrast to the utility function, which is shallow in that region.

In EUT, choices are based on probability weights of outcomes. In prospect theory, decision weights replace probability weights. Decision weights are a measure of an individual's psychological and emotional assessment of probabilities. Extremely low-probability events are given a weight of zero, whereas extremely high-probability events receive a weight of one. Individuals use a heuristic that results in assuming a tiny probability event as impossible, while a high-probability event is assumed to be a certainty.

However, individuals place too much weight on low-probability events, exaggerating the likelihood that the event will happen. Conversely, individuals place too little weight

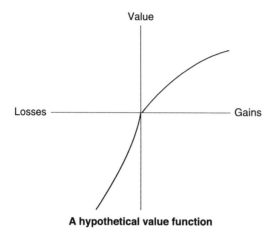

Figure 2.1 The Kahneman–Tversky value function.

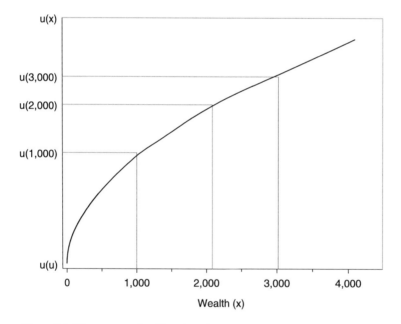

Figure 2.2 The expected utility function.

on moderate and high-probability events. When prospects are uncertain, individuals underestimate the likelihood of the prospect occurring.

In prospect theory, the value of each outcome is multiplied by a decision weight. Decision weights are subjective weights between prospects. They are not probabilities and do not obey probability rules.

Consider a prospect with two outcomes: x with probability p, and y with probability $1 - p$; where $x \geq 0 \geq y$. W is the initial level of wealth and the reference point. According to EUT, the value of this prospect is:

$$V = pu(W + x) + (1 - p)u(W + y)$$

According to prospect theory, the value of the prospect is:

$$V = \pi(p)u(x) + \pi(1 - p)u(y)$$

In the probability weighting function above, $\pi(p)$ is the decision weight and is not the same as probabilities in an expected utility function. The probability p has a decision weight of $\pi(p)$. Decision weights 'measure the impact of events on the desirability of prospects, and are not merely the perceived likelihood of these events'.[47] Probability and decision weight scales coincide such that $\pi(p) = p$ only if the expectation principle holds.

The probability weighting function overweights low probabilities and underweights high probabilities. The latter effect is more pronounced than the former. For example, in their experiments, Kahneman and Tversky found that people prefer a lottery ticket to the expected value of that ticket. On the other hand, people prefer a small loss that may be seen as the payment of an insurance premium, to a small probability of a large loss. Therefore, for low probabilities, $\pi(p) > p$. There is evidence to suggest that for all $0 < p < 1$, $\pi(p) + \pi(1 - p) < 1$ and the weighting function is not well behaved near the end points. This property is called subcertainty. Based on the relationship between $\pi(p)$ and p, a hypothetical weighting function can be drawn as shown in Figure 2.3.

(3) Framing

Kahneman and Tversky point out another psychological factor that counters the rationality assumption of MFT. Framing effects in decision choices arise when choices are put to an individual in different ways such as using different imagery and descriptions of the same problem highlighting different aspects of the outcomes. Research supports the proposition that decisions depend on the description and framing of choices. That decisions are affected by framing is not countenanced in EUT and EMH theory.

The feature of $\pi(p)$ in the weighting function explains decision choices due to framing. The major characteristic of the weighting function (Figure 2.3: a typical probability weighting function) is the overweighting of probability differences involving certainty and impossibility. For $\pi(1.0) - \pi(0.9)$ or $\pi(p0.1) - \pi(p0)$ are given greater weight than comparable differences in the middle of the scale, such as $\pi(p0.3) - \pi(p0.2)$.[48] For small p, π is generally subadditive such that $\pi(0.01) + \pi(0.06) > \pi(0.07)$. This property can lead to violations of dominance.[49]

The overweighting of outcomes that are obtained with certainty relative to outcomes that are merely probable also results in violations of EUT.

Take for example the following choices:

A: 24,000 for sure   B: 25% chance to win 100,000 and a 75% chance to win 0

C: −75,000 for sure   D: 75% chance to lose 100,000 and a 25% chance to lose 0

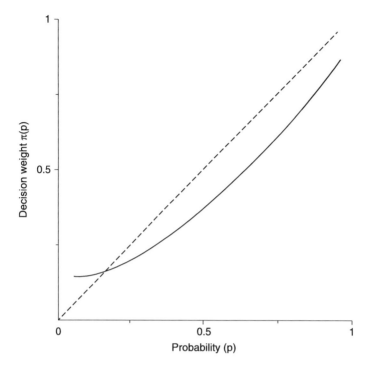

Figure 2.3 A typical probability weighting function.

More people choose the A and D combination than B and C combination even though the latter is stochastically dominant, such as superior, to the other prospect.[50] A and D, when combined, offer a 25 per cent chance of winning 24,000 and a 75 per cent chance of losing 76,000. The B and C combination offer a 25 per cent chance of winning 25,000 and a 75 per cent chance of losing 75,000. Instructions indicate to test subjects that the choice among A, B, C, and D is concurrent. Yet people tend to frame the choice into one from A and B and one from C or D. They did see the link between the two choices and derive a final wealth level from the relationship. However, when asked if they prefer the possibility of winning 25,000 instead of 24,000 and losing 75,000, all chose the more favourable amounts that were represented by B and C. Individuals are thus subject to perceptual or cognitive illusion.

Frames indicate information about an event, which is important in a world of uncertainty and imperfect information. When an event is positively or negatively framed, individuals read between the lines and attempt to extract extra information from the frames. A positive frame suggests a better choice than a negatively framed event.

Heuristics and biases

When there is a huge amount of information and much of it is complex, decision-making becomes a herculean task. Not only must the decision-maker consider the information that abounds but she must also make the correct optimization calculations.

Under these circumstances, humans tend to simplify the complex scenarios by relying on heuristics. Heuristics are information-processing shortcuts that people derive from experience. In everyday language, heuristics are rules of thumb. By their nature, heuristics are imperfect and, therefore, give rise to biases. Unsystematic biases average to zero across the population but the behavioural approach postulates that heuristics and biases are systematic and move prices away from fundamental values.

There are various reasons for using heuristics. One set of reasons is that decision-makers are unaware of the optimal solution to a problem, may not have the resources to find a solution, or may be using a formulaic solution unsuited to the problem. Another set of reasons is that decision-makers cannot get all pertinent information, may perceive the information incorrectly, or may have too much information that is ultimately overwhelming.

Kahneman and Tversky categorize heuristic behaviour in decision-making into three types: (1) representativeness (2) availability, and (3) anchoring and adjustment.[51] Slovic, Finucane, Peters, and MacGregor refine the categories further by compiling the work of a slew of researchers.[52] Slovic *et al.* include emotional factors as a general-purpose heuristic under the term 'affect heuristic'. Six general-purpose affect heuristics have so far been typified: (1) affect, (2) availability, (3) causality, (4) fluency, (5) similarity, and (6) surprise. In this section, we discuss representativeness, availability, anchoring, and adjustment and affect heuristics.[53]

(1) Representativeness

Representativeness is the overreliance on stereotypes. A stereotype is a standardized mental picture, an impression. When people have stereotypes of a group, class or type, they base their judgements on how much an outcome represents the stereotypical feature of the evidence. When people use the representativeness heuristic, probabilities are assessed on how much one object, A say, is representative of another object, B. If A is highly representative of B, the probability that A originates from B is judged to be high. The representative heuristic helps to evaluate the probabilities dealing with objects or processes A and B. The problem with the representative heuristic is that similarity should not affect the evaluation of probability. People should instead pay attention to prior probability or base rate. However, the representative heuristic results in people underweighting base-rate information. Their predictions, therefore, violate Bayes' rule.

In experiments, participants seem to ignore base-rate data and focus on stereotype characteristics. Kahneman and Tversky administered tests that required volunteers to give probabilities of whether an individual was an engineer or a lawyer.[54] The test subjects were given profiles of individuals consisting of thumb-nail descriptions. All subjects were presented with the same five descriptions. In the first part of the experiment, the subjects were informed there were 30 engineers and 70 lawyers in that group of 100. The experiment required subjects to indicate the probability that the individual described was an engineer or a lawyer.

One of the descriptions is as follows:

> Jack is a 45-year-old man. He is married and has four children. He is generally conservative, careful, and ambitious. He shows no interest in political and social issues and spends most of his free time on his many hobbies, which include home carpentry, sailing, and mathematical puzzles.
> The probability that Jack is one of the 30 engineers in the sample of 100 is ____%.

In a second part of the experiment, Kahneman and Tversky reversed the proportion of engineers to lawyers to 70:30 and conducted the experiment with a second group of subjects. The base rate or Bayesian prior corresponds to the relative proportion of engineers to lawyers. The description, such as that of Jack, corresponds to singular information. To correctly assess the probability that an individual among the 100 is either an engineer or lawyer requires the proper combination of Bayesian prior and singular information. Instead, most people focus on the singular information and significantly underweighted the base-rate information. People used the descriptions of individuals (such as that of Jack) and their own stereotypes of engineers and lawyers to form a probability number for every individual in the group of 100. The subjects largely underweighted the information about the proportion of engineers and lawyers in the population.

In another experiment, Kahneman and Tversky asked subjects to predict grade point averages (GPAs) of college students at the end of their freshman year based on descriptions that include: (1) GPA percentile at the early part of the year, (2) results of a test on mental concentration, and (3) a variable measuring sense of humour.[55] Again people tend to ignore base GPA percentile information and focus on the other singular information. Even if the GPA percentile is similarly high, people overestimate GPA predictions for those with positive descriptions and underestimate GPA predictions for those with negative descriptions.

Failure to allow for regression towards the mean is another bias associated with representativeness. This means people do not account for reversion of outcomes to averages. If the price of a security has been going up for some time, the belief is that the price of the security will continue to increase. Conversely, if the price of a security has been declining for some time, the prediction generally made is for the price of that security to continue declining in the future. Thus, people judge stocks that are 'winners' and 'losers' based on their historical prices.

In sum, the representative heuristic causes people to violate the laws of statistics in the major ways so that there is increased:

1   Insensitivity to prior probabilities or base-rate information. People tend to ignore base-rate information and rely more on the representativeness of the event alone.
2   Insensitivity to sample size. People make judgements based on the representativeness of the sample statistic rather than basing decisions on the size of the sample.
3   Misconceptions of chance and randomness. People impose patterns on random series. Related to this phenomenon is the 'law of small numbers', in which people place too much faith in the representativeness of a small number of observations.
4   Insensitivity to predictability. People make judgements based on the representativeness of the information presented ignoring the reliability of the information and the accuracy of the prediction.
5   Misconceptions of regression. Little account is given to the concept of 'reversion to the mean' so that exceptional performance is expected to follow by more exceptional performance rather than reverting to normal outcomes.

(2) Availability

When people need to estimate the frequency or probability of an event, they sometimes use the so-called availability heuristic. This heuristic refers to the overweighting of information that is easily recalled over rational calculation of probabilities using all information. By over-focusing on easily recalled associations, the main bias of availability is its extreme lack of sensitivity to sample size. Information that is dramatically available, such as in electronic and visual media, may reflect a small sample.

In a celebrated study, Tversky and Kahneman observed that participants overestimate the number of words that begin with the letter *r* but underestimated the number of words that have *r* as the third letter.[56] They postulated that the results were due to the ease of recalling words that begin with a certain letter over those that have a certain letter in the third position. In a related study, Gabrielcik and Fazio observed that exposing participants to subliminally presented words containing the letter *t* increased participants' estimates of the frequency of words beginning with *t*.[57]

In another study supporting the availability heuristic, Tversky and Kahneman presented test subjects with two lists: one with the names of 19 famous females and 20 non-famous males, and the other with 19 famous males and 20 non-famous females.[58] The subjects were then asked to estimate the proportion of female names to male names. In the first list, subjects estimated that there were more females on the list than males. In the second list, subjects estimated more males than females. Thus the famous female and male names were overrepresented in the recalled sample. Even with incentives for successful recall, subjects still overrepresented famous female and male names.

Later research supports Tversky and Kahneman's original thesis that it is the ease with which information is brought to mind rather than the recalled content that causes people to overestimate the frequency of an event, the likelihood of its occurrence, and its typicality.[59]

Schwartz describes two cases where the availability heuristic is applicable in financial markets.[60] First, the heuristic is associated with analysts and fund managers who favour securities that are high profile and the darlings of media attention. A successful fund manager with some knowledge of the availability heuristic will spurn these securities because their 'availability' is likely to lead to the companies being overvalued. Second, US investors tended to focus overwhelmingly on national rather than international stocks, particularly until the mid-1990s because of the availability heuristic. Consequently, investors missed out on profitable opportunities in Asian and emerging markets.

(3) Anchoring and adjustment

Anchoring and adjustment is a heuristic that involves adjustment of estimates of probabilities of events from some starting point (the anchoring point). It is a heuristic described by Tversky and Kahneman.[61] Anchoring is another shortcut to making decisions in a situation with complex and abundant information. The heuristic can be a useful way of making judgements. According to Tversky and Kahneman, 'people make estimates by starting from an initial value that is adjusted to yield a final answer [and] . . . adjustments are typically insufficient'.[62]

Thus, in the anchoring procedure, a salient but uninformative number is presented to subjects before they make a numeric judgement.[63] Subjects are asked, for instance, if the percentage of African countries in the United Nations (UN) is more or less than 10 per cent, a figure chosen at random. Then the subjects are asked to give their estimate of the target number. In this example subjects are instructed to indicate first if the 10 per cent is higher or lower than the actual quantity and then to estimate the value of the quantity by moving upwards or downwards from the given number. Different groups get different anchoring numbers. The median estimates of the percentage of African countries in the UN are 25 and 45 for groups receiving anchoring numbers of 10 and 65, respectively.

There are certain necessary conditions for anchoring effects to occur.[64] First, there must be attention to an anchor. The attention does not need to be from a comparative study as in the UN example given above. Subjects can be asked to do large computations. These subjects are then asked to estimate the number of, say, cancer incidences. Experiments find that the subjects who do large computations tend to give higher values for cancer incidences. Those who perform smaller computations tend to give lower estimates for cancer incidences. Second, the anchor and target value should be on the same scale. In situations where a target value is expressed in dollars, the anchor should also be expressed in dollars. Anchors have the most influence when they are relevant to the target value. Third, anchoring occurs even when the anchors have extreme or implausible values. Thus, anchors of up to 28 times the lottery expected value also produced anchoring.

Anchoring effects do not, however, require awareness of the anchor in order to occur. In studies, when asked if the anchor influenced their judgements, a vast majority of subjects said the anchor did not influence their judgements and yet their answers displayed anchoring effects. The relationship between knowing about an anchor and the anchor's effect is weak. Therefore, awareness is not necessary for anchoring. In addition, incentives also do little to reduce the anchoring effect. When subjects are offered an incentive for accuracy, their judgements were still affected by anchoring, although the subjects' ratings of the anchor's influence decreased.[65]

Anchoring and adjustment connote a cognitive process where people first focus on the anchor and then make a series of dynamic adjustments towards the final value. Experiments find that the adjustments tend to be insufficient and the final value is therefore, biased towards the anchor. There are a number of possible reasons for the inadequate adjustments. One reason is that people do not want to put in the effort, cognitively, to adjust adequately. Anchoring and adjustment need not go together. Research finds that adjustment is not necessary for the anchoring effect.

Anchors affect many judgement tasks such as evaluation of gambles, anticipation of future performance, and – most relevant to financial markets – estimates of risk and uncertainty.

Implications

In this chapter we have described prospect theory, heuristics, and biases such as representativeness, availability, and anchoring. From a categorical standpoint, we may view prospect theory as the counterpart to mean-variance theory in MFT. Applying heuristics and biases is the behavioural finance approach to asset pricing, and this approach is the counterpart to market efficiency in MFT.

(1) The Disposition Effect

The preference for avoiding losses over equivalent gains makes it more likely for people to engage in risky behaviour to prevent sure or highly probable losses. Consequently, people pay attention to sunk costs and, therefore, throw good money after bad. In investments this behaviour translates to holding on to poor performing corporations for longer than predicted by conventional finance. In contrast, neoclassical rational economic agents ignore sunk costs. The application of this principle of prospect theory to stock market behaviour also explains why investors tend to hold on to losing stocks for too long and sell winning stocks too soon. This propensity is called the disposition effect.[66]

Prospect theory's finding that people are risk-seeking in losses and risk-averse in gains helps explain this disposition effect. In circumstances of uncertainty, many people hold on to losing stocks hoping the value of these stocks will recover and move back to purchase price value (risk-seeking). Conversely, people will tend to sell relatively high-valued financial securities too quickly fearing the price of these securities will decline. In EUT and mean-variance models, rational economic agents will hold on to wining stocks to achieve further gains and sell losing stocks to prevent mounting losses. However, in a world where prospective risks are difficult to measure, ascertaining the correct time to sell or how long to retain a stock is not always clear. Future prices are not predictable nor is it easy to time the movements of security prices. In this scenario, behaving in accordance with prospect theory may be rational behaviour (utility maximizing). Research on the disposition effect still continues. Odean provides compelling evidence for the disposition effect among individual investors.[67]

(2) Equity premiums

Benartzi and Thaler apply prospect theory to the equity premium puzzle.[68] The difference between the historical returns of stocks and bonds is too high to be consistent with MFT. According to one estimate, the equity premium for US stocks over short-term government bonds averaged more than 6 per cent per annum from 1926–92. In the US from 1871 to 1993, returns from stocks easily dominated returns on bonds or Treasury bills. The opportunity cost as a result of this premium can be significant. For example if stocks yielded a rate of return of 8 per cent per annum while the rate of return of bonds was 2 per cent, the resulting 6 percentage point outperformance of stocks over a period of 30 years results in considerable monetary gain. A $100 investment in stocks will yield $1,006. The same investment in bonds over the same 30 years yields $181.[69] The puzzle is why rational investors will hold bonds given their underperformance relative to stocks. Risk aversion is not the answer because investors maximize utility over the long term and the relative risk differential between stocks and bonds is not large enough to explain the historical equity risk premium.

Benartzi and Thaler conclude the equity premium reflects 'myopic loss aversion'. According to prospect theory and the weighting function, individuals are sensitive to gains and losses relative to a reference point and weigh losses more than gains. If individuals are loss-averse as postulated first by Kahneman and Tversky, then they will demand a greater equity premium to invest in stocks if they characterize stocks as having a higher risk of loss than bonds. Olsen surveyed money managers and found that the managers display myopic loss aversion.[70]

(3) Portfolio construction

Kahneman and Tversky's studies indicate that people do not choose well-diversified portfolios. People ignore covariance among security returns and actually choose stochastically dominated portfolios that lie below the efficient frontier.

(4) Herding and bubbles

The MFT approach to market efficiency argues that prices of assets equal their fundamental values because people consider only fundamental values when choosing assets.

Prices are the aggregate of information of all investors in the market. However, as described above, behavioural finance postulates people use heuristics to assess assets. Given uncertainty and the existence of asymmetric information, a significant majority of people will make investment decisions based on herding, which reinforces the disposition effect. Herding, or crowd, behaviour generates large and deep swings in asset prices resulting in bubbles and busts. When there is imperfect and asymmetric information, investors rely on the market trend as a fast- and low-cost heuristic. The investor uses the crowd or market trend as a quick cognitive short cut believing the market may be better informed than a single individual.

Price bubbles are indicative of positive feedback trading. Thus, when the price of an asset goes up, investors buy more of the asset in anticipation of further price increases. This buying pushes the price of the asset up more, which in turn feeds the expectations of investors of future price increases. These expectations lead to further buying and further price increases. This process is the way a classic positive feedback mechanism works. Studies find people have expectations of price increases based on extrapolation of past price trends.[71] Home buyers in cities where house prices have risen rapidly in the past expect higher house price rises than home buyers in cities where house prices have been stagnant or declining. After the 1987 stock market crash, most sellers give as a reason for selling the fact that share prices were falling. They were expecting further price declines. During the dollar rise in the 1980s, forecasting agencies continued to make predictions of dollar appreciation in the following month while saying the dollar would depreciate in a year because of underlying fundamentals. Forecasting services were issuing buy recommendations while saying the dollar was overpriced on a fundamental basis. Schleifer concludes: 'Such trend-chasing short run expectations, combined with a belief in a long run return to fundamentals, are hard to reconcile with a fully rational model.'[72]

(5) Winners and losers

Following on the studies of representativeness, DeBondt and Thaler applied the hypothesis to studies of stocks to find out if people picked 'winners' and 'losers' based on historical price movements. Investors predicted that stocks that performed badly in the past would also perform poorly in the future (losers). Conversely, investors believed that stocks whose prices consistently rose in the past would perform well in the future (winners). DeBondt and Thaler found evidence consistent with this hypothesis.[73]

Based simply on the return from dividends, stocks should not exhibit the kind of volatility that is usually seen. Shiller has done extensive work on the excess volatility in stocks.[74] He concludes that at least over most of the twentieth century, dividends simply do not vary enough to rationally justify observed aggregate price movements. Stock prices are strongly correlated with the following year's earnings changes. This finding suggests a clear pattern of overreaction. According to DeBondt and Thaler, 'In spite of the observed trendiness in dividends, investors seem to attach a disproportionate importance to short-run economic developments'.[75]

DeBondt and Thaler's work support their thesis that stock markets overreact to unexpected and dramatic news events. Portfolios of prior losers outperform prior winners. Thirty-six months after the portfolios are constructed, the losing stocks earned about 25 per cent more than the winners, even though the latter are significantly more risky. These findings refute the weak form of the efficient market hypothesis as abnormal returns are possible based solely on historical prices.

Behavioural processes, such as representativeness, may explain overreaction in the stock market. When new data emerges about stocks it is presumed that people use Bayes' rule in reacting to new information. However, we have seen from the above discussion about heuristics that Bayes' rule is not an apt characterization of how people actually respond to new information. In revising their beliefs, individuals tend to overweight recent information and underweight prior or base-rate information (see representative heuristic above).

(6) Analyst stock recommendations and fund manager selection

The representative heuristic is a factor in stock recommendations by sell-side analysts. Studies show that analysts are not immune to the representative bias that good companies with good management are also good stocks.[76] Thus, well-managed companies are considered to be those whose stocks will outperform. However, if good management is relevant, the stock price should already reflect this characteristic. Analysts are more likely to make buy recommendations on stocks that tend to have positive price and earnings momentum, higher market/book rations and trading volume, greater past sales growth, and are expected to grow earnings faster in the future. However, such stocks tend also to be overvalued and to underperform.

Mokoaleli-Mokoteli, Taffler, and Agarwal test whether sell-side analysts are affected by behavioural bias when making stock recommendations. They conclude that analysts' recommendations are affected by various cognitive biases, including representativeness, as well as conflicts of interest in their new buy but not sell stock recommendations. Consequently, more than half of the new stock recommendations have negative abnormal returns over the following 12 months.[77]

Similarly, retail investors are affected by the representativeness heuristic in their selection of mutual funds. Are professional investors also affected in their selection of fund managers? Goyal and Wahal's research find that plan sponsors are not immune from the representative heuristic.[78] Investment plan sponsors tend to hire an investment manager if the manager has three years of outperformance. However, subsequent performance by the manager after hiring does not meet expectations because returns are not superior. Indeed, post-hiring abnormal returns do not differ significantly from zero. On the flip side, plan sponsors will tend to fire investment managers after three years of poor performance. Research finds that the three-year performance of these managers after their firing is superior and above those of the firms that replace them. In other words, if the plan sponsors had stuck with their original investment managers they would, at worst, not have performed differently from the newly hired managers. However, when fees and switching costs are taken into account, the fund under management may actually have done worse.

The same representative bias is seen in the selection process for investment managers through the use of investment consultants. Consultants derive a short list of managers based on prior performance (in itself a flawed criterion). These short-listed managers are then interviewed and selected based on a 'beauty contest'. Plan sponsors may conflate 'liking' the applicant fund manager with future good performance similar to the 'good management, good stock' representative bias. There is extensive evidence of the key role played by applicant attractiveness and appearance, as well as personality in the determination of which fund manager is hired.[79] These traits are not necessarily the ones related to superior fund returns.

2.3 Behavioural finance and ethics

Modern finance theory's narrow definition of rationality as profit maximization and its follow-on assumption that economic actors are solely self-interested gives no account to ethics and values. This failure to speak about values is a serious one and has had deleterious effects on the practice of finance, as we recently encountered in the 2008 global financial crisis. Empirically, historically, and theoretically speaking, MFT's assumption of the self-interested economic actor is just plain wrong. It is, however, deeply ingrained in the psyche of academics, practitioners, and the media. Indeed, the belief that all financial agents are relentlessly opportunistic is shown in Alan Greenspan's *mea culpa* when he bemoaned the fact that managers of financial institutions did not adhere to the tenets of 'enlightened self-interest'.[80] His dismay was not from a failure to recognize bankers would act in self-interest but a failure to recognize that bankers would act in such self-destructively opportunistic ways.

Dobson reminds us the presumption of opportunism and self-interest is not a historical one.[81] Adam Smith and David Hume had remarkably sophisticated views of the human psyche versus the impoverished view of *homo economicus* we hold today. The narrow view started with Marxism and continued into neoclassical economics that held sway in the twentieth century. Dobson gives two examples from Hume and Smith's writings that illustrate their recognition of the whole human psyche. David Hume wrote: 'The epithets sociable, good-natured, humane, merciful, grateful, friendly, generous, beneficent, or their equivalents, are known in all languages, and universally express the highest merit, which human nature is capable of attaining.' Adam Smith, who was a professor of moral philosophy, wrote:

> All members of human society stand in need of each other's assistance, and are likewise exposed to mutual injuries. Where the necessary assistance is reciprocally afforded from love, from gratitude, from friendship, and esteem, the society flourishes and is happy. All the different members of it are bound together by the agreeable bonds of love and affection, and are, as it were, drawn to one common centre of mutual good offices.[82]

Over a century or so, economics and later, finance lost touch with the basic human values that drive societies and markets. We have moved from a world view that includes moral sentiments to one in which moral sentiments have no rational place. However, MFT's narrow modelling of human behaviour does not change the reality on the ground. That is, two crucial ethical values underlie financial markets, ensuring their proper functioning – fairness and trust.

(1) Fairness

The validity of MFT's assumption that economic agents are profit maximizing and purely self-interested individuals, with no regard for community, is challenged by a growing body of empirical and experimental evidence to the contrary. One simple laboratory test to verify the validity of narrow self-interest is the ultimatum game. Results indicate people are not purely self-interested but instead are motivated by the principle of fairness.

The basic ultimatum game consists of two players. Player one is known as the proposer. She is given a significant amount of money and instructed to offer a portion of this money to a second player, the responder. Both proposer and responder know the amount given to the former. The responder may accept the proposer's offer, in which case both players receive their respective share of the money. The responder may also reject the proposer's offer. In this event, neither player receives any money.

According to MFT's assumptions of economic agents, the proposer should try to keep as much of the money as possible and give a nominal amount to the responder. If rational expectation is correct, then the responder will accept the offer because a small amount is better than nothing.

Yet, this outcome does not occur. Few act according to the conventional rationality model. The typical allocation is 20–50 per cent. Respondents offered less than 20 per cent generally reject the offer, acting irrationally because they prefer to take nothing than accept an offer that seems to them unfair. 'In other words, the principle of fairness has intrinsic value to them, and they are prepared to uphold that principle even in the face of a guaranteed material loss.'[83] An extremely unequal division offends our sense of fairness. We tend to refuse to participate in this unfair act.

We see this principle of fairness affecting the behaviour of even profit-maximizing firm. They have an incentive to act in a manner that is perceived as fair. Otherwise, the parties that the firms are dealing with will resist unfair transactions and punish unfair firms at some cost to themselves.[84] The firm that seeks to maximize shareholder wealth by treating others unfairly will fail in its objective. Successful firms know they must treat stakeholders fairly or the firms will be punished accordingly.

(2) Trust

Trust is a foundational pillar that supports thriving financial markets. The value requires two parties: the trustor, or the person doing the trusting, and the trustee, the person being trusted. The trustor makes herself vulnerable to the trustee, who can gain from exploiting that vulnerability. Trust requires that the trustee will not take advantage of the trustor to attain self-interested gains. The trustor must believe the person being trusted is not driven solely by self-interest. This belief goes completely against the assumptions of the rational expectations model. Yet, trust undergirds financial markets, a fact openly acknowledged by the CFA (Chartered Financial Analysts) Institute.

For the first time in its publication history, the 2010 tenth edition of *The Standards of Practice Handbook* of the CFA Institute has a section, immediately after the preface, dedicated to a discussion of ethics.[85] The title of the section is 'Why Ethics Matter'. The paragraph of the section talks about trust. 'Ethical practices instil public trust in markets and support the development of markets.'[86] It goes on to give examples of frauds and crimes that were perpetrated in financial markets and were discovered in the wake of the 2008 financial crisis. 'Each case has resulted in heavy financial losses and stained reputations. Equally important has been the terrible toll these actions have taken on investors' trust. Trust is hard earned and easily lost; corporations and individuals can safeguard themselves by committing to the highest standards of ethics and professional conduct.'

The ethics section of the CFA Standards of Practice Handbook ends with this admission: 'Markets function to an important extent on trust.'[87]

Yet, the rational expectations model of investors completely ignores the value of trust. According to assumptions of the model, investors are rational, self-interested actors, with the goal of maximizing profits for their own benefit. In this supposed environment, all investors must be extraordinarily careful not to be cheated or defrauded by other investors whose goal is to gain as much as possible for themselves. Investing requires high levels of investigating, checking, and knowledge of the law and other parties in the investment transaction. This amount of work would be onerous to the extent of deterring most investors. A 'rational expectations' investor will be continuously gathering, verifying, and analysing information to ensure her investments are safe. This level of work is not achievable or desirable. Yet, financial markets serve millions of investors every day. Logically, these investors cannot be the same ones modelled by rational expectations theory.

Apart from this argument based on logic that investors are not the stereotype given by rational expectations, there also is growing empirical evidence that trustworthiness is a foundation on which securities markets rest. There is a large amount of literature, both theoretical and empirical, exploring the phenomenon of trust in financial markets. In recent decades researchers around the world have run experiments to test the circumstances under which humans will trust others.[88] The game is called the trust game or the investment game.

In a typical trust game, one subject is given a modest amount of money. This player is called the trustor. The trustor may choose to give some, all or none of the money to another player, the trustee. The players are told that the money given to the trustee will be tripled. If the trustee receives the money from the trustor, she too has a choice. She may either keep all of the tripled funds for herself or send some or all of the funds back to the trustor.

The results of the trust game do not conform with results using rational expectations assumptions. People choose to trust others and trusted individuals tend to act in a trustworthy manner. Berg et al. carried out one of the first trust experiments.[89] In the study, consisting of 32 pairs of subjects, 30 trustors chose to invest with (such as send money to) the trustee. Twenty-four trustees sent back at least some of the funds they had received and most sent back more than they had originally received from the trustor, ensuring both parties gained from the investment.

These sorts of results have been replicated in subsequent experiments. The results indicate that trust may be an essential component for successful financial markets. Two tentative conclusions can be drawn from trust game studies. First, many people are willing to trust others, even strangers. People not only trust other people but also non-human entities such as computers, possibly institutions, or the market.[90]

However, trust is not invariable. Some entities are trusted (doctors and clergy, for example), while others are not (car salesmen and car dealerships). The willingness to trust a particular person or institution appears to depend on past experience. We build trust according to our experiences. In repeated transactions, trust levels for certain players decline because of previous untrustworthy actions of these players. This same result occurs in the gift exchange game, a variation of the trust game. Studies find that players assigned the role of trustor are far more willing to trust individuals who have proven themselves trustworthy in prior games.[91] Thus, people continue to trust and believe that it is safe to trust when they have favourable experiences with trustees. Conversely, violations of trust generally lead to players becoming unwilling to trust those deemed untrustworthy.

People participate in financial markets because they believe they can trust the system. If there are individuals and institutions that cheat, investors must believe these untrustworthy parties are the exception, not the rule. Investors must believe, on the whole, the system can be trusted. As of 2007, according to the US Census Bureau (2009), 91 million individual investors held a total of more than US$15 trillion in corporate bonds and equities, either directly or through pension and mutual funds. The financial markets thrive because these 91 million investors base their investments on trust. If, however, investors perceive the markets are rigged by big players, with the covert support of politicians and policy-makers, investors will no longer wish to participate in financial markets. Without investors, financial markets wither. We can now understand the statement in the CFA Standards of Practice Handbook that, 'Markets function to an important extent on trust'.[92]

2.4 Limitations of behavioural finance and further work

Behavioural finance demonstrates the invalidity of the first two arguments given by the efficient market hypothesis, such as the rationality of investors and the randomness of their trades. Shleifer provides evidence that disproves the third argument in support of EMH, such as arbitrage eliminates the influence of irrational investors on prices.[93] However, can behavioural finance provide predictive models on security pricing? There is no single unifying model in behavioural finance. Models exist for a particular theory of behavioural finance. For example, Shleifer attempts to give formal models on two aspects of pricing. He models underreaction and overreaction in prices, and price bubble formation. In the latter, he develops a model of arbitrageurs' trading in anticipation of irrational trading by noise traders as they chase prices in a positive feedback mechanism. The addition of rational traders can destabilize prices.

Schleifer's version of a price bubble model involves positive feedback investment strategies of a significant number of investors. These strategies cause price increases, and are then aggravated by arbitrageurs' anticipatory pumping up of the bubble. The model describes the formation of bubbles in three basic stages. First, an accumulation where informed investors purchase assets happens in anticipation of a future price increase. This stage is followed by the distribution stage, where informed investors sell the same but more expensive assets to investors pursuing the positive feedback investment strategies. Finally, the liquidation stage is when the bubble bursts and prices return to fundamental values. Schleifer admits the model is incomplete but it captures the reality of bubbles better than the alternative rational model, where prices keep growing. Neither model of price bubbles is complete or accurate. Each theory applies in different circumstances. Therefore, at a minimum, behavioural finance can complement modern finance theory.

There is an enormous amount of future work for behavioural finance to address questions that are as yet unanswered. The most intriguing problem for further research is risk. We still need to know how investors perceive risk and what factors influence these perceptions. Another piece of the risk puzzle that requires research is on how investors evaluate risk and subsequently style their investments.

Behavioural finance has shown empirically and through experimental research that markets are not efficient. A fruitful area of research is on whether market inefficiency matters and if it does what the implications of the inefficiency are. For instance, if markets are not efficient, then contrary to Modigliani and Miller's theory of the firm, capital structure is relevant.[94] Dividend policy will also begin to matter. Market inefficiency is therefore going to affect how the firm invests. For example, overvaluation of a firm may enable it to finance profitable projects it could otherwise not finance without imperfections in the capital markets. Some argue that the stock market bubble in Asia helped to finance private projects, thus leading to economic development and progress. On the other hand, when bubbles collapse the panic and economic destruction that ensues may have long-term social and economic costs. This has been the experience of the many burst financial bubbles around the world over the last 20 years.

The third area of research is on the role and efficacy of market regulation. Is government intervention a good or a bad thing? If the market is inefficient then regulatory intervention may be necessary to maintain the proper functioning of the market. If, on the other hand, markets are efficient, regulatory intervention merely serves to make the markets less efficient. Evidence suggests that countries with strong legal protections of minority shareholders and creditors have bigger and broader capital markets.

One crucial area of work that is still largely unexplored is how ethical and cultural values affect investors' view of risk, markets, and ultimately investment styles. This work would tie into policy and regulatory implications. Currently, markets are regulated *ad hoc*, with regulations arising as market failures occur. It may be an ideal but if regulations were to work together with instilling sound ethical values as widely as possible, can bubbles and debt crises be mitigated?

Notes

1 Emanuel Derman, *Models.Behaving.Badly.: Why Confusing Illusion with Reality can Lead to Disaster, on Wall Street and in Life* (New York, NY: Free Press, 2011).
2 Ibid.
3 Ibid.
4 Ibid.
5 G. W. Douglas, "Risk in the Equity Markets: An Empirical Appraisal of Market Efficiency," *Yale Economic Essays* 9, No. 1 (1969): 3–48.
6 William F. Sharpe and Guy M. Cooper, "Risk-Return Classes of New York Stock Exchange Common Stocks 1931–1967," *Financial Analysis Journal* 28, No. 2 (March–April 1972): 46–54.
7 Eugene Fama and R. MacBeth, "Risk, Return and Equilibrium: Empirical Tests," *Journal of Political Economy* 81, No. 2 (May–June 1973): 453–74.
8 Eugene Fama, and Kenneth R. French, "The Cross Section of Expected Stock Returns," *Journal of Finance* 47, No. 2 (June 1992): 427–65.
9 S. P. Kothari, Jay Shanken, and Richard G. Sloan, "Another Look at the Cross Section of Expected Stock Returns," *Journal of Finance* 50, No. 2 (March 1995): 185–224; Glenn Pettengill, Sridhar Dundaram, and Ike Matthur, "The Conditional Relation between Beta and Returns," *Journal of Financial and Quantitative Analysis* 30, No. 1 (March 1995): 101–15.
10 Eugene F. Fama and Kenneth R. French, "The Capital Asset Pricing Model: Theory and Evidence," *Journal of Economic Perspective* Vol. 18, No. 3 (Summer 2004): 25–46.
11 Frank K. Reilly and Keith C. Brown, *Investment Analysis and Portfolio Management* 7th ed. (Ohio: Thomson South-Western, 2003), 325–29.
12 Frank K. Reilly and Rashid A. Akhtar, "The Benchmark Error Problem with Global Capital Markets," *Journal of Portfolio Management* Vol. 22, No. 1 (Fall 1995): 33–52.
13 Reilly and Brown, 269.
14 Robert A. Levy, "On the Short-Term-Stationarity of Beta Coefficients," *Financial Analysts Journal* 27, No. 6 (November–December 1971): 55–62.
15 Thomas M. Tole, "How to Maximize Stationarity of Beta," *Journal of Portfolio Management* 7, No. 2 (Winter 1980): 45–9.
16 Jerome B. Baesel, "On the Assessment of Risk: Some Further Considerations," *Journal of Finance* 29, No. 5 (December 1974): 1491–94.
17 Edward Altman, B. Jacquillat, and M. Levasseur, "Comparative Analysis of Risk Measures: France and the United States," *Journal of Finance* 29, No. 5 (December 1974): 1495–1511.
18 Reilly and Brown, 260.
19 Meir Statman, "Betas Compared: Merrill Lynch vs. Value Line," *Journal of Portfolio Management* 7, No. 2 (Winter 1981): 41–4.

20 Frank K. Reilly and David J. Wright, "A Comparison of Published Betas," *Journal of Portfolio Management* 14, No. 3 (Spring 1988): 64–9.
21 James R. Thompson, L. Scott Baggett, William C. Wojciechowski, and Edward E. Williams, "Nobels for Nonsense," *Journal of Post Keynesian Economics* Vol. 29, No. 1 (Fall 2006): 3–18.
22 Thompson et al., 6.
23 W. C. Wojciechowski and J. R. Thompson, "Market Truths: Theory Versus Empirical Simulations," *Journal of Statistical Computing and Simulations* Vol. 76, No. 5 (2006): 385–95.
24 Thompson et al., 11–13.
25 Thompson et al., 12.
26 Harry M. Markowitz, "Market Efficiency: A Theoretical Distinction and So What?" *Financial Analysts Journal* (September–October 2005): 17–30.
27 Markowitz, 17–22.
28 Markowitz, 19.
29 Findlay, Williams, and Thompson, 93.
30 Findlay and Williams, 217.
31 M. C. Findlay, E. E. Williams, and J. R. Thompson, "*Why We All Held Our Breath When the Market Reopened*," *Journal of Portfolio Management* (Spring 2003): 91–100.
32 Findlay, Williams, and Thompson, 91–100.
33 F. Knight, *Risk, Uncertainty and Profit* (New York: Harper & Row, 1921).
34 J. M. Keynes, *The Treatise on Probability* (London: Macmillan, 1921).
35 M. C. Findlay and E. E. Williams, "Financial Economics at 50: An Oxymoronic Tautology," *Journal of Post Keynesian Economics* Vol. 31, No. 2 (Winter 2008–09): 213–26.
36 Findlay and William, 223.
37 Robert Kolb, "Ethical Implications of Finance," in *Finance Ethics*, ed. John R. Boatright (Hoboken, NJ: John Wiley & Sons, 2010).
38 Hersh Shefrin and Meir Statman, "The Contributions of Daniel Kahneman and Amos Tversky," *The Journal of Behavioral Finance* Vol. 4, No. 2 (2003): 54–8.
39 Robert Bloomfield, "Traditional Versus Behavioral Finance," in *Behavioral Finance: Investors, Corporations, and Markets*, eds. H. Kent Baker and John R. Nofsinger (Hoboken, NJ: John Wiley & Sons, 2010), 29.
40 Bloomfield, 30–1.
41 Daniel Kahneman and Amos Tversky, "Prospect Theory: An Analysis of Decision under Risk," *Econometrica* Vol. 47, No. 2 (March 1979): 263–92.
42 Kahneman and Tversky, 276–77.
43 Kahneman and Tversky, 277–80.
44 Kahneman and Tversky, 277.
45 Kahneman and Tversky, 269.
46 Morris Altman, "Prospect Theory and Behavioral Finance," in *Behavioral Finance: Investors, Corporations, and Markets*, eds. H. Kent Baker and John R. Nofsinger (Hoboken, NJ: John Wiley & Sons, 2010).
47 Kahneman and Tversky, 280.
48 Amos Tversky and Daniel Kahneman, "Rational Choice and the Framing of Decisions," *Choices, Values, and Frames*, eds. Daniel Kahneman and Amos Tversky, (Cambridge, UK: Cambridge University Press, 2000).
49 Dominance is a principle in EUT. If one option is better than another in one state and at least as good in all other states, the dominant option should be chosen. A slightly stronger condition, stochastic dominance, asserts that for unidimensional risky prospects, A is preferred to B if the cumulative distribution of A is to the right of the cumulative distribution of B (Tversky and Kahneman, 2000).
50 Shefrin and Statman, 55.
51 Daniel Kahneman and Amos Tversky, "On the Study of Statistical Intuition," in *Judgement Under Uncertainty: Heuristics and Biases*, eds. Daniel Kahneman, Paul Slovic, and Amos Tversky (Cambridge, UK: Cambridge University Press, 1982), 498–508.

52 Paul Slovic, Melissa Finucane, Ellen Peters, and Donald G. MacGregor, "The Affect Heuristic," in *Heuristics and Biases: The Psychology of Intuitive Judgment*, eds. Thomas Gilovich, Dale Griffin, and Daniel Kahneman (Cambridge, UK: Cambridge University Press, 2002).
53 Thomas Gilovich and Dale Griffin. "Introduction—Heuristics and Biases: Then and Now," in *Heuristics and Biases: The Psychology of Intuitive Judgment*, eds. Thomas Gilovich, Dale Griffin, and Daniel Kahneman (Cambridge, UK: Cambridge University Press, 2002), 1–18.
54 Kahneman and Tversky, 503.
55 Kahneman and Tversky, 498–508.
56 Amos Tversky and Daniel Kahneman, "Availability: A Heuristic for Judging Frequency and Probability," *Cognitive Psychology* Vol. 5 Issue 2 (1973): 677 – 95.
57 Adele Gabrielcik and Russell H. Fazio, "Priming and Frequency Estimation: A Strict Test of the Availability Heuristic," *Personality and Social Psychology Bulletin* Vol. 10, No. 1 (1984): 85–9.
58 Tversky and Kahneman, 498–508.
59 Norbert Schwarz and Leigh Ann Vaughn, "The Availability Heuristic Revisited: Ease of Recall and Content of Recall as Distinct Sources of Information," *Heuristics and Biases: The Psychology of Intuitive Judgment*, eds. Thomas Gilovich, Dale Griffin, and Daniel Kahneman (Cambridge, UK: Cambridge University Press, 2002).
60 Hugh Schwartz, "Heuristics or Rules of Thumb," *Behavioral Finance: Investors, Corporations, and Markets*, eds. H. Kent Baker and John R. Nofsinger (Hoboken, NJ: John Wiley & Sons, 2010).
61 Amos Tversky and Daniel Kahneman, "Judgment Under Uncertainty: Heuristics and Biases," *Science* 185, 4157 (1974): 1124–31.
62 Tversky and Kahneman, 1128.
63 Gretchen B. Chapman and Eric J. Johnson, "Incorporating the Irrelevant: Anchors in Judgment of Belief and Values," *Heuristics and Biases: The Psychology of Intuitive Judgment*, eds. Thomas Gilovich, Dale Griffin, and Daniel Kahneman (Cambridge, UK: Cambridge University Press, 2002).
64 Chapman and Johnson, 123–6.
65 T. D. Wilson, C. Houston, K. M. Etling, and N. Brekke, "A New Look at Anchoring Effects: Basic Anchoring and its Antecedents," *Journal of Experimental Psychology: General* 4 (1996): 387–402.
66 Hersh Shefrin and Meir Statman, "The Disposition to Sell Winners too Early and Ride Losers too Long," *Journal of Finance* 40, Issue 3 (1985): 777–92.
67 Terence Odean, "Are Investors Reluctant to Realize Their Losses?" *Journal of Finance* 53 (1998): 1775–98.
68 Nicolas C. Barberis and Richard H. Thaler, "A Survey of Behavioral Finance," in *Handbook of the Economics of Finance*, eds. George Constantinides, Milton Harris, and Rene Stulz (Amsterdam: North-Holland, 2003).
69 Morris, 205.
70 R. A. Olsen, "Investment Risk: The Experts' Perspective," *Financial Analysts Journal* 53 (1997): 62–6.
71 Andrei Shleifer, *Inefficient Markets: An Introduction to Behavioral Finance* (Oxford, UK: Oxford University Press, 2000).
72 Schleifer, 136.
73 Werner DeBondt, and Richard Thaler, "Does the Stock Market Overreact?" *Journal of Finance* 40 (1985): 793–805.
74 Robert Shiller, "Do Stock Prices Move too Much to be Justified by Subsequent Changes in Dividends?" *The American Economic Review* 71, No. 3 (1981): 421–36.
75 DeBondt and Thaler, 794.
76 Richard J. Taffler, "The Representative Heuristic," *Behavioral Finance: Investors, Corporations, and Markets*, eds. H. Kent Baker, and John R. Nofsinger (Hoboken, NJ: John Wiley & Sons, 2010).

77 Richard Taffler, 263–8.
78 Amit Goyal and Sunil Wahal, "The Selection and Termination of Investment Management Firms by Plan Sponsors," *Journal of Finance* 3, Issue 4 (2008): 1805–47.
79 Richard Taffler, 269–70.
80 Alan Greenspan, "Mea Culpa," *Financial Times* (7 January 2009): 1.
81 John Dobson, "Behavioral Assumptions of Finance," *Finance Ethics: Critical Issues in Theory and Practice* (Hoboken, NJ: John Wiley & Sons, 2010), 45–62.
82 John Dobson, 47.
83 John Dobson, 51.
84 Daniel Kahneman, Jack L. Knetsch, and Richard H. Thaler, "Fairness and the Assumptions of Economics," *Journal of Business* 59 (1986): 285–300.
85 CFA Institute, *Standards of Practice Handbook*, 10th ed. (2010).
86 CFA Institute, 1–5.
87 Ibid.
88 Noel D. Johnson and Alexandra Mislin, *Cultures of Kindness: A Meta-Analysis of Trust Game Experiments* (2008), accessed 27 August 27 2015, http://extranet.isnie.org/uploads/isnie2009/johnson_mislin.pdf.
89 Joyce Berg, John Dickhaut, and Kevin McCabe, "Trust, Reciprocity, and Social History," *Games and Economic Behavior* 10, Issue 1 (1995): 122–42.
90 Lynn A. Stout, "Trust Behavior: The Essential Foundation of Securities Markets," in *Behavioral Finance: Investors, Corporations, and Markets*, eds. H. Kent Baker and John R. Nofsinger (Hoboken, NJ: John Wiley & Sons, 2010), 513–22.
91 Stout, 518–19.
92 CFA Institute, 1–5.
93 Schleifer, 155–75.
94 Modigliani and Miller's theory states that the market value of the firm, holding its investment policy constant, is independent of the firm's capital structure. If the securities are correctly valued (market efficiency dependent) for their cash flows, then the combined market value of all the securities that the firm issues is equal to the present value of the firm's profits regardless of which securities are issued (see Shleifer, 2000, p. 184).

References

Shleifer, Andrei, *Inefficient Markets: An Introduction to Behavioral Finance* (Oxford, UK: Oxford University Press, 2000).
Tversky, Amos and Daniel Kahneman, "Rational Choice and the Framing of Decisions," *Choices, Values, and Frames*, eds. Daniel Kahneman and Amos Tversky (Cambridge, UK: Cambridge University Press, 2000).

3 Islamic finance

3.1 Introduction

Definition of Islamic finance

The theory and practice of finance according to Islamic principles is called Islamic finance. Islamic principles determine the objectives and the operations of Islamic finance. Modern finance theory informs today's conventional finance while ethical imperatives drive Islamic finance. The principles and prohibitions of Islamic finance are expounded in the *Shari'a*, or Islamic law.

Two features of Islamic finance distinguish the system from conventional finance. First, Islamic finance proposes a risk-sharing philosophy whereby the lender must share in the borrower's risk. According to the Islamic view, a non-Islamic, interest-based loan guarantees a return to the lender but the burden of risk falls disproportionately onto the borrower. This unequal distribution of risk where the borrower bears more than the lender is exploitative, socially unproductive, and economically wasteful.[1]

Second, the purpose of Islamic finance is to promote economic and social development, through specific business practices. Conventional finance has profit maximization as the goal, whereas Islamic finance is driven by ethical and religiously inspired goals as stated in the Shari'a.

History

Islam arose in the seventh century in the Arabian Peninsula. The holy book of Islam is the Holy Qur'an. Allah (the Arabic name for God) revealed the Holy Qur'an to his Prophet, Mohammed (peace be upon him), over the course of 23 years. The Prophet began receiving Allah's revelations in 610 CE and continued until his death in 632 CE According to the Qur'an, Allah chose Mohammed to be His messenger because of Mohammed's excellence. At age 40, Mohammed received his first revelation in a cave atop the Mountain of Light in Mecca, a city in Saudi Arabia. The Archangel Jibreel (Gabriel) appeared to Mohammed and ordered him to recite three times, 'Recite in the name of the Lord who creates!'[2] Mohammed, understandably fearful, and after some hesitation, repeated the words given to him by Jibreel. Thus was established the first chapter, or *surah*, of the Holy Qur'an, which was subsequently revealed over the years and is, even now, recited in an oral manner.

It is generally believed that Mohammed was illiterate. However, he employed many secretaries, who, with the help of other faithful Muslims, wrote down many of the revelations he received before he died.³ These secretaries, or scribes were known as 'revelation writers', many of whom were his companions (*sahabah*). While the revelations were not collected into one volume during the life of the Prophet, every revelation was memorialized in written form before his death. The Prophet's wives helped in this process.

When the Prophet passed away, no succession plans were in place. Two camps arose, each claiming its leader to be the successor to the Prophet. This early split led to the eventual formation of the Shi'ite and the Sunni sects. The Shias proclaimed Ali, the cousin and son-in-law of Mohammed, as the next leader. They believed succession should be based on blood-ties to the Prophet.

The Sunni sect had a majority of followers. They believed succession should be based on following the traditions, acts, words, and statements of the Prophet. The wisest, most pious, and noblest man would be leader. The Sunnis chose Abu Bakr as their first Caliph. This schism of Sunni versus Shia persists to this day. Despite this division in Islam's followers, a few decades after the death of the Prophet, Islam and its influence spread to the east from the border of China through North Africa and the Iberian Peninsula in the west. Today, the Sunnis account for roughly 85 per cent of all Muslims.

Muslim beliefs

Islam is a monotheistic religion. There is only one true God, Allah, who is omnipotent, omniscient, and omnipresent. Allah created the universe and everything in it. Muslims also believe in angels, devils, and Satan. There is life after death and the final resting place of a soul depends on his or her deeds in life. Paradise and Hell are akin to Christianity's Heaven and Hell. Again, like Christianity, there is the concept of Final Judgment. In the Battle of Armageddon, Christ fights and kills the Anti-Christ, and world peace ensues. After Armageddon, at the end of time, each soul faces a Final Judgment to go to Paradise or Hell. Whether a soul rests in Paradise or Hell depends not only on her earthly deeds but also on Allah's mercy.

Islam is built on five foundational obligations and practices. These foundations are the pillars of the religion. The five pillars of Islam are:

1 The profession of faith (*Shahada*)
2 Daily prayer (*Salat*)
3 Almsgiving (*Zakat*)
4 Fasting (*Sawm*)
5 Pilgrimage (*Hajj*)

These pillars are the essential religious duties required of every able, adult Muslim. The five pillars are distinct to Islam and constitute the core practices of the Islamic faith.

In saying the daily prayer, Muslims recite the profession of faith: 'I bear witness that there is no God but Allah and that Mohammed is his prophet.' This profession may be repeated at any time and in any place.

Daily prayers are performed five times daily, preceded by a ritual cleansing of the body. Believers face the Ka'aba, the ancient shrine in Mecca, stand, bow, and prostrate themselves, while reciting verses from the Qur'an, during prayers. The prayers are performed at the following times of day: dawn (*fajr* or *subh*), noon (*zuhr*), mid-afternoon (*asr*), sunset (*maghrib*), and evening (*isha*).

76 *Three finance paradigms*

Zakat, or charity, is obligatory for Muslims and is an expression of devotion to Allah. Every Muslim has a duty to care for the poor, orphans, and widows. Through zakat Muslims provide for the poorer sectors of society, purify their wealth, and attain salvation. The principle of zakat is infused into the practice of Islamic finance. In later sections, we learn that businesses and lenders must seriously consider forgiving debts under the principle of zakat if the borrower is in dire financial straits. Charity is expected of all Muslims, whether in the practice of business or in their personal lives.

Fasting takes place in the month of Ramadan, the ninth month of the twelve-month Islamic lunar calendar. The month of Ramadan is sacred because the first revelation is said to have occurred in this month. Ramadan officially starts when the new moon is sighted. During the entire month, Muslims cannot eat, drink, or have sexual intercourse from dawn till dusk. After the sun sets, however, Muslims partake of large feasts and may eat and drink till dawn the next day. By fasting Muslims are reminded of the misfortunes of the poor. Fasting fosters a sense of solidarity and mutual care for all in the community, regardless of social standing.

All Muslims are obligated to make a pilgrimage to Mecca at least once in their lives. This pilgrimage is known as the *hajj* and it must be embarked upon in the twelfth lunar month of the Islamic year. The hajj involves a set of detailed sequence of rituals undertaken over several days. All pilgrimage rituals take place in Mecca and the focus of the hajj is the Kaaba, also referred to as the House of God. The prophet Ibrahim is said to have built the Kaaba at God's command.

3.2 Shari'a

Shari'a is the religious law of Islam. There is no distinction between religion and daily life in Islam. Shari'a literally means the path, as shown by Allah, to be followed. The law covers every aspect of life including banking and finance. Shari'a is the ideal code of conduct for a Muslim, leading the way to a pure life. The sources of Shari'a are, in order of primacy:

1 The Holy Qur'an
2 The Sunnah of the Prophet
3 Ijma, and
4 Qiyas

Sources of Shari'a

(1) The Qur'an

The Qur'an is the supreme source of the Shari'a. It is both a religious and legal text. The word Qur'an means reading or recitation. It may be defined as 'the book containing the speech of God revealed to the Prophet Mohammed in Arabic and transmitted to us by continuous testimony'.[4] Muslims, therefore, believe the Qur'an contains the actual words spoken by God to his prophet, Mohammed. As such, the Qur'an is the authoritative and primary source of the Shari'a.

In sum, the Qur'an is the recorded words of God as spoken to the Prophet over the course of 23 years through the mediation of the archangel Gabriel. The Prophet received the first revelation in his forty-first year of life. The first *surah* (chapter) of the Qur'an begins: 'Recite in the name of thy Lord and Cherished who created man out of a (mere) clot of congealed blood. Proclaim and thy Lord is Most Bountiful.' (Surah 96: 1–3)

Over the course of the 23 years, the Prophet Mohammed received 114 surahs and 6,235 *ayat* (verses). In the last year of his life, the Prophet rearranged the order of the ayat within each surah and determined the sequence of the surahs.

While the Qur'an is the first and foremost textual reference for Shari'a, it is not exempt from ambiguity and vague terms. There is a need to discern meanings of these terms to apply them to real-world issues. The Qur'an is not unambiguous on all points and there remains a need for a 'guide to the Guide', which is the Sunnah of the Prophet as recorded in compilations of the hadith.[5]

(2) The Sunnah

Sunnah means a clear path and is used in the Qur'an to imply an established practice or code of conduct. While the Qur'an is the authoritative word on Islamic practice, there are instances when guidance for practical living is necessary. In such cases, Muslims turn to the Sunnah, which developed from the work of scholars over the ages who researched and recorded the details of the life of the Prophet. The Sunnah is therefore a collection of the acts, words, and judgments of the Prophet as well as the established practice of the Muslim community. The Hadith is the sayings of the Prophet while the rest, as a whole, is called the Sunnah. Technically, the Hadith is a part of the Sunnah and the two are often used interchangeably. However, there is a difference between the two. The Hadith is a record of the narratives and words of the Prophet. The Sunnah is the example or the law deduced from these recorded words of the Prophet. While the Qur'an is the primary source of the Shari'a, the Sunnah is the second most important source of the law.

The *mujtahid* (Scholar of Islamic Laws) must observe the order of priority between the Qur'an and Sunnah. When the mujtahid encounters a question of religious practice he first goes to the Qur'an for a solution. If he finds no guidance in the Qur'an for that particular problem, only then does he go to the Sunnah for a solution. With regard to the permissible forms of financial instruments and financial practice, scholars, therefore, go through the same process to determine Shari'a compliant financial transactions and products.

(3) Ijma (consensus)

Ijma refers to consensus of juristic opinions of the learned *ulema* (Islamic religious scholars), *fukaha* (Islamic legal scholars) of the *ummah* (Muslim community) after the death of the Prophet Mohammed. The ulema include the Companions of the Prophet and the learned *muftis* or *jurists*. Ijma did not take place when the Prophet Mohammed was alive because he alone was the highest authority on Shari'a. Consensus opinion probably first occurred when the Companions of the Prophet consulted each other on the interpretation and application of doctrines from the Qur'an. The Islamic community subsequently accepts the agreement of the ulema. After the death of the Companions, their Successors took on the task of forming consensus opinion on the Shari'a, using the past opinions of their predecessors. In turn, the descendants of these Successors formed more opinions basing their decisions on the consensus of the companions and the first line of successors. Thus, a historical record of ijma came into existence for the use of jurists and scholars. The use of ijma is not dissimilar to the method of case law practised in the US where precedents are set by previous court judgments. These legal precedents are consulted in determining judgments on new cases.

Unlike the Qur'an and Sunnah, ijma is not grounded directly on divine revelation. It is grounded on human reason and on universal acceptance of a particular opinion over a period of time. Once an ijma is established, it tends to become an authority in its own right. However, the establishment of an ijma is subject to some debate. Some argue ijma is not binding unless the entire Muslim community agrees to a particular interpretation after extensive discussion. As the ummah grew large, universal consensus has become almost impossible. Ijma may still develop regionally or by school but it may not be considered immutable until accepted by the entire ummah. When in the area of banking and finance, a transaction may be allowed in certain countries but not in others because there has been no universal agreement on the ijma pertaining to that particular transaction.

(4) Qiyas (analogical reasoning)

Qiyas means measuring, the length, weight, or quality of an entity. The term also connotes comparison of two equal or similar objects. Simply put, qiyas is analogical deduction. The method of qiyas is to compare a new case with one that is similar or analogous. The analogical cases or texts can be from the Qur'an, sunnah, or ijma. One moves on to qiyas only after exhausting the avenues of the Qur'an, sunnah, or ijma. In other words, Qiyas ranks fourth in terms of authority on the Shari'a.

Imam Abu Hanifah, the founder of the Hanafi School in Iraq, introduced the legal principle of qiyas.[6] During the Abbasids (CE 750–1258) period, Muslims were encountering new philosophical, scientific, and theological ideas from foreign lands. The people wanted to apply what they studied in foreign texts to Islamic jurisprudence. Abu Hanifah introduced the concept of qiyas because he wanted to keep the interpretation of Shari'a limited to pure Islamic principles.

It is acceptable to use qiyas to arrive at a logical conclusion in Shari'a as long as the conclusion does not violate the doctrines of the Qur'an or the sunnah.

(5) Ijtihad (individual reasoning)

Ijtihad is the use of human reason to interpret Shari'a. Qiyas is therefore a form of Ijtihad, although the latter is used specifically in legal contexts. One uses one's faculty of reason to arrive at a logical conclusion on a legal issue to deduce a conclusion about the effectiveness of a legal precept in Islam. Ijtihad is a method applied to the Qur'an, sunnah, qiyas, or ijma. Only specially educated religious and legal scholars engage in Ijtihad. In sum, Ijtihad is a process of independent legal reasoning. If the ummah accept the decision reached by Ijtihad, then the conclusion reached by Ijtihad becomes binding through ijma.

In the early years of Islam there was no restriction to scholars using ijtihad for interpreting the Qur'an and sunnah. However, Islamic scholars began to doubt if anyone could equal their predecessors in this process. Over time, scholars ceased using Ijtihad and independent reason was no longer accepted as a source of Shari'a. This occurrence is frequently referred to as the 'Closing of the Gate' to ijtihad. The Shi'ites view this closing with consternation because they believe Allah never leaves His people without guidance.[7] Within the Sunni tradition, the four schools hold the monopoly on interpretation.

The four schools

There are four major schools of Islamic jurisprudence that exist within Sunni Islam. First, there is the Maliki school, practised primarily in north and west Africa. Second is the Hanafi school, common in Turkic Asia. Third, the Shafii school found mainly in Egypt, East Africa, and South-East Asia. Fourth, the Hanbali school is dominant in Saudi Arabia. The schools are schools of jurisprudence. They are not analogous to the denominations of other religions such as Christianity. The schools focus more on matters of law than faith.

The differences among the Schools are not great. All four schools agree on the core principles of Islam such as the five pillars. All four also believe the Shari'a defines the content of the law, which in turn is determined by *fiqh*, or jurisprudence. The aim of fiqh is to regulate all of humanity's relations with Allah, separating acts into those that are permitted (*halal*) and those that are forbidden (*haram*), with several gradations between. Each School recognizes the validity of the other three, and any Sunni can choose to change schools.

3.3 Principles and ethics of Islamic finance

The purpose of Islamic finance

What is the purpose of finance? Answers vary depending on the financial theory of choice.

In conventional modern finance, the (unstated and not intentionally pursued) purpose of finance is to increase economic efficiency. This purpose is achieved through rational self-interest and profit maximization. Benefits to the community and the social good are by-products and unintended. In a free market, individuals make their own decisions, act rationally in their own self-interest and prefer to maximize profits. The behaviour of many individuals results in economic efficiency that consequently leads to prosperity and the material enrichment of society at large. Conventional finance is silent on the ethics of finance and on its teleology. Economic efficiency is not a stated or desired purpose. Efficiency simply is the outcome of all financial activity.

In contrast, the fundamental purpose of Islamic finance is derived from the Shari'a. The Shari'a, as we mentioned earlier, is the religious law Allah directly gave to his Prophet. As such, the purpose of Islamic finance is *ethically driven* because the aim of the Shari'a is also the aim of Islamic finance because finance is only one part of life and society. The objective of Shari'a is the happiness and wellbeing of the people in this worldly life as well as in the life Hereafter. Accordingly, the objective of Islamic finance is also the wellbeing of people in this life and in life Hereafter. *Islamic finance must contribute to the development and the good of the Islamic community*. How finance achieves this purpose is guided by principles written down in the Qur'an. Not surprisingly, therefore, the fundamental feature of Islamic finance is socio-economic and distributive justice. As Shari'a is the guide to Islamic finance, the latter contains a comprehensive system of ethics and moral values.

According to some Islamic finance scholars, Islam adopts a balanced approach between an individual's freedom and the wellbeing of society.[8] Society is served if the market is made more efficient through economic acts of self-interest, thereby leading to more transparent pricing and efficient allocation of resources. However, financial activities that cause social harm and do not aid social interests are not allowed, or halal.

Prohibitions

All business and financial contracts in Islamic finance must conform to Shari'a rules. Basic prohibitions in Islamic finance are:

1 Interest, or *riba*
2 Excessive risk, or *gharar*
3 Speculation, or *gambling*

(1) Prohibition against interest (riba)

There is little or no disagreement among Islamic scholars and legal scholars about the prohibition against interest. Making money from money is not Islamically acceptable and interest-based transactions are a sin. Primary sources of Shari'a (such as the Holy Qur'an and the Sunnah) are quite clear in condemning the practice. For example:

> Those who take Riba shall be raised like those who have been driven to madness by the touch of the Devil; this is because they say: 'Trade is just like interest' while Allah has permitted trade and forbidden interest. Hence those who have received the admonition from their Lord and desist, may keep their previous gains, their case being entrusted to Allah; but those who revert, shall be the inhabitants of the fire and abide therein forever.
>
> (Surah 275)

There are other verses in the Qur'an, which are equally clear about the sin of participating in interest-based transactions. Interest, or *riba*, is prohibited. Indeed, the prohibition of riba is the most significant one in Islamic finance.[9] The literal translation of riba is 'increase, growth, or accretion'.[10] Riba also means prohibited gain, juxtaposed in the Holy Qur'an to profits from sale. Riba is a form of unjustified enrichment, money used to make more money. Unjustified enrichment is forbidden.

Interest is any predetermined payment over and above the actual amount of principal of loans and debts, regardless of whether interest is charged on commercial or personal loans. Islam allows only one kind of loan and that is the interest-free loan, or the *qard al Hassan* (good loan). A strict reading of any gain above the principal may also mean the prohibition of indirect benefits that can potentially accrue to the lender.

A short history of interest

The rate of interest is a measure of the time value of money. In even more basic terms, interest is the rental price of money.[11] The practice of charging interest dates back to as early as the third millennium BCE during the Sumerian civilization. Wealthy landowners charged interest on loans of silver and barley. The inability of debtors to pay interest owed led to situations of virtual bondage to the extent that rulers of the times felt the need periodically to declare annulments of all debt servitude.[12]

Interest on loans was controversial in the Christian tradition for a long time. At the Council of Arles in 314 CE, clergymen of the Christian church were prohibited from taking interest on loans. This prohibition was repeated at the Council of Nicaea, 11 years later. The rules got tighter with passing years. Laymen were prevented from taking interest in 348 CE (Carthage), and again in 789 CE (Aix), 1179 (Lateran Council 3), and 1274 (Lyons Council 12).[13]

These repetitive prohibitions were to counter the habit of taking interest on loans that continued at regular intervals. Eventually, the Council of Vienna decided in 1311 that anyone who engaged in usury was a heretic. These prohibitions strengthened the financial role of the Jews. The Jews were further concentrated into the banking field by the additional constraint in some nations that would not permit them to engage in any other line of work.

The hard line against interest in the Christian community seems to have held firm until about 1500. It was not that interest was not being paid on loans prior to that time but simply that official notice had not been taken of it. In 1557 the burghers of Geneva appointed a committee to examine the situation. They concluded that for the avoidance of fraud, destruction, and ruination, the charging of interest ought to be allowed. Thus began the modern Western banking industry.

Interestingly, Adam Smith, the father of modern capitalism, was unwilling to let the interest rate float freely but instead supported state-imposed caps on the rate of interest. Smith's free market followers may be disappointed to know that Smith thought 5 per cent was the fair rate for any borrower in Great Britain to pay for a loan.[14] His opponent on this issue was Jeremy Bentham, who sought to persuade Smith to change his support for interest rate limits. Yet, the last edition of the *Wealth of Nations* to appear in Smith's lifetime, in 1789, left the usury passages defending state-set limits on interest.

Islamic views on money

The idea that money has a time value is a grounding principle of conventional modern finance. This concept has no meaning in Islamic finance. To many practitioners, those schooled in Western financial theories and academics, the idea of the time concept of money being meaningless is perplexing. Why does money not have a time value?

In the Islamic world view, money has no intrinsic value.[15] Money is a medium of exchange, not a commodity. Money is used for acquiring goods but does not possess intrinsic utility in itself.

Commodities may differ in quality and form but money has no qualities except as a measure of value and a medium of exchange.

Money does not have individual identity. One 10 dhiram bill is the same as any other. Every bill of a certain denomination is completely fungible with another bill of the same denomination. Products, in contrast, have individual identity. If a buyer contracts to buy house 'H', the buyer expects to buy house H and not house H1.

According to Islam, the role of finance is to promote socio-economic development within the mandate of preserving the Islamic State.

Islam does not distinguish between reasonable and exorbitant rates of interest because interest *per se* is forbidden. It is not the case that usury is forbidden while a 'market' rate of interest is allowed. Similarly, interest is forbidden no matter the use made of a loan, e.g., consumption versus production.

Opinions vary on the reasons for the ban on riba by Shari'a. Islamic scholars propose five reasons for prohibiting riba.[16]

1   Riba is unjust. This is one of the primary reasons for the prohibition of riba. Any contract involving riba is unjust to either borrower or lender. The Qur'an does not

explicitly say why it is unjust to charge an amount in excess of the principal. There can be little dispute that injustice and unfairness are not tolerable. The injustice of riba lies in the unequal relationship between lender and borrower and the unequal distribution of losses in a venture. If a business fails or loses money the person who used the loan to build the business suffers the loss. She receives no return for time and effort put into building the business. In contrast, the lender suffers no monetary losses but instead receives payment of both principal and accrued interest. In this way, riba is unjust. The Qur'an states that those who have problems making payments on their debts should have their obligations lessened. In addition, the lender cannot unilaterally impose additional fees for late payment on debt. Instead, a judge must consider the case of whether the debtor is under trying or extreme circumstances that make it difficult to make payments. For damages to be legitimate, they must be based on the claim of wilful breach of contract, and be decided by a judge.

2. Riba corrupts society. A passage of the Qur'an in chapter 30, 'Surah Rum', verses 37–41, support this reason for prohibiting riba. 'That which you give in usury in order that it may increase in other people's property has no increase with Allah ... Corruption does appear on land and sea because of (the evil) which men's hands have done ...'[17] This is the first mention of riba and the passage specifically links riba with corruption.

3. Riba implies the unlawful taking of property. This reason is supported in chapter four, 'Surah al-Nisa'. Jews were scolded for usury and 'devouring people's wealth by false pretences'. Interest on money is an unjustified creation of instant property rights. This type of enrichment is unjustified because interest is a property right claimed outside the legitimate framework of recognized property rights. As soon as a loan contract with agreed interest is signed, a right to the borrower's property is created for the lender.

4. Riba leads to negative growth. While riba increases money in quantitative terms, it does not generate growth in social wealth. We do not know for certain where interest earned goes. In contrast, charitable-giving is targeted at and transfers money to the poor and needy. Islamic economics argues that interest leads to inefficient allocation of society's resources and may contribute to the instability of the system. This misallocation occurs because in interest-based finance, creditworthiness of the borrower is the primary metric in loan decisions. In Islamic finance, the productive results of a business are the key metric because of the profit-sharing nature of the bank's investment. While conventional banking may reject a loan to high-return projects because the borrower does not meet credit-worthy measure, Islamic banking may invest in these projects. Therefore, the Islamic profit-sharing system is a more efficient allocator of resources. The bank is also more invested and interested in the project rather than only concerned with interest payments by the borrower. Interest-based systems force borrowers to pay their monthly interest payments, even if their circumstances are poorly suited for making repayments. Ultimately, forcing repayments without consideration of the borrower's circumstances exacerbates problems, resulting in default. Proponents of Islamic finance argue interest-based banking systems may accentuate downturns in the business cycle.

5. Riba demeans and diminishes the human personality. In one Surah (S2:275), the Qur'an illustrates the demeaning nature of 'those who devour usury'.[18] If a loan is required for the necessities of life, charging interest violates the nature of social life.

Those who have the resources and money should help and care for those in need. Charging interest affects a culture negatively by distancing that which is human and focusing on that which is monetary.

Ayub further adds, finance without riba promotes socio-economic and distributive justice. Intergenerational equity is more likely to result from banning interest. Distributive justice and socio-economic development are the most cited reasons for not allowing interest. Without interest, wealth will not accumulate in a few hands and 'circulate among the rich' (Holy Qur'an, 59:7). An interest-based financial system results ultimately in unrepayable debts, creating a wealthy class and another class of poor and oppressed.

As riba is prohibited, Muslims are not allowed to be creditors in a financial transaction, nor are they allowed to collect interest on bank deposits. Islamic finance promotes risk-sharing between the providers of funds (investors) and the users of funds (entrepreneurs). According to Islamic views, in conventional banking all risk is borne by the entrepreneur. The owner of the capital does not bear any risks associated with the failure of economic loss of a firm. Whether the firm succeeds or fails, the owner of capital is owed a pre-determined return. In Islam, this kind of unjust distribution of risk is not allowed. Instead, providers of finance in a business transaction are partners in the business and share in the profit and losses of the business. If the business is profitable, the partner who provides the finance shares in the profits. If the business makes a loss, the financing partner does not get any profits. If the business venture goes bankrupt, the investment is lost.

Interest on loans for productive purposes is prohibited because Islam does not consider it an equitable form of transaction. Money, in Islam, is only a medium of exchange, a way of valuing a thing. Money has no value *per se*, and should not be allowed to generate more money, via fixed interest payments, simply by being deposited in a bank or lent to someone else. Money is to be used for productive purposes such as business ventures or in building. Muslims are encouraged to spend and invest in productive investments and discouraged from keeping money idle. Hoarding money is not acceptable by Islamic standards.

When money is invested in a productive undertaking, the amount of profit that may be earned is not known with full certainty. Indeed the enterprise may even result in a loss. Therefore, to charge a fixed and predetermined rate of interest for such loans is not morally justified. Islamic justice demands the provider of capital to share the risk with the entrepreneur if the one with capital wishes to earn a profit. Capitalism considers capital as a factor of production, along with labour and land, each entitled to a return irrespective of profit or loss. In contrast, Islamic economics considers capital on par with enterprise.[19]

(2) Prohibition against excessive risk, or Gharar

Transactions that involve excessive risk are forbidden. *Gharar* refers to the uncertainty or hazard, caused by the lack of clarity with the price in a contract or exchange.[20] The literal translation of 'Gharar' is trick. Professor Mustafa Ahmad Al Zarqa of the University of Damascus offers the following definition of Gharar: '[Gharar is] the sale of probable items whose existence or characteristics are not certain, the risky nature of which makes the transaction akin to gambling.'[21]

A sale or any business contract that has an element of excessive Gharar is prohibited. The reason for prohibiting Gharar is not risk or uncertainty *per se* but as the definition above suggests, Gharar, in the sense of trickery and gambling involve unjust enrichment.

Prohibiting Gharar protects the weak from exploitation. The general financial or business instances when Gharar is present are:

1. The liability of or the payment from any of the contracting parties is uncertain or contingent.
2. Delivery of one or more of the products or services being bought or sold is not in the control of any of the contracting parties and is, therefore, uncertain.
3. Payment of one or more of the products or services being bought or sold is uncertain.
4. The sale of a product or service is not presently in the possession of the selling party.
5. Contracting parties to a sale or purchase do not know if the sale or purchase will actually take place.
6. The object of a legal transaction does not exist.

Gharar refers more to uncertainty than to risk as commonly used in financial terminology. The uncertainty pertains to the existence of the product or service in question, the rights of or benefits to the parties involved in the contractual relation, and the consequences of the contract. What of unknown objects, such as when the purchaser does not know what she has bought, or a seller does not know what she has sold? The Zahiri school of thought considers a transaction Gharar only when unknown objects are involved. The majority of jurists include both the unknown and the uncertain in calculating if a transaction is Gharar.

Every financial transaction involves some risk, such as currency risk, credit risk, legal risk, country risk, and political risk. While some transactions do not involve significant risk, others carry considerable risk. The Qur'an and literature on Islamic finance are not clear on the extent of risk allowed and, unlike Riba, do not have a great deal to say about Gharar. To ascertain which transactions or instruments are non-Shari'a compliant, scholars have taken on the task of differentiating between Gharar-e-Kathir and Gharar Qalil (too much and nominal uncertainty). Their decision on the matter is only those transactions involving too much or excessive uncertainty in respect of the product, service, or financial instrument, and their price in a contract should be prohibited.[22] Although Gharar is more difficult to define than Riba, there is now a consensus over the level of acceptable Gharar that makes a transaction Shari'a compliant. Thus, while any amount of Riba is prohibited, a certain degree of Gharar in the sense of uncertainty is acceptable in Islamic finance and business.

According to Ayub, future sales, suspended sales, and down payment sales all have the element of Gharar in their contracts. Options and futures, considered as very risky, are deemed as forbidden. So too are forward foreign exchange transactions, as forward exchange rates are determined by interest rate differentials. Whether short selling is prohibited in Islamic finance is still debated.

Short selling and Gharar

Short selling is the sale of an asset that the seller does not own and possibly does not even possess. The asset can be a stock, bond, commodity, currency, or other financial instrument. Typically, the short seller, such as a hedge fund, sells short a security, say Olam International, to a buyer. The short seller does not own any shares of Olam International and thus borrows the shares from a lender of securities, State Street Bank, for instance. The short seller has to pay a fee and interest to State Street and must eventually buy shares of Olam International to return to State Street. The goal is to buy the shares at a cheaper price than the price obtained from the short sale.

Clearly, Gharar is involved in the short selling-transaction.

1   It is uncertain if the short seller will make a profit. The short seller is betting the price of the security will fall in order to make a profit.
2   This bet (or gamble) involves a potentially unlimited liability. The price of the security could shoot up and wipe out the capital of the short seller.
3   There could be damage to the general stock market if short sellers depress the price of shares, thereby spreading panic.

In the various modes of Islamic financial transactions discussed in later sections, the seller is generally prohibited from selling an asset that she does not own and possess at the time of sale. The mechanism of short selling clearly steps over this prohibition. Thus, the Shari'a does seem to strongly incline against the practice of short selling.[23]

(3) Gambling or speculation

Gambling, or indulging in games of chance, is known as *Maisir* and *Qimar* in Arabic. Maisir refers to easily gained wealth by chance irrespective of whether the gain comes at the expense of another person's rights. Qimar means games of chance where one's gain is at the cost of another's loss.

In the Qur'an, it is maisir that is prohibited, but the Hadith literature discusses gambling under the general name of Qimar. According to jurists, qimar is an important kind of maisir. Both words are applicable to games of chance.

Gambling is a form of Gharar because the gambler is ignorant of the result of the gamble. The gambler may either win or lose his bet but he does not know the outcome. Islamic banks avoid conventional financial transactions that have elements of Qimar. For instance, conventional insurance is not Shari'a compliant because Islamic finance views conventional insurance as a gamble on whether something will happen. For instance, it is thought that life insurance is a bet on when one's life ends. Lotteries are common in the west for raising money for government. In the US, private companies administer and run lotteries under licence from state governments. The state gets a generous amount of taxes from these lottery operations. Under Shari'a, however, such lotteries are prohibited because they constitute gambling.

Other prohibitions with financial implications

Islam forbids its followers from consuming pork or pork products. This prohibition affects goods being traded or investments made. Muslims are not permitted to consume alcohol or illegal substances such as narcotics. For these reasons, these products cannot validly form the subject goods of a trade or transaction being conducted in accordance with Islamic finance. Similarly, if a company deals in activities, which are unethical according to Shari'a (e.g., pornography, prostitution, and weapons trading), then the company is not suitable either to participate in or be the subject of Islamic finance transactions. Using research and advice from Shari'a scholars, indexes have been formulated to screen stocks for Shari'a compliance. For instance, Dow Jones and FTSE have established dedicated Islamic indices. There is published information about which equities Muslims can trade in without breaching the requirements of their faith.

Ethical requirements

Islamic finance is not just compliance with a set of negative injunctions (avoidance) but also the active adherence to positive ethical principles (abidance) enunciated in the Shari'a. The Qur'an and Sunnah uphold the principles of justice, mutual help, free consent, and honesty on all contracting parties. It is a principle of Shari'a that Allah pardons acts against Him but does not pardon the harm done by a person to his fellow human beings or other animals. Therefore, giving people their due right is the cardinal principle of Islamic ethics.

The most important ethical principles in Islamic finance are:[24]

1. *Freedom to enter into contracts.* Islamic finance and economics allows the freedom to enter into contracts as long as the business or transaction is Shari'a compliant. A free market determines the price of freely exchanged goods and services. As common to free markets, the forces of demand and supply are responsible for setting prices. Thus, free markets and market pricing are not antithetical to Islamic finance and economics. Indeed, the Shari'a demands that prices are set fairly by the markets, with interference that leads to injustice. It is left to the businessperson to determine profit margins based on cost of goods sold and other expenses. However, ethics recommends moderation, contentment, and leniency. Most surprisingly, the Jeddah-based Council of the Islamic Fiqh Academy of the OIC (Organisation of Islamic Countries) recommends government should stay out of fixing prices. Government should intervene only when market failures and imperfections exist.
2. *Justice and fair dealing.* The rights and obligations of any person are neither greater nor lesser in any way than the rights and obligations of others. Rules, including business rules, are applicable to all. The Prophet spoke of the inviolability of human rights in the sphere of person, property, and honour.
3. *Honesty and Truthfulness.* According to the Shari'a, honesty, truthfulness, and care for others are the basic ethical 57principles Muslims should follow. Cheating others and telling lies is considered a great sin. A famous line in the Qur'an says: 'Fill the measure when you measure, and weigh with a perfectly right balance.' (17:35)
4. *Fulfilling contracts and paying liabilities.* The Qur'an uses as an example of a hypocrite, the person who does not fulfil his promises. There is strong agreement among contemporary scholars that business and financial promises signed in contracts are binding. The concept of promise is invoked in *Murabaha*, *Musharaka*, and other Islamic-based financial transactions (see section 3.5).
5. *Mutual cooperation and help for those in need.* The Islamic economic system stresses cooperation among players. Giving help to those in need is especially emphasized in the Holy Qur'an. The ethics of care logically extends to the prohibition of riba because of the harm the accumulation of riba may cause to those who are economically distressed.

3.4 Determination of compliance with Shari'a

Shari'a Supervisory Boards (SSB) are mandatory to ensure financial instruments and transactions are permissible according to Shari'a. SSBs are responsible for three main functions. First, the boards ensure the services and facilities financial institutions offer accord with Shari'a. Second, the boards guarantee the financial institution's investments and involvement in projects are Shari'a compliant. Third, the boards ensure the financial institution is managed according to Islamic principles. Most financial institutions retain (either independently or in-house) a panel of Shari'a scholars who are well versed in all the relevant schools of thought and who collectively reach a decision on issues posed to them. Such boards normally work for a fee. They then produce a certification of Shari'a compliance (known as a *fatwa* – literally meaning 'judgment') stating the documents, products, or services are Shari'a compliant.

The International Association of Islamic Banks (IAIB) enumerates the duties of the SSB as follows:[25]

1. Study previously issued Fatwa (religious rulings) to assess its constituency with Shari'a and, when appropriate, base its own rulings on these decisions.
2. Supervise the activities of the bank in order to guarantee conformity with the Shari'a.
3. Issue religious opinions on banking and financial questions.
4. Clarify legal religious rulings on new economic issues.

SSBs perform both supervisory and advisory roles to banks and other financial institutions. The supervisory roles entail reviewing the operations, investments, services, and products offered by the bank to ensure these elements are Shari'a compliant. In their advisory role, SSBs consult with banks to answer issues or concerns for a particular transaction or product. They offer constructive, creative, or alternative recommendations when necessary.

Supervisory role

SSBs and Shari'a advisers ensure financial institutions offer products and services that conform to Shari'a. For investment managers, this means investment products for clients such as mutual funds, passive funds, or exchange-traded funds are Shari'a compliant. For retail banks, SSBs evaluate the acceptability of products, such as savings accounts, time deposits, loans, and investments using their clients' deposits. Fund managers must invest only in securities classified as Shari'a approved by the Shari'a board. SSBs will, where appropriate, conduct audits of the portfolios of Islamic products sold by banks, to ensure there is continuing compliance with Shari'a.

SSBs review and endorse not only the products and services but also all relevant documents pertaining to the products and services. Before customers buy the bank offerings, SSBs look over prospectus, trust deeds, loan contracts, and other documents. Shari'a supervisors review operational and administrative matters. In these daily operational activities SSBs ensure that the practice and implementation of financial transactions accord with Islamic principles. There are always issues in everyday practice that textbooks or theory do not cover. SSBs should understand and resolve the issues. This responsibility requires close involvement with the actual practice and implementation aspects of financial transactions.

Advisory role

As the pace of financial change and practice is usually rapid, SSBs need to keep up with new transactions, products, and services. Thus, Shari'a boards advise financial institutions on developing innovative new products that are competitive and acceptable to all stakeholders. Some of the newer instruments requiring Shari'a compliant innovation are risk management, hedging tools, derivatives, and hybrid financing facilities. To meet these needs, Shari'a advisers have to conduct research on both Islamic law and financial practice.

Shari'a advisers, as keepers and scholars of Islamic knowledge, are the people expected to share their knowledge through educating and disseminating information to Islamic finance practitioners. Islamic financial markets are constantly growing and improving. Thus, education is continuous so that financial practitioners are up on their game and new entrants are also trained. As the Shari'a advisers possess the knowledge of *Mualamat* (practicalities of mundane daily life) as well as *Fiqh* (Islamic law), they are best placed to impart knowledge to practitioners and society in general.

Related parties of financial institutions in the Islamic financial market, such as legal counsels, auditors, and consultants, may seek advice on Shari'a matters from advisers. SSBs are expected to provide necessary assistance to ensure full compliance with Shari'a principles. Advisers must fully explain the basis for their particular decision and recommendation. These opinions must be supported by the relevant Shari'a jurisprudential literature from established sources.

Shari'a supervisory board expertise

As so much depends on the certification of Shari'a boards, those who make up the boards must be well-qualified Shari'a scholars. While there may be a divergence of opinions, banks tend to hire boards whose scholars are of the highest international reputation and integrity. There are a handful of well-known scholars from jurisdictions, such as Saudi Arabia, Kuwait, Bahrain, Pakistan, the US, and Malaysia. These scholars are the leading names in the field whose services are sought out by elite banks and financial institutions. Many of the scholars are regarded as pragmatic, possessing language expertise and knowledge of leading-edge issues in banking and finance. Of course, these scholars are also experts in Shari'a reasoning.[26]

Qualifications of Shari'a Board or committee members

Bank Simpanan Nasional of Malaysia offers Islamic Banking to its customers. The qualifications of some of its Shari'a Committee are given below.

Dr. Mohd Fuad bin Md Sawari (Chairman)

Dr. Mohd Fuad bin Md Sawari is currently an Assistant Professor at Department of Fiqh & Usul al-Fiqh, Kulliyyah of Islamic Revealed Knowledge and Human Sciences (IRKHS), International Islamic University Malaysia (IIUM). He obtained his first degree in Shariah from the Faculty of Shariah, Islamic Academy, University of Malaya, M.A. in Fiqh & Usul al-Fiqh from the Faculty of Shariah, University of Jordan, Amman, and Ph.D. in Fiqh & Usul al-Fiqh from the International Islamic University Malaysia. He is also one of the members of the

Shariah Advisory Board, Prudential BSN Takaful Berhad. His research interests are Islamic Law of Contract, Takaful, Islamic Legal Maxim, Electronic Commerce, and Principles of Islamic Jurisprudence (Usul Al-Fiqh).

Encik Zainudin bin Ismail

Encik Zainudin bin Ismail is currently a lecturer at Islamic Law Department, Ahmad Ibrahim Kulliyyah of Laws, International Islamic University Malaysia (IIUM). He obtained his B.A. (Hons) Shariah at Al-Azhar University, Egypt after which he received his Master of Comparative Laws at IIUM. Currently, he is pursuing his Ph.D. in Islamic Banking at IIUM. His areas of interest are Islamic Banking and Finance, Islamic Insurance (Takaful), Islamic Legal Maxims, and Principles of Islamic Jurisprudence.

Dr. Fauziah binti Mohd Noor

Dr. Fauziah binti Mohd Noor is an Assistant Professor at Ahmad Ibrahim Kulliyyah of Laws, International Islamic University Malaysia. She obtained her first degree in Shariah, Faculty of Shariah, Islamic Academy University of Malaya. Then she obtained her Master in Law (LLM) from the School of Oriental and African Studies at University of London, and a Ph.D. from University of Birmingham (Agricultural Law, Comparative Studies between Islamic Agricultural Law and the Malaysian Law). She is now a consultant at International Institute for Halal Research and Training, International Islamic University Malaysia (IIUM). Her areas of interest are Islamic Jurisprudence (Usul al-Fiqh), Islamic Banking, Islamic Family Law, and Islamic Land Law.

Source: Bank Simpanan Nasional Website (www.mybsn.com.my).

The Islamic Financial Services Board (IFSB)

The Islamic Financial Services Board (IFSB) is an international standard-setting organisation that promotes and enhances the soundness and stability of the Islamic financial services industry by issuing global prudential standards and guiding principles for the industry—broadly defined to include the banking, capital markets, and insurance sectors. The IFSB also conducts research and coordinates initiatives on industry related issues, as well as organises roundtables, seminars and conferences for regulators and industry stakeholders.

The IFSB is based in Kuala Lumpur, Malaysia, and began operating in March 2003. It serves as an international standard-setting body of regulatory and supervisory agencies that have a vested interest in ensuring the soundness and stability of the Islamic financial services industry, which is defined broadly to include banking, capital markets and insurance. In advancing this mission, the IFSB promotes the development of a prudent and transparent Islamic financial services industry through introducing new, or adapting existing international standards consistent with Shari'a principles, and recommending them for adoption.

> To this end, the work of the IFSB complements that of the Basel Committee on Banking Supervision, the International Organisation of Securities Commissions and the International Association of Insurance Supervisors.
>
> Source: Islamic Banking and Finance by World Savings Banks Institute/European Savings Banks Group, 2009.

3.5 Forms of Islamic finance I: profit- and loss-sharing-based transactions

Instead of lending money at a fixed rate of interest, the financier or banker forms a partnership with the borrower, sharing in a business venture's profits or losses. The principle of profit- and loss-sharing underlies this Islamic mode of financing. Two types of partnership exist: first, *Mudaraba*, which is a partnership or finance trusteeship; and second, *Musharaka*, which is a longer-term equity like arrangement. In both cases, the financial institution receives a share of the profits generated by the joint ventures.

Mudaraba

The Mudaraba is a profit- and loss-sharing model of business. One partner brings investment capital and the other provides sweat capital (effort). The former party is the owner of capital or financier, while the latter is the entrepreneur. In Arabic terms, the financier is called the *Rab ul-Mall* and the entrepreneur is the *Mudarib*. The *Mudarib* may also be known as the worker or the agent. Together the partners form a business enterprise whose profits are shared in a prearranged agreed amount among the partners. However, the loss is borne by the owner of capital while the entrepreneur simply receives no profits from the venture. In reality, Mudaraba is more like a profit-sharing partnership.

Islamic banks use the mudaraba mode of financing as their business model of operations. What conventional banking labels as depositors, Islamic banking calls investors. The Islamic bank is the entrepreneur in the enterprise because it puts in the effort and provides the management expertise. The investors in the enterprise are the depositors/customers of the Islamic bank. Instead of receiving interest on their deposits as conventional banking customers do, the depositors (investors) of Islamic banks receive a share of the profits from their deposits (capital). As discussed above, interest or riba is prohibited in the Shari'a. The bank, as the entrepreneur or agent in the mudaraba, does not share in the losses of the enterprise. The bank passes on this loss to the depositors, also known as investment account holders.

In the Mudaraba agreement, the owner of capital does not have the right to interfere with the management of the enterprise, which is the sole responsibility of the entrepreneur. The investors do have a say in the conditions, which ensure better management of their money. For this reason the mudaraba is sometimes called a sleeping partnership.

Structure of Islamic banks

Islamic banks are structured according to the mudaraba model of business. Using a two-tiered Mudaraba, the Islamic banking model consists of three entities: (1) the depositors who are the financiers/investors, (2) the bank, acting as an intermediary, and (3) the entrepreneurs, who require funds. On the first level of the two-tiered structure, the bank acts as the *Mudarib*, receiving investable funds from depositors, the *Rab ul-Mall* or financiers. On the second level, the bank becomes the *Rab ul-Mall* investing funds with entrepreneurs, who are the *Mudarib* at this level.

(1) The bank as Mudarib

The funds the bank receives from depositors are placed in unrestricted investment accounts. No constraints are placed on the bank in terms of investments the bank chooses. Naturally, the bank is not allowed to invest in activities prohibited by the Shari'a such as ventures involving pork or alcohol. The bank pools the profit from different investments, and shares the net profit with depositors, according to transparent and agreed amounts. In the event of losses, the depositors lose a proportional share or the entire amount of their funds. The bank shares profits with its investors according to an agreed ratio and not a fixed amount. A fixed amount renders the mudaraba void because the amount may not be achieved by the mudaraba venture. When the venture is profitable, funds are first deducted from profits to be set aside as capital. The *mudarib* has the right to use this capital for business-related expenses.

(2) The bank as Rab ul-Mall

The Islamic bank uses the money from its unrestricted investment accounts to invest in a venture managed by entrepreneurs who approach the bank for funding. The bank applies the restricted form of the mudaraba when it invests these funds with specified entrepreneurs. In the restricted mudaraba, the bank has the right to determine the type of activities, the duration and the location of projects, and to monitor investments. However, the bank cannot interfere with management, the daily operation of the venture, nor in a way that harms the venture. Profits to the bank as *Rab ul-Mall* are agreed upon with the entrepreneur. As with the agreement the bank has with its depositors, profits assigned to each party are based on a ratio and not a fixed amount.

The two-tier model of mudaraba financing replaces interest with profit-sharing on both the liabilities and the assets side of the bank's balance sheet.

Financing an Islamic bank

An Islamic bank is normally a joint stock company and receives financing from three sources.

1 Shareholders who provide equity receive dividends. The dividends come from profits, after expenses. The bank may retain profits after dividends to invest further in the business of the bank.
2 Depositors (investors) who place their funds with the bank and receive a pro rated amount of profits from the ventures in which their funds are invested. Rather than earning interest as depositors in conventional banks would, depositors in Islamic banks earn a portion of profits of the bank. In addition to unrestricted investment deposits, banks may also have restricted mudaraba investment accounts. These deposits are channelled to specific investment projects. Sometimes known as special

92 *Three finance paradigms*

investment accounts, depositors expect the money to be used in particular activities such as leasing and trade financing.
3   Depositors also may set up current accounts which pay no profits but from which funds can be withdrawn anytime. Banks may use current accounts to invest in ventures, keeping the profits from such ventures, but bearing the entire risk. The depositors are in effect making a loan to the bank whose repayment is guaranteed but does not receive any interest.

Reducing risks associated with mudaraba

As the Mudarib bears the risk of capital and profit loss, this form of financing is particularly risky from the point of view of a conventional banker. Under Mudaraba, financial losses are borne completely by the lender. The entrepreneur bears the risk of losing time and effort invested in the enterprise. This distribution effectively treats human capital and financial capital equally. To ameliorate the risks, many Islamic banks have developed less risky Mudaraba transactions:

1   Banks prefer to use Mudaraba with public limited companies (PLCs). This choice ensures greater transparency and oversight because PLCs have audited accounts and quarterly earnings reports.
2   Mudaraba contracts normally have guarantees that protect against loss due to negligence or mismanagement.
3   Banks tend to choose simple, common, open, and easily analysed economic activities for Mudaraba financing. For instance, financing a small business owner to expand retail space is a reasonably transparent activity.

Clearly, the difference between Mudaraba-based banking and conventional banking is not merely semantics. Conventional banks charge interest for the money loaned and are creditors. Islamic banks provide funding to clients to form partnership enterprises, and receive a share of the profits of these enterprises. The yield is not guaranteed in the profit-sharing mode and interest-based lending is not contingent on the profit or loss of lenders. Islamic banks are partners with their customers, while conventional banks are creditors to their customers. The risk of financial loss is borne mainly by the Islamic bank but falls most directly on the borrower in the case of conventional banking.

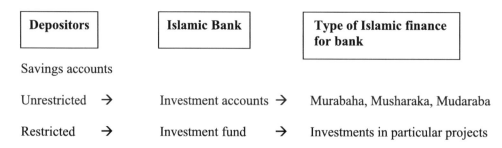

Figure 3.1 Islamic banking model.

Musharaka

The word *musharaka* means to share, or sharing. This Islamic mode of financing is in essence, a transaction where two or more partners have equity participation in a joint economic venture, share the profits according to prior agreement, and share the losses in proportion to the contributed capital.

The partners or shareholders in a musharaka contribute capital to and receive profits from the business venture. The amount of profits received by each partner depends on pre-agreed profit arrangements. In one form of musharaka, the constant musharaka, partners' share in the capital remains constant throughout the period of the venture. In another form of musharaka, the diminishing musharaka, a partner, normally an Islamic bank, agrees to transfer its share in the musharaka to the other partners. This transfer is done gradually so that the share of the bank's capital in the venture declines to zero and the other partner or partners have whole ownership of the business venture.

While partners in a musharaka share profits of the business venture in an agreed manner, losses must be shared according to the proportion of the capital contributions. This stipulation of loss-sharing in a musharaka is, therefore, Shari'a constrained.

There are two forms of musharaka. First, the *mufawada* is an unlimited, unrestricted and equal partnership. In the mufawada, every partner is equal in every respect, such as capital contributions, management control, privileges, and proportion of profits. Each partner is both agent and guarantor of the other. Second, the 'inan (shirkah al'inan) form of musharaka is not an equal partnership. Different partners have different rights, share of profits, and management control. In practice, the most common form of musharaka is the 'inan musharaka.

The musharaka form of financing is one of the purest modes of interest-free banking. However, in contemporary Islamic banking musharaka is rare. The reasons for its unpopularity are its complexity and relatively high level of risk. A bank cannot have ownership in and operational responsibility for a range of joint stock companies. It is also difficult for the bank to evaluate the status of the other partner or partners in the joint company. Calculating the profits at the end of the musharaka requires ascertaining the difference of the value of the venture at its end and at its beginning. This calculation is complex and risky.

Examples of musharaka

A general example of musharaka financing by Islamic banks is the use of musharaka in structuring a working capital facility for a company. The Islamic bank provides the funds to the company by depositing the amount in the client's account. The company accesses the funds whenever necessary. In the provision and access to funds, the working capital facility functions in the same way as a conventional facility. The difference lies in how the bank charges for the facility.

The Islamic bank does not charge interest. Instead, the bank debits an amount from the client's account based on a predetermined rate of profit. The amount is adjusted regularly, normally at the end of the quarter. At the end of each year, the profits of the company are calculated. If the profits due to the bank are more than the quarterly amount debited by the bank, then the difference is credited to a special reserve account the company creates in its books. On the other hand, if the profits due to the bank are less than the amount debited by the bank, then the client will reduce the amount of the excess payment in the special reserve account.

When the musharaka contract is terminated, such as when the working capital facility is closed, a final profit and loss account is prepared. The bank and its client share the balance of the special reserve account in the ratio agreed upon at the start of the contract. Should the company experience a loss, the special reserve account is reduced by the amount of those losses. If the amount in the special reserve account does not cover the loss, the client may ask the bank for a refund of the provisional profits previously paid to the bank. This risk of loss means it is vital a bank does a thorough due diligence of the client ensuring there is a track record of sustained profitability, before engaging in any musharaka contract.

Tejoori Musharaka Deal

Tejoori Limited, the investment company headquartered in Dubai and listed on the Alternative Investment Market in London, closed its musharaka agreement with Omniyat Properties Eleven.

Tejori took a 25 per cent equity stake in Omniyat Properties Eleven, giving the investment company a stake in land deals and projects valued at more than AED1bn (US$281 million) in Dubai Business Bay and Lagoons.

Under a musharaka arrangement, two or more parties combine either labour or capital and share in the profit or loss of the venture.

Sheikh Fawaz Bashraheel, chairman of Tejoori, said: 'The closure of this Musharaka agreement comes as we are announcing yet more transactions. We are now experiencing solid momentum and confirming Tejoori's commitment to both traditional and unique opportunities centred around the principles of Shari'a compliant investing.'

Omniyat Properties Eleven is a special purpose entity and part of Omniyat Holdings, which is also the holding company for Omniyat Properties, the real estate development company responsible for ongoing developments such as One Business Bay, The Binary, and the Square residential project. The developer has a special focus on creating technologically advanced properties and 'smart buildings' in the Middle East, with around US$735 million of projects currently underway.

Source: ArabianBusiness.com, 1 February 2007
(http://www.arabianbusiness.com/property-test/article/7068-tejoori-closes-musharaka-deal).

Problems with musharaka

The Islamic bank, as a partner or shareholder in a musharaka, may experience large losses. These losses will then be passed on to the bank's depositors. If the bank gets a reputation for poor investment decisions in musharaka ventures, then depositors will withdraw their money. To mitigate this problem, Islamic banks diversify their musharaka financing deals across many ventures. In addition, like conventional banks, Islamic banks must carry out careful due diligence on their musharaka partners. The upside of musharaka transactions is if profits are high, the bank, and therefore the depositors may enjoy higher returns than depositors who leave their money in conventional banks.

There is always a risk that the partner of an Islamic bank in a musharaka is dishonest and may not pay any returns to the bank, or may even claim a fictitious loss. The bank must install good auditing and management information systems to ensure their musharaka ventures are well monitored.

3.6 Forms of Islamic finance II: non-profit and loss-sharing-based transactions

Murabaha

The *murabaha* contract or financial transaction is also known as the cost-plus contract. The name implies the element of cost of a product or service and the element of a profit margin. The key feature of murabaha is that these pricing elements are known to both buyer and seller. In a typical murabaha contract, the seller agrees to provide a buyer a specific commodity. The seller discloses the actual cost incurred in acquiring the commodity, and adds the element of profit. The buyer can pay for the purchase in one payment or over several instalments but the buyer is cognizant of cost and profit margin and agrees to the purchase. If a person sells a commodity for a total price without reference to the cost, this is not murabaha, but musawamah.

The four general steps in a murabaha contract go as follows:[27]

Step 1: A buyer of a specific product asks a seller to purchase the product with the promise to buy this product at a profit. Shari'a scholars consider this move as an invitation to do business and not a firm commitment.
Step 2: If the seller accepts this invitation, she must then find the product, buy the product, and ensure the purchase is a legitimately contracted one.
Step 3: The seller contacts the buyer to inform her that the seller has purchased the product and has legitimate ownership of the product.
Step 4: The buyer may either reject the purchase of the product or buy the product. If the former, then the parties have entered into a murabaha contract.

Murabaha in finance

Cost-plus or murabaha transactions account for 80 to 95 per cent of all investments by Islamic financial institutions. The murabaha transaction is common in financing the purchase of assets, such as cars, houses, equipment, and replacing conventional lending, such as personal loans for car purchases, mortgages, and home equity loans. The bank finances the purchase of a good or asset by buying the item on behalf of its client and adding a margin before reselling the item to the client. For instance, if a bank customer wishes to buy a car under conventional banking, she simply applies for a car loan. The bank lends the customer the money. She then uses the money to purchase a car. In return for this service and for the use of its money, the customer agrees to pay a certain interest on the loan, over a specified period, to the bank.

In contrast, Islamic banking employs a murabaha contract to effect the transaction. The customer instructs the bank to buy the specified car, say, a red Toyota Corolla. The bank purchases the Corolla and has ownership of it for a short amount of time. The bank then almost immediately sells the car to the buyer at cost plus a mark-up. The buyer can pay for the car in one lump sum or over a period of time on an instalment basis.

Murabaha is Shari'a compliant because no interest on money is charged. The bank first acquires the asset and then resells it for a profit. Real goods are bought and sold and the transaction is not a mere exchange of money for money. In the process the bank is exposed to the risk of owning the asset, which may fall in price causing the client to reject the purchase at the originally agreed higher price. Thus, the bank shares in the risk of the transaction.

In practice the murabaha follows the steps as listed above. Often, when a client requires a specific asset, the bank appoints the client as its agent to purchase the asset on its behalf. In such instance, the two parties sign an agency agreement. The client then purchases the asset on behalf of the bank and takes possession of it as an agent of the bank. The client informs the bank it has purchased and has possession of the asset and at the same time, makes an offer at the agreed cost-plus price to purchase it from the bank. The bank accepts the offer and the sale concludes. Ownership of the asset transfers to the client.

The most essential element of the transaction is the bank continues to bear the risk from the time the asset is purchased by the client until the bank completes the sale to the client. Islamic scholars believe this feature of the murabaha distinguishes it from interest-based transactions. Another necessary feature of the murabaha is the purchase of the asset must be made from a third party. The purchase of an asset from the same person on a buy-back agreement is not allowed in the Shari'a.

Default

In the case of default by the client, the Islamic bank cannot increase the price. In conventional loans, interest will accumulate and the client is obligated to pay all accumulated interest. In Islamic finance, the bank and the client may make a prior agreement for the client to make a donation to a charity if she does not make a payment on a due date. This penalty discourages wilful delays by the client. The penalty is equal to the average rate of return for the mudaraba accounts of the bank. The amount recovered from the buyer cannot form part of the income of the bank. Instead, the penalty is given to a charitable purpose as the Shari'a board recommends. There is no penal interest such as conventional banks normally charge. Finally, the penalty clause in the murabaha agreement will not be enforced if the delay of payment is for reasons beyond the control of the client.

To be Shari'a compliant a murabaha transaction is obliged to follow three rules:

1. The asset must exist at the time of the sale. An item that has not come into existence cannot be sold.
2. The seller must own the asset at the time of the sale. If the seller does not own something that he subsequently sells, the sale is void.
3. The asset must be in physical or constructive possession of the seller when the seller sells to another person. Constructive possession means the rights of ownership belong to the seller even if she does not have physical possession of the object.

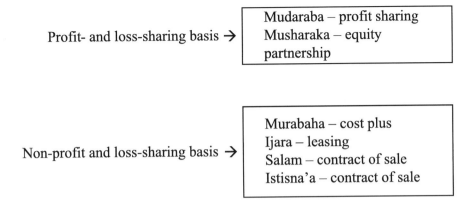

Figure 3.2 Types of Islamic finance.

Examples of Murabaha in practice

International Islamic Teams Up With QIB To Provide US$380 Million Finance Package For Nakilat

Qatar International Islamic Bank (International Islamic) signs a 'Murabaha' financing package of US$380 million for Qatar Transport Company (Nakilat) in partnership with Qatar Islamic Bank (QIB).

The package is split into US$200 million financed through International Islamic and US$180 million through QIB.

The joint arrangement is a big leap forward in enhancing cooperation between these two Islamic Finance institutions, as the market demand for Shari'a-compliant financial solutions continues to increase.

The signing ceremony took place at QIB's headquarter and signed by Ahmad Meshari, Acting Chief Executive Officer—QIB, Abdulbasit A Al-Shaibei, Chief Executive Officer—International Islamic, and Mohammad Ghannam, Managing Director—Nakilat, in addition to the presence of other senior officials from all parties for the signing ceremony.

Mr Al-Shaibei, commented, 'This Murabaha joint-financing partnership with QIB reflects a common interest in developing productive levels of co-operation for the benefit of both institutions involved but also, most importantly, for the benefit of the client, Nakilat'.

Source: *The Peninsula*, 13 August 2012
(http://thepeninsulaqatar.com/business/business-news/204645/qib-teams-up-with-qiib-for-nakilat-package).

Ijara

The term *ijara* means to give something to rent. Ijara activity is practically identical to conventional leasing and is probably the fastest growing financial activity of Islamic financial institutions.[28] The Western counterparts for ijara are operating leases and financial leases. The lessor leases an asset to a third party in exchange for a specified rent. The amounts of payments are known in advance and the asset remains the property of the lessor. In Arab terminology, the lessor is called the *mujir*, the lessee is called *mustajir*, and the rent payable to the lessor is called the *ujrah*.

Lease-purchase agreements are called the *ijara wa iktana*, and are more like the conventional financial lease. These specific leasing agreements allow the lessee to buy the asset at the end of the lease. To reduce the element of gharar, the price of the asset at the expiration of the lease cannot be predetermined.

Under the ijara scheme of financing, the financial institution purchases a real asset (perhaps according to the specifications of the lessee) and leases it to the client. The lessor and lessee determine the period of the lease, which may be from three months to five years or more. During the period of the lease the financial institution owns the asset but the physical possession of the asset and the right of use is transferred to the lessee.

To avoid gharar and riba, ijara differs in some minor ways from conventional leasing. Ijara is the sale of *usufruct* (the right of using another's property without ruining its substance) and therefore the rules of ijara closely follow those of ordinary sales. The usufruct is not a tangible thing but a series of future usage of an asset. This characteristic of ijara may increase risk or gharar. To mitigate gharar associated with ijara, Islamic law gives the lessee a broad scope to cancel the lease if the usufruct proves less valuable than expected. In return, the lessor is responsible for the maintenance and upkeep of the rental equipment. These elements of risk are components in making ijara acceptable within Shari'a.

Ijara is a popular mode of Islamic finance because it is easily compliant with Shari'a and acceptable to most Islamic scholars. There is no element of riba or gharar in ijara instruments. The Shari'a allows a fixed charge relating to tangible assets but not to financial assets. The financier is allowed compensation because she assumes the risks by converting financial capital into tangible assets. In addition, the financial institution has ownership of the asset during the term of the lease. This means the bank bears the risk of an economic recession or reduced demand for the assets.

As ijara is an established instrument of finance, there are standardized and easily usable ijara products available. Islamic leasing products are popular and competitive with conventional leasing because of their close similarities.

A summary of the main rules of Islamic leasing:[29]

1. Leasing is a contract where the owner of an asset transfers the usufruct of that asset to another for an agreed period, for an agreed sum of money.
2. The asset must have a use. Assets without usufruct cannot be leased.
3. Ownership of the leased asset must remain with the lessor. If an asset is consumed as a result of its use, this asset cannot be leased out. For example, items such as money, foods, and fuel cannot be leased.
4. The liabilities that arise from the ownership of the asset will be borne by the lessor. The liabilities that arise from the use of the asset will be borne by the lessee.

5 The time period of the lease must be clearly agreed.
6 The lessee must use the leased asset for the specified purpose.
7 The lessee is liable for damages to the asset caused by the lessee.
8 Benchmarking against LIBOR (London Interbank Offered Rate) is permitted.

> **Example of Ijara in practice**
>
> Bank Islam Malaysia provides lease purchase services.
>
> According to Bank Islam, its leasing facilities are termed 'Leasing-'. Leasing-i is a facility based on the Shari'a contract of Ijara, which allows the customer to lease equipment/commercial vehicles from Bank Islam on rental for the usage of equipment during the lease period. The total leased rental, which is fixed throughout the tenure, comprises the original cost of equipment and the Bank's profit margin.
>
> Source: http://www.bankislam.com.my/en/Pages/Leasing-i.aspx?tabs=2

Istisna'a

Shari'a rules on Islamic business and financing are clear in stating a seller of goods must have the goods in her physical or constructive possession. This rule has three corollaries. First, the good must exist at the time of a sale. Second, the seller must have ownership of the good. Finally, the seller also should have possession of the good. If the seller owns a good, but has not taken delivery herself or through an agent, she cannot sell it. Two types of financial transactions serve as exceptions to these Shari'a principles. The first is the case of *istisna'a* transactions, and the second is that of *salam* transactions.

The term istisna'a comes from *Sina'a*, which means to manufacture a specific commodity. Istisna'a is a contract of sale where the buyer asks the seller to manufacture, assemble, or construct a specified product to be delivered at a future date. The seller provides the raw materials. The price is determined before manufacturing begins. The bank acts as a middleman in this transaction. It offers financing for the specified product constructed, manufactured, or assembled. The bank adds a profit margin and sells the product to the customer. The buyer can pay for the agreed price later, either in one sum or in instalments. Istisna'a is the Islamic form of construction finance. For example, during the construction of a building, the buyer will make periodic payments according to the progress of the construction.

The contract can be made directly between the buyer and the builder or manufacturer, but typically an istisna'a is a three-party contract, where the bank acts as intermediary. A parallel, or back-to-back, istisna'a structure consists of two istisna'a contracts that form the basis of the three-party contract. In the first agreement, the client agrees to repay the bank on a longer-term schedule. This client/bank agreement contains detailed specifications for the asset being acquired. If the asset is an aeroplane, then the contract has a full description of the aeroplane to be built. The specifications may include names of contractors, estimates of costs, and suppliers of raw materials. The bank provides costs, profit margins, and the price it charges the customer. The second contract is between the bank and the supplier of the asset. The terms of the contract also gives specifications of the asset, the completion date, and the price of the asset. Under the second agreement, the bank, acting as a purchaser, makes progress instalment payments to the producer over a shorter period of time.

The bank makes its profit by adding a mark-up, which is the difference between the price the client pays the bank for the asset less the amount the bank pays for the same asset to the producer. This transaction is similar in structure and principle to the cost-plus transaction called murabaha, which we described earlier.

No overwhelming juridical and theological support exists for istisna'a as a Shari'a compliant form of financing.[30] The majority of religious schools argue istisna'a is inconsistent with Shari'a law. The exception is the Hanafi school, which bases its support on the practical need for project financing. Nevertheless, istisna'a is still a widely used form of financing among Islamic banks.

Istisna'a places the bulk of transaction risk on the bank. First, there is credit risk associated with its customer. Second, the bank is exposed to any failure on the part of the supplier of the asset. To mitigate the risk, the bank may take a performance bond from the manufacturer or contractor.

Example of Istisna'a in practice

Al Baraka Bank in Bahrain offers istisna'a transactions to its corporate clients. According to Al Baraka Bank among the types of deals that conform to istisna'a are:

1. The contracts in the nature of BOT (Build, Operate, and Transfer) can be categorised as istisna'a transactions. For example, the government may enter into a contract with a builder who will be repaid through toll collection over a specified period.
2. Istisna'a contract opens wide fields of application for the Islamic banks to finance the public needs and the vital interests of the society to develop the Islamic economy.
3. Istisna'a contract is applied in high technology industries such as aircraft industry, locomotive and ship building industries, in addition to the different types of machines made in factories or workshops.
4. The Istisna'a contract is also applied in the construction industry in the building of apartment buildings, hospitals, schools and universities.

Source: http://www.albaraka.bh/default.asp?action=article&ID=42

Salam

A salam is a contract whereby an asset or commodity is purchased or sold and the price is paid immediately, but delivery of the asset is deferred to a future date. The buyer is called *muslam*, the seller is the *muslam ileihi*, the cash price paid is *Ras ul Mall* and the purchased good is *muslam fihi*.

The origins of salam contracts are in agricultural commerce. Farmers make use of salam to get cash upfront from selling their agricultural products. In particular, small farmers need cash to live on before they harvest their produce. After the prohibition of riba, farmers could not take out loans. Instead, they were allowed to sell their agricultural products in advance of the harvest.

Exporters and importers in Arabia also used salam in their trade with buyers in other places. These traders needed financing to carry on the business of importing and exporting goods, but could not avail themselves of loans due to the prohibition of riba. Permission was given to these traders to sell their goods in advance. After receiving cash for the goods, traders had working capital for their ongoing businesses.

Salam is normally applicable only to fungible commodities. These are defined as commodities freely interchangeable with another in satisfying an obligation. Thus, soft commodities, such as rice, wheat, corn, and oil palms, are fungible commodities.

Islamic banks provide financing for salam contracts by either entering into two salam contracts or one salam contract and an instalment sales contract. The bank buys a commodity from a seller (the bank's client) and pays in advance. The date of delivery of the commodity is fixed according to the client's desired date. The bank then sells the commodity to a third party through a parallel salam contract or through an instalment payment sale contract. The parallel salam and sale contract is for the exact same quantity and description of the commodity as covered in the first salam contract. The second contract is signed after the first contract because the price must be paid immediately upon conclusion of the contract. The bank makes a profit through marking up the price of the product it sells to the buyer. The difference between the price paid to the seller and the price charged to the buyer is the profit margin. Thus, salam is also a cost-plus mode of Islamic financing.

The following rules apply to a salam contract:

1 The buyer must pay the price in full to the seller at the time of the sale.
2 The specifications of the quantity and quality of the commodity must be agreed upon to avoid gharar.
3 The contracting parties must agree on the date and place of delivery of the commodity.
4 Goods that are allowed under the salam contract should be fungible.
5 The commodity should be available at the time of expected delivery.
6 Salam is a forward sale and, therefore, not suitable for commodities that are sold and delivered on a spot basis.
7 Salam cannot be tied to a particular farm, field, or tree.
8 The buyer cannot contractually bind the seller to a buy-back, which can only be effected after delivery of the commodity.
9 A penalty can be agreed upon in the salam contract for the late delivery of the commodity. In accordance with Shari'a, the penalty must be donated to charity.
10 Each one of the parallel salam contracts is independent from the other. They cannot be tied together so the rights and obligations of the first contract are dependent on the rights and obligations of the parallel contract.

3.7 Islamic insurance: takaful

For a while, most did not think it possible to have an Islamic form of insurance. The main obstacle to developing Islamic insurance products was the Shari'a prohibition against risk, gambling, and interest. Conventional insurance contains significant measures of the three

Table 3.1 Summary table of forms of Islamic finance

Name of financing mode	Type of Islamic finance	Profits derived from	Main rules governing financing mode
Mudaraba	Profit and loss	Sharing of profits of business venture, more akin to partnerships	Amount of capital known at the start of contract. Capital owner bears the losses
Musharaka	Profit and loss	Equity participation in business venture	Capital existent and immediately available. Partners share in profits and losses according to agreed proportion
Murabaha	Cost-plus	Profit margin above cost	Subject of sale must exist, owned by, and in possession of seller at time of sale
Ijara	Cost-plus. Leasing	Rental of asset	Subject of lease must have a valuable use. Use of subject should not consume it. Purpose must be specified and adhered to
Istisna'a	Cost-plus. Bank is the intermediary between client and supplier	Manufacture, construction, or assembly of an asset. Payment in instalments. Construction financing	The asset must exist, owned, and possessed by the seller when sale is made
Salam	Cost-plus. Payment before delivery of goods or assets	Forward sales contract	The good or commodity must exist, possessed and owned by the seller when the sale is made

elements. There is no true antecedent to insurance in classical Islam. Especially troubling to Muslim scholars was life insurance, a gamble on matters of fate and divine will.

Remarkably, and a credit to the triumph of pragmatism, in recent years, Islamic doctrine has come to terms with most forms of insurance, including life insurance. Today, most Islamic banks have insurance subsidiaries. Business insurance is increasingly necessary in modern economies. The central principle of Islamic insurance is mutual guarantee (*takaful*) or solidarity.

Purpose

Islamic insurance is synonymous with a system of mutual help. The purpose of Islamic insurance is to help those facing difficulties through the cooperation of a group of individuals. In takaful, each participant contributes into a fund. The money in the fund is used to support other participants, each participant contributing enough to cover expected claims. Takaful is Shari'a compliant because it emphasizes unity and cooperation among participants, paying a defined loss from a defined fund. The basis of takaful is *tabarru'*, which means donation, gift, or contribution. This aspect makes takaful free from risk and gambling. Thus, the foundation of takaful is the concepts of mutual support, cooperation, and solidarity. Takaful is sometimes termed cooperative insurance with mutual agreement.

Formulation

The key parties in takaful are:

1 *Participants in the plan or pool*: the people who contribute to the mutual fund. Their monetary contribution is called their mutual contribution.
2 *Takaful operator*: a registered or licensed body or corporation. This body manages the fund according to Shari'a principles and provides financial stability.
3 *Insured individuals*: participants in the plan or pool (such as from the first point above) who face the risk and are helped by the fund.
4 *Beneficiaries*: those who benefit from the fund.

The pooled funds from participants are first, to help those in need, and then second, to earn profits. Contributions are normally divided into two funds. One is an investment fund and the other is treated as a charity according to the principles of tabarru'. This is a key difference between takaful operators and conventional insurance companies.

Takaful operations have at least four models: Ta'awun, mudaraba, wakala, and nonprofit. The Ta'awun model, in general, employs mudaraba in its daily transactions. The takaful operator and policyholder only share direct investment income. The policyholder receives 100 per cent of profits from the cooperative insurance and is entitled to distributions without any deductions. In contrast, the mudaraba model of takaful, policyholders, and the takaful operator share the profits in a ratio upon which they mutually agree. The ratio may be 50:50 or 60:40. The takaful operator shares in profits as well as favourable performance of investments. In the wakala model, the takaful operator does not share in profits from investments but instead charges a fee for services such as fund management fee or even a performance incentive fee. Finally, government and not-for-profit programmes tend to use the nonprofit model of takaful. Contributions to the takaful fund are entirely tabarru' (donation) from participants who wish to help the less fortunate members of their community.

Retakaful

Retakaful is akin to reinsurance. The goal also is to hedge risks through reinsuring original insured risks. Policyholders contribute to a takaful fund, buy takaful products such as general takaful, and pay an agreed premium to the takaful operator. The latter takes a portion of money from the takaful fund and, in turn, pays a premium to the retakaful operator to get reinsurance protection to spread its risks.

Retakaful does not differ in principle from takaful operations. In retakaful, participants are takaful operators instead of individuals. The retakaful operators are responsible for managing and investing the premiums paid by takaful operations on the basis of profit and loss sharing.

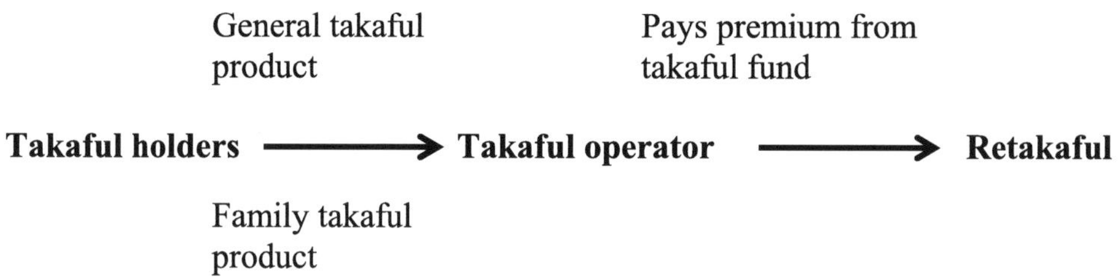

104 *Three finance paradigms*

```
                General takaful              Pays premium from
                product                      takaful fund

Takaful holders  ─────────▶  Takaful operator  ─────────▶  Retakaful

                Family takaful
                product
```

Figure 3.3 The Retakaful process.[31]

3.8 Sukuk and securitization

Sukuk (singular form *sakk*) are often wrongly termed as 'Islamic bonds', implying that the element of riba is associated with the instrument. The association with riba, is of course, strictly forbidden in Islamic finance and the more accurate English term for sukuk is *Shari'a compliant investment certificates*. The certificates represent an undivided beneficial ownership of, and return generated from, an underlying asset.[32] The sukuk holder has the right to receive a pro rata portion of the income stream of the underlying asset. For a sukuk to be Shari'a compliant, three criteria must be met. First, the sukuk must not pay interest or riba. Interest is forbidden, but profit is encouraged because of the sharing of risk. Second, the issuer must own the asset or assets it intends to utilize in any financing structure. Third, the company must not engage in any haram (forbidden) activities – notably, any related to pork, alcohol, gambling, armaments, and certain types of media activity.

The sukuk market has been growing at a rapid pace since the issuance of the first international sovereign sukuk by the Malaysian government in 2003. The size of the market has grown from US$336 million in 2000. The issuance of sukuk is forecast to top US$100 billion by the end of 2012. The first European sukuk transaction was a Euro100 million issue done by the German State of Saxony-Anhalt. Corporate entities also have entered the sukuk market, with multi-billion dollar issuances. For example, Nakheel issued a US$3.52 billion equity-linked sukuk. In the first six months of 2012, Malaysia issued more than 70 per cent of global sukuk, while Saudi Arabia was at the second spot with a 13 per cent share of the global issuance.[33]

In 2012, the global supply of sukuk was less than half that of investor demand and the gap may widen unless more institutions emerge capable of launching new issues. Estimates for demand for Islamic sukuk are some US$300 billion and is expected to grow to US$900 billion by 2017. The rise in demand is primarily a result of double-digit growth of the Islamic banking industry, and the increasing appetite for credible, Shari'a compliant, liquid securities.

Demand arises from both Islamic financial institutions and conventional institutions. The latter is showing increasing interest because of the European debt crisis and as sukuk products are backed by real assets. Liquidity is no longer a deterrent for non-Islamic investors because liquidity of sukuk is now comparable to conventional bonds of similar credit profiles.

Sukuk are increasingly being issued by non-Islamic entities. General Electric and Nomura have structured their bonds in a Shari'a compliant manner. The Republic of Ireland brought out a new sukuk issue of both sovereign and quasi-foreign to the market.

There are different types of sukuk depending on the nature of the financing structure of the underlying asset linked to the sukuk certificate. This chapter describes sukuk where the underlying financial transactions are based on ijara, musharaka, and mudaraba.

Securitization

Securitization is the pooling or repackaging of assets, generally illiquid, into tradable certificates of investment. Through securitization and the use of these certificates, or sukuk, ownership of assets is transferred to a large number of investors. The ownership of the securitized assets is transferred to a special purpose vehicle (SPV) or special purpose mudarabah (SPM). The vehicles are set up for the dual purpose of managing the assets on behalf of sukuk holders and for the issuance of investment certificates. The SPV as mudarib manages both the liabilities and assets of the issues. Sukuk holders earn any revenue generated by the project and/or capital appreciation of the assets involved. Sukuk are certificates of equal value representing undivided shares in the ownership of tangible assets, usufruct, and services, or assets of particular projects or specified investment activity.

The difference between sukuk and equity is the latter represents ownership of a company as a whole for an indefinite period of time. The former represents the ownership of specified assets for a particular period of time (generally between three months to ten years). *Sukuk, unlike bonds, do not receive interest but instead receive returns from cash flows from the use of assets.*

Main entities in Islamic securitization:

1   The originator or issuer of sukuk.
    The issuer sells its assets to the SPV and uses the realized funds. Issuers are mostly governments or large corporations. However, Islamic banks and non-banking institutions also issue sukuk.
2   The SPV manages the issue and the securitization process.
    It purchases the assets from the issuer, receiving the funds from sukuk holders to fund the purchase.
3   Investment banks are underwriters for the sukuk issue, and are paid by fees or commissions.
    The banks may form syndicates, spreading the risk when underwriting larger sukuk issues.
4   Sukuk holders, or subscribers, to a sukuk issue.
    Banks, individuals, central banks, or institutional investors may subscribe to securities issued by an SPV.

Other parties involved in securitization may be credit rating agencies, legal and tax counsel, auditors, and custodians.

Sukuk al-ijara

An *ijara* facility is essentially structured as a sale and leaseback. The party requiring funds sells equipment or other assets to the financier and leases the equipment back from the financier. In a sukuk al-ijara, the funding banks purchase an asset or pool of assets from the issuer and then lease the asset or assets back to the issuer on the agreed commercial terms. Sukuk al-ijara holders own certificates representing ownership of well-defined and known assets tied up to the lease contract. The rental payments by the issuer to the financiers are the returns payable to the sukuk holders. Sukuk al-ijara structures are often used in project financing, sovereign sukuk, and increasingly in corporate sukuk issues.

Payment of ijara rentals can be made before the beginning of the lease period, during the period, or after the period, based on mutual agreement. In the sukuk al-ijara, the funds raised may purchase assets, such as buildings or capital equipment, for the purpose of leasing them back to the ultimate users. These funds are called ijara funds. The ownership of the assets remains with the SPV. The SPV is created to purchase the assets and is the manager of the funds. In addition the SPV issues sukuk to investors and uses funds received in the issue to purchase the leased assets. The SPV receives rentals from the issuer of the sukuk (also the ultimate user of the assets) and distributes the rentals pro rata among the sukuk al-ijara certificate holders.

The lessor may sell the leased asset as long as the lessee may continue to enjoy the usufruct of the asset. The new owner (or owners) receives the rentals for the remaining period of the lease. A sukuk al-ijara certificate represents a certain proportional ownership of the leased asset. To be Shari'a compliant, the ijara certificates must represent real ownership of the leased assets and not just the right to receive rent. Thus, in line with all ijara financing, the owner of the leased asset assumes the rights and obligations of ownership. If the asset is destroyed, the sukukholder suffers the loss in proportion of her ownership. Expenses related to the basic characteristics of the asset are the responsibility of the owners, while the lessee pays for maintenance and operation expenses. Consequently, the expected returns from sukuk al-ijara may not always be completely fixed and predetermined.

Sukuk al-mudarabah

Sukuk al-mudarabah certificates represent projects or activities managed on the mudarabah mode of financing (see section 3.5). The issuer of the sukuk al-mudarabah is the mudarib (entrepreneur or working partner) in the partnership, the sukuk holders are the owners of the capital, and the funds from the sukuk issue are the capital for that mudarabah partnership. As the sukuk holders are the Rab al Mall, or the owners of capital in the mudarabah partnership, according to accepted terms of a mudarabah, the holders bear the risk of loss if there is one. Profits from the mudarabah partnership are distributed to the sukuk holders according to an agreed formula.

An SPV is set up to receive the funds collected from the subscribers of the sukuk al-mudarabah issue. The manager (normally an investment bank or banks) of the funds may invest in the issue and will get a profit for the capital contribution in addition to the share in the profits as mudarib. The prospectus for the issue must not guarantee a return from the capital or a fixed profit as that renders the sukuk non-Shari'a compliant. Instead, profit is divided as determined by the rules of Shari'a, as an amount in excess of the capital. A profit and loss account of the mudarabah-based project must be published and distributed to all sukuk holders.

Sukuk al-musharaka

This form of sukuk takes its structure from the musharaka or equity participation mode of financing described in section 3.5 of this chapter. The sukuk al-musharaka structure requires the formation of an unincorporated joint venture between the financiers and the issuer. The partners invest capital or services and share in the resulting profits and losses.

The issuer contributes assets to the musharaka joint venture; the sukuk holders contribute capital via an SPV. The capital enables the joint venture to buy the assets contributed by the issuer. Every sukuk holder receives a musharaka certificate, which represents the holder's proportionate ownership in the assets of the joint venture. The holders become owners of the joint venture according to the number of shares they have. Profit earned by the musharaka is shared according to an agreed ratio. Loss is shared on a pro rata basis. The sukuk al-musharaka is similar to sukuk al-mudarabah. The basic Shari'a rules relating to mudarabah also apply to musharaka certificates.

In general, the musharaka structure is more equitable and involves less risk for investors than the mudarabah structure for sukuk. The former involves both profit- and loss-sharing between the fund manager of the SPV and the sukuk holders, while the latter only allows for profit sharing with all losses being borne by the sukuk holders.

Sukuk al-salam

The sukuk al-salam is structured on the salam mode of financing (section 3.5). The salam contract is similar to a forward contract in conventional finance. The seller of a fungible commodity receives payment for the good for a forward delivery. The Islamic bank is the buyer of the commodity and may sell it on to another buyer in a parallel but independent salam contract or on an instalment contract.

Sukuk al-salam certificates are issued to obtain funds from subscribers to the issue to pay for a commodity in advance for delivery later. The seller of the salam commodity issues the certificates and the sukuk holders are the buyers of that commodity. In the parallel salam, the commodity is sold onward to another buyer. The holders of the sukuk al-salam are entitled to the salam commodity or the selling price at the time of delivery of the commodity.

Sukuk al-istisna'a

Section 3.5 describes the istisna'a mode of Islamic financing. Istisna'a financing is a contractual agreement for manufacturing goods, where cash payment is made either in advance or in the future, with the promise of future delivery of the manufactured goods. A parallel istisna'a is undertaken when the financing bank subcontracts the actual construction to a specific manufacturer with the required specialization.

In general, the sukuk al-istisna'a works as follows. The manufacturer (seller) issues the sukuk al-istisna'a certificates for a sum of money that is the sale price covering the cost of construction of the good as well as the profits. The subscribers or sukuk holders are the buyers of the good to be produced. In a parallel istisna'a, the funds from the sukuk subscription are immediately paid as a price to the manufacturer. Alternatively, a parallel istisna'a can involve the transfer of ownership of the manufactured item to the ultimate purchaser. In these cases, the istisna'a certificates are subject to the rules of disposing of debts and cannot be traded on a secondary market, but must instead be held to maturity.

Secondary trading of sukuk

Sukuk representing tangible assets or usufruct of such assets may be traded in the secondary market. Liquidity in the secondary market is a factor that will make a sukuk issue more desirable to investors. In the case of mudarabah and musharaka certificates, the sukuk holders are given the right to transfer the ownership by selling the sukuk in the securities market. The market value of the sukuk varies with the business rating and expected profits of the underlying project. If the sukuk creates a debt obligation, the certificates will not be tradable. Secondary market trading of sukuk al-salam certificates is not permissible because the certificates represent a share in the salam debt.

Example 1: Sukuk in international markets

QIIB Sukuk issue

Qatar International Islamic Bank (QIIB) rated A3/A- by Moody's and Fitch (both with stable outlook), successfully priced a US$700 million 5-year Sukuk issued at par with a 2.688 per cent annual profit rate, which will be settled semi-annually.

This transaction represents QIIB's first international debt capital markets issuance.

HSBC, QNB Capital and Standard Chartered Bank acted as Joint lead Managers and Joint Bookrunners, with Qatar Islamic Bank and CIMB Investment Bank, Malaysia, as Co-Managers on the transaction. The Trust Certificates are listed on the Irish Stock Exchange.

The success of the transaction comes on the back of an extensive marketing strategy aimed at introducing the QIIB credit story to international investors and included a comprehensive roadshow covering the Middle East, Asia and Europe.

The issue saw strong participation from investors, in particular from Asia and the MENA region. In terms of allocation, the geographic split stood at 50 per cent for Middle East, 30 per cent for Asia, and 20 per cent for UK/Europe/US Offshore investors. In terms of investor type, the transaction was distributed amongst a wide range of accounts.

Source: WN.com (http://article.wn.com/view/2012/10/14/14_10_12_Sheikh_Dr_Khalid_Huge_subscription_on_QIIB_Sukuk_ex/)

Example 2: Sukuk in international markets

UK Government issues sukuk

Britain became the first country outside the Islamic world to issue sovereign Sukuk on 25 June 2014. The size of the sukuk issue is £200 million, maturing on 22 July 2019. The profit rate on the sukuk was set at 2.036 per cent, in line with the yield on gilts of similar maturity. The British government sukuk uses the al-ijara structure, the most common structure for sovereign sukuk, with rental payments on property providing the income for sukuk holders. The sukuk is underpinned by three central government propertiesThe issue was sold to investors based in the UK and in Islamic financial centers around the world.

The issuance of sovereign sukuk is in line with Britain's goal to be the western hub of Islamic finance.

Source: gov.uk (https://www.gov.uk/government/news/government-issues-first-islamic-bond)

3.9 Issues in Islamic finance

The 'semantics' issue: interest disguised as profit margin

Murahaba makes up 75 per cent of Islamic banks' activities. Thus, most criticism of the authenticity of Islamic finance is levied mainly against the murabaha transaction.

Murabaha is criticized for being a conventional loan in disguise as a Shari'a compliant transaction. The interest is disguised through semantic games and other 'hiyal' (ruses). From a strictly economic standpoint – not considering legal, regulatory, or ethical, issues – murabaha transactions are comparable to interest rate transactions. For example, if the bank borrows MYR 100 at 8 per cent it will need to pay MYR 8 of interest to the lender. The bank then enters into a murabaha transaction with a client and charges the latter a mark-up of MYR 9 on a purchase of an asset that costs MYR 100. The bank earns MYR 1 in profits, but its mark-up is determined by the rate of interest.

Naturally, the use of the rate of interest for determining a halal (allowed) profit is not the most desirable method for determining the profit margin. Using an interest rate benchmark looks suspiciously like interest-based financing, dressed up differently. However, the fact remains the most important requirement for the validity of murabaha is that it is a genuine sale with all the Islamic requirements and necessary consequences. If a murabaha transaction fulfils all the conditions needed for compliance with Islamic law, merely using the interest rate as a benchmark for determining the profit of murabaha does not render the transaction invalid or haram (prohibited). The financial deal itself contains no interest. The rate of interest is used as a benchmark or indicator.

Using LIBOR

Benchmarking against LIBOR is permitted in Islamic financial transactions. Detractors question why the murabaha mark-up is based off fluctuating interest benchmarks such as LIBOR rather than on fixed predetermined mark-ups for the entire term.

One answer is that LIBOR is internationally accepted while there is still the absence of an internationally acceptable Islamic profit benchmark. This situation is not likely to be a permanent one because Islamic banking is becoming more common. As increasing numbers of people use Islamic financial products and services, it is likely that benchmarks for profit margins on murabaha will develop.

Growing acceptance and use of Islamic financial services also will ameliorate the other reason why LIBOR is now used as a profit margin benchmark. Currently, customers are worried they may pay a higher murabaha mark-up if it is fixed compared to the fluctuating benchmark-based interest charged by a conventional bank. Obviously the bigger the market for Islamic financing, the better and more efficient will be the pricing of the mark-up. Currently, there are relatively few Islamic banks compared to a vast number of conventional banks. Islamic banks wish to remain competitive in the global marketplace of all banks. To do so, these banks adjust their profit earnings to be as close to the market as possible. Hence, Islamic banks are simply basing profit margin decisions for murabaha transactions on prevailing market prices of comparable transactions such as interest-based loans.

Murabaha has negligible risk to financial institutions

While non-Muslims tend to criticize Islamic financial transactions as merely semantic games, it is Muslim scholars who are most likely to complain that murabaha is a low risk and short-term transaction. As the argument goes, the bank, using murabaha, does not share risk with the borrower. This feature of murabaha violates the mission of Islamic finance, which is to spread the risk between the financier and the user of funds. When the bank agrees on a profit margin with the customer, the risk to the bank is minimal. In addition, the purchased assets are guarantees, perhaps collateral the bank requires from its client. This combination of predetermined fixed profit and collateral means the bank takes on insignificant risk.

Liquidity problems

Islamic financial institutions lack deposit insurance programmes that reassure depositors and prevent runs on the banks. There is no ready and liquid secondary market or a central discount window. Opportunities for securitization are limited and there is no true Islamic interbank market to help fund daily liquidity. Conventional banks have the flexibility to manage their assets and liabilities by reselling loans to other financial institutions. These loans are repackaged into tradable securities, using the discount facilities of their central bank, or borrowing at interest.

Except for leasing, all other major Islamic financial instruments cannot be easily traded on the secondary market. Discounting debt obligations, such as selling debt at less than face value, usually raise riba-related issues. The buying and selling of financial obligations is still controversial. Islamic finance suffers from a lack of a true Islamic banking infrastructure and interbank market. In addition, Shari'a boards often disagree about which activities are permissible and the proper conduct of Islamic banking, making it difficult to coordinate and harmonize the industry. To many boards, an Islamic interbank market means the buying and selling of money – an uncomfortable concept – which makes the actualization of such a market unlikely in the near future. There are also disagreements and rivalries among Islamic communities, countries, and financial institutions that prevent the emergence of a true community of banks. Such a group can theoretically be similar to nineteenth-century clearing houses that can act as central regulator and even a lender of last resort.[34] Yet, at a time of increasing coordination among international financial institutions, Islamic financial institutions are lagging. However, there is progress in homogenization. For example, the Islamic Development Bank has increasingly taken up the role of lender of last resort to Islamic institutions.

Islamic finance in a world of conventional and interest-based finance

Islamic economics focus on the welfare of a community. One assumption of Islamic economics and, therefore, Islamic finance is that individuals behave altruistically and according to religious norms. In contrast, neoclassical economics and, therefore, modern finance theory assume individuals are rational self-interested agents, working for their own benefit. Thus, greed is by no means an aberration. The world of neoclassical economics is one of scarcity where, ironically, self-interest advances the greatest good.

Homo economicus is selfish and acquisitive. Homo Islamicus is just, socially responsible, altruistic.[35] Allah provides enough for everyone and scarcity is an unnatural condition caused by greed and avarice. Critics question whether the problem of scarcity is solved by the assumption of selfless behaviour. Economists do not think the Islamic view of human behaviour is realistic. Traditional Muslims see the principle of individual self-interest as glorifying greed and immoral.

Will the gap between these two economic and financial views narrow? There are increasing signs of a bridging of the gap. Modern Islamic economics is becoming more pragmatic and policy-oriented. The contrasts are now less stark. Hence, while capitalism views human beings as selfish, Islamic economics sees human beings as being both selfish and altruistic. Materialism is the supreme value for capitalism, but should be controlled under an Islamic economic system. Capitalism favours absolute private ownership but the Islamic economic system favours private ownership within a moral framework.[36] Islamic economics differs primarily from neoclassical economics to the extent the former adds an ethical and social dimension that the latter usually lacks. *Falah* is best translated as 'well-being', and is increasingly the centre of Islamic economics. Falah encompasses both moral as well as material wellbeing and refers to the welfare of the community. Warde goes as far as to say the homo economicus versus homo islamicus contrast is now largely irrelevant. Both represent ideals and are normative rather than descriptive. Indeed Warde argues there are obvious parallels between the guardians of the dogma in both Islam and economics. Both neoclassical economics and Islamic economics have the essence of theology.

> Just as those who inhabit a highly formalised world of perfect competition, perfect information, and perfect rationality seek to eliminate imperfections (such as the public sector, which in most countries accounts for nearly half of the Gross Domestic Product), so Islamic purists seek to eliminate selfish motives in a world dominated by altruism and virtue.[37]

Just as Islamic economics has its fundamentalists, so too does neoclassical economics.

Even if the contrast between fundamentals of Islamic finance and conventional finance is not irrelevant as Warde claims, the former is a growing market with attractive potential, while the latter has probably seen the peak of growth. Western investment banks are increasingly working with Muslim clerics to create a new range of financial products designed for Muslims. Muslim states are increasing their wealth and there is increased demand among the growing Muslim population in Europe and the US. Estimates of the size of the Islamic finance industry currently vary widely from US$800 billion to US$1 trillion. While there may not be agreement on the precise number, there is agreement that the business is expanding rapidly.

Notes

1 Ibrahim Warde, *Islamic Finance in the Global Economy* (Edinburgh: Edinburgh University Press, 2000).
2 Raj Bhala, *Islamic Law (Shari'a)* (New Providence, NJ: LexisNexis, 2011).
3 Bhala, 74–85.
4 Brian Kettel, *Introduction to Islamic Banking and Finance* (Chichester, UK: John Wiley & Sons, 2011).
5 Bhala, 286–309.
6 Kettel, 20.
7 Bhala, 332–8.
8 Muhammad Ayub, *Understanding Islamic Finance* (Chichester, UK: John Wiley & Sons, 2007).
9 Husam Hourani, "Three Principles of Islamic Finance Explained," *International Financial Law Review* (May 2005): 1.

10 Hourani, 1.
11 Joseph Persky, "From Usury to Interest," *Journal of Economic Perspectives* 21 (Winter 2007): 227–36.
12 Constant J. Mews and Ibrahim Abraham, "Usury and Just Compensation: Religious and Financial Ethics in Historical Perspective," *Journal of Business Ethics* 72 (2007): 1–15.
13 Andrew M. McCosh, *Financial Ethics* (Scotland, UK: Kluwer Academic Publishers, 1999).
14 Persky, 229.
15 Peter Koh, "Islamic Finance Moves on with Debut Eurobond," *Euromoney* (September 2003): 1.
16 Kettel, 39–42.
17 Kettel, 41.
18 Kettel, 42.
19 Ayub, 32–5.
20 Ayub, 75.
21 Bhala, 658–62.
22 Ayub, 75–6.
23 Bhala, 658–62.
24 Ayub, 64–9.
25 Kettel, 24.
26 Mustafa Hussain, "A General Introduction to Islamic Finance," in *Islamic Finance*, ed. Rahali Ali (London: Globe Business Publishing, 2008).
27 Kettel, 44.
28 Warde, 134.
29 Kettel, 89–90.
30 Kettel, 104.
31 Kettel, 136.
32 Bilal Aquil and Imran Mufti, "Innovation in the Global Sukuk Market and Legal Restructuring Considerations," in *Islamic Finance*, ed. Rahali Ali (London: Globe Business Publishing, 2008).
33 "Surge in Sukuk Demand Outpaces the Issuance," *Financial Times* (Monday 5 November 2012).
34 Warde, 199–200.
35 Warde, 44–8.
36 Muhammad Akram Khan, *An Introduction to Islamic Economics* (Islamabad: International Institute of Islamic Thought and Institute of Policy Studies, 1994).
37 Warde, 48.

References

Ayub, Muhammad, *Understanding Islamic Finance* (Chichester: John Wiley & Sons, 2007).
Bhala, Raj, *Islamic Law (Shari'a)* (New Providence, NJ: Lexis Nexis, 2011).
Kettell, Brian, *Introduction to Islamic Banking and Finance* (Chichester: John Wiley & Sons, 2011).

Part II
Practice of investment management

4 International financial instruments

4.1 Equity

Investors have many options when it comes to what they can do with their money. However, of all the opportunities, the most common securities investment involves corporate entity interests.[1] Corporate entity interests are ownership interests in a public corporation. Many different types of corporate entity interests exist that differ in rights; notably, cash flow, voting, and liquidation rights. The most familiar types include ordinary (common) stock and preferred stock, but also include warrants and convertibles.

Ordinary

An owner of ordinary stock has a right to cash flows in the form of dividends. The owners receive a residual share of the corporate profits. That is, they receive a proportion of the corporate profits only after all other ownership interests have been satisfied. Under the absolute priority rule, debt holders generally have first priority to corporate profit. Debt is a fixed claim against a corporation; it is a liability on its balance sheet that must be repaid. Preferred stockholders have next priority to profits. After ownership interests are satisfied (such as claims of debt and preferred stockholders), the residual profits, which may be more or less than those with a claim of debt or preferred stockholders, are proportionately allocated among common stockholders. Ordinary stockholders have the lowest priority and greatest risk. There is no guarantee an ordinary stockholder will be paid back in the form of dividends for her purchase of the stock. However, ordinary stock has the greatest potential for reward.[2]

Generally, in the case of a corporation with cash-intensive projects, a corporation may choose to not pay dividends. However, a common stockholder has the right to vote to elect a new board of directors that is more in tune with common stockholders' desires. Ordinary stockholders receive rights to liquidation. Similar to cash flow rights, debt holders have an absolute right to receive assets in liquidation before shareholders. Preferred shareholders have second priority, and ordinary shareholders have rights to remaining assets. In limited bankruptcy situations, shareholders may receive corporate assets that would otherwise go to higher priority security holders.[3] In addition, common stockholders enjoy liquidation rights. Similar to cash flow rights, common stockholders have residual liquidation rights.

Preferred

Preferred stock is a hybrid between common stock and debt providing a more senior nature like debt, with the ownership element of common stock. Generally, many corporations only issue preferred stock if they are a well-established corporation that needs infusion of capital. Another type is a new start-up company in need of quick investments of capital by outside investors.

Generally, investors are inclined to preferred stock because they have a fixed dividend with seniority over common stock. Although the dividend amount is fixed, it is an equity right. Therefore, failure to pay dividends does not result in default; the dividends are discretionary, and contingent on funds' availability. If the preferred stock is cumulative, the unpaid dividends accumulate each year. All accumulated dividends must be paid before any dividends can be paid to common shareholders. Conversely, non-cumulative preferred stock does not accumulate, and dividends that are not paid out to preferred stockholders are lost. Furthermore, other contractual provisions may be negotiated between investors and corporations. One notable example is participating preferred stock, where a stockholder may receive preference to dividends as well as a percentage of the common stock.

Preferred stock also has preferred liquidity rights. Preferred stockholders have second priority to a company's assets for any cumulated, unpaid dividends, and the contracted price of the share. Right to the assets is triggered only after debt holders have been repaid (for the above-mentioned reasons in the section about ordinary stock).

Commonly, preferred stock is not granted voting rights. However, in extraordinary situations, where a dividend is not paid for a certain number of quarters (generally two or three), then preferred stockholders will receive voting rights to elect a new board of directors.[4] Investors and companies may create other preferred stock contracts that specify for other rights not discussed here.

Others

There are many other types of equity securities. Two common examples are warrants and convertibles. Warrants are a financial instrument that may be used by an issuing company to entice investors to buy the underlying stock at a fixed price until an expiration date, or to reduce the interest rate that must be offered in order to sell the bond issue. In this sense, warrants are similar to options, allowing the holder special rights to buy securities. They are different from options in that warrants are issued and guaranteed by the issuing company, whereas the issuing company does not issue options. Generally, an option expires within months of issue, whereas a warrant's lifetime is measured in years.

There are two types of equity warrants: call and put warrants. A callable warrant offers investors the right to buy shares of a company from the company at a specific price at a future date prior to expiration. A puttable warrant, however, offers investors the right to sell shares of a company back to that company at a specific price at a future date prior to expiration.

Warrants are often attached to bonds or preferred stock, and there are usually secondary markets to buy and sell warrants. A holder may exercise the warrant when the holder informs the issuer of their intention to purchase the shares underlying the warrant. Warrant characteristics, such as its premium, gearing, expiration, and restrictions, are set shortly after the underlying bond has been issued. The premium sets out how much the holder will have to pay for shares purchased through the warrant as compared to buying shares through a secondary market. A warrant's gearing sets how much exposure a holder has to the underlying shares using the warrant as compared through the secondary market. The expiration date, which has been previously mentioned, also factors into the price of the warrant. The more time remaining until expiration allows for more time for the underlying security to appreciate, which increases the price of the warrant. Lastly, there may be restriction on exercising warrants. There are a variety of exercise restrictions, including the US style, which allows a holder to exercise a warrant any time before expirations, and the European style, which allows a holder to only exercise a warrant on the expiration date.

Convertible securities are used for investors that demand greater appreciation than bonds provide, and higher income than common stocks offer.[5] Convertibles are most commonly used in the form of bonds or preferred shares, which can be converted into common stock. Convertible bonds or convertible preferred shares pay regular interest to their holders, although generally at a slightly lower rate than standard bonds and preferred stock. Convertible securities can also include notes.

Generally, the holder of the convertible has discretion of whether and when to convert; however, in some cases the company has the right to determine when the conversion occurs, or condition conversion on the stock price appreciating to a predetermined level. A convertible security's conversion ratio, from convertible securities to common stock, may be fixed or based on the market. A fixed conversion formula may also include caps or other provisions to limit dilution. This method protects the company and the current common stockholders from risks of price decline. A market-based conversion formula is based on fluctuating market prices to determine the number of shares of common stock to be issued on conversion. In contrast with a fixed conversion formula, a market-based conversion formula protects the holders of the convertibles against price declines, while subjecting the company and current common stockholders to substantial risks.

This raises issues for potential convertible security purchasers that have difficulty in evaluating the convertibles, especially since many issuing companies do not have the strongest credit ratings.[6] Additionally, the global convertible bond market is relatively small. North America has the largest of the global convertible market with approximately 50 per cent, the whole Asian region representing 17 per cent, and Japan 8 per cent. Despite these downsides, most diversified portfolios contain convertible bonds. Holders like the hybrid debt and equity feature and the option to convert if beneficial.

4.2 Debt: sovereign, corporate, municipal

Bond basics

A bond is an instrument by which governments and companies can raise capital through issuance of loans to investors. Bonds in all forms are securities and, once issued, may typically be freely traded on the secondary markets previously discussed. Two distinctions are important to note between bonds and stock issued by a corporation to an investor: one being the relationship created by the purchase of the security. Owning a stock makes the holder a part owner of the company itself, whereas a bond creates a creditor/debtor relationship with the issuing corporation.

The second is the life of the instrument. A stock typically does not have any type of expiration., although there can be transfer restrictions placed upon both a stock and bond, and ownership of the stock stays with the purchaser as long as the company is in existence. In contrast, bonds typically have a set time in which the debt will be paid back to the creditor (maturity) and the date of maturity is specified on the bond along with, if any, interest payments to be made to the creditor and the frequency of said payments.

118 *Practice of investment management*

Generally, a bond has three parts that signify the value of the bond: the face value (par value) of the bond to be paid upon maturity, the maturity date, and interest payments to be made to the creditor in the time between issuance and maturity. These interest payments are known as coupons and are unique to each bond as they detail the number and frequency of payments to be made along with the interest rate attached to the bond. The interest rate (or coupon rate) can either be a fixed rate that is locked in at the securities issuance (fixed rate), or can fluctuate with the going market interest rate or some other designated marker (floating interest rate). The floating rate is often marked to the US Treasury Rate or the London Interbank Offered Rate (LIBOR). A simple equation will determine the annual coupon value of a bond:

$$\frac{(Face\ value\ of\ bond \times coupon\ rate)}{Number\ of\ annual\ payments} = Coupon\ value$$

$$\frac{(US\$10,000 \times 6\%)}{2} = \$300$$

(Note that Islamic bonds, or *sukuk*, are a distinct species of debt instrument that do not entail interest. They are discussed in Chapter 3.)

Bonds come in many forms with an infinite number of uses, but there are five particular securities within the bond market that will be discussed: Treasury bonds, municipal bonds, corporate bonds, and mortgage-backed securities (or asset-backed). A quick discussion of each of these securities is helpful to understand the distinction between them, how they relate to one another, and their relevance within the global and national bond markets.

Government bonds

Government bonds (Treasury bonds) are loans issued by a national government to individuals, companies, or foreign nations. These bonds are usually long-term debts that often exceed 10 years before the bond will reach maturity, and typically includes guaranteed interest payments at regular intervals. For example, the US Treasury issues 10 or 30 year bonds with semi-annual interest payments because national governments, especially ones with developed or healthy economies, are considered to be the safest bond investment. The typical interest rate for these debts is generally lower than other riskier debt securities. Often US Treasury rates are used as proxies for the risk-free rates used in capital asset pricing models (CAPM) (Chapter 1).

Municipal bonds

Municipal bonds are similar to Treasury bonds, except each are issued at the state or local governments or agencies. These bonds are usually issued to raise capital for state or agency projects, and are typically offered in two forms: general obligation bonds (which are backed by the state) and revenue bonds (backed by the expected revenue to be generated by the project). The interest received from these bonds is exempt from federal and state income tax, unless otherwise specified on the bond.[7]

Corporate bonds

Similar to Treasury and municipal bonds, corporate bonds are issued as a means of raising capital for the issuing corporation, and specify a maturity date and coupon rate. Unlike government and municipal bonds, the risk for corporations tends to be much higher due to the relatively volatile nature of corporate health. The increased risk of a corporation entering into bankruptcy tends to require a higher rate of interest for the bond, and some bonds are secured against bankruptcy through collateralized corporate assets. Corporate bonds are either secured or unsecured (called debentures, or subordinate debentures that have a lesser claim to recourse in the case of corporate bankruptcy).[8]

Mortgage-backed securities

After the 2008 recession, many investors cringe when they hear the term 'mortgage-backed security'. A mortgage is a fixed loan for a term of years that is originated by a bank (creditor) or other lending institution to a homeowner (debtor), and a mortgage can have either a fixed or floating interest rate. To reduce risk created by changing interest rates and default of debtors, banks began selling this risk on the open market through a process called securitization,[9] which creates a mortgage-backed security (also known as a pass-through).

Securitization occurs in several steps: (1) the bank or lender originates mortgages to home owners, (2) these mortgages, or rather the bank's claim to the interest rate and principal payments, are sold to a special purpose vehicle (SPV), a firm created to buy and pool mortgages, and (3) the SPV pools the mortgages together, then sells debt securities to investors to finance the purchase of the mortgages from the bank. For the end investor, the security purchased in the SPV is backed (secured) by the income generated from the pool of mortgages purchased from the banks. This practice is an excellent one when average home prices are increasing and owners are making their payments, but if the market takes a turn and a majority of the mortgages in the pool start defaulting then the SPV may begin to stop payments to investors.

4.3 ETFs, mutual funds, open-end, closed-end

ETFs

Exchange traded funds, or ETFs, are investment companies that are legally classified as open-end companies or unit investment trusts (UITs), but are not considered mutual funds. However, etf open-end companies and ETFs differ from traditional open-end companies and UITs.

ETFs issue shares in large blocks known as 'creation units'. ETFs are only available to investors through brokers and advisers. Investors, frequently institutions, purchase creation units with a basket of securities that mirrors the ETF's portfolio. Then the investor often splits it up and sells the individual shares on a secondary market.

Generally, ETF shares aim to achieve the same return as a particular market index. An ETF will invest in a selected market index, investing in all companies or a sample of securities from the index. An ETF price changes throughout the day, and is priced based upon its supply and demand in the secondary market. Generally, creation units may be redeemed by the ETF for securities within the ETF's portfolio. It is because of this limited redeemable power that ETFs are prohibited from calling themselves mutual funds.

ETFs are often used by institutional investors to make short-term, large bets on sectors such as oil and gold, although ETFs have been increasingly used for retirement accounts,

Mutual funds

Open-end investment companies, most commonly referred to as mutual funds, aggregate investment money from many smaller investors and reinvest the funds in securities. The money may be invested in a combination of stocks, bonds, short-term money-market instruments, or other assets that makes up the fund's portfolio. An individual investor will invest in a number of shares, with each share representing a proportionate ownership in the fund and the income the fund generates. The equity capital and assets of a mutual fund are increased when shares are sold and are reduced when the company repurchases the shares.

A prospectus is made available to all potential investors prior to sale. The prospectus includes a variety of details including the 'investment philosophy of the fund, assesses the risks in an actual investment, and discloses management fee schedules, dividend re-investment policies, share redemption policies, past performance, among other information'.[11]

Mutual fund shares cannot be purchased on a secondary market, but only from the fund itself or through a licensed broker. Price is calculated based on the funds approximate net asset value (NAV) per share plus any fees. When investors wish to sell their mutual fund shares, the investor can sell them back to the fund for the current NAV per share, and, of course subtracting fees the fund may charge. Mutual fund fees are a disadvantage to selecting a mutual fund. Fees such as sales charges, annual fees, and other expenses, as well as the possibility of paying taxes on any capital gains, must be paid regardless of negative returns.

Closed-end

Generally, closed-end investment companies, 'CEFs', issue shares in large quantities by licensed brokers. After shares are issued, the closed-end fund invests money from the initial public offering in accordance with the policy statement in the prospectus. However, unlike open-end companies, CEFs do not issue new shares to existing or new shareholders nor redeem shares from investors. After the public offering, shares can only be purchased or redeemed on a secondary market.

Since the 1960s, CEFs have offered two classes of common equity: income shares and capital shares. An equal number of income and capital shares are sold when first issued, but later sold separately in the secondary market. Generally, holders of income shares are entitled to their proportion of the fund's ordinary income, while holders of capital shares are entitled to their proportion of net assets at a specific maturity date.

Investment Advisers Act of 1940

The purpose of the Investment Advisers Act of 1940 was to protect investors against malpractice by persons paid for advising others about securities. The Act requires all individuals, partnerships, corporations, or other forms of organizations that engage in the business of advising on security investments to register with the SEC. Investment advisors are required to make broader disclosures than what is required under the Securities and Exchange Commission (SEC) Act of 1934, requiring disclosure of their education and all business affiliation in the last 10 years.[12] The Act provides a fiduciary duty on all investment advisers to their clients, subject to antifraud provisions, and restricted from making principal or agency cross-transaction among other regulations.[13]

However, many have taken the position that the Advisers Act is principally a disclosure statute. The Act sets out few specific prohibitions on conduct, and instead relies on broad proscriptions to prevent fraudulent conduct by investment advisers.[14] In reality, advisers must comply with a substantial number of standards of conduct the SEC has effectively imposed under the Act. These include maintaining various books and records and restricting advisory contract assignments, specific transactions, and forms of advertisements.

Investment Company Act of 1940

After years of abuse by investment companies, the *Investment Company Act of 1940* was an attempt to regulate the manipulative investment companies and prevent further abuse to investment company security holders.[15] The Act was written in the interest of investors and administered by the SEC. All investment companies were required to register with the SEC and make disclosures on fund risks, purposes, and performance. Generally, the Act provides for disclosure requirements, minimum voting control on key questions, and prohibition of certain practices that are fraudulent or tempt fraudulent behaviour.[16]

The Act relies on a composite of disclosure requirements. Disclosure requirements were expected to correct many of the problems within the investment industry. It was to further prevent investment companies from misleading their small individual investors. Thousands of individuals invested their savings in these purportedly expertly managed and diversified investments, only to find their funds were being used for the benefit of insiders.[17] Disclosure requirements only go so far, the Act recognizes this, and therefore prohibits self-dealing and reduces conflict of interest behaviour.

The SEC carries out enforcement of the Act through injunctive relief and criminal penalties. The SEC may suspend a company's registration if it fails to disclose information required or makes material misstatements. Additionally, the SEC may prohibit and supervise use of misleading names and sales literature.[18]

4.4 Foreign exchange spots and derivatives[19]

What types of foreign exchange (FX) instruments are traded, and how and where are they traded, not only in Asia, but also around the world? Any FX transaction is part for part, delivery of one currency against another currency. In effect, it is a payment for a payment. (It is not a sale of goods for a price, and thus does not trigger sales of goods law, such as Uniform Commercial Code Article 2.) 'Delivery' means the exchange of the funds being traded, almost always by electronic funds (wire) transfer.[20] That is, delivery is the crediting of the account of the counterparty for the amount of the counter-value. Thus, while delivery may be physical (such as in cash), that is rare. Almost invariably, delivery is effected through electronic debit and credit entries from the account of the originator of a payment with its bank (the originator's bank), through the international banking system (e.g., one or more intermediary banks), for the benefit of the account of beneficiary held at the beneficiary's bank.

Spots

The two basic types of FX transactions are 'spot' and 'forward'. Both transactions are straightforward and important, but as between the two of them, spots are more prominent.

In 2010, the average daily turnover of global FX spot transactions was approximately US$1.5 trillion, accounting for 37.4 per cent of all FX transactions.[21]

Participants in a spot transaction agree to buy and sell one foreign currency against another at the present market value such as the exchange rate for those two currencies. Further, they agree to settle the transaction in a matter of days (usually one, two, or three days). The standard settlement time frame is $T + 2$ days (where $T =$ trade date). There are exceptions to this standard $T + 2$ settlement. Examples include the spot market for US dollars and Canadian dollars (such as, USD/CAD) and US dollars against Mexican pesos (such as USD/MXN). Both settle on $T + 1$ day. Settlement on $T + 1$ is also called 'tomnext', which means 'tomorrow/next day' such as the day after the trade date, T.

Therefore, a spot FX transaction is one for nearly immediate delivery, unlike a forward or futures transaction, where delivery is deferred beyond a gap of two days. Spot FX trading occurs over-the-counter (OTC), not on an organized exchange.

By way of example, consider the following spot transaction:

Day 1 = Trade date, T.

Negotiations are done by dealers directly or their brokers.

Day 2 = Confirmation, $T + 1$.

Each side sends out written confirmations by telex or through the Society for Worldwide Interbank Financial Telecommunications (SWIFT), which is an international message transmission system incorporated in Belgium. Essentially, every significant financial institution in the international financial markets, and many less significant ones, is a SWIFT member. SWIFT has its own payment messages formats and security procedures (message authentication).

Day 3 = Value date, $T + 2$.

Settlement occurs, in the sense of delivery of the traded currencies. Delivery is by electronic credit entries in the appropriate bank accounts. Accordingly, $T + 2$ is the 'value date', because it is the day on which value (the currencies) is exchanged.

A spot transaction can be quoted in either currency, but will always include two sides. The first currency listed in the transaction is the base currency, while the second listed is the counter currency. For example, if a spot transaction is shown as USD/JPY 100, then for every US$1 dollar (the base currency) sold, a party receives 100 Japanese yen (the counter currency). Figure 4.1 depicts a hypothetical spot USD/JPY transaction.

As discussed further below, there is settlement, or *Herstatt*, risk associated with spot transactions. This risk refers to the possibility that one party to a spot deal has delivered the currency it is obligated to deliver to the counterparty, but before it receives delivery of the currency to which it is entitled, the counterparty fails. In other words, the first party has paid out, but not been paid.

In the hypothetical, JEH in Lawrence, Kansas buys cars from Honda of Japan to sell to its clients in the Midwest. The producer-exporter, Honda of Japan, needs to be paid in yen. To acquire yen, JEH enters into a spot transaction with BTM to receive yen in exchange for dollars. This transaction occurs over a period of three days (T for the trade date, $T + 1$ for confirmation, and $T + 2$ for exchange of value), and the currency will be traded at present (T) market value.

International financial instruments 123

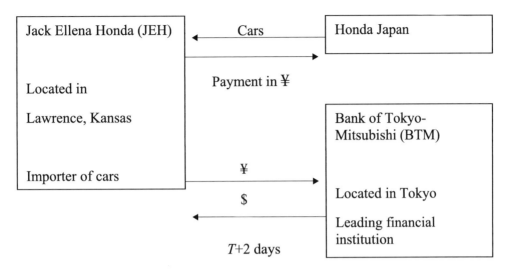

Figure 4.1 Hypothetical spot FX transaction.

Forwards

'Forward' connotes delivery of currency at some future date beyond two days (as two days would make it a spot transaction). Forward contracts are negotiated on Day 1 (T), but delivery can be any day in the future. It is possible for the delivery date to be as lengthy as five years in the future. However, it is more common for the delivery date to be $T + 30$, $T + 60$, or $T + 90$. The idea behind a forward transaction is to lock in a specific currency rate to hedge against possible future appreciation of that currency. In other words, a forward deal is a contract to buy or sell an asset (a particular foreign currency) on a future date, but at a price agreed upon today. Forward contracts are individually negotiated, hence the flexibility in the delivery date. Like spots, forwards are traded OTC, not on an organized exchange.

For example, on 1 June, a bank enters into a forward contract to buy the requisite amount of yen at ¥80/US$1, in anticipation of the yen appreciating, for delivery on 1 July ($T + 30$). If, in fact, the yen does appreciate in value during the 30 days, the bank will receive more yen per dollar than at the current (appreciated) market price. It is true that yen could depreciate during the 30 day time period. Then, the bank would receive less yen per dollar than the current market price.

Figure 4.2 presents a forward FX transaction. The figure is similar to that for a spot deal, with the exception of the delivery date, which occurs further into the future for a forward than for a spot.

Forwards involve settlement risk, or *Herstatt* risk, because there is a spot deal executed as part of the transaction. Forwards also involve credit risk and market risk. (Both are discussed in further detail below.) As to credit risk, if a counterparty to a forward FX deal fails to make its obligatory payment, then the remaining (and presumably solvent) party must go out and find a second counterparty (to replace the one that failed to make its obligatory currency payment). That second counterparty entails credit risk, as it might not make payment. As to market risk, FX rates may have moved against the remaining

124 *Practice of investment management*

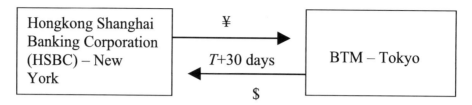

Figure 4.2 Hypothetical forward FX transaction.

bank, if and when it needs to replace its first counterparty that failed to make payment with a second counterparty.

Forward contracts also differ from spot deals in that they involve a forward rate. The forward foreign exchange rate is the rate that neutralizes interest differentials. Forward rates will be at a premium or discount. Interest rates determine forward rates, because they reflect the time value of money. During the pendency of a forward FX contract (e.g., 90 days), each of the two currencies involved in the contract can be invested in an interest-bearing asset denominated in the relevant currency.

For example, assume interest rates are 5 per cent in Australia and 10 per cent in Thailand. Obviously, there is a 5 per cent interest rate differential (IRD) in favour of the holder of a Thai asset. (The IRD is the difference in interest rate between two currencies in a pair.) Assume the spot rate of dollars to pounds is US$1.00 = £2. The spot rate must have an economic impact such that the holder of an interest-earning asset in Thailand loses 5 per cent. To achieve such an impact, the spot rate must take 5 per cent away from the investor converting from dollars to baht. The investor gets fewer dollars for the same amount of baht. Assume the Thai investor has £2. This investor must lose 5 per cent, hence it must get 95 cents in return.

On Day 1, the investor takes US$1.00 and converts it at the spot rate to receive £2. Six months later, on Day 180, the investor will take £2 and convert it at the forward rate, receiving US$0.95. Therefore, there is no incentive to engage in the transaction if the investor is seeking to earn a return based on the interest rate differential: the forward rate wipes out that differential.

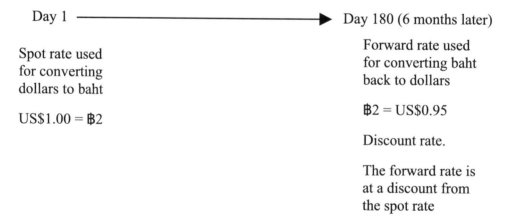

Figure 4.3 Hypothetical forward FX transaction.

In that sense, it might be said 'money does not follow interest rates'. However, that would be an overstatement. Money indeed does follow interest rates, at least under certain circumstances. For example, for reasons of market imperfections, the forward rate for a particular currency may be mispriced temporarily. Investors may see that a particular forward rate does not wipe out an interest rate differential, and seize on an opportunity to buy a higher interest-earning asset denominated in a foreign currency. Another example is if the investor can leverage an investment, e.g., borrowing foreign currency at a relatively lower interest rate, and using the borrowed funds to invest in a high-return asset.

It is critical to remember that when an investor enters into a forward FX deal on Day 1, two events occur: First, US$1.00 is converted into 2 baht on Day 1. Second, 2 baht are converted into US$0.95 for delivery six months hence. Therefore, the investor gains 5 per cent over six months on the IRD (10 per cent in Thailand versus 5 per cent in Australia.) But, the investor loses 5 per cent (5 cents) on the forward conversion. The forward rate exactly neutralizes the IRD.

These concepts can be put generally into the following statements about the relationship between interest rates, IRDs, and the forward rate:

- 'Interest rate premium means forward discount'
  On Day 1, suppose the spot rate is quoted at US$1.00 = ₤2 and IRD is 5 per cent in favour of baht-denominated assets. Then, the forward rate is quoted at a discount. This scenario is the same as the earlier example, with an IRD of 5 per cent (10 per cent in Thailand and 5 per cent in Australia).

  When the interest rate in the foreign currency is at a premium, then the forward rate for that foreign currency must trade at a discount from the spot rate, namely, 95 cents per 2 baht. It is that discount that wipes out the potential gain from the IRD.

  Day 1 ⟶ Future date

  Interest rate earned on assets denominated in foreign currency exceeds interest rate earned on assets denominated in domestic currency.

  The forward must be at a discount to the spot rate.

- 'Interest rate discount means forward premium'
  When the interest rate in the foreign currency is at a discount, then the forward rate is at a premium. Here, the potential loss incurred from a lower interest rate in the foreign currency is offset by a gain from the forward rate. This scenario would exist if spot rate is US$1.00 = ₤2 and IRD is 5 per cent in favour of dollar-denominated assets (10 per cent in Australia and 5 per cent in Thailand). The forward rate would be a premium over the spot rate of 105 cents per 2 baht.

  Day 1 ⟶ Future date

  Interest rate earned on foreign currency is less than the interest rate earned on assets denominated in domestic currency.

  The forward must be at a premium to the spot rate.

126 Practice of investment management

Generally, a forward FX rate can be calculated using a simple formula.

Assume:

a	=	currency of country A
b	=	currency of country B
i	=	interest rate
ia	=	interest rate in currency A such as the interest rate earned on an asset denominated in the currency of country A.
ib	=	interest rate in currency B such as the interest rate earned on an asset denominated in the currency of country B.

Further, there are 360 days in the investment year. 'Days' refers to the maturity period for an asset such as the number of days for the asset to mature in total.

Days equal 1 if the asset has a maturity of one year (360/360), and ½ if the asset has a maturity of six months (180/360).

With those assumptions, the formula is:

$$\text{Forward rate} = \text{Spot rate} \times \left[\frac{1 + ia \frac{(days)}{360}}{1 + ib \frac{(days)}{360}} \right]$$

Or, expressed in an intuitively easy fashion, via algebraic manipulation, the right-hand side denominator may be brought to the left-hand side:

The first term tells what return an investor will earn if the investor takes Australian dollars, converts them into a foreign currency, invests them in an asset denominated in the foreign currency for a fixed period, and then converts the principal and interest earned back to dollars at the end of the fixed maturity period.

$$(\text{Forward rate}) \times \left(1 + ib\left(\frac{(days)}{360}\right)\right) = (\text{Spot rate}) \times \left(ia\left(\frac{(days)}{360}\right)\right)$$

The second term tells the investor what its total return will be if it invests Australian dollars in an interest-bearing Australian asset.

The logic behind the formula can be understood by working from first principles. Assume:

- All exchange rates are expressed in Australian dollars per pound.
- The spot rate is £1 = US$2.00.
- The investment period is six months (180 days).
- The interest rate in the Australia is 5 per cent.
- The interest rate in the Thailand is 10 per cent.

The basic equation for figuring the total return from investing in an interest earning asset is:

$$\begin{aligned}
\text{Total return} &= (\text{Principal amount invested, } P) \\
&\quad + (\text{Interest earned on } P) \\
&= (P) + (P \text{ multiplied by interest earned for period}) \\
&= (P) + (P \cdot (i) \cdot \frac{(days)}{360}) \\
&= (P) \cdot (1 + 1 \cdot (i) \cdot \frac{(days)}{360})
\end{aligned}$$

(In the last step, P is factored out and put in front of the entire expression.)

Suppose an investor has ฿1, therefore $P = 1$ baht. The 1 baht is invested at 10 per cent for 180 days. The investment will earn:

$$\begin{aligned}
\text{Total return} &= 1 + (1 \cdot (0.10) \cdot \frac{(180)}{360}) \\
&= 1 + 0.05 \\
&= 1.05
\end{aligned}$$

At the end of 180 days, the investor will have 1 baht and 5 satang. (Observe this formula is the same as the denominator in the earlier formula.)

At the end of 180 days, the investor can convert the 1.05 baht back into dollars at the forward rate. What is the US dollar value of 1.05 baht in six months?

$$\begin{aligned}
\text{Dollar value} &= (\text{Forward rate}) \cdot (1.05 \text{ baht}) \\
&= \frac{(Dollars)}{(Baht)} \cdot (1.05 \text{ baht})
\end{aligned}$$

To solve, consider the alternative investment. Instead of investing 1 baht at 10 per cent, the alternative is investing US$2.00 at 5 per cent:

$$\begin{aligned}
\text{Total return} &= \$2.00 + \frac{(\$2.00 \times 0.005 \times 180)}{360} \\
&= \$2.00 + (0.05) \\
&= \$2.05
\end{aligned}$$

(Notice this formula is the numerator in the earlier formula.)

The forward rate will be the rate that sets these two amounts equal to each other. The equality reflects the fact arbitrageurs eliminate profitable opportunities from interest rate differentials, such as, market imperfection does not persist.

128 *Practice of investment management*

$$\frac{(Dollars)}{(Baht)} \cdot (1.05 \text{ baht}) = \$2.05$$

$$\frac{(Dollars)}{(Baht)} = \frac{\$2.05}{1.05 \text{ baht}}$$

Forward rate in dollars per baht = US$1.952 per baht.

Thus, the investor will get a higher interest return in Thailand. But, when the investment matures, the baht will be converted at a less favourable forward rate. The rate is less favourable in that each baht will fetch US$1.952 instead of US$2.00.

Finally, the formula involves putting the two sides together and inserting the numbers from the above example (forward rate is in dollars per baht):

$$(\text{Forward rate}) \cdot \left[฿1 + \left(฿1 \cdot (0.10) \cdot \frac{180}{360} \right) \right] = (\$2.00) \cdot \left[1 + \left(1 \cdot (0.05) \cdot \frac{180}{360} \right) \right]$$

$$(\text{Forward rate}) \cdot (1.05) = \$2.00 \cdot (1.025)$$

$$(\text{Forward rate}) \cdot (1.05) = \$2.00 \cdot (1.025)$$

$$(\text{Forward rate}) = \frac{\$2.05}{(1.05)}$$

$$= US\$1.952 \text{ per baht}$$

Futures

Futures emerged on 16 May 1972 as a financial innovation to facilitate foreign trading and investing. Futures were first traded on the International Monetary Market (IMM), an entity of the Chicago Mercantile Exchange (CME). Recall the demise of the Bretton Woods System that occurred in the 1970s. The creation of futures exchanges was in part in anticipation of the impending shift to the floating FX regime.[22]

A futures contract is a standardized contract between two parties to buy or sell an asset at a price agreed upon today (the futures or strike price). Delivery and payment are specified for a future date. That much is the same as a forward contract (though physical delivery on a futures FX contract is rare).

However, there are four main differences between a forward and futures contract:

1 Where they are traded:
    Forwards are traded OTC. Futures are traded on an exchange.
2 Individually negotiated versus standardized contracts:
    Forwards are individually negotiated contracts between parties and, therefore, can be tailored to the needs of the parties. Futures are standardized contracts that specify amount, quote the price in minimum increments, identify the nature and quality of the deliverable asset, set maturity and delivery dates, and define the delivery process.

3   Payment flows:
    Forwards, because they are OTC, do not require the buyer or seller to provide a collateral deposit for the transaction. Futures are traded on an exchange so it is actually the exchange, acting as a counterparty to both the buyer and seller (and because the exchange trusts neither the buyer, nor the seller, whereas both buyer and seller trust the exchange), which requires both parties to the transaction to 'post margin'. Margin is a collateral deposit that protects against the buyer or seller going bankrupt before the deal is settled. Therefore, exchanges (and clearing houses) in a futures deal assume the credit risk associated with each trade and ensure performance of the contract.[23] The difference in payment flows means in a forward that each party is exposed to the other (counterparty exposure), whereas for futures, the exposure lies with the exchange (and clearing house) such as the exchange is exposed to each party. (The possibility of exchange – or clearing house – failure exists, hence each party bears exchange – and clearing house – exposure. A variety of regulatory mechanisms are designed to minimize this risk.)
4   Delivery:
    The majority of forward contracts result in *actual* delivery of the asset (such as the foreign currencies being exchanged). The majority of futures contracts are closed prior to the agreed upon settlement date. The result is no physical delivery of the asset.

Options

An FX option, or currency option contract, gives the owner the right, but not the obligation, to exchange money denominated in one currency into another currency at a pre-agreed exchange rate on or before some date in the future. Most options trading is done OTC. There are two types of options: call options and put options:

1   A call option gives the owner (such as holder of the option) the right, but not the obligation, to buy, or call, a specified amount of an underlying asset at a fixed price (strike price or exercise price), on or before a set date in the future (expiration date or expiry). The owner buys that asset – foreign currency – from the seller (or writer) of the option.
2   A put option gives the owner (such as the holder of the option) the right, but not the obligation to sell, or put, a specified amount of an underlying asset at a fixed price (strike price or exercise price), on or before a set date in the future (expiration date, or expiry). The owner sells that asset – foreign currency – to the seller (or writer) of the option.

For example, suppose Jack Ellena Honda (JEH) anticipates, but is not sure of, a booming demand for Hondas on 1 December and is also concerned the yen will appreciate relative to the US dollar by 1 December. JEH has to import Hondas from Japan, and must pay the producer-exporter of the vehicles in Japan, such as Honda in Japan, for those cars in yen. Yet, JEH sells those Hondas in Kansas in dollars. That creates an income statement mismatch: its expenditure is in yen, but its revenue is in dollars. The concern of JEH is the yen might appreciate relative to the dollar, so its expenditures would rise.

So, to hedge this FX risk, JEH can purchase a call option for yen from the Bank of Tokyo-Mitsubishi (BTM). BTM is the seller of the option such as it writes the call option contract that JEH buys.

Under this contract, JEH has the right, but not the obligation, to buy yen from BTM at the strike price. JEH will exercise the option if that option is 'in the money', meaning the strike price allows JEH to get yen (to pay for the Hondas it imports from Japan) at a price denominated in dollars that is cheaper than the spot market price of yen against dollars.

In contrast, suppose JEH anticipates, but is not sure, of a booming demand for Hondas in Kansas on 1 December, and concerned the yen will depreciate relative to the dollar by 1 December. Here JEH faces the opposite income statement mismatch: its yen-denominated expenditures will fall, while its dollar-denominated revenues will rise. If that depreciation occurs, then JEH would be happy, as it were, because the cost of the vehicles falls (because JEH need not convert as many dollars into yen as before, as each dollar is worth more yen than before precisely because the yen has depreciated against the dollar).

Might JEH be able to profit from yen depreciation via a put option contract? Suppose JEH enters into a put option contract with BTM, which is the writer of that contract. Then, JEH will be entitled to sell yen against dollars at a higher than spot market price, if yen does depreciate against the dollar. BTM would lose money on the option, but JEH would have gained in the sense of selling an asset (yen) at a price higher than its spot market value. Of course, this particular hedge assumes JEH has sufficient yen in its account both to pay for the Hondas, and to sell to BTM.

A simple way to remember the difference between FX calls and puts is to think in terms of currency optimists versus pessimists. Buying FX calls is for optimists: they believe the spot market value of the currency of their option contract is going to rise, so they seek to lock in a cheaper value by buying a call option now. The writer of the call option has the diametric opposite view of the future direction of the spot market: it thinks the value of the relevant currency will fall, so the option will never be 'in the money', and thus go unexercised, allowing it to pocket the fee from selling the option.

Conversely, buying FX puts is for pessimists: they believe the spot market value of the currency of their option contract is going to fall. They seek to lock in a higher sales price for that currency by buying a put option now. Again, the writer of the put option has the diametric opposite view of the future direction of the spot market: she thinks the value of the relevant currency will rise. The writer of the put believes the option will never enter into the money, and thus go unexercised, leaving it with the fee from selling the option.

Currency swaps

A currency swap is a transaction that involves the exchange of principal and interest of a loan in one currency for an equal loan in another currency. Typically, Party A makes payments in currency B in exchange for Party B making payments in currency A. Currency swaps are traded OTC and serve to minimize foreign borrowing costs and hedge exposure to exchange rate risk. They are motivated by comparative advantage.

That is, Parties A and B face a balance sheet mismatch. Party A gets revenues from an asset denominated in currency A (e.g., an account or note receivable), but has a liability (e.g., an account or note payable) in currency B. Conversely, Party B earns revenues from an asset denominated in currency B, but bears a liability in currency A. To rectify the mismatch, the two Parties literally swap their payment obligations. Party A pays the liability of Party B, which is denominated in currency A. The asset and liability of Party A is then matched:

International financial instruments 131

both are in currency A. Likewise, Party B pays the liability of Party A, which is denominated in currency B. The asset and liability are then in the same currency; namely, B.

There are a number of motivations for entering into a currency swap, in addition to matching currency flows. Moreover, swaps are available for use by both sovereign and private entities so a party might enter into a currency swap:

- To benefit from its better credit rating in a foreign market
- To change a loan from one currency to another
- To change cash flow into or out of a foreign currency
- To hedge against exchange rate changes affect a loan
- To use proceeds of a loan denominated in one country's currency to meet currency needs in another county, or;
- To avoid capital or currency exchange controls in a particular country.[24]

For example, consider again the possibility of a currency swap between JEH and Honda of Japan.

JEH could send US dollars that it borrowed to Honda. In turn, Honda could send yen it borrowed to JEH. JEH would have borrowed dollars at the lowest possible rate, but needs to pay principal and interest in yen to Honda for vehicles. By getting yen from Honda, it matches this yen-based payment obligation. Likewise, Honda would have borrowed yen at the lowest possible rate, but has an obligation to pay principal and interest in dollars. By getting dollars from JEH, Honda matches this dollar-based payment obligation. Figure 4.4 shows these flows.

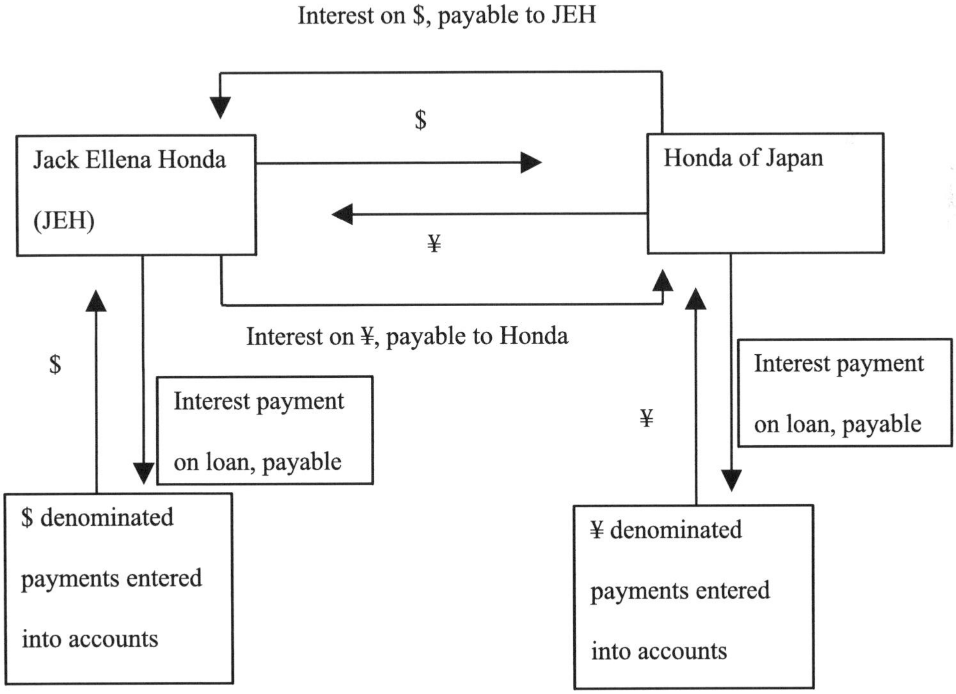

Figure 4.4 Hypothetical currency swap FX transaction.

Note that in a currency swap, the interest rates are fixed. Interest rate swaps involve exchanging fixed for floating interest rate payments. To be sure, there exist cross-currency interest rate swaps, which combine the features of both a currency swap and an interest rate swap.

An influential institution in the OTC derivatives market is the International Swaps and Derivatives Association (ISDA).[25] Headquartered in New York, ISDA also has offices in Washington, DC, London, Hong Kong, Tokyo, Brussels, and Singapore. ISDA has over 840 members, including regional banks, governments, corporations, law firms, exchanges, clearinghouses, and asset managers, located around the world. The mission of ISDA is to facilitate risk management for users of derivative products, such as currency swaps. It functions as a kind of self-regulatory organization (SRO).

To help manage credit and legal risk, ISDA publishes a *Master Agreement*, which is used by parties dealing in any of the asset classes in the OTC derivative market. Indeed, the *Agreement* is the most commonly used master contract for OTC derivative transactions in the world. ISDA last updated the *Master Agreement* in 2002 (the 2002 ISDA *Master Agreement*, or 2002 *Agreement*). The *Master Agreement* sets standard terms that apply to all transactions entered into between two parties. Therefore, new terms do not need to be re-negotiated each time the parties enter into a new transaction as the existing terms automatically apply.

Two versions of the *Master Agreement* exist. One is for parties transacting in the same currency and located in the same jurisdiction. The second is for parties transacting in multiple currencies, located in different jurisdictions. The entire contract consists of the master agreement, schedule, confirmations, definitions, and credit support annex.

Notes

1 Stephen Choi and A. C. Pritchard, *Securities Regulation: Cases and Analysis*, 3rd ed. (New York: Foundation Press, 2012), 3.
2 Ibid.
3 Ibid., 5.
4 Ibid., 7.
5 "Convertibles," Investopedia, accessed 13 May 2014, http://www.investopedia.com/terms/c/convertibles.asp.
6 Investopedia Staff, "Wonders of Convertible Bonds," *Yahoo! Finance*, accessed 12 May 2014, http://finance.yahoo.com/news/wonders-convertible-bonds-160000020.html.
7 Zvi Bodie, Alex Kane, and Alan J. Marcus. *Essentials of Investments*, 5th ed. (New York: McGraw-Hill/Irwin, 2004), 33.
8 Ibid., 36.
9 Ibid., 38–9.
10 "About ETFs," Bloomberg, accessed 14 May 2014, http://www.bloomberg.com/markets/etfs/etf_about.html.
11 Ibid., 11.
12 H. Lawrence Wisley, "The Investment Advisers Act of 1940," *Journal of Finance* 4, No. 4, (1949): 289.
13 Terrance O'Malley, "The Consequences of Investment Adviser Registration with the SEC," *Journal of Investment Compliance* 1, Issue 1, (2000): 47–54.
14 Barry P. Barbash and Jai Massari, "The Investment Advisers Act of 1940: Regulation by Accretion," *Rutgers Law Journal* 39.3 (2008): 627, accessed http://org.law.rutgers.edu/publications/lawjournal/issues/39_3/03BarbashVol.39.3.r_1.pdf.
15 Roy H. Steyer, "The Investment Company Act of 1940," *Yale Law Journal* 50 (1941): 440.
16 Ibid., 443.

17 "The Investment Act of 1940," *Columbia Law Review* 41 (1941): 269, 286.
18 Ibid., 288.
19 This section draws heavily on Raj Bhala, *Modern GATT Law*, Volume I, Chapter VI, Section VII (London: Thomson Sweet & Maxwell, 2013).
20 *Generally* Ernest T. Patrikis, Thomas C. Baxter, Jr., and Raj Bhala, *Wire Transfers* (Chicago, Illinois: Irwin/Probus, 1993) (discussing wire transfers of dollars and the legal rules governing them).
21 "Triennial Central Bank Survey of Foreign Exchange and Derivatives Market Activity in 2010," *Bank for International Settlements*, 17 September 2011, accessed www.bis.org/publ/rpfxf10t.pdf.
22 Tim Weithers, *Foreign Exchange: A Practical Guide to the FX Markets* (Hoboken, NJ: John Wiley & Sons, Inc., 2006), 129–32.
23 A prominent exchange is the Chicago Mercantile Exchange (CME), also called the 'Chicago Merc' or 'the Merc'. The CME, or any exchange, is in effect the buyer to the seller and the seller to the buyer in every trade conducted through the exchange. In October 2012, the CME Group FX exchange volume averaged 709,000 contracts per day. *See* www.cmegroup.com.
24 Jerold A. Friedland, *Understanding International Business and Financial Transactions* 3rd ed. (Newark, NJ: LexisNexis, 2010), 27.
25 "ISDA," accessed 13 May 2014, www.ISDA.org.

5 International financial markets

5.1 Introduction

This chapter details various global financial markets and how they interact. The markets discussed are:

1 Exchanges: global and emerging markets
2 Over the counter (OTC) markets
3 Hybrid markets
4 Dark pools
5 Bond trading.[1]

Associated with each of these markets is a clearing and settlement system (or systems). Interestingly, this system helps distinguish organized exchanges versus OTC markets. But, to begin, the fundamental concept of a 'market' should be recalled. What is a 'market'?

To answer, it is nothing more than a place for businesses and individuals to buy and sell goods, services, or intellectual property (IP).[2] A financial market is one in which the goods traded are investment instruments, such as securities (e.g., stocks or bonds), commodities, foreign exchange (FX), or derivatives, and the services traded are ones associated with those instruments, such as advice, ratings, clearing and settlement, and so forth.[3] The instruments and services may involve IP where a commercial or investment bank registers a copyright on the stock market research it publishes, or registers a mark on a particular type of service.

Accordingly, a potential participant in a market decides whether or not to participate in that market first by considering what it seeks to buy or sell. Thereafter, it acquaints itself with pertinent features of the market, which may encourage or discourage it to participate, or to seek substitute markets.

5.2 Exchanges: global and emerging markets

Introduction

An exchange is a centralized market in which financial instruments; that is, stocks, bonds, commodities, FX, or derivatives are bought and sold according to an organized set of rules. Those rules are determined by the exchange in which the financial instruments are traded. In turn, the rules are set within a legal framework, such as statutes, regulation, and judicial decisions.

Typically, two types of markets comprise an exchange: primary and secondary.[4] For example, suppose an investor seeks to purchase stock of the Korean multinational corporation Samsung Electronics, which is traded (*inter alia*) on the Korea Stock Exchange (KSE). Does the investor propose to buy the shares directly from the company? This type of purchase is one in the primary market.

Conversely, suppose an investor already holds Samsung equity, and seeks to sell it a year after purchasing it. The would-be seller must look to a new market with potential buyers. This market is a secondary one, allowing for transactions between businesses (including, of course, banks or investment companies) or individuals. Secondary markets are an essential element for a modern economy. Observe that the larger the number of ready, willing, and able buyers, the more liquid a secondary market is said to be. Liquidity is a virtue, in that it encourages investment simply because investors know they can sell their securities with ease in the future.

Moreover, through simple supply and demand principles, primary and secondary markets allow for prices to adjust to match the perceived value of the security traded. These prices are signals to actual and potential investors, and indeed the issuers of the securities, about the performance of the issuers, and the overall health of the sector, country, and region in which the issuers operate.

Traditional exchanges

Any company wishing to have its stock publicly traded must first meet the criteria of the exchange on which it seeks its stock to be bought and sold,[5] and also pay a listing fee to that exchange.[6] In an initial public offering (IPO), an issuer, such as a company, offers to sell its stock at a predetermined price to purchasers as a means of raising capital and increasing the liquidity of the issuer. Generally, the IPO is available to the general public, but in certain cases (e.g., with preferred stock), the floatation may be limited to select purchasers. Either way, any IPO is a primary market transaction.[7]

Subsequently, IPO purchasers may trade their securities on the secondary market. Brokers, mutual funds, and other financial institutions use the exchange to buy and sell securities already in the secondary market, or offered for the first time by the IPO investors. In other words, any trading after the direct purchase of a security from its issuer occurs in the secondary market, but both primary and secondary market transactions can and do occur on traditional exchanges.

Traditionally, stock was sold on an exchange floor (floor trading), with brokers taking calls from investors and making trades. The brokers can offer (such as sell) stock to investors at a certain price (known as the 'ask price'). They can also respond to offers from investors (such as buy stock) with their own price (called the 'bid price'). Indeed, they can do both, that is, buy and sell stock of the same issuer. In all such transactions, the agreed-upon price is recorded for the rest of the exchange to see. The prompt, public posting of the transaction price is a key indicator of market transparency, showing the current market value for any given stock. And, the floor traders serve as market makers, connecting buyers with sellers.

Transparency as to pricing distinguishes exchange from OTC trading, and dark pools. In OTC markets, bid and ask prices are apparent, but not final settlement prices, hence trading could be occurring at any point in between and including the bid and ask prices. In dark pool trading, as its name suggests, there is no public disclosure of bid, ask, or negotiated prices. Likewise, the nature of market making is different on a centralized exchange in comparison with OTC markets and dark pools.

Internet trading

The information technology (IT) revolution, specifically, the rise in internet trading, has led to increased efficiency and lower commission costs for investors. Before then, brokerage firms had to have several associates on the trading floor to make transactions. Since then, many sales occur online through the click of a mouse. These clicks, daily and nightly, by investors around the world, have forced these firms to specialize into two main classes: full service or discount brokers.[8]

Originally, most large brokerage firms were full service. That meant they provided investment advice, stock quotations, offered margin loans, and facilitated transactions. That also meant they charged high commission costs per transaction.

Now, discount brokers have discarded many of these additional services, and focus on quoting prices and completing trades using automated systems.[9] This simplification allows them to charge low, flat fees, or price their services at small percentages of the transaction at stake. Internet trading also allows for more efficient order aggregation, or 'bunching'. Bunching is the process whereby the firms pool a large number of small individual trades or odd-lot orders (orders of a security containing an amount less than the customary quantity for that security) together, and engage in only a few transactions per day, thus cutting down on trade execution costs.[10]

Online trading and National Association of Securities Dealers Automated Quotations (NASDAQ)

With the advent of the NASDAQ system and Internet trading, floor trading has become relatively less preferable. Electronic trading is faster, cheaper, more efficient, and even more certain, predictable, transparent, and precise, than floor trading. Many companies, especially those in the high-technology sector, such as Apple and Microsoft, have listed their stock on the NASDAQ alone, rather than on more traditional exchanges such as the New York Stock Exchange (NYSE).

Under the umbrella of the National Association of Securities Dealers (NASD), NASDAQ originated in 1971 as an electronic price quotation system, not actually sponsoring a trading platform, as part of the OTC market. That is, OTC market participants would take advantage of NASDAQ price quotations, as well as PinkSlips and OTC Bulletin Board (discussed below), to see bid and ask prices. In 1984, NASDAQ took the first step towards becoming the first electronic exchange with the creation of the Small Order Execution System (SOES). The system was originally limited to routing small traders' orders while it prohibited institutional entities from trading on their own behalf to market makers.[11] The October 1987 Stock Market crash and rapidly changing technology (e.g., the introduction of the NASDAQ Workstation in 1987 made the SOES available digitally to anyone with a PC) expanded the services SOES could provide.[12,]

SOES allowed small investors and market makers to submit offers, place bids, complete trades electronically, and automatically forward trade agreements to a clearing entity. The SOES is now largely unused due to the proliferation of modern trading platforms known as electronic communication networks (ECNs). Many of the largest exchanges in the world have followed the example set by NASDAQ, and have implemented their own ECNs. The NYSE is an example, as in 2005 it transitioned to a dual system, floor, and online trading.[13]

Developing versus developed economies

Before exploring global exchanges, it is first necessary to understand the environment in which regional exchanges exist. Is that environment a developing economy? What is the state of that economy? What is its political climate? Does the rule of law undergird that economy and, by extension, securities markets?

To help address these questions, it is useful to look at the way in which the World Bank categorizes countries. The United Nations Development Programme (UNDP) has technical economic criteria to define a 'least developed country', of which there are roughly 50. They are the poorest of the poor countries, and the essential criterion delineating them is an average *per capita* GDP of less than US$1.25 per day. But, what about the distinction between 'developed' versus 'developing' countries – how is that line drawn? Here the World Bank categories are useful.

The World Bank relies on two methods to categorize countries: (1) gross national income (GNI) *per capita*, and (2) geographic region.[14] The Bank uses GNI to make rank-order comparisons among countries, and group them by level of economic development. As intimated, the two broadest categories are (1) developing economies, and (2) developed economies.

The World Bank defines a 'developing economy' as one in which the annual gross national income is less than US$12,475.[15] Developing economies are further divided into (1) low income, (2) low-middle income, and (3) upper-middle income.

As to the second methodology, the World Bank applies it after or alongside the first. That is, once the Bank identifies a country as 'developing' based on GNI criteria, then it groups it by region. The Bank groups only developing, not developed, countries regionally.

Exchanges in developing economies

'Developing economy', or equivalently, 'developing country', are buzzwords in the investment world. (A related term, sometimes used interchangeably with the other two, is 'emerging market'.) By far, among the roughly 200 nations on earth, the largest number of them are in the category of 'developing country'. This category cuts across all regions. But the term 'developing economy' is imprecise: it does not have the same implication across all regions. A West Asian developing economy is not necessarily like one in South America, though the rubric is the same. The disparity between them may be striking.

What metric helps financial market players compare and analyse the likeness or lack thereof of different developing countries? Market capitalization, as well as GDP growth, is one answer.

Market capitalization, generally speaking, is a measure of the total value of all stock being traded on an exchange. It is the total number of shares being traded multiplied by the value of the shares, or mathematically:

Stock market capitalization	=	Total number of shares traded	+	Value of shares traded

Financial market players are accustomed to examining the trend of market capitalization within and across countries.

138 *Practice of investment management*

Growth is a healthy sign, whereas declines give pause for concern. Manifestly, liquidity; that is, the ability to buy and sell a security, is greater in a market with high and growing capitalization than in one that is small and shrinking (*ceteris paribus*, such as, all other factors held equal). Much attention in the past few decades has been spent on the BRICS countries (Brazil, Russia, India, China, and South Africa), which is for good reason. Table 5.1 shows stock market capitalization and GDP growth in the BRICS, as well as Indonesia and Mexico for comparative purposes.

Data in Table 5.1 show, for the selected countries, the growth in cumulative stock market capitalization (such as total market capitalization of all exchanges in a country) and aggregate GDP growth (reflecting the overall economic health of the country). Comparing these two statistics reveals the performance of exchanges (and, by proxy, the companies listed on those exchanges) in relation to the general economic performance. For example, the Mexican and Indonesian market capitalization growth rates were nearly double the corresponding national GDP growth rates, whereas South African market capitalization has grown more slowly than its GDP.

Obviously, there are three scenarios: market capitalization can grow faster, slower, or at roughly the same pace as GDP. What accounts for each scenario? Table 5.2 suggests some possible answers.

Table 5.1 provides a 'bird's-eye' view of growth in stock markets and economies over almost three decades. Table 5.2 offers possible explanations for the relative rates of growth. But how does this relate to the exchanges within these countries, and how does it affect potential investors? Table 5.3 answers this question, as well as how specific stock markets in the Asia-Pacific region, as well as Latin America, Africa, and the Middle East have performed. One way to see how they are performing is to compare these exchanges to their counterparts in other developing countries in various regions. Table 5.3 also asks how stock markets in the individual countries have performed (again measured by market capitalization) in a recent six-year period that spans the 2008 global economic turndown.

Regional fluctuations have the potential to affect these exchanges more than their counterparts in developed nations.

All of the exchanges listed in Table 5.3 exist almost exclusively within their respective countries, and are tied integrally to their respective economies. In contrast (as discussed later in this chapter), many of the largest exchanges in developed countries have expanded to include subsidiaries in other countries and regions. For example, the NYSE owns Euronext, and NASDAQ bought the OMX Group (also in Europe). So, by virtue of cross-border ownership, developed country exchanges tend to be more international in nature than their counterparts in developing countries.

That said, as a general proposition, there is a dichotomy concerning stock exchange performance that transcends the distinction between local versus cross-border ownership of an exchange. In normal times, when there is no economic, political, or national security crisis, stock market performance tends to reflect local conditions. Markets behave in a relatively decoupled fashion. But, when a crisis emerges, markets tend to be linked, if by nothing else than fear, greed, or both, and their performances are linked.

Developed country exchanges and international expansions

Setting aside questions of stock market performance, there have been three principal developments in recent decades in the exchanges of developed countries. First, the IT revolution has ushered in new ways of issuing and trading securities. Second, some

Table 5.1 Stock market capitalization, total GDP, and GDP growth in BRICS and selected other developing countries

Country	Stock market capitalization (in US dollars, billions) and growth					GDP and GDP growth (in US dollars, billions)				
	1993	1999	2005	2011	Percentage rate of growth in market capitalization (1993–2011)[16]	1993	1999	2005	2011	Percentage rate of GDP growth (1993–2011)[17]
China	40.60	330.70	780.76	3,389.10	8,248.00	440.50	1,083.28	2,256.90	7,318.50	1,561.40
Russia	0.02	72.21	548.76	796.38	3,981,800.00	435.06	195.91	764.00	1,857.77	327.00
India	98.00	184.61	553.07	1,015.37	936.10	284.19	464.34	834.22	1,847.98	550.30
Brazil	99.40	227.96	474.65	1,228.97	1,136.40	438.30	586.86	882.19	2,476.65	465.10
South Africa	172.00	262.48	565.41	855.71	397.50	130.41	133.18	247.05	408.24	213.00
Mexico	201.00	154.04	239.13	408.69	103.30	403.20	481.20	848.95	1,153.34	186.00
Indonesia	33.00	64.09	81.43	390.11	1,082.20	158.01	140.00	285.87	846.83	435.90

Table 5.2 Explaining relationships between growth in stock market capitalization and GDP

Scenario	Possible explanations
Growth in stock market capitalization *exceeds* GDP growth	1. Anticipated GDP growth (such as investors expect faster future economic growth); for example, because they see foreign direct investment (FDI) increasing, which in turn will bolster GDP growth. 2. Low interest rates, giving investors an incentive to buy stocks over interest-denominated assets (such as bonds). 3. Favourable foreign exchange rates whereby investors can purchase undervalued local currency and use it to pay for stocks. 4. Asset bubble, such as incentives are such that investors are encouraged to buy securities, notwithstanding relatively slower GDP growth.
Growth in stock market capitalization *trails* GDP growth	1. Anticipated GDP growth, such as investors expect slower future economic growth, and thus foresee sluggish corporate earnings. 2. High interest rates, giving investors an incentive to buy interest-denominated assets (such as bonds) over stocks. 3. Unfavourable foreign exchange rates, whereby investors face an overvalued local currency they need to pay for stocks. 4. Asset deflation, such as incentives, are such that investors are encouraged to sell securities, notwithstanding relatively faster GDP growth.
Growth in stock market capitalization *approximates* GDP growth	General balance among the factors mentioned above, such as expected growth in corporate earnings is roughly in line with anticipated GDP growth, monetary policy is appropriate, and exchange rates are properly aligned, there are no asset bubbles and no deflation.

exchanges have 'gone public'; that is, they have become publicly listed companies, as their owners have converted them from private entities.

Third, as intimated earlier, several exchanges have 'gone international'. Via mergers and acquisitions (such as M&A activity, usually with or of smaller exchanges), they have invested in exchanges outside of their home country jurisdiction, creating (for example) subsidiaries. As a result of these three developments, many developed country exchanges hardly resemble their former selves. The new, developed country-based exchanges, compared with their more regional brethren in developing economies, are now global both by geographic location and in reach.[18]

Table 5.4 highlights major M&A transactions and uncoupling events between 2006 and 2014 by developed country stock exchanges.

In 2007, the NYSE made a landscape-altering move when it merged with Euronext, a pan-European electronic exchange based in the Netherlands. As a result, NYSE Euronext became the first intercontinental stock exchange,[19] and a dominant player in global securities trading. With a market capitalization of over US$14 trillion (as of 2012) NYSE Euronext is over three times larger than NASDAQ, the second largest exchange in the world.[20] The NYSE–Euronext merger led to a domino effect of large, internationally prominent exchanges merging with or acquiring small domestic ones.

Table 5.3 Domestic equity market capitalization (in US dollars, millions) for exchanges in BRICS and selected other developing countries[21]

	Country	2006	2008	2010	2012	Percentage growth 2006–12
Americas						
BM&F Bovespa	Brazil	710,247.45	591,965.55	1,545,565.66	1,227,447.02	72.8
Columbia SE	Columbia	56,204.32	87,716.2	208,501.74	262,101.26	366.3
Mexican Exchange	Mexico	348,345.13	234,054.92	454,345.22	525,056.68	50.7
Asia Pacific						
Indian Sub-Continent						
Bombay (Bombay Stock Exchange (BSE))	India	818,878.58	647,204.77	1,631,829.54	1,263,335.5	54.3
NSE of India	India	774,115.6	600,281.63	1,596,625.26	1,234,491.96	59.5
Karachi	Pakistan	44,906.48	23,354.04	38,007.18	N/A	N/A
China						
Hong Kong Exchanges	China	1,714,953.25	1,328,768.47	2,711,316.16	2,831,945.86	65.1
Shanghai SE	China	917,507.53	1,425,354.02	2,716,470.22	2,547,203.79	177.6
Shenzhen SE	China	227,947.34	353,430.02	1,311,370.08	1,150,172.25	404.6
Southeast Asia						
Kuala Lumpur (Bursa Malaysia)	Malaysia	235,580.9	189,239.21	408,689.12	466,587.57	98.1
Indonesia SE	Indonesia	138,886.36	98,760.6	360,388.1	428,222.56	208.3
Philippine SE	Philippines	67,851.74	52,030.6	157,320.5	229,316.64	238.0
SE of Thailand	Thailand	140,161.28	103,128.24	277,731.74	389,756.32	178.1
Africa and Middle East						
Johannesburg	South Africa	711,232.32	482,699.98	925,007.15	907,723.2	27.6
Tehran	Iran	36,314.58	48,712.71	866,41.52	90,995.75	150.6
Dubai		N/A	38,543.92	54,200.95	33,377.41	N/A
Riyadh		326,900.00[22]	246,540.00[23]	353,409.59	373,374.75	14.2

Table 5.4 International expansion of developed country exchanges

Exchange (Home country of acquiror, year)	Market capitalization (US billions, as of July 2014)[24]	Public?	Subsidiaries/divisions (Country)
Intercontinental Exchange, Inc. (United States, 2013)	18.51 (NYSE)	Yes	Intercontinental Exchange, Inc.[25] – New York Stock Exchange (US) – NYSE Arca (US) – NYSE Amex Options (US) – NYSE Arca Options (US) – NYSE Bonds (US)
Merger of NASDAQ with OMX to produce NASDAQ OMX (United States, 2008)	6.51	Yes	The NASDAQ Stock Market (US) OMX:[26] – Armenian SE (Armenia) – Copenhagen SE (Denmark) – Helsinki SE (Finland) – Iceland SE (Iceland) – Riga SE (Latvia) – Stockholm SE (Sweden) – Tallinn SE (Estonia) – Vilnius SE (Lithuania)
Merger of the London Stock Exchange with Borsa Italiana S.p.A. (Great Britain, 2007)	4.43 (as of December 2013)[27]	Yes	LSE (Great Britain) Borsa Italiana S.p.A. (Italy)
Euronext becomes independent of ICE after IPO (Netherlands, 2014)	3.62	Yes	Euronext[28] – Euronext Amsterdam (Netherlands) – Euronext Brussels (Belgium) – Euronext Lisbon (Portugal) – Euronext London (Great Britain) – Euronext Paris (France)

At the time the merger was finalized, NASDAQ was in talks with the OMX group, a collective of Nordic and Baltic exchanges. Their merger transpired in 2008. The landscape changed in Europe, too, when the London Stock Exchange (LSE) purchased the largest Italian exchange, Borsa Italiana, in 2007. A 2010 proposal for the merger of the Singapore Exchange (SGX) and Australian Stock Exchange (ASX), which was rejected by the Australian Treasury in 2011, showed that M&A activity was not limited to Western exchanges.[29]

The landscape changed even more dramatically in 2013 when Intercontinental Exchange, Inc. (ICE) purchased NYSE Euronext to add to its already substantial portfolio of futures exchanges, central clearing houses, and OTC markets. With this acquisition, ICE became a player in nearly every area of the West's financial industry. Further upheaval quickly followed in June 2014 when Euronext issued an IPO and separated from ICE and the NYSE.

There are two unmistakable results of this kind of M&A activity. First, there is stunning concentration in the securities exchange business. Just four exchanges – NYSE, Euronext, NASDAQ OMX, and LSE – alone account for over 40 per cent of the stock market capitalization of the entire world. Second, this concentration is centred in the US and Europe. No non-Western stock exchange, or group of exchanges, has yet emerged to challenge at the global level what critics might view as an unbalanced playing field tilted in favour of neo-colonialist countries.

5.3 OTC markets

Exchanges, whether local, regional, or global in nature, consist primarily of two types of markets: primary and secondary. That also is true of the OTC market. If issuance and trading is not on an organized exchange, then there are only two other possibilities as to its venue: the OTC market, or dark pools.

As intimated, one aspect of OTC markets is identical to the secondary market: the equity, debt, or derivative instruments being traded have already come through the primary market, and are now traded publicly. The difference between the exchanges and OTC markets is in the process by which traded financial instruments change hands. Companies listed on an exchange must meet rigorous listing standards, and all final transaction prices are public information. Exchanges show in real time the value of a stock that the price sellers are willing to accept, and cost buyers will take on. That is not the case in the OTC market, as an understanding of OTC market history reveals.

History

The OTC market originated for the same reason most new markets come into being: money. From the late nineteenth century through the 1970s, major stock exchanges set (fixed) commissions on all trades. This presented a problem, as fixed commissions imposed a particularly heavy burden on traders engaged in a large number of transactions. They were the forerunners of what is now known as 'high-frequency traders' (HFT): they were unhappy with paying a fixed commission to organized exchanges regardless of the volume of their trading activity.

So, the large-volume players shifted their trading activity from exchanges to non-listed brokerage firms. Through such firms, these players traded exchange-listed securities, but avoided the fixed commissions of exchange trading. These players became what today commonly are 'market makers' (discussed later).

To facilitate price transparency, an organized exchange regulates the units in which a financial instrument is bought or sold (e.g., a price based on a lot of 100 shares). But, OTC markets afforded investors more flexibility than exchanges in the amounts traded, essentially allowing investors to buy or sell any volume amount of a security they wanted, with a price for each such amount. (So, for example, a price would be had for 27 or 163 shares, such as investors would not be restricted to 100 unit allotments).

Started in 1913, the National Quotation Bureau (NQB) provided a price quotation system, the Pink Sheets, as a means for market makers to record the going rates (that is, the bid and ask prices, such as the price a buyer offers and the price a seller seeks, but not the final agreed-upon transaction price) for securities on OTC markets.[30] Literally, 'Pink Sheets' were hard copy pieces of paper in pink colour, posted in prominent locations.

Today, the OTC Bulletin Board (OTCBB) rivals Pink Sheets, both offering ask/bid quotes for exchange-listed stocks, as well as those for companies that do not meet the requirements to be listed on a major exchange. 'Pink Sheets' still exist, but in electronic form, via a company with this name. Most penny stocks (such as a stock whose price is less than US$5, or a stock that is not traded on a large exchange), and high-risk stocks, are listed through the OTCBB or Pink Sheet services.[31] To this day, these services provide bid–ask spreads, but not final transaction prices.

So, today, on OTC markets, the ask prices offered by sellers and bid prices made by buyers are recorded on the OTCBB or Pink Sheet. But, the price at which an instrument is bought and sold may not be. Future legislation could require them to publish the latter, too.

Market makers

A 'market maker' is an individual firm or trader within the OTC market that buys, holds, and sells securities to investors or fellow market makers. It sets the price at which it is willing to sell (offer, or ask) and buy (bid), though these prices can differ depending on the second party. Market makers make deals among themselves to facilitate liquidity, offering different prices to one another than they would to investors. Such activity is analogous in commercial banking to inter-bank lending.

Like inter-bank lending, in which the interest rate on a loan a creditor bank charges to a borrower bank is lower than on a loan to a retail customer, with market making, the price at which one market maker offers a security to another market maker is likely lower than the price at which the first market maker would offer the security to an investor in the public at large. In both instances, the explanation lies in risk: commercial banks perceive each other, and market makers perceive each other as less risky than outside entities, but that is not always true.. There are then two tiers within the OTC market as there are in the commercial banking: transactions between a market maker and investor, and transactions between market makers.

Accordingly, a market maker acts as a transaction facilitator, buying securities from sellers and then turning around and selling those securities to investors looking to buy them. At its discretion, a market maker can stop trading in a particular security, and simply sit on the investments currently in its inventory.

Market makers come in many forms: from banks involved in currency exchanges, to private brokerage firms.[32] They generate revenue through the difference between their bid and offer, called the bid–offer or bid–ask, spread. In an OTC market, this spread is created by the market maker and amounts to a transaction cost for investors. With the rise of internet-based recording and distribution, and the availability of real-time data, the bid–offer spreads are much smaller than in the past. With this narrowing of bid–ask spreads towards a transaction price, many OTC markets more closely resemble exchanges. In other words, the traditional difference between an exchange and OTC market (other than in respect to organization and centralization); namely, the transparency of final transaction prices to which bids and asks converge is eroding.

OTC derivatives markets and 2007 financial crisis

A principal cause of the 2007–08 financial crisis came from within the OTC derivative markets. A 'derivative' is a complex financial instrument, but put simply it is a financial asset the value of which depends on an underlying instrument or item. That underlying instrument can be a stock, bond, commodity, or FX. For instance, a mortgage backed security (MBS), which is a particular species of asset-backed security (ABS), is a derivative because its value depends on the performance of the pool of mortgages on which the MBS is based. Principal and interest payments on underlying mortgages are passed from the mortgagors to the MBS holders. So, too, it is also with credit-card derivative securities, or automobile loan-backed securities, both of which are asset-backed securities.

So, a derivative is a contract between two parties with the terms determined by pertinent market conditions, such as interest or currency rates.[33] Simplistically, derivatives allow one party to separate its financial risk, and sell it to another party who is betting on the market to perform in a certain way.[34] So, a mortgage lender can (and does) sell its portfolio of mortgage loans to an investment bank that pools home loans into a special purpose vehicle (SPV), and issues MBSs based on them. The risk of default on the mortgage loan no longer is with the mortgage lender (the originator), but with the MBS investors.

As suggested, at their core, derivatives are contracts: they can come in any shape or size and need not be standardized to the extent necessary to be traded on exchanges, although some exchanges now allow standardized (futures or options) derivative contracts.[35] That makes the OTC market the largest facilitator for derivative trading. It is almost exclusively private, although the *Dodd–Frank Wall Street Reform and Consumer Protection Act* attempts to make changes to reporting and clearing requirements.[36]

Determining the value of derivatives can be difficult because they are contracts. One way to measure them is by their notional value, or the amount and number of payments specified in the contract. Because of the difficulty estimating their notional values, estimates of the size of the world's derivatives market vary. The consensus estimate (as of 2013) is that the notional value exceeds US$700 trillion. The value of derivatives being traded in OTC markets alone is estimated to be over US$650 trillion.[37] To put these figures in perspective, the entire world GDP (official exchange rate, as of April 2013), was US$71.83 trillion.[38] That is, the notional value of the derivative market is roughly ten times the entire global GDP.

There seems to be no end to the ingenuity of financial technologists to engineer new and ever-more complex derivatives. There are, for example, second-order derivatives, which are derivatives based on derivatives. Such innovations are not necessarily in accord with the common good, as many around the world found out in the aftermath of the 2007–08 financial crisis. Complex derivatives – too complex, indeed, for all but a handful of investment bankers such as Goldman Sachs who engineered them – played a role in the crisis. Notwithstanding such complexities, adhering to safe, sound principles was a problem. The MBS market was a case in point: pooled mortgages underlying MBS issuances included sub-prime mortgages. Some MBSs were backed by these high-risk loans, while others were blended with less risky loans into a new species of instrument called 'collateralized debt obligations' (CDOs).

OTC markets in Asia

When viewed regionally, the Asian OTC market, especially OTC derivatives, has grown by leaps and bounds in both size and complexity. Although this market accounts for only 8 per cent of all OTC derivatives outstanding globally, the notional value exceeded US$47 trillion after a 25 per cent increase from 2011 to 2012.[39] This trend is likely to continue; as the economies in the emerging markets continue to grow, and an increasing number of domestic businesses will use the local OTC derivatives markets for risk mitigation purposes.

However, this overall growth does not present a clear picture. Unlike Western OTC markets, which are highly integrated, OTC markets in Asia must be approached on a country-by-country basis. For example, the mature markets in Singapore and Hong Kong are relatively comparable to their Western counterparts, but in countries such as Vietnam the market may be all but non-existent. Excluding Japan, Singapore has become the regional trading hub, with roughly 40 per cent of all Asian trades conducted there.[40] Another difference between Western OTC markets and those in Asia – the make-up of the market. Forex derivatives trading is the largest sector of the OTC derivatives market, whereas Forex accounts for a much smaller share of volume in the West.

Following the 2007–08 financial crisis, the US and EU began implementing laws that required OTC derivatives to be cleared by a central clearing party, discussed in greater detail later in this chapter, and a similar push has been made in Asia. Although the implementation and goals may be similar, the effects may be quite different. Large, well-capitalized, multinational financial entities in the US and the EU have the capability to provide clearing and settlement services in multiple OTC markets located on different continents. In Asia, these entities are still developing and may not have these same capabilities. Additionally, the regulation of OTC derivatives is still in flux, and two outcomes are possible: (1) the Asia-Pacific nations will adopt a unified regulatory structure for clearing and settlement of OTC derivatives, or (2) the substance and implementation of these regulations will be left to the determination of each individual country. The first outcome should allow for greater trade and clearing and settle efficiency, which could lead to lower transaction costs. The second option would have the opposite effect, and could slow down the momentum gained since the crisis.

5.4 High-frequency trading

Origins and players

In 1998, the Securities and Exchange Commission (SEC) officially authorized the existence of electronic stock exchanges, and high-frequency trading (HFT) was born. HF traders use complex computer algorithms to exploit small inefficiencies in the markets, often trading on differences of mere pennies, but doing so tens of thousands of times per day. This computerized trading allows traders, which are often large firms such as Goldman Sachs, to execute transactions as quickly as 10 milliseconds per trade.[41] But, HF traders are by no means confined to Wall Street. One of the largest US HF traders is Waddell & Reed, based in Kansas City (Overland Park). And, HFT has spread to Asia.

Volume, speed, and effects

The significance of HFT cannot be overstated. In 2009, HFT hit a high in 2009, accounting for 61 per cent of trade volume in US stocks.[42] Since then, the importance of HFT has declined to the still extraordinary level of around 50 per cent of all volume in US markets. Simply put, the idea that small, individual retail investors, working with their local brokers via telephones to engage in value-based investing (such as picking an undervalued stock and holding it for the long run), predominant in US securities markets is akin to a Norman Rockwell painting: an accurate depiction of what once was, but a simpler, quaint era that is long gone.

Likewise, the speed with which HFT occurs cannot be overstated. HF traders aggressively seek the fastest possible connections to securities markets. It takes time to issue and execute purchase and sale orders through an electronic connection. Literally, the speed of the signal can make a difference between a profit or loss. Hence, for instance, HF traders seek to put their computers as close physically as possible to the computers of the exchange on which they trade; for example, in the same room, or a proximate one, such as the NYSE computers. As another example, HF traders may prefer a microwave connection to an exchange, as information is transmitted and received faster than via a fibre optic cable.

Manifestly, critics of HF traders note the ill effects HF trading has on average investors. They point to the disadvantage placed on them, and small- and medium-sized firms, which lack the ability to have their own supercomputer housed within the NYSE to perform HF trades. HF traders have technologies in place to spot trends in demand for a security before slower investors do, and algorithms to act on those trends before the slower investors.

So, HF traders are able to buy a security at a low price, before the price rises, and then sell high thousands of times, before the demand for that stock is satiated. For example, suppose a stock starts the day at $30.00 per share, and ends the day at $35.00. HF traders can spot the upward trend, and exploit it many times over. They can buy the stock at $30.00, and sell it at $30.02, then buy it at $30.03, and sell it at $30.05, and so on, with successive iterations to the top end-of-day price. Average investors simply lack the computer linkages, and algorithms to trade such large volumes, on such thin spreads, so many times in one day.

Indeed, some HF traders have the ability to cancel a purchase or sale offer rapidly, and make a new one at a better price. In the hypothetical above, suppose an HFT program puts out a sale offer at $30.02 but, within a fraction of a second thereafter, the program sees the price has risen, or is headed to $30.03. The program automatically cancels the $30.02 sale offer, and issues a new offer at $30.03. From a legal perspective, depending on the applicable Contract Law, the first offer has not been accepted, so it is revocable up until acceptance. Yet, from a securities regulation perspective, might such behaviour be tantamount to market manipulation? After all, revocation of the first sale offer in favour of a new one at a higher price may be a device to increase demand for the security in question; that is, a way to inflate the price of the security artificially. (Of course, the hypothetical can be put in the reverse direction, leading to a crash in prices.)

Dramatic gyrations

To be sure, the idea of trading securities on the basis of a computer program is not new. In the 1980s, such activity was called 'program trading', and was widely thought to be a cause of the October 1987 stock market crash in which the Dow Jones Industrial Average (DJIA) plummeted 507 points in one day. More recently, HFT has been linked to the May 2010 'flash crash', when the DJIA gyrated wildly in four hours, falling roughly 1,000 points (9 per cent of the market index), only to recover within minutes. Even if HFT is not the initial cause of such events, there seems to be little doubt that it exacerbates the drama. The computer algorithms perceive that one or more securities are being sold, so HF traders rush to dump before others, and before each other, thus worsening market declines.

The extremely large number of transactions allows these firms to exploit the small inefficiencies for large gains. A prime example was HFT of Broadcom stock, detailed by Charles Duhigg of the *New York Times*.[43]

In this case, Intel reported large gains overnight, and savvy traders prepared to buy a large quantity of small bundles of Intel stock in anticipation of a hike in the stock price. However, the HFT traders were able to exploit a regulatory loophole that allowed exchanges to rout orders to some traders before others. This split second advantage was all that the supercomputer powered HFT traders needed, and they began buying up vast quantities of Intel stock. By agreeing to orders and then promptly cancelling them (all within hundredths of a second), the traders were able to gauge the highest price the market would bare. They repeated this arbitrage behaviour in successive iterations, making profits off of tiny spreads in a large volume of transactions. Finally, when the stock hit that price ceiling, the HFT traders began selling the stock back. The slower traders were constantly buying at a higher price than they would have paid had the playing field been even.

HF traders aspire to capitalize on any inefficiency with respect to any stock, that is, any information suggesting a stock can be bought at a lower price and quickly flipped out at a higher price.

Undermining efficient markets hypothesis?

Clearly, HF traders paid the theory that securities markets are efficient. If the efficient markets hypothesis (EMH) were true, then all material publicly available would be incorporated instantaneously in the price of a security, and opportunities for arbitrage would not exist. (Likewise, asset price bubbles would be impossible.) Indeed, the whole idea securities regulations ought to ensure a level playing field among investors through transparency and disclosure rules misses the mark: that playing field is tilted when one investor has a high-speed computer link to get orders executed, while another works with less sophisticated technologies.

That said, advocates for HFT applaud the rise in high-speed trading, saying it makes securities markets more efficient. After all, HFT increases market liquidity, by virtue of the large volume participation of HF traders. In turn, HFT makes trading cheaper, as it drives down the liquidity cost borne by investors. Continuous HFT also provides even greater transparency than occurs through orthodox securities regulation disclosures. That is because of the second by second (or thousandths of a second) value of a stock, which shrinks market spreads. In other words, the value of information conveyed in traditional ways is priced in minutes, hours, or days. HFT gives information a value in fractions of a second.

This value is redolent of intra-day interest rates such as charging a debtor an interest rate based on a debt (e.g., a bank account overdraft) incurred in less than a 24-hour period. The Federal Reserve first priced these 'daylight overdrafts' in 1985.[44] With regard to both HFT on information in fractions of a second, and intra-day interest rates, the idea is that the time value of money is compressed: money has a value in small splices of time. And, both are possible because of the IT revolution of the 1980s.

Another way to put the above points is to consider the distinction between arbitrage and market making. As presented above, the computer algorithms concocted and used by HFT traders look for and exploit minor price discrepancies within and across markets. Therefore, what is happening is nothing more than arbitrage: buying low and selling high. But, might the more accurate characterisation be market making? HF traders argue that is their strategy: using thousands of orders per day to establish buy or sell limit orders to set their bid–ask spread.[45] The average, end investors purportedly benefit from HFT operations, as the decreased cost in liquidity and lowered market spread makes it cheaper for the final buyer.[46] In other words, HF traders argue they are not evil geniuses seeking to make a quick profit, but rather are salubrious market makers, contributing to the cadre of ready, willing, and able buyers and sellers.

HFT and dark pools

Interestingly, there are links between HFT and dark pools. HFT may have been one factor in the trend towards dark pools (discussed below). Investors sought to be able to move blocks of securities without the value of a security being affected during the transaction. Further, investors in dark pools felt they could avoid front running by HFT. As soon as orders to buy or sell a security were placed, HFT computers would detect them, and place their own large, fast orders, thus bidding up or down the price, and through their speed, effectively running in front of the initial non-HFT orders.

So, dark pools are a kind of safe harbour from HFT. Of course, average investors do not have access to this harbour. While they can invest in dark pool funds, the typical 'boats', as it were, in this harbour are large ones.

Avoidance of HFT was the first link between it and dark pools. But (as discussed below), some dark pools actually use HFT for their benefit. For instance, a dark pool may use HFT to buy a large block of stock at a favourable price, and then sell smaller pieces of that pool to investors in the pool.

HFT risks, flash crashes, and circuit breakers

HFT does not come without risks. As in OTC trading, with HFT the high degree of liquidity provided by market makers potentially leads to disastrous consequences should market makers withdraw from trading. The liquidity HFT firms provide means they are ready, willing, and able to buy or sell large volumes of securities. Indeed, that they can and do make markets in such a broad, deep manner is an argument in their favour. But, suppose one or more of the firms suddenly decide to cease trading in a particular security. That might happen because of a market irregularity that the HFT computer algorithms detect. The liquidity those HFT firms had been providing dries up, and a so-called 'flash crash' occurs, such as on 6 May 2010. Further, as the algorithms of some HFT firms see the price of a security begin to drop, they may accelerate sales, and thus exacerbate the crash, before exiting the market.

So, two possibilities exist: some firms will cease trading immediately and entirely, while others will execute a few trades, before exiting the market. There is even a third possibility: still other firms will widen their bid–ask spreads, offering to buy at lower prices, and sell at higher prices. All three reactions reduce market liquidity, and all of them can manifest within just 20 minutes.[47]

To offset these possibilities, and maintain market liquidity, regulatory mechanisms called 'circuit breakers' have been installed in some organized exchanges.[48] The basic idea of a circuit breaker is to call a halt to trading in a security if the swing (up or down) in the price of that security rises or falls by a defined percentage. For instance, a 10 per cent fall in the price of Apple equities would trigger a pause of trading in that stock. The pause may last a short period, even only a few seconds. In particular, the US SEC has a circuit breaker that lasts for five minutes. It is triggered if the price of a security changes by more than 10 per cent in the previous five minutes.

During the pause, the HFT algorithms reset, and prepare to re-enter the market in a normal manner. After all, HFT computers operate based on reliable price data presented to them swiftly to make markets with narrow bid–ask spreads. A circuit breaker-induced pause cuts off the interaction between computers and price data, forcing the computers to reset. And, the pause is the time needed for the security to regain its actual, or true, value, and thereby allow for trading to resume based on correct data.

So, circuit breakers may help prevent market collapses associated with flash crashes but they are not perfect. In August 2012, they failed to keep the HFT firm Knight Capital from losing over US$440 million in less than an hour due to an errant algorithm.[49]

Regulatory reforms and future of HFT

Reform in the US and Europe has faced an uphill climb in putting into place regulations and guidelines that place reasonable disciplines on HF traders and techniques. Transaction speed limits and resting periods between trades are two of the most hotly contested proposed additions to extant regulation. Many reform opponents believe such additions would place an undue burden on HFT, and force firms to migrate from US and European exchanges towards exchanges in third countries that are less strictly controlled. Simply put, opponents raise the spectre of a loss of liquidity, plus job and income losses, caused by differential regulatory structures. Recall what Thomas Jefferson (1743–1826) said of merchants: 'Merchants have no country. The mere spot they stand on does not constitute so strong an attachment as that from which they draw their gains.'[50]

The same may be said of HF traders. Fearful of their loss to other countries, US and European politicians have been chary of enacting significant reforms.

In this void, lawmakers have shifted their focus to tracking transactions themselves. For example, with the 2014 adoption of *Markets in Financial Instruments Directive II* (*MiFID II*), the European Union (EU) requires HF traders to be registered, use special flags on trades that originate from an algorithm, and potentially limits the ratio of executed to unexecuted trades.[51] *MiFID II* may not help to prevent flash crashes, nor errant algorithms from bringing down entire companies, but it could help prevent abuse and market manipulation.

MiFID II follows legislation drafted in Germany in 2013; namely, the *Act for the Prevention of Risks and the Abuse of High Frequency Trading* (*HFT Act*). This Act added to the existing German legal definition of market manipulation the transmission of orders through algorithmic trading if such trading is not for the purpose of trading *per se*, but rather for a purpose to:

> [1] disrupt or delay the functioning of the trading system or are suitable to do so;
>
> [2] hinder the determination of 'real' purchase or sell orders in the trading system or are suitable to do so;
>
> [3] or create an incorrect impression of the offer or demand regarding a financial instrument or are suitable to do so.[52]

In effect, the German Act differentiates between legitimate or proper, and illegitimate and improper, algorithmic trades. Another way to put the point is the Act sets any algorithmic trade fitting within one of the above-quoted three prongs as unethical and illegal market manipulation trades.

International financial markets 151

The prospect of harsher regulation, while in doubt, has left an impression on HF traders and non-HF traders alike. HF traders are eager to fend off such regulation (otherwise they must make good on their threat to exit the US and EU for, say, Japan). Non-HF traders, such as commercial banks participating in the FX, are upset at HF traders:

> High-frequency trading has become an increasingly significant part of the foreign-exchange market in recent years, and it now [as of April 2013] makes up about 40 per cent of all trading, nearly double the share in 2007 . . . These firms have been able to pump out orders and snap up prices at such speed that they have nibbled away at banks' large orders and made it difficult for them to complete large trades at the price they want.[53]

Under pressure from banks, which are the largest players in the FX market, HF traders have acquiesced to certain measures that fall short of outright government intervention, and banks have pushed them to do so.

Consider the FX market, which has witnessed what might be dubbed the most assertive mini-self-regulatory movement by trading platforms. Banks were frustrated at limits caused by HF trading on their ability to make large trades at suitable prices (a frustration parallel to that of investors in securities markets seeking to move large blocks of shares). So, in August 2013, Electronic Broking Services (EBS) and other platforms announced that they were implementing methods to rein in HFTs.[54] For instance, EBS replaced the traditional 'first in, first out' method of executing orders with a protocol that batches incoming trades every few milliseconds, and then executes the trades within that pool at random.[55] In consequence, banks should not need to race against HFT firms by committing huge funds to establish computers and algorithms to trade as fast as those firms.[56]

None the less, governmental and market-based regulatory reforms have proceeded slowly, and arguably with little real progress. It is difficult to predict the future of HFT regulation in the US and Europe, although the trend has been towards more, if tepid, frameworks. In turn, it is impossible to predict accurately expansion of HFT in Asia, other than to affirm that such expansion almost surely will proceed. There is a disparity from one Asian country to the next as to both the (1) legal prohibitions placed on HFT and (2) economic viability of the practice.

Some countries, such as Japan and Australia, are at one end of a spectrum. They already are well acquainted with HFT. Japanese and Australian (along with Indian) regulators have begun investigating possible safeguards. In Japan, HFT accounts for roughly 70 per cent of trade volume on the Tokyo Stock Exchange.[57] At the other end of the spectrum is Hong Kong. There, HF trading is virtually non-existent, due to trade tariffs on transactions, in addition to trading fees.[58] Such tariffs (e.g., HK$0.50 payable to the Hong Kong Stock Exchange on each purchase or sale of a security) and fees (e.g., 0.005 per cent per side of the consideration of a transaction, rounded to the nearest cent) wipe out narrow margins of profit, making HF trading unviable.[59]

5.5 Dark pools

Despite the malevolent connotation associated with their name, 'dark pools', are simply a new iteration of an OTC market. Like the OTC market structure (discussed earlier), a dark pool is a trading forum for exchange-listed securities. Usually in the pool, a price for a security is determined by the going bid–ask rate for that security in the OTC market. For example, suppose an investor wants to sell 100 shares of a company that is listed on the NYSE. Rather than sell the shares transparently on the NYSE, it sells them in a dark pool. Presumably, the sale price in this off-exchange transaction is the same as it would have been on the NYSE. But that is just a presumption: the pool is dark, connoting that bid and ask prices are not disclosed, although final transaction prices are revealed. In other words, in a dark pool, only the two parties, buyer and seller, see what price each party seeks.

So, the key difference between (1) traditional OTC markets and organized exchange and (2) dark pools is the information available to the investment community before a trade occurs. On exchanges and OTC markets, the investing public has the ability to see two facts not available to prospective investors in a dark pool. First, with regard to exchanges and OTC markets, any prospective investor can see all of the listed bid–ask prices for a given stock from each market maker. If that price is not to their liking from one maker, then they can seek a better price with another. Second, any prospective investor can gauge market liquidity by seeing how many market makers are providing bid or ask prices. Obviously, the larger that number, the deeper that liquidity. Because both facts are apparent, exchanges and OTC markets are called 'lit', meaning that prospective investors have the light to see bid–ask prices and possible counter-parties.

In contrast, within a dark pool, only the parties to the specific transaction at issue have knowledge of the price and quantity of the security to be traded, or even whether there are interested buyers and sellers in the security at all. Hypothetically, Trader A could be selling 1 million shares of Apple with Trader B, but not know if there are other potential buyers or sellers, should Trader A wish to buy back the Apple securities in Apple. Conversely, other potential investors in the same dark pool as Traders A and B do not even know of the existence of A and B.

Notably, it is often the case the operator of the dark pool is privy to all information about the Pool, such as bid, ask, and settlement prices for all securities, and the number and identity of investors. That asymmetric knowledge leads to ethical and legal dilemmas (discussed later).

History of dark pools and rationales for their existence

Dark pools have seen a rapid shift in size, complexity, and scope since 2007. It is important to understand their history, and the early rationales for participating in them, so as to put this burgeoning market in perspective.

Not surprisingly, like the driver for other financial markets, money propelled innovation of the dark pool. Large financial institutions such as investment banks, pension funds, and insurance companies have always faced a dilemma when attempting to buy or sell a large block of securities: how to sell the security in a timely manner, without impacting the market? When a security is traded on the open market, the trade itself affects the value of that security.

To illustrate, suppose a financial institution posts a limit order to sell one million shares of a stock at $10 per share is a signal to the market that those shares soon will be gone from the market, thus lessening liquidity in that stock.[60] (As the order is a limit one, the financial institution will sell at no less than $10 per share.) A short seller, seeing the institutional sale order, might place an order to short sell the security at, for instance, $9.90. One scenario could be the stock price goes up past $10, in which case the short seller has limited its loss to 10 cents per share – because the short seller could cover its position by buying the shares from the financial institution at $10 per share. A second scenario could be the stock price gets to $9.90, but not beyond, and then falls. The short seller could cover its position at a price below $9.90, thus garnering a profit. But the sales order of the institutional investor went unfilled, because the limit price of $10 was never reached.

The point from this illustration is that when an order for a large block of securities is posted, it has the potential to drive the value of that stock up (if a buy order) or down (if a sell order). By posting the order for a large block of securities, the financial institution 'tips its hand', and risks either the price going against it, or being front-run.[61] The risk of front running has become a greater issue with the rise in HFT, because HF algorithms can detect the direction in the price of a security before the rest of the market has time to react.

One solution to this problem, which is not generally considered a dark pool practice, is the use of an 'iceberg' order. As its name connotes, an 'iceberg' order means a large order is placed, but only a small portion of the order is visible to the public. The party placing the order specifies a 'display quantity' to be shown transparently. Once that quantity is filled, the order recycles through to the end of the line, and continues until all of the 'display quantity' orders fill the total block order that had been placed originally. This method keeps the non-display quantity orders waiting to be fulfilled invisible from would-be short sellers, or HFT algorithms. But, this method takes extra time for each order to be executed and the remainder to recycle back through, plus it entails the additional cost of transaction fees associated with each individual order.[62]

All combined, the problem of market impact via signalling an order, the consequent risk of front running, and the unsatisfactory nature of iceberg orders, were an incentive for dark pools. So, in the 1980s, dark pools were created as a means to trade large quantities of securities, without impacting the market before the transaction was complete.[63] They allowed for completion of a large order in a single transaction, and thereby the locking-in of a specific price for the security, and the avoidance of excessive delays and transaction fees. Financial institutions began trading among one another in private, without any signal being given to the market at large, prior to the completion of the transaction. Until 2007, this practice remained mostly unchanged.

Regulation NMS and increased prominence of dark pools

In 2007, the US SEC passed Regulation NMS (National Market System). Regulation NMS forever altered the scope of dark pools. The Regulation was intended to create greater competition among exchanges. Essentially, it allowed individual investors to skip trading on exchanges, if they could find better prices off-exchange at a quicker pace. While market participants had transacted through OTC markets, some of the risks (e.g., front running) mentioned earlier were present in them, too. Dark pools afforded greater privacy than OTC markets.

In brief, Regulation NMS provided for the legal foundation for individual trading in dark pools, which by definition meant trading off an exchange, and not on an OTC market. Broker-dealers began setting up private pools, market making for individual investors as well as financial institutions. Some of the largest broker-dealers in dark pools are familiar Wall Street names: Goldman Sachs (specifically, the Sigma X division), Knight Capital (the company that lost 440 million in less than an hour), Barclays Capital, Credit Suisse, and Merrill Lynch.

This increase in the breadth of investors led to a dramatic increase in the volume of trading in dark pools at the expense of the formal exchanges. In 2005, the value of trading in dark pools equalled 5 per cent of the total volume of all stock trading in the US. By 2013, the figure rose to 12 per cent.[64] The rise of dark pool trading was highlighted again in January 2013, when the daily trading volume of the NYSE (900 million trades) was surpassed by the combined trading volume of 19 of the dark pools in the US (roughly 920 million trades daily).[65] The bottom line is that stocks in the US are increasingly being traded privately, and dark pools are the key vehicle for private trading.[66]

There are several explanations for the dramatic increase in trading in dark pools. The first is the means by which broker-dealers attract investors, with the two most prominent methods being 'payment for order flow', also known as internalization, and 'indications of interest'. Internalization occurs when operators of a dark pool pay a retail broker to direct orders to be routed to the pool before the broker sends those orders to an exchange, thus giving the pool the opportunity to deal with investors before the orders ever make it to the general investing public on exchanges. Indications of interest are pieces of information sent to potential investors that contain pieces of information about a specific security available within the pool, sometimes containing nothing more than the ticker name of the stock. Both methodologies indeed have brought into dark pools new investors, such as a new clientele, investors that were unlikely to have ever participated in dark pools.

A second reason for the increased prominence of dark pools is a shift in status and sentiment among average investors. They have become more knowledgeable about, and are more willing to enter into, dark pool trading. Investors have responded to the decreased volatility of prices on exchanges, arguably in part due to HFT, which has led to the narrowing of exchange bid–ask spreads.[67] With less volatility and slimmer spreads, investors have time to seek out other buyers and sellers in a dark pool – there is no rush to sell on an exchange. Additionally, investors have become less fearful that the price of their security may change while seeking a counter-party within the pool.

There is a third reason for the rise of dark pools: costs. Many broker-dealers have lowered their transaction costs through use of HFT techniques. They buy a block order of a security, separate the block into quantities of securities desirable to smaller investors, and resell the securities in a short period of time.[68] This decrease in transaction costs allows a broker-dealer to charge lower trading fees in a dark pool than those imposed on exchanges, and the HFT techniques inherently create a higher volume of trades.

Dark pool trading and potential ethical issues

The process of trading in a dark pool is similar to that used on exchanges and OTC markets. Dark pools use crossing networks, as opposed to the ECNs owned by exchanges. These crossing networks match buy and sell orders, but do not direct them on to an exchange. Until the trade is completed, extraneous parties are completely closed off from the information about the existence of the order, and thus about its terms.[69] The network often matches orders at the half-way point between the bid–ask spread to facilitate a transaction. If the two parties come to an agreement, then the transaction and price of the security traded (but not the parties) are listed on the consolidated tape as required for any NYSE or AMEX traded securities by the Consolidated Tape Association, the governing body in charge of information collection and dissemination.[70]

Dark pool trading thus far has been difficult to regulate and track, due to the heavily veiled nature of the practice. There is potential for ethically and legally questionable practices to occur. Individuals can try to 'game' a dark pool. For instance, they can place multiple small orders to detect if a large order in a given security is available, and then front-run that security.

Additionally, a potential ethical issue exists when the creator or operator of a dark pool, such as a broker-dealer, uses 'indications of interest' to attract investors. This broker-dealer is the only entity within the pool that can see the entire waterfront and body of water, such as all of the participants, and all of their buy and sell interests. No particular investor has the breadth or depth of information that the creator-operator does. In other words, asymmetric information lurks in dark pools, disfavouring regular participants.

Finally, a potential conflict of interest besets broker-dealers that establish and run dark pools. They have an inherent interest in facilitating transactions for the continued existence of the pool. Many of these broker-dealers are investment banks, hedge funds, and HFTs (or institutions bearing all these identities). The primary goal of such firms is to make a profit for their clients, some of which are participants in the pool. Armed with full information because they operate the pool, they may be tempted to share key data with favoured clients in the pool. For example, they might tip off a client in the pool that a non-client, also in the pool, is keen to sell a large block of shares. Passing such data amounts to insider trading and market manipulation. Simply put, operating a pool with full knowledge about it, but also having clients in the pool, creates considerable opportunity for abuse.

Current regulation, proposed changes, and prosecution[71]

This section draws heavily from Christopher Mercurio, Dark Pool Regulation, *Review of Banking & Financial Law*, 33 (2013): 69–77.

As discussed above, Regulation NMS made it possible for Dark pools to become mainstream trading avenues. However, an earlier regulation, to be covered shortly, had a greater impact on dark pools in terms of regulatory oversight. Remember, dark pools operate using trading platforms that are independent of formal exchanges; in the US, regulators have classified these platforms as alternative trading systems (ATS). In 1998, the SEC enacted Regulation ATS, which required that all ATS trading platforms, including dark pools, to register as broker-dealers. This is important because both the SEC and the Financial Industry Regulatory Authority (FINRA) have the power to regulate broker-dealer activities.

Additionally, Regulation ATS increases order display and trade execution requirements when the trade volume of a stock traded on an ATS is greater than '5 per cent of the average daily trading volume' of that stock on an exchange.[72] For example, assume that 10 million shares of Coca-Cola are traded per day on average. Now, assume that an institutional investor is looking to sell its 700,000 shares of Coca-Cola in order to decrease its risk. Selling the 700,000 shares on an open exchange is not ideal due to the risk of being front run by HFTs, so the institutional investor elects to use Goldman Sachs' Sigma X dark pool. If the full 700,000 is traded that day, then the 5 per cent threshold has been exceeded, and Sigma X must alter the platform to conform with Regulation ATS.

Greater scrutiny has been placed on dark pools following the 2007–08 financial crisis, and regulators are contemplating proposed rules that would 'shed at least more surveillance light and perhaps public light on dark pools'.[73] FINRA has proposed several rules such as: (1) a rule which grants FINRA access to broker-dealers' trade information, which FINRA would use to discern between dark pool and non-dark pool trades, and (2) a rule requiring broker-dealers to pass incoming trades on to exchanges unless a better price is available through the broker-dealer (this approach has already been adopted by regulators in Canada, and Australia has implemented a disclosure requirement regime).[74]

The SEC took a different approach in 2009 via a proposed rule that would lower the 'daily trading volume' threshold from 5 per cent to 0.25 per cent, but was abandoned after the proposal failed to gain any traction.[75] The parties opposing these rules claim that such rules will give exchanges a competitive advantage over dark pools, increase transaction costs, and hamper their ability to execute trades.

Though the push for regulatory reform in the US has come to a standstill, the SEC and other government entities have not been completely idle. In 2012, eBX LLC, a broker-dealer, settled allegations brought by the SEC for US$800,000. The SEC alleged that eBX gave Lava Trading, a unit of Citigroup, access to customer trade information for Lava Trading's benefit.[76] On 6 June 2014 the SEC charged Liquidnet Inc., a New York-based dark pool, with sharing confidential customer trading information; the allegations were settled for US$2 million. On 9 June 2014 the SEC announced that it was conducting a probe to determine whether LX, a pool owned by Barclays PLC, and other pools had engaged in improper disclosure practices, preferential treatment for certain clients, and failure to protect client information.[77] Finally, on 25 June 2014, the Attorney General of New York sued Barclays for securities fraud. The allegations claimed that Barclays' marketing lied to customers about the significant presence of HFT traders, that a predatory HFT firm was the largest entity in the pool, misrepresented its order routing process, and favoured HFTs.[78]

5.6 Bond markets

Bond markets generally

Bonds and other debt securities are financial instruments that are freely traded through organized exchanges and OTC markets (discussed earlier). These debt securities markets are enormous, surpassing US$78 trillion in 2013.[79] (That figure roughly equals the size of 2013 world GDP.) The process of a bond reaching the market begins with an issuer, either a corporation, bank, or government entity, which looks to take on long-term debt in return for capital to finance current or future projects.

Often a bond issuer seeks to assume billions of dollars (or local currency equivalent) in debt to finance economic activity, yet it may be imprudent or impracticable simply to raise that amount by an IPO of equities. A variety of financial, economic, political, and legal issues influence the choice of equity versus debt financing.

Bonds are underwritten using similar methodologies as for stocks. Most prospective issuers of debt securities lack the reputation and wherewithal to tap directly into private investors, though of course 'blue chip' corporations can and do use short-term (usually unsecured) instruments like commercial paper. Most prospective issuers need a middle man between them and investors. An underwriter plays that role.

Typically, underwriters are syndicates of investment banks, or other institutional investors, which make bulk debt purchases from the issuer. When buying the bonds, underwriters effectively take on the risk of reselling the debt securities on a secondary market. With some governmental issuances that are particularly large, an auction for the underwriting is held for the underwriting services, resulting in multiple underwriting institutions, as no one of them can assume this risk in respect of the entire IPO amount.[80] For the underwriter, the profit comes from the difference between the price at which the underwriter (1) purchases the bond from the issuer, and (2) sells that security on the secondary market. Especially with certain governmental bonds like US Treasury Bonds, which are highly sensitive to interest rate fluctuations due to their extended duration, underwriters must be sensitive to trends in the market.

Consider the following illustration. An underwriter purchases US$1 million in 10-year bonds at an interest rate (the coupon rate) of 6 per cent. But, before the underwriter can resell the bonds, interest rates for 10-year bonds increase to 7 per cent. They increase by virtue of secondary market trading in similar bonds of the same maturity: there is an inverse relationship between the price and yield of a bond, so an increase to 7 per cent means 10-year bond prices on the secondary market fell, which in turn must have occurred because selling pressure exceeded buying pressure. The rise to 7 per cent means investors seek to purchase bonds with a higher interest rate, as it will entail a higher yield. In turn, the underwriter will have to decrease the asking cost for the bond, such as sell the bonds at a lower price, because it has a lower coupon rate. Conversely, if market rates on 10-year bonds based on secondary market trading were to drop to 5 per cent, then the underwriter could charge more per bond, because demand in the primary and secondary markets for a bond paying 6 per cent interest rate would grow.

Once a bond is issued through underwriters, or directly to the public if not underwritten, it is a tradable security on a secondary market. Nearly all bond trading volume occurs through OTC markets, such as traditional OTC markets or dark pools (discussed earlier). There are two prominent exceptions: standardized corporate bonds that are traded on formal exchanges (covered earlier); and the two-tier system instituted in China (discussed below).

Bond market dimensions

The US boasts the most prominent bond markets, accounting for 45 per cent of the market capitalization of bond markets around the world, with a value exceeding 37 trillion dollars in 2013. Notwithstanding the 2008 global financial crisis, intense political partisanship and paralysis in Congress, and even a credit downgrading, US Treasury debt instruments, exceeding US$10 trillion outstanding,[81] are still considered one of the safest long-term securities. That is because of the relative stability of the US economy. It also is because of the post-Second World War preference among foreign investors for bonds denominated in dollars, given the relative stability of the greenback and ease with which it is traded internationally, and the use of the dollar to facilitate foreign company entry into the US.

Not surprisingly, the US has been the key driving force in the globalization of bond markets. With global trading in dollar-denominated bonds, bond markets have become more inter-connected. Dollar-denominated bonds traditionally have had highest annual net issuances globally. But, the rise of the EU and viable alternatives in emerging Asian markets have led investors to shift to bond markets where there are relatively higher bond yields to be had. A feature of the globalization of bond markets, in addition to cross-border trading, is what determines investor interest to buy or sell bonds: studying prices and yields of different types of bonds, denominated in different currencies. So, for example, in 2012 the largest group of bond issues outstanding by currency was denominated in the *euro*.[82] Traditionally, yen has been the second most favoured denomination, but new economic policies instituted by the Japanese government have led to a reduction in outstanding yen bonds (discussed below).

With regard to Treasury securities, they fall into three maturity classes: long-, medium-, and short-term. Bonds have maturities of 10 years or more, Notes are of 1–5 years maturity, and Bills are less than a year (making them money market instruments). Similarly, debt issued by other sovereign governments is of varying maturities.

Asian bond markets

Asian bond markets have seen dramatic growth since the 1997–99 Asian financial crisis. Non-existent or merely dormant seedlings before the turn of the millennium, these markets have become influential, with investors across the globe seeking high yields that have become uncommon with bonds issued in mature, sluggish Western markets. In 2012, the Asian bond market exceeded US$18 trillion, accounting for roughly 22 per cent of the global market. While the US remains the dominant individual bond market by sheer size, between 2000 and 2012 the growth rate of the Asian market doubled that of the US: 257 per cent,[83] and 125 per cent, respectively.[84]

Note that Asian countries here include China, Hong Kong, Indonesia, Japan, South Korea, Malaysia, Philippines, Singapore, Thailand, and Vietnam. Removing Japan from the mix alters the figures substantially. Excluding Japan increases the growth figure to over 1,100 per cent.

After the 1997–99 crisis, there has been a concerted effort to develop a structured, liquid, and stable bond market in Asia. Many different regulations and initiatives have been introduced, such as the Asian Bond Market Initiative in 2003, in an attempt to further this goal. Two trends have developed: an increase in bond issuances denominated in local rather than foreign currency; and the emergence of a corporate bond market outside of Japan.

Government and corporate bond markets

Since 2000, a prominent trend in world bond markets has been the rise of government bonds; that is, sovereign debt, denominated in local currency rather than foreign currencies. Prior to 1997, developing countries expanded through issuance of government debt in foreign currencies; that is, sovereign bonds primarily denominated in dollars. But, that behaviour obviously entailed increased FX and interest rate risk.

Why? Put simply, a sovereign government, say Malaysia, receives tax revenues in local currency, *ringgit*. It uses those revenues to make timely payment of principal and interest to investors. If those investors hold bonds Malaysia issued in foreign currency, such as US dollars, then Malaysia faces two problems: currency and interest rate risk. First, the value of the *ringgit* may have depreciated relative to the currency in which the debt instrument is denominated (e.g., it takes 4 *ringgit* instead of 3.5 to fetch 1 dollar). Second, the interest rate (if adjustable) Malaysia owes on the bonds is that of another country, well beyond the control of Bank Negara (the Malaysian central bank).

To avoid these risks, some Asian developing country governments increasingly have issued bonds in their own currency. In 1999, the value of total government bonds in local currency outstanding (excluding Japan) was worth US$346 billion,[85] and by 2012 it was roughly US$4.2 trillion. However, least developed countries such as Vietnam still issue sovereign bonds denominated in foreign currency. It has little choice until the *dong* becomes an attractive currency for non-Vietnamese portfolio investors in which to hold assets. To attract foreign investors, such bonds are discounted (such as face value prices are lower), and coupon rates and yields are higher, due to the increased currency risk (the bond is denominated in a soft currency) and default risk (the issuing government is perceived as a potentially dubious credit risk).

The 1997–99 Asian financial crisis was exacerbated in part by the relative non-existence of a corporate bond market in Asia, other than that of Japan. Banks, often owned by a national government, were the only domestic source of credit for corporations that needed to finance expansion. Yet, the balance sheets of state-owned or controlled banks were weak, saddled with currency and interest rate mismatches, different terms of maturity for assets and liabilities, and many non-performing loans (NPLs). So, foreign investors withdrew support from banks and non-banks alike. Banks needed recapitalization, and were hardly in a position to lend to businesses. Businesses needed capital to endure, much less expand, but with credit from local banks evaporating, and foreigners unwilling to lend, they had just two choices: an IPO of equity or debt. The former was unfeasible, as equity markets had collapsed. The latter was impossible, because there were no Asian bond markets, and few Asian companies were strong enough to float debt (or equity) on a US or European exchange.

To make matters worse, many such companies were export-oriented, and the currency of their countries had been pegged to the US dollar. With the crisis, the dollar strengthened relative to local currencies, but the official peg remained. So, the cost of Asian exports rose such as adjusting upwards in local currency with the dollar because of the peg. Put differently, by design, the peg blocked the normal operation of a flexible exchange rate: allow the local currency to depreciate, and thus permit Asian exports to become cheaper in dollar terms. With that blockage, Asian companies did not experience a boost in export revenues, putting them in worse peril.

Gradually, as the crisis receded, the corporate bond in Asia grew for three reasons. First, governments, such as that of China, began to allow greater free market activity. Second, local companies saw their self-interest at stake in having alternatives to bank loans to raise capital as a means to diversify their risk.

Third, Asian companies appreciated that corporate bonds issued in a given foreign currency can ease entry into the market and protect against currency exchange rate risk. To show the rapid growth in corporate issuances: in 1999 Japanese corporate bonds outstanding, valued at US$1.21 trillion, accounted for 94.6 per cent of all Asian corporate bonds outstanding. In 2012, the value of Chinese corporate bonds outstanding passed Japanese ones, which made up less than 30 per cent of the market, with South Korea a close third. The graph in Figure 5.1 depicts the growth in the total outstanding value of Asian sovereign (government) and private (corporate) issued in local currency since 1999.

Offshore bond markets: foreign bonds

The primary focus of the above discussion covers the types of bonds and rationales for their issuance. That discussion is foundational to understanding and investing in any bond market. Typically, issuers and investors alike 'start local', in that they think first about issuance or investment in their domestic bond market, with instruments denominated in local currency. For some issuers and investors, the domestic market and home-country currency are sufficient to satisfy their needs and risk preferences.

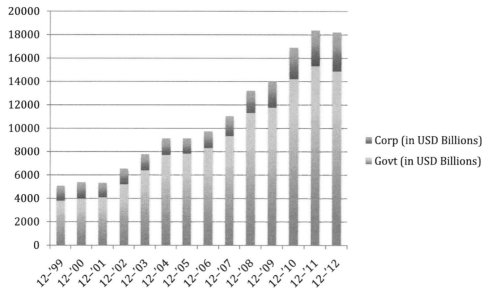

Figure 5.1 Asian local currency (LCY) bond market (in US$ billions).

However, frequently, a local market cannot meet the needs of an issuer, nor does it offer attractive investments to match the risk profile of an investor. These inadequacies can stem from a number of factors. First, the domestic market may be illiquid. There may be an insufficient number of ready, willing, and able investors, with the requisite purchasing power, to invest in the issuer's bonds. That is especially true if the banking sector is weak. In some mature bond markets, the US for example, roughly '85 per cent of the trading in key segments of the bond market' are executed by institutions.[86]

Or the change in supply in demand created by the issuance may have a marked effect on price. Another problem may be low interest rates (for natural or artificial reasons), which make an issuance unappealing to an investor. Still other impediments could be unfavourable exchange rates, high exchange rate volatility, or global disfavour towards the local currency, all of which make an issuance denominated in the local currency unattractive. Relatedly, an issuer (such as a US company) may be seeking to enter or expand in a foreign market (such as China) the currency of which (yuan) is not available in the local (such as the US) market. In such an instance, issuance of bonds in the US denominated in the Chinese currency would be impossible, compelling the issuer to look offshore – in particular, to China – as the issuing market.

Offshore markets and foreign bonds offer a solution to an issuer in need, as well as a diverse array of attractive investment opportunities for local investors. An 'offshore market' is a market for a security denominated in a currency outside of the home country of that currency. For example, buying and selling of bonds denominated in US dollars outside of the US constitutes an 'offshore market', as the trading activity is outside, or off the shores of, the US. Such bonds, logically, are called 'offshore bonds'.

A 'foreign bond' is a debt security issued in a particular domestic market by a non-domestic entity. For instance, a Chinese company issuing a bond in the US denominated in dollars is floating a 'foreign bond', because that company is not a US one. Note that foreign bonds can be issued and traded in offshore markets. For example, if the bond of the Chinese company issued in the US is denominated in yuan, then that bond is 'foreign', and is traded in a market outside of China.

In sum, whether a domestic local market meets a need or not, failing to consider the offshore and foreign bond options are opportunities wasted.

Offshore bond markets: Eurobonds

Sovereign and corporate entities might look to raise funds in foreign bond markets for the reasons outlined above, but they also have the choice of doing so in the currency of their home country, or in a foreign currency. Both categories of issuers have incentive to issue foreign bonds to minimize exchange rate risk (such as the risk a foreign currency will appreciate or depreciate relative to the value of another or other currencies). Foreign bonds help alleviate this risk by matching both sides of the balance sheet of the issuer.

That is, if an issuer has an asset (giving it a stream of revenue such as an account receivable on its balance sheet) in a foreign currency, then it can float bonds in that currency to create a corresponding liability (a stream of obligatory principal and interest payments recorded on its balance sheet as a note payable). Suppose, for example, a Japanese auto company selling cars in India earns revenues denominated in Indian rupees from those sales. Its home country currency is yen, so issuing bonds in yen would create a balance sheet mismatch (setting aside all other features of the balance sheet). If it did so, and if the rupee depreciates relative to the yen, then the company will need a larger number of rupees to convert them into the requisite amount of yen to pay off its yen-denominated principal and interest obligations. Simply put, the value of its rupee-denominated asset stream has fallen relative to the value of its yen-denominated liability. The obvious solution is for the company to issue bonds denominated in rupees.

Consider another example. Suppose a British company seeks to finance new production facilities in Thailand valued at 10 million baht. It could obtain a loan from a Thai bank denominated in pound sterling such as an offshore pound loan. If it did so, then the corporation would have liabilities of £10 million (the loan) and assets of 10 million baht (the production facilities).

The baht might appreciate against the pound. This appreciation would mean the corporation would require fewer baht to pay off its fixed pound obligation. But, what if the baht depreciates relative to the pound? Then the corporation would need more baht to pay off a sterling-denominated loan. To manage this risk, the corporation could sell some of its Thai-based production facilities, but that would likely be an unappealing option. (The sale price might be beneath the cost the corporation incurred to build the facilities, and in any event the baht raised from the sale would translate into fewer pounds, because of the depreciation of the baht.)

If the corporation proceeded with the sterling-denominated loan, then it might hedge the possibility of a baht-pound depreciation with a derivative instrument, such as a FX option or future. Yet, the corporation has another financing possibility: issue bonds denominated *in baht. A bond issuance in baht by the British* corporation would guard against this risk; the corporation matches the currency of its assets (production facilities in Thailand) and liabilities (payments of principal and interests to bond holders). So, a 10 million baht bond issuance creates a liability of 10 million (to be paid in baht), which the corporation could use to finance 10 million in assets (denominated in baht). Currency risk is negated, because appreciation or depreciation of the baht against the pound affects liabilities and assets equally.

Of course, other species of risks are not eliminated. Foreign bonds carry the same interest rate risk concerns as other traditional bonds. Issuers must be sensitive to trends in both domestic and foreign interest rates. A change in the rate, post-issuance, represents the opportunity cost of securing the debt at a lower interest rate.

If a private or sovereign entity believes a bond issuance in a foreign currency is the optimal method of securing financing, then it must determine if issuance in the desired foreign currency is available. Issuances denominated in the currency of a country with a free market, open currency policies is a simple solution for acquiring substantial funds to be used for financing operational expenses. The most common type of bond chosen for this purpose is the Eurobond.

The term 'Eurobond' is a generic one. It refers to a bond issued in a market, and denominated in a currency, other than that of the home country of the issuer. So, in the above examples, Indian rupee bonds issued by a Japanese corporation on a securities market outside Japan, baht-denominated bonds issued by a UK company outside the UK are Eurobonds. As still another illustration, the Swiss food products corporation, Nestlé, issues 10 million yen-denominated bonds spread across the NYSE, Australian (ASX), Hong Kong (SEHK), Bombay (BSE), and Korea (KRX) stock exchanges to fund ongoing operations in Japan. These instruments are 'Eurobonds', and more specifically, 'EuroYen' bonds.

To be clear, the terms 'Eurobond' and 'foreign bond' are not synonymous. Both terms are captured by the general rubric 'offshore bond'. But, a 'foreign bond' is a bond issued by an entity of one country (e.g., the US) in the market and currency of another country (e.g., Japan and yen). In Table 5.5, an example is a Samurai bond: it is a yen-denominated bond, issued in Japan by a non-Japanese entity. In effect, a 'foreign bond' simply is a foreigner issuing a bond in a local market. In contrast, a 'Eurobond' is a bond issued by an entity of one country (e.g., the US) in a currency outside of the home country of that currency (e.g., yen), and a market other than that home country (e.g., not Japan).

Eurobonds are issued and traded like normal bonds, although typically a minimum issuance of US$50 million is required[87] for regulatory purposes if not investor interest. This activity across national exchanges comprises the global Eurobond market.

Note the prefix 'Euro', followed by the currency in which the instrument is denominated (e.g., EuroYen), does not mean the bond is issued only on European exchanges. Rather, the prefix is a historical one dating from around the 1970s. The first offshore bonds were Eurodollar bonds, that is, bonds denominated in US dollars issued in Europe. Today, the term 'Eurobond' could apply to an instrument issued in the Middle East, or Indian Subcontinent, but not Europe.

Often bonds issued outside of the home country of the designated currency are not subject to the laws and regulations of that home country, or at least are subject to fewer such controls from that country. After all, the bonds are offshore, so jurisdiction asserted by that country would be extraterritorial, and thus possibly controversial. Accordingly, Eurobond issuers may face fewer compliance issues than their contemporaries within the home country of the same currency.

Consider a Japanese company issuing bonds denominated in US dollars on the LSE (a EuroDollar bond). Because the issuance is outside of the US, the US authorities, such as the SEC, do not have jurisdiction to enforce regulatory compliance, as they clearly would if the bonds are issued on a US exchange. The Japanese corporation has an incentive to issue on an exchange outside the US (e.g., LSE, ASX, or BSE) as legal compliance is very expensive, often prohibitively so.

Table 5.5 lists details of common offshore debt instruments (both foreign and Eurobonds), along with possible regulatory schemes imposed by the country of the currency in which the issuance is denominated.

A bond issuance denominated in a currency where the home country has restrictive outflow policies, such as China, may be unavailable or prohibitively difficult. From the Communist Revolution through the mid-2000s, foreign corporate bond issuance denominated in renminbi ('people's money', RMB, or yuan) was non-existent under China's tightly controlled monetary policies. Bank loans were often the only form of financing, and had to be in transacted in hard currencies like the dollar – not RMB.

Table 5.5 Types of offshore bonds

Name	Currency (Issuance)	Country (Issuance)	Country (Issuer)	Subject to regulation by country whose currency in which the bond is denominated?
Eurobond	Any (other than issuer's local currency)	Any (other than issuer's)	Any (other than issuer's)	Possible, depends on country of currency issued
Eurodollar	USD	Any (other than US)	Any (other than US)	Little regulation, not under regulation by Federal Reserve
Yankee	USD	US	Any (other than US)	Subject to SEC regulation
Shogun (Geisha)	Any (non-yen)	Japan	Any (other than Japan)	High standards for issuers, administrative burdens, tax rate
Samurai	Yen	Japan	Any (other than Japan)	
Dim sum	Renminbi	China, HK, LSE (as of 2012)	China, Any	Heavily regulated by Chinese government, issuance approval required
Panda	Renminbi	China	World Bank, Asian Development Bank, (plans for future expansion to private entities)	Only two issuances (evolved from Japanese Samurai bonds), funds could not be repatriated out of China
Kimchi	Non-*Korean won*	Korea	Any (other than Korea), also issued by Korean entities	Financial companies prohibited from purchasing if the issuer plans to convert the proceeds into won[88]
Arirang	*Korean won*	Korea	Any (other than Korea)	N/A
Formosa	Non-*new Taiwan dollar*	Taiwan	Any (other than Taiwan)	Minimum BBB rating, may not be issued in renminbi

Plans of the Chinese government to internationalize gradually the yuan has entailed loosening of iron-fisted controls over currency. In 2007 the first RMB-denominated bonds – named 'dim sum bonds' in reference to the popular Cantonese restaurant cuisine – were issued outside of Mainland China. The issuances were strictly controlled and only allowed in Hong Kong, which has been a testing ground for relaxed currency policies. Additionally, in 2011 McDonald's (MCD) became the first non-HK foreign entity to issue dim sum bonds (issued in Hong Kong), followed by the China Construction Bank becoming the first issuer of dim sum bonds on the LSE in 2012.[89]

Offshore bond markets for investors

Much like issuers described above, institutional (e.g., index and hedge funds, banks) and individual investors seek to maximize profit and minimize risk. An issuer may look abroad when its home country market lacks desirable financial or risk-abating opportunities, so should investors too. Much of the reasoning for entering a foreign bond market (e.g., mitigating exchange and interest rate risk) applies to both parties, and should not be viewed as exclusive to issuers or investors. Additionally, foreign bond markets present opportunities for investors to reduce risk through diversification while seeking higher profits.

As described in Chapter 4, bond yields determine the profitability of a bond purchase. The simple calculation for bond yield is the coupon rate divided by the price of the bond. That is:

$$Bond\ yield\ (simplified) = \frac{Coupon\ rate}{Bond\ rate}$$

Manifestly, there is an inverse relationship between the yield of a bond and price of that bond.

For example, assume a US Treasury 10-year bond sells for a par value of $500 with a fixed coupon of $50. The yield of that bond is 10 per cent. But suppose the demand for those bonds on the market increases (such as there is an excess of buyers over sellers at the par value). The market equilibrium price of the bonds increases to $555. Then, the yield must fall to 9 per cent. It now costs more to purchase the bond and attain the same coupon rate, so it makes sense that the bond will become less desirable to investors. Conversely, if the bond price drops to $445, then the yield must increase to 11 per cent. Both results follow from the arithmetic formula above.

Another way to understand bond prices yields is in terms of trade-offs. Suppose a $500 Treasury bond pays a coupon rate of 10 per cent. At that point, its yield also is 10 per cent (as per the above example). Now assume, thanks to monetary policy changes, interest rates rise. Consequently, new bonds are issued at 11 per cent. The investor seeks to sell its 10 per cent coupon bond in the secondary market. Can the investor get $500 for it? No, because no one would pay $500 for a bond earning 10 per cent given that interest rates have risen to 11 per cent. So, the bond would have to sell at a discount; that is, at a price below $500. What would that price be? The answer is $445. Why? Because at that price, the bond sold in the secondary market offers the same yield, 11 per cent, as does a new bond with a coupon of 11 per cent.

Conversely, suppose the investor buys the same $100 Treasury bond with a 10 per cent coupon rate issued at par value with a yield of 10 per cent. In this hypothetical, however, the US Federal Reserve has adopted a program to decrease interest rates so as to encourage lending following the 2008 financial crisis. Following the institution of this program, bonds are being issued with an interest rate of 9 per cent. These new bond issuances have a yield of 9 per cent. Now, market investors will seek bonds with higher interest rates leading to a rise in the demand for the 10 per cent interest rate bond. The holder can now demand a premium, raising the bond price up to the point where the yield will equal that of the newly issued bonds (the holder may not be able to set the price higher because the yield would then be less than that of the new bonds, and buyers will seek alternative investment opportunities). To match the 9 per cent yield, the holder sets the price at $545. The bond holder must also consider the trade-off between selling or continuing to hold. If the holder sells, but wishes to purchase 10 per cent bonds in the future, then she will also have to pay a premium.

An investor unsatisfied with current bond yields available in the local market may look abroad for higher yields. A typical search would cover bond yields in developing countries. Such countries often issue bonds (indeed, must do so) with coupon rates relatively higher than those in developed countries in order to attract investors. This phenomenon was reinforced, if not partly caused, by the US Federal Reserve policy of holding interest rates artificially low following the 2008 great recession. The so-called 'quantitative easing' increased demand for non-Western bonds.

The facts are that higher yields may be found outside the conventional Western financial markets. The J.P. Morgan EMI Global Diversified Index (emerging markets index) had an annualized rate of return nearly double that of investment quality bonds in the US over a 10-year period ending in 2013.[90] Additionally, certain countries of the 10-member emerging countries of the Association of South East Asian Nations (ASEAN), such as Indonesia, have experienced credit rating upgrades over the same decade.[91] Investors regard many ASEAN country bonds as relatively low risk, lower than the technical credit rating, and thus discount ratings that are less than 'triple A', or ones not 'investment grade'.[92]

Interestingly, anticipated exchange rate changes render investors eager to buy debt in emerging markets. To be sure, exchange rates are a source of risk (namely, a depreciation in the currency in which a foreign bond is denominated relative to the currency of the home country of the investor) and prompt risk-reduction strategies. But investors see opportunities in growing economies to increase the value of their bond portfolios over time. Consider the following example.

Suppose Investment Group A uses US dollars to purchase bonds of a Thai corporation denominated in baht, specifically, 10 million baht worth of those bonds. The investor anticipates the baht will appreciate relative to the dollar. After 24 months, the baht has appreciated by 8 per cent relative to the dollar. Group A sells the bonds, receiving baht, and converts the bonds on the spot FX market to dollars. Group A thereby experiences an 8 per cent gain in addition to the two annual coupon payments it received. The opposite scenario could have occurred: an economic downturn during the two-year period, resulting in the depreciation of the baht relative to the dollar, in which case Group A would experience a loss from selling the bonds and translating the proceeds into dollars (unless, of course, it hedged this currency risk).

Manifestly, investors must be wary of the economic environment when purchasing a foreign-entity issued bond. They must also monitor political events with Thailand and the instability it suffered in 2013–14 a case in point. Many bonds issued by sovereign or private entities in emerging economies carry high coupon rates due to the increased risk of default, or systematic weaknesses within the country, which are both the catalyst for and exacerbated by economic downturns. Relatedly, governmental upheaval can lead to nationalization of businesses and industries, leaving bond holders with few satisfactory means of recourse. Argentina and Iran, among others, furnish plenty of examples.

Investors enter a foreign bond market not only for higher yields, but also to reduce their risk. Investment in foreign bonds gives a portfolio diversity, which means risk in the portfolio is spread geographically across different economic and political environments. Such spreading helps decrease the variance of returns in the portfolio from one year to the next.

There are two aspects of risk to be distinguished here: non-diversifiable and diversifiable. Risks that cannot be avoided, such as systematic and market risk, are 'non-diversifiable'. They affect all investments in some way. By definition, it is not possible to ameliorate significantly these risks simply by holding bonds from a larger number of foreign countries. For instance, during the 2008 financial crisis, almost regardless of the country of issuance of bonds, bond investors suffered losses.

In contrast, risk in a portfolio (usually associated with the securities or investments themselves and the issuers) that can be mitigated by including many different investments is 'diversifiable'. The goal is to avoid the 'all eggs in one basket' scenario: if an investor has a portfolio entirely made up of MCD's bonds, and its defaults, then the investor has lost the entire value of the investments. But, if the investor diversifies, then while it incurs a partial loss, the portfolio retains most of its value. The same logic applies to bonds issued in different countries. A portfolio diversified with foreign bonds incurs less risk than one made entirely of bonds from one country. Should an economic downturn occur in that country, the first portfolio incurs losses only from investments tied to the local economy, whereas the second incurs losses across its entirety. An added benefit of diversification is a decrease in variance of annual returns. It is an oversimplification, but a diverse portfolio averages the expected annual returns of the investments to give a reliable output from one year to the next.

5.7 Clearing and settlement systems

Definition of clearing and settlement

Before clearing and settlement (C&S) occurs, there must be a transaction agreement between two parties. The possible subjects of the underlying purchase and sale contracts are endless: a used car, stock, bonds, derivatives, FX, an overnight loan, and so on. 'Clearing' is a pre-settlement activity. It is the transfer and confirmation of information between a buyer–payer and seller–payee. Essentially, clearing is the tallying of who owes what to who, and for which transaction.

'Settlement' refers to the actual transfer of funds (usually via electronic funds transfer) between the financial institution of the payer and financial institution of the payee. Settlement discharges the obligation of the payer's financial institution to the payee's financial institution in regard to the payment order. 'Final' settlement, by definition, is unconditional and irrevocable, such as the buyer–payer cannot claw back funds credited to the account of the seller–payee, even if the subject matter of the contract is non-conforming with the terms of that contract. Rather, the buyer must pursue other remedies against the seller.

C&S is essential to the existence of a modern economy. Indeed, it is akin to the plumbing in a building: occupants in the building, like investors in a financial market, expect the plumbing, or C&S system, to work accurately and efficiently. When the plumbing backs up, as when a C&S operation or system fails, there is chaos.

A traditional example of a C&S system pertains to check clearing. For example, suppose Alice (the payor or drawer) writes a check to her neighbour, Ben (the payee or drawee), for the purchase of his used car. In a modern cheque clearing system, Alice can take possession of the car the same day knowing Ben will receive his payment when he deposits the cheque with his bank (the payee, or depositary bank).

When Ben deposits that check, he receives a provisional credit to his account equal to the stated amount of the cheque. His bank then submits a payment request to the Federal Reserve's FedWire Automated Clearing System (ACS). Alice's bank (the payor's or drawer's bank) receives the payment request from Ben's bank through the FedWire ACS. Alice's bank makes payment, and debits the amount from Alice's account. The credit to Ben's account becomes final.

These actions occur electronically within seconds. In the US, a Federal Reserve Bank acts as the third party (an intermediary bank) between commercial banks that are members of the Federal Reserve System. Their doing so ensures Ben's bank receives payment from Alice's bank. Without such a third party, banks would be reticent to accept cheques from other banks with which they were unfamiliar or that may not be able to pay, such as they would be disinclined to take on the credit risk of the other banks. (Recall that banks do not actually hold their client's funds in distinct accounts.) Figure 5.2 clearly illustrates the details of this transaction.

Without such clearing systems, modern business could not operate; sellers could not deliver goods until receiving payment, because the sellers' bank would have no guarantee of being repaid. In this example, two processes are occurring: clearing, in the sense of the banks determining who owes what to who; and settlement, meaning the credit of funds to an account.

This same process happens on the international level in a wide variety of contexts, such as large value electronic (or 'wire') funds transfers, FX, and financial instrument transactions. Indeed, each such market has its own C&S systems.

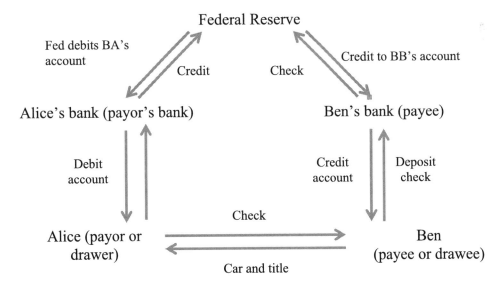

Figure 5.2 Federal Reserve payment system.[93]

C&S also occurs among sovereign central banks. The Bank for International Settlements (BIS) acts as a 'Federal Reserve' for the central banks of its member countries. Its mission is to '[act] as a prime counterparty for central banks in their financial transactions' and '[serve] as an agent or trustee in connection with international financial operations'.[94] The Asian Clearing Union, headquartered in Tehran, Iran, provides similar services for its member countries.

Clearing and settlement of stocks and bonds

Traditionally in securities transactions, banks engaged in clearing, while the parties (buyer and seller) settled among themselves by the physical transfer of paper-based (such as 'certificated') stocks or bonds. This method worked, but could not keep up with the rise in globalization and the sheer size of today's markets. Moreover, it became less relevant as stocks and bonds became uncertificated, that is, held in book entry electronic records of banks. So, today, sophisticated clearing systems exist that help make complex financial markets operate more efficiently (e.g., by lowering transactions costs) with less risk (e.g., by reducing fraud risk associated with physical certificates).

Less than 5 per cent of brokerage firms have an internal clearing system, while the rest must use clearing houses.[95] A clearing house is a third-party facilitator between two of its members such as two client brokerage firms. The clearing house plays the vital role of assuming the risk of the buyer of a security by guaranteeing payment to the seller of that security. The clearing house becomes the contractual counter-party firm to the seller, and then to the buyer, meaning that it buys the security from the seller, and essentially instantaneously sells the security to the buyer. In doing so, the clearing house makes sure the information in the transaction, submitted by the buyer and seller, matches before assuming the risk. If there is a discrepancy, then the clearing house sends the trade back to the firms.

Note the importance of the capital base of the clearing house. Securities buyers and sellers enjoy the reduced credit and insolvency risk of dealing directly with one another on C&S matters by having the clearing house as their counter-party. For example, suppose the seller of stock encounters credit or insolvency problems after agreeing to sell that stock to a buyer. The risk of non-delivery of the stock is borne by the clearing house, not the buyer. The clearing house is the seller's counter-party, hence it stands in the position the buyer would otherwise have been in. Practically speaking, that means the clearing house is legally obligated to provide the stock to the buyer – whether or not the seller delivers stock to the clearing house. But what if the clearing house has credit problems, or goes bankrupt?

That question raises systemic risk concerns, because failure of the clearing house to deliver securities to thousands if not millions of buyers would have knock-on effects. So, the capital adequacy of the clearing house is crucial. It must be well-capitalized to deal with losses and absorb shocks. Clearing houses also hedge their own risks. They hold securities in inventory, and place hedges to cover market risk; that is, fluctuations in the price of their inventoried stocks or bonds. In brief, while clearing houses are not regarded as the glamorous part of high finance, and sometimes dismissed as part of the 'back office' of the international financial system, they are essential.

In the US, the Depository Trust and Clearing Corporation (DTCC) runs an ACS that performs its functions similarly to FedWire, the automated clearing system used by Federal Reserve Banks for bank clearing. DTCC, and other C&S organizations, also facilitate settlement of transaction. DTCC holds the stocks and bonds of many member firms and exchanges, and then records transfer of ownership. This recordation is part of a payment scheme called 'Delivery-versus-Payment', or 'DvP'. As its name suggests, payment is made to the seller only after the security is delivered to the buyer.[96] The less common 'delivery-versus-delivery', or 'DvD', system is used when two parties 'trade' one set of securities for another. The only difference between DvP and DvD is in the consideration: DvP entails delivery of funds against a security, while DvD is delivery of one security against another. In both cases, the deliveries are contemporaneous, if not simultaneous; that is, one is not supposed to occur far later than the other.

DvP and DvD systems create a streamlined process wherein millions of transactions cleared everyday, payment is transferred, new ownership is recorded, and notice of the successful completion of each deal is sent to the parties – all within a few seconds. Table 5.6 lists several major regional clearing houses and the financial instruments for which they provide C&S services.

It must be stressed that each clearing house operates under a unique set of laws and rules. They must be researched carefully to appreciate fully how a particular clearing house operates. For example, under US law, foreign clearing houses providing futures or options swaps or contracts services within the US must register with the Commodity Futures Trading Commission (CFTC) to provide C&S services for those products.[97] Additionally, they must comply with the core principles as set out in 7 USC. 7a-1(c)(2).

Clearing and settlement of derivatives

The global financial crisis that commenced in 2007 had marked effects on a wide array of security instruments. Most of the blame was directed at the derivatives market, which consequently has seen the most regulatory changes. Before the crisis, derivatives clearing occurred through a bilateral clearing process, which the European Central Counterpart Ltd. defined as a clearing process wherein it was incumbent on the parties to a transaction to 'make their own arrangements to reduce their exposure to each other's default'.[98] In other words, with bilateral clearing, there was no centralized clearing organization to standardize and oversee derivatives C&S operations.

Following the crisis, the US and EU overhauled C&S operations in the OTC derivatives market through major regulatory reforms such as the Dodd–Frank Act and European Infrastructure Regulation (EMIR), respectively. Former CFTC Chairman Gary Gensler summarized the intent of the reform legislation in the context of the swap market, over which the CFTC has oversight:

> The Wall Street reform bill will – for the first time – bring comprehensive regulation to the swaps marketplace. Swap dealers will be subject to robust oversight. Standardised derivatives will be required to trade on open platforms and be submitted for clearing to central counterparties. The Commission looks forward to implementing the Dodd–Frank bill to lower risk, promote transparency and protect the American public.[99]

In the US, the Dodd–Frank Act conferred upon supervisory authorities, such as the CFTC broad oversight of derivatives clearing organizations (DCOs), and other financial market utilities (FMUs).

Table 5.6 Major regional clearing houses

Region	Country	Clearing house	Financial instruments cleared and settled
Asia	Japan	Japan Securities Clearing Corporation[100]	Listed products – Equities, bonds, futures, options, OSE-FX OTC products – Japanese government bonds, credit default swaps, interest rate swaps
	China	China Securities Depository and Clearing Corporation[101]	Equities, bonds, cheques, currency
	Hong Kong	Hong Kong Securities Clearing Company[102]	Securities, derivatives, OTC derivatives securities, funds
	India	BOI Shareholding Ltd.[103]	Equity, corporate and municipal debt instruments'
		National Securities Clearing Corporation Ltd.[104]	American depository receipts, ETFs, and unit investment trusts
	Korea	Korea Securities Depository[105]	Market – Equity, government and corporate bonds OTC – Equity, government and corporate bonds
	Australia	ASX[106]	ASX Clear – Shares, warrants, ETFs ASX Clear (Futures) – Futures, options, OTC products
Europe		European Multilateral Clearing Facility[107]	– Equities, depository receipts, ETFs, currency ETCs
		LCH.Clearnet[108]	– Listed commodities, OTC commodities and freight, OTC credit default swaps, OTC interest rate derivatives, listed derivatives, equities, fixed income, OTC foreign exchange
North America	Canada	Canadian Depository for Securities[109]	Exchange and OTC – Equities, debt, money market transactions, derivatives
	Mexico	Contraparte Central de Valores de México[110]	– Securities and derivatives
	United States	DTCC[111]	– Equities, government/municipal bonds, mortgages backed securities
South America	Brazil	BM & FBOVESPA[112]	– Equities, derivatives, bonds

Section 5b(a) of the *Commodity Exchange Act* (*CEA*) sets forth a registration requirement, making it illegal to clear covered derivatives without formal registration with the CFTC. When registering, Section 5b(c)(2) of the *CEA* sets forth 'Core Principles' with which an applicant CDO must comply. Section 5b(c)(2)(A) states:

> (A) IN GENERAL. – To be registered and to maintain registration as a derivatives clearing organisation, an applicant shall demonstrate to the Commission that the applicant complies with the core principles specified in this paragraph. The applicant shall have reasonable discretion in establishing the manner in which it complies with the core principles.

The list of core principles includes: financial resources, participant and product eligibility, risk management, system safeguards, and reporting.

In Europe, the EMIR contains a requirement that all 'clearing eligible' derivatives be cleared through a European Securities Market Authority (ESMA)-registered Central Clearing Counterparty (CCP). In March of 2014 the ESMA published the first 'Public Register for the Clearing Obligation Under EMIR'.[113] The regulation in the EU, as in the US, is still in flux. But substantial change has occurred in derivatives market operations, and it is likely that it will continue to be ever-more heavily regulated.

Clearing and settlement of FX[114]

Unlike standard derivatives and other exchange-traded securities, there is no single or central FX marketplace. This decentralization means the process of clearing and settling foreign currencies, which is important in all markets, is a challenge in FX markets. The process must be objective, promote market efficiency, and mitigate risk. But how can these goals be achieved when there is no single market location and, therefore, no single clearing and settlement service? The answer is there exists a kind of 'centralized decentralization' of clearing and settlement services, which are (in theory, at least) well capitalized and regulated.

While clearing and settling usually go hand in hand, technically they are two distinct steps in the overall process of finalizing an FX transaction. Clearing is a pre-settlement activity. It is the transfer and confirmation of information between a payer and payee. Settlement is the actual transfer of funds (usually via electronic funds transfer) between the financial institution of the payer and financial institution of the payee. Settlement discharges the obligation of the payer's financial institution to the payee's financial institution in regard to the payment order. Final settlement is unconditional and irrevocable.[115]

Today, the parties involved in an FX trade usually do not clear and settle transactions bilaterally because of the direct and indirect risk involved in clearing and settlement (such as *Herstatt* risk, discussed below). Rather, clearing houses handle these processes. Clearing houses are organizations that act as a third party in FX contracts. On a daily basis, clearing houses net the daily trades of their member, and require the members to post collateral. Clearing houses also centralize trade reporting, thereby increasing transparency on OTC derivatives markets. Three of the larger and more prominent clearing houses include LCH.Clearnet, CME Group, and InterContinental Exchange.

Currently, no single central clearing house exists for the FX market. However, there is a push, led by the US through the July 2010 Dodd–Frank Act,[116] to centralize clearing for FX instruments classified as swaps.[117] By March 2014, the CFTC mandated that interest rate swaps be cleared through a registered clearing house, with anticipated regulation to cover OTC FX options as well.[118] Regulating OTC derivatives clearing is not limited to the West, however. The Shanghai Clearing House began clearing renminbi interest rate swaps on 2 January 2014 following China's commitment to clearing all standardized OTC derivatives at the G20 Pittsburgh Summit in 2009.[119]

Following clearing, settlement is often conducted through a standard PvP system. In a PvP settlement, the payment instructions of both parties are settled simultaneously, thereby reducing Herstatt risk, which arises whenever there is a gap between settlement of one obligation against another. Today, the CLS Group (formerly Continuous Linked Settlement) is the market standard for FX settlement. CLS uses PvP through the bank accounts of CLS members, in conjunction with local real-time gross settlement (RTGS), to settle FX transactions and mitigate risk.

Notes

1. Islamic bond (Ṣukūk) markets are covered in a separate chapter.
2. "Market," *Investopedia*, accessed 28 August 2014, http://www.investopedia.com/terms/m/market.asp.
3. The term 'goods' in reference to securities is not used in the legal sense of a 'good' under Article 2 of the US Uniform Commercial Code (UCC). Typically, commercial codes contain special sections and provisions for investment instruments, and such instruments are governed by Securities Law.
4. Geoffrey A. Hirt and Stanley B. Block, *Fundamentals of Investment Management*, 10th ed. (New York: McGraw-Hill, 2012), 27.
5. "Listing Standards – US Standards," *NYSE Euronext*, accessed 15 April 2013, http://usequities.nyx.com/regulation/listed-companies-compliance/listings-standards/us.
6. For example, on the New York Stock Exchange (NYSE), US$100,000 is the listing fee (as of March 2013) for a domestic issuer the total shares outstanding of which at the time of listing is less than or equal to 30 million. http://usequities.nyx.com/regulation/listed-companies-compliance/listings-standards/us.
7. "Stock Exchange," *Wikipedia*, accessed 15 April 2013, https://en.wikipedia.org/wiki/Stock_exchange.
8. "Brokerage Firm," *Wikipedia*, accessed 5 April 2013, https://en.wikipedia.org/wiki/Brokerage_firm.
9. Geoffrey A. Hirt and Stanley B. Block, *Fundamentals of Investment Management* 10th ed. (New York: McGraw-Hill, 2012), 54.
10. "Bunching Definition," *Investopedia*, accessed 10 September 2014, http://www.investopedia.com/terms/b/bunching.asp; Stephanie M. Monaco and Lawrence P. Stadulis, "Current Issues Relating to Investment Adviser Trade Aggregation and Allocation," *Morgan, Lewis & Bockius LLP* (2000), 2, accessed 10 September 2014, http://www.morganlewis.com/pubs/ebe9da6b-370d-4853-9e8f23899f3b6f48_publication.pdf; "General Information on the Regulation of Investment Advisers," *Securities Exchange Commission*, accessed 10 September 2014, http://www.sec.gov/divisions/investment/iaregulation/memoia.htm; "Odd Lot Definition," *Investopedia*, accessed 10 September 2014, http://www.investopedia.com/terms/o/oddlot.asp.
11. "SOES (Small Order Execution System)", *FinancialWeb*, accessed 26 August 2014, http://www.finweb.com/investing/soes-small-order-execution-system.html. SOES was created to give smaller traders (such as non-institutional entities) easier access to the OTC market. Prior to the introduction of SOES, small investors faced difficulty making trades due to the relatively small size of the trade sought.
12. Through 1987, orders were predominantly submitted via telephone, but market liquidity dried up during the 1987 crash when market makers stopped answering the phones.

"NASDAQ," *Wikipedia*, 14 April 2013; Jeffrey W. Smith, James P. Selway, and D. Timothy McCormick, "The Nasdaq Stock Market: Historical Background and Current Operation, NASD Working Paper 98–01," *NASD Economic Research Department* (1998), 8, accessed 26 August 2014, https://cobweb.business.nd.edu/Portals/0/MendozaIT/Research/Shared%20Documents/Nastraq/Nasdaq%20Stock%20Market%20Historical%20Background%20and%20Current%20Operation.pdf.

13 "New York Stock Exchange," *Wikipedia*, accessed 15 April 2013, https://en.wikipedia.org/wiki/New_York_Stock_Exchange.

14 "How we Classify Countries," *The World Bank*, accessed 15 April 2013, http://data.worldbank.org/about/country-classifications.

15 "World Bank Atlas Method," *The World Bank*, accessed 15 April 2013, http://data.worldbank.org/about/country-classifications/world-bank-atlas-method.

16 "Market Capitalization of Listed Companies (current US$)," *The World Bank*, accessed 15 April 2013, http://data.worldbank.org/indicator/CM.MKT.LCAP.CD/countries?display=default.

17 "GDP (current US$)," *The World Bank*, accessed 15 April 2013, http://data.worldbank.org/indicator/NY.GDP.MKTP.CD.

18 "Company Overview," *NYSE Euronext*, accessed 26 August 2014, http://www.nyx.com/who-we-are/company-overview. (The NYSE lists around 8,000 companies, representing over 55 different countries.)

19 "NYSE Euronext," *Wikipedia*, accessed 15 April 2013, https://en.wikipedia.org/wiki/NYSE_Euronext.

20 "World Exchanges Monthly Report for 2014," *World Federation of Exchanges*, accessed 25 August 2014, http://www.world-exchanges.org/statistics/monthly-reports.

21 All information (except as otherwise noted) was retrieved at http://www.world-exchanges.org/statistics/annual-query-tool. The data was found by using the following options: US$ as the currency, equity as the instrument, and domestic market capitalization as the indicator.

22 "Saudi Stock Exchange (Tadawul) Annual Review – 2006," Market Information Department, Tadawul, accessed 26 August 2014, http://www.tadawul.com.sa/static/pages/en/Publication/PDF/Annual_Report_2006_English.pdf.

23 "Saudi Stock Exchange (Tadawul) Annual Review – 2008," Tadawul, accessed 26 August 2014, http://www.tadawul.com.sa/static/pages/en/Publication/PDF/Annual_Report_2008_English.pdf.

24 "Singapore Exchange," *Wikipedia*, accessed 17 September 2014, http://en.wikipedia.org/wiki/Singapore_Exchange#Merger_talks.

25 "ICE at a Glance," *InterContinental Exchange*, accessed 26 August 2014, https://www.theice.com/publicdocs/ICE_at_a_glance.pdf.

26 "OMX," *Wikipedia*, accessed 22 February 2013, https://en.wikipedia.org/wiki/OMX.

27 "Top 10 Largest Stock Exchanges," ChinaDaily.com.cn, accessed 27 August 2014, http://www.chinadaily.com.cn/business/2014-04/29/content_17472002_4.htm.

28 "Euronext," *Wikipedia*, accessed 4 August 2014, https://en.wikipedia.org/wiki/Euronext.

29 "Singapore Exchange," *Wikipedia*, accessed 17 September 2014, http://en.wikipedia.org/wiki/Singapore_Exchange#Merger_talks.

30 "History of OTC Markets Group Inc," OTC Markets, accessed 10 August 2014, http://www.otcmarkets.com/history-pink-otc.

31 Hirt and Block, 39; "Penny Stock," *Investopedia*, accessed 27 August 2014 http://www.investopedia.com/terms/p/pennystock.asp.

32 "Market Maker," *Wikipedia*, accessed 21 March 2013, https://en.wikipedia.org/wiki/Market_maker.

33 "Derivatives," Office of the Comptroller of the Currency, accessed 25 August 2014, http://www.occ.gov/topics/capital-markets/financial-markets/trading/derivatives/index-derivatives.html.

34 "Derivative (finance)," *Wikipedia*, accessed 14 April 2013, https://en.wikipedia.org/wiki/Derivative_(finance).

174 *Practice of investment management*

35 "Exchange-Traded Derivative Contract," *Wikipedia*, accessed 15 April 2013, https://en.wikipedia.org/wiki/Exchange-traded_derivative_contract.
36 For example, clearing houses providing clearing services for futures/options swaps or contracts must register with the CFTC. Public Law Number 113–42, Stat. 7 USC. § 7a-1.
37 Steve Denning, "Big Banks and Derivatives: Why Another Financial Crisis Is Inevitable," *Forbes* (8 January 2013), accessed 15 April 2013, http://www.forbes.com/sites/stevedenning/2013/01/08/five-years-after-the-financial-meltdown-the-water-is-still-full-of-big-sharks/.
38 "Field Listing: GDP (official exchange rate)," *Central Intelligence Agency, The World Fact Book*, accessed 15 April 2013, https://www.cia.gov/library/publications/the-world-factbook/fields/2195.html.
39 Paul J. Davies and Jeremy Grant, "OTC Trading Reform Threatens Asian Markets," FT.com, accessed 17 September 2014, http://www.ft.com/cms/s/0/6b6d30b8-b0a9-11e2-9f24-00144feabdc0.html.
40 Ibid.
41 Bezinga, "What is High Frequency Trading?" *Nasdaq*, 9 April 2013, accessed 18 November 2014, http://www.nasdaq.com/article/what-is-high-frequency-trading-cm235032#.UXVg_yv70Vl.
42 "Declining US High Frequency-Trading," *The New York Times*, 15 October 2012, http://www.nytimes.com/interactive/2012/10/15/business/Declining-US-High-Frequency-Trading.html.
43 Charles Duhigg, "Stock Traders Find Speed Pays, in Milliseconds," *The New York Times*, 24 July 2009, accessed 18 November 2014, http://www.nytimes.com/2009/07/24/business/24trading.html?ref=highfrequencyalgorithmictrading.
44 "Payment System Risk," *Federal Reserve*, accessed 27 August 2014, http://www.federalreserve.gov/paymentsystems/psr_overview.htm#tocI.
45 "High-Frequency Trading," *Wikipedia*, accessed 7 May 2013, https://en.wikipedia.org/wiki/High-frequency_trading.
46 Charles Jones, "The Reality of High-Frequency Trading," *Politico*, March 2013, accessed 20 March 2013, http://www.politico.com/story/2013/03/correcting-the-record-on-high-frequency-trading-89082.html.
47 "Futures Sale Spurred May 6 Panic as Traders Lost Faith in Data," *Bloomberg*, 1 October 2010, www.bloomberg.com/news/2010-10-01/automatic-trade-of-futures-drove-may-6-stock-crash-report-says.html.
48 "SEC Approves Rules Expanding Stock-by-Stock Circuit Breakers and Clarifying Process for Breaking Erroneous Trades," United States Securities and Exchange Commission, 2010, accessed 25 August 2014, www.sec.gov/news/press/2010/2010-167.htm.
49 Halah Touryalai, "Can Knight Capital Be Saved?" *Forbes*, 2 August 2012, accessed 7 May 2013, http://www.forbes.com/sites/halahtouryalai/2012/08/02/can-knight-capital-be-saved/.
50 Thomas Jefferson, quoted in Brainy Quote, accessed 25 August 2014, www.brainyquote.com/quotes/quotes/t/thomasjeff138493.html#WpV73xOOWqcC8Vmd.99.
51 "Two-Speed Future for High-Frequency Algorithmic Trading," *EuroMoney*, n.d., accessed 19 May 2013, http://www.euromoney.com/Article/3204810/Two-speed-future-for-high-frequency-algorithmic-trading.html.
52 "Germany's New High-Frequency Trading Act," *Baker & McKenzie*, n.d., accessed 19 May 2013, http://www.bakermckenzie.com/files/Publication/837d847c-b132-40d7-b638-fecb6b858cb9/Presentation/PublicationAttachment/155464bb-d225-4498-a4b3-03971b885f33/AL_GermanyHighFrequencyTradingAct.pdf.
53 Ira Iosebashvili, "EBS to Rein in High Frequency Traders," *The Wall Street Journal*, 29 April 2013, accessed 15 August 2014, http://online.wsj.com/article/SB10001424127887323528404578453183303289790.html.
54 Wanfeng Zhou and Nick Olivari, "Exclusive: EBS Take New Step to Rein In High-Frequency Traders," *Reuters*, 23 August 2013, accessed 27 August 2014, http://www.reuters.com/article/2013/08/23/us-markets-forex-hft-idUSBRE97M0YJ20130823.
55 Stephen Foley, "High-Frequency Traders Face Speed Limits," *CNBC*, 29 April 2013, accessed 23 August 2014, www.cnbc.com/id/100682552.

56 Linette Lopez, "What The Heck Is A Dark Pool And Why Are People Trading In Them?" *Business Insider*, October 2012, accessed 27 August 2014, www.businessinsider.com/what-is-a-dark-pool-2012-10.
57 Justin Lee, "High-frequency Trading No Threat to Financial Markets, Regulators Find," *Risk.net*, 22 April 2013, accessed 27 August 2014, www.risk.net/asia-risk/feature/2263010/highfrequency-trading-no-threat-to-financial-markets-regulators-find.
58 "Hong Kong Exchanges and Clearing," *World Federation of Exchanges*, 19 November 2013, accessed 26 August 2014, www.world-exchanges.org/member-exchanges/key-information-/hong-kong-exchanges-and-clearing.
59 Ibid.
60 "Market Impact," *Wikipedia*, 19 July 2014, accessed 28 August 2014, https://en.wikipedia.org/wiki/Market_impact.
61 Lauren Lyster, "Dark Pools: What Are They And Should You Be Concerned?" *Yahoo! Finance*, 19 April 2013, accessed May 19, 2013, http://finance.yahoo.com/blogs/daily-ticker/dark-pools-concerned-164905843.html.
62 "Dark Liquidity," *Wikipedia*, last modified 1 May 2013, accessed 20 May 2013, https://en.wikipedia.org/wiki/Dark_liquidity.
63 Linette Lopez, "What The Heck Is A Dark Pool And Why Are People Trading In Them?" *Business Insider*, October 2012, accessed 17 October 2013, http://www.businessinsider.com/what-is-a-dark-pool-2012-10.
64 Linette Lopez, "GASPARINO: Mysterious Dark Pools Are Seeing More Trading Action Than The NYSE For The First Time Ever," *Business Insider*, March 2013, accessed 19 May 2013, http://www.businessinsider.com/more-trading-in-dark-pools-than-nyse-2013-3.
65 Ibid.
66 Nathaniel Popper, "As Market Heats Up, Trading Slips Into Shadows," *The New York Times*, 31 March 2013, accessed 19 May 2013, http://www.nytimes.com/2013/04/01/business/as-market-heats-up-trading-slips-into-shadows.html?pagewanted=all&_r=0.
67 Ibid.
68 Brent Radcliffe, "Should You Be Afraid Of Dark Pool Liquidity?" *Investopedia*, 6 Oct 2009, accessed 19 May 2013, http://www.investopedia.com/articles/trading/09/dark-pool-liquidity.asp.
69 "Crossing Network," *Wikipedia*, last modified 27 April 2013, accessed 20 May 2013, https://en.wikipedia.org/wiki/Crossing_network.
70 "Consolidated Tape Association," *Wikipedia*, last modified 14 February 2013, accessed 20 May 2013, https://en.wikipedia.org/wiki/Consolidated_Tape_Association.
71 Christopher Mercurio, *Dark Pool Regulation*, 33 REV. BANKING & FIN. L. 69, 69–77 (2013).
72 Ibid., 71 (citing Christina Davilas, *New Dark Pool Regulation On the Horizon*, LAW360, http://www.law360.com/articles/450159/new-dark-pool-regulation-on-the-horizon).
73 Christina Davilas, "New Dark Pool Regulation On the Horizon," *Law360.com*, 14 June 2013, accessed 17 September 2014, http://www.law360.com/articles/450159/new-dark-pool-regulation-on-the-horizon (quoting FINRA CEO Richard G. Ketchum).
74 Ibid.
75 Ibid.
76 Jenny Strasburg and Scott Patterson, " 'Dark Pool,' SEC Settle," *The Wall Street Journal*, 4 October 2012, accessed 17 September 2014, http://online.wsj.com/news/articles/SB10000872396390444223104578034413566549332.
77 Scott Patterson and Jean Eaglesham, " 'Dark Pools' Face New SEC Probe," *The Wall Street Journal*, 9 June 2014, accessed 17 September 2014, http://online.wsj.com/articles/dark-pools-face-new-sec-probe-1402356915.
78 Stephanie Russell-Kraft, "NY AG Sues Barclays Over Dark Pool Fraud," *Law360.com*, 25 June 2014, accessed 17 September 2014, http://www.law360.com/articles/551825/ny-ag-sues-barclays-over-dark-pool-fraud; Scott Patterson and Andrew R. Johnson, "New York Attorney General Sues Barclays Over Stock-Trading Business," *The Wall Street Journal*, 25 June 2014, accessed 17 September 2014, http://online.wsj.com/articles/new-york-attorney-general-plans-lawsuit-against-barclays-1403723283.

79 Sean Kidney, "9 Useful Facts about the Global Bond Market," *Climate Bonds*, 27 February 2013, accessed 20 May 2013, http://www.climatebonds.net/2014/05/9-useful-facts-about-global-bond-market.

80 Jason Van Bergen, "Basics of Federal Bond Issues," *Investopedia*, 26 August 2012, accessed 20 May 2013, http://www.investopedia.com/articles/basics/04/052104.asp.

81 "US Bond Market Issuance and Outstanding: Quarterly Data to Q1 2013," The Securities Industry and Financial Markets Association (SIFMA), accessed 25 June 2013, http://www.sifma.org/research/statistics.aspx.

82 "BIS Quarterly Review, June 2013," *Bank of International Settlements*, accessed 25 June 2013, http://www.bis.org/publ/qtrpdf/r_qa1306.pdf.

83 US Bond Market Issuance and Outstanding: Quarterly Data to Q1 2013," The Securities Industry and Financial Markets Association (SIFMA), accessed 25 June 2013, http://www.sifma.org/research/statistics.aspx.

84 "Historical Growth of Asian LCY Bond Market," *AsianBondsOnline*, accessed 15 July 2013, http://asianbondsonline.adb.org/regional/data/bondmarket.php?code=LCY_in_USD_Local_Total, visited July 15, 2013.

85 Ibid.

86 Geoffrey A. Hirt and Stanley B. Block, *Fundamentals of Investment Management*, 294.

87 Singh Permjit, "The Ins and Outs of Corporate Eurobonds," *Investopedia*, 2009, accessed 23 September 2013, http://www.investopedia.com/articles/bonds/09/issuing-a-corporate-eurobond.asp.

88 Song, Jung-a, "Seoul Takes Kimchi Bonds off the Menu," *Financial Times*, 19 July 2011, accessed 18 November 2014, http://www.ft.com/cms/s/0/b7153548-b1e0-11e0-a06c-00144feabdc0.html#axzz3jlqF55xj.

89 "Dim Sum Bond," *Wikipedia*, last modified 5 July 2013, accessed 23 September 2013, https://en.wikipedia.org/wiki/Dim_sum_bond.

90 Thomas Kenny, "Introduction to Emerging Market Bonds," *About.com*, accessed 18 November 2014, http://bonds.about.com/od/bondinvestingstrategies/a/Introduction-To-Emerging-Markets-Bonds.htm.

91 Teresa Kong, "Why Invest in Asia Bonds?" Matthews Asia, March 2012, accessed 18 November 2014, http://matthewsasia.com/perspectives-on-asia/asia-insight/article-497/default.fs.

92 Ibid.

93 Image is taken from slides presented by Terri D. Thomas, JD-SVP, Legal Department Director Kansas Bankers Association, 610 SW Corporate View, Topeka, KS 66615.

94 "About BIS," *Bank for International Settlements*, accessed 18 November 2014, http://www.bis.org/about/index.htm?l=2.

95 John L. Teall, *Financial Trading and Investing* (Amsterdam: Academic Press, 2013), 46.

96 "Principles for Financial Market Infrastructures," *Bank for International Settlements and International Organization of Securities Commissions* (April 2012): 8, accessed 18 November 2014, http://www.bis.org/publ/cpss101a.pdf.

97 "Clearing Organizations," *U.S. Commodity Futures Trading Commission*, accessed 28 August 2014, http://www.cftc.gov/IndustryOversight/ClearingOrganizations/index.htm.

98 "What is Clearing?" *EuroCCP*, accessed 18 November 2014, http://euroccp.com/qa/clearing-ccp%E2%80%99s/what-clearing.

99 "Dodd-Frank Act," *CFTC*, accessed 18 November 2014, http://www.cftc.gov/lawregulation/doddfrankact/index.htm.

100 "Basic Structure of Clearing and Settlement," *Japan Securities Clearing Corporation*, accessed 26 August 2014, http://www.jscc.co.jp/en/cash.html.

101 "China," *Asia eTrading*, 15 October 2009, accessed 27 August 2014, http://asiaetrading.com/industry/clearing/china/.

102 "Clearing Services," *HKEx*, accessed 27 August 2014, https://www.hkex.com.hk/eng/prod/clr/ClearingService.htm.

103 "Clearing House Activities," *BOI Shareholding Ltd.*, 2007, accessed 27 August 2014, http://boislindia.com/Clearinghouse.html.

104 "National Securities Clearing Corporation," *DTCC*, accessed 27 August 2014, http://www.dtcc.com/about/businesses-and-subsidiaries/nscc.aspx.

105 "Settlement," *Korea Securities Depository*, accessed 27 August 2014, https://www.ksd.or.kr/eng/static/EB0102010000.home?menuNo=93.

International financial markets 177

106 "Clearing," *ASX*, accessed 27 August 2014, http://www.asx.com.au/services/clearing.htm.
107 "Company Info," *EuroCCP*, accessed 28 August 2014, http://euroccp.com/content/company-info.
108 *LCH.Clearnet*, accessed 28 August 2014, http://www.lchclearnet.com/en/home.
109 "Clearing and Settlement," *CDS*, accessed 28 August 2014, http://www.cds.ca/cdsclearinghome.nsf/Pages/-EN-Clearingandsettlement?Open.
110 "Services," *CCV Grupo BMV*, accessed 28 August 2014, http://www.contraparte-central.com.mx/.
111 "Clearing Services," *DTCC*, accessed 28 August 2014, http://www.dtcc.com/clearing-services.aspx.
112 "Clearing and Settlement," *BM & FBOVESPA*, accessed 28 August 2014, http://www.bmfbovespa.com.br/en-us/services/post-trade-services/clearing-and-settlement/clearing-and-settlement.aspx?idioma=en-us.
113 "European Market Infrastructure Regulation (EMIR)," *Market Structure Partners*, accessed 18 November 2014, http://www.marketstructure.co.uk/european-legislation/european-market-infrastructure-regulation/#2014.
114 This section draws heavily on Raj Bhala, *Modern GATT Law*, Volume I, Chapter VI, Section VIII (London: Thomson Sweet & Maxwell, 2013).
115 *Clearing and Settlement*, accessed www.credfinrisk.com/clearing.html.
116 Dodd-Frank Wall Street Reform and Consumer Protection Act, Public Law, 111th Congress, HR 4173, 21 July 2010, 111–203.
117 Tom Osborn, "Clearing Houses Move Their FX Pieces Into Place," *Financial News*, 29 November 2012, accessed 27 August 2014, www.efinancialnews.com/story/2012-05-14/clearing-houses-move-their-fx-pieces-into-position.
118 Mike Kentz, "Corrected–Refile–US Regulator Nears New FX Clearing Guidelines," 13 March 2014, accessed 27 August 2014, http://www.reuters.com/article/2014/03/13/derivatives-cftc-fx-idUSL2N0MA1R220140313.
119 http://www.risk.net/asia-risk/news/2323246/shanghai-clearing-house-becomes-fifth-in-asia-to-start-otc-clearing.

6 International financial players

6.1 Introduction

This chapter explains and analyses the major players in international financial markets, or global financial system (GFS). The GFS is the 'interplay of financial companies, regulators and institutions operating on a supranational level'.[1] In particular, those players are:

1 Commercial banks
2 Investment banks
3 Broker dealers
4 Investment managers
5 Central banks
6 International organizations.

More such players exist, and many of them are far larger than at any time since the end of the Second World War. In recent decades, their growth, along with the values and volumes of the transactions in which they engage, has far outstripped growth in the underlying 'real' economy. That is because the players have adapted to – indeed, they have driven – rapid cross-border capital flows, and pushed down capital market barriers.

They have also created a dizzying array of complex financial products. If one word had to be selected to characterize the GFS, 'complex' would be a good choice. Complexity in the GFS renders it nearly impossible for countries to supervise the players and their deals in a coordinated, real-time manner. Thanks to their large size, rapidly shifting, cross-border nature, and technically intricate transactions, they typically outpace traditional, jurisdictionally based regulators. No global financial supervisor has yet been agreed to by sovereign states to act as an all-powerful authority, though there are coordinating bodies (such as the Basle Supervisors Committee) and supranational organizations (like the European Central Bank) pertinent to subsets of countries.

Notably, a major financial crisis has occurred at least once every three years since 1970.[2] Whether that history might have been different had there been a centralized GFS supervisor is uncertain. What is known is that domestic and international supervisors try to anticipate the next crisis, but often do so by writing rules industry-wide that respond to the previous debacle. Consequently, new legal regimes suffer from three defects. First, they are $t - 1$, where t stands for time, meaning they are one step behind the players.

Second, the laws themselves, piled one on top of another, are a complex web of details. Third, not uncommonly, some rules bespeak the phenomenon of regulatory capture, whereby the interests of the regulated govern the regulators. In turn, the rules, including *sui generis* provisions (such as ones for individual commercial or investment banks), do little to boost safety and soundness in the GFS.

6.2 Commercial banks

General definition

A commercial bank is a bank that provides services to the general public and companies. Such services include accepting deposits, making business and consumer loans, and offering basic investment products like savings accounts and certificates of deposit. A traditional commercial bank has physical branches with tellers, safe deposit boxes, vaults, and automated teller machines (ATMs).

However, some commercial banks do not have any locations for consumers to procure services. They require consumers to complete all transactions by phone or internet. Typically, these kinds of banks pay higher interest rates on investments and deposits, while charging lower fees.

Sources of income

Traditionally, a commercial bank makes money off of the spread (difference) between interest rates paid on deposit and interest rates received on loans. A bank raises funds by taking deposits (which are a liability on its balance sheet). With those funds (or a percentage thereof, based on applicable bank regulatory lending limits), the bank makes loans to businesses or individual borrowers (which are an asset on its balance sheet). The bank generates revenues on these transactions by paying a lower interest rate to depositors and higher interest rate to borrowers. Typically, the spread is at least 2.5 per cent.[3] Manifestly, then, a commercial bank acts as a financial intermediary, connecting borrowers and lenders by accepting money and loaning funds.

In addition, a commercial bank also generates significant fee-based income; that is, revenues from services they provide for a fee. A quintessential example in international finance is trade finance, whereby commercial banks earn fees for issuing letters of credit (L/Cs), or guaranteeing payments from importers to exporters. Credit and debit cards are another common example of fee-based transactions. The fee usually amounts to 1.7 per cent of the transaction, for which the merchant pays.[4] Additionally, commerce banks are able to make money off service fees. Still other routine fee-based services are ATM access for non-customers, coupon/bond redemption, electronic banking, foreign currency exchange, and providing safe deposit boxes.

Beyond lending and fee income, there is a third prominent, and controversial, category of sources of commercial bank revenue: investment instruments. A bank may generate considerable income – and, sometimes, crushing losses – from underwriting and dealing in stocks, bonds, foreign exchange (FX), and derivatives. Whether the bank does so depends heavily on whether it can do so, based on the applicable legal and regulatory regime governing bank activities.

6.3 Commercial bank activities

1933 US Glass–Steagall Act

Before the stock market crash of 1929, commercial banks were allowed to engage in the investment business, and did so to dangerous degrees with disastrous consequences. Their investment banking activities included underwriting corporate stock issues, which guaranteed they would furnish a sum of money by a definite date to a business or government in return for an issuance (floatation) of stock or bonds by that business or government entity.[5] Additionally, commercial banks established security affiliates that owned less than a majority of the common stock of companies, and also held floating rate bonds. A floating rate bond is a debt instrument, the interest rate on which parallels market interest rates.

As a result, commercial banks took on too much risk with depositor funds. Banks made unsound loans to companies in which those same banks had invested. They even encouraged their clients to invest in the stock of companies for which they were acting as underwriters, or in which they were investing themselves using depositor funds.[6]

This improper banking activity is regarded as the main culprit of the stock market crash of 1929, which triggered the Great Depression. To be sure, some historians believe these unsafe activities had little effect on the already devastated US economy. Nevertheless, as a result of the Wall Street crash, nearly 5,000 banks closed, and the global Great Depression ensued. International trade protectionism, coupled with competitive currency devaluations (collectively referred to as 'beggar-thy-neighbour policies'), exacerbated the problem.

In response to the economic turmoil, the US Congress passed the Glass–Steagall Act in 1933.[7] The Act gave the Federal Reserve System (which had been created in 1913 by the *Federal Reserve Act*[8]) tighter regulation of national banks. The Act also created the Federal Deposit Insurance Corporation (FDIC) to insure bank deposits with a pool of money collected from banks. Most importantly, the new law separated commercial banks from investment banks.[9]

With the Glass–Steagall Act, commercial banks could no longer underwrite securities, and investment banks could no longer engage in the business of receiving deposits. The only exceptions were for the US Treasury and federal agency securities, and municipal and state general obligation securities. They were considered safe instruments, with the backing of the full faith and credit of their governmental issuer, thus justifying the exception. Commercial banks came to use Section 20 of the Act, creating 'Section 20 subsidiaries', in which they could do a limited amount of underwriting and dealing in so-called bank eligible securities. The bank itself supposedly was protected from risk arising from the securities activities of its section 20 subsidiary by firewalls, or 'Chinese walls'. With this separation, or 'wall', between commercial and investment banking, the Act helped to restore the confidence of the US public in the banking system. Significantly, only commercial banks had direct access to the lender of last resort functions of the Federal Reserve, and the FDIC only insured their deposits up to US$100,000.

Additionally, bank restrictions expanded with the passing of the *Bank Holding Company Act* in 1956.[10] This Act restricted bank holding companies that owned two or more banks from engaging in non-banking activity. Here, then, was a second separation justified on safety and soundness grounds: a wall between finance and commerce. Titanic conglomerates like those built by J.P. Morgan and John D. Rockefeller were a thing of the past, as a bank and an industrial company could not be under the same corporate roof. The potential for conflict of interest was obvious, and analogous to that between commercial and investment banking activities before the Glass–Steagall Act. The non-bank unit (such as the investment bank or industrial company) could pressure the commercial bank to make loans to it, and underwrite and deal in its securities. Additionally, under the Bank Holding Company Act, a bank holding company could not acquire banks in another state.[11]

Ironically, however, the separation between commercial and investment banking also created problems. First, by restricting the activities of banks, banks could not diversify risks in a broad portfolio of activities. Law and regulation channelled them into limited activities, thus potentially making their risk profiles worse.[12] Banks and pro-bank commentators argued that by allowing commercial banks to spread themselves across a range of activities, in moderation, risks to individual banks, and the banking system generally, would be reduced.

Second, US commercial banks felt at an international competitive disadvantage *vis-à-vis* banks from foreign countries with universal banking (such as no separation between commercial and investment banks). Those banks, such as from Germany, grew larger and more powerful empires than did their 'handicapped' US counterparts. During the 1980s and 1990s, both arguments were made with greater force, leading to the erosion and eventual removal of the Glass–Steagall wall.[13]

On 6 April 1998 the largest merger in world history occurred by the exchange of US$70 billion in stocks between a commercial bank and an investment company. The merger created what is now known as Citigroup, the largest financial services company in the world. The two merged companies were Citicorp, the parent of giant Citibank, and Travelers, owner of the Salomon Smith Barney investment business.[14]

With the Glass–Steagall Act still in place, the merger was carefully structured to conform to its strictures. Obviously, the Act had been put in place to prevent just this type of merger.[15] Yet, the Federal Reserve approved the merger, with strict conditions. One basic condition was the merged Citigroup would have two years of life, with the potential for three one-year extensions if approved by the Federal Reserve Board. Once the life span elapsed, Citigroup would have to divest itself of Travelers, unless the *Bank Holding Company Act of 1956* was amended.

Predictably, immediately after announcing the merger, Citicorp and Travelers went to work lobbying in Washington, DC. The companies feared the necessary statutory changes would not happen in time, and company share prices, which fell, would plummet. Yet, over a year after approval by the Board, Congress repealed the Glass–Steagall Act. Citigroup never had to divest itself of Travelers.

1999 US Gramm–Leach–Bliley Act

After decades of fighting against the Glass–Steagall Act, opponents such as Citigroup prevailed in late 1999, when Congress passed the Gramm–Leach–Bliley Act, known more euphemistically as the *Financial Services Modernization Act*.[16] It took over 20 years, and over US$300 million in lobbying, to rid the financial industry of what it regarded as an outdated law.[17]

The Gramm–Leach–Bliley Act made significant changes to the Glass–Steagall Act, effectively repealing part of it. The new Act removed barriers between commercial banks, investment banks, and insurance companies, thus permitting consolidation among any of the three financial services. Its purpose was to foster competition in the financial services industry by providing for the affiliation of banks, securities firms, and other financial service providers. Concomitantly, consolidation would lead to larger, more powerful US financial institutions better positioned for global competition against universal banks. Thus, following the 1999 passage of the Act, many banks consolidated via the creation of new bank holding companies.

However, in the 2008 financial crisis, many of the ostensibly 'blue chip' names ran into trouble. Bank holding companies for Bear Stearns, Goldman Sachs, Lehman Brothers, Merrill Lynch, and Morgan Stanley faced serious problems, and created systemic risks to one degree or another.[18] Their names remain notorious among large swathes of the US public, and the public in other countries. That is for good reason. Their risky banking practices cost US taxpayers around US$12 trillion in bailouts to these bank holding companies.[19]

Significantly, Sanford Weill, co-founder of Citigroup and instigator of the Gramm–Leach–Bliley Act, regrets the decision to repeal the Glass–Steagall Act, saying it was a mistake to tear down the barrier between commercial and investment banks.[20] Ironically, his logic is the same as that from the 1930s when the Act was passed: banks took excessive risks with depositor funds. John Reed, co-founder of Citigroup, and David Komansky, former Chief Executive Officer (CEO) of Merrill Lynch, have also spoken about the causal link between the repeal of the Act and global financial crisis. Albeit after they retired, all three of these experienced financial leaders expressed dismay at the effect of the Gramm–Leach–Bliley Act on the domestic and international economy.

US Volcker Rule

This disquiet has grown exponentially since the global economic slump of 2008. With the passing of the 1999 Gramm–Leach–Bliley Act, and the erasure of the line between commercial and investment banking, financial institutions are able to transact across multiple products and markets, thereby incurring risks that are sometimes unsafe and unsound, and even engage in unfair business practices, to boot. Their reply; namely, that they have appropriate risk-monitoring systems in place, and have boosted capital against losses, is met with scepticism reinforced by episodic crises at one bank or another (such as massive trading losses), or one scandal or another (such as fixing the London Inter-Bank Offered Rate [LIBOR], or money laundering).

Sceptics also point out that allowing a financial institution to grow to a size that it purportedly is too big to fail can create a moral hazard problem: If such a bank knows it will get a bailout from a government, then what incentives does it have to control risks in the first place? This point has generated a robust debate about whether having so-called 'systemically important financial institutions' (SIFIs), which are deemed *a priori* to be too big to fail because of their significance to the financial system, is prudent. To what extent should a large financial institution be entitled to rely on the lender-of-last-resort functions of a central bank, such as the Federal Reserve?[21] And, if large aggregations of financial power are permitted, then surely the institutions involved should have a 'living will'; that is, a plan for their demise.

Another, complementary, response to the concern that financial institutions have grown too large under the Gramm–Leach–Bliley Act is the Volcker Rule, whose namesake is Paul Volcker (1927–), former President of the Federal Reserve Bank of New York (1975–79) and Chairman of the Board of Governors of the Federal Reserve System (1979–87). The *Rule* limits the size of institutions by regulating certain activities and addresses in part the too-big-to-fail problem.

The Volcker Rule places trading restrictions on financial institutions by separating investment banking, private equity, and proprietary trading (colloquially called 'prop trading') from commercial banking. It is similar to, but not identical with, the Glass–Steagall Act wall. Its gist is that no commercial bank could trade securities for its own prop trading account. The goal of the Rule is to reduce conflicts of interest, and bar them from simultaneously playing the role of adviser to and creditor of a client. Separating the different types of financial business practices in which a company may engage ideally makes financial institutions more transparent and more effectively monitored.[22]

The Volcker Rule was added to the *Dodd–Frank Wall Street Reform and Consumer Protection Act*, which Congress passed, and President Barack H. Obama signed in 2010, in the wake of the 2008 financial crisis. Originally, the Rule was to be implemented in July 2012, but regulatory agencies are still in the process of drafting it. The Rule was expected to be complete within the first few months of 2013, but the resignation of Chairman Mary Schapiro further delayed matters. The House Financial Services committee was to look to implement the Rule as early as December 2013.[23]

Universal banking

Figure 6.1 summarizes the rather seesaw history of the Great Crash of 1929, 1933 Glass–Steagall Act, 1999 Gramm–Leach-Bliley Act, and the Volcker Rule passed in 2010. Evidently, from this chart and the preceding discussion, the metaphor of a 'wall' dividing commercial and investment banks is somewhat misleading. Rather than just two possibilities, 'yes–no' or 'on–off', there is a spectrum of banking.

At one end of the spectrum there is universal banking. This German-style model allows universal banks to provide a multitude of financial services. Unlike in the US under the Glass–Steagall Act, these banks include both commercial and investment services, but, to be sure, they are not required to do so. Many smaller banks specialize in a particular area of services.

Supporters of universal banking argue diversification has many benefits for universal banks. They allow banks to offer the full range of services to their clients. Banks are therefore able to diversify by avoiding excessive concentration in a narrow range of activities. Additionally, universal banking stimulates competition among banks that offer a wide variety of services. Indeed, with more banks offering underwriting and dealing services, the supply curve of such services shifts out. That, in turn, means a larger quantity of inexpensive capital is available to industry to help promote growth (via underwriting activities), and securities markets are more liquid (via dealing activities).

There is a historically well-founded concern that banks engaged in securities activities will behave in unsafe, unsound ways, putting customer deposits at risk, especially if those deposits are government insured (given the perverse incentive created by the moral hazard problem). Banks are in the position to leverage customer assets against risk investments.[24] In other words, the interests of depositors who look to their financial institution for its commercial banking services, and those of the institution in respect of securities activities, are not necessarily aligned.

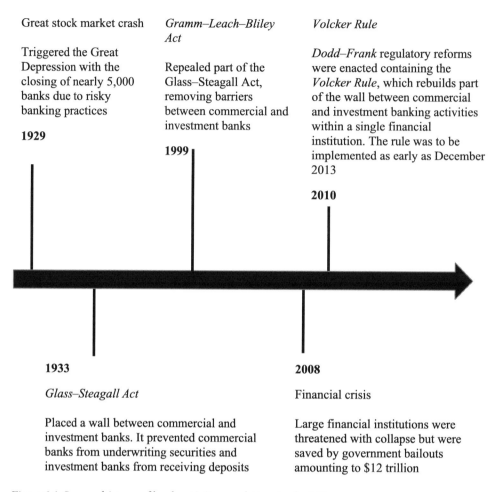

Figure 6.1 Seesaw history of bank activity regulation in the US.

Universal banking and Hong Kong

Generally speaking, the post-Second World War trend among financial institutions in countries that do not have any regulatory distinction between investment and commercial banks has been in favour of universal banking.[25] European nations are an example, which have spawned universal banking giants such as BNP Paribas of France, Deutsche Bank of Germany, and UBS of Switzerland.

Hong Kong historically has had a universal banking model. Hong Kong banking and monetary authorities; namely, the Hong Kong Monetary Authority (HKMA), have sought to create a light-handed regulatory scaffolding in which one-stop shops for financial services flourish. These shops meet the range of needs from the most simple, routine retail deposit transactions, to the needs of sophisticated conglomerates operating in multiple jurisdictions, such as trade finance, capital raising, and risk hedging. However, since the global financial crisis, Hong Kong authorities have put on new regulatory disciplines. As of 2009, banks are now required to adhere to protection measures in addition to those of the Hong Kong's Securities and Futures Commission (SFC). The new requirements mandate a physical separation of the investment and commercial banking activities, an audio recording of the sales process, and a 'two day pre-investment cooling off period' for inexperienced investors.[26]

Hong Kong authorities expect (*inter alia*) the post-2009 regulations will help prevent negative effects, such as those that followed the Lehman Brothers minibonds scandal. In 2008, Lehman sold 'guaranteed minibonds' to over 47,000 individuals in Hong Kong. That is, Lehman sold minibonds to local Hong Kong banks, which then sold them aggressively to their clients.[27] Yet, these minibonds were complex, high-risk structured products. Months later, in September 2008, when Lehman Brothers unexpectedly collapsed, and so could not make good on its guarantees of the minibonds, the minibond holders were left unable to look to Lehman to recoup the full value of their holdings. Luckily, the Hong Kong government proposed a plan to buy back the minibonds, giving investors a partial recovery.[28]

Still, the Hong Kong minibond case is yet another illustration – this one arising in Asia – of problems concerning universal banking. Had the Hong Kong banks not been able to peddle the minibonds, the case might not have arisen, and the Hong Kong government might not have been put upon to clean up a mess originating on Wall Street. Hence, this (and other) cases impelled Hong Kong authorities to rethink their long-standing approach of letting financial institutions roam relatively freely on the spectrum of banking activities, without entirely abandoning the universal banking model.

Narrow banking

On the opposite side of the spectrum from universal banking is narrow banking. A narrow bank, also called a safe bank, is a financial institution that issues demandable liabilities and invests in assets that have little to no nominal interest rate and credit risk.[29] A narrow bank has built-in safety measures to reduce drastically potential risk and, in turn, the need for banking insurance.

On the liability side of the balance sheet of a narrow bank, the safety measures include not lending deposits, and paying lower interest rates to depositors. On the asset side, the measures include investing only in liquid and safe government bonds. For the entire balance sheet, the bank operates within a regulatory framework characterized by higher scrutiny and restrictions.[30]

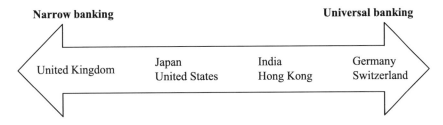

Figure 6.2 Narrow and universal banking country spectrum.

6.4 Investment banks

General definition

Investment banks specialize in activities that businesses rarely are willing or able to perform on their own; namely, raising capital by selling securities such as stocks and bonds to the investing public. Investment banks underwrite and distribute new security issues in the primary market, more commonly known as an initial public offering (IPO). An investment banker (or, in reality, an army of such bankers and their lawyers) advises the issuing company on the price and terms of a security, and then guarantees the sale while overseeing distribution through brokerage firms. It does so under a legal framework concerning disclosure of all material information about the issuer in the offering documents, such as those in the US Congress enacted *Securities Act 1933 (1933 Act)*.[31]

Investment bankers can, and also do, trade securities for the account of their investment bank, so-called proprietary trading, that is, dealing for the benefit (or loss) of the institution. Such trading, along with trading on behalf of investment customers on a brokerage basis, occurs in the secondary market. This market, like the primary one, operates under a legal framework, such as the US *Securities Exchange Act of 1934 (1934* Act), aimed at transparency and against market manipulation and insider trading.[32]

Still another prominent, and highly lucrative, activity of investment bank concerns corporate structures. They facilitate mergers and acquisitions (M&As), reorganizations, and broker trades.[33] Finally, depending on the applicable legal framework (namely; whether it permits universal or near-universal banking), investment banks may also operate as commercial banks. A few notable bank holding companies (BHCs) with investment and commercial banking subsidiaries include Citigroup, Bank of America, and J.P. Morgan Chase.

Unlike these BHCs or their commercial bank subsidiaries, investment banks generally are subject to less regulation. Investment banks are less burdened, but not entirely unencumbered, with restrictions on maintaining capital adequacy ratios and introducing new products. The Securities and Exchange Commission (SEC), Commodities Futures Trading Commission (CFTC), Financial Industry Regulatory Authority (FINRA), and US Treasury are the regulatory bodies that supervise investment banks.[34] The regulatory authorities (*inter alia*) ensure registration documents for IPOs meet disclosure standards and monitor secondary market trading. Additionally, they subject investment banks to net equity rules and monitor certain types of proposed new products.

Disclosure

There are three ways (discussed below) to sell a newly issued security and thereby raise capital for the issuing entity. However, regardless of which method is used, before any IPO can 'go public', a key legal requirement must be met: disclosure.

Why do securities laws like the Securities Act of 1933 require an issuer to file a prospectus? The touchstone of securities law is 'disclosure'. Securities market supervisors like the US SEC, and those in Asian countries, require disclosure about the issuer. They seek to make investors aware of the risk of a publicly offered investment. Transparency, or metaphorically the fresh light of the sun shining on the books and records of the issuer, allows them to become aware of those risks. And full disclosure of all material facts protects the issuer from liability for non-disclosure. Note that the hallmark of commercial banking supervision is not 'disclosure', but 'safety and soundness', which (*inter alia*) capital adequacy rules address.

Accordingly, mandated disclosure in a prospectus includes a description of the business of the issuer, names and addresses of the officers of the issuer, the salaries and business histories of those officers, and the ownership positions of each officer. Additionally, the prospectus must provide a description of the offering, price, selling discounts given to the underwriter (e.g., if an IPO price is US$100, and the underwriter obtains the securities from the issuer at US$85, then its discount is 15 per cent, which is in addition to, and distinct from, its underwriting fee), date, use of proceeds, description of the underwriting, financial information, risks to buyers, and any legal proceedings in which the issuer is involved at the time of the IPO.[35] Notably, under the 1933 Act, it also includes an SEC disclaimer.

6.5 Investment banking activities

Underwriting

The first method in respect of IPOs is underwriting, which is the most common method used to sell securities and raise capital for corporations. The issuer hires an investment bank to underwrite, or guarantee, the securities to be sold, thus assuming the risk of unsold securities. Once the underwriting agreement is finalized between issuer and investment bank underwriter, the latter is legally obliged to sell the securities.

The 'underwriting spread' is the difference in the amount an underwriter has to pay the issuing company for its securities, or the selling discount price (e.g., US$85), and the amount the underwriter receives from selling the securities in the public offering (e.g., US$100). The underwriter also earns a fee for its services. If the securities are viewed favourably in the market, for instance, then the underwriter will be able to sell the securities at the planned price (e.g., US$100). These stocks or bonds will be well received by investors, as manifest in their purchase of them at that offering (IPO) price. However, suppose the underwriter misjudged the optimism the market would have for the IPO, or suppose conditions associated with the issuer, equity or bond markets, or the local or global economy changed dramatically. Then the underwriter bears the cost of holding on to the unsold securities until they can be sold favourably in the future (if ever).

In some IPOs, an underwriting investment bank enters into an agreement to give a selling firm the option to buy the securities at a fixed price. This selling firm is a third party, distinct from the underwriter, which is responsible for distributing the IPO to investors. For example, the selling firm might be a stock brokerage company holding accounts of retail investors. The underwriter agrees to sell to the brokerage company a portion of the IPO, if the brokerage company is interested – and it will be, if its clients are keen on the IPO. Assuming the brokerage company agrees to buy an allotment of the IPO stock or bonds on behalf of its clients, then the underwriter has the certainty and predictability – before the IPO actually occurs – the securities in the allotment are spoken for. In other words, the underwriter has eliminated the risk of unsold securities, with regard to that allotment, and thus raised capital for the issuer as originally planned.

Underwriting example

To illustrate several of the aforementioned precepts, consider the following hypothetical example. Suppose the Bangalore, India-based company, United Breweries Holdings

Limited, maker of the famed Taj Mahal beer, seeks to raise capital through an equity offering, the proceeds of which are to fund a production facility in Malaysia. United Breweries hires Daiwa, the Japanese securities firm based in Tokyo as underwriter. Daiwa commits to selling 100 shares of United Breweries equity on the Bombay Stock Exchange at a per share price of $10.

In return, United Breweries agrees to give Daiwa 100 shares at a $9 discounted price. Daiwa accepts and pays this price, believing market sentiment will enable it to sell the stock in the market at $10 or higher. Daiwa assumes the risk of selling the stock, and delivers payment of $900 to United:

$$(\$9 \text{ per share}) \cdot (100 \text{ shares}) = \$900$$

If Daiwa is able to sell the stocks at $10, then it will make a profit of $100:

$$(\$10) \cdot (100) = \$1,000 - \$900$$
$$= \$100$$

However, if Daiwa is able to sell the United Breweries shares for only $9 per share, then it makes no profit. Rather, it breaks even (abstracting from any transactions costs, which if accounted for would mean it incurs a loss):

$$(\$9) \cdot (100) = \$9000 - \$900$$
$$= \$0$$

If the stock were sold for under the discounted price, then obviously Daiwa would lose money on the floatation.

Before any competent underwriter is able to consider the profit it expects to make, it must fulfil the solemn responsibility of advising the issuing firm on an appropriate price for the planned security offering. The underwriter works conjointly with the issuer to determine that price. The duo must carefully balance a price that maximizes the capital raised for the issuer against a price that makes the security liquid. Underpricing the security means the entire allotment sells, but for less capital than the issuer could have enjoyed. Overpricing the security means only a portion of the allotment (or, in theory, none of it) sells, and also results in a sub-optimal amount of capital.

To price the offering correctly, the underwriter and issuer consider supply and demand conditions in the target market. On the supply side, they will think about how many comparable investment vehicles have been brought to market recently. For example, in the United Breweries case, have five other alcoholic beverage producers issued stock on Indian exchanges in the last six months? If so, then investors may be saturated, or supersaturated, with equity from this sector. Unless Daiwa can make a credible pitch to investors that the United Breweries offering is not substitutable with the five earlier ones, that the company is truly distinct from the other issuers, Daiwa may have to advise its underwriting client to accept a reduced per share price.

On the demand side, Daiwa will seek indications of interest in United Breweries stock. The indications of interest estimate demand by the number of shares subscribed. A subscription is a non-binding commitment to purchase equity or debt instruments. Once a price is agreed upon, and registered by the relevant securities regulator (such as the

SEC), underwriters call these subscribers to confirm their orders. If demand is high, then the issuer and underwriter may decide to raise the price, and reconfirm the new price with subscribers. Once the underwriter and issuer are certain they will sell all of the securities, they close the offering.

After the offering is closed, the underwriter purchases all the securities from the issuing company at the discounted price, less the underwriting fees it charges the issuer. Then, the underwriter sells the securities to the subscribers that are still willing to buy the stock or bonds at the offering price. As for any securities not purchased by the subscribers, the underwriter must find other investors to purchase them, or the underwriter must keep them.

Obviously, the above-described process is the primary market, in which funds flow among issuers, underwriters, and IPO investors. After securities are sold in the primary market, they begin trading in the secondary market, whereas in a secondary market, trading occurs between investors. Secondary markets include the New York Stock Exchange (NYSE) and the National Association of Securities Dealers Automated Quotations (NASDAQ), which also function as primary markets. In secondary markets, securities prices fluctuate with market supply and demand, with general market environment conditions, and with factors specific to the issuer of the security in question. All such determinants of the secondary market price of a security may add to, or detract from, the liquidity in the market for that security. Liquidity is measured by how quickly an asset can be converted for cash at its fair market value (FMV). That is, it reflects the number of ready, willing, and able sellers and buyers of an asset: the more there are of them, the faster the asset can be sold for cash at FMV.

In addition to selling a security via an IPO, underwriters usually agree to ensure a stable FMV in the secondary market by purchasing or selling that security. Underwriters do so by diversifying the distribution of that security throughout the market. When widely distributed, the security is not as vulnerable to changes in the market, and thus its price not as volatile compared to the security being held by only one or a few stockholders.

Best efforts

The second, and less common, methodology is an investment bank may sell securities on a best-efforts basis. The issuing entity, usually a corporation or government, assumes the risk of taking back any securities not sold after a predetermined time. Manifestly, best-efforts placement is less risky for an investment bank than underwriting, as it makes no guarantee it will hold securities on its books if there is insufficient market demand for them. However, the best-efforts method is not commonplace. Typically, it is used when the issues are too risky for investment banks to accept the risk of loss associated with the equity or debt instruments.

Direct sale

The third way to raise capital through the selling of newly issued stocks or bonds is for the issuing corporation or government to sell securities directly to the public. The issuing process is long, complex, and presumes the issuer has a strong network of connections among investors. In house security issuance divisions can be expensive to operate, while investment banks specializing in IPOs charge issuing firms a fraction of the cost of those operations. Consequently, issuers use this method infrequently, in favour of underwriters. However, investment banks can and do earn huge underwriting fees, which if sufficiently high could be an incentive for the issuer to go directly to the market. Indeed, for certain securities and issuers, such as commercial paper issued by 'blue chip' companies, direct, private placements occur.

Syndicates

Often, an underwriter of large issues distributes the risk of loss of holding unsold securities on its books by forming a group called a 'syndicate'. Generally, the larger an offering, the more investment bank participants there are within the syndicate to divide up and allocate between, thereby spreading the risk. In the US, once a syndicate is formed, the Securities Act of 1933 mandates the issuing firm file a prospectus (as it must when no syndicate is involved).[36] Each participant in a syndicate receives an underwriting commission and selling discount for taking on the risk for underwriting. Here again, it earns an underwriting spread, plus a fee.

Shelf registration

While investment banks may distribute securities through underwriting, best efforts, or syndicates, they also have the option of so-called 'shelf registration'. Shelf registration allows an issuing firm to register its securities with the appropriate securities regulator (such as the SEC), and sell the securities as needed in the future. Shelf registration is more popular with bond than equity offerings.

The metaphor is apt: the securities are 'on the shelf', ready for sale, when conditions warrant. That is, this technique is useful when market uncertainty prevails. The legal process of registration is complete, so as funds are needed or when market conditions turn favourable, the securities can move swiftly to the market. Note that investment banks are able to buy portions of a shelf issue, and immediately resell securities to clients.

Private placements

An issuing company may decide to raise capital through private placements instead of the traditional methods previously mentioned. Private placements are not as common, making up only 20 per cent of the funds raised for companies, compared to public offerings which make up 80 per cent. In a private placement, a company sells a large block of stocks or bonds to a small number of selected investors such as a large bank, insurance company, pension fund, or mutual fund. An issuing company may find its investors directly, or decide to find them through an investment banker. The incentive for investors is generally a higher yield; however, the pitfall is a non-existent or limited secondary market.

In the US, private placements do not have to be registered with the SEC. Unlike a public offering, a private placement is offered to a few, selected investors. The SEC often waives the need for a prospectus, so detailed financial information is not disclosed. However, the private placement must be genuinely private to meet the private offering exemption. There cannot be any general solicitation or advertisement.[37]

M&As

Apart from underwriting, investment banks also participate in M&As. A 'merger' is a fusion of two companies, mutually deciding to become a single company.[38] When a company takes over another company and becomes the new owner, this is called an 'acquisition'. However, the line between a merger and an acquisition has become increasingly unclear. Rarely do companies of about the same size 'merge' as equals. But, there is a negative connotation with the classification of 'acquisition'. So, although most same-size company deals are technically 'acquisitions', the terms of the agreement allow the acquired firm to categorize the deal as a 'merger' of equals.

Investment banks are at the heart of M&A activity. They play the vital role of advising companies about potential mergers or targets for acquisition. Companies look to M&As, as distinct from organic (endogenous) growth, as an opportunity to extend their customer base, expand to new regions, and provide superior and diversified products and services.

For these benefits to flow, businesses in an M&A deal have to assimilate, while eradicating redundant operations and active inefficiencies.[39] Often it is difficult to integrate when company culture and strategic direction are not complementary or aligned. Investment banking advice can be essential in M&A to ensure not only the numbers in spreadsheets are compelling, but also that any merger or acquisition will be strategically beneficial and further the long-term goals of the parties.

Advising often begins with the M&A division of an investment bank producing a pitch book of financial information to promote to a potential client. That division focuses on specific industries and maintaining relationships with corporations. Once it has a potential M&A client, the product coverage division in the same investment bank specializes in finding the financial products the client needs. These products range from advice on trading suggestions, to evaluating risk, to structuring complex derivatives.

In addition to the globally prominent companies Table 6.1 lists, there are many boutique investment banks that specialize in M&As. Examples include Lazard, Greenhill, Evercore, and Gleacher.

Traditionally, M&As are the most lucrative service an investment bank provides. This activity generates not only huge fees, but also a sizeable percentage of the value of each M&A transaction. Corporations rely heavily on investment bank expertise, particularly when hundreds of billions of dollars are at stake. The Mannesmann (German conglomerate) and Vodafone AirTouch merger in 2002, for example, resulted in a US$202.8 billion merger.

Table 6.1 Top 10 global merger and acquisition advisers[40]

Company	Country	2011 (billions)	2012 (billions)
Goldman Sachs	United States	$ 664.077	$ 661.958
J.P. Morgan	United States	$ 503.506	$ 508.679
Morgan Stanley	United States	$ 494.117	$ 441.744
Citigroup	United States	$ 482.813	$ 337.922
Barclays	United Kingdom	$ 424.500	$ 363.598
Deutsche Bank	Germany	$ 409.330	$ 293.259
Credit Suisse	Switzerland	$ 405.799	$ 405.62
Bank of America–Merrill Lynch	United States	$ 391.681	$ 394.372
Rothschild	Switzerland	$ 236.737	$ 167.672
UBS	Switzerland	$ 232.919	$ 292.531

192 *Practice of investment management*

6.6 Asian investment banks

Growth trends

A once US-dominated list of investment banks now is increasingly cosmopolitan. Asian Financial Markets have grown and are likely to continue in that trend, so concomitantly Asian financial institutions are ever more prominent. For instance, in 2013, Japan's Daiwa Securities became the first Asian investment bank to be recognized as a global winner of *Global Finance*'s annual rankings. Daiwa Securities was voted as the most creative international bank in the world in 2013. Additionally, in 2013, China International Capital Corporation was voted the best investment bank for infrastructure deals.[41] China International Capital Corp also underwrote the largest initial public offering (IPO) on record in the world (as of July 2011).[42] It raised US$22.12 billion for the Agriculture Bank of China.

Table 6.2 Best Asian investment banks[43]

Asian country	2010	2011	2012	2013
Australia	UBS Investment Bank	UBS Investment Bank	Macquarie	Macquarie
China	China International Capital Corp	China International Capital Corp	China International Capital Corp	China International Capital Corp
Hong Kong	N/A	N/A	HSBC (Hong Kong Shanghai Corporation)	HSBC
India	Kotak Mahindra Bank	Morgan Stanley	State Bank of India	Citi
Indonesia	Mandiri Sekuritas	Mandiri Sekuritas	Mandiri Sekuritas	Mandiri Sekuritas
Japan	Nomura	Daiwa Securities	Daiwa Capital Markets	Nomura
Kazakhstan	N/A	Halyk Finance	Halyk Finance	Kazkommerts Securities
Malaysia	N/A	N/A	N/A	CIMB
Mongolia	N/A	N/A	Eurasia Capital	Optima Capital
Philippines	N/A	N/A	N/A	BDO Capital & Investment Corp
Singapore	N/A	Standard Chartered	Standard Chartered	DBS (Development Bank of Singapore)
South Korea	Samsung Securities	Bank of America–Merrill Lynch	Samsung Securities	Daewoo Securities
Taiwan	Fubon Financial Holding	Fubon Financial Holding	Fubon Financial Holding	Grand Cathay Securities
Thailand	N/A	N/A	N/A	Siam Commercial Bank

Asian financial markets emerged from the global financial crisis that commenced in 2008 stronger than markets in the US, and certainly in Europe. Many Asian governments responded to the 1997–99 Asian Financial Crisis with sound fiscal and monetary policies, attractively high interest rates, and openness to trade and foreign direct investment (FDI). They also sought to combat corruption, or what was dubbed 'crony capitalism'. To be sure, the 2008 global financial crisis hit Asian economies, but by then Asian markets had recovered from the crisis of a decade earlier thanks partly to these structural economic and legal reforms. Additionally, Western corporations continued to be attracted to the lower underwriting fees in Asian capital markets.

As Figure 6.3 shows, after the 2008 crisis, pre-tax profits of banks in the Asia-Pacific region rose dramatically, as a percentage of total pre-tax bank profits of the largest 1,000 banks (gauged by Tier One capital) in the world. The increase was 35 percentage points, or 185.2 per cent, in four years. Moreover, in 2011, banks domiciled in the Asia-Pacific region earned over half of the total income (53.9 per cent) generated by the largest 1,000 banks in the world. That year also found four out of five of the most profitable banks in the world were Chinese, accounting for a third of the profit in the region.[44]

Special prominence of Hong Kong

Of Asia's many appealing and intriguing financial markets, the Hong Kong Stock Exchange (HKSE) is worthy of mention. Ever since the economic reforms in mainland China triggered by Deng Xiaoping in 1978, the HKSE has played a strategic role for companies seeking to tap Chinese investment funds, and for Chinese companies to tap foreign capital. In other words, the HKSE has long been prominent not only in association with the success of Hong Kong itself, but also as a gateway for global investors into China, and for China to global investors. Overseas (and Hong Kong) companies seeking to build or

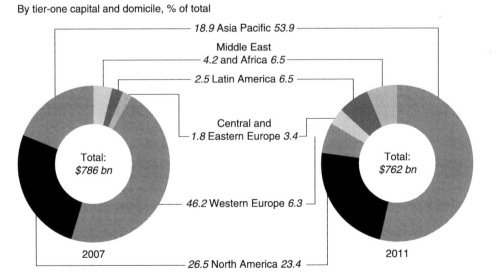

Figure 6.3 Pre-tax profits of 1,000 largest banks in world[45.]
Source: *The Banker Top 1000*.

expand operations on the mainland, or simply to tap new wealth on the mainland, saw the HKSE as a venue to do so. Conversely, mainland companies seeking foreign capital to fund domestic or overseas expansion saw the HKSE as an obvious market for IPOs.

To be sure, the HKSE faces competition from the Shenzhen and Shanghai stock exchanges. Nevertheless, the HKSE remains the fifth largest stock exchange in the world. It is the second largest stock exchange in Asia, in terms of market capitalization, next to the Tokyo Stock Exchange.[46] Not surprisingly, many US companies listed on its stock exchanges eagerly awaited listing on the HKSE. However, US shares listed on the HKSE generally were far too expensive for most local investors. It was a tedious legal process for companies to break the stocks into smaller denominations, and therefore was too expensive to execute. The costs outweighed the benefits of a new market of investors.

In 2011, J.P. Morgan perceived the need to disaggregate US shares on foreign stock exchanges, and created the service for US companies to do so. J.P. Morgan devised a new legal structure for companies listed in the US to list their companies on the HKSE. Companies such as Coach finally were able to offer one Hong Kong Depositary Receipt (HDR), representing one-tenth of a Coach share. Coach is one of the many US companies leading the way for other companies seeking to diversify globally by raising capital on the HKSE.

6.7 Broker-dealers[47]

Definition

A broker-dealer is a person, company, or other organization in the business of buying and selling securities for its own account or on behalf of its customers. 'Broker-dealer' is a term used in financial services regulations to describe brokerages, because most act as agents or principals. A broker-dealer acts as a broker, or agent, when it executes orders on behalf of clients.

In contrast, a broker-dealer acts as a dealer, or principal, when it trades for its own account. Securities bought on behalf of the firm may be sold to clients, to other firms, or enter into the holdings of the brokerage firm. Many broker-dealers are independent firms, but others are subsidiaries of commercial banks, investment banks, or investment companies.

Full service brokerage

Within the financial industry there are two kinds of brokers: full service and discount. Full service brokers are also known as financial consultants (FCs) or account executives (AEs). They fulfil several important functions, including advising customers about investment alternatives, holding securities for safekeeping, extending margin loans, facilitating trading activities, and publishing investment research.

Prepared reports and forecasts are essential to the functions of full service brokers. A full service broker relies on research staff to provide financial analysis and make buy–sell recommendations. Brokers use this information to make suitable investment suggestions based on their client's income, portfolio, risk tolerance, investment objectives, and overall financial situation. That research may be provided by the same financial institution for which the broker works (such as Bank of America–Merrill Lynch), or may be provided (typically for a fee) by third-party institutions.

Full service brokers reserve more judgement when a customer agrees to a discretionary account. With a discretionary account the broker holds the authority to make buy and sell decisions on behalf of the customer. However, the broker is limited to pre-specified securities on which the customer has agreed. Despite the prior agreement, there are concerns with this arrangement. Full service brokers may be tempted to 'churn', or trade excessively, with the unsafe and unsound goal of generating commissions for themselves, regardless of the best investment decisions for their client. Churning is illegal under the securities laws of many countries, yet still occurs. Clients with discretionary accounts must remain aware of the risk of churning, and remain proactive by monitoring their broker relationship to prevent unnecessary trading.

Discount brokerage

Discount brokerage entails a more straightforward relationship than full service brokerage. Discount brokers provide some, but not all of the services of a full service broker. They simply buy and sell securities, hold securities for safekeeping, offer margin loans, and facilitate trading activities. Unlike full service brokers, the only securities information discount brokers provide are price quotations.

It is becoming increasingly popular for discount brokers to be located in investment banks. As previously mentioned, investment banks are moving towards one-stop financial shops, going beyond underwriting securities, and M&A deals. Consistent with this trend, investment banks are adding discount brokerage services to the range of services they provide to customers.

Rise of online brokerage

Since the information technology (IT) revolution of the 1980s, with the integration of computers into everyday life, the brokerage industry has changed substantially. A potential investor simply needs a computer and internet access, and she can trade online. With ease, an investor can create an account, review the online brokerage company's procedures and fees, and begin trading. The service is convenient and efficient. An investor can initiate a trade, and in less than a minute the trade is completed and confirmed. So, in addition to full or discount brokerage, customers have the additional option of direct access to securities markets through an online brokerage service.

Many bank holding companies have begun offering online broker services in an attempt to target a new market of clients. The number of trades completed online is rising exponentially each year, and is expected to continue to increase. Furthermore, the internet has provided investors with instant access to information previously not readily available to the public. An increasing number of self-educated investors are able to trade independently from the comfort of their home without unnecessary costs and services.

In exchange for using online brokerage services, customers pay a commission on every transaction made by the broker on their behalf. Generally, an online brokerage company receives a small price per share (e.g., $0.02 per share). However, regardless of the trade size, generally there is a minimum charge (e.g., $20). Lower prices may be advertised by brokerages, but these prices generally are for larger amounts of shares traded. Limited (such as small volume) orders are far more expensive.

Pricing brokerage services

In choosing among full service, discount, or online brokerage, customers also need to take into account the prices of different types of brokerage services. A full service broker provides complex financial reports and other services, but for a higher price than a discount broker. A discount broker charges only 25–75 per cent of the commission typically charged by a full service broker. An online broker charges even less than a discount broker.[48]

Another way brokers are able to generate income, if they are also dealers, is through the bid–ask spread. The bid–ask spread is the difference in the amount the dealer purchased the securities (bid) and the increased amount for which the dealer sells the securities (ask):

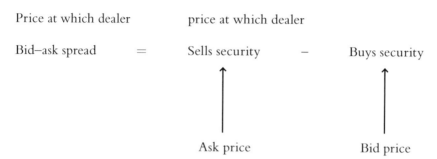

Some brokers collect only a fee in the form of the bid–ask spread, and do not charge a commission.

Broker licensing

In order for a stockbroker in the US to be licensed to sell or take orders of investment securities on behalf of their clients, or for their own account, the broker must meet certain requirements. The requirements are established by the Securities Exchange Act of 1934 and apply to anyone engaged in the business of effecting transactions in securities for the account of others.

Four requirements must be met for an individual to be a registered stockbroker. First, she must pass either the Series 7, or the Series 7 and Series 63 exam. The Series 7 licence is for a general securities representative, also known as a stockbroker or investment representative. Alternatively, to become a Uniform Securities Agent, she must complete the Series 7 and Series 63 contemporaneously. A Uniform Securities Agent entitles a holder to solicit orders for any type of security in a particular state of the US. The Financial Industry Regulatory Authority (FINRA) manages Series 7 and Series 63 testing. The three additional requirements include being registered with the SEC, a member of the Financial Industry Regulatory Authority (FINRA), and employed by or associated with a broker-dealer firm.[49]

6.8 Investment managers[50]

General definition

An investment manager, also called an asset or portfolio manager, is a person or organization that buys and sells securities for a designated portfolio. There are two sides to investment management work. An investment manager may make either investment decisions for clients, or manage the asset and liability (deposit and loan) portfolio of a financial institution. The former type of activity entails work for individual clients, including private wealth management for high net worth persons. The latter type of activity includes work for mutual funds, pension funds, hedge funds, and other institutional investment vehicles.

When an investment manager makes financial decisions for a client, the manager uses the investment objectives and constraints of a client to create a portfolio. Portfolios are designed according to the risk tolerance, time frame, and investment objectives of an investor. Asset managers aim at maximizing the expected return, and minimizing the risk, of that portfolio.[51]

Two of the most basic considerations are the amounts of money the client wishes to invest, and risk she is prepared to assume. Generally, the amount of risk correlates with the rate of return. However, portfolio diversification in a variety of assets mitigates some of the risk.

An investor must also decide whether she wishes to assume a long- or short-term orientation. An investment manager for a short-term trader uses financial analysis reports that come from market indicators and charting. The investment manager uses the reports to buy stocks or bonds that are intended to go up, and may plan, for example, to liquidate if there is a five-point increase. It is important to consider that a short-term trader, while hypothetically able to make money off of small point increases or decreases, pays considerably more in commission fees than a long-term investor. Long-term investors aim at finding well-established, sound companies with securities to buy and hold. Hence, they search for value, looking for an undervalued stock they can obtain at a low price, and 'ride' it as it increases in value over one or more years. One advantage of the buy-and-hold approach is capital gain taxes are minimized.

Portfolio managers work for investment management firms.[52] These firms range in size from large multidisciplinary firms to small offices consisting of only a couple of people. Boutique investment management firms often specialize and advertise the great passion of their manager for markets and investing. However, with smaller firms, the risk profile of a risk profile may not match the investment vehicles those firms offered. Some firms follow what might be called a 'multidisciplinary approach', to accommodate all investors, employing multiple asset classes and styles, domestic and foreign, traditional and alternative.

Tax considerations

Taxes are another aspect many high tax-bracket investors must consider in determining their investment objectives. These considerations vary from country to country, and year to year. For example, in the US in 2003, long-term capital gains, or gains on securities that are held for over a year, were taxed at a lower percentage than ordinary dividends. A differential between taxation of dividends as ordinary income (a higher tax rate) and capital gains (a lower tax rate) creates an artificial incentive in favour of investing in equities *vis-à-vis* other financial instruments (simply because of the lower taxes on capital gains than on returns to those other instruments).

However, since 2011, both dividend and capital gains on stock are taxed at a maximum rate of 15 per cent. Consequently, investors in high tax brackets now are able to consider more options besides standard municipal bonds with no taxable interest, real estate with depreciation, investments that offer tax credits, and long-term capital gains. In brief, taxes are factors investment managers must consider insofar as they bear on investment objectives of their client.

Portfolio management tools

Investment managers have a range of tools at their disposal to pick securities for the portfolios they manage. They use technical analysis to create a portfolio with a balance of risk and return that matches the goals of the client. Investment managers receive reports from internal analysts, as well as external analysts from investment banks. These reports often give asset managers ideas for client portfolios, which is why asset managers spend most of their day sifting through and perusing these lengthy materials.

A portfolio manager also spends time talking to company managers, and visiting their facilities, studying industries, and monitoring macroeconomic trends and the international political economy. Special note should be made of interviewing managers and checking their operations. The sad fact is some company managers stretch the truth, or even lie, to promote the stock of their companies to fund managers. The prudent portfolio manager knows to 'never trust management'. An eyeball-to-eyeball meeting can help ferret out trustworthy from dubious management. Further, visiting the premises of a company, be it a palm oil plantation in Malaysia, an air conditioning manufacturer in Thailand, or a financial services firm in Indonesia, helps a portfolio manager understand the potential risks and rewards of an investment in that company. Through all such work, the goal of the fund manager is to find the right financial instrument issued by the right company in the right country at the right time. After all, that is what the client, be it individual or institutional, pays for via fees.

As indicated, an investment manager may be responsible for the portfolio of an institution. That portfolio represents a vehicle into which multiple individuals, sometimes tens of thousands of them across many countries, put their savings in the hope of obtaining a return. That return comes from the work of the manager in investing those savings wisely in securities, employing the same kinds of tools a manager for an individual portfolio uses. So, for example, at its peak in the late 1990s, roughly 35,000 investors held shares in the Merrill Lynch Dragon Fund, a Far East (excluding Japan) fund valued at roughly US$1.5 billion. Technical charts, research reports, manager interviews, and company visits, plus reviewing industry and macroeconomic, and international trends, were the key methodologies for running that fund.

Monitoring and adjusting portfolios

Like an investment manager for an individual client portfolio, an institutional fund manager may buy and sell securities day to day and, indeed, night to night, as trading may occur on a 24/7 basis. Monitoring the portfolio constantly is essential, as performance of the fund is measured by both short- and long-term metrics and published widely.

Clearing and settlement issues

Clearing and settlement problems can and do arise. An investment manager must ensure all securities purchases and sales are cleared and settled in an accurate, timely fashion. Transactions are settled in multiple ways, depending on the nature of the financial instrument and market on which it is traded. As a general matter, for equities traded on a US securities exchange, the regular way (RW) requires a client pay for a stock on the third business day after the transaction (T), or $T + 3$. Similarly, the seller must have the security ready for delivery by that third business day after the transaction.

In contrast, suppose registration of newly purchased securities in an Egyptian company is held up for 30 days because of inefficiencies on the Cairo Stock Exchange. The fund manager must work with her team, and the clearing and settlement agents, to fix such problems, and thereby assure that the fund does not accumulate unwanted cash. Investors obviously do not choose a fund to hold a cash balance – that is a function of their personal bank account. Simply put, if money is not in a stock or other financial instrument, then it is not working for investors. Finally, the fund manager and her lawyers are responsible for reporting findings to clients and regulatory bodies such as in the Securities Exchange Commission in the US or the Financial Services Agency in Japan.

Loss prevention

Markets change rapidly and substantively; therefore, investment managers are required to monitor frequently their portfolios and make adjustments to ensure the level of risk is appropriate. They must have a loss prevention strategy in place. A loss prevention strategy is not comprised solely of buying 'blue chips', because even investments in well-established, financially sound companies such as blue chips do not always protect against market losses. (The same may be said of Chinese 'red chip' stocks.) Rather, a sound investment strategy may include parameters for buying and selling, diversification, and hedging techniques. Some strategies are more appropriate than others, though no strategy perfectly prevents disaster.

Performance measurement

Asset managers may also be able to prevent losses by measuring the performance of her investments by market indexes. Simply seeing how well her portfolio is doing against an appropriate benchmark may trigger needed adjustments. Those benchmarks are market indexes. These indexes are likely to be capitalization-weighted, which means the amount of each security held in the index fluctuates, according to the ratio of its market capitalization against the total market capitalization of all securities in the index.

Investment managers use complex strategies to track in real time the constant changes of an index. Asset managers also use sophisticated performance measures, such as the capital asset pricing model (CAPM), which is a pillar (albeit a discredited one) of modern finance theory. (The CAPM is discussed in Chapter 1.) Performance measurement is critical in evaluating whether an investment manager succeeds in meeting expectations. Performance reports are prepared and delivered to clients every quarter.

Note that along with these performance reports, asset managers prepare and distribute client portfolio reports and management information reports. These reports contain data on investment performance, daily transactions, a valuation of each account, and other performance or management reporting.

Fund manager compensation

Depending on the nature of the client (individual or institutional) and portfolio (individual account, mutual fund, pension fund, hedge fund), asset managers are compensated in various ways. These include a flat hourly rate, salary plus bonus (if warranted), commission on transactions, or percentage of the assets under management (AUM). Commissions on transactions are a traditional, large source of income for investment firms. However, it is becoming more popular for asset managers to charge fees based on a percentage of the AUM of a client. 'AUM' is a financial term denoting the market value of all the client's funds being managed by a financial institution. For example, a client with a US$10 million portfolio that is managed by an investment manager that charges 1 per cent would pay US$100,000 in fees. The amount of fees fluctuates with the performance of the portfolio.

Asian financial managers

Similar to investment banks, asset management firms in Asia have increased in number and size (measured by AUM). Within five years, from 2006 to 2011, there was a significant increase in the number of Asian asset management firms in the Top 500 Asset Manager Firms in the World.[53] In this short period, the three Japanese firms in the Top 50 expanded to seven in 2011. Such trends are expected to continue.

6.9 Central banks[54]

A central bank, also known as a reserve bank or monetary authority, is a public institution that generally issues currency, functions as the bank for a government, and regulates the credit and payments system. Its primary purpose is to manage the nation's money supply through interest rates, reserve requirements, and acts as a lender of last resort to the banking sector during a financial crisis. Additionally, a central bank may also have supervisory powers to oversee the commercial banking (including payments) system within its respective country.

In response to the bank panic of 1907, the US Congress passed the Federal Reserve Act to stabilize the economy and banking system. The Act created the Federal Reserve System in 1913.[55] The Federal Reserve System consists of 12 banking districts, with a Reserve Bank in each: Atlanta, Boston, Chicago, Cleveland, Dallas, Kansas City, Minneapolis, New York, Philadelphia, Richmond, St. Louis, and San Francisco. The Federal Reserve System, also known as the Fed, has had its powers and responsibilities altered and increased since its creation in 1913 by several acts passed by Congress, including the 1933 Glass–Steagall Act, 1956 Bank Holding Company Act, 1999 Gramm–Leach–Bliley Act, and 1977 *Federal Reserve Reform Act*. Technically, the Board of Governors of the Federal Reserve System (such as the 'Board') is an independent agency of the US government. The 12 Federal Reserve Banks are instrumentalities of this agency.[56]

Of the 12 Reserve Banks, New York is the most important, in part because of its location in one of the three most significant global financial centres (along with London and Tokyo). Additionally, the New York Fed is home to the largest vault of monetized gold in the world, a result occurring from the Second World War era when countries moved their gold reserves out of the path of invading Nazi armies.

The 2008 international credit crisis is a more recent example of why central banks must closely regulate commercial banks.[57] The threat of collapse of large financial institutions had a ripple effect on the economy, affecting more than just those directly connected. It created declines in international trade, housing markets, and economic activity. The Federal Reserve sought to prevent banks from closing their doors in the US, and thus avoid a rerun of what happened after the 19 October 1929 stock market crash.

The primary regulator of a commercial bank depends on the type of charter of the bank. The Office of the Comptroller of the Currency (OCC, or Comptroller), an independent bureau within the US Department of Treasury, regulates nationally chartered

International financial players 201

banks. State-chartered banks are regulated primarily by the Federal Deposit Insurance Corporation (FDIC), if they are not members of the Federal Reserve System, or by the Fed it they are members. The Fed, however, has ultimate regulatory authority in that under the Bank Holding Company Act, it regulates bank holding companies.

Supervision of regulated financial institutions

In addition to having a primary federal regulator, a state-chartered bank is regulated by an agency of the state in which it is chartered, such as a Department of Banking. That agency is responsible for restricting the amount of interest a bank charges for loans, auditing the bank, evaluating the financial performance of the bank, and ensuring the bank complies with all applicable regulations. A state-chartered bank has the option to belong to the Federal Reserve System, the central bank of the US.

Many state-chartered banks decide to join the Federal Reserve System. Their motivations for doing so may vary, but can include direct access to payments systems (like Fedwire, used for electronic funds transfers). State-chartered banks that are Federal Reserve members are supervised by the Fed,[58] which may enhance their access to capital, as investors regard them as well regulated.

The FDIC, created in 1933 during the Great Depression via the *Banking Act*, regulates any bank that carries FDIC insurance. It is a US government corporation operating as an independent agency.[59] The FDIC offers depositor insurance, guaranteeing that the funds of any single depositor are protected up to US$250,000 in the case of a bank failure.[60] This independent agency also monitors insured banks for safety and soundness. Indeed, 'safety and soundness' is the touchstone of all banking regulation, and a mantra frequently used by regulators to justify their decisions.

Note the rather confusing US system of overlapping supervisory authority. Almost all state-chartered banks are either members of the Federal Reserve System or have FDIC insurance. Therefore, most state-chartered banks are regulated or supervised by the federal government. What about non-state-chartered, such as, national, banks?

A bank that wishes to be exempt from regulation by a state banking authority logically would choose to apply for a national charter. The Comptroller supervises nationally chartered banks.[61] Significantly, in addition to supervising national banks, the OCC also monitors branches and agencies of foreign banks in the US.[62]

Wholesale versus retail payment systems

A payment system is an operational network that links bank accounts and uses cash substitutes for monetary exchange. The network provides a wide range of payment services to financial institutions and the government, which are then offered to their customers. Those customers are account holders ranging from large businesses to modest individuals. The purpose of a payment system is to provide a convenient way for a customer, a payor or obligor, to transfer funds from its account in its bank to the account of another customer, the payee or oblige. Note that the payor and/or payee can be a bank, as banks settle obligations between themselves via a payment system.

It is important to appreciate that the account of the payee need not be held at the same bank as that of the payor. If both accounts are at the same bank, then the payment transaction is a simple 'in house' transfer. More typically, however, the accounts are at different banks. When they are, then the banks of the payor and payee are connected through third-party banks; that is, an inter-bank network referred to as correspondents. So, payment transactions routinely are executed through correspondent banks, everyday across countries and around the world, often in large amounts.

A primary objective of a central bank is to ensure payment systems function smoothly, and systemic risk is minimized. Ideally, a payment system should be like well-functioning plumbing: users should not notice any backlogs or failures. This metaphor connotes that when problems arise, a financial institution can face severe difficulties, even collapse, and the knock-on effects to the real economy can be disastrous.

After all, when payment system risk materializes, payors cannot transfer funds to payees. In turn, those payees, which had been counting on receiving funds, cannot fulfil their obligations. There is a linked chain of payor-1/payee-1/payor-2/payee-2/payor-3/payee-3/payor-4 collapses. When the payment system fails, the link breaks, and downstream payors/payees collapse like dominoes. Imagine those payors/payees as businesses needing to fulfil wage and salary obligations to employees. When those employees go unpaid, they, in turn, cannot pay their bills. Thus, the manifestation of payment system risk easily can become a problem of systemic risk.

Central banks have different methods to ensure the safety and soundness, as well as the efficiency, of their payment systems. The degree of involvement by a central bank in the payment system has long been a subject for controversy, and remains so.[63] The payment system and regulations of one country may not work for the characteristics and economy of another. Central bankers analyse the design and operation of payment systems, comparing models from other countries to see what might help their financial system and economy. Put differently, strong payment systems are a hallmark of a developed economy, whereas weak systems are not only commonplace in developing and least developed countries, but also a cause of their underdevelopment. Weak systems, or their outright failure, result in inefficient use of financial resources, participant losses, and erosion of public confidence. Underlying transactions in the real economy either do not occur because of the inability to make payments for them, or occur inefficiently, as via barter. Simply put, there is an integral direct relationship between the health of a payment system and economic growth.

In the US, the Federal Reserve is involved in wholesale and retail payment systems. A wholesale payment system transfers large dollar values using electronic technologies, while a retail payment system is used for the majority of mostly low-value transaction payments. The quintessential wholesale payment system transaction is the electronic funds transfer (EFT), commonly called a 'wire transfer'. Paper-based cheques are illustrations of a retail payment system instrument. Individuals, companies, and public authorities are payees and payors in both systems. Note that commercial, but not investment, banks are involved in both systems.

Cheques

Aside from cash withdrawals, cheques are the traditional method consumers use to access their bank accounts to make or receive a payment. A cheque is a payment order, and a negotiable instrument, which instructs payment of money from a bank account of the payor (also called the 'drawer') to the account of the payee (also known as the 'beneficiary'). The cheque contains the monetary amount, date, names of the payor and payee, payer's signature, payer's account number, and name and routing number of the paying commercial bank (the payee, or drawer's, bank).

A cheque can clear and settle through direct presentment at the payor's bank. A correspondent commercial bank will settle the cheque by using accounts on its books, a clearing house, or other intermediaries. Many clearing houses offer processes and systems for imaging, transferring, archiving, and retrieving cheques.

In 1959, the routing and account number of the payee (drawer's) bank were printed at the bottom of the cheque in magnetic ink character recognition (MICR), hence the name 'MICR line'. The MICR line permitted high-speed readers to process a cheque quickly. This method revolutionized the previously tedious methods of Sort-A-Matic and Top Tab Key. The Sort-A-Matic method sorted cheques by hand, placing them in dividers numbered 00 to 99 based upon the first two digits. The cheques were removed, and different piles were sorted into dividers by the third and fourth digits. This process was repeated until the cheques were completely sorted. The Top Tap Key method punched holes in the top of each cheque representing the values of the digits. Metal keys were used to move the cheques by their punched holes until they were sorted.

As technology evolved, so too did cheques. In the mid-1990s, many countries enacted laws allowing for cheques truncation, where physical cheques were converted into an electronic format to transmit to a clearing house or the payor's bank. Cheque truncation reduced overall costs and cut delays in processing. Fraud prevention furthered the evolution of the cheque by incorporating micro-printing, security-screened designs, and multi-stained security paper to protect against alteration and duplication. With these anti-fraud measures, large banks were able to reduce cheque fraud cases by more than 80 per cent.[64]

Even with electronic cheque format and fraud protection, the volume of cheque payments peaked in the mid-1990s and continued to decrease thereafter. In the US, paper cheques collected by the 12 Federal Reserve Banks have declined 11–12 per cent per year.[65] Consumers have traded their cheque books for more convenient payment methods, such as credit, debit, and stored value cards. Moreover, to cut their own processing costs, commercial banks encourage their customers to use electronic payments over paper-based cheques, for instance, by not offering free chequing accounts, or not paying interest on those accounts.

Cash[66]

For their retail transactions, US consumers use cheques and debit cards to transfer the most amount of money. But they use cash more widely than any other payment settlement methodology. Central banks have a unique statutory obligation to issue new, and destroy old, currency, ensuring an amount of currency in circulation commensurate with economic needs.

How exactly does the Federal Reserve affect the money supply? This answer is the subject of a course in money and banking. Essentially, the Fed has three tools:

1 Open-market operations (OMOs)
  To increase the money supply, the Federal Reserve can purchase US Treasury Securities from commercial banks, and a portion of those funds the Fed pays them for those instruments may be loaned by them. Conversely, the Fed can decrease the money supply by selling Treasuries to commercial banks. The result is a decrease in liquidity, and thus in loanable funds, as the banks pay the Fed with funds.

204 *Practice of investment management*

2   Discount rate
    To encourage borrowing, the Federal Reserve can influence interest rates downwards. To discourage it, it may drive up interest rates. The key to rate is the discount rate, which is the interest rate the Fed charges to a commercial bank when that bank borrows from the 'discount window' at its regional Federal Reserve Bank.
3   Reserve requirements
    Commercial banks holding accounts with the Federal Reserve must keep a certain (small) percentage of their funds on deposit as required reserves. If the Fed increases the reserve requirement, then banks must increase the deposited amount to meet the higher level. The result is they have less loanable funds available. Conversely, if the Fed decreases the reserve requirement, then commercial banks are more liquid, and can increase lending. Note the Fed rarely uses this tool.

Overall, then, any central bank increases or decreases the money supply by increasing or decreasing funds in bank deposits; that is, by injecting or withdrawing liquidity from the banking system. Once money is deposited in a commercial bank, that bank is able to loan out a high percentage of that money. If the loaned money is also deposited in the same or another bank, then the bank receiving the deposit may loan out a high percentage of that money, and so forth. This process is a multiplier effect based on a fractional reserve system. In effect, the more money being deposited means the more money in circulation.

Wire transfers

A wire transfer is a transfer of funds across an electronic network. Figure 6.4 shows a simple wire transfer. The electronic network links multiple banks, which may be located in different jurisdictions. Money is transferred via a rolling system of debits and credits through bank accounts held by the linked banks. The accounts of payors are debited (such as funds are deducted), while the accounts of payees are credited (such as funds are added). A wire transfer allows a single individual or entity to pay funds to other individuals or entities in a rapid, secure manner. Electronic debits and credits roll across bank accounts around the world almost instantaneously, and the risk of interloper fraud (such as payments being intentionally misdirected by a thief) is low.

Not surprisingly, therefore, most commercial banks offer wire transfer services, for a fee, of course. Wire transfers account for the largest value movements of funds. For instance, every day in the US, trillions of dollars are transferred electronically; meaning the equivalent of the entire gross domestic product (GDP) of the country crosses the wires every few days.

The payment transaction begins with a sending bank, also called the 'sender' or 'originator's bank' (as the payor holding an account at that bank is the 'originator'), collecting the international bank account number (IBAN), a business identifier code (BIC), and the amount of the transfer. The sending bank transmits a message, through a secure system such as Fedwire, to the receiving bank, sometimes called the 'receiver'. The receiving bank obtains instructions for payment and settlement. Note the receiving bank may be an intermediary bank, if it is not the bank at which the payee – that is, the beneficiary – holds an account. If it is, then it is the beneficiary's bank.

Generally, it takes several hours at a minimum to transfer funds from the sender's account to the receiver's account, such as from the payment instruction from the originator to acceptance of a payment order by the beneficiary's bank on behalf of the beneficiary.

International financial players 205

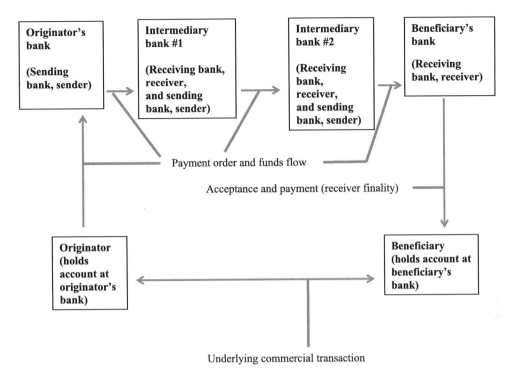

Figure 6.4 Basic wire transfer.

However, a central bank wire transfer system often has a real-time gross settlement (RTGS) system. An RTGS system transfers funds from one bank to another in 'real time' and on a 'gross' basis, which means there is nearly no waiting period, and transactions are settled as soon as they are processed. Lastly, the sending and receiving banks settle the transaction either through a reciprocal account with each other or through a correspondent bank.

All sending and receiving banks, such as, the originator's bank, beneficiary's bank, and any intermediary bank or banks, in the transfer process collect a fee. Typically, the sending bank collects a fee separate from the funds being transferred, while the receiving bank simply deducts fees from the money being transferred. Fees vary from bank to bank, but generally sending banks charge more for sending a wire than a receiving bank does for receiving one. International wire transfers are usually more expensive than domestic ones.

Article 4A of the Uniform Commercial Code (UCC.) is the statute (enacted into State laws) in the US governing wire transfers.[67] Federal Reserve Regulation J governs electronic funds transfers using the system of the Federal Reserve Banks; namely, Fedwire.[68] Three points about this body of law are vitally important.

First, under the Receiver Finality Rule, once a beneficiary bank accepts a payment order on behalf of the beneficiary, the funds are irrevocably those of the beneficiary. The originator cannot try to 'recall', 'retract', or 'unwind' the wire transfer, which it might do in the event of a dispute in the underlying contractual obligation (such as the sale of goods) between the originator (buyer) and beneficiary (seller). Acceptance by the beneficiary's bank results is a final, irrevocable credit to the account of the beneficiary.

The second point follows logically from the first. As with letter of credit, in a wire transfer, banks do not want to get involved in disputes over sales of goods or services between originators and beneficiaries. In letter of credit law, the independence principle essentially protects them from having to do so. So, too, is it with wire transfer law. Banks are under no obligation to check whether, for example, a beneficiary (seller) shipped non-conforming goods to an originator (buyer). Simply put, wire transfer law stresses the continuation of funds – keep the dollars moving, as it were. Hence, wire transfers are sometimes referred to as 'push' payment methodology, as funds are pushed out of one account into another via a rolling system of electronic debits and credits. In contrast, paper cheques are a 'pull' system, whereby a payee pulls money out of the account of the payor.

Third, in 1992 the United Nations Commission on International Trade Law (UNCITRAL) approved a Model Law on International Credit Transfers. This Model Law borrowed heavily from, and adapted, principles in Article 4A and Regulation J, including the Receiver Finality Rule. Countries around the world are free to look at the Model Law with a view to developing or enhancing their own wire transfer rules.

Formulation and implementation monetary policy

Monetary policies are the actions of a central bank, currency board, or other regulatory committee to control the supply of money. The main objective of monetary policy is price stability, though in some countries (including the US) the central bank is also responsible for setting monetary policy with a view to full employment (meaning an allowance for frictional and structural unemployment). In the US, the Federal Reserve Act of 1913 assigns the Federal Reserve the responsibility of setting monetary policy.[69] Through the Act, the Federal Reserve controls three tools of monetary policy: reserve requirements, discount rate, and OMOs.

Monetary policy is set by the Federal Open Market Committee (FOMC), which consists of all of the Board of Governors of the Federal Reserve System, plus the Presidents of five of the 12 Federal Reserve Banks. The President of the Federal Reserve Bank of New York is a permanent fixture among those five individuals, reflecting the unique importance of both the New York Fed and New York as international financial centres.

First, reserve requirements are the percentage of total deposits a bank must hold on site in cash or in deposits at the relevant Federal Reserve Bank. Raising a reserve requirement is contractionary, as commercial banks need to keep more funds on deposit with a Reserve Bank to meet them. Conversely, cutting the reserve requirement is expansionary, as they can hold less on deposit, and use the excess funds to lend to borrowers. Accordingly, reserve requirements allow central banks to implement actions and policies that affect financial market performance, money, credit creation, and economic conditions generally.[70] The existence of reserves also permits efficient financial markets to function and process end-of-day settlement of hundreds of billions (if not trillions) of dollars' worth of transactions.[71]

The Federal Reserve typically does not conduct monetary policy through reserve requirements. Altering them is a blunt-edged tool, possibly with unintended consequences. Among others, former Federal Reserve Bank of New York President E. Gerald Corrigan, in a classic 1982 article, entitled 'Are Banks Special?', notes monetary policy may not be dependent on the reserve requirements. He argues they are incompatible with a strong yet adaptable banking and financial system, and change will be needed in the future. While alternative schemes that depart from traditional bank reserve concepts exist, overwhelming evidence is lacking to demonstrate that an alternative system undoubtedly would work more efficiently.[72]

Second, the discount rate is the interest rate a Federal Reserve Bank charges a commercial bank or depository institution (DI) for a loan from the Bank. Commercial banks and DIs may seek short-term loans, approximately one to three weeks, at the Fed's lending facility, logically called the 'discount window'. The discount rate level influences the practices and reserves of an actual or prospective borrower. An increase in the discount rate has a direct, inverse effect on a bank or DI's money supply. If the discount rate is higher, then the bank or DI will refrain from transactions that may require emergency short-term loans from the Fed. That is, it will be hesitant to reduce its excess reserves, thus extending fewer loans. Conversely, a reduction by the Federal Reserve in the discount rate may stimulate banks and DIs to borrow and, in turn, lend profitably at a premium over that rate.

Lastly, the Federal Reserve purchases and sells securities to implement monetary policy, referred to as open market operations (OMOs). Those securities are US Treasury obligations.

OMOs are the primary tool by which the Federal Reserve conducts monetary policy, and all OMOs are done at the Open Market Desk of the New York Federal Reserve. OMO objectives historically serve the purpose of adjusting the supply of reserve balances to keep the federal funds rate near the FOMC target goal. The Fed Funds Rate is a very influential interest rate in the US, as it is the interest rate depository institutions lend funds maintained at the Federal Reserve to another depository institution overnight.[73]

The Federal Reserve has expanded its use of OMOs to create a Maturity Extension Program and Single-Tranche Term Repurchase Agreement. These programs have placed substantial downward pressure on long-term interest rates.[74] Since the 2008 global financial crisis, OMOs have helped support economic activity by making financial conditions more accommodating.[75] Obviously, purchases by the Federal Reserve of Treasury securities via OMOs evidence expansionary monetary policy, as banks receive loanable funds when they sell the Federal Reserve those securities. Conversely, purchases by the Federal Reserve of Treasuries are a form of contractionary monetary policy, reducing funds commercial banks have on hand to lend to borrowers.

Formulation and implementation of foreign exchange policy (FX)

FX policies are the measurement a country's central bank takes to support its national currency and ensure financial stability. Central bank FX activities include monitoring and analysing global financial market developments, managing currency reserves, and occasionally intervening in currency markets.

First, central banks actively monitor and analyse international financial markets to understand developments and identify possible problems. The factors they examine are wide-ranging, including financial market conditions, financial stability risks, monetary policy, economic expectations, and political issues. By studying prices, trading activity, long-term trends, and underlying motivations, central banks develop an accurate picture of the international financial landscape.

Second, a central bank holds currency reserves in a variety of foreign currencies, foreign government securities, and other foreign currency-denominated assets. Generally, it is the central bank that holds the reserves, although in some countries finance ministries or sovereign wealth funds (SWFs) may hold them.[76] The most common reserve currency is the US dollar, but most reserves also hold the European Union (EU) euro, the UK pound sterling, and the Japanese yen.

Third, financial policies include occasional direct or indirect interventions in an FX market. Most developed countries that practise sound fiscal policy seldom intervene in a currency market. A central bank only becomes involved if it believes it is essential to support or alter the price of the country's currency against another or other currencies.

To resist movement in the exchange rate of its currency, a central bank may buy or sell foreign exchange reserves to stabilize the currency exchange. A country can avoid depreciation (or appreciation) of its currency by buying (or selling) the domestic currency and accumulating (forfeiting) FX reserves. To push up the price of its currency, a central bank buys that currency, selling another or others out of its reserves. To drive down the price of its currency, it sells its own currency in return for (and thus accumulating in its reserves) another or other currencies.

These central bank actions are official FX interventions, and they are direct. Indirect intervention is more subtle: a central bank may let it be known through communications with banks that it prefers to keep a certain exchange rate. Alternatively, a central bank might operate not via its own traders on its FX desk, but through agents, such as it may place buy or sell orders at private banks. Note that a central bank also may use FX reserves to calm disorderly markets, or insure against liquidity losses and disruptions to capital market access. In both cases, the central bank is not targeting an exchange rate, but rather seeking to exert psychological influence on markets to stabilize them.

6.10 International organizations

Two main types of international organizations exist – international non-governmental organizations (INGOs) and intergovernmental organizations (IGOs). An INGO is a private organization that is international in scope. Its goal is to relieve suffering, promote the interests of the poor, protect the environment, provide basic social services, or undertake community development. Generally, an INGO focuses on either projects and operations or influencing governmental policy within countries. However, if an INGO is large enough, then often it integrates components of both, such as the World Bank.

In contrast, an IGO is established by a treaty and comprises of mostly sovereign states or other IGOs. IGOs have a wide variety of goals and a range of scopes. Some, such as the United Nations (UN), are general; others, such as the Association of Southeast Asian Nations (ASEAN), are regional in focus, while others are still limited in subject matter jurisdiction, like the International Monetary Fund (IMF), an economic organization.

IMF

The IMF was founded in 1944 at the Bretton Woods Conference, in New Hampshire, US. The IMF was created to help reconstruct international payment systems after the Second World War (1939–45), working to improve the economies of the then 29 founding countries. By 2014, that number had expanded to 188 member countries.[77]

Originally, the IMF was designed to implement a par value system that, in turn, was supposed to stabilize world currency values against one another. A currency was fixed in its price in comparison to other countries' currencies, with little fluctuation. However, in the 1970s the par value system began to crumble, and the IMF *Charter* was amended in 1978 to eliminate the par value system.

Consequently, the IMF role had to evolve if it was to justify its continued existence. Following the Latin American Debt Crisis of 1982, the IMF increased its scope to lend money to countries with balance of payment (BOP) problems. Currently, the IMF focus is on promoting 'international economic cooperation, international trade, employment, and exchange rate stability'.[78]

To ensure stability in the international system, the IMF has three primary functions: to monitor the global economy and member countries' economies, to lend money to countries with BOP problems, and to provide technical assistance to members. Since the 1980s, IMF loans have become increasingly conditional and, therefore, controversial, requiring countries to agree to economic and financial policies to receive funding. Three of the most common conditions are on money supply, government borrowing, and financial regulation. However, they may also contain conditions on providing social safety nets and environmental protection. Notably, the importance of IMF lending is vastly diminished in relation to raising funds through private capital markets: the entire loan portfolio and lending capacity of the IMF is a fraction of what is available through the other players mentioned in this chapter.

To become a member of the IMF, a country must first agree to pursue policies that promote economic growth and reasonable price stability, avoid manipulating exchange rates for an unfair competitive advantage, and provide the IMF with information about its economy. Note that currency manipulation has been a point of contention in international trade negotiations, particularly between the US and China, with the Americans alleging the Chinese systematically undervalued the yuan against the dollar to boost Chinese exports to the US, and discourage its imports into China.

With regard to each member, the IMF is mandated to keep surveillance of that member in relation to the international monetary and financial system, the currency unions (if any) in which the member participates, along with economic developments in the region of the member. The IMF also gives assessments of the economic and financial developments within each member, and makes appropriate recommendations.

Countries may receive an assortment of technical assistance and training from the IMF. The goal is to improve economic policy design and implementation. About 80 per cent of the IMF's technical assistance is to low- and lower-middle-income countries that have high amounts of debt and need poverty-reducing programmes for their citizens.[79] The technical assistance takes the form of implementing monetary and financial policies, fiscal policy and management, compilation, management, dissemination, and improvement of statistical data, and advising on economic and financial legislation.[80]

The IMF receives its source of lending through member contributions. At the time a member joins the IMF, the countries economic and financial system is assessed, and is assigned a quota. The 'quota' determines the contribution of capital the country must provide to the IMF, the corresponding voting power, and the borrowing limits from the IMF. The IMF is based upon a weighted voting system with its leadership resting in its Board of Governors. The Board is made up of all member countries. Additionally, there is an Executive Board made up of 24 members appointed by those member countries with the largest quotas: the US, Japan, Germany, France, and the UK. Voting is conducted based upon the basic votes granted to all members, and additional votes determined by the quota.

World Bank

The World Bank was also founded as a result of the international ratification of the Bretton Woods Agreement in 1944. Its purpose was to facilitate post-Second World War reconstruction and development, including in Europe. The Bank is notoriously known as the largest development bank in the world, though it provides only around US$30 billion in loans and assistance – a pittance in relation to private sector financial flows. The World Bank began as a single institution, the International Bank for Reconstruction and Development (IBRD), but has since expanded to five unified international organizations with the goal of reducing poverty through 'inclusive and sustainable globalization'.[81]

The World Bank generally is known for the IBRD and the International Development Association (IDA). However, the World Bank Group consists of three other entities: the International Finance Corporation (IFC), the Multilateral Investment Guarantee Agency (MIGA), and the International Centre for Settlement of Investment Disputes (ICSID). Participation within these different entities varies, though a majority of the 188 World Bank Group members participate in all five World Bank Group organizations (127 members). All 188 members participate in the IBRD.[82]

The IBRD issued its first loan in 1947 to France for US$250 million. Since its founding, the IBRD has sought to reduce poverty by providing loans, as well as guarantees, risk management services, and analytical and advisory services to middle-income and creditworthy low-income countries. The IBRD is financed by capital raised from issuing bonds to private sector investors. The capital raised is then lent through hard loans to developing countries for projects. When interest and principal are paid back, the IBRD uses the money to pay the bondholders.

Similarly, the IDA makes grants and loans to member countries; however, it provides interest-free loans, called 'credits', to the poorest countries. The IDA provides debt relief through the Heavily Indebted Poor Countries (HIPC) Initiative and the Multilateral Debt Relief Initiative (MDRI). Since its founding in 1960, the IDA has supported 108 countries and created positive change for 2.5 billion people.[83] Together, the IDA and IBRD complement each other by providing an assortment of services to assist each country's specific needs.

In contrast, the IFC concentrates on sustainable growth through a developing country's private sector. The IFC provides a developing country's private sector with investment services and products including loans, equity, trade finance, structured finance, and syndications to clients in over 100 countries. Additionally, it offers advice, problem solving, and training in overcoming obstacles to companies and other organizations.

The World Bank Group's MIGA operates to promote FDI in developing countries. It attracts investors and private insurers into otherwise overlooked developing countries. MIGA provides political risk insurance guarantees to investors and lenders, guaranteeing their investments against non-commercial risks. Since MIGA was founded in 1988, it has issued over US$24 billion in political risk insurance for projects all over the world.[84]

Lastly, ICSID removes major obstacles to the free international flow of private investment, by providing facilities for conciliation and arbitration of international investment disputes. ICSID is well known in the international community with its 140 members, frequent use, and repeated references to its arbitration facilities in investment treaties and laws.

Like the IMF, the World Bank has a weighted voting system consisting of a Board of Governors and a Board of Executive Directors. The Board of Governors is the principal governing body, consisting of all member countries. The Board of Executive Directors is a 12-member body elected by all members. Weighted voting is based upon the share the member was allowed to subscribe to upon gaining membership, and the amount of money contributed.

Notes

1 "Definition of Global Financial System," *Financial Times Lexicon*, accessed 27 March 2014, http://lexicon.ft.com/Term?term=global-financial-system.
2 "The Global Finance Regime," *Council on Foreign Relations*, 25 June 2013, accessed 10 June 2014, http://www.cfr.org/financial-regulation/global-finance-regime/p20177.
3 Mike Konczal, "What Are You Worth to Your Bank?" *The Washington Post*, 6 April 2010, accessed 20 March 2013, http://voices.washingtonpost.com/ezra-klein/2010/04/what_are_you_worth_to_your_ban.html.
4 Ibid.
5 "Glass–Steagall Act (1933)," *The New York Times*, accessed 20 March 2013, http://topics.nytimes.com/top/reference/timestopics/subjects/g/glass_steagall_act_1933/index.html.
6 Reem Heakal, "What Was the Glass–Steagall Act?" *Investopedia*, 26 February 2009, accessed 20 March 2013, http://www.investopedia.com/articles/03/071603.asp.
7 Public Law Number 91-607, 84 Stat. 1766, codified at 12 U.S.C. Sections 1841-1850.
8 Public Law Number 63-43, 38 Stat. 251, codified at 12 U.S.C. Section 226.
9 "Glass-Steagall Legislation," *Wikipedia*, accessed 20 March 2013, https://en.wikipedia.org/wiki/Glass%E2%80%93Steagall_Legislation.
10 Public Law Number 89-485, 80 Stat. 136, codified at 12 U.S.C. Section 1841.
11 "The Bank Holding Company Act of 1956," *Duke Law Journal* 7.1 (Durham, NC: Duke Law, 1956): 1–24, accessed 21 March 2013, http://scholarship.law.duke.edu/cgi/viewcontent.cgi?article=1637&context=dlj.
12 Reem Heakal, "What Was the Glass–Steagall Act?" *Investopedia*, 26 February 2009, accessed 20 March 2013, http://www.investopedia.com/articles/03/071603.asp.
13 This erosion occurred partly through a series of successful applications made by commercial banks to the Federal Reserve, which allowed the banks to expand the activities of their Section 20 subsidiaries.
14 "The Long Demise of Glass–Steagall," *Frontline*, 8 May 2003, accessed 21 March 2013, http://www.pbs.org/wgbh/pages/frontline/shows/wallstreet/weill/demise.html.
15 For more detailed explanations of this merger and the Federal Reserve conditions, *see* Michael P. Malloy, *International Banking*, 3rd ed. (Durham, NC: Carolina Academic Press, 2013); Hal S. Scott, *International Finance: Law and Regulation*, 3rd ed. (London, UK: Sweet & Maxwell, 2012).
16 Public Law Number 106-102, 113 Stat. 1445, codified at 15 U.S.C. Section 6801.
17 "The Long Demise of Glass–Steagall," *Frontline*, 8 May 2003, accessed 21 March 2013, http://www.pbs.org/wgbh/pages/frontline/shows/wallstreet/weill/demise.html.
18 "Glass–Steagall and the Volcker Rule," *American Enterprise Institute*, 10 December 2012, accessed 22 March 2013, https://www.aei.org/publication/glass-steagall-and-the-volcker-rule/.
19 Bartlett Naylor, "Here's the Real Deal on the Volcker Rule," *Huffington Post*, 18 December 2012, accessed 21 March 2013, http://www.huffingtonpost.com/bartlett-naylor/volcker-rule_b_2317541.html.
20 Christine Harper, "Breaking up Banks Won't Make Them Safer, Ex-Senator Says," *Bloomberg Business*, 26 July 2012, accessed 22 March 2013, http://www.bloomberg.com/news/articles/2012-07-26/breaking-up-banks-won-t-make-them-safer-ex-senator-says.
21 This question implicates the corporate structure of a financial institution, namely, whether it is held by a bank holding company under the 1956 *Bank Holding Company Act* and, therefore, ultimately subject to Federal Reserve supervision.
22 "Volcker Rule," *Investopedia*, accessed 22 March 2013, http://www.investopedia.com/terms/v/volcker-rule.asp.
23 John Light, "What's Going on with the Volcker Rule," *Moyers & Company*, 7 December 2012, 22 March 2013, http://billmoyers.com/2012/12/07/whats-going-on-with-the-volcker-rule/.

24 Gregory S. Davis, "Has Anyone Seen Glass or Steagall?" *Investopedia*, 18 September 2008, accessed 22 March 2013.
25 "Universal Banking Together, Forever?" *The Economist*, 18 August 2012, accessed 22 March 2013; Georg Rich and Christian Walter, "The Future Of Universal Banking," *CATO Journal* 13, No. 2, (Fall 1993): 310–11, accessed 11 June 2013, http://object.cato.org/sites/cato.org/files/serials/files/cato-journal/1993/11/cj13n2-8.pdf.
26 Norman T. L. Chan, "Hong Kong's Perspective," Keynote address, Asian Banker Summit, Hong Kong, 7 April 2011.
27 "Proposal for Resolution of Mini-Bond Issue," *Hong Kong Democratic Foundation*, November 2008, accessed 24 March 2013, http://www.hkdf.org/pr.asp?func=show&pr=178.
28 "Bankruptcy of Lehman Brothers," *Wikipedia*, accessed 30 March 2013, https://en.wikipedia.org/wiki/Bankruptcy_of_Lehman_Brothers.
29 George Pennacchi, "Narrow Banking," *Annual Review of Financial Economics* Vol. 4 (2012), accessed 3 April 2013, https://business.illinois.edu/gpennacc/GPNarrowBankARFE.pdf.
30 "Narrow Banking," *Wikipedia*, accessed 20 March 2013, https://en.wikipedia.org/wiki/Narrow_banking.
31 15 U.S.C. Section 77a.
32 15 U.S.C. Section 78 *et seq.*
33 "Investment Banking," *Investopedia*, accessed 3 April 2013, http://www.investopedia.com/terms/i/investment-banking.asp.
34 "Complete Guide to Corporate Finance: Introduction – Types of Financial Institutions and Their Roles," *Investopedia*, accessed 4 April 2013, http://www.investopedia.com/walkthrough/corporate-finance/1/financial-institutions.aspx.
35 "Underwriter," *Investing Answers*, accessed 4 April 2013, http://www.investinganswers.com/financial-dictionary/insurance/underwriter-873.
36 15 U.S.C. Section 77a.
37 Thomas J. Morgan, "Raising Capital – What You Don't Know Could Hurt You," *The National Law Review*, 6 March 2013, accessed 5 April 2013, http://www.natlawreview.com/article/raising-capital-what-you-don-t-know-could-hurt-you.
38 "Mergers and Acquisitions," *Wikipedia*, accessed 15 April 2013, https://en.wikipedia.org/wiki/Mergers_and_acquisitions.
39 "What Makes an M&A Deal Work?" *Investopedia*, 17 June 2008, accessed 20 April 2013, http://www.investopedia.com/articles/financial-theory/08/ma-deal.asp.
40 "Investment Banking Scorecard," *The Wall Street Journal*, accessed 20 April 2013, http://graphics.wsj.com/investment-banking-scorecard/.
41 Chris Giarraputo, "World's Best Investment Banks 2013," *Global Finance*, 22 February 2013, accessed 20 April 2013, https://www.gfmag.com/awards-rankings/best-banks-and-financial-rankings/worlds-best-investment-banks-2013.
42 Michael Shari, "Investment Banking in Asia," *Global Finance*, 6 February 2012, accessed 21 April 2013, https://www.gfmag.com/magazine/february-2012/investment-banking-in-asia.
43 "World's Best Investment Banks 2012," *Global Finance*, 17 February 2012, accessed 20 April 2013, https://www.gfmag.com/awards-rankings/best-banks-and-financial-rankings/worlds-best-investment-banks-2012.
44 Philip Alexander, "Top 1000 World Banks 2011," *The Banker*, 30 June 2011, accessed 21 April 2013, http://www.thebanker.com/Top-1000-World-Banks/Top-1000-World-Banks-2011.
45 "Bank Profits Head East," *The Economist*, 3 July 2012, accessed 21 April 2013, http://www.economist.com/blogs/graphicdetail/2012/07/daily-chart-0.
46 "Hong Kong Stock Exchange," *Wikipedia*, accessed 17 April 2013, https://en.wikipedia.org/wiki/Hong_Kong_Stock_Exchange.
47 This discussion draws from the following sources: Geoffrey Hirt and Stanley Block, *Fundamentals of Investment Management* (New York: McGraw-Hill/Irwin, 2003), 34–9; Zvi Bodie, Alex Kane, and Alan Marcus, *Essentials of Investments*, 5th ed. (New York: McGraw-Hill/Irwin, 2003), 80–6.
48 Zvi Bodie, Alex Kane, and Alan Marcus, *Essentials of Investments*, 5th ed. (New York: McGraw-Hill/Irwin, 2003), 80.

49 Investopedia, "Differences Between Stockbrokers, Investment Advisors, and Financial Planners," *Forbes*, 20 March 2013, accessed 20 April 2013, http://www.forbes.com/sites/investopedia/2013/03/20/differences-between-stockbrokers-investment-advisors-and-financial-planners/.
50 This discussion draws from the following sources: Zvi Bodie, Alex Kane, and Alan Marcus, *Essentials of Investments*, 5th ed. (New York: McGraw-Hill/Irwin, 2003), 361–66; Geoffrey Hirt and Stanley Block, *Fundamentals of Investment Management* (New York: McGraw-Hill/Irwin, 2003), 565–83.
51 "Portfolio (Finance)," *Wikipedia*, accessed 23 May 2013, https://en.wikipedia.org/wiki/Portfolio_(finance).
52 Under US States Securities Law, there is an important and technical distinction between an 'investment manager' and an 'investment company'. The pertinent laws are the 1940 *Investment Company Act* and 1940 *Investment Advisors Act*.
53 "The World's Largest Asset Managers," *Pensions & Investment and Watson Wyatt* (2006), PDF file.
54 This discussion draws on the following sources: Michael P. Malloy, *International Banking*, 3rd ed. (Durham, NC: Carolina Academic Press, 2013); Hal S. Scott, *International Finance: Law and Regulation*, 3rd ed. (London, UK: Sweet & Maxwell, 2012).
55 Stephen D Simpson, "The Banking System: Federal Reserve System," *Investopedia*, accessed 14 April 2013, http://www.investopedia.com/university/banking-system/banking-system10.asp.
56 12 U.S.C. Section 263.
57 Stephen D. Simpson, "The Banking System: Commercial Banking – How Banks Are Regulated," *Investopedia*, accessed 14 April 2013, http://www.investopedia.com/university/banking-system/banking-system6.asp.
58 12 U.S.C. Section 36.
59 Public Law Number 73-66, 48 Stat. 162, codified at 12 U.S.C. Section 227.
60 12 U.S.C. Section 1813.
61 12 U.S.C. Section 36.
62 12 U.S.C. Section 36.
63 "Payment Systems: Central Bank Roles Vary, but Goals Are the Same," *US General Accounting Office: Report number GAO-02-303*, 25 February 2002, accessed 26 March 2014, http://www.gao.gov/assets/240/233724.pdf.
64 "Frequently Asked Questions About Checks and the Check Payments System," *Check Payment Systems Association*, accessed 12 June 2013, http://www.cpsa-checks.org/i4a/pages/index.cfm?pageid=1.
65 Barbara S. Pacheco, "The U.S. Retail Payments System in Transition: Federal Reserve Iniatives," *Federal Reserve Bank of Kansas City*, August 2006, accessed 11 June 2013, https://www.kansascityfed.org/publicat/psr/Briefings/PSR-BriefingAug06.pdf.
66 This discussion draws on the following source: "Monetary Policy," *Federal Reserve Bank of Richmond*, accessed 27 March 2014, https://www.richmondfed.org/faqs/monetary_policy.
67 U.C.C. Law § 4a (1997).
68 12 C.F.R. Section 210.
69 Federal Reserve Act of 1913.
70 E. Gerald Corrigan, "Are Banks Special?" *Federal Reserve Bank of Minneapolis: Annual Report Summary*, 1 January 1983, accessed 27 March 2014, https://www.minneapolisfed.org/publications/annual-reports/are-banks-special.
71 Ibid.
72 Ibid.
73 "Federal Funds Rate," *Investopedia*, accessed 27 August 2013, http://www.investopedia.com/terms/f/federalfundsrate.asp.
74 "Open Market Operations," *Board of Governors of the Federal Reserve System*, 6 February 2013, accessed 27 March 2014, http://www.federalreserve.gov/monetarypolicy/openmarket.htm.
75 "Credit and Liquidity Programs and the Balance Sheet," *Board of Governors of the Federal Reserve System*, 7 January 2013, accessed 27 March 2014, http://www.federalreserve.gov/monetarypolicy/bst.htm.

76 Linda Goldberg, Cindy E. Hull, and Sarah Stein. "Do Industrialized Countries Hold the Right Foreign Exchange Reserves?" *Current Issues in Economics and Finance* 19, 1 (2013), accessed 11 June 2013, http://www.newyorkfed.org/research/current_issues/ci19-1.pdf.
77 "List of Members," *International Monetary Fund*, 13 June 2012, accessed 27 March 2014, https://www.imf.org/external/np/sec/memdir/memdate.htm.
78 "International Monetary Fund," *Wikipedia*, accessed 5 June 2013, https://en.wikipedia.org/wiki/International_Monetary_Fund.
79 "Technical Assistance," *International Monetary Fund*, accessed 7 June 2013, http://www.imf.org/external/about/techasst.htm.
80 Ibid.
81 "About the IMF," *International Monetary Fund*, accessed 7 June 2013, http://www.imf.org/external/about.htm.
82 "World Bank," *Wikipedia*, accessed 8 June 2013, https://en.wikipedia.org/wiki/World_Bank.
83 "What is IDA?" *The World Bank*, accessed 8 June 2013, http://www.worldbank.org/ida/what-is-ida.html.
84 "Who We Are: Overview," *Multilateral Investment Guarantee Agency*, accessed 8 June 2013, https://www.miga.org/who-we-are.

References

Bodie, Zvi, Alex Kane, and Alan Marcus, *Essentials of Investments*, 5th ed. (New York: McGraw-Hill/Irwin, 2003).

Hirt, Geoffrey and Stanley Block, *Fundamentals of Investment Management* (New York: McGraw-Hill/Irwin, 2003).

7 Security analysis

7.1 Introduction

This chapter describes the process of analysing a company's stock. The ultimate aim of security analysis is to discover if an investor should buy, sell, or hold the stock.

First, the investor must evaluate and scrutinize the financial statements of the company. Financial statements consist of the balance sheet, income statement, cash flow statement, and statement of shareholders' equity. Familiarity with accounting and accounting terms is a useful skill in financial statement analysis. The equity analyst must be able to read and analyse a financial statement with a high measure of facility because the character of a company is captured in the numbers in these statements. The chapter teaches the student how to do ratio analysis of financial statements and describes the most relevant ratios used for analysing a stock.

Second, the investor needs to do an analysis of a stock on three levels. She must do careful analysis and research on; the company, the industry in which it operates, and economy in which it operates. This chapter guides the student to do equity research on these three levels.

7.2 Financial statements

There are four main financial statements:

1. Balance sheets
2. Income statements
3. Cash flow statements
4. Statements of shareholders' equity.[1]

Balance sheets show the financial standing, in terms of assets and liabilities, of a company at a particular point in time. Income statements show the profit or loss and expenditures of a company over a range of time, usually a quarter or a year. Cash flow statements show the amount of money flowing in and out of a company over a period of time. Lastly, the statement of shareholders' equity shows the changes in the interests of the company's shareholders over time.

Financial statements have detailed information about the financial position and performance of a company used to calculate financial ratios. The statements are vital for stock analysis as a means to find out the health of a company in terms of its asset/liability position, its profitability, and its cash flows.

Balance sheet

The balance sheet is a snapshot of the company's financial position at a point of time, usually the end of the fiscal year or the end of a quarter. It shows the value of assets, liabilities, and shareholders' equity. A company owns assets typically consisting of physical property such as; factories, machinery, inventory, and equipment. Assets also include non-physical property, such as trademarks and patents. Other assets are cash and investments of the company.

Liabilities are the funds owed by the company to other entities. These owed funds may be different obligations such as loans from banks, money owed to suppliers, compensation owed to employees, other costs, and taxes. A company has current liabilities (accounts payable or short-term borrowings), and long-term liabilities (fixed debt), and owners' equity (preferred stock, common stock, and retained earnings).[2]

Shareholders' equity is also known as capital. It is the measure of how much the owners of the company, that is, the shareholders, have in the company. After all assets are sold and liabilities paid off, the company is left with capital that belongs to the shareholders.

The formula that summarizes the balance sheet is given as:

$$Assets = Liabilities + Shareholders'\ Equity$$

Therefore, a company's assets must equal the total of liabilities plus shareholders' equity.

A balance sheet lists the assets on the left side and the liabilities and shareholders' equity on the right side. Current assets are property, such as inventory, likely to be sold within the year. Non-current assets are things a company uses to produce its goods and services and are unlikely to be sold within a year. They include fixed assets such as plant and machinery.

Income statements

The income statement shows the profitability of a company. It lists the revenues and the expenditures of the company over a period of time (a quarter or a year). In contrast to a balance sheet that is a picture of the financial position at a fixed point in time, the income statement has the flow of sales, expenses, and earnings during a range of time. The bottom line of the income statement usually shows the company's net earnings or losses.

Most income statements include a calculation of earnings per share or EPS. This calculation shows how much money shareholders earn for each share of stock they own. EPS is the total of net income divided by the number of outstanding shares of the company.

Statement of cash flows

A cash flow statement accounts for a company's inflow and outflow of cash. While the balance sheet is a snapshot of what the company owns or owes and the income statement shows the profitability, the cash flow indicates how much cash a company generates. The latter shows changes over time rather than absolute dollar amounts at a point in time.

The bottom line of a cash flow statement is the net increase or decrease in cash for the period. Generally cash flow statements are in three main parts:

1 Cash flows from operating activities
2 Cash flows from investing activities
3 Cash flows from financing activities.

The sum of the cash flow from these three activities is the net change in the cash position of the company. This number should equal the difference in the cash balance between the ending and the beginning of the balance sheet.

Cash flow from operating activities

This section of the cash flow statement analyses cash flow from net income or losses. Net income from the income statement is adjusted for any non-cash items such as; adding back depreciation expenses and adjusted also for any cash used by other operating assets and liabilities (working capital items).

Cash flow from operating activities = Net income + Non-cash revenue and Expenses + changes in net working Capital items

Cash flow from investing activities

Cash flow from all investing activities generally includes purchases or sales of long-term assets, such as property, plant, equipment, and investment securities. If a company buys a robot for its car manufacturing plant, the cash flow statement reflects this activity as a cash outflow from investing activities because it used cash. If the company sells its equity in a subsidiary, such as from its investment portfolio, the money from the sales is a cash inflow from investing activities. The cash flow from investing activities is the change in gross plant, and equipment plus the change in the investment account. The changes are positive if cash flows in and negative if cash flows out. The dollar changes in these accounts are calculated using the two most recent balance sheets. In general, most companies have negative cash flows from investments due to substantial capital expenditures.

Cash flow from financing activities

This section of the cash flow statement shows cash flow from all financing activities; typically cash from stock and bonds sales or borrowings from banks. Repaying a bank loan uses cash and shows up as a cash outflow. Dividend payments to shareholders are a financing cash outflow.

Summing up the totals from operating, investing, and financing activities is the net increase or decrease in the company's cash. An analyst can use several cash flow measures to determine the health of a company.

Cash flow from operations includes traditional cash flow (net income plus depreciation expense and deferred taxes), but adjusted for changes in current assets and liabilities that use or provide cash. For example, an increase in accounts receivables means cash is supporting this increase, or the company did not collect all the sales reported. The changes in current assets and liabilities add or subtract from the cash flow estimated from the traditional measure of cash flow.

Free cash flow considers three additional items because they are essential to the operations of a company:

1 Capital expenditures
2 The disposition of property and equipment
3 Dividends.

These three items are subtracted from cash flow from operations:

Free cash flow = cash flow from operations − capital expenditures − disposition of property and equipment − dividends

Free cash flow represents the cash a company is able to generate after paying money to maintain or expand its asset base. Free cash flow is important because a company requires cash to take advantage of opportunities that enhance shareholder value such as developing new products and making acquisitions.

7.3 Financial ratios

The numbers given in financial statements are useful to obtain a general view of the health of the company. From these statements we glean knowledge about the debt, assets, liabilities, shareholders' equity, and cash flow of the company. To sharpen our picture of the company's financial position we use financial ratio analysis.

Financial ratios are relative comparisons between individual items in financial statements. Investors calculate a plethora of ratios from information on financial statements and then use them to evaluate a company. Again, by themselves, these ratios have limited value because they do not tell us how the company stands over time, versus its peers, its competitors, the general industry in which it is located, and the economy in which it operates. We need to compare any ratio with other similar companies, the median, or average of the industry, and the median or average of the market in general. Therefore, only relative financial ratios are relevant and of use in security analysis.

For example, a common ratio is the P/E ratio or the price earnings ratio, derived by dividing the price of a company's stock by the earnings per share of the same company. Using the P/E ratio and comparing it in a variety of ways, we are able to make some inferences about the company. First, we note the P/E ratio uses two numbers, the price comes from the market and the earnings is from the income statement. The P/E ratio of, say, Cheung Kong Holdings is 12 times. What inferences can we draw from this number? Not much by itself but more in relation to other entities.

Second, we must choose the entities to which we compare the P/E ratio of Cheung Kong Holdings. The company is a Hong Kong listed company and is a conglomerate. It has holdings in telecommunications, property, retail, and utilities. It is in the top 10 largest market capitalization stocks in the Hong Kong Stock Exchange. There are four relative comparisons to make to better evaluate Cheng Kong as an investment. The comparisons are with:

1. The broad Hong Kong market
2. The conglomerates industry
3. Cheung Kong's major competitors within the industry
4. Cheung Kong's own performance over the past years.

Most relevant financial ratios

To help in thinking about financial ratios it is best to categorize them into groups. In general, the categories are liquidity ratios, operating performance ratios, leverage ratios, and growth ratios. The following is a breakdown of the most common ratios under each of the categories.

Liquidity ratios

This category of ratios assesses the ability of the company to meet future short-term financial obligations. The ratios compare calls on the company in the form of accounts payable or notes payable to the cash or current assets of the company.

Current ratio

The ratio measures the relationship between current assets to current liabilities.

$$\text{Current ratio} = \frac{\text{Current assets}}{\text{Current liabilities}}$$

Quick ratio

This ratio gives a better picture of the ability of the company to meet current obligations with the most liquid assets. Inventories are not included because they may be difficult to sell quickly.

$$\text{Quick ratio} = \frac{\text{Cash} + \text{Marketable securities} + \text{Receivables}}{\text{Current liabilities}}$$

Cash ratio

This measures the most liquid of assets against the current liabilities to gauge if a company can meet its current liabilities with, basically, cash on hand.

$$\text{Cash ratio} = \frac{\text{Cash and marketable securities}}{\text{Current liabilities}}$$

Receivables turnover

This ratio measures the liquidity of the accounts receivable by assessing how often the company's receivables turnover. This gives a sense of the average collection period. The faster the accounts are paid, the sooner the company can cover current liabilities.

$$\text{Receivables turnover} = \frac{\text{Net annual sales}}{\text{Average receivables}}$$

Inventory turnover

This ratio gives an idea of how quickly inventories turnover. From the ratio, we also get an implied processing time.

$$\text{Inventory turnover} = \frac{\text{Cost of goods sold}}{\text{Average Inventory}}$$

Operating performance ratios

Performance ratios indicate the operating efficiency and operating profitability of a company. Operating efficiency is a measure of how well a company uses its assets and capital by evaluating how much sales are generated by assets and by capital. Operating profitability ratios are a means of assessing the profits as a percentage of sales, assets, and capital employed.

Gross profit margin

This ratio is a comparison of gross profit (net sales minus the cost of goods sold) to net sales.

$$\text{Gross profit margin} = \frac{\text{Gross profit}}{\text{Net sales}}$$

Operating profit margin

Operating profit is gross profit minus sales, general and administrative (SGA) expenses.

$$\text{Operating profit margin} = \frac{\text{Operating profit}}{\text{Net sales}}$$

Net profit margin

This ratio compares net income to sales. Net income is earnings after taxes but before dividends on preferred and common stock.

$$\text{Net profit margin} = \frac{\text{Net income}}{\text{Net sales}}$$

Return on total capital

This ratio compares the earnings to all the capital of the company – debt, preferred stock, and common stock. Earnings are the net income from continuing operations before dividends but after interest paid on debt. This measure gives a sense of how well the company used its capital employed to obtain earnings.

$$\text{Return on total capital} = \frac{\text{Net income} + \text{Interest expense}}{\text{Average total capital}}$$

Return on total equity

This ratio, commonly used in acronym form ROE, is well known and frequently used. It is a useful way of gauging how efficiently the company uses its equity to get earnings. All equity including preferred stock is considered.

$$\text{Return of total equity} = \frac{\text{Net income}}{\text{Average total equity}}$$

Leverage ratios

When a company takes on debt, in general, it increases its risk levels. The measures of debt or leverage in a company help assess the financial risks the company has taken in order to increase earnings.

Debt/equity ratio

The proportion of debt indicates the firm's capital compared to other sources of capital such as stock and retained earnings. A higher proportion of debt increases the volatility of earning and the probability the company will not be able to make interest payments. A higher debt ratio increases the financial risk of a company but it also increases the earnings of a company. The debt used in calculating this ratio includes all long-term fixed obligations, including subordinated convertible bonds. The equity is the book value of equity and includes preferred stock, common stock, and retained earnings.

$$\text{Debt/equity ratio} = \frac{\text{Total long-term debt}}{\text{Total equity}}$$

Long-term debt to total equity ratio

This ratio indicates the proportion of long-term capital derived from long-term debt. Long-term capital includes all long-term debt, preferred stock, and total equity.

$$\text{LT debt to LT capital ratio} = \frac{\text{Total long-term debt}}{\text{Total long-term debt}}$$

Interest coverage

This ratio relates the flow of earnings available to meet required interest and lease payments. A higher ratio indicates lower financial risk.

$$\text{Interest coverage ration} = \frac{\text{Income before interest and taxes (EBIT)}}{\text{Debt interest charges}}$$

Cash flow coverage ratio

Cash flow coverage of fixed financial costs =

$$\frac{\text{Traditional cash flow} + \text{Interest expense} + \frac{1}{3}\text{Lease payments}}{\text{Interest expense} + \frac{1}{3}\text{Lease payments}}$$

Comparative ratio analysis

Financial ratios by themselves tell us little. Their value is enhanced when used in comparison with ratios of companies in the same industry, in the same market, and in different countries. We compare any particular ratio against the median or average of the value of the same ratio in the three segments. If the ratio of the company is better than the industry or market median, then it warrants further investigation. Better can mean the ratio may be higher or lower than industry median, depending on the ratio in question. For example, free cash flow per share is an indicator of how much cash a company has and how much cash it burns. If the industry median is say, HK$1.00 but the company has a free cash flow per share of US$1.50, the stock investor should take a closer look at the company. It also is useful to compare the ratio across a period of time to discover the trend. For instance, we can see that a company is becoming more financially risky when the interest coverage ratio increases over a five-year period. In contrast, we note that operating margins are increasing over time, indicating the company is becoming more operationally efficient. In this particular case, the analyst would then investigate further. If the debt/equity ratio of the company is low compared to the industry median, then the company seems less financially risky. The analyst would then ask why there is less debt and look at other ratios to get a more complete picture of the company.

Analysis of financial statements gives the stock analyst a picture in her mind of the company's financial operations and its financial structure. The use of financial statements is a first pass at analysing a company. If the company seems viable and not overwhelmed by seemingly intractable financial problems, then the analyst can move on to carry out a further and more in-depth investigation into the company to determine if the company's securities, whether equity or bonds, are worthwhile investments. If, at first glance, the financials of a company are so attractive, the analyst will be moved to get finer details as soon as possible.

Financial ratios are useful but have their limitations. The statements are, of course, backward-looking and report on the assets, liabilities, and equity of a past date. The profits, revenues, and cash flows are from a past range of time. However, this 'stale' information is nevertheless still useful because it helps the analyst to assess future developments on the company. The analyst must draw a more complete picture of the company by finding out more about the quality of the company's management team; its business strategy, the industry environment, and other macro- and micro-economic factors.

Combining financial statement analysis with other data of this sort, the analyst then arrives at a decision on whether to invest in the company.

Financial ratios are, therefore, invaluable for stock valuation models. Analysts spend a large amount of time developing these models based upon present value of cash flows or relative valuation for a stock. All valuation models take into account expected growth rates of earnings, cash flows, dividends, and the required rate of return of the stock.

7.4 Valuations

The purpose of doing a valuation on a company's issued securities is to determine the attractiveness of the security as an investment. As the term 'valuations' imply we are trying to place a value on the security. At the fundamental level of security analysis is the determination of whether to buy, hold, or sell a security. In general, the single most important factor in this choice is how we value a security and how that value measures up against its market price. Obviously, we prefer to buy the security when its calculated value is below its market value and, conversely, we sell the security when its valuation is above market value.

The two main techniques of valuing a stock are:

1   Discounted cash flow (DCF) methods
2   Relative valuation methods.

Both methods have their strengths and limitations and ideally, they should be used together to enable the analyst to have a broader, deeper view of the stock. They have some factors in common. Both need a required rate of return because this rate is the discount rate in discounted cash flow calculations. The two techniques also are affected by the estimated growth rate of the variable (e.g., dividends, earnings). Often companies in specific industries are best analysed using one or the other method of valuation because of the nature of the businesses. For example, a utility is best analysed using the DCF method because of its relatively stable stream of earnings, while a relative valuation method is usually more suitable for an internet company.

DCF methods

We expect a stock to provide a stream of returns during the holding time. DCF methods entail finding the value of a stock using the present value of some measure of cash flow such as dividends, operating cash flow, and free cash flow. Thus, the three DCF models are:

1   The dividend discount model (DDM)
2   Present value of operating cash flows
3   Present value of free cash flows.

All DCF models presume the value of any security is the present value of its expected cash flows according to the formula:

$$V_s = \sum_{t=1}^{n} \frac{CF_t}{(1+r)^t}$$

Where:

V_s = value of stock

n = life of the asset

CF_t = cash value in period t

r = the discount rate

DCFs are useful in giving an idea of the current market valuation of a stock. The DCF value has added informational worth when compared with the DCFs of the aggregate market, the appropriate industry, and with other stocks in the industry. It is important to understand that current market valuations provided by the DCF method do not give an indication of whether the market or industry is itself over- or undervalued. If the aggregate market value may be overly high, comparing the DCF of the stock to this overvalued market makes the stock more attractive than it may actually be. It is necessary for accuracy,

DDM

The DDM of a stock is the present value of all future dividends given by the formula:

$$V_s = \frac{D_1}{(1+r)} + \frac{D_2}{(1+r)^2} + \frac{D_3}{(1+r)^3} + \cdots + \frac{D_\infty}{(1+r)^\infty}$$

$$= \sum_{t=1}^{n} \frac{D_t}{(1+r)^t}$$

Where:

V_s = value of common stock s

D_t = dividend during period t

r = required rate of return of stock s

Holding periods

One year

Assume the holding period of the stock is one year. In this case, we need to know:

1. The expected dividend at the end of the one-year period
2. The selling price for the stock at the end of the year
3. The required rate of return.

$$V_s = \frac{D_1}{(1+r)} + \frac{P_{s1}}{(1+r)}$$

If the holding period is one year, the value V_s is the dividend payment in year 1 plus the sale price of stock s at the end of year 1.

It is general practice to derive the expected dividend from the past dividend payout of the company. If, in the past year, the dividend payout was 50 per cent and forecast earnings for the coming year is HK$10 per share, then the dividend is estimated at HK$5 per share.

We can estimate the selling price of the shares of the company at the end of the year by applying the DDM. We receive dividends for year one. The expected selling price is the value of all remaining dividend payments. Another way to estimate the final selling price of the shares after a year is to use the earnings multiplier model. Multiply the future expected earnings for the stock by an earnings multiple. We estimate the earnings multiple based on forecast of growth in the company, its sector, and the economy.

To determine the required rate of return for stocks, we normally use the risk-free rate plus a risk premium we place on the stock. One-year Treasuries are a good proxy for the risk-free rate, especially because we are looking at a one-year holding period. If one-year Treasuries are yielding 1.5 per cent and we believe the risk premium of the stock is 5 per cent, then the required rate of return for stock is 14 per cent.

Multiple year

It is often necessary to determine the value of the stock of a company in a scenario where the holding period is many years. We forecast the dividend payments and the sale price of the stock multiple years into the future.

Assume the holding period is five years. Again, we need to estimate the dividends paid for each of the five years and the selling price of the stock at the end of the period. We usually forecast dividends based on the past trend of dividend growth. If dividends have been growing by a certain dollar amount each year, say HK$1 per year, and the dividend paid last year was HK$5, then years one to five of the dividend stream will be as follows: HK$6, HK$7, HK$8, HK$9, and HK$10. This type of dividend estimate is easier to compute than using dividend payout estimations. In the case of the latter, earnings estimates must also be forecast as dividend payout is a function of earnings.

The sale price, P, of the stock at the end of the five-year period is computed in the same way we do for the one-year holding period; that is, using the DDM. We need to forecast the dividend growth for the stock beginning five years from the present time.

We can use the five-year Treasury bond rate as the required rate of return:

$$V_s = \frac{D_1}{(1+r)} + \frac{D_2}{(1+r)^2} + \frac{D_3}{(1+r)^3} + \frac{D_4}{(1+r)^4} + \frac{D_{s5}}{(1+r)^5}$$

$$P_s = \frac{D_5}{(1+r)} + \frac{D_6}{(1+r)^2} + \cdots + \frac{D_\infty}{(1+r)^\infty}$$

Which becomes the DDM formula:

$$\sum_{t=1}^{n} \frac{D_t}{(1+r)^t}$$

Infinite period

We often wish to value the company based on the assumption we hold the stock for a long enough time for the period to be considered as infinite. In this case we use the formula for the infinite period model. In this model, we assume the dividend growth is constant for an infinite period such as 10 per cent per year for infinity.

$$V_s = \frac{D_0(1+g)}{(1+r)} + \frac{D_0(1+g)^2}{(1+r)^2} + \cdots + \frac{D_0(1+g)^n}{(1+r)^n}$$

Where:

V_s = value of stock s

D_0 = dividend payment in the current period

g = the constant growth rate of dividends

r = the required rate of return on stock s

n = the number of periods assumed to be infinite

This infinite constant growth rate model is simplified to the following expression:

$$V_2 = \frac{D_1}{(r-g)}$$

The value of s is highly dependent on the assumed growth rate of dividends and the number we use for required rate of return. The spread between the required rate of return (r) and the expected constant growth rate of dividends is a significant determinant of the value of the stock. A decline in the spread leads to an increase in the value of the stock, V. Conversely, an increase in the spread causes a decrease in V.

Present value of operating free cash flows (PVOFCF)

In calculating the PVOFCF we estimate the value of the company by discounting the total operating free cash flows prior to paying interest to debt holders but after deducting capital expenditures. The discount rate used in this DCF method is the weighted average cost of capital of the company.

The formula for calculating PVOFCF is:

$$PVOFCF_s = \sum_{t=1}^{n} \frac{OFCT_t}{(1+WACC_s)^t}$$

Where:

$PVOFCF_s$ = value of the stock of company s

n = number of periods assumed as infinite

$OFCF_t$ = operating free cash flow in period t

$WACC_s$ = weighted average cost of capital for company s

Present value of free cash flows (PVFCF)

To calculate PVFCF, free cash flow is defined as:

Operating cash flow less:

– debt payments (interest and principle)

– capital expenditures used to maintain asset base

We call this form of cash flow free because it is the cash left after paying off debt and using funds for capital expenditures. Free cash may be thought of as the cash flows available to equity owners. As such the discount rate used in PVFCF is the company's cost of equity and not the WACC.

$$PVFCF_s = \sum_{t=1}^{n} \frac{FCF_t}{(1+r_s)^t}$$

$PVFCF_s$ = value of the stock of company s

n = number of periods assumed as infinite

r = discount rate

FCF_t = free cash flow in period t

Relative valuation methods

This method of valuation compares the price of a stock with an estimated value calculated using earnings, cash flow, book value, or sales. The resultant ratio values such as P/E are then compared to the values of the same ratios for the industry in which the company is located, the economy in which it operates, and the relevant market aggregate. Relative valuation methods, therefore, measure the stock price relative to variables affecting the stock value such as earnings, as well as comparing the ratios relative to the ratios of other entities.

Price/earnings ratio (P/E)

This is a commonly used ratio in security analysis. It is simple to compute and gives a quick view on the value of the stock. The *P/E* is a measure of how much we are paying for a dollar of expected earnings per share. The formula is:

$$P/E = \frac{\text{Current market price per share}}{\text{Expected earnings per share}}$$

The expected earnings are normally the estimated earnings during the following 12-month period. A stock of a company, call it S, which trades at 12 times earnings, means we pay HK$12 for every HK$1 per share earned.

Is a *P/E* of 12 an attractive valuation for a company's stock? This question can only be answered when we compare the valuation against the valuation of other entities.

Relative to market and industry P/Es

If the *P/E* of the aggregate market, the Hang Seng Index, is 15 times, the *P/E* of the stock S, at 12 times, is obviously lower. This lower relative value indicates the stock is undervalued versus the market. The analyst would drill deeper into the stock fundamentals to find out why the stock is undervalued. Often there are good reasons for the undervaluation.

1. The company has low earnings growth versus the market because it is a mature company operating in a mature industry.
2. There are doubts about the quality of management of the company.
3. The company is associated with business risk such as high cash burn (using cash at a high rate) or high debt levels.
4. The company is a conglomerate and has revenues coming from many areas of operation. The discount to the market P/E exists because of difficulties in ascertaining earnings due to its spread of businesses
5. The company has most of its revenues deriving from a utility function such as power generation.

If point (5) is true for the company, then it becomes necessary to compare the P/E of the company with the average or median P/E of the industry group. If the median P/E of the industry comprising companies that derive most of their revenue from power generation is 14 times, then the company is also undervalued versus its peers, as well as against the market. This result makes the company an attractive investment on first review. Note the importance of getting the comparative industry group as accurate as possible. If we had compared company S against the group containing all companies whose revenues derived mostly from power generation and water provision, the group would not be fully comparable.

Lower market and industry P/E

If the P/E of the market is eight times and the stock S trades at a prospective P/E of 12 times, the stock is overvalued versus the market. Again there are several reasons for the overvaluation:

1. The stock is a high-growth stock operating in a new market where there are few competitors.
2. The stock is highly liquid and a popular holding of investors.
3. The stock has predictable earnings growth.

An analyst or investor will not necessarily reject the stock as an investment simply because it is overvalued versus the market. We should find out more, such as the degree of overvaluation, the earnings growth of the company, the sustainability of its position in the industry, and its balance sheet strength. The P/E ratio gives us one benchmark for the company, but it is rarely sufficient to get a complete picture of the stock. Other relative valuations are useful to give us a fuller view of the stock.

Another way to see the P/E ratio is to invert it by dividing the earnings per share by current share price. The resultant ratio is called the earnings yield. This ratio tells us how much return (on a per-share basis) the stock's shareholders earned over the past 12 months.

$$\text{Earnings yield} = \frac{\text{Earnings per share}}{\text{Current share price}}$$

The dividend yield is how much the company actually returns to the shareholder in cash. While not all earnings may be paid to the shareholder, the retained earnings of a company still belong to the shareholder, and may be used for reinvestment into future growth opportunities.

Earnings yields are often used to compare with bond yields to ascertain the attractiveness of a share versus returns from a bond. In comparing the alternatives, the key factors to consider are: growth rate, earnings predictability, and the current fixed-income rates. The earnings yield of a stock should be higher than the bond yield, because of the greater unpredictability of earnings of a company versus the predictability of interest from a bond. The higher risk, justifies a higher yield.

The price to earnings growth ratio (PEG)

The price to earnings growth ratio is also known as the PEG of a company. This ratio is the measure of how much we are paying for the earnings growth of a company. While a high P/E ratio may make a stock look expensive, factoring the company's growth rate to get the stock's PEG ratio gives a more complete picture. In the example above, company S has a P/E of 12 times. The market has a P/E of eight times. The stock of company S seems overvalued versus the market. However, the earnings growth rate may be extraordinary and investors are willing to pay for this pace of earnings. But just how much are investors paying for rapid earnings growth of company S? The formula for price to earnings growth ratio is:

$$PEG_s = \frac{P/E_t}{EG_{t+1}}$$

Where:

P/E_t = the P/E of the stock in period t

EG_{t+1} = expected earnings growth rate for the company s

The lower the PEG ratio, the more a stock may be undervalued given its earnings growth rate. All things being equal, the PEG ratio of fast-growing companies should be lower than the PEG ratio of low-growth companies, even though the P/E ratio of the former is higher. If the P/E of S is 12 times and the expected earnings growth rate is 30 per cent, then its PEG is 0.4 times. Whether a PEG is undervalued or overvalued depends on the industry and company type. A broad rule of thumb is a PEG ratio of less than one is attractive. We also need to differentiate between historical and forecast growth rates. If a company's growth is changing to faster rates and deviating from its historical trend, then using historical growth rates does not give an accurate PEG ratio. If we use forecast growth rates, the term used is 'forward PEG'. If historical numbers are used, then the term is 'trailing PEG'.

The price to cash flow (PCF) ratio

This ratio measures the price we pay for cash flow per share. Cash flow is less easy to manipulate than earnings per share and is important in credit analysis. Companies may have high earnings per share, but have negative cash flow over many periods. This is sometimes a red flag about a company's rate of cash burn.

The formula for price to cash flow is:

$$P/CF_s = \frac{P_t}{CF_{t+1}}$$

Where:

P_t = price of the stock in period t

CF_{t+1} = the expected cash flow per share for company s

The main variable that affects P/CF is the expected growth rate of cash flow of a company. The specific cash flow used is typically earnings before interest expense, taxes, depreciation, and amortization (EBITDA), but it will depend on the nature of the company, and the industry in which it operates. Free cash flow may be a better measure of performance for a particular industry, while operating cash flow may be more appropriate for another industry.

Price to book value (P/BV) ratio

This ratio is particularly popular among value investors who are sceptical about forecasts of earnings growth. These types of investors do not believe forecasts are necessarily accurate, and prefer to use historical figures such as book value to value a company. For instance, the book value of a bank is a good indicator of intrinsic value because most bank assets, such as loans and bonds, have a value equal to book value. Fama and French discovered a significant inverse relationship between P/BV ratios and excess return for a cross section of stocks.[3] The formula for P/BV ratio is:

$$P/BV_s = \frac{P_t}{BV}$$

Where:

P_t = price of the stock in period t

BV = estimated historical book value per share for firm s

The historical book value is often the latest quarter's book value per share and is calculated as:

Book value = Total assets − Intangible assets and liabilities

A simplified way to find BV is to use the original value of common stock issued, plus retained earnings, minus dividends, and stock buybacks. BV is a good indication of the value of a stock because it is a proxy for the liquidation value of the shares. In many cases, stocks trade at or below book value. In general, we prefer a stock with a lower P/BV because it is an indication that the stock is undervalued. It can also mean there is something fundamentally wrong with the company. As with other ratios, the P/BV varies according to industry and market.

If a company is experiencing a period of cyclical losses, it may not have positive trailing earnings or operating cash flows. In some cases, the analyst has low visibility of the company's future earnings prospects. Therefore, it is difficult to compute P/E or P/CF ratios. In such cases, the P/BV ratio is one way to value a stock.

Enterprise value to EBITDA

Enterprise value or EV gives us an idea of how much a business is worth. In other words EV tells us how much it would cost an acquirer to buy another company. The measure is useful in comparing companies with different capital structures because the value of a company is unaffected by its capital structure. To buy a company, an acquirer assumes the acquired company's debt, and receives all its cash. Acquiring the debt increases the cost to buy the company, but the cash reduces the cost of acquiring the company.

$$\text{Enterprise value} = \text{Market capitalization} + \text{Debt} - \text{Cash and short-term investments}$$

Debt includes both long- and short-term debt. The market value of debt should be used to calculate EV, but in practice the book value of debt is used. Cash and equivalents include marketable securities and items marked as available for sale securities.

Clearly, EV is a modification of market capitalization (number of shares outstanding × current share price). The EV gives more information than the market capitalization because financial analysts use the metric to arrive at a value of a company views as a going concern.

The EV to $EBITDA$ ratio is a measure of the value of the company, not just equity. This ratio is usually more valid for comparisons across companies than the P/E ratio. Like the P/E ratio, the $EV/EBITDA$ ratio is a measure of how expensive a stock is.

$$\text{Enterprise value multiple} = \frac{\text{Enterprise value}}{\text{EBITDA}}$$

Where:

$EBITDA$ = earnings before interest expense, taxes, depreciation and amortization

The EV multiple is a rough measure of how long it takes for an acquisition to earn enough to pay off the cost of acquisition, assuming no change in $EBITDA$. By looking at $EV/EBITDA$ instead of market capitalization, investors get a better sense of whether a company is undervalued.

7.5 Stock analysis

The type of stock valuation technique we apply to a stock of a company depends on the type of company and the industry in which it operates. Analysts use the discounted cash flow methods or relative valuation methods to determine the value of a stock. The purpose of stock analysis is to help decide if it is worth paying the market price for a particular stock. This requires comparison of the intrinsic value of a stock with its market value. A company may have superior financials, growth prospects, and excellent management. However, these very factors may lead to the market overpricing the stock of the company. Investors push up the price due to high demand for such a high-quality company. In the end, the demand pushes the stock price so that the intrinsic value of the stock is below the market price resulting in the stock being overvalued. In contrast, a boring company with steady but low growth may command little market attention. Consequently, demand for its stock is low, leading to undervaluation if the intrinsic value exceeds market price.

Companies can broadly be categorized according to their growth and earnings profiles into:[4]

1. Slow-growth companies
2. Consistent growth companies
3. High-growth companies
4. Cyclical companies
5. Turnarounds
6. Asset plays.

Slow-growth companies are at or near the top of their industry or product life cycle. Companies in this group tend to pay regular and relatively high dividends because of few internal investment opportunities for retained earnings. These companies may be valued by using the discounted cash flow method, in particular the dividend discount method.

Consistent growth companies have faster earnings growth than slow-growth companies. The earnings grow in a consistent manner characteristic to the type of company. Investors find this predictability desirable. However, the earnings consistency is most likely already priced into the stock price. Investors should look at the current *P/E* ratio of the company in relation to its industry and the market. A comparison should be made of the current valuation, versus its historical trends, versus industry, and market. Investors should be keenly aware of any possibility for a change in the trend of the company's earnings growth.

Fast-growth companies tend be operating in new, innovative industries. They also tend to be smaller, aggressive companies with high-earnings growth potential (20–25 per cent per year). These companies are on the steep slope of the earnings growth curve because they are new, have a novel competitive advantage, or are taking away market share from established rivals. These companies are higher risk because their stock price may fall at the first sign of negative earnings surprises. Analysts will tend to use *P/E* ratios and *PEGs* to determine the value of high-growth companies.

Cyclical earnings growth companies are generally engaged in businesses that are subject to the rise and fall of the business cycle. Investors should base earnings forecast on the economic environment and growth, as well as the company's internal conditions.

Turnaround companies are those that have weaknesses and financial problems but encounter external opportunities that may allow them to recover from the difficult times. As with high-growth companies, these companies are also risky investments because the hoped for opportunities may not materialize or management is unable to execute well to take advantage of the opportunities. Investors need to do a thorough investigation of the management capabilities, strategic plans, financials, and key external factors that will impact on a successful turnaround.

Asset plays are companies with valuable assets hidden on the balance sheet. Examples of such assets are holdings of property, trademarks, or patents. A typical valuation method to employ in valuing asset plays is to determine BV/share and compare this intrinsic value to the market price per share of the stock.

Applying valuation methods

As noted earlier in this chapter, there are two main valuation approaches in stock analysis. Each approach has several different techniques or methods that may be applied.

A. Discounted cash flow approach comprising:

1   The dividend discount model
2   Present value of operating cash flows
3   Present value of free cash flows.

B. Relative valuation approach comprising:

1   P/E ratio
2   PEG ratio
3   P/CF ratio
4   P/BV ratio.

We apply some of these techniques to find the value of Tencent Holdings, a highly traded stock listed on the Hong Kong Stock Exchange.

Stock analysis of Tencent Holdings

Tencent is a Chinese internet company founded in November 1988 with its headquarters in Shenzhen. Currently, its major business includes social networks, online games, online advertising, and E-Commerce transactions. Products include the well-known instant messenger Tencent QQ and mobile chat service app WeChat/Weixin. Both products have helped Tencent's continued expansion into smartphone services. In 2004 the company was listed on the main board of the Hong Kong Stock Exchange. Tencent derives a large proportion of revenues from developing and offering online games. The company is a growth stock because the company is in a new industry and a leader of the group. Research analysts value Tencent using mostly P/E ratio relative (to peer group, to its historical trading range, to growth metrics such as PEG). No analyst uses P/BV because this valuation method does not give much information. A few analysts use a Sum of the Parts (SOTP) because some of Tencent's businesses make very little money (social network and payment) but are actually worth a lot. A stock like Tencent will probably move more based upon milestones (monetization of social network, for instance) than on any other parameter.

Table 7.1 Tencent Holdings: income statement

Tencent Holdings Ltd. (HK:700)

In Millions of the reported currency, except per share items.	Template: Period Type: Currency:	Standard Annual Reported Currency			Restatement: Order: Conversion:	Latest Filings Latest on Right Historical	

Income Statement

For the Fiscal Period Ending	12 months Dec-31-2009	Reclassified 12 months Dec-31-2010	Reclassified 12 months Dec-31-2011	Restated 12 months Dec-31-2012	12 months Dec-31-2013	LTM 12 months Sep-30-2014
Currency	CNY	CNY	CNY	CNY	CNY	CNY
Revenue	12,398.5	19,570.8	28,305.8	43,528.0	59,815.0	72,914.0
= Value-added Services	–	–	–	35,718.0	44,985.0	–
+ E CommercE Transactions	–	–	–	4,428.0	9,796.0	–
+ Internet Value-added Services	9,530.7	15,482.3	23,042.8	–	–	–
+ Mobile and Telecommunications Value-added Services	1,905.6	2,715.9	3,270.8	–	–	–
+ Online Advertising	962.2	1,372.5	1,992.2	3,382.0	5,034.0	–
Other Revenue	41.5	0.1	0.2	366.0	622.0	2,010.0
= Others	41.5	75.3	190.3	366.0	622.0	
Total Revenue	**12,440.0**	**19,646.0**	**28,496.1**	**43,894.0**	**60,437.0**	**74,924.0**
Cost Of Goods Sold	3,889.5	6,320.2	9,928.3	18,207.0	27,461.0	30,422.0
= Cost of Revenues	–	–	–	–	27,778.0	–
– Asset Writedown	–	–	–	–	(317.0)	–
+ Cost of Revenues	3,889.5	6,320.2	9,928.3	18,207.0	–	–
Gross Profit	**8,550.5**	**13,325.8**	**18,567.8**	**25,687.0**	**32,976.0**	**44,502.0**
Selling General & Admin Exp.	2,607.8	3.8	7.2	10,760.0	15,683.0	20,717.0
= Advertising Expenses	8.7	116.3	–	1,998.0	3,894.0	–

+ Advertising Expense	—	—	—	—
+ Net Rental Expense	—	—	4.9	16.0
+ Net Rental Expense	0.5	—	—	—
+ Net Rental Expense	—	3.7	—	—
+ Selling and Marketing Expenses	581.5	945.4	2,994.0	5,695.0
− Advertising Expenses	8.7	116.3	—	—
− Advertising Expenses	—	—	1,998.0	3,894.0
− SBC (Gen. & Admin. Exp.)	—	—	(1,733.0)	(2,777.0)
+ General and Administrative Expenses	2,026.3	2,836.2	1,013.0	1,786.0
− Net Rental Expense	—	—	7,766.0	9,988.0
− SBC (Gen. & Admin. Exp.)	0.5	4.9	8.0	16.0
− Net Rental Expense	—	—	1,013.0	1,786.0
+ Selling and Marketing Expenses	—	3.7	—	—
R & D Exp.	—	1,920.9	—	—
Depreciation & Amort.	—	—	—	—
Other Operating Expense/(Income)	0.1	0.1	—	—
= Other Gain/(Loss), Net	(58.2)	38.1	—	(32.0)
− Gain (loss) On Sale of Assets	(3.0)	15.9	420.8	904.0
− Interest and Investment Income	—	0.9	708.5	(87.0)
− Gain (Loss) from Sale of Investments	(1.7)	—	(243.0)	509.0
− Gain (Loss) from Sale of Investments	11.9	(18.0)	—	267.0
− Gain (loss) On Sale of Assets	—	—	(1.7)	(6.0)

(continued overleaf)

Table 7.1 Continued

Income Statement

For the Fiscal Period Ending	12 months Dec-31-2009	Reclassified 12 months Dec-31-2010	Reclassified 12 months Dec-31-2011	Restated 12 months Dec-31-2012	12 months Dec-31-2013	LTM 12 months Sep-30-2014
Currency	CNY	CNY	CNY	CNY	CNY	CNY
− Gain (Loss) on Sale of Business	–	–	–	–	189.0	–
Other Operating Exp., Total	**2,673.3**	**3,726.5**	**7,262.8**	**10,760.0**	**15,651.0**	**21,059.0**
Operating Income	**5,877.2**	**9,599.4**	**11,304.9**	**14,927.0**	**17,325.0**	**23,443.0**
Interest Expense	–	(35.0)	(72.5)	(327.0)	(394.0)	(707.0)
= Interest Expense	–	(35.0)	(72.5)	(327.0)	(394.0)	
Interest and Invest. Income	136.0	255.9	484.8	1,243.0	1,823.0	1,744.0
= Interest Income	136.0	255.9	469.0	836.0	1,314.0	–
+ Interest and Investment Income	–	–	15.9	–	–	–
+ Interest and Investment Income	–	–	–	407.0	509.0	–
Net Interest Exp.	**136.0**	**220.9**	**412.3**	**916.0**	**1,429.0**	**1,037.0**
Income/(Loss) from Affiliates	22.2	75.8	(190.0)	(80.0)	171.0	(90.0)
= Share of Profit/(losses) of Associates	22.2	72.4	(24.3)	(54.0)	213.0	–
+ Share of Profit/loss of Associates and a Jointly Controlled Entity	–	3.4	(165.7)	(26.0)	(42.0)	–
Currency Exchange Gains (Loss)	(2.0)	16.2	108.0	(21.0)	310.0	310.0
= Currency Translation Gain/(Loss)	(2.0)	34.2	108.0	(21.0)	310.0	–
+ Currency Translation Gain/(Loss)	–	(18.0)	–	–	–	–

Other Non-Operating Inc. (Exp.)	—	—	—	—	—	(506.0)
EBT Excl. Unusual Items	**6,033.5**	**9,912.3**	**11,635.3**	**15,742.0**	**19,235.0**	**24,194.0**
Impairment of Goodwill	—	—	—	—	—	—
Gain (Loss) On Sale Of Invest.	11.9	—	465.5	(692.0)	180.0	904.0
= Gain (Loss) from Sale of Investments	—	—	—	(699.0)	—	—
+ Gain (Loss) from Sale of Investments	—	—	708.5	—	—	—
+ Gain (Loss) from Sale of Investments	—	—	(243.0)	7.0	267.0	—
+ Gain (Loss) from Sale of Investments	11.9	—	—	—	—	—
Gain (Loss) On Sale Of Assets	(4.7)	0.9	(1.7)	1.0	183.0	2,125.0
= Gain (loss) On Sale of Assets	(3.0)	—	—	—	—	—
+ Gain (loss) On Sale of Assets	—	0.9	—	—	—	—
+ Gain (loss) On Sale of Assets	(1.7)	—	—	—	—	—
+ Gain (Loss) on Sale of Assets	—	—	(1.7)	1.0	(6.0)	—
+ Gain (Loss) on Sale of Business	—	—	—	—	189.0	—
Asset Writedown	—	—	—	—	(317.0)	(317.0)
= Asset Writedown	—	—	—	—	(317.0)	—
Other Unusual Items	—	—	—	—	—	—
EBT Incl. Unusual Items	**6,040.7**	**9,913.1**	**12,099.1**	**15,051.0**	**19,281.0**	**26,906.0**
Income Tax Expense	819.1	1,797.9	1,874.2	2,266.0	3,718.0	5,041.0
= Provision for Income Tax	819.1	1,797.9	1,874.2	2,266.0	3,718.0	—
Earnings from Cont. Ops.	**5,221.6**	**8,115.2**	**10,224.8**	**12,785.0**	**15,563.0**	**21,865.0**

(continued overleaf)

Table 7.1 Continued

Income Statement

For the Fiscal Period Ending	12 months Dec-31-2009	Reclassified 12 months Dec-31-2010	Reclassified 12 months Dec-31-2011	Restated 12 months Dec-31-2012	12 months Dec-31-2013	LTM 12 months Sep-30-2014
Currency	CNY	CNY	CNY	CNY	CNY	CNY
Earnings of Discontinued Ops.	–	–	–	–	–	–
Extraord. Item & Account. Change	–	–	–	–	–	–
Net Income to Company	**5,221.6**	**8,115.2**	**10,224.8**	**12,785.0**	**15,563.0**	**21,865.0**
Minority Int. in Earnings = Minority Interest (After Tax)	(66.0) (66.0)	(61.6) (61.6)	(21.7) (21.7)	(53.0) (53.0)	(61.0) (61.0)	(4.0)
Net Income	**5,155.6**	**8,053.6**	**10,203.1**	**12,732.0**	**15,502.0**	**21,861.0**
Pref. Dividends and Other Adj.	–	–	–	–	–	–
NI to Common Incl Extra Items	**5,155.6**	**8,053.6**	**10,203.1**	**12,732.0**	**15,502.0**	**21,861.0**
NI to Common Excl. Extra Items	**5,155.6**	**8,053.6**	**10,203.1**	**12,732.0**	**15,502.0**	**21,861.0**
Per Share Items						
Basic EPS	0.57	0.89	1.12	1.39	1.69	2.38
Basic EPS Excl. Extra Items	0.57	0.89	1.12	1.39	1.69	2.38
Weighted Avg. Basic Shares Out.	9,008.2	9,084.8	9,094.8	9,140.0	9,160.0	9,192.3
Diluted EPS	0.56	0.87	1.1	1.37	1.66	2.34
Diluted EPS Excl. Extra Items	0.56	0.87	1.1	1.37	1.66	2.34
Weighted Avg. Diluted Shares Out.	9,236.4	9,304.9	9,292.7	9,315.0	9,340.0	9,358.8

	Mar-28-2011	Mar-25-2012	Mar-28-2013	Mar-31-2014	Nov-12-2014
Normalized Basic EPS	0.41	0.68	0.8	1.07	1.31	1.64
Normalized Diluted EPS	0.4	0.66	0.78	1.05	1.28	1.62
Dividends per Share	0.07	0.09	0.12	0.16	0.19	0.19
Payout Ratio %	7.7%	7.9%	8.2%	8.7%	9.5%	8.1%
Shares per Depository Receipt	1.0	1.0	1.0	1.0	1.0	1.0
Supplemental Items						
EBITDA	6,363.9	10,378.6	13,239.4	17,364.0	20,696.0	27,919.0
EBITA	5,958.0	9,708.8	12,031.1	15,484.0	18,212.0	25,012.0
EBIT	5,877.2	9,599.4	11,304.9	14,927.0	17,325.0	23,443.0
EBITDAR	6,453.7	10,498.7	13,587.3	17,987.0	21,579.0	NA
As Reported Total Revenue*	12,440.0	19,646.0	28,496.1	43,894.0	60,437.0	74,924.0
Effective Tax Rate %	13.6%	18.1%	15.5%	15.1%	19.3%	18.7%
Current Domestic Taxes	NA	NA	NA	NA	NA	152.0
Total Current Taxes	494.4	1,127.4	1,863.9	1,747.0	3,607.0	3,759.0
Deferred Domestic Taxes	NA	NA	NA	NA	NA	1,171.0
Total Deferred Taxes	324.8	670.5	10.3	519.0	111.0	1,282.0
Normalized Net Income	3,705.0	6,133.6	7,250.3	9,785.8	11,960.9	15,117.3
Filing Date	Mar-28-2011	Mar-25-2012	Mar-28-2013	Mar-31-2014	Mar-31-2014	Nov-12-2014
Restatement Type	NC	RC	RC	RS	O	O
Calculation Type	REP	REP	REP	REP	REP	LTM
Supplemental Operating Expense Items						
Advertising Exp.	8.7	116.3	NA	265.0	1,117.0	NA
Selling and Marketing Exp.	581.5	945.4	1,920.9	2,994.0	5,695.0	7,767.0
General and Administrative Exp.	2,025.9	2,832.5	5,278.2	7,758.0	9,972.0	12,934.0
R&D Exp.	1,242.7	1,724.6	2,798.3	4,352.0	5,314.0	6,940.0
Net Rental Exp.	89.8	120.1	347.9	623.0	883.0	NA
Imputed Oper. Lease Interest Exp.	–	12.2	23.7	145.3	216.1	–
Imputed Oper. Lease Depreciation	–	107.9	324.2	477.7	666.9	–
Stock-Based Comp., G&A Exp.	–	–	–	1,013.0	1,786.0	1,786.0

(*continued overleaf*)

Table 7.1 Continued

Income Statement

For the Fiscal Period Ending	12 months Dec-31-2009	Reclassified 12 months Dec-31-2010	Reclassified 12 months Dec-31-2011	Restated 12 months Dec-31-2012	12 months Dec-31-2013	LTM 12 months Sep-30-2014
Currency	CNY	CNY	CNY	CNY	CNY	CNY
Stock-Based Comp., Unallocated	321.4	495.8	814.8	–	–	530.0
Stock-Based Comp., Total	**321.4**	**495.8**	**814.8**	**1,013.0**	**1,786.0**	**2,316.0**

* Occasionally, certain items classified as Revenue by the company will be re-classified as other income if it is deemed to be non-recurring and unrelated to the core business of the firm. This field shows Total Revenue exactly as reported by the firm on its consolidated statement of income.

Note: For multiple class companies, per share items are primary class equivalent, and for foreign companies listed as primary ADRs, per share items are ADR-equivalent.

Table 7.2 Tencent Holdings: balance sheet

Tencent Holdings Ltd. (HK:700)

In Millions of the reported currency, except per share items.	Template: Period Type: Currency:	Standard Annual Reported Currency				Restatement: Order: Conversion:	Latest Filings Latest on Right Historical	

Balance Sheet

Balance Sheet as of:	Dec-31-2009	Dec-31-2010	Dec-31-2011		Restated Dec-31-2012	Dec-31-2013	Sep-30-2014
Currency	CNY	CNY	CNY		CNY	CNY	CNY
ASSETS							
Cash And Equivalents	6,043.7	10,408.3	12,612.1		13,383.0	20,228.0	33,454.0
= Cash and Cash Equivalents	6,043.7	10,408.3	12,612.1		13,383.0	20,228.0	33,454.0
Short Term Investments	5,310.2	11,725.7	13,716.0		13,806.0	19,623.0	17,195.0
= Short-term Deposits	–	–	–		–	–	17,195.0
+ Term Deposits	–	–	–		–	–	–
+ Term Deposits With Original Maturities of Over Three Months	5,310.2	11,725.7	13,716.0		13,806.0	19,623.0	–
Total Cash & ST Investments	**11,353.9**	**22,134.0**	**26,328.1**		**27,189.0**	**39,851.0**	**50,649.0**
Accounts Receivable	1,229.4	1,715.4	2,020.8		2,354.0	2,955.0	4,293.0
= Accounts Receivables	1,229.4	1,715.4	2,020.8		2,354.0	2,955.0	4,293.0
Other Receivables	110.5	135.2	413.4		942.0	1,351.0	–
= Other Receivables	–	–	–		353.0	1,131.0	–
+ Other Receivables	–	89.4	143.4		589.0	220.0	–
+ Other Receivables	53.5	45.8	270.0		–	–	–
+ Other Receivables	57.1	–	–		–	–	–
Total Receivables	**1,339.9**	**1,850.6**	**2,434.2**		**3,296.0**	**4,306.0**	**4,293.0**

(continued overleaf)

Table 7.2 Continued

Balance Sheet

Balance Sheet as of:	Dec-31-2009	Dec-31-2010	Dec-31-2011	Restated Dec-31-2012	Dec-31-2013	Sep-30-2014
Currency	CNY	CNY	CNY	CNY	CNY	CNY
Inventory	–	–	–	568.0	1,384.0	154.0
= Inventories	–	–	–	568.0	1,384.0	154.0
Prepaid Exp.	174.8	306.2	1,685.8	2,816.0	3,876.0	7,660.0
= Prepaid Expenses	35.5	85.8	405.9	1,640.0	1,454.0	–
+ Prepaid Expenses	95.4	121.0	483.6	–	–	–
+ Prepayments, Deposits and Other Receivables	–	–	–	503.0	1,031.0	–
+ Prepayments, Deposits and Other Receivables	373.6	487.9	2,211.9	3,878.0	5,365.0	7,660.0
− Prepaid Expenses	35.5	85.8	405.9	1,640.0	1,454.0	–
− Other Receivables	95.4	121.0	483.6	353.0	1,131.0	–
− Other Current Assets	73.9	46.5	112.7	503.0	1,031.0	–
− Other Receivables	14.4	89.4	143.4	589.0	220.0	–
− Other Receivables	53.5	45.8	270.0	120.0	138.0	–
− Other Receivables	57.1	–	–	–	–	–
Restricted Cash	0.2	1,036.5	4,942.6	2,520.0	4,131.0	6,696.0
= Restricted Cash	200.0	1,036.5	4,942.6	2,520.0	4,131.0	6,696.0
Other Current Assets	0.1	46.5	112.7	120.0	138.0	–
= Other Current Assets	73.9	46.5	112.7	–	–	–
+ Other Current Assets	14.4	–	–	–	–	–
+ Other Current Assets	–	–	–	120.0	138.0	–
Total Current Assets	**13,156.9**	**25,373.7**	**35,503.4**	**36,509.0**	**53,686.0**	**69,452.0**
Gross Property, Plant & Equipment	3,527.4	5,205.0	8,702.7	12,151.0	16,753.0	–
= Buildings	1,299.1	1,368.5	1,731.9	2,358.0	2,800.0	–
+ Leasehold Improvements	90.4	130.3	385.6	586.0	873.0	–
+ Leasehold Improvements	–	–	(0.0)	–	(1.0)	–
+ Construction in Progress	105.8	386.9	158.7	534.0	2,041.0	–

+ Machinery	1,955.3	3,185.9	6,159.2	10,494.0
+ Machinery	68.8	125.8	255.1	541.0
+ Machinery	8.1	7.6	12.6	47.0
+ Machinery	–	–	(0.3)	(43.0)
+ Machinery	–	–	(0.0)	1.0
Accumulated Depreciation	(0.9)	(1.5)	(2.7)	(6,019.0)
= Accumulated Depreciation	(904.5)	(1.5)	(2.7)	(6,019.0)
Net Property, Plant & Equipment	**2,623.0**	**5,203.5**	**7,937.0**	**10,734.0**
		6,043.6		**11,037.0**
Long-term Investments	972.5	5,272.1	8,838.9	36,114.0
= Investment in Joint Venture	–	–	–	–
+ Long-term Deposits	–	–	10,892.0	11,420.0
+ Available-for-sale Investments	–	–	–	–
				68,501.0
				18.0
				13,735.0
+ Investment in Associates	477.6	1,070.6	4,433.4	12,170.0
+ Held to Maturity Investments	341.4		7,310.0	
+ Term Deposits				–
+ Investments in Jointly Controlled Entities		74.5	61.9	35.0	9.0
					4,931.0
+ Long-term Investments – Equity Method Investments				–
				49,817.0
				46,931.0
+ Equity Method Investments	153.5	4,126.9	4,343.6	5,633.0
+ Available-for-sale Financial Assets				12,515.0	46,931.0
Goodwill	62.2	302.7	2,615.8	2,929.0	2,552.0
= Goodwill	62.2	302.7	2,694.7	3,013.0	2,698.0
+ Goodwill			(78.9)	(84.0)	(146.0)
Other Intangibles	241.8	758.4	1,653.4	2,584.0	2,422.0
= Goodwill and Intangible Assets					5,153.0
					4,331.0
+ Land Use Rights	0.0	230.9	794.0	871.0	822.0
+ Accumulated Amortization of Intangible Assets	(0.1)	(208.1)	(644.8)	–	–

(continued overleaf)

Table 7.2 Continued

Balance Sheet

Balance Sheet as of:	Dec-31-2009	Dec-31-2010	Dec-31-2011	Restated Dec-31-2012	Dec-31-2013	Sep-30-2014
Currency	CNY	CNY	CNY	CNY	CNY	CNY
+ Accumulated Amortization of Intangible Assets	(0.0)	(17.1)	(193.1)	(887.0)	(919.0)	–
+ Accumulated Amortization of Intangible Assets				(265.0)	(950.0)	–
+ Accumulated Amortization of Intangible Assets				(243.0)	(292.0)	–
+ Gross Intangible Assets		258.2	258.2	–	–	–
+ Gross Intangible Assets			(3.1)	–	–	–
+ Gross Intangible Assets			(1.5)	–	–	–
+ Gross Intangible Assets				(3.0)	(3.0)	–
+ Gross Intangible Assets				(2.0)	(2.0)	–
+ Gross Intangible Assets	196.8	222.1	1,355.1	1,510.0	1,386.0	–
+ Gross Intangible Assets	14.5	42.4	282.6	797.0	1,441.0	–
+ Gross Intangible Assets				403.0	420.0	–
+ Capitalized/purchased Software				1.0	(7.0)	–
+ Capitalized/purchased Software	257.8	377.8	629.7	915.0	1,125.0	–
+ Capitalized/purchased Software	(107.8)	(146.8)	(260.3)	–	–	–
+ Capitalized/purchased Software				(436.0)	(648.0)	–
+ Capitalized/purchased Software			(0.3)	–	–	–
+ Capitalized/purchased Software						
Loans Receivable Long-Term	54.7		15.8	50.0	–	–
= Loans Receivable Long-term	54.7			–	–	–
+ Loans Receivable Long-term			15.8	50.0	–	–

Deferred Tax Assets, LT	301.0	219.0	198.1	169.0	431.0	289.0
= Deferred Income Tax Asset	301.0	219.0	198.1	169.0	431.0	289.0
Other Long-Term Assets	93.6	224.4	1,935.4	1,208.0	1,296.0	1,463.0
= Prepayments, Deposits and Other Receivables	—	—	—	—	—	1,194.0
+ Investment Properties	68.0	37.2	—	22.0	—	269.0
+ Prepayments, Deposits and Other Receivables	80.3	445.4	2,187.6	1,236.0	1,296.0	—
Other Receivables	—	258.2	—	—	—	—
– Other Long-term Assets	—	—	258.2	575.0	840.0	—
– Other Long-term Assets	—	—	510.4	97.0	37.0	—
– Other Long-term Assets	54.7	—	458.0	244.0	—	—
– Loans Receivable	—	—	15.8	50.0	—	—
Long-term						
– Other Long-term Assets	—	—	945.1	270.0	419.0	—
+ Prepayments, Deposits and Other Receivables	—	—	2,187.6	1,236.0	1,296.0	—
Other Receivables	—	—	258.2	575.0	840.0	—
– Other Long-term Assets	—	—	510.4	97.0	37.0	—
– Other Long-term Assets	—	—	458.0	244.0	—	—
– Other Long-term Assets	—	—	15.8	50.0	—	—
– Loans Receivable	—	—	—	—	—	—
Long-term						
– Other Long-term Assets	—	—	945.1	270.0	419.0	—
+ Prepayments, Deposits and Other Receivables	—	—	2,187.6	1,236.0	1,296.0	—
Other Receivables	—	—	258.2	575.0	—	—
– Other Long-term Assets	—	—	—	97.0	—	—
– Other Long-term Assets	—	—	—	244.0	—	—
– Other Long-term Assets	—	—	15.8	50.0	—	—
– Loans Receivable	—	—	—	—	—	—
Long-term						
– Other Long-term Assets	—	—	—	270.0	419.0	—
+ Prepayments, Deposits and Other Receivables	—	—	—	1,236.0	1,296.0	—
Other Receivables	—	—	—	—	—	—
– Loans Receivable	—	—	—	50.0	—	—
Long-term						
Total Assets	**17,505.8**	**35,830.1**	**56,804.4**	**75,256.0**	**107,235.0**	**155,895.0**

(continued overleaf)

Table 7.2 Continued

Balance Sheet

Balance Sheet as of:	Dec-31-2009	Dec-31-2010	Dec-31-2011	Restated Dec-31-2012	Dec-31-2013	Sep-30-2014
Currency	CNY	CNY	CNY	CNY	CNY	CNY
LIABILITIES						
Accounts Payable	696.5	1,380.5	2,244.1	4,212.0	6,680.0	7,441.0
= Accounts Payable	696.5	1,380.5	2,244.1	4,212.0	6,680.0	7,441.0
Accrued Exp.	1,330.7	2,096.4	2,525.0	3,679.0	5,148.0	541.0
= Other Taxes Payable	217.0	225.2		540.0	593.0	541.0
+ Accrued Expenses	846.3	1,337.6	1,478.4	2,222.0	3,085.0	–
+ Accrued Expenses	267.4	533.6	731.6	873.0	1,440.0	–
+ Accrued Expenses			315.0	44.0	30.0	–
Short-term Borrowings	202.3	5,298.9	7,999.4	983.0	2,284.0	1,356.0
= Short-term Bank Borrowings	202.3					–
+ Borrowings				1,077.0	2,589.0	–
– Current Portion of Long-term Debt				94.0	305.0	125.0
+ Loans Payable Current			7,999.4	–	–	1,231.0
+ Borrowings		5,298.9		–	–	
Curr. Port. of LT Debt				94.0	305.0	3,197.0
= Notes Payable				–	–	1,843.0
+ Current Portion of Long-term Debt				1,077.0	2,589.0	2,710.0
– Loans Payable Current				–	–	125.0
– Loans Payable Current				983.0	2,284.0	1,231.0
Curr. Income Taxes Payable	85.2	341.1	708.7	420.0	1,318.0	1,123.0
= Income Taxes Payable	85.2	341.1	708.7	420.0	1,318.0	1,123.0
Unearned Revenue, Current	1,736.0	2,760.6	5,016.3	8,115.0	11,841.0	14,953.0
= Deferred Revenue	1,736.0	2,760.6	5,016.3	8,115.0	11,841.0	14,953.0
Other Current Liabilities	512.3	1,144.5	2,510.3	3,162.0	5,691.0	14,966.0

= Derivative Financial Instruments	—	18.0	—	—	—	—
+ Other Payables and Accruals	1,626.1	2,997.8	5,014.3	6,301.0	10,246.0	14,966.0
− Accrued Expenses	846.3	1,337.6	1,478.4	2,222.0	3,085.0	—
− Accrued Expenses	267.4	533.6	731.6	873.0	1,440.0	—
− Other Current Liabilities	71.9	841.1	1,840.9	2,487.0	4,045.0	—
− Accrued Expenses	265.1		315.0	44.0	30.0	—
− Other Current Liabilities	175.2		253.0	40.0	11.0	—
− Other Current Liabilities		285.5	395.4	635.0	1,635.0	—
+ Other Payables and Accruals	1,626.1	2,997.8	5,014.3	6,301.0	10,246.0	—
− Accrued Expenses	846.3	1,337.6	1,478.4	2,222.0	3,085.0	—
− Accrued Expenses	267.4	533.6	731.6	873.0	1,440.0	—
− Other Current Liabilities	71.9		1,840.9	2,487.0	4,045.0	—
− Accrued Expenses	265.1		315.0	44.0	30.0	—
− Other Current Liabilities	175.2		253.0	40.0	11.0	—
− Other Current Liabilities			395.4	635.0	1,635.0	—
+ Other Payables and Accruals	1,626.1		5,014.3	6,301.0	10,246.0	—
− Accrued Expenses	846.3		1,478.4	2,222.0	3,085.0	—
− Accrued Expenses	267.4		731.6	873.0	1,440.0	—
− Accrued Expenses			315.0	44.0	30.0	—
Total Current Liabilities	**4,563.1**	**13,022.0**	**21,183.3**	**20,665.0**	**33,267.0**	**43,577.0**
Long-Term Debt				9,623.0	12,464.0	29,744.0
= Borrowings				2,106.0	3,323.0	5,537.0
+ Long-term Notes Payables			3,733.3	7,517.0	9,141.0	24,207.0
Unearned Revenue, Non-Current						3,732.0
= Deferred Revenue						3,732.0
Def. Tax Liability, Non-Curr.	370.0	967.2	939.5	1,312.0	1,441.0	2,176.0
= Deferred Income Tax Liabilities	370.0	967.2	939.5	1,312.0	1,441.0	2,176.0

(continued overleaf)

Table 7.2 Continued

Balance Sheet

Balance Sheet as of:	Dec-31-2009	Dec-31-2010	Dec-31-2011	Restated Dec-31-2012	Dec-31-2013	Sep-30-2014
Currency	CNY	CNY	CNY	CNY	CNY	CNY
Other Non-Current Liabilities	274.1		1,859.8	1,508.0	1,600.0	1,272.0
= Long-term Payables	274.1		1,859.8	1,508.0	1,600.0	–
– Derivative Liabilities – Non Current			671.0	1,138.0	1,297.0	–
– Other Non-current Liabilities	248.4			104.0	99.0	–
– Other Non-current Liabilities				97.0	37.0	–
– Other Non-current Liabilities				169.0	167.0	–
+ Long-term Payables				1,508.0	1,600.0	–
– Derivative Liabilities – Non Current				1,138.0	1,297.0	–
– Other Non-current Liabilities				104.0	99.0	–
– Other Non-current Liabilities				97.0	37.0	–
– Other Non-current Liabilities				169.0	167.0	–
+ Long-term Payables				1,508.0	1,600.0	–
– Derivative Liabilities – Non Current			671.0	1,138.0	1,297.0	–
+ Long-term Payables				–	–	1,272.0
+ Derivative Liabilities – Non Current	248.4			1,138.0	1,297.0	–
+ Derivative Liabilities – Non Current				–	–	–
Total Liabilities	**5,207.1**	**13,989.3**	**27,716.0**	**33,108.0**	**48,772.0**	**80,501.0**

Common Stock	0.2					—
= Common Stock – Par Value	0.2		0.2			—
Additional Paid In Capital	1,244.4	1,100.3		2,846.0		—
= Additional Paid in Capital	1,244.4	1,100.3		2,846.0		—
Retained Earnings	10,590.8	17,873.8		52,886.0		—
= Retained Earnings	10,520.5	17,795.2	1,950.9	52,224.0	2,880.0	—
+ Retained Earnings	57.9	66.2	27,228.6		38,852.0	—
+ Retained Earnings	12.4	12.4	26,710.4		38,269.0	—
+ Retained Earnings			505.8	650.0	571.0	—
			12.4	12.0	12.0	—
Treasury Stock						—
Comprehensive Inc. and Other	343.1	2,782.7	(715.8)	2,213.0	(434.0)	2,311.0
= Other Reserves						3,623.0
+ Other Reserves	(166.4)	1,919.7	409.3	3,746.0	816.0	—
– Equity Equivalent	20.0					—
– Equity Equivalent	(6.2)					—
– Equity Equivalent	(250.5)	1,821.1	587.3	4,236.0	1,411.0	—
– Comprehensive Income			(31.6)	48.0		—
– Retained Earnings	57.9	66.2	505.8	(68.0)	(20.0)	—
– Retained Earnings	12.4	12.4	12.4	650.0	571.0	—
– Retained Earnings			107.2	12.0	12.0	—
– Deferred Compensation				310.0	212.0	—
Expenses						
+ Other Reserves	(166.4)					
– Equity Equivalent	20.0					
– Equity Equivalent	(6.2)					
– Equity Equivalent	(250.5)					
– Retained Earnings	57.9					
– Retained Earnings	12.4					
+ Other Reserves	(166.4)					
– Retained Earnings	57.9					
– Retained Earnings	12.4					
+ Comprehensive Income		1,821.1	587.3	4,236.0	1,411.0	—
+ Comprehensive Income				48.0		—
+ Deferred Compensation			107.2			—

(continued overleaf)

Table 7.2 Continued

Balance Sheet

Balance Sheet as of:	Dec-31-2009	Dec-31-2010	Dec-31-2011	Restated Dec-31-2012	Dec-31-2013	Sep-30-2014
Currency	CNY	CNY	CNY	CNY	CNY	CNY
+ *Deferred Compensation Expenses*	703.6			212.0	310.0	–
+ *Share-based Compensation Reserve*		1,199.7				–
+ *Shares Held for Share Award Scheme*	(123.8)	(258.1)	(606.9)	(667.0)	(871.0)	(1,312.0)
+ *Accumulated Currency Gain/Loss*			(31.6)			–
+ *Accumulated Currency Gain/Loss*				(20.0)	(68.0)	–
Total Common Equity	**12,178.5**	**21,756.9**	**28,463.8**	**41,298.0**	**57,945.0**	**74,786.0**
Minority Interest	120.1	83.9	624.5	850.0	518.0	608.0
= Minority Interest	120.1	83.9	624.5	850.0	518.0	608.0
Total Equity	**12,298.7**	**21,840.9**	**29,088.3**	**42,148.0**	**58,463.0**	**75,394.0**
Total Liabilities And Equity	**17,505.8**	**35,830.1**	**56,804.4**	**75,256.0**	**107,235.0**	**155,895.0**
Supplemental Items						
Total Shares Out. on Filing Date	9,042.4	9,110.8	9,110.0	9,169.9	9,213.0	9,243.0
= Ordinary Shares	9,042.4	9,110.8	9,110.0	9,169.9	9,213.0	9,243.0
Total Shares Out. on Balance Sheet Date	9,042.4	9,110.8	9,110.0	9,169.9	9,213.0	9,243.0
= Ordinary Shares	9,042.4	9,110.8	9,110.0	9,169.9	9,213.0	9,243.0
Book Value/Share	1.35	2.39	3.12	4.5	6.29	8.09
Tangible Book Value	11,874.5	20,695.8	24,194.7	35,785.0	52,971.0	69,633.0
Tangible Book Value/Share	1.31	2.27	2.66	3.9	5.75	7.53
Total Debt	202.3	5,298.9	11,732.8	10,700.0	15,053.0	34,297.0
Net Debt	(11,151.5)	(16,835.1)	(14,595.4)	(16,489.0)	(24,798.0)	(16,352.0)

Debt Equivalent Oper. Leases	718.8	960.8	2,783.1	4,984.0	7,064.0	NA
Total Minority Interest	120.1	83.9	624.5	850.0	518.0	608.0
Equity Method Investments	477.6	1,145.2	4,495.3	7,345.0	12,179.0	46,949.0
Inventory Method	NA	NA	NA	Avg Cost	Avg Cost	NA
Buildings	1,299.1	1,368.5	1,731.9	2,358.0	2,800.0	NA
Machinery	2,032.2	3,319.3	6,426.6	8,673.0	11,040.0	NA
Construction in Progress	105.8	386.9	158.7	534.0	2,041.0	—
Leasehold Improvements	90.4	130.3	385.6	586.0	872.0	—
Full Time Employees	7,515	10,692	17,446	24,160	27,492	26,284
Filing Date	Mar-28-2011	Mar-25-2012	Mar-28-2013	Mar-31-2014	Mar-31-2014	Nov-12-2014
Restatement Type	NC	NC	NC	RS	O	O
Calculation Type	REP	REP	REP	REP	REP	REP

Note: For multiple class companies, total share counts are primary class equivalent, and for foreign companies listed as primary ADRs, total share counts are ADR-equivalent.

Table 7.3 Tencent Holdings: cashflow statement

Tencent Holdings Ltd. (HK:700)

In Millions of the reported currency, except per share items.	Template: Period Type: Currency:	Standard Annual Reported Currency			Restatement: Order: Conversion:	Latest Filings Latest on Right Historical	
For the Fiscal Period Ending	12 months Dec-31-2009	12 months Dec-31-2010	12 months Dec-31-2011	Restated 12 months Dec-31-2012		12 months Dec-31-2013	LTM 12 months Sep-30-2014
Currency	CNY	CNY	CNY	CNY		CNY	CNY
Cash Flow							
Net Income	**5,155.6**	**8,053.6**	**10,203.1**	**12,732.0**		**15,502.0**	**21,861.0**
Depreciation & Amort.	405.9	669.9	1,208.3	1,880.0		2,484.0	2,907.0
= Depreciation of Fixed Assets and Investment Properties	–	–	1,208,261.0	–		–	–
+ Depreciation from Notes	405,301.0	668,580.0	–	1,880.0		2,484.0	–
+ Depreciation from Notes	575.0	1,280.0	–	–		–	–
Amort. of Goodwill and Intangibles	80.8	109.4	726.2	557.0		887.0	1,569.0
= Depreciation/Amortization Charge of Intangible Assets	131,897.0	–	–	733.0		1,106.0	–
+ Amortization of Intangible Assets	–	–	–	733.0		1,106.0	–
– Amortization of Software Assets	51,109.0	–	–	176.0		219.0	–
– Amortization of Intangible Assets	79,213.0	–	–	–		–	–
– Amortization of Intangible Assets	1,575.0	–	–	–		–	–
+ Depreciation/Amortization Charge of Intangible Assets	131,897.0	–	–	–		–	–

– Amortization of Software Assets	51,109.0	—	—	—	—	—
– Amortization of Intangible Assets	—	—	—	—	1,106.0	—
+ Depreciation/Amortization Charge of Intangible Assets	—	109,411.0	726,221.0	—	—	—
Depreciation & Amort., Total	**486.7**	**779.3**	**1,934.5**	**2,437.0**	**3,371.0**	**4,476.0**
Other Amortization	51.6	3.7	4.9	184.0	235.0	235.0
= Amortization of Land Use Rights	—	3,724.0	4,925.0	8.0	16.0	—
+ Amortization of Software Assets	51,109.0	—	—	176.0	219.0	—
+ Amortization of Leasehold Land and Land Use Rights	466.0	—	—	—	—	—
(Gain) Loss From Sale Of Assets	4.7	(0.9)	1.7	(1.0)	6.0	6.0
= Gain/(Loss) on Disposal of Fixed Assets	3,043.0	(883.0)	1,694.0	—	6.0	—
+ Loss on Disposals of Intangible Assets	1,654.0	—	—	—	—	—
(Gain) Loss On Sale Of Invest.	—	—	(465.5)	692.0	(180.0)	(180.0)
= Gain on Disposals/deemed Disposal of Associates	—	—	(708,486.0)	—	—	—
+ Gains on Disposal of Investees	—	—	—	(7.0)	(267.0)	—
+ Impairment Provision for Available for Sale Financial Assets, associates and Joint Ventures	—	—	243,000.0	699.0	87.0	—
(Income) Loss on Equity Invest.	(22.2)	(75.8)	190.0	80.0	(171.0)	(171.0)
= Share of Losses of Joint Venture	—	—	—	26.0	42.0	—

(continued overleaf)

Table 7.3 Continued

Cash Flow

For the Fiscal Period Ending	12 months Dec-31-2009	12 months Dec-31-2010	12 months Dec-31-2011	Restated 12 months Dec-31-2012	12 months Dec-31-2013	LTM 12 months Sep-30-2014
Currency	CNY	CNY	CNY	CNY	CNY	CNY
+ Share of (Profits) Losses of Associates	(22,206.0)	(72,359.0)	24,255.0	54.0	(213.0)	–
+ Share of Losses/(profits) of Jointly Controlled Entities	–	(3,399.0)	165,731.0	–	–	–
Stock-Based Compensation	321.4	495.8	732.7	905.0	1,168.0	1,168.0
= Share-based Compensation Expense	321,422.0	495,772.0	732,691.0	905.0	1,168.0	–
Other Operating Activities	294.6	714.9	(420.5)	(1,107.0)	(1,472.0)	(4,414.0)
= Net Income (Loss)	65,965.0	61,584.0	21,748.0	53.0	61.0	–
+ Exchange Gain/loss	1,953.0	(34,189.0)	(108,042.0)	21.0	(310.0)	–
+ Interest Incomes	(136,014.0)	(255,922.0)	(468,990.0)	(836.0)	(1,314.0)	–
+ Dividend Income	–	–	–	(407.0)	(509.0)	–
+ Income Tax (Benefit)	819,120.0	1,797,924.0	1,874,238.0	2,266.0	3,718.0	–
Expense						
+ Cash Income Tax Paid – Operating Activities	(456,448.0)	(872,435.0)	(1,836,263.0)	(2,225.0)	(3,118.0)	–
+ Losses from Derivative Financial Instruments	–	–	96,790.0	21.0	–	–
+ Losses from Derivative Financial Liabilities	–	17,964.0	–	–	–	–
Change in Trad. Asset Securities	329.8	–	–	–	–	–
= Financial Assets Held for Trading	329,804.0	–	–	–	–	–
Change in Acc. Receivable	(246.0)	(483.7)	(250.7)	(267.0)	(606.0)	(606.0)
= Accounts Receivable	(245,977.0)	(483,712.0)	(250,693.0)	(267.0)	(606.0)	–
Change In Inventories	5.5	–	–	(301.0)	(815.0)	(815.0)
= Inventories	5,483.0	–	–	(301.0)	(815.0)	–

Change in Acc. Payable	247.5	478.3	827.6	1,689.0	2,036.0	2,036.0
= Accounts Payable	247,454.0	478,330.0	827,573.0	1,689.0	2,036.0	2,036.0
Change in Unearned Rev.	1,053.8	1,024.6	2,253.1	3,098.0	3,728.0	3,728.0
= Deferred Revenue	1,053,833.0	1,024,570.0	2,253,098.0	3,098.0	3,728.0	3,728.0
Change in Other Net Operating Assets	715.4	1,329.4	(1,652.7)	(712.0)	1,572.0	1,572.0
= Restricted Cash	—	—	(1,850,652.0)	(640.0)	(1,611.0)	—
+ Long-term Payable	(43,331.0)	(179,804.0)	—	—	—	—
+ Prepayments, Deposits and Other Receivables	36,892.0	(51,936.0)	(2,630,368.0)	(2,255.0)	(940.0)	—
+ Other Tax Liabilities	113,045.0	9,942.0	(45,689.0)	397.0	52.0	—
+ Other Payables and Accruals, and Other Taxes Payable	608,788.0	1,551,226.0	2,873,982.0	1,786.0	4,071.0	—
Cash from Ops.	**8,398.4**	**12,319.3**	**13,358.1**	**19,429.0**	**24,374.0**	**28,896.0**
Capital Expenditure	(788.8)	(1,488.2)	(4,059.7)	(3,657.0)	(4,788.0)	(3,783.0)
= Purchase of Fixed Assets, Construction in Progress and Investment Properties	(788,824.0)	(1,488,220.0)	(4,059,717.0)	(3,657.0)	(4,788.0)	—
Sale of Property, Plant, and Equipment	0.6	1.6	0.6	4.0	17.0	17.0
= Proceeds from Disposal of Fixed Asset	595.0	1,574.0	599.0	4.0	17.0	—
Cash Acquisitions	(0.9)	(387.1)	(1,444.4)	(435.0)	4.0	4.0
= Payment for Acquisition of Non Controlling Interests in a Non Wholly Owned Subsidiary	(717.0)	(118,260.0)	—	—	—	—
+ Proceeds/(payments) for Business Combinations, Net of Cash Acquired	(140.0)	(268,852.0)	(1,444,442.0)	(435.0)	4.0	—
Divestitures	—	—	—	—	203.0	203.0
= Proceeds from Disposals of Subsidiaries	—	—	—	—	203.0	—
Sale (Purchase) of Intangible assets	(32.0)	(758.4)	(794.3)	(1,182.0)	(1,293.0)	(1,293.0)
= (Purchases) of Intangible Assets	(31,950.0)	—	—	—	—	—

(continued overleaf)

Table 7.3 Continued

Cash Flow

For the Fiscal Period Ending	12 months Dec-31-2009 CNY	12 months Dec-31-2010 CNY	12 months Dec-31-2011 CNY	Restated 12 months Dec-31-2012 CNY	12 months Dec-31-2013 CNY	LTM 12 months Sep-30-2014 CNY
+ Payment for Land Use Rights	–	(456,555.0)	–	–	–	–
+ Purchase/prepayments of Land Use Rights	–	–	(5,950.0)	(313.0)	(93.0)	–
+ Purchase/prepayments of Intangible Assets	–	(301,831.0)	(788,375.0)	(869.0)	(1,200.0)	–
Invest. in Marketable & Equity Securt.	(4,138.3)	(8,836.4)	(7,420.7)	(15,095.0)	(14,306.0)	(14,306.0)
= Purchases of Available-for-sale Financial Assets	(68,782.0)	(2,179,096.0)	(1,706,752.0)	(557.0)	(3,651.0)	–
+ Payments for Investment in Joint Venture	–	(71,143.0)	(194,915.0)	–	(9.0)	–
+ Payments for Held-to-maturity Investments	(341,795.0)	–	–	–	–	–
+ Proceeds from Disposals of Interests in Associates	–	–	–	111.0	155.0	–
+ Payment for Interest in Associates	(148,417.0)	(511,967.0)	(3,528,714.0)	(3,668.0)	(4,456.0)	–
+ Payments for Term Deposits with Initial Term of Over Three Months	(4,212,396.0)	(6,530,237.0)	(7,979,595.0)	(29,513.0)	(22,295.0)	–
+ Proceeds from the Redemption of Held to Maturity Investments	68,346.0	341,410.0	–	–	–	–
+ Receipt from Maturity of Term Deposits with Initial Term of Over Three Months	564,729.0	114,662.0	5,989,298.0	18,532.0	15,950.0	–

Net (Inc.) Dec. in Loans Originated/Sold	—	—	—	—	—
Other Investing Activities	(65.4)	(546.5)	(1,636.2)	4,095.0	1,029.0
= Cash Dividend and Interest Received – Investing Activities	116,162.0	219,937.0	415,055.0	626.0	536.0
+ Cash Dividend and Interest Received – Investing Activities	—	15,338.0	20,000.0	440.0	551.0
+ Receipt From/(payment For) Loan Made to a Related Party	18,394.0	—	—	—	—
+ Payments for Loans to Joint Ventures	—	—	(15,764.0)	(34.0)	(38.0)
+ (Loan Advanced)/repayment of Loan to Associates and Jointly Controlled Entities	—	54,700.0	—	—	—
+ Refund Of/(payments For) Restricted Cash	(200,000.0)	(836,457.0)	(2,055,486.0)	3,063.0	—
+ Proceeds/(payments) for Loan to Associates	—	—	—	—	(20.0)
Cash from Investing	**(5,024.8)**	**(12,015.0)**	**(15,354.8)**	**(16,270.0)**	**(19,134.0)**
Short Term Debt Issued	202.3	5,298.9	6,682.8	982.0	2,320.0
= Short-term Debt Issued	202,322.0	5,298,947.0	6,682,837.0	982.0	2,320.0
Long-Term Debt Issued	—	—	3,760.9	5,983.0	4,693.0
= Long-term Debt Issued	—	—	3,760,928.0	3,768.0	1,847.0
+ Long-term Debt Issued	—	—	—	2,215.0	2,846.0
Total Debt Issued	**202.3**	**5,298.9**	**10,443.8**	**6,965.0**	**7,013.0**
Short Term Debt Repaid	—	(202.3)	(3,765.9)	(8,024.0)	(986.0)
= Short-term Debt Repaid	—	(202,322.0)	(3,765,941.0)	(8,024.0)	(986.0)
Long-term Debt Repaid	—	—	—	—	(1,328.0)
= Long-term Debt Repaid	—	—	—	—	(1,328.0)
Total Debt Repaid	**—**	**(202.3)**	**(3,765.9)**	**(8,024.0)**	**(2,314.0)**
Issuance of Common Stock	165.4	199.2	159.7	238.0	308.0
= Exercise of Common Options/warrants	165,448.0	199,249.0	159,729.0	238.0	308.0
Repurchase of Common Stock	(178.2)	(477.7)	(1,485.7)	(141.0)	(1,603.0)
= Repurchases of Shares	(74,570.0)	(310,222.0)	(1,047,033.0)	(20.0)	(1,325.0)

(continued overleaf)

Table 7.3 Continued

Cash Flow

For the Fiscal Period Ending	12 months Dec-31-2009	12 months Dec-31-2010	12 months Dec-31-2011	Restated 12 months Dec-31-2012	12 months Dec-31-2013	LTM 12 months Sep-30-2014
Currency	CNY	CNY	CNY	CNY	CNY	CNY
+ Payment for Purchase of Shares for Share Award Scheme	(103,618.0)	(167,519.0)	(438,714.0)	(121.0)	(278.0)	–
Common Dividends Paid	(396.1)	(639.3)	(838.3)	(1,108.0)	(1,468.0)	(1,761.0)
= Dividends	(554,604.0)	(639,264.0)	(838,290.0)	(1,108.0)	(1,468.0)	(1,761.0)
+ Common Stock Dividends Paid	–	–	–	–	–	–
– Special Dividend Paid	(158,458.3)	–	–	–	–	–
Total Dividends Paid	**(396.1)**	**(639.3)**	**(838.3)**	**(1,108.0)**	**(1,468.0)**	**(1,761.0)**
Special Dividend Paid	(158.5)					
= Special Dividend Paid	(158,458.3)					
Other Financing Activities	(32.1)	(66.7)	(140.5)	(316.0)	(228.0)	–
= Dividends Paid to Non-controlling Interest	(32,088.0)	(66,723.0)	(56,531.0)	(117.0)	(73.0)	15,877.0
+ Proceeds from Capital Injection from a Minority Interest	–	–	9,800.0	22.0	5.0	–
+ Payment for Acquisition of Non Controlling Interests in Non Wholly Owned Subsidiaries	–	–	–	(179.0)	(160.0)	–
+ Payment for Derivative Financial Instruments in Relation to Short-term Borrowings	–	–	(93,761.0)	(42.0)	–	–
Cash from Financing	**(397.1)**	**4,112.1**	**4,373.0**	**(2,386.0)**	**1,708.0**	**16,793.0**
Foreign Exchange Rate Adj.	(0.7)	(51.9)	(172.5)	(2.0)	(103.0)	(65.0)
= Foreign Exchange Rate Effect on Cash and Cash Equivalents	(692.0)	(51,881.0)	(172,490.0)	(2.0)	(103.0)	–
Net Change in Cash	**2,975.8**	**4,364.6**	**2,203.9**	**771.0**	**6,845.0**	**14,851.0**

Supplemental Items

Cash Interest Paid	NA	NA	NA	NA	NA
Cash Taxes Paid	456.4	872.4	1,836.3	2,225.0	3,118.0
Levered Free Cash Flow	5,545.5	6,935.6	4,445.6	14,179.4	21,577.4
Unlevered Free Cash Flow	5,545.5	6,957.4	4,491.0	14,383.8	22,019.3
Change in Net Working Capital	(1,833.4)	(1,925.7)	474.8	(6,259.4)	(5,416.4)
Net Debt Issued	202.3	5,096.6	6,677.8	(1,059.0)	2,944.0
Filing Date	Mar-28-2011	Mar-25-2012	Mar-28-2013	Mar-31-2014	Nov-12-2014
Restatement Type	NC	NC	NC	RS	O
Calculation Type	REP	REP	REP	REP	LTM

P/E ratio

Most analysts think Tencent is one of the best positioned Chinese internet companies to benefit from the mobile internet growth trend. Mobile game sales are forecast to increase rapidly with one forecast of 87 per cent growth in 2015. PC online game sales will grow steadily and online advertising sales will post high levels of growth driven by mobile video advertising. Tencent's eCommerce business will also grow strongly because the company has built out the infrastructure for this part of the business.

To arrive at a *P/E* ratio, we require an earnings per share (EPS) figure which means we need to know historical earnings as well as future forecast earnings. A *P/E* based on historical earnings is called a historical *P/E*. To derive the current *P/E* based on future earnings forecast we need to make earnings forecast. We therefore need to develop an earnings model.

Earnings models can be simple or they can be extremely detailed. In the example of a simple earnings model given in Table 7.1, the revenues are broken down according to the business division. It is important to know the gross profit margins and operating profit margins in order to find operating and net profits. The gross profit margin is the revenues minus cost of goods sold divided by revenues. To find gross profit margins, we may use historical gross profit margins and change the figure according to new information we may have obtained about the company and its products.

For example, the company may have raised the price of its products without incurring any increase in the cost of goods sold. The price increase should result in an increase in gross profit margins. Similarly, operating profit margins are derived from past numbers, adjusted for any changes to the company, its products and other relevant factors.

From Tables 7.4 and 7.5, we are able to calculate the *P/E* ratios as follows:

Historical *P/E* based on 2013 EPS:

$$P/E = \frac{104.70}{1.83}$$
$$= 57.2X$$

Table 7.4 Simple earnings model for Tencent Holdings

Rmb mn	2012 A	2013A	2014E	2015E	2016E
Total revenue	43,894	60,437	81,152	98,407	115,942
Value added services	35,718	44,985	65,797	84,296	100,110
Social networks	11,919	13,020	19,300	24,821	29,631
Online games	23,798	31,965	46,496	59,475	70,479
Online advertising	3,383	5,033	6,724	9,782	12,812
E-Commerce	4,427	9,796	7,450	3,051	1,638
Others	365	621	1,178	1,275	1,381
Gross profit	25,686	32,658	48,334	62,686	76,037
Gross profit margin (%)	58.5	54	59.6	63.7	65.6
EBITDA	18,430	21,719	32,543	43,205	53,544
Adj. OPM (%)	36.0	30.0	34.6	39.0	41.6
Net income	14,286	17,063	23,805	32,121	40,674
Reported diluted EPS (RMB)	1.37	1.66	2.55	3.25	4.15
Adj. diluted EPS (RMB)	1.53	1.83	2.60	3.53	4.47
Adj. diluted EPS growth (%)	30.5	19.2	42.3	35.8	26.5

Share price HK$: 132.30
Share price RMB: 104.70

Table 7.5 Financial and valuation metrics for Tencent Holdings

	12/13A	12/14E	12/15E	12/16E
Revenue (RMB mn)	60,437	81,152	98,407	115,942
EBITDA (RMB mn)	20,565	31,231	41,631	51,655
Net profit (RMB mn)	17,063	23,805	32,121	40,674
EPS (RMB)	1.83	2.60	3.53	4.47
EPS growth (%)	19.2	42.3	35.8	26.5
ROE (%)	34.4	36.6	37.1	34.0
Net debt/equity (%)	Net cash	Net cash	Net cash	Net cash
P/E (X)	57.2	40.2	29.5	23.3
P/B (X)	16.7	13.2	9.2	6.7
EV/EBITDA (X)	46.6	30.8	22.5	17.5
Dividend yield (%)	0.90	0.22	0.29	0.29

Where:

Price = 104.7 RMB
2013 EPS = 1.83 RMB

Current *P/E* based on 2014 Estimated EPS

$$P/E = \frac{104.70}{2.60}$$
$$= 40.2X$$

Where:

Price = 104.7 RMB
2015 EPS = 2.60 RMB

The *P/E* ratios of Tencent Holdings in 2013, 2014, 2015, and 2016 are 57.2X, 40.2X, 29.5X and 23.3X, respectively. The ratio falls over the next few years, which is an attractive characteristic in terms of valuation. Note however, the *P/E* ratios of future years are based off earnings forecasts. If these forecasts are wrong then the stock may become either more expensive in the future (if actual earnings are lower than expected) or cheaper (if actual earnings are higher than expected). Thus, comparing the *P/E* ratio on a time relative basis, a declining *P/E* ratio makes the stock look attractive because the trend implies increasing earnings growth.

PEG of Tencent for 2015:

$$PEG = \frac{29.5}{39.8}$$
$$= 0.7X$$

Where:

P/E for 2015 = 29.5
EPS growth for 2015 = 39.8 per cent

262 *Practice of investment management*

The *PEG* of Tencent is less than one, a desirable valuation in *PEG* terms generally.

It is not uncommon for securities analysts to give a target price for a stock. The target price or *TP* is higher than the current stock price; that is, if the analyst thinks the stock is a buy. The *TP* is an estimate of where the stock price will be, say, in 12 months based on the compound annual growth rate (CAGR) of earnings and the *PEG*. Thus, it is not unusual for an analyst to give a *TP* of HK$155 for Tencent, given its current price of HK$132. Using the financials in Table 7.5, a TP of HK$155 implies a 35.1X 2015 *P/E* and a 23.9X 2016 *P/E*. The *P/E* multiples are justified because an earnings CAGR of about 22 per cent is high and driven by strong growth in the mobile search market and social media advertising. These levels of *P/E* multiples are also reflective of the multiples in the industry domestically and globally.

Sum of the parts valuation

Some financial analysts may use a sum of the parts (SOTP) valuation technique on Tencent Holdings because some of the company's businesses, such as the social network and payment systems, make very little money but are actually worth a lot if sold off.

An SOTP valuation is, therefore, determining the value of a company by breaking up its various businesses and giving each a value. This method measures how much each division would be worth if it was broken up and spun off or acquired by another company. We then sum up the value of all these divisions, thus arriving at a sum of the parts valuation. This technique is sometimes used to value young technology companies because they are worth more than the sum of their parts. This means the value of the tech company's divisions could be worth more if they were sold to other companies.

For a company with different business segments, each segment is valued using different types of multiples appropriate for that particular segment. The types of multiples often used for SOTP valuation include; revenue, EBITDA, EBIT, or net income. A DCF analysis may also be useful when forecasted results are available.

Each segment of a company may be valued using a different type of trading or transaction multiple depending on the type of business in which it is engaged. For example, Division A may be valued using a certain multiple of EBITDA, say 4X; Division B may be valued using a multiple of revenue say 3X; and Division C may be valued using a multiple of net income, say, 10X.

$$\text{SOTP} = \text{Segment A (4X EBITDA)} + \text{Segment B (3X Revenue)} + \text{Segment C (10X Net income)} - \text{Net debt}$$

In the case of Tencent Holdings, to simplify the calculation, we use the *P/E* multiple to determine the value of each of the company's divisions. The results are shown in Table 7.6. We estimate the *P/E* multiple each division is likely to be valued at based on comparable businesses in the market and, if applicable, globally. For example, online games and value-added services are estimated to be worth a multiple of 18X *P/E* based on 2015 net profit of HK$28,170 million.

$$\text{Valuation of online games and VAS} = 18 \times 28{,}170$$
$$= \text{HK\$507{,}062m}$$

Table 7.6 Sum of the parts valuation for Tencent Holdings

HK$m	Valuation basis	Valuation metrics	Multiple	Valuation
Online games + VAS	PE 2015E	HK$28170m 2015 Net Profit	18X	507,062
Mobile game	PE 2015E	HK$10181m 2015 Net Profit	37X	376,697
Online Advertising	PE 2015E	HK$7503m 2015 Net Profit	70X	525,210
Net cash		HK$56,715		56,715
Total valuation (HK$m)				1,465,684
Number of Shares (m)				9,334
Value per share (HK$)				$157

We carry out the same calculations for the other divisions and sum up the total of each division, less net debt (in this case we add the cash). The SOTP value of Tencent Holdings is HK$1,465,684 million. If we divide this sum by the number of shares of the company, we arrive at a per share value for Tencent Holdings of HK$157.

This value is higher than the current share price of HK$132 and, therefore, we may conclude the stock of Tencent Holdings is undervalued from a SOTP valuation standpoint.

7.6 Industry analysis

Tencent Holdings' destiny is somewhat dependent on the future of the industry to which the company belongs. If the industry is growing at a healthy pace, this bodes well for Tencent. On the other hand, a mature industry with declining growth has a different type of impact on the company. It is, therefore, vital to investigate and analyse the industry as part of the research on a company's future especially with regard to earnings.

First, we need categorize the company correctly and break down its component businesses so we can do an industry analysis of each business.

Tencent belongs to the sector broadly labelled technology, media, telecommunications or TMT. The revenues for Tencent come from four main sources:

1 Value-added services
2 Social networks
3 Online games
4 Online advertising.

The growth in revenues for Tencent is forecast to derive from its mobile internet and mobile eCommerce businesses. The industry sector relevant to Tencent is therefore the internet sector in general and the mobile internet sector in particular. It is important to compare the P/E and other relative valuation metrics to the *P/E*s and similar metrics of other companies in this same industry. The comparison should be made with companies operating in the same market; that is, the Chinese market and also with those operating in the region (Asia) and globally.

Questions to consider in doing an industry analysis

The purpose of carrying out an industry analysis is ultimately to discover if the company under investigation is a good investment. The analyst needs to find out more about the structure, and determine the competitive and financial strength of the company being analysed.

Knowledge of the industry in which a company is situated gives us more information about the company itself. A company does not operate in isolation. Other companies supply it with materials and inputs for its products. The company has employees whose wages are determined by the market for labour in the industry. Most importantly, the company has competitors and customers for its products or services. Therefore, it is vital to find out more about these factors and how they affect the revenues and operations of a company.

There are some standard queries in any industry analysis.

1. Market for the product/service

The nature of the market: growing, stable, saturated, or declining.
  Customer profile: demographics, preferences, and income levels.
  In terms of market and customer profiles for Tencent we find that:

- China's mobile games market is growing rapidly driven by innovations in mobile technology, smartphones migration, and availability of faster networks. Within the online game sector, industry experts expect the mobile games sector to enjoy the fastest growth.
- E-Commerce is likely to grow rapidly. The Chinese online shopping market is forecast to grow at a CAGR of 36 per cent from 2013–16, driven largely by the strong growth in mobile internet and changes in the shopping behaviour of consumers. China's online shopping penetration rate is expected to increase from 8 per cent in 2013 to 14.5 per cent in 2016.
- With increasing popularity of the mobile payment capabilities, the percentage of mobile game players willing to pay for mobile games either on a subscription basis or virtual items purchases is increasing at a high rate. Analysts expect the percentage of mobile game players to trend up strongly as more mobile games launch, and internet companies get aggressive in monetizing the games after years of heavy investment.
- China's online shopper penetration is lower than many other countries. There were 302 million internet shoppers in China in 2013 accounting for 48.9 per cent of total internet users. The percentage in the US is 63.8 per cent.

2. Competitors

One of the most salient issues when investigating competitors is the size of their market share. The other issues worth looking into are the products competitors make, to which market segment of the industry they cater, and the strengths and weaknesses of each competitor.
  Looking at Tencent's competitive environment we find that:

- Tencent was the biggest games developer with 15.7 per cent market share in 3Q14, followed by Locojoy, Playcrab, and Yinhan. Smaller developers make up the remaining 51.2 per cent of the market. There is likely to be consolidation in this market. Traditional games developers like Tencent are transforming themselves into mobile game developers and will enjoy a competitive advantage because of name brand recognition.

3. Suppliers and inputs

What are the main inputs into the product or service? If the company is dependent on a particular commodity, and costs are sensitive to the price of the commodity, then an analysis must be made on the price trends for that commodity. For example, an airline is very much dependent on the price of oil. Any rise or fall in the latter will have a proportionate effect on the profits of the airline. This is why airline analysts study research on the oil market.

Tencent is, therefore, one of the best positioned Chinese internet companies to capture the mobile internet growth trend. The company has a well-structured ecosystem comprising online games, mobile games, social platforms, instant messaging, Apps store, online advertising, and E-Commerce capabilities

Looking at the peer group valuation comparison in Table 7.7, we note that Tencent is somewhere in the middle of the valuation range of its peers. The cheapest *P/E* is Sina's at 7X 2016 earnings. Sohu has the highest *P/E* at 53X 2016 earnings. However, SINA and Perfect World (7.2X *P/E*) are both far smaller companies in market capitalization terms compared to Tencent. The latter is, therefore, more likely to be an institutional holding and more liquidly traded. We may conclude that Tencent is not overvalued versus its peer group especially considering its PEG.

7.7 Economic analysis

After completing a thorough analysis of the company's industry sector, we move on to look at the economic environment in which it operates. Questions to consider in doing an economic analysis are:

1. What stage of the business cycle is the economy in? Is the economy currently in recession, just coming out of a recession, entering into a recession, or at the peak of the business growth cycle? As the economy enters a recession, consumption is

Table 7.7 Peer group valuation comparison

	Mkt Cap (US$M)	P/E(X) 2015	P/E(X) 2016	PEG(X) 2015
Tencent	137,103	29.5	23.3	0.7
Baidu	78,214	22.5	16.0	0.7
Alibaba Group	269,049	38.7	27.2	1.1
Sohu	2,017	N/A	53.5	N/A
Qihoo	7,519	14.6	10.5	0.4
YY	3,716	16.8	12.2	0.5
NetEase	12,912	12.8	10.9	0.8
Sina	2,520	10.7	7.0	0.4
Perfect World	952	8.4	7.2	N/A

likely to decline, which may hit the revenues of a company. If the company is in a recession-resilient industry such as a utility, the profits are less likely to be impacted by falling consumer spending. As an economy enters recession or if it is in recession, utilities tend to maintain a more or less steady stock price because their profits are less impacted by the state of the economy. Consumer stocks, however, are dependent on consumer spending and profits are likely to be hit on the downside by a slowing economy. Conversely, when the economy is entering into a recovery phase and pulling out of a recession, consumer stocks tend to move up strongly in price while utilities will lag in performance.

2   How long is this stage of the business cycle expected to last? If an investor is willing to hold on to a stock through the various business cycles this question is not particularly relevant. However, for an investor who trades stocks and looks at the business cycle as an important investing metric, then it is important to keep monitoring the economy's progress.
3   Is the economy in which the company operates a developed economy, an emerging market or a middle market economy? In general, certain sectors do especially well in emerging markets such as infrastructure, real estate, and consumer durables. This is because these sectors are not yet saturated but are instead at the takeoff stage. For example, India has a need for roads, railroad stock, electrical generation, capital equipment, and housing. The country is only at the takeoff stage of economic development where demand in most sectors of industry is high. In contrast the US is a developed country that has reached saturation point in many sectors. Growth exists in selective industries such as technology and services.
4   What are the demographics of the economy? It is said that demographics is destiny. Is the population of the country an ageing one like Japan or a young one like India? An ageing population requires more health care services and goods while a young population requires housing, consumer durables, and non-durables.
5   What is the trend of the country's currency rates, inflation rates, and interest rates? These metrics are important to analyse and monitor.

In the case of Tencent Holdings the economic considerations are as follows:

- Real consumption in China is likely to grow strongly in the next three years. Consumption was about 35 per cent of China's GDP in 2013, much lower than many Organization for Economic Co-operation and Development (OECD) countries. Increasing real income levels of Chinese consumers has become a major driver for the rising contribution of consumption to the economy. This contribution is forecast to continue increasing as the government sets policies to restructure the economy from one dependent on fixed asset investments to one more balanced between consumption and investment.
- The economy is showing signs of significant structural changes. The pace of urbanization has slowed. This slowing means that there is less labour available in urban areas.
- The job market remains tight despite a growth slowdown in China in 2014. The forecast is for the labour market to remain tight. The tightening of labour supply is due to both slowing urbanization and ageing of the population. China's labour force declined by 3.7 million in 2014. Thus, wages are not declining but are instead rising. Household disposable income per capita is likely to continue to outperform

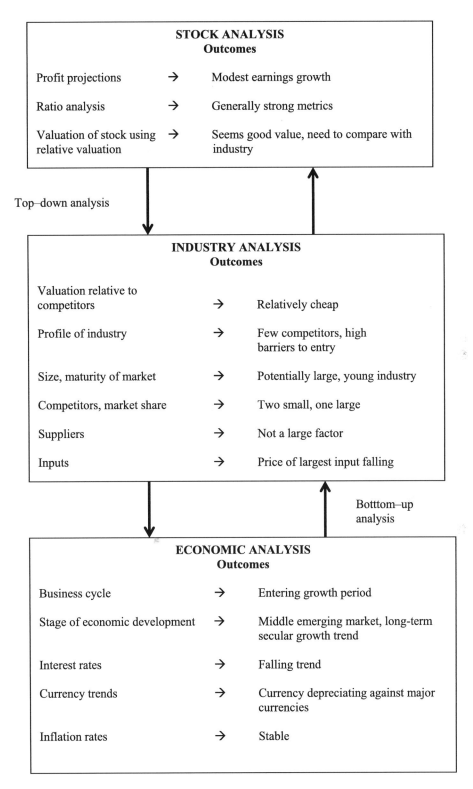

Figure 7.1 Top-down and bottom-up investment analysis.

268 *Practice of investment management*

GDP growth. This trend together with social security reforms is likely to boost consumption but may put some pressure on corporate profitability.
- Due to a slowing property market and economy, the People's Bank of China (PBOC), China's central bank, is likely to continue its easing of interest rates. In addition, weak inflation data may induce the central bank to cut rates further.

These economic considerations help determine the attractiveness of Tencent as an investment. First, the government directed rebalancing of the Chinese economy from investment- to consumption-led is a positive macro factor for Tencent. Ultimately, the company produces a consumption item. Second, the increase in household income is also positive because people have more disposable income to spend on consumption and entertainment—Tencent's products fall into both categories. Third, if the PBOC eases rates and increases liquidity into the economy, the likely result will again be a rise in incomes through a rise in asset prices. This promotes the wealth effect, which again is again positive for Tencent.

7.8 Tying the different analyses together

Depending on whether an investor has a 'top-down' or a 'bottom-up' investment style, the sequence of analysis will start from stock, industry to economy (bottom-up) or economy, industry, stock (top-down). If at each stage of the analysis a stock is seen as an attractive investment, then the investigation should continue on to the next stage. In practice, all three analyses are usually carried out more or less at the same time.

A much simplified example of the process of analysing a stock is illustrated in Figure 7.1.

Based on the generally positive outcomes of the analyses of the stock, its industry, and the economy, the stock of Tencent Holdings seems to merit a 'buy'.

Students should note that such easy decisions on investment are unusual. Not all metrics are aligned the same way and point in the direction of either a buy or a sell. It is more likely the case that some metrics will show the stock as attractive while others will be negative. The analyst has to do more granular research, going in-depth into more metrics, and developing innovative metrics to provide greater illumination into the investment quality of the stock. After all the analysis is done, the analyst must decide which of the data outcomes is most important, ranking them in order of priority. If the most important metric is positive, but the least important is negative then the former trumps the latter. In the end, security analysis is probably more art than science.

Notes

1 "Beginner's Guide to Financial Statements," *US Securities and Exchange Commission*, accessed 28 January 2015, www.sec.gov/pubs/begfinstmtguide.htm.
2 Frank K. Reilly and Keith C. Brown, *Investment Analysis and Portfolio Management*, 7th ed. (Mason, OH: Thomson South-Western, 2003).
3 Reilly and Brown, 391.
4 Ibid., 541.

Part III
Ethical issues in Asian investing

8 Overview of ethical theories – philosophy

8.1 Introduction

How do people evaluate moral issues and choose the right actions? In almost every situation where moral values are in question, people can use reason and apply ethical theories. In a perfect world, people using reason and ethical theory work through an ethical problem in a thorough and objective way as possible. However, a meticulous and comprehensive assessment is not always done or frequently possible. Yet, there is a systematic and rigorous way for humans to determine the right ethical choices. Contrary to current conventional attitudes and beliefs, we do not need to flounder in a confusion of emotions or shrug helplessly amid what (wrongly) seems to be a plethora of opposing cultural mores.

In this chapter, we discuss the moral theories available as frameworks for assessing ethical issues. The theories are applied in all areas of life and can therefore be applied in finance. These theories are secular; that is, the foundation of morality in these theories is not religiously based. There is little metaphysical or other-worldly aspects to these frameworks; rather, they derive from the world in which we live. The underlying foundation for ethics in these theories are human reason, the consideration of the good for humans, social communities, and human flourishing. The next chapter gives an account of ethics grounded in religions, specifically, Judaism, Christianity, Islam, and Buddhism.

8.2 Utilitarianism

Utilitarianism is an ethical theory that evaluates the rightness of an action according to the resulting consequences of that action. The motives for the act are not taken into account. How the act is done, or the character of the actor also does not matter. What is important for determining if the act is ethical or not ethical is the consequence of the act. For this reason, utilitarianism is a sub-genre of ethics known as consequentialism. In its simplest form utilitarianism derives from the 'principle of utility', a phrase first proposed by Francis Hutcheson.

> **Principle of utilitarianism**
>
> In any situation where there is a moral choice, act in a way that results in the greatest happiness for the greatest number of people.

Classical utilitarianism possess these three principles:

1 Actions are judged right or wrong solely on the consequences of the actions.
2 To assess consequences, only the amount of happiness or unhappiness created is considered.
3 Each person's happiness counts the same.

The English philosopher, Jeremy Bentham, was the first to set out the theory of utilitarianism. For Bentham, happiness is simply measured by the amount of pleasure attained and pain avoided. John Stuart Mill refined the theory by giving degrees of value to pleasure and pain. Henry Sidgwick became one of the theory's most successful advocates. Utilitarianism in its various forms continues to command the attention of philosophers and is one of the most widespread and influential ethical theories.

Bentham wanted to develop a scientific method of ethics. Instead of basing ethical choices on fickle and subjective emotions as the philosopher David Hume suggested, Bentham proposed an evaluative system that was essentially quantitative and objective. Society is a collection of individuals and what is right for society depends on achieving the happiness of as many of those individuals as possible. The quantitative aspect of the theory involves counting these numbers as well as obtaining a measure of the amount of happiness attained. For Bentham, happiness was purely the measure of intended pleasure and the absence of pain. If the final balance is more pleasure than pain, then the act should be done. If the final balance is more pain than pleasure, then the act should not be done. This focus on measuring happiness, as defined by Bentham, shows the depth of Bentham's insistence on ethics as a quantitative analysis of physical pleasure and pain. The whole calculus is a matter of numbers derived from hard data.

The objective aspect of the theory comes from the notion that each person counts equally and everyone has an equal right to happiness, irrespective of her situation. In Bentham's version of utilitarianism, happiness is measured in terms of:

1 its duration
2 its intensity
3 its certainty or uncertainty
4 how near and immediate it is
5 how free from pain it is
6 whether it is likely to lead on to further pleasure.

The last element of Bentham's utilitarian calculation is the 'extent'. This factor refers to the number of people who are affected by any action. Each action is good or bad according to its predicted results in generating the maximum amount of happiness, shared between the maximum number of people.

Bentham's definition of happiness is completely based on pleasure. However, not all pleasure is of equal value. John Stuart Mill refined Bentham's definition of happiness as pure physical pleasure by assigning degrees of quality to pleasure. For Mill, the quality of pleasure is just as important as the quantitative aspects, and perhaps even more important. For example, Mill prefers pleasures of the mind to those of the flesh. Mill lists a hierarchy of pleasures from best to least good as follows:

1 Moral pleasure
2 Intellectual pleasure

3   Imaginative pleasure
4   Sensual pleasure

While Mill differentiates emotional and physical pleasures and assigns degrees of quality to pleasure, he does not depart from Bentham in equating happiness with pleasure. The idea that pleasure is equivalent to the one ultimate good and pain is the ultimate evil is termed 'hedonism'. Hedonism is attractive because it is simple and it is plausible what makes us happy is that which gives us pleasure.

Mill also went further than Bentham, proposing a form of utilitarianism that accommodates rules. Over time, two major forms of utilitarianism developed. One is rule utilitarianism and the other is act utilitarianism.

Act utilitarianism

Bentham's version of utilitarianism is known as act utilitarianism. The consequences of each individual act are taken into account. Even if the act may seem similar to other acts, the act must still be subject to the utilitarian test. For the circumstances in which the act is carried out may be different. The people affected by the act and their preferences also may differ.

Rule utilitarianism

A type of utilitarianism in contemporary circles is called rule utilitarianism. This particular form tries to give universality in moral guidance. Rule utilitarianism attempts to give universality by introducing a rule of behaviour between the actor and the consequences of her act. For example, the rule that one should always tell the truth is a way of obtaining the greatest happiness for the greatest number. Without this rule, no one will be able to trust another person to tell the truth. Society cannot function properly without trust and, therefore, truthfulness is a principle society requires.

Rules reduce arbitrariness in moral decision-making. Evaluating every act and its consequences to decide if the act is right introduces a degree of arbitrariness.

> I promise to pay the college student who mowed my lawn $50. However, I do not pay him, breaking my promise. However, I reason that by donating the $50 to Save the Children, more happiness will be obtained by a greater number of people. It is right not to pay the college student even though I promised I would.

If only consequences matter, we are capable of creating circumstances in which a bad action will have the best consequences.

Rule utilitarianism does not involve judging every particular action by the principle of utility. Instead, there is a set of optimal rules, derived from a utilitarian viewpoint. The rules come out from the question, 'What rules should be followed to maximize happiness?' A rule is promulgated not for its own sake but because a rule such as truth telling is of great utility, essential for the effective functioning of human society. Individual acts are judged right or wrong according to whether they are acceptable or unacceptable by this set of rules. Using the standards of rule utilitarianism, I would be wrong to not give the college student the $50 because it is wrong to not fulfil a promise.

Using human reason, rules against violating people's rights, lying, and cheating can be established. Following the rules promotes the general happiness. Acts are judged by whether they conform to the rules and not by their utility. The advantage of rule utilitarianism is it makes use of the accumulated experience of many generations about which kinds of actions will have good or bad consequences. We do not need to calculate the consequences of every single action from beginning to end.

Rule utilitarianism is not radically different from act utilitarianism. It may be viewed as a version of utilitarianism that gives quick decision rules, or 'rules of thumb'. Rules are convenient guidelines and have three distinctive benefits:

1   Following the rules saves time.
2   Following the rules precludes bias and special pleading.
3   The rules encapsulate generations of experience with acts and their consequences.

The rule utilitarian approach, therefore, does not require us to forecast consequences of a set of actions. The history of humanity provides the data to determine consequences of acts such as lying, cheating, or promise breaking.

Framework for applying utilitarianism[1]

It is helpful to have a working framework to use when we wish to apply utilitarian analysis to an ethical question. While the framework given here is by no means completely comprehensive, it is a starting point for further and deeper evaluations, if necessary.

1   *The act*: state the action we are considering, for example: selling mortgages that do not require the mortgagee to have proof of income. Should we do this act or should we not? Stating the act should be done clearly, completely, and as honestly as possible. The action should be stated in morally neutral language so we do not anticipate or colour the outcomes.
2   *Specify the parties affected*: identify those who will be affected, directly or indirectly by the act. This step also requires projecting the effects of the action outwards from the immediate environment of the act.
3   *The consequences*: list all the good and bad consequences for those who are directly and indirectly affected. Proceed as far into the future as feasible when considering the consequences. Assign probabilities to the different possible outcomes to give a more complete picture.
4   *The calculation*:

    a   For those directly affected, consider all the good consequences versus all the bad consequences. Use the criteria Bentham provides: duration, intensity, nearness, and possibility of further good or bad. Consider also, as Mill suggests, the relative value of the good or the bad consequences.
    b   For those indirectly affected, the same weighing of good versus bad consequences must also be done.
    c   Finally, the good and bad consequences for society as a whole must be weighed.

5   *The decision*: sum up all the good and the bad consequences. If the good consequences are greater than the bad, then the action is ethical. If the bad consequences are greater than the good, then the action is not ethical.

6   The iterations:

   a   Are there any alternatives to the action being considered? Instead of simply choosing to carry out or not carry out an action, think about another option to the chosen action that may be as effective.
   b   Compare the results of other options to the act under evaluation. The action resulting in the most good or the least bad (if no option produces more good than bad) among the alternatives is the ethically right action to take.

Applying the utilitarian framework in the case of bank bailouts

We may use this framework in the case of an actual financially relevant action taken by the US government during the height of the 2008 global financial crisis.

Consider the bailout of the big money centred banks such as Morgan Stanley, Goldman Sachs, and J.P. Morgan in 2008. Is it right to use government, such as taxpayers' money, to rescue banks that are private corporations?

From the example in Table 8.1, we note the utilitarian approach does not require mathematically precise calculations. It is not possible to get this type of precision when dealing with the morality of actions. In a vast majority of cases, the consequences of an action are obviously good or bad. The example given here is more complex and difficult than the usual cases. It may be true there is less certitude about the decision being correct.[1] In this case, we should be ready to revise the decision if we find the calculation is mistaken. This is not a defect of the theory but a statement of the human condition and the nature of morality.[2]

Common criticisms of utilitarianism

1. Ethical acts according to utilitarian calculations may not be just

Utilitarianism can justify making decisions that violate a person's human rights. What may be considered good for some people can violate rights of others. An example of this problem is a wealthy person who needs an organ transplant. If the wealthy person offers to donate a large sum of money to a charity to help thousands in exchange for being the top of the list for an organ transplant, utilitarianism says the wealthy person should be placed at the top of the list. Why? Because more good results from the wealthy person receiving the organ than would result if the next person on the list receives the organ. However, the next person on the list for the organ has the right to receive the organ first, and it seems unfair for the wealthy person to use her wealth as an advantage. Justice does not depend on the consequences of an action. Justice is giving each person her due and treating people equitably.

RESPONSE

Advocates of utilitarianism will say the utilitarian calculation was not done properly in the cases where justice seems to be miscarried. What will become of the organ donation system if it is discovered the rich can buy their way to being first in line for organ donations? Trust breaks down and there will be far fewer organ donors. People do not want to donate organs into a system that is corrupt. The organ donor system disintegrates as a result. The consequences from a wealthy recipient buying his way to being first in line for an organ are more bad than good.

Table 8.1 Steps in utilitarian analysis

Steps in a utilitarian framework of analysis	Applying the framework to the bailout of banks
1. The act	
• State the act under consideration	The government providing capital to the largest banks when these banks are under a state of financial stress
2. The ones affected:	
• Directly	Bank employees, shareholders, creditors, customers, government
• Indirectly	Taxpayers, other banks, banking system, vendors to banks
3. The consequences	
• To those directly affected	
• Good consequences	Bank employees remain employed, shareholders do not lose as much money, creditors do not lose as much money, customers do not lose their money, government does not have to pay unemployment benefits to those who lose their jobs
• Bad consequences	Government must deal with moral hazard problems in the future. Banks will take on risk knowing the government will bail them out because they are perceived to be too big to fail. Without bankruptcy, banks will evaluate risk incorrectly. Banks will continue to overcompensate their employees. There will not be a change to the existing banking culture that caused banks to overextend themselves
• To those indirectly affected	
• Good consequences	Other weak banks will not be threatened with depositors and investors losing confidence and withdrawing funds
• Bad consequences	Taxpayers must pay for banks' mistakes, when they did not benefit economically from the banks' successes
• To society	
• Good consequences	The national and global banking system does not seize up causing possible collapse of the financial system. A deep depression is avoided
• Bad consequences	Losing tax dollars that can be spent elsewhere. A probable consequence is a cut in spending on other government projects such as infrastructure or welfare
4. The calculation	
• Good consequences versus bad	
• To those directly affected	The action seems to produce more bad than good
• To those indirectly affected	The action seems to produce more bad than good
• To society	The action seems to produce the more good than bad
5. The decision	The action produces good for a greater number of people (society)
6. The iteration	
• Alternatives?	Instead of giving capital to banks, help homeowners under threat of foreclosure

This response that the utilitarian calculation is not done on the right time frame or does not take into account all affected does not satisfy most critics. Some advocate the use of both utilitarian and justice-based principles. In most cases, the utilitarianism works well. However, when utilitarian principles seem to go against justice, then the principle of justice should take precedence. The justification for the joint approach is that it produces more good overall. In other words, the justification is utilitarian.

2. Unrealistic goal of impartiality

Another problem with utilitarianism is that it requires an impartial decision-maker. Total impartiality does not allow special relationships like friends or family. The decision-maker naturally considers the good of people close to her before more distant stakeholders. The celebrated train dilemma illustrates the impartiality problem. Suppose you can save a train load of people heading for a collapsed bridge by pulling a switch to re-route the train. In doing so, your wife and children will certainly die because they are in the path of the train if it takes the alternate route. Many will not knowingly sacrifice their family for strangers. But utilitarianism forces the decision-maker to weigh the overall good. Depending on the number of people on the train one may have to sacrifice the family.

RESPONSE

The example above is, of course, an extreme moral dilemma. The benefit of utilitarianism is that it removes the problem of special treatment and favouritism such as nepotism. The theory ensures each human is measured the same as another.

3. Happiness does not necessarily equate to rightness

Another criticism of utilitarianism is that it answers the question 'what decision is right?' by answering 'what decision brings about the most good, pleasure, or happiness?' But the questions are not the same. It does not necessarily and logically follow that the answer to one question will be the answer to the other. The argument is especially pertinent when applying act utilitarianism and thinking only to the consequences in the immediate future. For example, we can use utilitarianism to justify lying to another person to avoid immediate negative consequences of hurting feelings or damaging the relationship. But if no one ever provides truthful answers to tough questions, adverse long-term consequences can result. The lie leads to further bad decisions made from ignorance or bad information, leading to far more dire consequences.

RESPONSE

Contemporary utilitarians have largely rejected hedonism such as pleasure and pain. Instead, the focus is on the values of all sorts of things, such as artistic creativity and friendship, for their own sakes. Right actions are those that increase the world's supply of these valuable things. Others say we should act to maximize the satisfaction of people's preferences.

4. A full utilitarian calculation is impossible

No one has the time to do a full utilitarian calculation of all the consequences of an act before acting. We will inevitably miss out some who are indirectly affected or even directly affected. There is no time to do a full utilitarian calculation. In terms of consequences, we do not have the ability to discern their full measure. Furthermore, no way exists to know how far into the future we should extend to include all effects of an action.

RESPONSE

This criticism is often true. However, utilitarianism does not require a calculation before every act. This is why we have rule utilitarianism. In human history, there are multiple cases of great similarity. We know it is wrong to cheat on financial transactions because we know the bad consequences of cheating nearly always outweigh the good consequences. Knowing the process and reasoning behind utilitarianism give us a means of arriving at a decision regarding the morality of cheating. We know why it is wrong. We are not at a loss of reasoned moral argument to support the immorality of cheating.

8.3 Duty-based (deontological) theories

Another secular moral theory is the duty-based, or deontological, theory. *Deon* is the Greek word for duty. The theory of deontology states we are morally obligated to act in accordance with a certain set of principles and rules regardless of outcome. Thus, deontology is in direct contrast to consequentialism, which postulates whether an action is right depends on the consequences of the action. In religious deontology, the principles derive their foundation or basis from divine commandment so that under religious laws, we are morally obligated not to steal, lie, or cheat. Thus, deontological theories and duties have existed for many centuries. Immanuel Kant, deontology's celebrated proponent, formulated the most influential form of a secular deontological moral theory in 1788. Unlike religious deontological theories, the rules (or maxims) in Kantian deontology are grounded in human reason.

Deontological theories hold some acts are always wrong, even if the act leads to an admirable outcome. Actions in deontology are always judged independently of their outcome. An act can be morally bad even if its outcome is favourable. Kantian deontology holds that moral rules or laws are absolute. For example, Kant argues that lying is wrong under any circumstances. Instead of appealing to theological reasons, Kant instead appeals to human reason – reason always forbids lying.

> **Deontological or duty-based ethical theory:**
>
> We are morally obligated to act in accordance with a certain set of principles and rules regardless of outcome.

The will

Kant's moral theory is grounded on the exercise of the will. The will is the agent that creates value. A person does her duty in following the moral law because of a good will. The only way moral goodness can exist is for rational creatures to act from a good will. Humans apprehend how they should act according to the moral law and act from a sense of duty, driven by will. Having a good will is an attitude, rather than just a way of behaving. When we act on moral obligations, we are working out our will. In choosing to act morally, a person is exercising an inner freedom in following a sense of purpose and destiny.

The hypothetical imperative versus the categorical imperative

Hypothetical imperatives tell us what to do to achieve certain desires. If I am hungry, then I will eat some food. If I want to go to a good college, I will study hard. We will do a certain action if the action fulfils a particular desire we possess. If we do not possess the desire, then we do not need to take that course of action.

Moral obligations, in contrast, do not depend on particular desires. The form of a hypothetical imperative is, 'If you want x, then you ought to do y'. However, the form of a moral imperative is, 'You ought to do y'. The moral requirement is categorical: You ought to tell the truth, no matter what your desires are. The moral rule is not: You ought to tell the truth, if you want to be a good person. We are all obligated to act according to a moral rule.

The question then is why are we are obligated to act according to a moral rule. Kant argues it is possible to have hypothetical 'oughts' because we have desires. In a similar vein, it is possible to have categorical oughts because we have *reason*. Every rational person must accept that categorical oughts are obligatory, without exception. Categorical oughts are grounded in the principle called the categorical imperative, which is binding on rational agents because the agents are rational.

The three formulations of the categorical imperative

There are three formulations of Kant's categorical imperative. The three formulations can be seen as three views or perspectives on Kant's moral law.

The first formulation

The first formulation is:

> *Act only according to that maxim by which you can at the same time will that it should become universal law.*

The categorical imperative is a first-order principle that informs us if an act is morally permissible. The categorical imperative provides a simple, logical test of whether a rule is moral. When considering an act, we may use the following steps to determine if the act or rule behind the act is moral:

1. Think about the rule the act falls under. This rule is the 'maxim' of the act.
2. Next, consider if you are willing for the maxim to become a universal law. Should all people follow the maxim at all times?
3. If so, then the maxim is sound, and the act is acceptable.
4. If not, the act is not permissible.

Take the case of borrowing money. Mei needs money and has to borrow the money from a friend or a bank. To borrow the money, Mei must promise to repay the loan otherwise no one will lend the money. Yet, Mei knows she will not be able to repay the loan. Should Mei make a false promise to get the loan? Using the steps above:

1   The maxim will be: Whenever you need a loan, promise to repay it, even if you know you cannot.
2   Should this maxim become universal law? No. The maxim will be self-defeating because when it becomes universal law, no one will believe such promises. Therefore, no one will make loans based on these false promises.
3   Therefore, this act is forbidden.

The second formulation

The second formulation of the categorical imperative is:

> *Act so that you treat humanity, whether in your own person or in that of another, always as an end and never as a means only.*

People have intrinsic worth because they are rational agents, who are free and able to make their own decisions guided by reason. This intrinsic worth gives dignity to every human. As everyone possesses human dignity, morality requires we treat humans as an end and never as a means. To treat people as an end requires we treat them with respect. We should not manipulate or use people for our own purposes.

Let us return to the case of Mei who is desperate to borrow the money from a friend. She knows she cannot repay the loan. Is it right if Mei tells her friend she can repay the loan just to get the money? In telling her friend she can repay the loan, Mei is of course lying. In the above example, we used the act of lying to borrow funds against the first formulation of the categorical imperative. The test showed the act to be unethical.

We can also test whether it is ethical to tell a lie that Mei can repay the loan when she knows she cannot, in order to get a loan against the second formulation of the categorical imperative.

Is lying to a friend to get money from her permissible?

Lying to a friend to get something is to use the friend as a means to an end. You are manipulating your friend. Therefore, this act is not permissible.

On the other hand, if Mei tells her friend the truth, that she will not be able to repay the loan, Mei allows her friend to decide based on full disclosure and information. She can consult her own values and wishes, use her reason and choose freely. Thus, she is not a means to Mei's end but is instead treated with respect as a human being.

Notice, treating people as an end requires us to respect them as thinking beings and not force them to act against their will. They should be able to decide on their own volition. Kant is clear that laws, which are meant to protect people from themselves, such as wearing crash helmets, should be questioned.

The third formulation

The third formulation of the categorical imperative is:

> *Act only so that the will through its maxims could regard itself at the same time as universally lawgiving.*

This formulation is not written in an easily understood way. Roughly translated, the third formulation says that as autonomous and rational beings, humans will freely agree to abide by moral laws. However, those laws must accord with universal reason. In a nutshell, moral rules must be acceptable to rational beings.

As ends in themselves, human beings are not subservient to anyone else. Each human being determines the moral law and agrees to abide by the moral law freely. However, even though each person gives herself the moral law, she cannot prescribe anything she wants. The moral law legislated by each person must conform to reason and its demands. Reason is the same for all rational beings. Therefore, we give ourselves the same moral law.

Once again, we can apply this third formulation of the categorical imperative to Mei and her money problems to discover whether the rule, 'Whenever you need a loan, promise to repay it, even if you know you cannot' is moral. Mei should ask herself if the commands of the rule are acceptable to all rational beings acting rationally. She must consider the action not only from the point of view of the person doing the act, but also from the viewpoint of the receiver of the act. Mei's friend, a rational being, will not want to be lied to about Mei's ability to repay the loan. No rational being will want to be lied to. From Mei's side, as a rational being, she accepts limitations on what she is permitted to do.

Framework for applying deontological ethics

1. *The act:* state the action we are considering. For example, selling a risky financial security to a client to help a friend. This friend is a trader at another bank, who mistakenly bought too much for his trading book.
2. *Find a principle or rule that applies to such an action:* if there is, then follow that principle or rule because we have a moral duty to do so. For example, if your act involves cheating someone, then the principle 'Do not cheat others' applies in this instance and it is your moral duty to not cheat the person.
3. *If uncertain about the principle, go through the three categorical imperatives:*

    a   Should all people follow the same principle at all times without contradiction to adherence to the principle?
    b   Does the act treat the person as an end and not a means to an end?
    c   Would all rational people freely accept the act because it accords with reason?

    If the answer to the three questions is yes, then the act is ethical. If any question is answered with no, then the act is not ethical.
4. *Does the principle under which the act is subsumed conflict with other principles?* Sometimes, it may seem as if the act is right according to one principle but wrong if analysed under another principle (see 'Conflicts between rules' below). A renowned example is the hypothetical case of the runaway slave. A slave runs away from his owner, knocks on your door and asks you to hide him. You do so. Later, the owner comes to your house, and asks if you have seen the slave. Do you lie to the owner, or do you tell the truth and give up the slave? A conflict between two principles seems to exist in this hypothetical: (1) Do not lie, and (2) Do not harm others. If you lie to the slave owner you go against principle (1). If you do not lie and give up the slave you go against principle (2) because giving up the slave will lead to his losing his freedom, thus harming him.

5 *Discuss, use reason and good judgement to decide which principle to uphold:* in the case of the runaway slave, it is more important that you uphold principle (2) because it prevents harm (psychological and physical) to another person. You protect the person you promised to keep from harm, thus also upholding another principle: keep your promises.

Applying the deontological framework using the principle of fiduciary duty

The principle of fiduciary duty is one that applies to many financial professionals. A fiduciary is responsible for the care of another person's property or assets. Financial professionals, who are responsible for helping their clients, have as their primary duty to do the best for their client. In other words, a financial adviser has a fiduciary duty to her client. A director of a company has a fiduciary duty to shareholders of that company.

Simply put, a fiduciary duty is the duty to act solely in the best interest of the client. This duty includes not advancing the financial professional's personal interests.

You are a financial adviser and you manage the small portfolio of a new client. You advise your client on what stocks to buy and sell in her portfolio. You have done your research and you have read some research about a certain stock, Dive. The stock does not seem like a good one to own. The stock fundamentals are poor, in your opinion, and in the opinion of many experts in the field.

Your best friend works with you in the same company. He is in a more senior position. He has been your best friend since high school. He was instrumental in getting you hired at your current company. You were the best man at his wedding. You are his daughter's godfather.

Your best friend made a mistake and just bought millions of dollars of Dive on the company's books. He may lose a lot of the company's money because the price of Dive is likely to fall soon. He needs to get rid of the stock quickly. He asks you to advise your clients to buy as much Dive in their portfolios as possible. He will sell to your clients the Dive stocks that he just bought so he can get them off the company's books. He will ask you to especially call your new client because she is new and your relationship with her is not as deep as the one you have with your best friend.

Do you strongly recommend to your clients to buy Dive in order to help your best friend, who is also your senior in rank in the company, to get out of this situation? Or do you advise your new client not to buy Dive, based on your honest opinion and those of many other experts?

Use the principle of fiduciary duty: act solely in the best interest of your client. Do not put your interest ahead of your client's. This principle trumps the request of your friend to help him out, even if he is your best friend.

You tell your friend you cannot advise your new client to buy Dive because doing so will not be in the best interest of your client. Even though he is your friend, he is also a financial professional and he should know the principle of fiduciary duty. As a friend he should understand that you are following a professional duty. Discuss this with him.

At first, he may be so stressed by his mistake he will be angry with you. Later, when he is more rational, he should understand your position. He should understand you might have saved him from committing a bad mistake. If you had bought Dive for your client and its stock price fell a lot, and if people discovered you did it to save your friend from making a loss for the company, then the publicity and possible legal consequences could be bad.

Criticisms of Kant's deontological theory

1. The categorical imperative is a formal rule without content

Note the categorical imperative does not tell you the content of your moral obligations. It does not actually give any rule on lying, killing, or any act. The categorical imperative is the most general principle possible. We test second-order maxims or moral rules against the three formulations of the categorical imperative to find out if the rules are moral. If the rule passes the test of the three formulations, then it is moral. If the rule does not pass all three tests, then the rule is immoral. Thus, moral rules such as 'Do not lie' or 'Do not kill' pass the test of the three formulations of the categorical imperative.

The difficulty in determining the precise formulation of a maxim is the criticism levelled at Kant's use of the categorical imperative to derive maxims. How we articulate the moral rule is important. In Mei's situations, she may have devised a moral rule like, 'Lie about your ability to repay a loan in order to get a loan, when you cannot pay the rent on your house'. Even with this formulation of the moral rule that applies in Mei's situation, we find that the moral rule does not pass the second test. Mei is still treating her friend as a means to an end and not as an end in herself. She is not respecting her friend's human dignity and, therefore, the rule is not moral.

Yet, it is not always easy to state accurately the rule of an action or to test it. People are tempted to articulate a rule that favours their particular situation so the rule passes the three tests. Honesty and impartiality are required. The renowned Oxford philosopher, Elizabeth Anscombe, argues the categorical imperative is useless without some guidance as to how to formulate rules.

2. Conflicts between rules

Circumstances exist when second-order principles that tested successfully against the three formulations may conflict. Such conflicts pose a moral dilemma. A common example of a conflict of moral rules is the dilemma of the battered wife and her murderous husband. The wife runs away from the husband who she believes will kill her. She tells you she is going to her mother's house to hide. The husband comes by and asks you where the wife is. You believe if you tell the truth, the husband will kill his wife. However, if you lie, you will be breaking the moral rule of not lying. What should you do?

There are two ways to resolve the dilemma. The first is to make an exception to one of the rules in conflict to give a resolution to the conflict. For instance, we construct the rule allowing a person to lie to save the life of a person. We test the rule with the exception against the three formulations of the categorical imperative. If the rule passes the tests, then the rule is moral. We may make exceptions in both the conflicting rules and test both rules with their exceptions to find out which is right. However, the answer may not always be obvious and we may need to give arguments to justify the correct rule.

The second way out of a moral dilemma is to view each of the conflicting rules as *prima facie* moral rules.[3] A *prima facie* rule is one that is binding in general. When only one *prima facie* rule applies in any particular situation, then we are morally bound to obey the rule. However, when several *prima facie* rules apply, or when we cannot fulfil every one of them, then not all of the rules are morally binding. The actual moral duty that is binding in the multiple rule situation is the one that is appropriate in that particular case. We decide which is the morally binding rule by seeing which takes precedence. Reasons must be given why one rule takes precedence over the other or others.

In the case of the murdering husband, the moral rule, 'Do not aid in murdering a person' trumps, 'Do not lie'. The reason is clear: a human life is measured against harming someone in a non-life-threatening way. The rule that takes precedence, 'Do not aid in murdering a person', therefore, is the rule we have a moral duty to follow.

When moral principles clash, it is often difficult to decide which takes precedence. In these cases the individual and society should carefully and as objectively as possible consider the various arguments in support of opposing views. When a clear decision is not possible, then the position with the strongest argument should be chosen.

8.4 Justice theories

Justice is an ancient concept. For Plato, justice is knowing the right balance of emotions, reason, and appetites within an individual, and knowing the right place of oneself and others in society. For Aristotle, justice is the supreme and complete virtue because justice is the sum of all virtues. He distinguishes two particular types of justice: distributive and corrective justice. Distributive justice deals with distribution of honour, wealth, and other items. Distributions count as just if equal persons receive equal shares. Clearly, just distributions require a determination of worth of the persons and worth of the thing being distributed.

Corrective justice is concerned with restoring the equality between people when one has wronged the other. In this case the worth of the person does not matter. What does matter is correcting the difference of what is lost by the victim to the perpetrator. Corrective justice seeks to restore equality by taking away the perpetrator's gain and restoring it to the victim.

From the brief discussions above, we may conclude that justice, in the broadest terms, is giving each person her due, treating equals as equals, and unequals unequally.[4] Aristotle distinguishes two types of justice described above, but there are other forms of justice.

1. *Compensatory justice*: Compensating someone for a past injustice or making good some harm suffered in the past. People must be fairly compensated for their injuries by those responsible for them. Just compensation is proportional to the loss inflicted on a person.
2. *Retributive justice*: This form of justice is punitive because it is the punishment due to someone who breaks the law or has committed harm to others. The punishments must be fair and just. In general, relevant criteria for deciding the level of punishment are the seriousness of the crime and the intent of the criminal.
3. *Procedural justice*: This form of justice concerns fair decision procedures, practices, or agreements and is relevant in the fair resolutions of disputes. There must be fairness and transparency in the processes by which such decisions are made. Fair procedures are deemed necessary to have equitable outcomes. This form of justice is important in the concept of due process in law.
4. *Commutative justice*: This form of justice belongs in the sphere of transactions and is relevant to finance and business. Commutative justice calls for fundamental fairness in all agreements and exchanges between individuals or private social groups.
5. *Distributive justice*: This form of justice is largely as Aristotle describes. In contemporary usage, distributive justice concerns the distribution of benefits and responsibilities, in contemporary terms, by the state.

Commutative justice is most commonly associated with business and financial transactions because it refers to fairness in exchange of goods or services. Sellers are expected to set fair prices for their goods and not gouge the customer. To ensure fair pricing in transactions, there must first be full informational disclosure to both buyer and seller. Second, both parties must enter into the transaction freely and not be coerced. Third, both parties should see some benefit from the transaction.

While commutative justice is most directly relevant to business and financial transactions, the other types of justice also apply to finance, particularly in the aftermath of the financial crisis upon the discovery of fraudulent, illegal, and unethical practices perpetrated by banks and other financial services companies.

For example, in the case of the London Interbank Offered Rate (LIBOR) manipulation by several international banks, compensatory and retributive justice is applicable. Barclays Bank was fined US$453 million, RBS US$612 million, and UBS a staggering US$1.5 billion. British and US regulators levied these fines on the banks as compensatory justice. In addition, class action suits are now under way against the banks, accusing them of manipulating LIBOR and increasing the amount of interest paid by a wide swathe of borrowers. The amounts these banks are likely to pay in the event of the lawsuit going against them will be in the hundreds of millions, if not billions. We can argue the sums of dollars banks are paying is just compensatory amounts because of the loss suffered by those harmed through LIBOR manipulation. However, if we disagree on whether compensatory justice was served, there is likely to be agreement that retributive justice was not served.

No bank or banker has been charged, arrested, tried, or sentenced for his part in the global financial crisis. This discrepancy has left most of the public in Europe and the US questioning if retributive justice has been served. Is compensatory justice sufficient in, say, the LIBOR case? Do the banks that were fined simply view the fines as a cost of doing business and go on to the next profitable, but unethical transaction?

Theories of justice

Justice is giving each person her due, treating equals as equals, and unequals unequally. The forms of justice are:

1 Compensatory justice
2 Retributive justice
3 Procedural justice
4 Commutative justice
5 Distributive justice

John Rawls and distributive justice

There are different ways to distribute the benefits and burdens in society. For instance, should the strong and powerful get the most benefits while the weak and powerless receive what remains? This type of distribution describes the plutocratic society ruled and enjoyed by the elites. This type of society is rather like the dystopian society of the *Hunger Games*, a series of novels by Suzanne Collins. Another model of distributive justice is the communist model, where everyone theoretically gets an equal share of benefits and shoulders an equal amount of the burdens of society. The Soviet Union and The People's Republic of China are examples of countries that attempted to follow the precepts of communism. While there have been and are instances of a working plutocracy, there has been no instance of a pure, working communist nation.

John Rawls (1921–2002) proposed an influential model of distributive justice. Rawls wanted to design a theory that is an explicit alternative to utilitarianism because the latter treats people in the aggregate and does not consider the distinction between persons. The theory of justice Rawls develops takes the question of how rights and duties, benefits, and burdens are to be fairly distributed between members of a society.

Rawls is both a social contract theorist and a Kantian. Social contract theory explains how a group of people form a society and holds that people agree, either explicitly or implicitly, to a particular system of governance where each person has certain responsibilities and rights. The social contract also specifies how people should treat one another. John Hobbes and John Locke were the earliest proponents of social contract theory. In their view, people are willing to give up certain freedoms in order to enjoy peace and the protection of their rights by the state. John Rawls uses the contractarian approach in his theory of justice as his theory posits people enter into a social contract when they agree to the principles of justice that govern society. He bases his idea of justice on a social contract.

Rawls is a Kantian because his theory may be seen as a way of applying the third version of the categorical imperative. You will recall the third version of the categorical imperative says that as autonomous and rational beings, humans will freely agree to abide by moral laws. Those laws must, however, accord with universal reason. In other words, moral rules must be acceptable to rational beings. Rawls argues that his theory of justice stands on principles of distributive justice that are acceptable to all rational persons. The principles are universal, respect the dignity of all persons, and are rationally acceptable to everyone. Thus the principles meet Kantian requirements of the categorical imperative. How do we arrive at the principles of justice that will determine the distribution of the good and the bad in a society? Rawls suggests a unique and creative way of deriving these principles of distributive justice.

The veil of ignorance and original position

Imagine everyone in a society is behind a 'veil of ignorance'.[5] This situation is the state of nature in which we find ourselves. Rawls calls this state the 'original position of equality'.[6] Rawls's original position is not an actual situation in any time period in the past or present. It is instead a 'hypothetical situation'[7] we adopt when we put on the veil of ignorance. Behind this veil, we theoretically do not know our status in society. We do not know if we are rich or poor, sick or healthy, attractive or ugly. We do not know our intelligence level, talents, race (e.g., Chinese, Indian, Malay), or gender.

From this original position where hypothetically everyone is equal, rational, and mutually disinterested, we choose the principles of justice for the society we wish to have. Our rationality and self-interest determines our choice. Presumably, we wish for what is best for ourselves. Hence, we opt to support the most disadvantaged in society, as we do not know if we fall into this forlorn category. Rawls believes most of us are risk-averse and will assume we will be the most disadvantaged in society. Based on this risk aversion, we will choose the society that best suits the most disadvantaged in society. According to Rawls, from the original position, we choose two principles of justice.

First principle of justice

The first principle of justice is the *principle of equal liberty*:

Each person is to have an equal right to the most extensive basic liberty compatible with a similar liberty for others.[8]

The reason everyone in a society who is behind the veil of ignorance agrees to this first principle of justice is because no one knows her position in society. We will rationally choose the principle of equal liberty because no one wants to be treated poorly in the event of being in a disadvantageous position. The first principle means that each person has a right to the same level of liberty as everyone else. The basic liberties are rights to freedom of thought and conscience, freedom of speech and assembly, and the right to vote and to stand for office. The first principle, therefore, gives a prominent place to the ideal of rights. In a Rawlsian state, the equality principle guarantees each citizen equal political freedom, protection of the law, and equal treatment before the law. No matter a citizen's wealth, health, intelligence, talents, ethnicity, religion, gender, age, etc., she is entitled to the same rights and liberties due to each and every person in the society. This first principle of justice is the ideal and takes precedence over the second principle.

The second principle of justice

The second principle of justice concerns the distribution of wealth and power and is called the *equality of opportunity principle*:

Social and economic inequalities are to be arranged so that they are both

a   to the greatest benefit of the least advantaged and
b   attached to offices and positions open to all under conditions of fair equality of opportunity[9]

The second principle upholds that everyone should be as well off as possible. Rawls understands that any society has inequalities. However, in a Rawlsian society, the inequalities are to the advantage of the least well off. Structures and policies that make some people better off than others can only be justified if they also make the least advantaged person better off than she will otherwise be.

The second part of the second principle of justice is uncontroversial and generally accepted. This part calls for equality of opportunity and access to all positions and offices. Thus, for example, a person cannot be discriminated against getting a job because she is a woman. We all want to be able to have access to and the opportunity to obtain jobs, political appointments, and other positions in society.

The first part of the second principle of justice, however, is more controversial. This part says that inequality in society is tolerable so long as the society – its institutions, policies, politics, economic systems – is arranged so that the arrangements benefit the least disadvantaged. In other words, under the second principle, a society cannot have systems that benefit only the elite and continue to help them fare better if the systems offer no benefit to the most disadvantaged. For example, take two different societies. Everyone in the first society, Xanadu, is equal and the measure of well-being for each person in that society is 20. In the second society, Orbis, there exists inequality, but the measure of well-being in that society ranges from 30 to 50. According to the first part of the second principle of justice, we will be acting rationally and in line with Rawls's theory if we choose Orbis. Although people are not all equal in Orbis, everyone is better off than the people in Xanadu. The worst off in Orbis will have a well-being measure of 30, which is better than the well-being score of 20 in Xanadu. The first part of the second principle of justice, therefore, allows for inequalities of success, as long as everyone is better off because of the success.

The second principle has critics who either think the principle is too strong or too weak. Those who say the principle is too strong argue that there is no injustice if those who are more hardworking, talented, intelligent, and driven receive more rewards. Their success should not be conditioned by arrangements that also produce benefits for the least advantaged group in society. Those who think the principle is too weak argue that the rich and powerful are able to arrange society and its systems to benefit themselves most and yet the least advantaged get only a little progress. For example, in the past two decades, inequality has grown in many countries around the world, in particular the US and China. If we adhere to Rawls's theory these inequalities are just fine because while the rich have become richer, the poor have become less poor. However, critics argue the rich are getting far richer in percentage terms than the poor who have only advanced a small degree in percentage terms. To critics of the second principle of justice, growing and immense inequality is not acceptable if a society is to be a just society.

Rights

The oldest basis of human rights or the justifiable moral claims to which humans are entitled by virtue of being human, arise from religion, and in particular Christianity. God confers inviolable rights to humans. These God-given rights, such as the right to freedom and the right to life, are called natural rights.

In secular versions of human rights, the notion emerges from Kant's moral theory. The second formulation of the categorical imperative states, 'Act so that you treat humanity, whether in your own person or in that of another, always as an end and never as a means only'. This second formulation means we must respect human beings as ends in themselves because every human being has dignity and is therefore deserving of respect. Respect for people involves respect for their liberty and autonomy. Every person has a right to pursue her own ends through her own free action. Accordingly, Kant puts great emphasis on the notion of human rights. Kant writes, 'There is nothing more sacred in the wide world than the rights of others. They are inviolable'.[10] A Kantian ethic insists, therefore, that rights cannot be violated simply for the sake of promoting desirable ends, whether for oneself or for others.

The idea of rights has been developed most fully by recent political philosophers. The notion of rights is inherent in Rawls's theory of justice. The first principle of Rawlsian justice is that 'Each person is to have an equal right to the most extensive basic liberty compatible with a similar liberty for others'. This means that people have a right to liberty and comports with Kant's view on rights to autonomy. The second principle of justice states that people have a right to equal access to positions and opportunity. The right to liberty includes the freedom of speech and conscience, freedom to own and control one's own body, or the freedom to dispose of one's property.

Ronald Dworkin, a legal philosopher, who has written extensively on rights, is critical of utilitarianism because the theory does not take into account the role of rights in its moral calculation. Utilitarianism requires maximization of preferences of all individuals in a particular situation. However, if an individual's preference violates the rights of others (e.g., to discriminate against non-whites), the utilitarian must still consider that preference in the calculation. Dworkin thinks rights have priority and override ordinary utilitarian calculations.

Robert Nozick agrees with Dworkin's criticism of utilitarian approaches. For Nozick, rights are what he calls 'side constraints'.[11] Nozick emphasizes the contrast between utilitarianism and a 'rights' approach. Utilitarianism is a moral system in which moral goals or ends serve to guide actions. In contrast, rights do not tell us what to aim for but instead function as side constraints on action. We are limited in what we can do to other people in pursuit of our own goals. His view on rights echoes Kant's. In particular, the Kantian principle that individuals are ends and not merely means underlies the side constraint upon our actions. Nozick agrees with Kant that the status of human beings as ends and not just means rests on their ability to shape their lives and, ultimately, give meaning to their own lives. Nozick rejects the idea of aiming to minimize the total extent of the violation of rights even though it may be necessary to violate some people's rights in order to achieve this goal.

Nozick does not give a full list of rights and why people should have them. He does say we have a right not to be a victim of physical aggression. This extends to the right of the person not to be coerced in many ways by the state. For Nozick, a state cannot coerce citizens to act in some way that fulfils the utilitarian goal of general welfare of the country, to redistribute justice, or implement greater social equality. States cannot justifiably tax citizens to improve the positions of the less well off. The tax is a violation of the rights of those who are taxed. He argues that only a minimal state, whose role is limited to protecting people's rights, is justified.

Applying justice theory

Insider trading

If most individuals who enter the global financial market agree to a social contract in which fairness and distributive justice are key features, the contract and conflicting values must be managed and handled appropriately in order for the market to work properly. Hersh Shefrin and Meir Statman state that fairness in financial markets means 'all parties have equal access to information relevant to asset valuation but are entitled to nothing more'.[12] This definition certainly implies that the use of inside information is unfair, but this is not the whole story. Several factors and conflicting rights affect justice in financial markets, such as informational efficiency and asymmetries, freedom from coercion, and freedom from one's own ignorance, among others.[13]

Shefrin and Statman contend that legalizing insider trading may actually increase the efficiency of stock market prices and that there is an 'efficiency/fairness frontier' in which 'choices ... involve reductions in efficiency to increase fairness' and vice versa.[14] One conflict of rights in financial markets is the right to true informational efficiency versus the right to equal information for all traders. However, informational efficiency is fulfilled by disclosure. Further, Shefrin and Statman argue that if insider trading is legalized, novice traders will no longer be under the false impression that it is rare because it is illegal, making them more able to protect themselves. However, the authors remind us that if insider trading is legalized, many individuals will choose not to participate, thereby creating adverse effects such as illiquidity. Investing will no longer be 'a fair game of skill, [where] winners and losers are expected ... trading on inside information is unfair because it conveys a non-skill based advantage to the trader'.[15]

However, those who possess insider tips and wish to trade based on that information might feel they have a right to be exempt from the coercion of disclosure that facilitates equal information.[16] Nevertheless, the social contract of market investing holds certain rights above others, and the right to equal information is first priority for many participants. In the US, the widely accepted 'fiduciary duty' rule under the *Insider Trading Sanction Act* of 1984 and the *Insider Trading and Securities Fraud Act* of 1988 states that inside information must be disclosed or heavy penalties will be administered.[17]

According to Kolb, distributive justice becomes an issue in this context because of the risk associated with investing in financial instruments.[18] The act of investing may impose costs on others in a morally relevant way. Kolb's outlook on risks in financial markets somewhat coincides with Hobbes's theory of justice, of those who bear socially useful risks, few accept those risks to promote the benefit of society. The transfer of such risks needs to be managed according to distributive justice, since most investors determine the riskiness of their own portfolios in a fair market. When risk transfer involves informational asymmetries, deceit, or unequal positions of power, ethical dilemmas result. Insider trading is an example of an informational asymmetry in which risks can be transferred from a knowledgeable to an unknowledgeable party, subjecting the unknowledgeable to a degree of risk that would not normally be acceptable. Kolb contends that, 'when we transfer, manage, or avoid risk, we seldom pause to ask what has happened to the risk that we have escaped . . . Transferred risk does not truly disappear, but remains to harm others'.[19] Besides the question of fair risk distribution, insider trading is a violation of justice in the context of modern finance theory.

The assumptions of modern finance theory are that 'investors are rational, are risk averse, possess homogenous expectations regarding the distribution of future investment returns . . . and are utility maximizing with utility being a positive function of expected return and a negative function of risk'.[20] Although investors realize that everyone is generally risk-averse and profit-maximizing, involuntarily bearing risk as a result of insider trading can cause people to withdraw from the market to avoid being treated unfairly, which puts limits on the basic assumptions of modern finance theory. Additionally, modern finance theory is violated because expectations of returns have been disturbed, and 'informational asymmetry gives rise . . . to discussions [that] usually focus on the returns the insider can garner by exploiting the inside information'.[21] Given this perspective, neither the libertarian nor the egalitarian concepts of justice suit the finance industry, but just deserts theories stating that hard-working analysts deserve their profits do match the social contract of the stock market.

Decisively, insider trading is unjust under Rawls's veil of ignorance, because those who have inside information should choose not to use it based on the uncertainty of which position they will ultimately hold. Therefore, by not exercising their advantageous position, they will protect their own interests as well as the interests of those who would potentially be subject to a violation of distributive justice. It is postulated that under the veil, many market participants share this same view and will abide by the social contract of modern finance theory in order for justice to predominate. Also, inside traders will attempt to avoid finding themselves at the mercy of someone else with inside information. According to Rawls's theory of justice, insider trading is largely unethical. However, there are no guarantees and no absolutes in evaluating ethical decisions from a justice theory perspective.

8.5 Virtue ethics

Virtue ethics is an ethical tradition that dates back to ancient Greece. The tradition was the dominant moral philosophy during the classical period. We encounter Plato expounding on virtue ethics in his dialogues. The most famous virtue ethicist and perhaps the starting point of discussion for most virtue ethicists is Aristotle. In the *Nicomachean Ethics*, Aristotle refines and formulates a well-developed theory that is a prototype for contemporary virtue ethics.

Virtue ethics refers to an approach to ethics that has as its central focus the judgement of character. A person's character is made up of all her virtues and vices. A person who is honest will generally act honestly even if tempted to do otherwise. Virtues are character traits Aristotle calls dispositions. A disposition, to be honest, is instilled when young through regular practice. By constantly choosing to act honestly, the disposition to be honest eventually forms into habit. This habitual honesty develops into a character trait and becomes part of a person's character. This same process of habituation applies to other virtues such as generosity, courage, and moderation. The person who possesses the virtues and practices them is the virtuous person.

The focus on a person's character means the virtue ethics approach is agent-centred (such as the decision on whether an act is right or wrong depends on the person who does the act) rather than act-centred (the rightness of the act depends on the act itself and does not take into account the character of the person performing the act). The alternate focus on the agent differentiates virtue ethics from utilitarian and deontological ethics, both of which are act-centred. There are three versions of this agent-centred focus.[22] First, the moderate version views most of morality as connected with character, although some actions can be evaluated independently of virtue. Second, the reductionist version has all judgements of rightness being reducible to judgements of character. Lastly, there is the replacement version, where the virtuous notions gain priority by default, after the deontic concepts have been eliminated.

All three versions of virtue ethics are formulated through the idea of a virtuous character – the moral goodness of persons is determined by the virtues they possess. Instead of asking, 'what should I do?' as deontological and utilitarian ethics do, virtue ethics consider what sort of person the moral agent should be and what sort of life she should lead. This question is not answered by consulting principles, norms, or policies that apply to situations. Rather, the question is answered by considering the person's character along with other morally salient features of the situation. According to most virtue ethics theories, the virtuous do not act virtuously for the sake of being virtuous. An honest person tells the truth because she loves the truth.[23] The virtuous person expresses who they are when they act, and in acting, they develop their characters. While the moral evaluation of the person is different from the moral evaluation of an action, nevertheless, the evaluations are related. A virtuous person refrains from immoral acts. So for instance, a truthful person does not lie, and an honest person does not cheat.

Virtue ethics

Virtue ethics is an approach to ethics that focuses on the judgement of character. This emphasis on a person's character means the virtue ethics approach is agent-centred – the decision on whether an act is right or wrong depends on the person who does the act. In contrast, utilitarianism and deontological ethics are act-centred – the rightness of the act depends on the act itself and does not take into account the character of the person performing the act.

Deontological and utilitarian theories have the notion of right and wrong acts. The theories represent our legalistic approach to ethical thinking. There is an emphasis on rules and laws, implying correct answers to ethical questions. By contrast, according to virtue ethics, especially in the replacement version, the recommended method in ethics is an Aristotelian one, in the sense that we can expect no precise answer to practical questions. Virtuous people may therefore arrive at different answers to the same practical problem. Of course, this then raises the question that Schneewind writes about: If two allegedly virtuous agents strongly disagree, one of them (at least) must be morally defective.[24]

Virtues

What then is a virtue? *Arete* is the Greek word for virtue and can also be translated as 'excellence'. Aristotle's definition of virtue is that it is a state (*hexis*) of one's character.[25] This is equivalent to the definition of virtue as a 'character trait'. A *hexis*, or character trait, is a settled state that involves reason and emotion. A person is honest and does honest deeds 'readily, eagerly, unhesitatingly, scrupulously, as appropriate'.[26] Each of the virtues involves getting things right, for each involves practical wisdom (or in Greek *phronesis*), which is the ability to reason correctly about practical matters. For Aristotle (some contemporary philosophers disagree), all virtues are morally good. (For example, Rosalind Hursthouse, a renowned virtue ethicist, gives the example when benevolence is not a virtue – someone could be honest and generous 'to a fault', or her benevolence may lead to breaking a promise she should have kept in her desire to prevent other's hurt feelings.)

For Aristotle a virtue is the 'mean between extremes', something more than the Greek emphasis on moderation. Aristotle is clear that the excess or deficiency of a virtue is not the virtue itself. Virtue is the mean between excess and deficiency. Courage is the mean between timidity and recklessness. Temperance is the mean between gluttony and prudishness. To judge what is the mean requires reason and knowledge – these excellences are the guides to our virtues.

David Hume (1711–76) is one of the two important modern virtue theorists. The other, who has special significance to business and the free enterprise system, is Adam Smith (1711–76). Both defended a portrait of human nature in which 'sympathy' and 'fellow-feeling' play roles as important as self-interest. For Hume and Smith, virtues are important because they are both useful and pleasing. In Smith's *Theory of the Moral Sentiments*, published before the (currently viewed) capitalist manifesto, *Wealth of Nations*, he places great store on the two basic virtues of modern market society – justice and benevolence. Followers of Adam Smith's economics often ignore his ethics, but the economics is not workable without the ethics.

There is another ancient virtue ethicist who has been more influential than Aristotle, Hume, or Smith. Confucius (551–479 BCE) is the foremost Chinese proponent of virtue ethics, emphasizing virtues such as good upbringing, good habits, and good instincts. Confucius taught the way to universal harmony (Tao) through right action (Jen) in harmony with others (Yi). The virtues, particularly the virtue of, 'filial piety', are central to this vision.

According to Aristotle, Confucius, Smith, and Hume, virtues are cultivated responses and actions, which may at the time require no deliberations whatsoever.[27] While deontology may require some reasoning for us to act on principle, and utilitarianism encourages the calculation of utilities, the manifestation of virtue seems to require little or no thought. A virtuous person acts on a virtue naturally as the circumstance arise. The truly honest person, for example, does not need to think about acting honestly. She never even considers lying. The virtues, accordingly, do not require deliberation. Indeed, too much deliberation; for example, should I give a loan to a friend who needs monetary assistance, is evidence one does not have the virtue of generosity. Virtues may blur the distinction between altruism and selfishness, a duality often discussed by moral philosophers. A generous person may act generously, not because of concern for the well-being of others, but because she may simply be generous and/or take pride in being generous. To be generous is to act and be motivated by generosity, but no further claim needs to be given to distinguishing self-interest, altruism, and concern for others.[28]

Hursthouse, who is an adherent of the Aristotelian version of virtue ethics, gives a general way to determine virtues. She neatly summarizes the premises that underlie the virtue ethics approach to right action in the following way:[29]

> P.1. An action is right if and only if it is what a virtuous agent would characteristically (such as, acting in character) do in the circumstances.
> P.1a. A virtuous agent is one who has, and exercises, certain character traits, namely, the virtues.
> P.2. A virtue is a character trait that . . .

The second premise, P.2., is completed by giving a list or a criterion. In the *Second Enquiry Concerning the Principles of Morals*, David Hume completes P.2. such that: A virtue is a character trait that is useful or agreeable to its possessor or to others. Hursthouse completes P.2. in an Aristotelian manner: a virtue is a character trait that a human being needs for *eudaimonia*, roughly translated as happiness (see below).

Eudaimonia, *flourishing or happiness*

According to Rosalind Hursthouse, '[A] virtue is a character trait a human being needs for *eudaimonia*, to flourish or live well'.[30] *Eudaimonia* is a Greek word that roughly translates as 'happiness', 'flourishing', or 'well-being', although each translation has its drawbacks. Happiness, in its contemporary understanding, connotes something subjective. Flourishing does not have this subjectivity problem but its drawback is that we may have a mistaken idea of what flourishing consists of, such as pleasure, for instance. Well-being does not have a corresponding adjective, and is therefore clumsy to use. Hursthouse proposes that the notion of *eudaimonia* is close to the idea of 'true (or real) happiness', or 'the sort of happiness worth having'.[31] We would want this sort of happiness for our children for their own sakes.

Eudaimonia is an expression of a form of naturalism. In other words, we can (to a certain extent) use an account of human nature to base our understanding of virtue. The virtues are those character traits that make a human being a good human being. Human beings need those character traits to live well as human beings, to live a good, characteristically human life.

> Ethical evaluations of human beings as good or bad are taken to be analogous to evaluations of other living things as good or bad specimens of their kind. The analogy is instructive, because it reveals that several features of ethical evaluation thought to be peculiar to it, and inimical to its objectivity, are present in the quasi-scientific evaluation even of plants.[32]

Criticisms of virtue ethics

Relativism

Virtue ethics generally begins within an established tradition or culture that uphold traits that are admired in that tradition or culture. This cultural aspect of virtues gives rise to the criticism that virtue ethics is relativistic. Relativism is the idea that there may be very different virtues in different societies. How are we to decide which virtues are true?

Indeed, different virtues are lauded in, say, Homeric Greece, versus the medieval period of Thomas Aquinas, versus the Confucian era and contemporary corporate Asia. However, it does not follow that there are not some non-relative virtues. These virtues are found in every human society or institution, just because, as Hursthouse argues, we are human. Thus, we consider trustworthiness and honesty to be virtues because they are crucial to almost any human interchange. The non-relative virtues are essential in all societies because of their necessity in order for us to cooperate and live together. We need to supply society with the necessities of life, protect society from others who would harm and from natural disasters. All this suggests that there are non-relative virtues, perhaps with local variations and interpretations, such as courage, honesty, generosity, and congeniality. In business, trustworthiness and cooperation are particularly important non-relative virtues because they undergird any form of market or non-market society.

Applying virtue ethics

Financial markets and the virtues

Finance and the proper functioning of free markets require at least some basic virtues to allow them to work at full efficiency amid the larger society in which the markets operate. A market at odds with the needs of and interests of the rest of society cannot exist for long.

Finance is a specialized function in the general field of business. When one thinks of markets working efficiently, one instantly thinks of how trust underlies the very structure of all markets. Instilling trust in markets requires a general belief that participants are honest. Why would anyone trade with or through someone else who is not honest?

Honesty is, therefore, one of the most important virtues in finance. We require honesty in executing trades, drawing up financial agreements, dealing with customers and other companies. There needs to be transparency in financial transactions. Lying is unacceptable. What is special to virtue ethics is that there is no need to search for the general criterion for proper honesty. A virtuous person possesses the motives and habits of honesty and thinks in terms of fairness of the situation, what information is appropriate to the relationship and the occasion, and does what an honest person would do.

Courage is an essential virtue for the truly great financier. In finance, courage takes on a number of forms, ranging from the willingness to assume risk (e.g., in investing or trading) to the virtue of moral courage. The latter involves a willingness to take a principled stand, even when there are serious threats to the individual's position, job, or prospects.

Temperance in finance refers to moderation and prudence in desires. Not being greedy is perhaps the first and foremost among financial virtues. Typically, it is because of greed that people lie, cheat, and act unfairly. The history of financial crises is full of examples of greed being the catalysing element in a chain of causation that leads to financial collapse. A temperate approach to demands and desires allows the limits imposed by the other virtues, such as honesty, to come more clearly in focus.

Applying virtue ethics: the case of Rajat Gupta and insider trading[33]

Rajat Gupta was an Indian American businessman who was the Managing Director of management consultancy McKinsey & Company, and a business leader in India and the US. Rajat Gupta also served as Corporate Chairman, Board Director or Strategic Adviser to Goldman Sachs, Procter & Gamble, and American Airlines, and non-profit organizations, The Gates Foundation, The Global Fund, and the International Chamber of Commerce.

Rajat Gupta was convicted in June 2012 on insider trading charges. He was sentenced in October 2012 to two years in prison, an additional year on supervised release, and ordered to pay US$5 million in fines. His trial began on 22 May 2012. On 15 June 2012, Gupta was found guilty on three counts of securities fraud and one count of conspiracy.

The primary parties affected are Rajat Gupta, McKinsey & Company, Goldman Sachs, Raj Rajaratnam, Galleon Group, Warren Buffet, and the US equity markets. Other parties indirectly affected are family and friends of Rajat Gupta, employees at McKinsey & Company and Galleon Group, investors in Goldman Sachs and its creditors, and government and officials involved with the case.

The transactions

In September 2008, Warren Buffet agreed to pay US$5 billion to Goldman Sachs in exchange for preferred shares in the company. This news was likely to raise the share price of Goldman Sachs and was not to be announced and made public until the end of day. Less than a minute after the board approved the Buffet purchase, Rajat Gupta called his long-time friend Raj Rajaratnam, a hedge fund manager and billionaire founder of the Galleon Group. Once Rajaratnam got the information, he immediately bought shares of Goldman Sachs. Next day, when the stock market opened, Raj Rajaratnam made nearly US$1.2 million in profits as the shares of Goldman Sachs increased in price. The Securities and Exchange Commission (SEC) estimates the tip leaked by Rajat Gupta generated profits and avoided losses of more than US$23 million.

Ethical analysis

Would a virtuous person have leaked the information to Raj Rajaratnam?
Rajat Gupta showed a failure of character:

- *Integrity:* Integrity is honesty and truthfulness, or accuracy, of a person's action. Rajat Gupta did not act with integrity in dealing with his company Goldman Sachs, where he served on the board of directors. Instead, he gave away insider information for personal benefits.
- *Trust:* Rajat Gupta broke the trust to other Directors on Goldman's Board and to other people with whom he had business relations. His actions affect the relationship with McKinsey & Company.
- *Fairness:* Rajat Gupta's actions are not fair for two reasons. First, other investors who do not have the information on Buffett's deal are at a disadvantage. Second, he used the information entrusted to him to benefit himself and Rajaratnam.

- *Honesty:* He was not honest with Goldman Sachs and his fellow board members to whom he implicitly, as a board director, promised not to share inside information.
- *Self-control:* If Rajat Gupta had self-control, he would not have leaked inside information to Rajaratnam for personal gain.

Gupta was commended by people who knew him as a person who helped others. He was very active in providing medical and humanitarian relief to developing countries. Born to humble circumstances, he became a pillar of the consulting community and a trusted adviser to the world's leading companies and organizations. A word that was used repeatedly in media coverage for Rajat Gupta during his trial was '*respected*'. In the past, alas, much less so now, we assume that people in leadership positions are virtuous. However, instances like the Rajat Gupta insider trading case and other financial scandals remind us that the assumption is perhaps not well-founded.

As a professional, the good manager strives to achieve a moral excellence that includes honesty, fairness, prudence, and courage. To improve moral character we may install tighter government regulations, better systems and processes in financial institutions, enhanced corporate governance, and better awareness of customer rights. Yet, a root of the problem is not addressed: not teaching financial ethics in business schools, where moral decision-making should be the core lesson. If business schools provide future financial managers with a proper ethical education, there is a chance that financial situations like Rajat Gupta may be less frequent.

Notes

1. Richard T. De George, *Business Ethics*, 6th ed. (Upper Saddle River, NJ: Pearson Prentice Hall, 2006).
2. De George, 63–6.
3. De George, 87–8.
4. De George, 97.
5. John Rawls, *A Theory of Justice* (Cambridge, MA: Harvard University Press, 1971).
6. Rawls, 17.
7. Rawls, 12.
8. Rawls, 53.
9. Rawls, 83.
10. Immanuel Kant, *Lectures on Ethics*, trans. Louis Infield (New York, NY: Hackett Publishing, 1981), 193–94.
11. Robert Nozick, *Anarchy, State, and Utopia* (New York, NY: Basic Books, 1974).
12. Hersh Shefrin and Meir Statman, "Ethics, Fairness and Efficiency in Financial Markets," *Financial Analysts Journal* 49, No. 6 (November–December 1993): 21–9.
13. Ibid., 21–8.
14. Ibid., 23.
15. Ibid., 28.
16. Ibid., 22.
17. Ibid., 27.
18. Robert W. Kolb, "Risk Management and Risk Transfer: Distributive Justice in Finance," *Journal of Alternative Investments* (Spring 2011): 90–8.
19. Ibid., 91.
20. Ibid., 94.
21. Ibid., 95.
22. Meir Statman, "The Cultures of Insider Trading," *Journal of Business Ethics* 89 (May 2009): 51–8.

23 Stan Van Hooft, *Understanding Virtue Ethics* (Chesham, UK: Acumen Publishing, 2006), 11.
24 J. B., Schneewind, "The Misfortunes of Virtue," *Virtue Ethics*, eds. Roger Crisp and Michael Slote (Oxford, UK: Oxford University Press, 1997), 200.
25 Rosalind Hursthouse, *On Virtue Ethics* (Oxford, UK: Oxford University Press, 1999), 11.
26 Ibid.
27 Robert C. Solomon, "Business Ethics and Virtue," *A Companion to Business Ethics*, ed. Robert E. Frederick (Oxford, UK: Blackwell Publishing, 2003).
28 Ibid.
29 Hursthouse, 28–9.
30 Ibid., 10.
31 Ibid.
32 Ibid., 21.
33 "Applying Virtue Ethics: The Rajat Gupta Case," *Seven Pillars Institute for Global Finance and Ethics*, 11 February 2013, accessed 19 June 2014, http://sevenpillarsinstitute.org/morality-101/applying-virtue-ethics-the-rajat-gupta-case.

References

Brown, Montague, *The Quest for Moral Foundations: An Introduction to Ethics* (Washington DC: Georgetown University Press, 1996).
De George, Richard T, *Business Ethics*, 6th ed. (Upper Saddle River, NJ: Pearson Prentice Hall, 2006).
Rachels, James and Stuart Rachels, *The Elements of Moral Philosophy*, 6th ed. (New York, NY: McGraw-Hill, 2010).
Thompson, Mel, *Ethical Theory* (Abingdon, Oxford: Hodder & Stoughton, 1999).

9 Overview of ethical theories – religion

9.1 Introduction

What is the relation of religion and religious ethics to economic life? There are a couple of hypotheses on the issue.[1] First, there is the hypothesis closely associated with Karl Marx. Materialist philosophers and economists both in the East and West hold the view that human motivations are obviously and decisively based on materialist interests. The control of the means of production determines aspects of economic systems. The fittest will survive. There is, of course, the influence of evolutionary psychology on this view. Religion played a role in the early stages of human economic history, but religion and religious ethics no longer play a role in shaping economic, and therefore, financial life.

Another, more congenial and realistic view to religion's relation with economics is associated with the legacy of Max Weber. This view holds that religious convictions of people strongly affect their behaviour and character. This effect, in turn, has consequences for the development and fate of nations, including their economic culture. Humans are more than simply driven by material motivations. They have spiritual and ideal interests that impact upon their economic decisions. Religion shapes the moral life of the people who form a society. Some religious orientations encourage people to form corporations to create wealth for the community. Religious ethics urges people to develop principles of morality to regulate open societies.

Clearly, the author holds the latter view and this chapter is a concise guide to the world's major religions and their ethical doctrines. The chapter describes the major tenets and ethics of Buddhism, Christianity, Hinduism, and Judaism. Islam is not covered, as there is a comprehensive description and analysis of the religion, its ethics, and its approach to finance in Chapter 3. In this chapter, for the other religions just listed, there is a general overview of each one via sections on history, doctrine, metaphysics, and ethics. The sections on ethics focus on a religion's ethical attitudes to the main aspects of finance such as wealth, charity, debt, conduct of business, and economics. Notably and in contradiction to cultural moral relativists, the major religions have remarkably similar ethical positions on these sub-areas of finance.

9.2 Buddhism

Buddhism is the practice of the Buddha's teachings, also known as the Dharma. The philosophy is sometimes called a middle way between the extremes of sensual indulgence and profound self-mortification. The founder of Buddhism is the Buddha Shakyamuni, born Siddhartha Gautama, a prince and son of the ruler of the Sakyas in north India. The

Buddha's birth date is not certain but specialists generally agree to sometime in the fifth century BCE.

Siddhartha Gautama lived a privileged and sheltered existence, lacking experience and, therefore, an understanding of human suffering. When Siddhartha stole away from the palace as a young adult, he saw for the first time an old man. On further outings from the palace, Siddhartha saw a sick man and then a decaying corpse. The encounters were life changing. Siddhartha decided to leave the comfort and wealth of his environment to seek the answer to how we end human suffering.

Siddhartha travelled around, initially as an ascetic. He found severe self-denial too extreme, hindering rather than helping spiritual awakening. He chose a simple life of few possessions, a meal a day, and a simple shelter as a better way for reaching enlightenment. It is said Siddhartha became the Buddha when he became enlightened in Benares under a pipal tree, now known as the Bodhi tree. From then on, Siddhartha became the Buddha or the Awakened One, and started teaching the Buddhist path to others.

Buddhist schools

The very early tradition of Buddhism is called Theravada Buddhism. The principles practised are close to those that are practised by the early followers of the Buddha. This school is prominent and has a large presence in Southeast Asia, especially Sri Lanka, Thailand, Burma, and Cambodia.

Mahayana (the Greater Vehicle) Buddhism is a later school that developed in Nepal, China, Korea, and Japan. The Tantrayana (the Esoteric Vehicle) arose in Tibet and Mongolia. In this chapter, we focus on the teachings common to all these schools of Buddhism, particularly the ethical teachings.

Fundamental Buddhist precepts

1. The Three Jewels

Technically, a person becomes Buddhist when she decides to take refuge in the Three Jewels and when she generates *bodhicitta*, the Sanskrit term for compassion. To take refuge in the Buddhist sense is to entrust your spiritual wellbeing to the Three Jewels because you become entirely convinced of their validity. The Three Jewels of Buddhism are:

1. The Buddha – the Enlightened One or the Awakened One, the founder of Buddhism, and the giver of the teachings.
2. The Dharma – the teachings of the Buddha. These are given in a series of books known as the *Sutras*, or *Suttas*. The earliest Sutra is the *Dhammapada*. One of the last is the *Lotus Sutra*.
3. The *Sangha* – the community of Buddhist practitioners.

2. The Four Noble Truths

The four noble truths are a diagnosis of and a prescription for a cure to the human condition. According to Buddhism, it is a natural fact of life that each of us seeks happiness and avoids suffering. The Four Noble Truths distinguish two sets of causes and effects: those causes that produce suffering, and those that produce happiness. The ultimate aim of the Truths is to attain happiness and overcome suffering.

1. The Truth of the existence of suffering (*dukkha*). A person whose mind is undisciplined and untamed is in the state of suffering. Those who live with attachment and desire of physical objects, thought processes, and sensory experiences are bound to suffer.
2. The Truth of the origin of suffering. The root cause of suffering is ignorance – ignorance of the true nature of reality.
3. The Truth of the cessation of suffering. This truth tells us that liberation from suffering is possible.
4. The Truth of the path. This truth gives us the true path to liberation from suffering. The path is called the Eightfold Path.

3. The Eightfold Path

The third noble truth is that there is a way to be liberated from suffering. If we accept that liberation is an achievable goal, the fourth truth deals with the true path. Liberation is gained through the realization of the ultimate nature of reality. According to Buddhist belief, the ultimate nature of reality is emptiness (see below). The intuitive realization of emptiness leads to the attainment of cessation (of suffering).

Knowledge of emptiness is obtained both through experience (empirical knowledge) and through an intellectual understanding developed through inference. Experiential knowledge is gained through meditation, but experiential knowledge of emptiness is not possible without an intellectual understanding of emptiness.

An important point to note is that achieving liberation or awakening is a three-level process. It is not possible to achieve liberation without practice of the first level, which is to act morally. Hence, the three levels of training are: training in morality, concentration or meditation, and wisdom or insight.

Why is morality important in the path towards enlightenment? Success in reaching awakening is dependent on single-pointedness of mind and penetrative insight. To have a union of these two factors, one must possess mindfulness and mental alertness, and be able to apply these capacities. The two capacities of mindfulness and mental alertness will only develop successfully if we live an ethically sound life. Hence, the three trainings of morality, meditation, and wisdom are connected to each other. The Buddhist meditator transitions from one stage to another.

The above explanation gives a brief background to the structure and reasoning behind the Eightfold Path. The first two elements of the Eightfold Path trains towards wisdom, the middle three are directed to moral development, and the last three are to develop mental concentration.

1. *Right understanding*: the practice of right understanding involves knowing the ultimate nature of reality, which is emptiness. It requires an understanding of suffering, the law of cause and effect, and impermanence, including the impermanence of the individual self.
2. *Right thought*: the practice of right thought involves the purification of the mind and heart and the growth of thoughts of unselfishness and compassion. The latter is the root of action.

3   *Right speech*: the act of right speech requires the discipline of refraining from lying, offensive speech, or gossiping.
4   *Right action*: the performance of right action requires refraining from harm to living things, stealing, misuse of senses, wrong speech, and taking drugs or alcohol.
5   *Right livelihood*: to have a right livelihood is to have a worthwhile job or way of life that avoids harm or injustice to other beings.
6   *Right effort*: the practice of right effort is the use of mental discipline to prevent desires, hatred, and ignorance from arising. Instead, the Buddhist practitioner of the Dharma should encourage what is good.
7   *Right mindfulness*: this involves total attention to the present moment, to the present activities of the body, and mind.
8   *Right concentration*: the practice of right concentration is the training of the mind in the stages of meditation.

4. The 10 non-virtuous actions

The 10 non-virtuous actions are already given within the elements of the Eightfold Path. The Buddha requested people to refrain from these non-virtuous actions:

1   Killing
2   Stealing
3   Sexual misconduct
4   Lying
5   Divisive speech
6   Offensive speech
7   Senseless speech
8   Covetousness
9   Malice
10 Wrong views

The Buddha also requested people to practise positive moral virtues. The virtues fall into three groups:[2]

1   Virtues of conscientiousness: veracity, truthfulness, and righteousness.
2   Virtues of benevolence: loving-kindness, compassion, sympathetic joy, and equanimity.
3   Virtues of self-restraint: self-control, abstinence, contentment, patience, celibacy, chastity, and purity.

Metaphysics

Enlightenment or awakening

For Buddhists, enlightenment is an awakening to ultimate truth and reality. The path to awakening requires three practices: acting morally, practice of meditation, and developing wisdom so as to come to a true understanding of the ultimate truth of reality. Through awakening, a practitioner sees clearly the true nature of reality and the true nature of reality is emptiness. This liberation from delusions and ignorance leads to the end of suffering, whose root cause according to the third Noble Truth is ignorance.

Enlightenment is liberation for the Buddhist and the primary goal of practice. Liberation is the freedom from cyclic existence or the cycle of rebirth. We realize a short-term aspiration to attain favourable rebirth by understanding the law of causality, but the long-term aim (and this may take a multitude of lifetimes) of complete liberation comes from a deep realization of the empty nature of reality. Either way, what binds us to cyclic existence is karma.

Karma

Karma is 'one particular instance of the natural causal laws that operate throughout the universe where, according to Buddhism, things and events come into being purely as a result of the combination of causes and conditions'.[3] Karma involves intentional action and therefore an agent. Our actions are the causes of resulting events, which then cause further actions, resulting in further events. This chain of causation arises from the interdependent nature of reality, a fundamental principle of Buddhism. This principle is common to every Buddhist school. All conditioned things and events in the universe come into being only as a result of the interaction of causes and conditions. Every being is connected to another because everything arises from the coming together of the many factors from which they are constituted. It is dependence upon other factors that causes anything to come into being. Buddhists believe entities do not have independent or intrinsic identities of their own. Every being's identity is contingent on the interaction between our perception and reality.

A deep understanding of the interdependent nature of reality in terms of causal dependence helps us appreciate the notion of karma, and the karmic law of cause and effect that governs human actions. According to the law, suffering results from negative actions, thoughts, and behaviours. Our experiences, either in one's current consciousness or in a future one, depend on the causes and conditions that correspond to the result. In a nutshell, karma is the doctrine that teaches, 'what you sow you shall reap', whether in this life or future rebirths when the consequences of karma happen.

Emptiness

The purpose of understanding emptiness is the attainment of liberation or awakening. The understanding of dependent origination, and a deep insight into the principle shows the way every object and event is a result only as a combination of many factors. They have no independent or autonomous existence. Deep apprehension of the principle of dependent nature of reality also gives the Buddhist, at the subtlest level, an insight into the Buddhist view of the empty nature of reality. To understand emptiness is to realize that beings and events do not have inherent or intrinsic existence. Everything is a result of mind and a myriad of causal factors.

Moral precepts

The moral precepts are given in the middle three elements of the Eightfold Path and more clearly repeated in the 10 non-virtuous actions, and in the virtues Buddha encouraged people to practise. All the virtues arguably emanate from the single most important virtue of Buddhism, which is compassion.

Cultivating compassion

The entire teaching of Buddha is founded on compassion, according to no less authority than the Dalai Lama.[4] Compassion is the very foundation of the Dharma. The practice of enhancing a good heart, and developing an altruistic mind is aimed at deepening a Buddhist's understanding of compassion, and stirring the compassionate potential that exists within every human being. There is no stipulation on how we exercise compassion because our choice depends on the context.

Buddhist ethics and finance

Wealth

The Buddhist belief in non-attachment informs its practitioners to be detached from wealth and wealth accumulation. However, the Dharma does not call for complete and painful self-denial. Buddhism is a middle way between extremes and the Buddhist attitude to wealth is one example of this approach. The principle of non-attachment does not mean that Buddhism's approach to wealth is a simple opposition between non-attachment and material prosperity. As humans, we have needs of basic food, clothing, and shelter. To know what is materially enough is wisdom that comes from Buddhist practice. Too much wealth and too many possessions lead people to spend all their time preserving and guarding them, while in a state of anxiety of losing them.

Non-attachment is to see things as they truly are, according to the dharma. This view is to recognize the self as a conditioned reality and to reject self-indulgent cravings as harmful illusions. A non-attached orientation towards life does not mean a rejection of all material possessions. A Buddhist has a practised attitude towards reality no matter her economic position. To be non-attached is to possess and use material things, but not to be possessed or used by them.

A person should earn wealth through skilled and earnest endeavour. Buddha encourages the layperson to contribute to his economic stability by earning wealth in a just manner, saving, and living within one's means. The layperson has a right to property and to accumulate wealth to ensure a decent way of life for the family. The right livelihood factor in the Eightfold Path requires eschewing any mode of livelihood based on trickery or greed. Increasing one's wealth is fine, but to be blind to moral considerations, to participate in tricks, frauds, and lies is to not practise Buddhist morality.

Charity

The Buddhist view on finance is that wealth is first used for looking after family and friends, and then in ethical investment in business. Excess wealth, if there is any, is to be given to charitable causes and to the support of the sangha. Generosity (*dana*) is one of the most important virtues for the layperson. Giving generously to charity demonstrates the person is not unhealthily attached to wealth and possessions. Giving to the three jewels is particularly meritorious.

The Buddhist emphasis on compassion and generosity translates into acts of giving – to the poor and to those in need. The Buddhist attitude to the responsibilities of society, to the welfare of others, may be summed up in this paragraph from the Cakkavatti Sihanada Sutta: 'Thus because one is forced to act desperately because one is poor, poverty became widespread, and from this stealing increased, from the spread of stealing violence grew, and from the growth of violence the destruction of life became common.'[5] Helping the individual in poverty also helps maintain a stable and peaceful society.

Economic ethics

A Buddhist text or Sutra tells the story of a line of rulers, each one governing according to the Dharma, justly, and with righteousness. One ruler in the line stops giving to the needy. As a result of this poverty arose for the first time in ages. Consequently, stealing arises. When a thief is caught, the ruler, upon hearing the thief stole because of poverty, gives the thief goods to support himself, and his family. When others hear of this, stealing increases. The ruler makes an example of the next thief by executing him. This then leads to thieves arming and killing those who they rob, for then there are no witnesses.

In another story, the Buddha tells of a rich and powerful king who wants to have a good rebirth and seeks advice on how to attain this goal. His priestly adviser points out that the country had a high property crime rate. The priest goes on to say that executions and other forms of corporal punishment lead to more violent crimes. His alternative is to grant grain and fodder to those who cultivate crops and keep cattle, grant capital to traders, and give proper living wages to those in government service. Such a policy would lead to greater government revenues, tranquillity in the country, and 'the people, with joy in their hearts, will play with their children and dwell in open houses'.[6] The king carries out this advice and the country indeed became calm and peaceful.

The key message of the two texts is that a government or ruler who allows poverty to develop will see the country riven by social strife. Indeed the poor should be exempt from taxes and kings should lend capital at no interest to subjects in need of it for trading. This form of government support for the economy is not considered inappropriate in Buddhist philosophy.

Debt

There does not appear to be a prohibition on debt and interest in the Buddhist scriptures and interpretations. Many of Buddha's comments on business and economics are found in his conversations with Anathapindika (he who gives food to the poor and powerless).[7] Anathapindika was a contemporary of the Buddha and one of the major characters in Buddhism. His original name was Sudatta and he was a banker.

In a discourse with Anathapindika, the Buddha mentions debt is to be avoided. If debt is necessary, however, one should pay off the debt as soon as possible. The Dharma does not prohibit debt, nor do the teachings consider lenders to be acting immorally in making loans.

Conduct of business

The Buddha gave specific ideas on running a company in the Sigala Sutra in which he talks about relationships with employees.[8] Employers should assign work commensurate with the abilities and capacities of workers. Adequate wages should be paid and medical needs provided. Employers and managers should grant bonuses occasionally.

The employee is also responsible for acting morally when working in a business. She should be diligent, not lazy, honest (no cheating of the employer), obedient, and earnest in her work. Moreover employment is a two-way contract. Both employer and employee have duties they are obligated to fulfil. The Buddhist teaching on work and employer/employee relations is rather modern considering the period in which it was written. At that time, fair wages was a revolutionary idea, as was the concept of providing medical care.[9]

9.3 Christianity

A Christian is one who is a follower of Jesus Christ. The Christian faith rests on two key beliefs: the existence of one God and that Jesus is the Son of God, and the Saviour or Messiah (The Anointed One).

Jesus was born in Bethlehem, during the time of Herod, to Joseph and Mary. According to the gospels of Matthew and Luke, Mary was a virgin when Jesus was conceived and she was 'found to be with child from the Holy Spirit' (Matthew 1:18; Luke 1:35). He lived as a carpenter's son for much of his 33 years of life. As a young adult, Jesus went to be baptized by the prophet John the Baptist and shortly thereafter he started his ministry, teaching God's word at about the age of 30 and gathering a group of disciples who followed him on his journeys around Galilee.

Jesus was arrested when he travelled to Jerusalem for Passover. His final ministry in Jerusalem is sometimes called the Passion Week and begins with his triumphal entry into Jerusalem. After his arrest, Jesus is tried, found guilty, and sentenced to death by crucifixion. He was crucified and died on a Friday. On the Sunday after, Jesus is resurrected and appears to his disciples over a 40-day period, after which he ascends to Heaven.

The Christian faith is a strongly ethical one. The authority behind Christian ethics is the Old Testament and the New Testament of the Bible. The Old Testament is seen as preparing for and being fulfilled, and in many respects negated by the ministry of Jesus. The New Testament is a witness to the life, death, and triumph over death of Jesus, and to the new community. The New Testament consists of 27 different writings (including Gospels, Acts, Letters, and the Book of Revelation). The four gospels of the New Testament are the narratives of the life, death, and resurrection of Jesus Christ. The term, 'gospel' means 'good news'. Each of the four gospels presents a particular perspective on Jesus' teaching. For Roman Catholic Christianity, authority for moral issues is also found in the Magisterium, the teaching authority of the Catholic Church. The Magisterium is the authentic interpretation of the Word of God by the Pope and the bishops in communion with him.

There are five broad traditions of Christianity:

1 The Orthodox. This segment is primarily in eastern Europe and Russia.
2 The Roman Catholic. This segment is by far the most numerous.
3 The Lutheran.
4 The Calvinist or Reformed.
5 The Anglican and its larger offshoot, Methodism.

There are hundreds of other churches such as Baptists, Quakers, and Presbyterians. Most of these churches are categorized under 'Protestants'. Christian ethics is the term commonly used in Protestant circles, whereas in Catholic ones the more common term is moral theology. There is no essential difference in subject matter between these terms. Both are concerned with the two basic issues in ethics; how to act from the right motive, and how to find what is the morally right action in particular circumstances.

Metaphysics

The crux of Jesus's teaching concerns the Kingdom of God. Jesus' life, death, and resurrection overcame the human condition. Christian tradition holds humanity had fallen from a state of grace in which it was created. Humanity, in the beginning of its time enjoyed a perfect relationship with God. The fallen state is in the broad Christian tradition referred to as Original Sin. Often called The Fall, the belief in Original Sin is an indication of the separation of God and creation. However, once human beings realize that God loves them, no matter how bad they may be, humans can respond with gratitude and joy. The Christian does not earn the love of God by being good – this gives them power over God. As each person realizes and accepts God's love, the person is able to respond by trying to live in accordance with God's commands. This process is known as sanctification.

Christian identity relies on each person coming to a personal recognition of the presence of God in her life, experiencing the sense and power of God's love, and then responding to the love. The importance of the personal recognition of the love and power of God varies according to the church. Some churches, such as the Protestant ones, place a greater emphasis on personal interpretation of God's word. Others, like the Roman Catholic Church, while still stressing the importance of a personal commitment, look to the guidance and leadership of the Church.

Christian ethics

While some may propose the New Testament includes a plurality of ethical stances, rather than one uniform position, all will concur the New Testament authors agree on two main issues:[10]

1. All moral commitments depend on a prior acceptance that God came into the world as Jesus of Nazareth in order to redeem the world from original sin. This affirmation of faith is the foundation for any ethical orientation. Ethics is understood as a way of imitating Christ.
2. The love of God and the love of neighbours are intimately linked in one commandment, which represents the core of Christian ethics (Mark 12:30–1).

This agreement comes from all four Gospels (Matthew, Mark, Luke, and John), and also from St. Paul's Letters to the Corinthians.

The conduct appropriate for a Christian who enters the Kingdom of God is in some measure at the level of natural morality, such as the Golden Rule: 'Always treat others as you would like them to treat you' (Matthew 7:12).[11] Some of the ethical teachings are radical. For instance, there is no limit to the forgiveness for injuries (Matthew 18:21), not on the grounds it will win over the offender but because it corresponds to God's forgiveness of us. Jesus also commands his followers to love their enemies – a radical enjoinder in those times in which he taught – not because loving one's enemies is a way to persuade the enemy but because God loves his enemies. In addition, there is no restriction on the love one gives to one's neighbour (Luke 10:29). A fundamental belief is that God loves people unconditionally. This all powerful, all-embracing love is demonstrated through the life, death, and resurrection of Jesus. Love in word, will, and action is stressed, even as a condition of knowledge (Luke 17:17).

Jesus' teachings emphasize the importance of loving one's neighbour as oneself. To love one's neighbour means being responsible for fellow human beings, because they are made in the image of God. Christians are to act according to the Golden Rule and treat neighbours the same way they wish to be treated. Both the Old and the New Testaments stress the love of others. When more than two people are involved there should be fairness in how they are treated. Questions of corrective and distributive justice, therefore, underlie the New Testament.[12] The issues of fairness, justice, and love are related in Christian tradition.

In determining whether a moral decision is a Christian one, the question to ask is if the decision is in accordance with the law of love. This consideration in moral decision-making stands supreme in the Christian tradition. Again, Christian ethics begins with God's love for the world (John 3:16) and Jesus' life. Jesus gave his followers a new commandment that is the new covenant for the Christian religion, taking precedence over the old commandments of the Old Testament. He says to his disciples: 'I give you a new commandment: love one another; as I have loved you, so you are to love one another. If there is this love among you, then all will know that you are my disciples' (John 13:34). The emphasis of loving one's neighbour is continued by St. Paul in his observation that 'All [commandments] are summed up in one rule, "Love your neighbour as yourself"'. Paul also defines the love that is central to Christian morality:

> Love is patient; love is kind and envies no one. Love is never boastful, nor conceited, nor rude; never selfish, not quick to take offense. Love keeps no score of wrongs; does not gloat over other men's sins, but delights in the truth. There is nothing love cannot face; there is no limit to its faith, its hope and its endurance.
> (1 Corinthians 13:4–7)

Imitating Jesus and fulfilling the law of love are for Christians, ways of trying to reach the ideal standard of Christian morality.

Christian ethics and finance

Wealth

Pope Francis points to the root causes of current economic and social troubles as man's relationship with money and the acceptance of its power over man and society. Perhaps Pope Francis has the best pithy statement of the Christian view on wealth: 'Money has to serve, not to rule.' In saying this, the Pope reiterates the view of the Church on matters of money. Money cannot be elevated so that it has power over people and society. Instead, money should serve ends that promote human dignity and the common good. In terms of the individual, accumulating and possessing money should not be the end goal of work.

All forms of work have intrinsic dignity. The Christian belief in the dignity of work has its origins from Jewish attitudes. Work is honourable as well as a necessity. At the same time burdensome work is seen as a consequence of the Fall and the disobedience of God. However, work also is consecrated by Jesus' work as a carpenter (Mark 6:3).

Clearly, Jesus was not a wealthy man, nor did he come from a wealthy family. He often criticizes those who had or sought after great wealth. Money makes it difficult to love

God with all of one's heart. Wealth focuses the mind on earthly things, not on the Kingdom of God. Hence the pertinent phrase: 'You cannot serve God and Mammon' (Luke 6:13). From the New Testament the author of the Letter to Timothy writes: 'The love of money is the root of all evil things' (1 Timothy 6:10). Finally one of Jesus' most famous sayings is: 'It is easier for a camel to pass through the eye of a needle than for a rich man to enter the Kingdom of God' (Mark 10:24, 25).

One interpretation of this saying is, Jesus is drawing attention to the responsibilities the wealthy have in their stewardship of the earth and its people. Wealth is a form of stewardship, which means responsibility and caring. Money and wealth are not good or bad. How we use wealth determines the moral weight of money. The wealthy and those with means have a responsibility to use their resources wisely to care for God's world and make it a better place.

Charity

One of the responsibilities of stewardship is taking care of the poor. Jesus lived in a world where there were many poor people. He spoke much about the poor and the theme recurs frequently in his teachings. All Christians have a duty to care for the poor according to their means. Jesus says the right hand does not know what the left hand is doing in giving charity (Matthew 6:2–4). Christians in an affluent society have the responsibility of not giving into the temptations that wealth presents. Additionally, Christians should think and act compassionately towards the poor. They cannot ignore the needy using the excuse the poor and downtrodden are lazy and irresponsible. This attitude goes against Jesus's teaching which says the way we treat others is the way we treat him (Matthew 23:31–46).

In the Gospels, Jesus frequently encounters and helps the needy. He often speaks of the needs of the poor, the disabled, and those who are at a particular disadvantage such as widows and orphans. Paul and other New Testament writers demonstrate how the care of the needy is an accepted part of Christianity. Indeed, charity is one of the three Christian virtues: '. . . and now lives faith, hope, charity, these three; but the greatest of these is charity' (1 Corinthians 13:13).

It is universally understood that the basic obligations of a Christian include the requirement to make charitable donations. Over the centuries Christians have met this obligation. Calvin's view on charity went beyond the obvious obligation of giving to the poor. Some redistribution of wealth through ready employment and fair wages is necessary. It is equally important to eliminate practices that threaten the wellbeing of the badly impoverished. Specifically, Calvin condemned speculation, hoarding, and profiteering on essential commodities, especially food.[13]

Debt

In the early Church, interest on lending was forbidden, not unlike the current case with Islam. At the Council of Arles in 314 CE, clergymen of the Christian church were prohibited from taking interest on loans. The prohibition is upheld in the Council of Nicaea, 11 years later.

With passing years, the rules on usury became tighter. Laymen were prevented from taking interest at the Council of Carthage in 348 CE, in the Council of Aix in 789 CE, the Third Lateran Council in 1179, and in the Second Lyons Council in

1274. Finally, in 1311 the Council of Vienna condemned anyone who engaged in usury as a heretic.[14]

The prohibition against usury held firm until about 1500 when the Lateran Council of 1515 accepted a motion that Franciscans had not been sinning when they charged a fee for their loans to the poor. The Burghers of Geneva appointed a committee in 1557 to examine the question of usury. They concluded that for the avoidance of fraud, destruction, and ruination, the charging of interest ought to be allowed.[15] With this decision, the modern banking industry thus began. It is now an accepted Christian view that lending on interest is a permissible activity provided the rate of interest charged is a reasonable reflection of the risks involved.

Conduct of business

There is general agreement among Protestants and Catholics that business is not a bad enterprise. The person engaged in business should gain profits. However, she should do so by legal means and without harming others or herself. Christian tradition holds speculation, hoarding, and profiteering on essential commodities, especially food, as morally unacceptable. The reason behind the poor view taken on speculation and hoarding is clear: these activities damage community members least able to cope with rising food prices.

The economy is a system to serve humanity to live well. Pope Benedict writes:

> Profit is useful if it serves as a means towards an end that provides a sense both of how to produce it and of how to make good use of it. Once profit becomes the exclusive goal, if it is produced by improper means and without the common good as its ultimate end, it risks destroying wealth and creating poverty.[16]

Economic development is meant to produce real growth, benefit everyone, and is genuinely sustainable.

In reference to general management issues, the religions largely are in agreement. Christian ethical standards call for the payment of a decent living wage, a theme of Christian writing down the centuries. The same sentiment is expressed in other Holy books. Honest dealing, giving full measure, accurate scales and weights, are all endorsed (2 Corinthians 13:7; Proverbs 16:11; Philippians 2:3–4).[17]

Christian economics

Christian tradition also has a high degree of concern for the poor. Feeding the hungry is an ethical imperative of the Catholic Church, as it is for Protestants. Thus, the Church encourages the development of a network of economic institutions capable of guaranteeing regular access to sufficient food and water for nutritional needs. Christianity promotes eliminating structural sources that cause hunger and poverty. Thus, it calls for investment in infrastructure, particularly in rural areas, and equitable agrarian reform.[18]

Social justice requires the adoption of economic policies that do not increase disparities of wealth. Pope Benedict states that countries should prioritize the goal of access to steady employment for everyone.[19] The Church is most concerned about the rights of workers and the abandonment of social welfare policies because of the single-minded pursuit of profits and economic efficiency. Christianity warns against the inhumanity of consumerism and an economic system that exalts free markets and denies a truly humane goal.[20]

The Catholic Church has been vocal about the effects of untrammelled markets, consumerism, and materialism on the individual and society. The Church warns against the mistaken conviction that the economy is autonomous and the market is value-free. 'In the long term, these convictions have led to economic, social, and political systems that trample upon personal and social freedom and are therefore unable to deliver the justice that they promise.'[21] The current Pope Francis calls for global financial reform that respects human dignity, helps the poor, promotes the common good, and allows states to regulate markets. He stresses the importance of ethics in finance, and 'for financial reform along ethical lines that would produce in its turn an economic reform to benefit everyone'.[22] For the Christian tradition, the economy should serve the common good, provide employment opportunities, help those in need, especially the poor, and allow humans to attain their full realization.

9.4 Hinduism

Unlike other major world religions, a central authority or canon that derives from one spiritual entity or one scripture does not define Hinduism. In practice, Hinduism is polytheistic and sectarian. There is no central doctrine that forms the essence of the faith, no one supreme God, no Holy Prophet, and no one holy book. Supreme authority rests in an invisible creative force, sometimes referred to as God or Brahma, but also as the impersonal Brahman, an 'all-pervading, self-existing power'.[23] However, Brahma is not prominent in Hindu worship. The divine appears in a great number of incarnations. Indeed, Brahman manifests as atman, the essence or principle of life or the Self, on earth.

The Vedas are the earliest Hindu religious texts. The work consists of volumes of myth, poetry, and sacrificial injunction, derived from oral composition that spans over a millennium. The Rig Veda is one of the oldest in the Vedas and is likely to have been composed in the second millennium BCE. The Upanishads are more recent (post-500 BCE). Hindus treat the sacrificial hymns of the Vedas as revealed truth or heard knowledge. A Prophet did not receive this sacred knowledge, but instead an undefined group of ancient wise men or sages received the truths. This makes the origins of Hindu religion difficult to identify and has important consequences. For instance, belief in the sanctity of the Vedas is not a prerequisite for being a Hindu. In any case, almost all the Hindu schools and sects (of which there are a multiplicity) recognize the supreme authority of the Vedas.

The Vedas tell of the creation and the formation of castes or social classes of humanity. According to the Hindu tradition, the world is not an independent, or objective reality. Universal order is constructed by ritual performance. Rituals and sacrifices, therefore, take a primary place in the practice of the religion according to the early Vedic tradition. Hindu society consists of classes formed by the sacrifice of gods, creating the Brahman (priestly caste), the warrior, the merchant, and the servant castes. Within each of these main castes (varna) are more subdivisions of the castes; so much so that it is said there are hundreds of Hindu castes. Every human, plant, and animal has a place in the tightly woven, hierarchical world.

To be moral, to act rightly, is to realize one's place in the constituted cosmos.

Metaphysics

Dharma is the established norm, the moral, social, and cosmological order in Hindu tradition. The term also envelops concepts of religion, duty, and righteousness. Dharma, as duty, emphasizes the systemic duty of every person to act, in every life situation, in such a way that righteousness is achieved. Dharma evolved from the classical period of Hinduism (500 BCE–c. 200) to become a theory of obligations of an individual according to his or her caste and stage of life (ashrama).

While parts of the Vedas emphasize the importance of ritual and sacrifice, within the Vedic corpus, the Upanishads reject the ritual and promote a contemplative turn. In the Upanishads, moksha, or release from the cycle of reincarnation – rebirths and deaths (termed 'samsara'). Karma guides the human soul through the succession of rebirths determined by the actions taken in one's life. A person becomes virtuous through virtuous action and wicked through wrong action (Upanishad 4.4.5). Moksha is achieved by meditation and contemplation of the true nature of self and the world. This Upanishadic vein of Hinduism posits that a person must experience and realize the underlying unity of the world, expressed in terms of the identity of Self (Atman) and the highest Reality (Brahman).

Thus, Hinduism has two strains of thought woven together in practice. First, there is the model of behaviour guided by rituals and sacrifices as written in the Vedas. Second, there is the life lived towards the pursuit of attaining the knowledge of the unity of Atman and Brahman – that Atman and Brahman are one. This is the ascetic, contemplative, and meditative life, aimed at attaining a mystical knowledge beyond the material and temporal.

The weaving together of the two strands of Hindu thought is expressed in the *Dharmasutra*, a volume with extended treatises on the nature of moral life. It is a Hindu text that applies the performance of public rituals to the everyday activities of the Brahman householder. The Sutra literature speaks of a moral life rooted in the Brahman householder's ritual activities directed towards the gods, ancestors, and cosmos. The Hindu cosmos endlessly cycles through four great ages that tend towards moral disorder. The current age in which we live is the last and most morally dissipated. Through each stage of the cosmos the duties of men are different. Similarly, there are four stages in an ideal human life, with each stage requiring the application of different moral codes.

The first stage starts with the life of a student, learning the Vedic texts from his teacher. In classical Hindu theory the lowest caste group, the servants or shudras, as well as females, are not allowed to enter this stage. Impurity is a major reason. Shudras and females are denied access to the scriptures and to formal education in them.

The individual grows older and moves to the second stage of life that involves marriage, fatherhood, and being a householder. In the second stage of life, the Hindu takes part in the maintenance and development of society, including procreation. Women, in classical theory, do not seem to be given much importance in the system, despite their crucial role in the procreation aspect of a householder's duty. In both these stages, the Hindu acts correctly and performs the necessary rituals required of a priestly householder.

In the final stages of a Hindu's life cycle, he is to concentrate on achieving moksha, or release from the cycle of rebirth. He does this by entering a life of solitude, gradually withdrawing from society (third stage), and then becomes a full renunciant who single-mindedly pursues self-knowledge. By realizing the ultimate identity of Self and Reality, Manu declares: 'he who sees the Self in all living beings through the Self/achieves equanimity toward all and approaches Reality, the highest step' (Manu, 12.125). As the Hindu goes through the four stages of life, he follows at each stage a different morality. This contextual aspect of morality leads many to question if Hinduism has a moral theory based on universal values.

Hindu ethics

The debate is on whether within Hinduism there exists a moral philosophical theory, in the sense of a body of developed moral theory. Of course, Hindu religious texts contain proposals concerning how to live, how to act, and what sort of person to be. However, it is not clear if there is a system of well-developed Hindu ethics because Hindu philosophy does not offer a substantial amount of rigorous or extended discussions on philosophical ethics.[24]

Hindu ethics appears to lack universality. In other words there are few ethical doctrines, precepts, or principles that apply to all humans. Weber explains this lack (except for the few absolute and general prohibitions – particularly the killing of cows) of universality by pointing to the doctrine of karma. What we are is a result of our previous deeds in past lives. Karma, as understood in the Hindu tradition, is the cause of the Hindu caste system, where humans are ranked in a complex and detailed hierarchy that determines the social status and profession of individuals. Whether one is a merchant or a street cleaner depends on the caste into which one is born. Hence, in Hinduism, there are different 'ethical codes for different status groups which not only differed widely but were often in sharp conflict'.[25] Caste explains why Hindu ethics does not have a universal human nature from which to deduce ethical decrees. Ethics is contextual and context is largely a matter of caste.

Within the *Dharmasutra* is an important text, often translated as 'The Laws of Manu'. The priestly elite composed the text around the turn of the Common Era or earlier. The focus of the text is providing a model for human moral behaviour – not a universalist model such as we see in say, Kant (see Chapter 8), but many models according to the presumed innate differences of human beings. The 'Laws of Manu' gives a self-proclaimed authoritative account of the ethics for different stages of life and social caste. Manu focuses on the specific duties and obligations of the three upper or 'twice-born' castes, with occasional references to lower social groups, including women.[26] Attention is paid to ritual and rites for each stage of life, of which there are four for the male Brahmin.

Manu is also adamant about the innate tendencies and activities of each social class. Social and moral order can only be maintained when there is a separation of distinct groups and people and earthly things. Manu does accord some universal values to the four classes of humans. His decrees contain 10 virtues: contentment, forgiveness, self-restraint, non-anger, non-appropriating, purity, sensual control, wisdom, self-knowledge, and truth.[27] Yet the overwhelming theme in the book of Manu is that particular classes are obliged to perform particular duties. To be moral, is therefore, to particularize.[28]

In addition, each stage of a Hindu's life requires him to follow a different moral code. In the first stage as a student, the Hindu must perform rites and rituals, obey his teacher, and be diligent in his study. In the second stage as a married householder, with meaningful work and a family, the Hindu should fulfil his ritual and reproductive debts to ancestors, gods, and sages. He must have an ethic of self-restraint and sensory control to guide his actions. This ethic is developed even more when the Hindu enters the third stage of life; that of a solitary contemplative in search of spiritual liberation. In the fourth stage of complete renunciant, the Hindu follows an ethic of complete asceticism and disregard for the material.

Work

The Hindu caste system is a hierarchical model of division of labour in society. Accordingly, the Brahmins are priests and teachers. They continue the tradition of learning and provide links with the divine realm. The Kshatriyas are kings, local rulers, and soldiers. In other words, the contemporary parallel is government ministers and elected officials. Kshatriyas are the leaders and protectors of society. The third caste is the Vaishyas. These are mainly farmers, traders, artisans, and others who work by looking after the socio-economic aspects of society. The lowest caste is the Sudra caste. The Sudras are low-status artisans, agricultural, and manual labourers. Generally, they inhabit the servile world. Below the Sudras are the various outcaste groups called 'the Untouchables',who are engaged in 'unclean' professions.

In the past, caste mobility was almost non-existent and forbidden. By requiring a Hindu to follow his particular dharma, and promising a better rebirth, the caste system justifies the status quo, and precludes revolutions of the poor and oppressed. However, in modern times there is much evidence of upward mobility in India. Although, the traditional system is still rigid and unfair, it does permit mobility through persistence and effort. In addition, there are government-mandated affirmative action programmes benefiting lower castes and Untouchables.

In modern India, capitalist philosophies have many followers in the upper classes. A consequence of India's history as a British colony and its eventual independence, socialist, and communist ideologies are strongly represented, especially among intellectuals and populist politicians.

Charity

Charitable giving ranks highly among good deeds a Hindu may do. Individuals may make special efforts to gain merit for good works in order to attain a better rebirth. Charity, through making donation for good purposes, and doing some form of social work count as good works. All Hindu religious leaders seem to emphasize this aspect. Mohandas Gandhi devoted time to his spinning wheel, spinning cloth for the poor and to a variety of aspects of social work. It behoves a Hindu to give several hours a week to the care of others. There is, however, little thought given to intentions behind actions so that one only does good work to get benefits for a better rebirth. Charitable thought and deed is not an integral part of a person's behavioural pattern. Buddhism has much more to say on the importance of intention as a key factor in karma.

Wealth

The pursuit of wealth and power has a place in the legitimate aims of Hindu life.[29] While there is a significant spiritual and ascetic turn in Hinduism, there are times when a Hindu is required to be primarily concerned with power. The ideal, however, is a balanced approach because excessive concern for wealth, both its acquisition and its use, is negative. In the Upanishads, there are many passages that say man is not to be satisfied with wealth alone. Additionally, the acquisition of wealth should be done in a righteous way.

In the classical model the first stage of a Hindu's life is one of humility as the student learns from his teacher and lives simply. In the second stage of life, the householder is actively engaged in gaining wealth because other parts of society depend on him. Thus, those in the other three stages of life derive support from the householder especially for their material needs.

9.5 Judaism

Judaism is one of the oldest, living religions on the planet. To be Jewish is to belong to a people and a historical community. Jewish history is marked by a relationship with God and persecution by rulers of the lands on which the Jews, often called the people of the Book, settled. The Book refers to the Torah, which besides containing laws also gives details of the early history of the Jewish people. The Jewish religion has two main sources of authority: the Torah and the Talmud.

Jewish religious tradition starts from the Torah that consists of the first five books of the Bible. These books are: Bereshit (Genesis), Shemot (Exodus), Vayikra (Leviticus), Bamidbar (Numbers), and Devarim (Deuteronomy). Within the Torah are laws and commandments such as 'Honour your father and your mother' (Exodus 20:12). These laws are just the beginnings of an extensive system of rules and laws known as the Oral Torah. These laws have been debated and interpreted for centuries to the present day. The largest encyclopaedia of these debates is the 18-volume Talmud. This collection of laws and their interpretations include the thoughts and teachings of over a 1,000 rabbis over a 1,000 years up to about the fifth century CE. The Talmud, in its larger and more authoritative Babylonian version, contains 63 tractates (comprising 17 volumes in the Soncino English translation).

Authority

Much of the Talmud is halakhic in nature. The Halakha is the accepted consensus as to the proper course of action or ruling. Halakha or Jewish law is codified norms of Torah-based behaviour that encompasses civil, criminal, and moral law as well. The laws were written centuries ago and require continual interpretation because of contextual changes over time. When a body of rulings has built up, they will then be considered by a scholar specialized in the subject. The scholar may determine the assessment of the majority as accurate. Even so other rabbis need not accept the scholar's view and the Halakha will simply not accord with their own view. Eventually, as consensus grows on the correct way to act in a given situation, this consensus view becomes Halakha. For instance, when the electric light was first invented, a debate arose as to whether turning electric lights was allowed on Shabbat (the Jewish holy day). Traditional law forbids lighting a fire on Shabbat. Each rabbi rules on this question and the majority or consensus decision is the Halakha. On this issue of the electric light the Halakha forbids turning on or off electric lights on the Shabbat.[30]

Conservative Jews take the Halakha into consideration when addressing new issues or situations and give Halakha rulings occasionally. Reform and Liberal Jews do not consider themselves to be of the Halakhic tradition, but will bear the Halakha in mind when interpreting laws. They use other methods and hold the belief that each Jew has the autonomy to decide for herself the right action in a given situation. Thus, in the electric light case, Reform or Liberal Jews are not likely to follow the Halakha of turning on or off electric lights on the Shabbat. In general, the Jewish tradition cultivates an atmosphere of debate and argument when considering the laws. The Torah is profound and deserves study by human rationality and ingenuity to arrive at legitimate interpretations. Consequently, Jewish culture values study, articulate discussion, and free thinking that result in responsible action within the community.[31]

Laws

The Genesis narratives contain the seven laws of the descendants of Noah: (1) the establishment of a judicial system in society, and six prohibitions against (2) blasphemy, (3) idolatry, (4) the wanton destruction of human life, (5) adultery, incest, homosexuality, and bestiality, (6) robbery, and (7) eating the flesh of a living animal. These seven laws are presented in the Talmud and precede the laws of the covenant. The laws are called the Noachide laws and are some of the earliest in Jewish history. Remarkably, the laws are regarded as pertaining to all human beings because of the general rabbinic belief that humans are capable of understanding and respecting moral norms governing civilized life.

Despite the Noachide laws being prior in time, they probably take second place in terms of their importance for Jewish ethics. First in importance are the narratives concerning the Exodus and the Covenant at Sinai. At Mount Sinai, God revealed his will to Moses through the law. Together, the Noachide and Sinaitic laws constitute the central story of the Jewish ethical tradition. Some key motifs emerge from the Exodus and Sinaitic covenant and as such are central to the Jewish ethical tradition:[32]

1. *The importance of redemption and social justice*: The Jews were slaves and oppressed in Egypt, but they were freed through God's redemption of his people. In doing so, God demonstrated his power, justice, righteousness, and compassion. For these reasons, the Jews agree to obey God and his commandments. There is a strong social justice strain throughout Judaism because of their history of oppression and slavery. The commitment to social justice characterizes all expressions of Jewish ethics from the ancient to the modern period.
2. *Transforming ethics to law*: Jewish tradition commonly converts ethical norms to legal (Halakhic) requirements. The ethics of the covenant at Mt. Sinai after the Exodus from Egypt is expressed as law. The laws are meant to be authoritative and to govern the conduct of all members of the community. The core of this legal corpus is the 613 commandments identified in Jewish scripture. The Jewish faith has a major ethical conviction that for moral requirements to be taken seriously, they must be made into law so the community members realize adherence to moral rules are expected and non-adherence will be subject to punishment.
3. *Autonomy to interpret revealed law*: As noted in the section on Halakha, Jewish tradition gives enormous autonomy for interpretation of the Mitzvot because of the high respect given to human reason. According to tradition, direct communication from God came to an end in the prophetic period. From that time forward, Jews have been using their reason to rationally interpret revealed law that represents

God's will. While Jews are encouraged to interpret the law, there is never a question about whether humans can create or discover new laws. They cannot. The law is complete in its revealed content. Nevertheless, there are countless ways for morally creative interpretation of the law that comes out from new contexts and changing moral sensibilities.

4 *Study and obedience*: In rabbinic tradition, study of the law entails obedience to it. No one can study the law and be completely detached from its content. However, study by itself without the following deed is empty. The very essence of Jewish ethics is based on the principle that the divine commandment must be converted into a deed.

Ethics

The reason for humans to treat each other well is because it is God's will. This is one of the basic contributions of Judaism to the Western religious tradition.[33] According to rabbis, one worships God through decent, humane, and moral relations with one's fellows. The underlying foundation for behaving morally and the demand that God makes upon humankind to treat each other properly is the biblical teaching that man is created in the image of God (Genesis I: 27). As human beings are created in the image of God, it is clear that to reach the highest level of perfection, humans should become as similar to God as possible. Jews are commanded to act in certain ways. It is through the achievement of moral perfection that Jews imitate God and thus fulfil their destiny as individuals created in the image of God.[34]

Social justice

The commitment to social justice in the Jewish tradition is seen in the extensive body of legislation requiring compassion for the poor, the sojourner, the widow, and the orphan. Having experienced conditions of being marginalized and oppressed, the Jews are expected to have an insight into how evil those states are and to help others, especially fellow Jews out of these states. In addition, Jews are asked to avoid practices that create new suffering for the powerless among them.

The urging for social justice is not confined to the Exodus narratives. The Pentateuch has numerous commandments, or Mitzvot, pertaining to providing for the poor, such as tithing harvests (Deuteronomy 14:28–9) and the cancelling of debts in the Sabbatical year of release (Deuteronomy 15:1–2). In the prophetic writings, social justice is vital. When the Israelites fail to help the poor as they promised to in the covenant with God, they incur God's wrath. In the era of the Jewish diaspora when Jews moved to urban centres and spread out to different lands, rabbis felt it necessary to write a new set of rulings and norms focused on the commitment to social justice. So extensive were social justice requirements among the diaspora that Jewish communities took the form of modified welfare states with compulsory levies and trustees taking care of the poor and needy.[35]

Charity and wealth

No moral norms or laws prohibit the accumulation of wealth. There is guidance on how to use wealth. Jews have generally been poor for much of their history. The collective memory of slavery in Egypt is an important motivation for being economically independent. Rather than serve another master, wealth provides the ability to serve God. Thus, as with other religions discussed in this chapter, wealth, on its own, is not regarded as evil. Wealth is an aspect of life about which one should be careful. If you find yourself getting too rich, do not take this too seriously (Psalm 62:10). Be watchful of yourself, so that you do not become greedy and envious (Ecclesiastes 5:10–12). Most importantly, a wealthy person, while not denying any material comforts to herself or her family, should serve the community.

The Hebrew word for charity is also the word for justice, *Tzedaka*. It is not a leap to infer the Jewish concept of charity is closely aligned with its concept of justice. The idea of charity is not only about generosity but more about the simple justice of the 'haves' giving to the 'have nots'.[36] According to the Code of Jewish Law, a person should give up to a fifth of her wealth to the poor. A tenth of wealth is the average amount and anyone who gives less than this percentage is called ungenerous. However, the Code does say that a person should not give so much as to make it difficult to live well.

Maimonides, one of the greatest rabbis in Jewish tradition, speaks of eight levels of charity.[37] At the highest level is to support a fellow Jew by giving a gift or loan, or entering into a partnership with the person. The second level is to give to the poor without knowing who receives the gifts and who gives the gifts. Not knowing the recipient means the gift is one for the sake of Heaven. The story is told of an 'anonymous fund' in the Holy Temple in Jerusalem. There the donors gave in secret and the poor received in secret. The third level of charity is when the giver knows the identity of the recipient, but remains anonymous to the person receiving the charity. The fourth level is when the recipient knows the donor but the donor does not know the identity of the recipient. The fifth level is when the giver gives to the poor person directly and before being asked. The sixth level is when one gives to the poor person after being asked. The seventh level is when one gives insufficiently but still gladly and willingly. The last level is when a giver gives unwillingly.

Work

The value of work is stressed repeatedly in the Talmud. For instance, one phrase in the Talmud says, 'No labour, however humble, is dishonouring'.[38] Many of the Pharisees were manual workers such as carpenters or charcoal burners. Both the Talmud and the Torah contain discussions of wage and employment ethics. Some ethical rules in the books include:

- Creditors are not allowed take possession of the tools of a person's trade in payment of a debt.
- Employers are not allowed to withhold payment from an employee for work performed.
- An employee is allowed to resign from work at any time, because God pronounced, 'I did not free you from slavery to become slaves to others' (Bava Metzia 10a).

In the Talmud, the relationship of the worker and God is the primary focus such that humans work in the service of God, the Master, 'Know before whom you are toiling and who your employer is who will pay you the reward of your labour' (Pirke Avot 2:19–21). The implication of this primary work relationship is, in the workplace, the individual has first allegiance to the ethical values as given by God, and then secondarily, the rules as given by the employer. If there is a conflict, God's ethical rules should trump an organization's or a boss's. The importance of following the prescribed Jewish ethics in work is seen when the first question a person is asked when presented for Life in the World to Come[39] is, 'Were you faithful in business?' (Shabbat 31a). This faithfulness in business includes the virtue of honesty, but it also means compliance with the ethical level of behaviour beyond which the law requires. The rabbis note that more than 120 of the Mitzvot (precepts or commandment of the Jewish law given by God) in the Torah are related to work, business, and employment. Behaviour in these fields, therefore, is a key test of a person's moral and ethical standards.[40]

9.6 Summary and conclusion

There is no significant difference in the ethical views of the major religions towards key features of finance. All religions discussed in this chapter and in Chapter 3 on Islam hold work as a dignified pursuit on condition the work is done in an honest and fair way. Honesty and fairness are two virtues frequently upheld in the conduct of business. Employers are asked to pay a fair day's wages, and employees are asked to earn these wages without cheating their employers. Similarly, wealth and money in themselves are not disparaged. Religious traditions admonish their followers only if they become overly attached to wealth. People do not exist for money. On the contrary, money exists to help people. Spending all of one's time and mental efforts accumulating money takes one away from spiritual endeavours and growth.

Charity is greatly encouraged by all religions studied in this book. Some religions, such as Islam, even prescribe a certain percentage of income to be donated to charity. In terms of contributing to society, the general view is that using one's ability in work that contributes to the development of society and to the common good is to be encouraged. We all have an obligation to contribute to social justice in society so that the least advantaged are helped. Below is a table summarizing the ethical positions of religions on key aspects of finance. Checks in the boxes under a specific religion indicate its precepts align with the stated principle listed in the respective headings. All the major religions agree on the conduct, the role, and the attitude to money and charity. The only disagreement is on whether interest on loans should be prohibited. Islam does not allow interest. However, all religions take the stand that excessive interest on loans is unethical.

An observation of Table 9.1 clearly shows there is more common ground in religious ethics pertaining to finance than assumed. To argue that we cannot utilize the principles of religious ethics when conducting the activity of finance because each religion has its own values that differ from another's is unsound. Indeed, the practice of finance may be a lot more ethical if practitioners were encouraged, rather than looked askance at, to delve into their own religious-based ethical resources when exercised by moral issues at work.

Table 9.1 Ethical stands of major religions on key aspects of finance

Religions	Fairness and honesty in the conduct of business	Pay fair wages to employees and fair work from employees	Acceptable to be rich but do not be obsessed about money	Business is noble so long as the venture is not engaged in unethical actions	Business should make community as a whole better off	Charity is encouraged. Take care of the poor. In giving charity, you do not need to impoverish yourself	Lending: Interest is prohibited	Usury: Excessive interest is prohibited	Trustees have a duty to care for assets well and never use the assets for oneself
Buddhism	✓	✓	✓	✓	✓	✓	✗	✓	✓
Christianity	✓	✓	✓	✓	✓	✓	✗	✓	✓
Hinduism	✓	✓	✓	✓	✓	✓	✗	✓	✓
Islam	✓	✓	✓	✓	✓	✓	✓	✓	✓
Judaism	✓	✓	✓	✓	✓	✓	✗	✓	✓

Notes

1. Max L. Stackhouse, "Economics," *The Blackwell Companion to Religious Ethics*, ed. William Schweiker (Oxford, UK: Blackwell Publishing, 2003), 455.
2. Padmasiri De Silva, "Buddhist Ethics," *A Companion to Ethics*, ed. Peter Singer (Oxford, UK: Blackwell Publishing, 1993), 64.
3. Dalai Lama, *A Simple Path* (New York, NY: Harper Collins Publishers, 2009), 89.
4. Dalai Lama, 89.
5. Peggy Morgan, "Buddhism," *Ethical Issues in Six Religious Traditions*, eds. Peggy Morgan and Clive A. Lawton (Edinburgh, UK: Edinburgh University Press, 2007), 80.
6. Peter Harvey, *An Introduction to Buddhist Ethics* (Cambridge, UK: Cambridge University Press, 2000), 198.
7. Andrew M. McCosh, *Financial Ethics* (Norwell, MA: Kluwer Academic Publishers, 1999), 80.
8. McCosh, 84.
9. Ibid.
10. Jef Van Gerwen, "Origins of Christian Ethics," *The Blackwell Companion to Religious Ethics*, ed. William Schweiker (Oxford, UK: Blackwell Publishing: Oxford, 2003), 204.
11. Ronald Preston, "Christian Ethics," *A Companion to Ethics*, ed. Peter Singer (Oxford, UK: Blackwell Publishing, 1993), 95.
12. Preston, 98.
13. McCosh, 51.
14. McCosh, 52.
15. McCosh, 54.
16. Pope Benedict XVI, *Caritas in Veritate* (San Francisco, CA: Ignatius Press, 2009).
17. McCosh, 58.
18. Pope Benedict XVI, 51–2.
19. Pope Benedict XVI, 62.
20. Pope Francis, "Pope: Financial Reform Along Ethical Lines," *The Vatican Today*, 16 May 2013, accessed 24 March 2015, http://www.news.va/en/news/pope-financial-reform-along-ethical-lines.
21. Pope Benedict XVI, 66.
22. Pope Francis, "Pope: Financial Reform."
23. Roy W. Perret, "Hindu Ethics?" *The Blackwell Companion to Religious Ethics*, ed. William Schweiker (Oxford, UK: Blackwell Publishing, 2003).
24. Perret, 323.
25. Max Weber, *The Religion of India* (New York, NY: Free Press, 1958).
26. Perret, 334.
27. Purusottama Bilimoria, "Indian Ethics," *A Companion to Ethics*, ed. Peter Singer (Oxford, UK: Blackwell Publishing, 1993), 49.
28. Perret, 335.
29. Werner Menski, "Hinduism," *Ethical Issues in Six Religious Traditions*, eds. Peggy Morgan and Clive A. Lawton (Edinburgh, UK: Edinburgh University Press, 2010), 27.
30. Clive A. Lawton, "Judaism," in *Ethical Issues in Six Religious Traditions*, eds. Peggy Morgan and Clive A. Lawton (Edinburgh University Press: Edinburgh 2010), 169.
31. Lawton, 169.
32. Ronald M. Green, "Foundations of Jewish Ethics," *The Blackwell Companion to Religious Ethics*, ed. William Schweiker (Oxford, UK: Blackwell Publishing, 2003), 169.
33. Menachem Keller, "Jewish Ethics," *A Companion to Ethics*, ed. Peter Singer (Oxford, UK: Blackwell Publishing, 1993), 84.
34. Keller, 85.
35. Green, 170.
36. Lawton, 182.
37. "Maimonides' Eight Levels of Charity," *Chabad.org*, accessed 20 November 2013, http://www.chabad.org/library/article_cdo/aid/45907/jewish/Eight-Levels-of-Charity.htm.
38. Lawton, 180.

39 The World to Come generally refers to three states. The first is the world after the End of Days when the virtuous are resurrected. The second is the world of immortal souls following the time of resurrection. The third is the heavenly world inhabited by righteous souls upon death. Believing in one way of the World to Come does not necessarily mean not believing in the other two ways.
40 Lawton, 181.

10 Ethical issues in investment management

10.1 Introduction

This chapter discusses major ethical topics in the investment management business, a part of the business commonly called the 'buy side' in finance. This is the side where mutual fund management, private banking, hedge fund management, and private equity reside. It is the area in finance that involves asset management, or management of clients' money and funds.

Multiple ethical issues obviously arise in asset management. This chapter covers the main, most topical issues that investment managers and analysts are most likely to encounter in their daily work. The topics are: (1) insider trading, (2) market manipulation, (3) market timing, (4) management fees, focusing on hedge fund and mutual fund fees, and (5) ethical issues related to managing Shari'a compliant funds. Each section describes the nature of the activity, gives examples of empirical studies of the activity and provides an ethical evaluation of the activity.

10.2 Insider trading

What is insider trading?

The phrase 'insider trading' includes both legal and illegal conduct. The legal form of insider trading is when corporate insiders (such as officers, directors, and employees) buy and sell stock in their own companies. In the US when corporate insiders trade in their own securities, they must report their trades to the Securities and Exchange Commission (SEC).

Illegal insider trading refers generally to the trading of stock of publicly held corporations, in breach of a fiduciary duty or other relationship of trust and confidence, while in possession of material, non-public information about the stock. Those who give such information, or 'tippers', the people who use the information to trade the stock, or 'tippees', and those who misappropriate such information for stock trading, are all violating insider trading laws.

The key elements to consider when deciding whether an act constitutes insider trading are:

1 The information must be both material and non-public.
2 The trader has violated a fiduciary and/or legal duty to a corporation and its shareholders.

3   The source of the information has a fiduciary and/or legal duty, and the one who trades on this information knows the source is violating that duty.

Some examples of insider trading are:

1   Officers, directors, or employees of a corporation trade the securities of the corporation after learning significant, confidential corporate developments such as an earnings downgrade or upgrade, a fall in customer orders, or a merger with another corporation.
2   Friends, business associates, family members, and other tippees, or recipients of information, of corporate officers, directors, and employees who traded the securities after receipt of information.
3   Employees of companies who provide services to the corporation and have been given material non-public information, then trade on the information.
4   Government employees who learned of such information because of their position in government.

In the US, statutory authority from section 10b of the *Securities Exchange Act* of 1934 governs insider trading rules. Based on this authority, the SEC enacted Rules 10b-5 and 14e-3, which it applied to impersonal stock exchange transactions beginning in 1961.

Most European countries enacted insider trading regulations in the early 1990s with Italy and Denmark in 1991, Austria in 1993, and Spain and Germany in 1994. The European Union (EU) updated its regulation with the introduction of the Market Abuse Directive (MAD) in 2003. MAD prohibits primary and secondary insiders to engage in the following acts:

1   Using their inside information in conducting a transaction
2   Disclosing the inside information to a third party
3   Recommending a transaction to a third party.[1]

Primary insiders are those with direct access to information because of their positions as corporate insiders, e.g., executives, employees, and directors. Primary insiders are also persons with access to inside information due to their employment, profession, or duties, e.g., lawyers and consultants. Secondary insiders are those who are not primary insiders, but who possess inside information and they know (or ought to know) it is inside information disclosed in a breach of a fiduciary duty.

Trading on privileged insider information is lucrative. Empirical studies examining the profitability of reported legal insider trading clearly show insiders earn abnormal returns. Studies of illegal insider trading by Cornell and Sirri report an abnormal return of 5.4 per cent during the month insiders were trading.[2] Meulbroek finds insiders earn abnormal returns of about 3 per cent on the day of the insider trade.[3]

Reasons why insider trading is unethical

Insider trading is unethical for many good reasons. After the global financial crisis, several high-profile cases of insider trading were prosecuted in the US. The most publicized and biggest insider trading cases were the Raj Rajaratnam, Rajat Gupta, and SAC cases.

These prosecutions were carried out to deter future insider trading activity. Why did prosecutors and regulators feel it necessary to deter this type of trading? Indeed, many free market and market efficiency proponents argue that insider trading should not be illegal because the activity actually leads to more efficient price discovery. This argument is an economic and utilitarian argument that takes into account only one aspect of the utility calculation. In contrast, there are a number of good arguments why insider trading is unethical.

Fairness

Critics of insider trading often use the argument based on fairness to support the claim that insider trading is unethical. Fairness does not require that all parties should possess the same information. Markets function well and with credibility when some players have superior information and trade on the information to make profits. The information is obtained through work and time spent on analysing companies and economies. The rewards from superior information obtained through effort gives incentives to seek out new information. In other words, fairness is not an issue when investors gain supernormal profits due to skill, hard work, and just pure luck.

Fairness does, however, require all to have equal access to information. Thus, the availability of information is not due to lack of effort but to lack of access. All information must be available to everyone for use in the market. How investors use and what they make of the information determines success in the markets. In today's financial markets, information is readily available if one is willing to spend time and effort obtaining and analysing the information. There is no shortage of channels, from social media, to trade journals, analyst reports, and everything else on the World Wide Web. However, insider information is not available on any of these channels, no matter how hard one works to obtain the information. Instead, the information is released only to particular individuals in their organizations. These individuals are those identified in section 10.2: officers, directors, employees of corporations; their friends, business associates, family members, and other tippees; and employees of companies who provide services to corporations that have the inside information. Why should these individuals be able to profit from information that is not available to everyone else? The fairness argument rests on the fact that these individuals make supernormal profits by trading the inside information because of their position and not because of their own skill, experience, or effort. Most consider the positional advantage unfair. Werhane analogizes insider trading to a game of poker where some players have marked cards.[4] Poker players may have different skill and knowledge levels, distinctions not considered in any way unfair. A game played with a marked deck, however, gives certain players an unfair advantage over others. By analogy, insider trading is like playing poker with a marked deck.

Fiduciary duty

Nearly everyone deemed an insider is likely to have a fiduciary duty to serve the interests of the corporation and its shareholders. Employees who may legally trade on insider information may spend more effort on pursuing their own interests rather than the interests of shareholders and the corporation. The corporation itself may attempt to tailor its release of information for maximum benefit to insiders. More importantly, the opportunity to engage in insider trading may undermine the relation of trust essential for business organizations.

Courts in the US agree with the judgment that insiders in corporations have a fiduciary duty to serve shareholders and are in breach of this duty if they trade on the information gained as a corporate insider. The *US Supreme Court in US* v. *O'Hagan* upheld the fiduciary duty argument for corporate insiders. O'Hagan was a partner in a Minneapolis law firm advising the British company, Grand Metropolitan, in a hostile takeover of the US company, Pillsbury Company.[5] O'Hagan tricked a fellow partner into revealing details of the takeover and made a profit of US$4.3 million through trading Pillsbury stock and stock options.

The appellate court ruled that O'Hagan did not engage in insider trading because he had no fiduciary duty to Pillsbury. Although O'Hagan misappropriated confidential information from his law firm, he did not perpetrate a fraud against it or Grand Metropolitan. O'Hagan would have been guilty of insider trading only if he were an insider of Pillsbury.

The US Supreme Court overturned this lower court ruling in a six-to-three decision. The highest court affirmed the misappropriation theory. According to the decision, a person commits securities fraud when she 'misappropriates confidential information for securities trading purposes, in breach of fiduciary duty owed to the source of the information'. In other words, an insider does not need to be a person in a company or one who is directly providing services to the company whose stock is traded; even a person not directly working with the company, but is in an organization providing a service to either the bidder or the target of the tender offer. Therefore, people entrusted with information and who trade on this information are considered by the law to be misappropriating – or stealing – the information.

Reasons insider trading should be legal

The principal and most favoured reason given by proponents who argue that insider trading is not unethical is the market efficiency argument.

The market efficiency argument

The argument rests on a theory of modern finance called the efficient market hypothesis (as discussed in Chapter 1, the term 'model' is probably more accurate than 'hypothesis'), or EMH. According to the EMH, all information is captured in the price of a security. The existence of insider trading laws means we have only the semi-strong form of the EMH. This form of EMH states that prices reflect all public information but not privately held information. Efficient pricing requires market participants to know as much information as possible. Insider trading is trading that depends on the use of non-public, material information. The information has an impact on the fundamental value of a stock and is 'crucial' for the evaluation of a stock price.[6] Releasing the information will automatically imply the price of a stock moves closer to its fundamental value. By definition, then, insider trading will increase market efficiency.

In sum, proponents for making legal insider trading say that market efficiency increases because insider trading releases information early into the market and moves prices closer to the real values of stocks.

Empirical studies

Meulbroek examines the transactions of 320 individuals charged with insider trading by the SEC from 1980 to 1989. According to Meulbroek's results, in 81 per cent of all cases, insider trading resulted in quick price changes reflecting the insider information. Cornell and Siri's study seem to corroborate Meulbroek's results, as does Chakravarty and McConnell's work. Atkas *et al.* examine legal insider trading. Their findings lead them to conclude that insiders do contribute significantly to faster price discovery on insider trading days. These empirical studies bolster the case of market efficiency proponents who say that many insider trading events help to increase information efficiency in markets.

The managerial incentive argument

The second reason for allowing insiders to profit from their private information is that it encourages a more creative and productive risk-taking breed of managers. These individuals are attracted to work for the firms. Indeed, by allowing employees and officers of the company to trade on inside information, the agency problem is actually ameliorated to a certain extent. Agency issues arise when the utility functions of managers do not coincide with those of shareholders. The separation between ownership and control in publicly listed companies is a main cause of agency issues. The divergence of interests between shareholders and managers means the latter may not necessarily do what is best for the owners of the corporation. Agency problems result in management decisions that may not maximize shareholder value.

Proponents of legalizing insider trading argue that the inclusion of insider information as part of the remuneration scheme of corporations helps to align the interest of the shareholder with those of managers. Legalizing insider trading means the company can allow managers to use inside information to trade for profit. This profit is considered a part of the managers' overall compensation package. The theoretical support for giving companies the right to allow managers to use inside information is based on the efficient allocation of rights. The property rights of a company are best left to be allocated by the company. Coase shows property rights will be allocated to their highest-valuing user.[7] Legal restriction of insider trading is not the best way to allocate information because there is no uniform legal rule that can find the party who values the information the most. Indeed, a uniform legal rule that bans insider trading displaces efficient contracts with inefficient regulatory solutions.

However, there are problems associated with insider trading as a compensation scheme. For instance, managers may focus on short-term price movements to exploit insider trading opportunities. Managers may create false information causing share price movements beneficial to their own trades but detrimental to shareholders. In addition, managers may choose risky projects to increase the volatility of stock prices to gain profits based on insider information.

Some authors brush these worries aside by arguing that the same problems arise out of equity-linked compensation schemes.[8] Yet, executive stock options have not been eliminated. Just because these remuneration methods have not been eliminated does not mean they are optimal. Similarly, the benefits of legalizing insider trading and allowing managers to act on insider information do not necessarily outweigh the downsides noted above.

Applying the arguments in a utilitarian framework

The utilitarian evaluation weighs the positive consequences versus the negative consequences of insider trading. The consequences measured should cover a broad array of interests including societal benefits or costs.

On the benefits side of a utilitarian analysis and, as noted above, empirical research shows security prices will better and faster reflect the fundamental value by incorporating the private information due to the transactions of insiders. Faster and efficient price discovery improves the optimal allocation of scarce financial resources at a fair price. This is a central function of stock markets in an economy. Another positive arising from efficient information dissemination and price discovery is that insider trading creates one more channel for conveying information. This is important because some market information is diffuse and complex, arguably not easily given in a public announcement. Sometimes information pertaining to valuing an asset or revenue stream is not channelled effectively. In such cases, insider trading can act as an efficient replacement for public disclosure.[9]

The second benefit espoused by insider trading proponents is the increase in market liquidity that comes from the activity. The evidence on this issue is mixed as Kyle predicts less liquid stock markets while Grossman and Holden, and Subrahmanyam predict markets will be more liquid. Different results come out from the different assumptions about the relative importance of insiders, liquidity traders, noise traders, or market makers.

The third benefit of insider trading is the incentives managers have to take risks and, therefore, possibly increase the shareholder value of the company. Not unlike other stock compensation schemes, if managers are allowed to trade on inside information, they are likely to engage in activities that will benefit the stock price of the company, such as increasing sales through innovative schemes or embarking on revenue-generating projects. Managers know the revenues generated by these projects before other investors. They use this knowledge to trade the company's stocks before the information is public and make profits from this insider trading. Thus, the argument goes, insider trading by corporate executives results in enhancing shareholder value.

Market efficiency is not an ethical argument but an economic one. Economic arguments about market efficiency give much weight to the positive outcomes of faster and better price discovery for traded securities, but little to the adverse consequences of legalized insider trading. What are the negative consequences of insider trading? These arise from the belief that the market is rigged. Investors are likely to perceive the stock market as an unlevel playing field and be less inclined to participate. The lack of participation may lead to two poor outcomes: (1) a fall in the volumes traded in markets that may lessen the efficiency of price discovery, and (2) a belief financial markets are structured for the privileged few, which leads to disillusionment with the financial and perhaps economic system. In addition, investors may feel they have to adopt costly defensive measures. Eventually volumes will fall as will market liquidity. The market is left to the use of professional investors and high-frequency traders such as computer trading.

When those who advocate for insider trading measure its benefits and costs, they surmise that it is actually difficult to find damage done by insider trading.[10] They put stress on the informational gains, which lead to better prices guiding capital formation in the economy. Yet, the evidence that insider trading does not harm liquidity and volumes is not conclusive. This lack of evidence is mainly because insider trading is illegal and it is difficult to set up a controlled situation to measure the effects of legalized insider

328 *Ethical issues in Asian investing*

trading. Crucially, proponents of insider trading argue for the benefits solely through the lens of modern finance theory, ignoring other models of analysing markets and investors such as behavioural finance.

Applying behavioural economics to insider trading

The concept of trust is absent in modern finance theory and yet that feeling or virtue is of prime importance in business and financial relationships. Market efficiency proponents of insider trading seem assured that by improving the efficiency of the security market, the confidence of a rational investor in the security market will not be damaged. For the (mythical) rational investor, it is irrelevant if the insider trader earns abnormal profits. What is important is that market prices reflect every piece of information. Note the assumption that it is a 'rational investor' who does not mind unfair, abnormal profits. This 'rational investor' is one who is rational in one sense only: her sole utility preference is profit maximization and her sole motivation is self-interest. As discussed in the chapter on behavioural finance (Chapter 2), this archetypal investor does not exist. The conclusion rational investors in the security market are unfazed by insider trading is unsound because the assumption investors are rational, in the neoliberal economic sense is wrong.

Applying behavioural finance to insider trading gives us different conclusions from those using modern finance theory. We described the ultimatum game in Chapter 5. Results of this game indicate people are not purely self-interested, but instead are motivated by the principle of fairness. A quick reminder of the ultimatum game:

Two players participate in this game. Player 1 is the proposer and is given a large sum of money. Player 2 is the responder. The proposer offers a certain amount of her initial funds to the responder. The responder can either accept or reject the offer. If the responder rejects the offer, both players lose the initial sum of money. If the responder accepts the offer, both players keep their respective shares.

If both players are 'rational' agents, the proposer should offer to share a small percentage of the initial sum, perhaps 5 per cent. A rational economic agent will accept the offer because the small amount is better than a zero amount.

However, results of this experiment across cultures and time show this type of rational expectation behaviour is largely absent. The typical allocation is 20–50 per cent. Responders who are offered less than 20 per cent generally refuse the offer. This behaviour surely does not accord with the rational expectations model. Players are instead driven by the concept of fairness. Responders prefer to take nothing rather than accept an offer that seems to them unfair. Thus, the principle of fairness has intrinsic value to them, and they are prepared to uphold the principle even in the face of certain monetary loss.

Apply the result of the ultimatum game on insider trading and it is not a leap to infer that investors will view gains made from such activity as unfair enrichment. Market participants not in the privileged position to gain from insider trading are then likely to reject the market and withdraw. Players will do so despite the arguments that insider trading increases the speed of price discovery, leading to more efficient pricing of securities and benefiting the market as a whole. As long as there are people not benefiting from insider trading and who view gains from insider trading as unfair, there is the strong likelihood that these people will not participate in the securities markets. This result is contrary to the expectations of those who that argue investors will not lose confidence in the market because they are 'rational agents' interested only in profit maximization and driven by self-interest. In other words, from a behavioural finance standpoint, insider trading will result in loss of trust and lower liquidity in the market.

If we weigh the above outcome against the benefits of insider trading propounded by market efficiency advocates, there is a significant measure of doubt whether the utilitarian calculation comes out in their favour. Thus, the ethics of insider trading should not be considered only using modern finance theory. Rather, behavioural finance theory should supplement the ethical analysis of insider trading.

10.3 Market manipulation

While there is debate about the ethics of insider trading, there is little disagreement about market manipulation being wrong. Widespread agreement exists that market manipulation is bad for markets. Indeed, one of the reasons the US Congress established the SEC in 1934 was to eliminate stock market manipulation. Yet, there is no generally accepted definition of market manipulation. Indeed, because market manipulation is an old practice, dating as far back as the first organized trading exchanges, the lack of a generally agreed definition of the term is surprising.[11] The Corporations Law in Australia, the *Securities Exchange Act* 1934 in the US, and the Market Abuse Directive in the EU prohibit market manipulation, but none of these laws attempt to define manipulation precisely. The task of defining manipulation is largely left to the courts based on each particular case.

Boatright defines market manipulation as involving, '[T]he buying and selling of securities for the purpose of creating a false or misleading impression about the direction of their price so as to induce other investors to buy or sell the securities'.[12] Thel uses the term 'manipulation' to mean trading undertaken with the intent of increasing or decreasing the reported price of a security.[13] Applying the term to large numbers of uninformed traders, Jarrow uses market manipulation to mean a trading strategy that generates positive real wealth with zero risk.[14] Cherian and Jarrow define manipulation as trading in such a way as to influence the share price to the advantage of the trader or traders.[15] In general, the aim of manipulation is to deceive others through the creation of false or misleading appearances.

Forms of market manipulation

Putnins draws a useful taxonomy of market manipulation.[16] At the broadest level, manipulation is categorized into (1) runs, (2) contract-based manipulations, and (3) market power techniques. Within these categories are three main ways to manipulate, which are: trade-based, information-based, or action-based. In the form of manipulation, known as a run, the manipulator takes either a long or a short position in a stock. He then inflates or deflates the price of the stock, at the same time increasing liquidity in the stock. The final step in a run entails reversing the manipulator's position at the inflated or deflated price. Runs that inflate a stock's price are often called 'pump-and-dump' manipulation. The manipulator changes the price of the stock by techniques such as spreading rumours or false information into the market. A common feature of runs is that the manipulator profits from the manipulated market by causing investors to buy or sell a stock to move its price up or down.

The contract form of manipulation requires a contract or market external to the manipulated market. For example, a trader may buy an options contract on a particular stock and then manipulate the price of that stock to profit on the options position. In contrast to a run, the contract form of manipulation does not require inducing other investors to trade at manipulated prices.

The third broad group of manipulation techniques is moving the market through use of market power. The manipulator may gain market power by, say, taking a controlling position in the supply of an asset or security. Like the contract form of manipulation, power-based techniques are more mechanical in nature than runs. However, like the runs-based technique, contract manipulation gets its profit by exploiting participants of the manipulated market.

Allen and Gale break down these three general classifications of manipulation to (1) trade, (2) information, and (3) action-based manipulation.[17] First, there is trade-based manipulation. This involves influencing the price of a stock through trading. For example, a trader or group of traders makes transactions that are publicly seen in the market, to give the impression of high-volume trading activity or price movements. The trader buys and sells the security in order to change the price of the security in a series of 'wash sales'. High-frequency trading (HFT) firms have been accused of performing this kind of market manipulation. Consider the case of Trillium Capital.

Trillium Capital is an HFT firm in New York engaged strictly in HFT trades. Trillium entered many trades that were considered non-bona fide because Trillium had no intention of following through on these orders. Trillium placed the orders to deceive the market into thinking that there was a large amount of activity happening in certain securities. These orders induced other traders to trade based on the untrue impression of demand or supply created by Trillium. Before these false trades were entered, Trillium had limit positions. These orders were executed as a result of their traders creating buy- or sell-side demand that moved the prices in certain directions. Once the real trades were executed, Trillium immediately cancelled their non-bona fide trades and profited from their limit orders.[18] These types of trades are illegal and cause market movements or prompt market activity that otherwise would not happen if these HFT traders had not manipulated the market to their advantage.

Second, there is information-based manipulation. This form of manipulation requires a manipulator to disseminate false information or rumours about a company to inflate or deflate its price. The spreading of untrue information through media and the Internet is commonly known as 'hype-and-dump'. The intent is to drive up the price of a stock and then sell the stock when the price is high. Alternatively, spreading bad news about a stock to depress its price is called 'slur-and-dump'. Fund management companies or hedge funds that rely on short selling as a primary means of investment may engage in this form of manipulation. An infamous case of information-based manipulation is the London Interbank Offered Rate (LIBOR) scandal perpetrated by several international banks.

LIBOR is a benchmark rate that indicates the 'lowest perceived rate' at which a LIBOR contributor bank can obtain unsecured funding in the London interbank money market for a given maturity, in a given currency. The coordinated manipulation of LIBOR affected about US$300 trillion of transactions globally. In 2012, a number of banks were accused of manipulating this key interest rate. Banks allegedly submitted artificially high or low LIBOR quotes to profit from their own trading positions. The banks also wished to give an impression of higher creditworthiness to the market. If banks could only borrow at a higher rate than others, it would be an admission that the market viewed them as less creditworthy.

Third, there is action-based manipulation. This form of manipulation requires action on the part of the manipulator to affect the value or perceived value of a company. For instance, manipulators use a technique called 'marking the close' or 'closing price manipulation'. They buy or sell securities at or shortly before the close of the market to alter the closing price. 'Marking the open' is similar, but involves influencing the opening price rather than the closing price.[19] This technique works particularly well for stocks that are not liquid (does not trade in large volumes), because their prices are easily moved by a larger than usual volume of trades. The price distortions are particularly harmful because of the widespread use of closing prices.

Window dressing

Marking the close can be used on the last day of the month or the quarter when performance of mutual funds, hedge funds, and other types of pooled assets are measured. By pushing the price of the stocks in a portfolio up at the end of the trading day, the performance of the fund is made to look more favourable for the quarter or for the month. Indeed, fund performance looks better for the one- and five-year period of measurement. Marking the close manipulation when used by fund managers is also known as 'window dressing'.

Empirical support suggests window dressing is rather more common than acknowledged. Studies show stock prices in US equity markets spike in the last half-hour before the close, and the intensity increases on quarter-end days.[20] An astounding 80 per cent of funds beat the Standard & Poor's (S&P) Index on the last trading day of the year, but only 37 per cent do so on the first trading day of a new year. Carhart *et al.* attribute these extraordinary results to manipulation by fund managers.[21] Another study supports the findings of the previous study. Gallagher *et al.* find fund managers tend to purchase illiquid stocks in which they have overweight positions on the last day of the quarter.[22] Poor performing managers are more likely to manipulate prices. In Pakistan's main stock exchange, researchers find evidence of pump-and-dump market manipulation.[23] Brokers can earn at least 8 per cent higher returns on their own trades. Market timing or liquidity provision cannot account for this level of higher profits.

Emerging markets are particularly prone to market manipulation. The annual returns appear to be in the range of 50–90 per cent higher than the average investor.[24] These levels of returns act as strong motivators for traders to resist robust regulation in order to continue extracting these high rents.

Ethical evaluation of market manipulation

Manipulation harms others and has negative consequences

The effect of market manipulation by use of any of the techniques described above is to push the price of a security away from its fundamental value.[25] For example, in the information-based form of manipulation false information released by the manipulator pushes the security price below or above its fundamental value. At the moment manipulation takes place, market efficiency decreases. In general, information seekers are good for the market, but manipulators reduce market efficiency. The presence of more information seekers makes it possible for manipulators to pool with the informed parties and profit from trading with the information seekers. Aggarwal and Wu find that the

332 *Ethical issues in Asian investing*

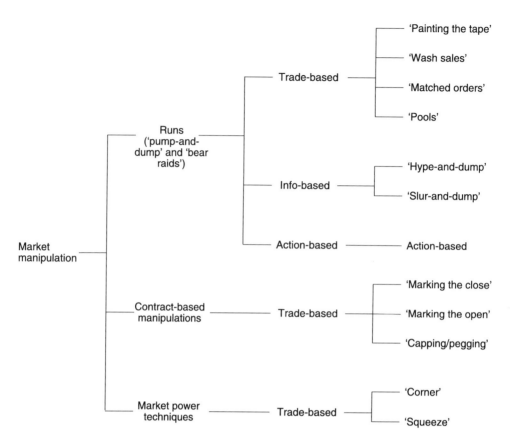

Figure 10.1 Categorization of market manipulation techniques.
Source: Talis J. Putnins (2011).

more information seekers trade with manipulators, the more they lose.[26] This in turn causes information seekers to leave a market they perceive to be highly manipulated and in which they are likely to make fewer profits. Thus, Aggarwal and Wu conclude market manipulation can drive away information seekers and make the market inefficient. In the extreme, there will be no information seekers and the market is inefficient in regard to information. With manipulators present in the market, models predict prices do not converge to the true value of the stock. A higher probability of market manipulation decreases market efficiency. From the efficiency point of view, therefore, market manipulation does harm to the market and is unethical.

Manipulation is unfair

Manipulative practices enable the manipulators to profit at the expense of another segment of the investment community; for instance, HFT traders by using trade-based methods such as the spoofing or stuffing profit at the expense of slower, low-tech traders. From a fairness perspective, manipulators get an unjust advantage from the rest of the market.

10.4 Market timing

Market timing is the practice of trading large amounts of securities for short periods of time to benefit from anticipated temporary changes in security prices.[27] To trade in and out of individual securities is costly because of the commissions a trader will incur. Brokers charge a small amount for each purchase and sale of a security. Market timing may not pay off well for individual stocks but trading costs are eliminated if market timers trade in mutual funds instead. Many classes of mutual funds do not have up-front or back-end fees. In addition, diversified funds often reflect the composition of the broader market.

Market timing of international funds based on time differences is an easy, attractive way to make profits. Being in different international time zones, Asian markets, such as the Singapore Stock Exchange or the Japanese Stock Exchange, close half a day earlier than the US market. Mutual funds that are specialist portfolios of Asian stocks continue to trade in the US market based on the previous day prices of Asian stocks. A market timer will buy an Asian mutual fund if share prices on the Asian markets close sharply up. The fund traded in the US will not reflect these higher prices, but will be priced according to the closing prices the previous day in Asia. Then the market timer will sell the same fund a day later when the selling price finally reflects the high closing prices.

Late trading is a special case of market timing. Orders are placed after the market closes in the US. Traders can use information released during the day that will negatively or positively impact share prices. Late trading is a sure bet because the information is known, but the closing share prices do not reflect the new information yet. It is like betting on the winner of the World Cup when the champions are already known. Late traders, therefore, have an unfair advantage over other investors in the market. For this reason, late trading is illegal in the US and prohibited by the *Investment Company Act Rule* 22c-1.

In contrast, market timing is legal as long as the mutual fund sponsor permits it. The practice is ethically questionable because only a few favoured clients are allowed to engage in this type of transaction, harming others who are not permitted to trade on the same terms. This unequal treatment of investors violates the fiduciary duty of a fund sponsor who is obligated to act in the best interest of all clients.

The case of Canary Capital

Canary Capital was a New Jersey-based hedge fund charged with investing the money of the Stern family. The fund, headed by Edward J. Stern, had market timing agreements with 30 mutual fund companies. From 1998 to the end of 2002, Canary Capital outperformed the market return by a substantial amount. For instance, in 1999, the S&P 500 index rose 20 per cent while Canary earned 110 per cent. In 2000 and 2001 Canary showed returns of 50 per cent and 29 per cent, respectively compared to the market averages of −9 per cent and 13 per cent for the same years.

Among the mutual fund companies who had market timing agreements with Canary were Nations Funds, a unit of Bank of America, Pimco Advisors, Bank One, Janus Capital, Alliance Capital Management, Invesco, and Strong Capital Management.[28] The management of these fund companies was aware of Canary's purchases of their mutual funds and permitted them as long as the hedge fund kept other assets with the investment management company. Yet, Canary's trading is the type explicitly prohibited in the funds' prospectuses.

The fund group that had the most cooperative agreement with Canary was the Bank of America. The Bank provided Canary with its own electronic trading terminal, installed in Canary's office, so trades could be entered as late as 6:30 p.m. This direct access allowed Canary to disguise their trades as Bank of America's own trades. The bank provided a credit line of US$300 million to Canary and the portfolio holdings of its mutual funds for Canary to replicate in order to engage in short selling of its mutual funds.

To be fair, many mutual fund companies rejected the requests of market timers. Fidelity declined to do business with them. The fund companies that did welcome market timers negotiated secret arrangements with hedge funds. They were allowed to buy and sell a predetermined amount of money from the mutual fund. In return, the market timing firms deposited an agreed amount of funds to the fund management companies. These funds generated a steady amount of fees and were usually placed in low-risk money market or government bond funds. Sometimes they would be placed in hedge funds run by the fund managers.[29]

Canary Capital also managed to engage in short selling of the mutual funds. It developed a market instrument that replicated the holdings of a mutual fund and shorted this instrument. To do this, the firm needed to know the holdings, such as the securities held in the portfolio of the mutual fund, which it could not get from the quarterly public reports. The holdings in these reports usually do not reflect the most current list of holdings. To obtain the most up-to-date holdings list, Canary struck deals with mutual fund companies whereby the latter would provide the list at any time.[30] This agreement allowed preferred investors but not others to short mutual funds.

The market timing scandal came to light because a former employee of Canary blew the whistle on the unethical activities. Noreen Harrington called the New York State Attorney General's office. The subsequent investigation led to Canary and to the mutual fund companies.

As part of the settlements with the federal SEC and the New York Attorney General Eliot Spitzer, eight trustees of the Bank of America's Nations Funds left the board. The bank agreed to pay US$250 million in restitution and US$125 million in fines. Canary Capital paid a fine of US$40 million, and Eddie Stern agreed to cooperate with prosecutors. He provided information about the mutual fund companies with which he had market-timing agreements. In 2003 and 2004, 25 mutual fund organizations were charged or investigated for illegal trading activities. Most of these mutual fund companies entered into large settlements and compensated investors for their losses.[31] In addition to the damage in reputation, some companies faced significant redemptions of funds.

Ethical evaluation of market timing

Market timing is not illegal but there are three clear ethical problems with the practice: harm caused to investors, violation of the fiduciary duty of a fund's management and board, and unfair treatment of investors.

First, market timing cheats other investors in funds by loading them with additional trading fees that hurt total return. In contrast, market timers gain material benefits. There are several ways in which total return is diminished.

1. Trading in and out of funds in large amounts over short periods increases trading and other overhead costs.

2   Big redemptions resulting from selling of fund shares require a fund manager to keep higher levels of liquidity in the portfolio to meet these redemptions. Consequently, the performance of the fund is hurt in rising markets because the higher cash levels act as a drag to performance. Cash tends to have much lower returns than equity or even bonds.
3   Frequent short-term trading in and out of funds may cause a fund manager to apply less than optimal portfolio strategies.
4   Selling securities in a fund to meet redemption demands of market timers may result in capital gains and subsequent higher taxes that impact all fund investors.
5   When the performance of a fund rises sharply, market timers buy into the fund to participate in the rising performance. However, the new money into the fund dilutes its performance and hurts long-term investors.

Second, directors and management of mutual fund companies have a fiduciary duty to their investors. This means putting the interest of their clients first. The people in authority violate their fiduciary duty when they allow market timing in mutual funds. Mutual funds are independent entities with their own board of directors. The board contracts with the mutual fund management company and the latter becomes an agent hired by the directors of a fund to administer or advise the fund. Thus, the board of directors in particular has a fiduciary duty to the shareholders, who are also the investors of a mutual fund. It is the board's duty to safeguard the interest of shareholders. However, the management of the mutual fund company also has a fiduciary duty to the investors of the fund because investing and managing the money best serves its clients.

Third, if market timing is offered to a few select investors as was the case for the Bank of America and Canary Capital, then it is obviously unfair to the other investors who do not have the opportunity to engage in short-term rapid trading. In addition, other investors are usually unaware of the favourable treatment a mutual fund gives to market timers. Hiding information in this way violates the principle of transparency, a principle that is crucial for markets to be fair and open. The SEC has pushed mutual fund companies to clearly state their position on market timing. In 2003, New York Attorney General Eliot Spitzer deemed market timing, in many circumstances, to be a fraudulent activity on the part of the mutual fund organization. Spitzer contended that firms allowing clients to trade more frequently than the formal fund prospectus allowed were committing fraud. The failure of fund companies to stop mutual fund investors from market timing, given the formal stated position on the issue, is a direct misrepresentation of a firm commitment to long-term shareholders and is actually deemed illegal by the SEC.

10.5 Fees

Hedge fund fees

Hedge funds are lightly regulated limited partnerships. The reason hedge funds are not subject to regulation falls under two exemptions under the *Investment Company Act* of 1940. First, funds that limit the number of investors to 100 are exempt from the 1940 Act. Second, after 1996, funds that only have investors who are 'qualified' are exempt from regulation under the same Act. Qualified investors are informed and sophisticated and, therefore, not in need of the protections offered by the 1940 Company Act.

Albert Winslow Jones started the first hedge fund in the US in 1949. The performance of his fund was above the average mutual fund and attracted the attention of media and then the investing community. There followed a period of explosive growth of hedge funds. The end of the 1969 bull market and the oil price recession of 1973–74 killed off the industry, but only temporarily. Interest in hedge funds reignited with Julian Robertson's Tiger Fund that produced average returns of 43 per cent (after expenses and fees) from 1980–86. During the bull market of 1980s and 1990s the number of hedge funds grew to nearly 1,000 by the early 1990s.

In 1992, George Soros and his Quantum Fund became world famous for taking on the Bank of England and winning. Soros earned as much as US$1.8 billion by shorting the British pound and going long the Deutschmark. Hedge funds took on an invincible aura after that episode in their history. Yet, only after a few short years, another hedge fund, long-term capital management (LTCM) almost collapsed with global repercussions. The reason LTCM did not was due to the bailout orchestrated by then Federal Reserve Chairman, Alan Greenspan. Banks were more or less ordered by Greenspan to not act on the margin calls they had on LTCM. John Meriweather, the former head of Solomon Brother's bond trading unit, started the hedge fund. Its managers included two Nobel laureates for economics, Myron Scholes and Robert Merton. Their purported genius, however, did not prevent them from making the wrong bet on the direction of the Russian ruble. The hedge fund lost US$4.6 billion in less than four months following the 1997 Asian financial crisis and the 1998 Russian financial crisis. Without the Federal Reserve, directed forbearance of the banks these losses and the interconnected trades may have brought down (or at least have done major damage) to global financial markets. Ultimately, the positions were liquidated, reportedly at a small profit to those who participated in the bailout.[32] Hedge funds have continued to grow in numbers since then, with a brief hiatus after the 2008 Great Financial Crisis (GFC).

Regulation

A number of hedge funds closed as a result of the GFC. However, despite a short-lived requirement that hedge fund operators register as investment advisers (for a six-month period in 2006), there has been no widespread regulation of the hedge fund industry. Their activities 'remain shrouded from public scrutiny, which occasionally is punctuated by the story of a large speculative gain or loss'.[33] After the GFC, there was discussion about requiring hedge funds to register and provide more information to appropriate regulators. This idea died quietly, no doubt with the help of the industry and its lobbyists.

Although hedge funds are legally defined as investment companies, they are exempt from the 1940 Securities Act. The exemption is set forth in sections 3(c)1 and 3(c)7. A 3(c)1 fund cannot have more than 100 accredited participants. A 3(c)7 fund need only register its securities if participants exceed 499 in number. An accredited investor is defined as having a minimum net worth of US$1 million, or a minimum income of US$200,000 for the prior two years. The presumption is that wealthier investors are sophisticated and knowledgeable about risks associated with offerings of unregistered securities. In the past, hedge funds were not allowed to have organized sales effort, although word-of-mouth communication of the offering is permitted.

The prohibition against general hedge fund solicitation was lifted under the 2012 Jumpstart Our Business Startups (JOBS) Act. The funds are still private investment funds that remain restricted to accredited investors. In fact the SEC makes it clear that hedge funds must ensure that the sales are made only to accredited investors.

> The final rule permits issuers to use general solicitation and general advertising to offer their securities if, among other things, issuers take reasonable steps to verify 'accredited investor' status, and all purchasers of the securities are accredited investors – meaning that, at the time of the sale of the securities, they fall within one of the categories of persons who are accredited investors, or the issuer reasonably believes that they do. Determination of the reasonableness of the steps taken to verify that an investor is accredited is by an objective assessment by an issuer, and in response to comments, the final rule provides a non-exclusive list of methods that issuers may use to satisfy the verification requirement for individual investors.[34]

Some hedge funds have taken advantage of the new freedom to advertise by taking out space in periodicals and journals as well as posting commercials on their websites. However, hedge funds have not generally taken full advantage of the ability to advertise, fearing that they will open themselves up to closer scrutiny by regulators and more frequent audits.[35]

Fee structure

The lack of regulation is one of the three *L*s that distinguish hedge funds from other investment funds. The other two *L*s are 'lock-up' and 'leverage'. Hedge funds usually lock-up investors' funds for a significant period of time, between six months to as many as three years. The lock-up helps hedge funds invested in illiquid securities. In addition, not moving invested funds in and out of the hedge fund improves performance. Another way hedge fund performance is enhanced is through the use of leverage. In contrast to mutual funds, hedge funds regularly use leverage, such as debt, to increase returns.

The push to increase performance is motivated by the fee structure of a typical hedge fund. Hedge funds follow the now famous '2 and 20' fee structure. First, there is a 2 per cent management fee based on the net assets of the fund. Second, there is the 20 per cent contingent incentive fee calculated as a percentage of the fund's net returns, and may be subject to a hurdle rate or high-watermark provision. In the case of a hurdle rate, the performance fee is paid only on returns in excess of some hurdle rate, say, the Treasury Bill rate or the return on a chosen benchmark index. With the high-watermark, a hedge fund must recover any losses (return to the last high-watermark) before incentive fees can be charged.

Example

A hedge fund in Singapore has S$100 million under management. It produces a net return of 10 per cent in year 1. Its total fees in year 1 are calculated thus:

2 per cent management fee	=	S$2 million
Net returns	=	S$10 million
20 per cent incentive fee on net returns	=	S$2 million
Total fees	=	S$4 million

In year 2 the fund makes a negative return of S$5 million. Its total fees are 2 per cent of 105 million, or S$2.1 million, with no contingent incentive fee.

In year 3 the fund makes a positive return of S$15 million. Its management fees are 2 per cent of S$120 million, or S$2.4 million. Its contingent incentive fee is based on 20 per cent of S$10 million (S$2 million) because it can only charge the fee after recovering any losses to return to the last high-watermark (S$110 million). Its total fees in year 3 are S$4.4 million.

Total fees for years 1–3 for this hypothetical hedge fund = S$10.5 million.

In terms of performance, over the same period, the fund made its investors $(10–5+20) million, or S$25 million. Of the S$25 million in returns, investors paid out S$10.5 million – roughly 42 per cent of total returns!

Dan McCrum of the *Financial Times* calculates hedge fund fees paid by pension funds from 2008–14.[36]

Public pension funds contribute around 20 per cent of hedge fund assets and private funds about 19 per cent.

In 2014, Hedge Fund Research's (HFR) estimate for total hedge fund assets under management equalled US$2.7 trillion.

In 2014, the amount of hedge fund assets that comprise public pension funds equalled US$540 billion.

In 2014, the amount of hedge fund assets that comprise private pension funds equalled US$500 billion.

Pensions (public and private) started in 2008 with about US$630 billion invested in hedge funds.

From 2008–14, returns for pension funds from their hedge fund investment were about US$156 billion. (Over the same period trustees invested another US$260 billion for hedge funds to manage.)

2008–14 investment returns   =   US$156 billion

Conservatively assume that the hedge funds charged the pension funds an average of 1.6 per cent management fee and an 18 per cent performance fee.

For simplicity McCrum takes 1.6 per cent of the year-end assets under management totals, and 0.8 per cent of the 2014 figure.

The amount of management fees paid out by pension funds in the six-and-a-half-year period is US$77 billion, or about half of the investment gains received.

2008–14 management fees paid at 1.6 per cent   =   US$77 billion

Returns were negative in 2008 and 2011. To take into account the high watermark condition, in calculating performance fees, McCrum did not count any performance fees from 2008 onwards until the hedge funds in aggregate made back their losses, which was sometime in 2010. Similarly, management fees were not calculated for 2011 and 2012. This method probably undercounts the performance fee element.

Assume performance fees were paid on a gain of 7.1 per cent above the high watermark in 2010. In 2012 performance fees were paid on a gain of 0.8 per cent above the previous high water point.

The estimate for performance fees paid is equivalent to US$40 billion over the six years.

2008–14 performance fees paid at 18 per cent of returns   =   US$40 billion

Here are the results:

From 2008–14
Amount given to hedge fund by pension fund trustees   =   US$800 billion
Investment returns to pension funds   =   US$156 billion
Total fees paid to hedge fund managers   =   US$117 billion

For public sector funds, government workers handed over about US$400 billion, paid US$68 billion, to make gains of US$95 billion. These returns are hardly impressive for the average government pensioner. Pension fund managers are, therefore, not doing their fiduciary duty of looking after their clients' best interests when investing in hedge funds. Thus, investing pension fund money through hedge funds over 2008–11 is ethically questionable.

Mutual fund fees

The hedge fund industry is an obvious example of high fees charged to clients. It is less apparent that mutual fund fees are high as well. Their fee levels are not in the bright spotlight as hedge fund fees. Yet, there are pertinent problems with mutual fund fees.

The mutual fund industry has grown enormously over the past 60 years. In 1945 the industry ran US$882 million of fund assets. Compare this amount to the US$15 trillion in 2013 and it is obvious the industry has grown impressively. In fact, this is a compound annual growth rate of 16 per cent. If the industry had matched the 7 per cent nominal growth rate of the US economy, assets under management (AUM) would be US$50 million today.[37]

With the explosion of AUM, the culture of the mutual fund industry has changed from an industry engaged primarily in the profession of serving investors to a highly focused marketing business aimed at successful salesmanship.[38] The purpose of the industry has changed as well, from that of serving the interests of shareholders to serving the interests of managers and distributors of funds.

Before the 1930s, fees were charged as a percentage of the investment income received in interest and dividends. The level of fees was therefore low. In the new era of mutual fund investing, value rather than cost drives the market. Beginning in the 1960s, new managers discovered that they could charge much more than the old-line companies offering mutual funds (banks and insurance companies) because investors expected higher fees to mean superior performance. Mutual fund companies thus started to implement a structure of mutual fund fees that steadily increased expenses for investors.

Mutual fund fee structures

Mutual funds charge two primary types of expenses and fees: ongoing expenses and sales loads. Ongoing expenses cover the cost of managing the portfolio including salaries of managers, fund administration, daily accounting and pricing, shareholder services such as call centres, distribution charges known as 12b-1 fees, and other operating costs. These expenses are added together in a fund's expense ratio. This ratio is calculated by expressing the fund's annual expenses as a percentage of total assets managed by the fund.

Distribution fees or 12b-1 fees are a way for mutual funds to charge investors to compensate financial professionals (such as financial consultants, brokers, and financial advisers) and other financial intermediaries. These are asset-based fees. Investors pay indirectly for the services of these financial professionals and other financial intermediaries. Fund companies may also use 12b-1 to pay for a fund's advertising and marketing.

Investors pay sales loads when they purchase mutual funds through brokers or financial advisers. These loads are a way for fund management companies to pay financial advisers for selling their mutual funds. There are three types of sales loads: front-end loads paid at the time of share purchase, back-end loads paid when shares are redeemed, and level loads charged to the investor over time. Investors who buy mutual fund shares without the assistance of a financial adviser generally use no-load funds. Front-end load shares are predominantly Class A shares. The load usually decreases as the size of an investor's initial purchase rises. Back-end load shares are primarily Class B shares. Loads in this class of shares include a contingent deferred sales load (CDSL). Investors who hold their fund shares for more than a specified number of years do not pay the CDSL. The charge is, therefore, a way to encourage investors to be long-term holders of shares. Level-load shares are generally Class C shares that do not have front-end loads. Investors pay the CDSL if they sell their shares within a year of purchase.

No-load share classes have no front-end load or CDSL and have 12b-1 fees of 0.25 per cent. Investors purchase no-load funds through employer-sponsored retirement plans, mutual fund supermarkets, discount brokerage firms, bank trust departments, and mutual fund sponsors.

Investment returns versus fees

How has the average mutual fund investor fared after paying mutual fund fees? Studies reveal a minority of actively managed mutual funds outperforms the stock market index. Table 10.1 shows the reality of how few funds have outperformed their indices after adjusting for survivorship bias over the 15 years to year-end 2011.

Clients are often overly optimistic about the expected performance of their mutual funds. Even though no major manager has done so, the average US institutional client expects its chosen group of active investment managers to outperform annually after fees by 100 basis points. Corporate and public pension funds are nearly as optimistic, while endowments and unions are slightly more optimistic.[39] Little evidence exists to back these hopeful high expectations of returns.

According to Eugene Fama, who carried out a study of the performance of all domestic mutual funds with at least 10 years of results, after factoring for costs, only the top 3 per cent of managers outperform the index enough to cover those costs.[40] Despite all the effort and research, active managers can only keep up with low-cost passive index funds.

Table 10.1 Percentage of funds that outperformed their benchmarks after adjusting for survivorship bias, 1997–2011

Market cap	Value funds (%)	Growth funds (%)
Large	43	24
Medium	0	3
Small	30	22

On the other hand, based on Fama's study, we can expect the other 97 per cent of active managers to underperform the index. Only 3 per cent of active managers beating their chosen markets is not far from what would be expected in a purely random distribution. Viewed from the perspective of statistical chance, Charles Ellis, a well-known proponent of index funds, notes:

> [T]he odds of 97 to 3 are, frankly, terrible – particularly when risking the real money that will be needed by millions of people in retirement or to help finance our society's most treasured educational, cultural, and philanthropic institutions. The long-term data repeatedly document that investors would benefit by switching from active performance investing to low-cost indexing.[41]

In addition, research shows that in the years after a manager performs well, he is as likely to underperform the following year. The performance of managers after a good year takes on a random distribution. There is no significant pattern in mutual fund performance over time. The top 20 per cent of US equity funds, according to risk-adjusted returns in one year, did not show any consistency of performance in the following five years. If the top funds demonstrated consistently superior risk-adjusted returns, a significant majority should remain in the top 20 per cent. However, approximately 17 per cent of returns of these funds were dispersed evenly across performance categories, indicating a random outcome.

Despite the known research evidence on the cost of mutual fund fees and active manager performance, the move to index funds has been gradual although the pace has been increasing in recent years.

The ethics of mutual fund fees

Taking advantage of investor ignorance

It is not inherently wrong to charge high fees and produce poor net returns to investors. It is wrong to do so without being open and completely transparent about fees and performance. This information should be presented in a form easily understandable by the average, non-sophisticated investor. While fund management companies give more information on performance, using that measure to differentiate their products, they do not give clear and simple information on fund expenses and fees. This is because it is generally the case that a sophisticated investor is more likely to take greater account of fund costs. Investors with more knowledge tend to invest in lower cost funds. On the other hand, investors with lower levels of financial sophistication are less sensitive to costs. This is particularly true of costs that are deducted from assets during the calculation of daily returns. Performance of mutual funds is presented net of operating expenses. Consequently, investors easily overlook fund expenses.

In addition, studies show the funds with extra loads charge higher management and custodial fees and pass on greater total expenses than no-load funds.[42] Investors in load and no-load funds show different price sensitivity. Management companies are apparently taking advantage of the different price sensitivities and financial sophistication of investors. The higher management fees do not translate into better performance. Yet, managers who sell load funds obtain a higher gross return, which compensates for higher operating expenses. The higher gross returns are not used for the benefit of the shareholder but for the benefit of the financial institutions to which the funds belong. The potential exists for fund management companies to charge higher fees to the part of the customer base that is less price-conscious. The lack of cost sensitivity may be due to the lack of shareholder financial sophistication in load fund companies. The clients for sales loads funds are small investors in funds characterized by having a high number of shareholders. These funds are in the main offered by banks.

Crespo concludes, '[H]igher fees reflect higher profitability for the fund company, and an unethical behavior since profits are based on taking advantage of the lower level of financial sophistication of the investor'.[43] When companies use market segmentation to offer different levels of customer services, this may be beneficial to customers. However, if market segmentation is used to extract greater fees and charges from investors with lower financial acumen, this act causes some concern in terms of ethics.[44] In sum, it is unethical to take advantage of a consumer's financial ignorance.

Maximizing profits for fund company over doing well for customers

Another ethical issue with mutual fund fees is that it appears fund companies are run for the benefit of the companies rather than for customers. The average investor in an equity mutual fund earned an annualized return of 5.8 per cent over the 1996–2005 period versus 9.1 per cent for the S&P 500 Index. Besides high transaction costs and fees, mutual fund performance is also hobbled by fund managers' determination to maximize assets under management in order to capture the attractive economies of scale the business offers.

The change in focus from client to fund company came about through a change in law. Before 1958, fund management companies in the US were small, private firms that were barred from selling their own shares to outside investors. After 1958, public ownership of mutual fund companies was allowed in the US. Shares of mutual fund companies were offered in initial public offerings. Banks and insurance companies acquired privately held management companies. Focus shifted from client first to earnings and return on capital. Asset gathering became the priority and trading of portfolio holdings became more frequent. To increase AUM, behaviour of participants changed from trying to deliver long-term performance through the value approach to the cheerleading, 'yes you can' encouragement of fund managers, investment consultants, and other participants who make their living as advocates of active management.[45]

Fairness: performance should justify fees

If a management company is charging high fees, one should expect commensurate high performance. Yet, from the previous discussion, this type of fair exchange of fee for performance is not empirically demonstrated. Consider a 1 per cent management fee. If the future equity returns are 7–8 per cent, then 1 per cent of assets quickly becomes nearly 12–15 per cent of returns. The cost looks even worse if we compare the returns of an actively managed fund to an index fund. Ellis puts it as follows:

> [T]he informed realist's definition of the fee for active management is the incremental fee as a percentage of incremental returns after adjusting for risk. That fee is high – very high. If a mutual fund charging 1.25% of assets also charged a 12b-1 fee of 0.25% and produced a net return of 0.5% above the benchmark index each

year – an eye-popping performance – the true fee would be very nearly 75% of the incremental return before fees! Because a majority of active managers now underperform the market, their incremental fees are over 100% of long-term incremental, risk-adjusted returns. This grim reality has largely gone unnoticed by clients – so far.[46]

Thus, it can be argued that there is an unfair exchange between the customer and her fund management company. To put it bluntly, mutual fund customers are overpaying for services rendered to them.

10.6 Managing Shari'a compliant assets

Maqasid al-Shari'a means the objective and the rationale of the Shari'a, or Islamic Law. The underlying tenet of Shari'a is to protect and preserve the public interest in all aspects and segments of life.[47] This broad purpose encompasses the concepts of compassion and the pursuit of a just society for all. In particular, Shari'a stresses the importance of aiding the poor and weak. Indeed, the Arabic word *Maslahah* (public interest) is synonymous with *Masqasid*.

As Islamic finance is based on the Shari'a, the former should, therefore, also be driven by the same purpose of justice, cooperation, and mutual support within the family and society at large. One of the biggest challenges of the Islamic finance industry is to create products and services that comply with the Shari'a and still be competitive and profitable.

How do we determine if a financial contract is Shari'a compliant? The majority of Islamic scholars agree in principle that an Islamic financial product is Shari'a compliant if the contract is valid in its legal form as well as its substance. In other words, a financial contract is valid if it meets all Islamic contractual conditions and requirements and has real intention or substance based on the purpose behind the Shari'a.

Thus, a financial institution should design a Shari'a compliant financial instrument or transaction with the intention of fulfilling the underlying purpose of Shari'a. The institution should ask, 'Does this instrument or transaction contribute to preserving the public interest and help produce a just society?' Shari'a compliance for asset managers means investing in securities that first, meet this overarching purpose, and second, that do not participate in any *haram* (forbidden) activities proscribed by Shari'a. Obviously, investing in the securities of companies involved with gambling and the manufacture and sale of pork products or alcohol does not meet with the standards of Shari'a. Less obvious is investing in sukuk bonds that ostensibly and legally abide by Shari'a precepts, but may not be designed in the spirit of Islamic Law and premised on its objectives. In such cases, asset managers of Shari'a compliant funds should be wary of investing in these technically sound, but substantively questionable, securities.

For example, recent innovations in equity-based sukuk are troubling from a Shari'a compliance standpoint. Sukuk or Islamic bonds have two basic features. First, the capital cannot be guaranteed. Second, the periodic returns depend on actual profits made from investing the funds obtained from selling the sukuk. The higher risk of equity-based sukuk may be unattractive to risk-averse investors who wish a greater certainty of return associated with conventional bonds. Equity-based sukuk are those based on *mudarabah* (partnership), *musharakah* (joint-venture), and *wakalah* (agency) transactions. Both musharakah and mudarabah sukuk do not represent debt receivables, but rights in specific investment projects or assets. The characteristics of mudarabah and musharakah-based sukuk (see Chapter 6, section 6.8) may not meet the risk appetite of investors who expect capital preservation and more assured returns of conventional bond instruments. To attract more investors, equity-based sukuk have evolved more into debt-based obligations with various 'credit enhancements' and strategies introduced to the mudarabah and musharakak sukuk structures. These enhancements ensure greater capital protection and periodic returns similar to conventional bond instruments.

One type of mechanism is the liquidity-facility arrangement where the entity that needs the sukuk funding (obligor) undertakes to pay the returns to sukuk holders if there is insufficient cash to pay the expected periodic returns.[48] This liquidity is normally provided either in the form of a loan or other Shari'a compliant facility, such as *tawarruq*. For example, a sukuk raised MYR 500 million and the expected return is 7 per cent. However, in the first year the actual return is only 5 per cent. The obligor provides the additional 2 per cent by way of a liquidity facility to ensure the sukuk holders get the 7 per cent return.

The purchase undertaking at a fixed formula is another credit enhancement mechanism. Here the obligor promises at maturity, or in the event of a default to buy back, the sukuk holder's interest in the partnership assets at par/face value (outstanding principal plus accrued but unpaid profit), regardless of whether their value exceeds that of their face value. For example, a sukuk raises MYR 500 million with a five-year maturity and an expected profit of 7 per cent each year. At the end of the fifth year, the obligor buys back the sukuk holder's share at the price of MYR 500 million plus the 7 per cent return (for the fifth year).[49]

Another credit-enhancing mechanism is the non-distribution of expected profit constituting event of default. This is sometimes known as the non-payment clause. If the obligor fails to pay profit (or any amount due), it will be considered a default. These examples of credit enhancements resemble conventional bond features. The innovations aim to achieve the same economic outcome as conventional bonds.

Not surprisingly, the Shari'a Board of Accounting and Auditing Organization for Islamic Financial Institutions (AAOIFI) criticizes these credit enhancement innovations, suggesting the enhancements are not congruent with Shari'a principles. In these structures there is a promise in the repurchase of assets and shares from sukuk holders at a certain agreed price to ensure the principal remains intact. This amounts to a guarantee of return of capital at maturity.

The various arrangements and commitments in these credit enhancements, in themselves, are Shari'a compliant. However, when they are used in conjunction with the whole process of sukuk issuance, these commitments are devices to ensure capital preservation and a predictable return on investment to make sukuk compatible with conventional bond and debt instruments. While the credit enhancements are legal from a Shari'a standpoint, they do not uphold the principles of Shari'a and Islam. They maintain the legality of the form but neglect the legality of the substance of Shari'a. In such cases, the asset manager should consult the findings of Islamic jurists and the AAOIFI to ascertain the ethics of purchasing these forms of investments.

Notes

1 P. J. Engelen and L. V. Liedekerke, "Insider Trading," *Finance Ethics: Critical Issues in Theory and Practice*, ed. John R. Boatright (Hoboken, NJ: John Wiley & Sons, Inc., 2010), 201.
2 B. Cornell and E. Sirri, "The Reaction of Investors and Stock Prices to Insider Trading," *Journal of Finance* 47 (1992): 1031–59.

3 L. Meulbroek, "An Empirical Analysis of Illegal Insider Trading," *Journal of Finance* 47 (1992): 1661–99.
4 P. H. Werhane, "The Indefensibility of Insider Trading," *Journal of Business Ethics* 10 (1991): 729–31.
5 John Boatright, *Ethics in Finance*, 3rd ed. (Malden, MA: John Wiley & Sons, Inc., 2014), 188.
6 Engelen and Liedekerke, 202.
7 R. Coase, "The Problem of Social Cost," *Journal of Law and Economics* 3 (1960): 1–44.
8 Engelen and Liedekerke, 211.
9 Engelen and Liedekerke, 205.
10 Engelen and Liedekerke, 207.
11 Talis J. Putnins, "Market Manipulation: A Survey," *Journal of Economic Surveys* 26, No. 5 (2011): 952–67.
12 Boatright, 176.
13 S. Thel, "$850,000 in Six Minutes – The Mechanics of Securities Manipulation," *Cornell Law Review* 79 (2004): 219–98.
14 R. A. Jarrow, "Market Manipulation, Bubbles, Corners, and Short Squeezes," *Journal of Financial and Quantitative Analysis* 27 (1992): 311–36.
15 Putnins, 954.
16 Putnins, 955.
17 F. Allen and D. Gale, "Stock Price Manipulation," *Review of Financial Studies* 5 (1992): 503–29.
18 Courtney Comstock, "Huge: First High Frequency Trading Firm is Fined For Quote Stuffing and Manipulation," *Business Insider*, 13 September 2010, accessed 31 March 2015, www.businessinsider.com/.
19 Putnins, 956.
20 M. Carhart, R. Kaniel, D. Musto, and A. Reed, "Leaning for the Tape: Evidence of Gaming Behavior in Equity Mutual Funds," *Journal of Finance* 57 (2002): 661–93.
21 Carhart *et al.*, 682.
22 D. R. Gallagher, P. Gardener, and P. L. Swan, "Portfolio Pumping: An Examination of Investment Manager Quarter-End Trading and Impact on Performance," *Pacific-Basin Finance Journal* 17 (2009): 1–27.
23 A. Khwaja and A. Mian, "Unchecked Intermediaries: Price Manipulation in an Emerging Stock Market," *Journal of Financial Economics* 78 (2005): 203–41.
24 Khwaja and Mian, 210–20.
25 Engelen and Liedekerke, 203.
26 R. K. Aggarwal and G. Wu, "Stock Market Manipulations," *Journal of Business* 79, No. 4 (2006): 1915–53.
27 Boatright, 122.
28 Ibid., 124.
29 Ibid.
30 Ibid.
31 Ibid., 125.
32 S. C. Anderson, "Closed-End Funds, Exchange-Traded Funds, and Hedge Funds," *Innovations in Financial Markets and Institutions* 18, Springer Science+Business Media (2010): 89.
33 Anderson *et al.*, 89.
34 Norm Champ, "Current SEC Priorities Regarding Hedge Fund Matters," *The Securities and Exchange Commission*, 12 September 2013, accessed 22 September 2014, http://www.sec.gov/News/Speech/Detail/Speech/1370539802997#.VCG-gku4nHg.
35 Alexandra Stevenson, "With Ban on Ads Removed, Hedge Funds Test Waters," *DealBook, The New York Times*, 20 February 2014, accessed 22 September 2014, http://dealbook.nytimes.com/2014/02/20/.with-ban-on-ads-lifted-hedge-funds-test-waters/?_php=true&_type=blogs&_r=0.
36 Dan McCrum, "The Obscene Cost of Hedge Funds," *FT Alphaville, Financial Times*, 17 September 2014, http://ftalphaville.ft.com/2014/09/17/1974492/the-obscenecost-of-hedge-funds/.

37 John C. Bogle, "The Mutual Fund Industry 60 Years Later: For Better or Worse?" *Financial Analysts Journal* (January–February 2005): 15–24.
38 Bogle, 15.
39 Charles D. Ellis, "The Rise and Fall of Performance Investing," *Financial Analysts Journal* 70, No. 4 (July–August 2014): 14–23.
40 Eugene Fama and Robert Litterman, "An Experienced View on Markets and Investing," *Financial Analysts Journal* 68, No. 6 (November–December 2012): 15–19.
41 Ellis, 18.
42 R. M. Crespo, "Spanish Mutual Fund Fees and Less Sophisticated Investors: Examination and Ethical Implications," *Business Ethics: A European Review* 18, No. 3 (July 2009): 224–40.
43 Ibid., 238.
44 Ibid.
45 Ellis, 15.
46 Ibid., 17.
47 A. W. Dusuki, "Do Equity-based Sukuk Structures in Islamic Capital Markets Manifest the Objectives of Shari'a?" *Journal of Financial Services Marketing* 15, No. 3 (2010): 203–14.
48 Dusuki, 209.
49 Ibid., 210.

Part IV

Legal issues in Asian investing

11 Overview of international securities regulation

11.1 Introduction

Globalization allows companies and investors to raise and earn money around the world. Issuers go wherever necessary to raise money and grow their businesses. Investors are less parochial and willing to put their money in markets that offer the best returns, regardless of locality. US investment managers allocate larger portions of their portfolios to international issues.

Investors can basically trade around the clock. But to say that there is one 24-hour market is not altogether correct. There are three or four markets that operate in different overlapping time zones. The markets in London, New York, and Tokyo are the biggest markets, which transact billions of dollars on a daily basis. There is no real legal definition for international securities and therefore regulators, issuers, and investors are left to mine through domestic laws and informal organizations to find the legal landscape of international securities.

11.2 International securities transactions

Chapter 4 describes the type of instrument traded in financial markets: stocks, bonds, and hybrids. To recap:

1. Stocks represent an ownership claim on an enterprise, but offer no guaranteed or fixed rate of return.
2. Bonds are debt instruments, which yield a fixed rate of return to the investor who is a creditor of the bond issuer.
3. Hybrid securities have a mix of the features of stocks and bonds.

There are two basic ways to understand international securities transactions, which are the 'how' and the 'where' of transactions.[1] The 'how' dimension deals with the issue of how funds are transferred. There are three possibilities:

1. *Financial intermediaries*: Financial intermediaries are entities such as commercial and investment banks that stand between the seller and buyer of a financial instrument or the borrower and lender of funds.
2. *Organized securities markets*: Organized securities markets allow sellers and buyers of financial instruments to link up directly (or through a broker or series of brokers). The instruments traded on these markets are registered or listed with the appropriate governmental or other official bodies that, in turn, regulate the

participants in the markets. There is a well-known central market, or floor, such as the Stock Exchanges in Tokyo, Singapore, Kuala Lumpur, and Shanghai.

3   *Over-the-counter (OTC) or informal markets*: OTC markets also allow sellers and buyers, or borrowers and lenders, to link up directly. However, there is no commonly recognized central meeting point. There are in certain cases central clearing organizations that participants use to clear and settle their trades and to provide services such as netting of trades. These markets are dispersed and participants communicate by telephone, fax, and computer. The markets for foreign exchange and swaps are examples of such markets.

In the 'where' dimension, the location or jurisdiction of the transfer is considered. There are again three possibilities:

1   *Domestic*: In a domestic transaction, both the buyer and seller, or the borrower and lender, are from the same country, they negotiate and conclude their transaction in their home country, and the transaction is denominated in that country's currency.
2   *Semi-international*: In a semi-international transaction, there is at least one aspect of the deal that is not domestic. For example, the buyer and seller (or borrower and lender) may be from different countries. Goldman Sachs's New York office might sell China Telecom stock on the New York Stock Exchange (NYSE) to the Hong Kong office of the Deutsche Bank. Both the buyer and seller may be from the same country, but the transaction is executed on an organized securities market located abroad. Goldman in New York might sell China Telecom stock on the Hong Kong Stock Exchange to Merrill Lynch's New York office. Still another example, both buyer and seller may be from the same country but the transaction is denominated in a foreign currency. For instance, Goldman and Merrill, both in New York, might engage in a currency swap involving foreign exchange denominated in yen and pounds. In general, when people use the term 'international' financial transaction, a more careful analysis reveals that there is a significant domestic component to the deal. The legal complexities involving a partial international transaction are significant.
3   *Pure international*: In a pure international transaction, every aspect of the deal has an international flavour. Few transactions qualify for this category. Examples of some that do are the issuance of Euromarket instruments, such as Eurocommercial paper, and international syndicated loans. The term 'Euromarket', or more generally, 'offshore market', refers to a market for a financial instrument denominated in a currency that is different from the currency that serves as a means of payment (such as legal tender) in the place where the market is located. For example, dollar-denominated commercial paper in London is Eurocommercial paper because the paper is denominated in dollars yet the market is in England. Similarly, there is a large offshore market for US Treasury securities. Treasuries are the largest and most liquid type of financial instruments in the world. US Treasury securities, which of course are dollar-denominated, are traded on a 24-hour basis in offshore centres such as Tokyo and London.[2] The legal complexities involving a pure international transaction are considerable.

11.3 International regulation of securities

Regulation of securities occurs across the world and is a complex landscape for issuers and investors. Securities are offered throughout the world with investors trading billions of dollars of stocks daily. The US is the predominant securities market in the world, but issuers and investors raise and invest money worldwide. Foreign issuers who engage in offerings in the US also offer their securities to investors in other countries. Likewise, US issuers raise capital at home and overseas.

'Internationalization' used to mean foreign companies coming to the US to offer their securities. Now, it also means US companies leaving the US to raise money. We must expect that with such transactions there are a plethora of regulatory hurdles in different countries. There are no standardized laws internationally for securities regulations but different securities laws in each country. The International Organization of Securities Commission (IOSCO) attempts to fill the gaps between regulatory schemes. IOSCO creates standards and policies to allow investors and issuers a standardized environment in international securities markets.

International Organization of Securities Commissioners (IOSCO)

IOSCO is an international body established in 1983, which regulates 95 per cent of the world's securities markets in over 110 jurisdictions.[3] IOSCO develops, implements, and promotes adherence to internationally recognized standards for securities regulation. It works with the G20 and the Financial Stability Board (FSB) on the global regulatory reform agenda.[4]

IOSCO is an informal organization, which does not have any formal status in international law. It does have significant influence in financial markets across the globe. The organization's core objectives are:

1. To cooperate in developing, implementing, and promoting adherence to internationally recognized and consistent standards of regulation, oversight, and enforcement in order to protect investors, maintain fair, efficient, and transparent markets, and seek to address systemic risks.
2. To enhance investor protection and promote investor confidence in the integrity of securities markets, through strengthened information exchange and cooperation in enforcement against misconduct, and in supervision of markets and market intermediaries.
3. To exchange information at both global and regional levels on their respective experiences in order to assist the development of markets, strengthen market infrastructure, and implement appropriate regulation.[5]

Two IOSCO Committees conduct the vast majority of IOSCO's work. They are the Technical Committee and the Emerging Markets Committee.[6] The Technical Committee does the policy work and makes recommendations to the President's Committee for the adoption of new policies. The Emerging Markets Committee is not directed towards policy formation but to advance the effectiveness of emerging markets by providing support to such markets through the institution of principles and standards and providing guidance programmes.[7] The other important Committee for IOSCO is the President's Committee, which decides on the adoption of new policies. The President's Committee is composed of all the Presidents or Chairs of the ordinary and associate members of IOSCO. The President's Committee meets once a year in an annual conference, which is held at a different location every year.

IOSCO has three categories of members: ordinary, associate, and affiliate. There are

117 general members made up of the national securities commissions in their respective jurisdictions including the US Securities and Exchange Commission (SEC) and Commodity Futures Trading Commission. There are 12 Associate members, that are usually agencies or branches of government, other than the principal national securities regulators, and includes the European Securities and Market Authority. IOSCO also has 75 Affiliate members coming from self-regulatory organizations including stock exchanges or international bodies such as the International Monetary Fund (IMF) and the World Bank.[8]

In 2002, IOSCO formulated and adopted a Multilateral Memorandum of Understanding (MMoU) Concerning Consultation and Cooperation and the Exchange of Information.[9] This MMoU creates a standardized process by which securities regulators, who are IOSCO members, can obtain information from other member securities regulators for enforcement purposes. The MMoU provides a framework of procedures to prevent securities fraud as securities regulators can exchange information necessary to facilitate the enforcement of a wide range of domestic laws. International Securities Regulations suffered from a lack of information sharing in multi-jurisdictional transactions. The MMoU attempts to fix this problem by allowing authorities to make information requests when necessary.

Under the MMoU, authorities can make information requests when they are in the process of investigating offences related to:

1. Insider trading and market manipulation
2. Misrepresentation of material information and other fraudulent or manipulative practices relating to securities and derivatives
3. Solicitation and handling of investor funds, and customer orders
4. The registration, issuance, offer, or sale of securities and derivatives
5. The activities of market intermediaries, including investment and trading advisers who are required to be licensed or registered, collective investment schemes, brokers, dealers, and transfer agents
6. The operations of markets, exchanges, and clearing and settlement entities.[10]

Under the terms of the MMoU, securities regulators can provide information and assistance, including records:

1. To facilitate reconstruction of securities and derivatives transactions that can include the records of funds and assets transferred into and out of bank accounts related to these transactions
2. That identify the beneficial owner and controller of the account
3. The amount purchased or sold at the time of the transaction, the price of the transaction, and the individual and the bank or broker and brokerage house that handled the transaction
4. Taking or compelling a person's statement or, where permissible, testimony under oath, regarding the potential offence.[11]

The MMoU allows for securities commissions to exchange information and attain relevant information to help prosecute securities fraud. There are currently 101 signatories to the MMoU, which includes the SEC in the US, the Securities and Exchange

Board of India, the Financial Services Agency of Japan, and the Financial Conduct Authority of the UK.[12]

Principles of IOSCO

There are 38 basic principles of IOSOC consistent with the objectives of securities regulation. In general, the principles aim to reduce systematic risk and to protect investors, ensuring that markets are fair, efficient, and transparent.

1 **Principles relating to the Regulator**

   a   The responsibilities of the Regulator should be clear and objectively stated.
   b   The Regulator should be operationally independent and accountable in the exercise of its functions and powers.
   c   The Regulator should have adequate powers, proper resources and the capacity to perform its functions and exercise its powers.
   d   The Regulator should adopt clear and consistent regulatory processes.
   e   The staff of the Regulator should observe the highest professional standards, including appropriate standards of confidentiality.
   f   The Regulator should have, or contribute to, a process to monitor, mitigate, and manage systemic risk, appropriate to its mandate.
   g   The Regulator should have, or contribute to, a process to review the perimeter of regulation regularly.
   h   The Regulator should seek to ensure that conflicts of interest and misalignment of incentives are avoided, eliminated, disclosed, or otherwise managed.

2 **Principles for self-regulation**
   Where the regulatory system makes use of Self-Regulatory Organizations (SROs) that exercise some direct oversight responsibility for their respective areas of competence, such SROs should be subject to the oversight of the Regulator and should observe standards of fairness and confidentiality when exercising powers and delegated responsibilities.

3 **Principles for the enforcement of securities regulation**

   a   The Regulator should have comprehensive inspection, investigation, and surveillance powers.
   b   The Regulator should have comprehensive enforcement powers.
   c   The regulatory system should ensure an effective and credible use of inspection, investigation, surveillance, and enforcement powers and implementation of an effective compliance programme.

4 **Principles for cooperation in regulation**

   a   The Regulator should have authority to share both public and non-public information with domestic and foreign counterparts.
   b   Regulators should establish information sharing mechanisms that set out when and how they will share both public and non-public information with their domestic and foreign counterparts.

c The regulatory system should allow for assistance to be provided to foreign Regulators who need to make inquiries in the discharge of their functions and exercise of their powers.

5 Principles for issuers

a There should be full, accurate, and timely disclosure of financial results, risk and other information, which is material to investors' decisions.
b Holders of securities in a company should be treated in a fair and equitable manner.
c Accounting standards used by issuers to prepare financial statements should be of a high and internationally acceptable quality.

6 Principles for auditors, credit ratings agencies, and other information service providers

a Auditors should be subject to adequate levels of oversight.
b Auditors should be independent of the issuing entity that they audit.
c Audit standards should be of a high and internationally acceptable quality.
d Credit rating agencies should be subject to adequate levels of oversight. The regulatory system should ensure that credit rating agencies whose ratings are used for regulatory purposes are subject to registration and ongoing supervision.
e Other entities that offer investors analytical or evaluative services should be subject to oversight and regulation appropriate to the impact their activities have on the market, or the degree to which the regulatory system relies on them.

7 Principles for collective investment schemes

a The regulatory system should set standards for the eligibility, governance, organization, and operational conduct of those who wish to market or operate a collective investment scheme.
b The regulatory system should provide for rules governing the legal form and structure of collective investment schemes and the segregation and protection of client assets.
c Regulation should require disclosure, as set forth under the principles for issuers, which is necessary to evaluate the suitability of a collective investment scheme for a particular investor and the value of the investor's interest in the scheme.
d Regulation should ensure that there is a proper and disclosed basis for asset valuation and the pricing and the redemption of units in a collective investment scheme.
e Regulation should ensure that hedge funds and/or hedge funds managers/advisers are subject to appropriate oversight.

8 Principles for market intermediaries

a Regulation should provide for minimum entry standards for market intermediaries.

b There should be initial and ongoing capital and other prudential requirements for market intermediaries that reflect the risks the intermediaries undertake.
c Market intermediaries should be required to establish an internal function that delivers compliance with standards for internal organization and operational conduct, with the aim of protecting the interests of clients and their assets and ensuring proper management of risk, through which management of the intermediary accepts primary responsibility for these matters.
d There should be procedures for dealing with the failure of a market intermediary in order to minimize damage and loss to investors and to contain systemic risk.

9 Principles for secondary markets

a The establishment of trading systems including securities exchanges should be subject to regulatory authorization and oversight.
b There should be ongoing regulatory supervision of exchanges and trading systems, which should aim to ensure that the integrity of trading is maintained through fair and equitable rules that strike an appropriate balance between the demands of different market participants.
c Regulation should promote transparency of trading.
d Regulation should be designed to detect and deter manipulation and other unfair trading practices.
e Regulation should aim to ensure the proper management of large exposures, default risk, and market disruption.
f Securities settlement systems and central counterparties should be subject to regulatory and supervisory requirements that are designed to ensure that they are fair, effective, and efficient, and that they reduce systemic risk.

11.4 Inbound transactions

Foreign companies looking to invest in US securities markets have to follow US securities laws. An inbound transaction is an offering or an issue of securities by foreign companies in the US. For example, a company like Singapore Airlines does not want to be restricted to raising funds by issuing securities on the Singapore Stock Exchange. It would also like to have access to the enormous savings of Americans, for example, by issuing stock on the NYSE. Foreign companies who wish to do so are subject to SEC rules and regulations on disclosure requirements.

The most significant laws that foreign businesses have to be aware of when accessing the US capital markets are the *Securities Act of 1933*, which is referred to as the *Securities Act*, and the *Securities Exchange Act of 1934*, which is referred to as the *Exchange Act*. The fundamental mandate of the 1933 Act is that 'an issuer of securities is required to register with the SEC specific securities to be sold to the public in a particular plan of distribution'.[13] The general rule, to which there are exceptions discussed below, is that 'no public offering of securities may be made in the US by the issuer of those securities or by a person who controls, is controlled by, or is under common control with, the issuer until a registration statement relating to the offering has been filed . . .'.[14] The Exchange Act of 1934 created the SEC and built upon the basis of the 1933 Act.

The registration process

There are three phases in the registration process, which are the pre-filing period, the filing period, and the post-effective period. The distinctive focus of the registration process is on the actions the issuer can take to market its securities to the investment community. The SEC throughout the process regulates the amount of promotional activity in which an issuer can engage to sell its securities. The SEC does this as a measure to protect certain investors from gaining an unfair advantage.

The pre-filing period spans the period before the foreign issuer transmits a registration to the SEC for its approval. During this period, it is impermissible for the issuer to offer the securities that it plans to issue to potential buyers. No public offering of securities may be made in the US until a registration statement is filed with the SEC pursuant to the 1933 Act.

The filing period begins the moment the registration statement is filed with the SEC and ends when the SEC declares that statement effective. During the filing period, the SEC reviews the registration statement submitted to it and comments on it. The issuer responds with appropriate amendments. The issuer can offer the securities to potential buyers 'orally or through use of the preliminary prospectus which forms part of the registration statement, but no sales may be made until the registration statement is declared effective by the SEC'.[15] In other words, the issuer is permitted to market its securities using oral communications or preliminary prospectus statements. If sale is confirmed during this period the issuer must deliver to the purchaser a copy of the final form of the prospectus.

The post-effective period covers the time when the SEC is satisfied with the registration statement and any amendments to it. The issuer is then entitled to request the SEC to declare the registration effective. Once the SEC has declared the registration statement effective, the issuer is free to market its securities to the investment community. The period is essentially the time when the securities are actually being sold in the primary market.

Registration statements

For a foreign issuer to offer its securities in the US capital markets it must register its securities with the SEC. Domestic US issuers use Forms S-1, S-2, and S-3 but foreign issuer have different forms to file when registering securities. There are three basic forms, which foreign issuers may file to register their securities: Form F-1, F-2, and F-3. All foreign companies must file one of the three forms to register with the SEC. Canadian companies are the exception because they file a Form F-10.

Form F-1 is the most basic of the three forms. Non-Canadian foreign private issuers that issue securities in the US for the first time use Form F-1. The only way for a first-time issuer to avoid this form is to qualify for a private placement or commercial paper exemption. Form F-1 presents significant hurdles to new foreign companies. There are several noteworthy features of Form F-1:

1. *Description of securities*: Predictably, the issuer must describe the securities being offered and the terms of the offering, explain the purpose to which the proceeds of the offering will be put, and state the plan for distributing the securities.
2. *Disclosure about business*: The issuer must also describe its business and disclose information about the nature of its business activities and any material country risks of which investors are unlikely to be aware. Such risks could include 'dependence

upon a few major customers or suppliers, governmental regulation, expiration of material contracts or rights, unusual competitive conditions, cyclicality of the industry, and anticipated raw material or energy shortages'.[16]

3 *Five year record/three year record disclosure*: Requirements concerning business disclosure and financial forms are particularly burdensome for first-time foreign companies registering their securities in the US. A company must describe the general development of its business over the past five years and provide a breakdown of its total revenue during the past three years by categories of business activity. It must provide audited balance sheets for each of the last two years and audited income statements for each of the last three years. In addition, the foreign entity must provide selected financial data for each of the last five years such as revenue, income, assets, and long-term liabilities. In the management discussion and analysis ('MD and A') portion of Form F-1, the issuer must discuss its financial condition and changes therein for each of the last three years. Therefore, a company that has a track record of less than five years cannot fulfil this requirement and, therefore, is barred from entering the US capital market.

4 *Accounting practices*: The requirements regarding financial statements, which are set forth in Regulation S-X, pose further difficulties for many foreign issuers – new and established – because of the insistence on using accounting practices that are consistent with US generally accepted accounting principles (GAAP).

5 *Blackout periods*: Another financial statement requirement that may be difficult for foreign entities leads to 'black out' periods during which the US capital market is closed to such entities. Audited balance sheets that are older than six months are considered stale and unacceptable. In their place, unaudited interim financial statements must be submitted. 'This requirement has had a significant impact on the ability of non-US issuers which publicly release financial statements on a semi-annual basis only. In view of the time required to prepare such financial statements, this requirement has had the effect of creating "blackout periods" during which the public capital markets in the US have been unavailable to such issuers'.[17]

6 *Auditors*: The SEC will not accept just any 'audited' financial statement from a foreign issuer. Rather, the accountants that perform the audit must be acceptable to the SEC. Here, the key concept is 'independent'. The SEC requires that the auditors be completely unrelated to the audited company. This means that no one who works for the accounting firm can hold any direct or materially indirect interest in the securities of the issuer, serve in any capacity (e.g., promoter, underwriter, voting trustee, director, officer, or employee) with the issuer or affiliate of the issuer, or perform services for the issuer that are incompatible with auditing it, such as preparing the issuer's books and records.

7 *Other disclosure requirements*: Both new and established foreign entities may find other disclosure requirements burdensome. For example, they must provide information about control of the issuer by a parent company and shareholders who hold 10 per cent or more of the issuer's shares. In some business cultures, including the Middle East and the Far East, the control relationships may be complex and some controlling pieces may wish to remain confidential.

Form F-2 is used by non-Canadian foreign private issuers, which are 'reporting companies' and have filed annual reports on Form 20-F pursuant to the 1934 Act. In other words, it is used by foreign entities that have already issued securities in the US on at least one previous occasion. There are some additional technical requirements for eligibility to use Form F-2:

1. The issuer must have been a reporting company for three years.
2. Alternatively, the issuer must:

   a. Have filed at least one annual report on Form 20-F.
   b. Either have outstanding voting common stock worth at least US$300 million or be issuing investment grade debt securities.
   c. Finally, the issuer must not have defaulted on any of its financial obligations during the last year.

These requirements make it difficult for a foreign entity that has not been a reporting company for three years to use Form F-2. If the entity is small or its currency is weakly valued against the US dollar, then its market capitalization may not reach $300 million. An additional feature of the $300 million requirement is that all of the outstanding voting common stock must be held by non-affiliates of the issuer. Yet, in many countries, including those in the Far East, it is common for companies to raise capital by selling securities to affiliates or related parties. The US rule discriminates against companies that engage in such practices. An investment grade rating is one of the top four ratings from a US rating agency, like Standard & Poor's (S&P).

It may be difficult for a small foreign company to receive an investment grade rating on its debt securities – even if it is highly creditworthy – because it is small and located overseas. However:

> as a practical matter, acceptable ratings from the two major statistical rating agencies in the US, Moody's Investors Service, Inc. and Standard & Poor's Corporation, are virtually essential for the successful marketing of investment grade securities in the US public debt market at competitive interest rate levels.[18]

Form F-3 is also available to a non-Canadian foreign private issuer that has been a reporting company for at least three years and has not been involved in any defaults in the last year. Form F-3 incorporates by reference the material disclosed in Form 20-F and only recent material changes need to be disclosed on Form F-2. Form F-3 is similar to Form F-2 but has two major distinctions between the use of Forms F-2 and F-3.

First, Form F-3 can be used only in connection with the offering of specific types of securities.

1. It can be used to register an offering for cash of investment-grade non-convertible debt securities. In other words, the issuer must be offering bonds that are not convertible to stock, and the bonds must receive one of the top four ratings from a US rating agency.
2. Form F-3 can also be used to register an equity offering. But, that offering must be made only to existing shareholders if the issuer already has $300 million outstanding voting shares that are held by non-affiliates. The $300 million threshold and non-affiliated holder requirements may pose the potential problems for foreign companies discussed above.

3   If the offering is not of investment-grade non-convertible securities or of equity to existing shareholders, then Form F-3 can be used where the issuer has disclosed supplemental financial information in its Form 20-F pursuant to the 1934 Act.

The second principal difference between Forms F-2 and F-3 concern delivery to the investment community. When Form F-3 is used, the issuer is not required to deliver the forms that are incorporated by reference (namely, 1934 Act Forms 20-F and 6-K) with the prospectus. Purchasers of securities of a foreign issuer that has used Form F-2 to register its securities must receive a copy of all incorporated filings with the prospectus that relates to these securities. Therefore, the F-2 issuer has a greater burden in terms of the number of documents that must be transmitted to purchasers than the F-3 issuer. This makes Form F-3 more attractive than Form F-2.

Foreign private issuer

A foreign company looking to enter the US capital markets may gain access to them by receiving foreign private issuer status. Foreign private issuers cannot be governments of other countries and are subjected to a test promulgated under the Securities Act. A foreign company that wants to gain foreign private issuer status is subjected to a two-part test:

1   *The shareholder test*: Issuer has 50 per cent or less of its outstanding voting securities held of record by US residents; or
2   *Shareholder and business contacts test*: Issuer has more than 50 per cent of its outstanding voting securities held of record by US residents, but does not have any one of the following:
    a   Majority of its executive officers or directors are US citizens or residents,
    b   More than 50 per cent of its assets are located in the US, or
    c   The business is principally administered in the US.[19]

If an organization can receive the foreign private issuer status, it can receive benefits to access the capital markets in the US. The SEC has made certain special accommodations for foreign private issuers, not available to domestic issuers. These include:

1   File a Form 20-F rather than a Form 10-K, which has later filing deadlines, less demanding disclosure requirements, and less demanding filing requirements.[20]
2   Confidential filings for first time issuers.[21]
3   No quarterly filing requirements.[22]

Exempt offerings

The costs and delays associated with registering securities under the 1933 Act, whether in connection with a conventional offering or a shelf registration, are incentives for foreign entities to seek to raise capital in the securities market without undergoing the registration process. The principal means of avoiding registration requirements is to qualify for a statutory or regulatory exemption. An offering that so qualifies is frequently referred to as an 'exempt offering' and the securities are called 'exempt securities'. In all exempt cases, filing a registration statement with the SEC is unnecessary. The main exempt offerings are:

1   Rule 144A
2   Regulation D
3   Regulation S
4   The private placement exemption under Section 4(2) of the 1933 Act.

Private placement exemption: the Section 4(2) Exemption

Under Section 4(2) of the 1933 Act, offers and sales of securities that are made 'in transactions by an issuer not involving any public offering' are exempt from registration statement requirements. It is available to both foreign and US issuers. The statutory language does not limit the exemption to non-public offerings in the US or to US citizens or residents. However, the SEC would have little interest in an offshore non-public offering, or one where the offerees were foreign citizens or residents. Accordingly, the language is construed as applicable only to non-public offerings that are made in the US or to US citizens or residents.

Disclosure is the fundamental concept behind the 1933 Act, yet disclosure is relevant only in certain contexts. Where securities are offered to a large number of investors, or where the investors differ in their level of financial acumen, disclosure is presumably beneficial. In contrast, if the securities are offered to a small number of sophisticated institutional investors, then it is unlikely that information disclosed in a registration statement will significantly help the investors. Professional investors employ an army of investment analysts and strategists to obtain and digest information about companies around the globe that seek to tap into the US market. They do not need the SEC staff to act as a watchdog for them – if they cannot get the information they want about a foreign company issuing securities, then they will eschew those securities. Thus, 'The underlying principle . . . is that the [private placement] exemption should be available only in those cases in which the offerees and purchasers of the securities do not require the protection of Securities Act registration'.[23]

The 1933 Act does not delimit the scope of the Section 4(2) exemption. Whether a foreign or US issuer qualifies for a Section 4(2) private placement exemption depends on four broad factors:

1   *Number of offerees*: The securities can be offered only to a small number of offerees and no general advertising about the issuance is allowed. However, if high quality securities are offered only to financially sophisticated institutional investors, then a large number of offerees is permissible.
2   *Availability of information*: The information that would have been provided in a registration statement should be known by, available to, or provided to the offerees but it does not have to be registered with the SEC. To meet this requirement, issuers prepare a private placement memorandum, which furnishes information about the issuer and the securities being offered.
3   *Nature of the offerees*: 'The offerees and purchasers must be capable of evaluating the merits and risks of the investment (possibly with the help of a qualified adviser).'[24]
4   *Prevention of resales*: Because the private placement is by definition designed to be a distribution of securities to a limited number of investors, there must be some mechanism to ensure that the initial investors do not resell their securities, thereby creating a secondary market for the securities and expanding the distribution of the securities. The securities must not be distributed broadly or to persons that do not qualify for the relevant exemption (such as Rule 144A or Regulation S).

Rule 144A

Rule 144A is designed to enhance the secondary market liquidity of privately placed securities and thereby lower the cost of issuing such securities. The rule allows for foreign companies to make private placement sales without the registration requirement that the SEC mandates on other sales of securities. These sales are reserved for buyers who are perceived to have expertise in the marketplace and therefore require less protection than the general public. The securities issued under Rule 144A can only be sold to Qualified Institutional Buyers ('QIBs') as the investors. A QIB owns and invests on a discretionary basis at least $100 million in securities of issuers. These can be mutual funds, banks, trust funds, or an entity owned by a qualified investor. Issuers can avoid certain stringent liability rules with private placement offerings, but are still subject to Rule 10-b5 antifraud liabilities.[25] There are four fundamental requirements set forth in Rule 144A.

1. *The non-fungibility of the securities*: the unregistered securities must not be the same as any class of securities of the same issuer that are currently publicly traded on any US exchange or in the over-the-counter market (such as quoted on NASDAQ).
2. *Qualified institutional buyers*: Essentially, the term is meant to capture sophisticated institutional investors. Any institution that owns and invests at least $100 million is a QIB if it has full discretion to invest the funds (*i.e.*, it does not act in a fiduciary capacity such as a trustee and operates with no or limited freedom) and if it invests in securities issued by companies that are not affiliated to the QIB.[26]
3. *Notice*: The issuer must provide to prospective purchasers evidence that the securities being offered are exempt from 1933 Act registration requirements under Rule 144A. This requirement speaks of the issuer taking 'reasonable steps' to provide notice.
4. *Information*: The final requirement concerns disclosure of information about the issuer. The issuer must furnish prospective investors and any existing holders with information about itself; namely, its business, products, and services, and its financial statements for the portion of the previous two years that it has been in operation. The information must be 'reasonably current', which means that it must meet the requirements of the issuer's home country or principal trading market of the issuer's securities.

Regulation D

One of the most prevalent exemptions used to offer securities without registering with the SEC is Regulation D. Rules 504, 505, and 506 are the most important rules under the regulation that provide three exemptions for companies to offer securities without bearing registration costs and liabilities. Rule 504 allows companies to sell up to $1 million dollars in securities in a 12-month period without registering securities. Rule 505 allows organizations to sell up to $5 million in securities in a 12-month period with restrictions on the number of purchasers and a ban on general solicitation of the securities.

Rule 506 allows sellers of securities to sell an unlimited number of securities to accredited investors and to 35 additional non-accredited investors who meet a sophistication requirement. The sophistication requirement in Rule 506 requires purchasers to have knowledge and experience in financial and business matters and be capable of evaluating the merits and risks of the investment. The considerations for the sophistication requirement are wealth and income, experience, education, present investment status, and the performance on an investment.

The Rules 505 and 506 exempted securities are mostly sold to accredited investors. These are usually large investors who the SEC believes have enough knowledge about the financial markets to make their own decisions without oversight from the SEC. The term 'accredited investor' is defined under Rule 501 of Regulation D as:

1   Banks, insurance companies, registered investment companies, business development companies, or small business investment companies
2   Employee benefit plans, within the meaning of the *Employee Retirement Income Security Act*, if a bank, insurance company, or registered investment adviser makes the investment decisions, or if the plan has total assets in excess of $5 million
3   Charitable organizations, corporations, or partnerships with assets exceeding $5 million
4   Directors, executive officers, or general partners of the company selling the securities
5   Businesses in which all the equity owners are accredited investors
6   Natural persons who have individual net worth, or joint net worth with the person's spouse, that exceeds $1 million at the time of the purchase, excluding the value of the primary residence of such person
7   Natural persons with income exceeding $200,000 in each of the two most recent years or joint income with a spouse exceeding $300,000 for those years, and a reasonable expectation of the same income level in the current year; or a trust with assets in excess of $5 million, not formed to acquire the securities offered, whose purchases a sophisticated person makes.

Regulation S

Regulation S provides foreign (as well as US) companies with an exemption from 1933 Act registration requirements. Regulation S applies to securities that are offered outside of the US, so called 'offshore offerings', where there are no sales or directed selling efforts made to persons in the US. Under this Regulation, offers and sales of securities occurring outside the US are not subject to the registration requirements of Section 5 of the 1933 Act.

Fundamentally, Regulation S is about the extraterritorial application of the 1933 Act. It delimits the reach of the Act's registration requirements. The general principle that underlies the Regulation is that Section 5 of the 1933 Act does not apply to offers and sales of securities that occur outside the US.[27] It is important to realize that both the sale and the offer relating to that sale must be made outside of the US.[28] Regulation S

> is based on a territorial approach to Section 5 of the Securities Act . . . . The territorial approach recognizes the primacy of the laws in which a market is located. As investors choose their markets, they choose the laws and regulations applicable in such markets.[29]

Regulation S can be used in tandem with one of the exemptions discussed above. Under Regulation S, a foreign issuer can engage in an offshore public offering and avoid 1933 Act registration. Relying on one of the other exemptions, the foreign company can

Table 11.1 Regulation D

	Rule 504 (§3(b))	*Rule 505 (§3(b))*	*Rule 506 (§4(2))*
Aggregate offering price	≤$1 million (504(b)(2), 501(c))	≤$5 million (505(b)(2)(i), 501(c))	No limit on amount
	Prior 12 mo. and during offering aggregation w/§3(b) offerings and w/§5(a) violations	Prior 12 mo. and during offering aggregation w/ §3(b) offerings and w/ §5(a) violations	
Number of purchasers	No limit on purchasers	≤35 purchasers (505(b)(2)(ii), 501(a), 501(e))	≤35 purchasers (506(b)(2)(i), 501(a), 501(e))
			Sophistication requirement (506(b)(2)(ii), 501(h))
Resale limitation	Freely transferable – Except 502(d) applies where offering fails to meet state requirements	Resale limitation (502(d), 502(b)(2)(vii), Rule 144)	Resale limitation (502(d), 502(b)(2)(vii), Rule 144)
Integration with other offerings	Integration (502(a))	Integration (502(a))	Integration (502(a))
Mandatory information	None	Information disclosure (502(b)) (to non-accredited investors)	Information disclosure (502(b)) (to non-accredited investors)
Manner of offering	Unrestricted – Except 502(c) applies where offering fails to meet state requirements	No general solicitation (502(c)) (But see Rule 135c)	No general solicitation (502(c)) (But see Rule 135c)
Other	Rule 503 (Form D) Rule 508	Disqualification (see 505(b)(2)(iii)) Rule 503 (Form D) Rule 508	Rule 503 (Form D) Rule 508
Excluded issuers	Not '34 Act Co. Not Investment Co. Not Blank Check Co.	Not Investment Co.	None

issue securities in the US – for example, these can be privately placed. Foreign issuers are able to engage in a multi-jurisdictional offering that includes the US without registering securities under the 1933 Act. Alternatively, securities of a foreign issuer that have been previously privately placed can be sold offshore without registration under the 1933 Act by virtue of Regulation S. This would enhance the liquidity of the privately placed securities, as they would be purchased not only by QIBs but also by overseas persons.

The scope of the exemption provided by Regulation S is limited to Section 5 of the 1933 Act. Other provisions of that Act, principally those in Section 11, 12(2), and 15, concerning fraud are applicable to a foreign issuer that qualifies for the Regulation S exemption. That is, the extraterritorial application of the anti-fraud and other rules of the 1933 Act are not limited by Regulation S.[30] US courts will continue to apply the antifraud rules according to either the 'conduct test' or the 'effects test'.[31] Under the conduct test, a court examines whether significant conduct occurred in the US.[32] Where conduct occurs outside the US, a court will look to whether that offshore conduct has a significant effect within the US or on the interests of US investors.[33] Either the conduct or the effects test can support jurisdiction of US courts.

Two safe harbours are set forth in Regulation S. A transaction, which meets all of the conditions of either of these, is deemed to occur outside the US and, therefore, not subject to the registration requirements of Section 5 of the 1933 Act. The first is called the 'issuer safe harbour' while the second is known as the 'resale safe harbour'. These safe harbours are non-exclusive, which means that they are 'not intended to create a presumption that any transaction failing to meet their terms is subject to Section 5'.[34]

Two general conditions apply to both safe harbours and must be satisfied to avoid application of the 1933 Act. First, the offer and sale must be an 'offshore transaction'. For both safe harbours, this means that no offers can be made to persons in the US. However, the further interpretation of the term 'offshore transaction' differs depending on the safe harbour in question. With regard to the issuer safe harbour, it means that the buyer is outside the US at the time the buy order is originated (or, at least, the seller reasonably believes this is so) or that the sale is made on an established foreign securities exchange.[35] In contrast, the additional meaning in the context of a resale safe harbour is somewhat different. The buyer must be outside the US when it originates the buy order (or the seller must reasonably believe this to be the case) or, alternatively, the sale must be made in a designated offshore securities market and the sale transaction must not be pre-arranged with a buyer in the US.[36]

Second, no 'directed selling efforts' are allowed in the US. In other words, the issuer must not attempt to sell its securities in the US. Specifically, a 'directed selling effort' is any activity that is 'undertaken for the purpose of, or that could reasonably be expected to result in, conditioning of the market in the United States for the securities being offered'.[37]

1   *Issuer safe harbour*: This safe harbour applies to offers and sales by issuers and distributors.[38] A 'distributor' is 'any underwriter, dealer, or other person who participates, pursuant to a contractual arrangement, in the distribution of the securities offered or sold in reliance upon Regulation S'.[39] To qualify for the issuer safe harbour, not only must the 'offshore transaction' and 'no directed selling efforts' requirements be met, but also certain additional conditions must be satisfied. The precise conditions depend on the categories of securities being offered. There are three categories of securities offerings: an overseas directed offering, offerings by US reporting companies, and offerings that fall within a residual category.
2   *Resale safe harbour*: This safe harbour applies to anyone other than an issuer or distributor (or affiliate or agent thereof).[40] For anyone other than a dealer, a securities professional, and officers and directors of the issuer, there are no condi-

tions that must be met to qualify for the resale safe harbour other than the two general requirements discussed above.[41] However, for dealers (or persons receiving payment – such as a concession or fee – for selling securities) the resale safe harbour is available only if two additional conditions are met. First, the seller must not know that any offeree or buyer of the securities is a US person. Second, if the seller knows that the purchaser is a securities professional, then it must transmit a confirmation to the purchaser that contains restrictive language regarding the securities. Each of these requirements poses burdens that we have seen and criticized before. The seller is legally obligated to know its offerees and purchasers and guarantee that they fall within the relevant legal requirements.

Disclosure requirements

The SEC requires disclosure of certain types of information from public companies that are offering securities to the US market. Disclosure requirements are in place to allow the investing public to be able to make informed decisions. There are three basic disclosure documents for public companies. First, is the Form 8-K, which is filed when important events occur within a company that are of importance to investors. Second, is the Form 10-K, which is filed annually with the SEC, and which has the most stringent and extensive disclosure requirements. Third, is the Form 10-Q, which is filed quarterly and it usually provides earnings reports from quarter to quarter.

Form 8-K is a disclosure requirement to update investors when specific occurrences happen within the organization. The events that require current disclosures usually fall into one of these categories:

1. *Registrants business and operations*: This includes new and terminated contracts entered into by the organization, which are significant.
2. *Financial information*: Acquisition or disposition of assets over 10 per cent.
3. *Securities and trading*: delisting or transfer of listing.
4. *Matters related to accountants and financial statements*.
5. *Corporate governance and management*: includes departure or election of directors and principal officers and amendment to articles or bylaws.
6. *Asset-backed securities*.
7. *Regulation FD*: Any disclosure the issuer elects to disclose through Form 8-K has to comply with Regulation FD. Rule 100 of Regulation FD states the basic rule for selective disclosure, which is whenever an issuer or a person acting on its behalf discloses material non-public information to a certain number of enumerated persons, the issuer must make public disclosure of that same information simultaneously (for intentional disclosures); or promptly (for non-intentional disclosures).
8. *Financial statements and exhibits*.

The Form 10-K is filed annually and requires the most extensive disclosure by public companies. The SEC requires companies to provide complete disclosure on the following information.

1. Description of business
2. Description of properties

3 Legal proceedings
4 Market for common stock
5 Management discussion and analysis of financial condition and results of operation
6 Directors and officers
7 Executive compensation
8 Security ownership of certain beneficial owners and management
9 Certain relationships and related transactions
10 Principal accounting fees and services.

Table 11.2 Types of issuing companies

	Non-reporting	*Non-seasoned*	*Seasoned*	*WKSI*
Eligibility	First time registrants under Securities Act	Reporting company for 1 year + do not satisfy Form S-3; or WKSI not current and timely in filings to does not satisfy	Eligible to use Form S-3 for a primary offering of its securities (a) $75m float requirement	Eligible to use Form S-3 for a primary offering of its securities + either (a) >$700 million of common equity worldwide market value by non-affiliates, or (b) Issued $1 billion aggregate principal of non-convertible securities in reg. offerings in past 3 years
Requirements	File Form S-1	File Form S-1	File Form S-1 or File Form S-3	File Form S-1 or File Form S-3
Pre-filing safe harbours	Rule 139 Rule 163A Rule 169	Rule 139 Rule 163A Rule 168	Rule 139 Rule 163A Rule 168	Rule 139 Rule 163A Rule 168 163
Preliminary prospectus	Yes	Yes	Yes	Yes
Free writing prospectus	No	No	Yes	Yes
Tombstone	Yes	Yes	Yes	Yes
Roadshow	Yes	Yes	Yes	Yes
Rule 138	No	Yes	Yes	Yes
Rule 139 Industry Report	No	No	Yes	Yes

11.5 Outbound transactions

An outbound is where an investor or issuer purchases or sells stock in countries other than its home country. For example, a US company may have its stock issued and traded in both the US and foreign securities exchanges. In outbound transactions an investor buys the US company in a foreign securities exchange where the company offers its stock.

Limitations to outbound stock

The laws of the investor's home country may inhibit the investor's ability to purchase financial assets overseas. These serve as a constraint on the free flow of capital. For example, suppose India does not allow Indian citizens and residents to obtain more than $500 worth of foreign currency. This means that Indians can buy only $500 worth of US securities; with the remainder of their rupee savings, they are forced to invest in assets in India. More generally, any foreign exchange control operates as a constraint on capital flows because investors from the country that enacts the control cannot obtain the foreign currencies they need to purchase assets denominated in the foreign currencies. While there are no foreign exchange controls in the US, there are constraints on the ability of US investors to buy certain assets. For example, US citizens are not allowed to purchase new Eurobond issues.[42]

The regulations of overseas stock markets are also relevant to an outbound investor. There may be limitations on the extent to which foreigners can hold shares in domestic companies. Frequently, countries do not want foreigners to hold a majority stake in local companies. Thus, for instance, companies in China issue two classes of shares – class A and class B. Class B shares are non-voting and designed for foreigners.

Investors will also seek rapid clearing and settlement of trades. 'Clearing' refers to 'the process whereby the trades are compared, matched, and confirmed'.[43] It involves 'capturing the trade data, comparing the buyer's and seller's version of the data, and guaranteeing that the trade will settle once the data match'.[44]

'Settlement' is the process whereby parties to trades fulfil the obligations they are under – generally a 'delivery' of the securities by the seller and payment of the agreed price by the buyer'.[45] It involves the exchange of funds and/or financial instruments between the trading parties. 'Those who owe money and/or financial instruments make payments or deliveries. Those who are owed money and/or securities receive the funds or securities'.[46] Slow clearing and settlement systems are unappealing to foreign investors because they impede rapid trading.

Suppose an investor purchases shares in the Aswan Dam Company on the Cairo Stock Exchange on day 1 and that it takes 30 days for the trade to clear and settle and for the registration of the stock in the investor's name to occur. Suppose further the investor seeks to sell the stock on day 7. Whether the Exchange can accommodate these two deals in such a short time is unclear, and the investor may justifiably be concerned that money to pay for the stock or money earned from the stock sale will be lost. She may also fear that the ownership interests in the stock will not be properly transferred.

Capital adequacy

Capital adequacy rules include statutory and regulatory laws requiring regulated financial firms to keep levels of capital comparative to assets to foster the protection and soundness of the organization and the financial system.[47] Capital adequacy regulation aims to reduce costs connected with financial institution failures. The regulation reaches this goal by fostering a loss cushion with reasonable assurance and imposes a risk tax in the form of a capital charge for riskier business lines.[48]

Regulators impose these capital requirements to ensure firms have an available 'cushion' or buffer to absorb unexpected losses without threatening the ability of the institution to satisfy claims of depositors (in the case of banks), insurance policy holders (in the case of insurers), or clients (in the case of broker-dealers), or the systemic integrity of the financial system. In its simplest form, the capital requirement consists of a minimum ratio of capital that is defined to include equity (assets minus liabilities) and in some cases other add-ons thought to possess equity-like features, such as subordinated debt-to assets. Thus, as a firm's equity declines, so does its capital ratio, which may result in noncompliance with the capital adequacy regime and a need to raise new capital.[49]

The net capital rule gauges the adequacy of a broker-dealer's capitalization by reference to availability of liquid assets to satisfy the obligations of its customers. Specifically, firms must elect either to '(a) maintain aggregate indebtedness at a level' not in excess of 'fifteen times net capital' (the 'basic test') or '(b) maintain minimum net capital equal to not less than two per cent of "aggregate debit items"'.

In 2004, the SEC offered to these broker-dealers the option of opting out of the net capital rule system and entering the new consolidated supervised entity (CSE) regulatory regime of consolidated groups. Under the CSE Program, broker-dealers with at least $5 billion of capital would be permitted to avoid the net capital rule entirely, and instead subject themselves to an alternative net capital program resembling Basel II.

A qualifying broker-dealer could become a CSE by applying for an exemption from the SEC standard net capital rule. CSE groups would have to '[c]alculate a group-wide capital adequacy measure consistent with the international standards adopted by the Basel Committee' and 'maintain an overall . . . capital ratio of not less than the Federal Reserve's 10 per cent 'well-capitalized' standard for bank holding companies'. Firms were to maintain tentative net capital at a level above $1 billion and net capital above $500 million at all times.

11.6 The Volcker Rule

In the aftermath of the 2008 financial crisis, governments across the world have turned a spotlight on their respective financial industries in search of flaws within domestic and global financial systems. The light glared harshest on the banks, condemned publicly for their reckless relationships with the 'shadow banking system', and demand for reform was swift.[50]

Two regulatory frameworks quickly emerged in Basel III and the *Dodd–Frank Wall Street Reform and Consumer Protection Act* (Dodd–Frank).[51] Both of these frameworks established minimum capital requirements for banks in the belief that greater liquidity reserves should decrease systemic risk, dampen future shocks to the system, and prevent another liquidity crisis.[52] Dodd–Frank went a step further via the implementation of the Volcker Rule, prohibiting banks from engaging in proprietary trading activities and acquiring or sponsoring non-banking investment institutions.[53]

Background

Although the Volcker Rule is a modern approach to regulating a complex financial system, its foundation is built on concepts that trace back to the Great Depression and the

New Deal. In the late 1920s, public confidence in the banking system wavered. Bank runs occurred across the country as depositors, fearing their bank would be the next to fail, attempted to pull money out. More banks were forced to close, being unable to borrow from one another to pay out deposits, and the cycle continued until the system collapsed in 1933. Banks, who took the brunt of the blame, were accused of improper lending and disclosure practices, as well as manipulating the stock market through affiliate firms.[54]

The Banking Act of 1933 (commonly known as the *Glass–Steagall Act*, or *Glass–Steagall*) reigned in bank autonomy by recognizing, and erecting a wall between, two distinct bank entities: depository and investment banks. Furthermore, it prohibited depository banks from investing in securities for their own account, as well as affiliating with investment banks.[55]

Over the next 60 years, legislation and court cases attacked the wall, weakening its once rigid restraints on banking activity. Then, in 1999, the *Gramm–Leach–Bliley Act* removed the non-affiliation prohibition, allowing depository banks to join with investment institutions under the umbrella of financial holding companies.[56] Over that time the financial system evolved into a creature never imagined in 1933. Following the 2008 crisis, many believed reviving Glass{-}Steagall was the only solution to protecting banks from themselves. The Volcker Rule is an attempt to re-institute the basic principles of the original Glass–Steagall Act.[57]

Creation of the Volcker Rule

The Volcker Rule is named after the man who championed its creation, former Federal Reserve chairman Paul Volcker, and is the implementation of Section 13 of the *Bank Holding Company Act* 1956 (BHC Act) as amended. Section 13 charges financial regulators with the task of jointly adopting a rule to 'promote and enhance the safety and soundness of banking entities', and in November 2011 an initial Rule proposal was released.[58] However, the Final Rule was not adopted until 10 December 2013 due to an intense debate. Over 17,000 comments were submitted in response to the initial proposal between regulators and the banking industry.[59] The Final Rule can be viewed as consisting of two elements: (1) entities governed by the Rule, and (2) activities that are prohibited for those entities.

Banking entities

Volcker's two 'prohibitions' are, in effect, limits placed on the investment activities and relationships in which banking entities may participate. Therefore, it is important to understand the scope of the institutions covered under 'banking entities'. The term refers to any company that is, or controls, an insured depository institution (IDI) and any affiliate or subsidiary thereof.[60] An IDI is 'any bank or savings association the deposits of which are insured by the [FDIC]'.[61] The expansive nature of this definition has global ramifications due to the Rule's extraterritorial reach, and is discussed further below.

Prohibition on proprietary trading

Congress determined the first activity that needed addressing was proprietary trading, which is the purchase, or sale, of financial instruments by a banking entity for that entity's trading account (such as any account used by the entity for the purpose of gaining a profit or benefit from short-term resale, arbitrage, price movements, or hedging activities).[62]

The debate over Volcker's implementation has primarily focused on the ban on proprietary trading; regulators insist that these speculative high-risk trading activities led to 'losses within large trading positions [that] were in fact a contributing factor for some of our most systemically important institutions' needing a government bailout.[63] Additionally, supporters of the prohibition argue that proprietary trading is in dissonance with the true functions banks should engage in; banks are incentivized to act in their own best interest, rather than the interests of customers, because the profits to be gained from such activities are so great.

The counter-argument points to a lack of conclusive evidence that proprietary trading caused, or had a significant impact on, the financial crisis, and the prohibition was included to appease populist wishes.[64] Interestingly, although banks have fought the rule with tooth and nail, many began closing down their proprietary trading desks over a year before the Rule's implementation.[65]

Activities exempt from the definition of proprietary trading

Activities considered as necessary banking functions are exempt from the above definition of proprietary trading. The full list of exempt activities can be found in Table 11.3. This necessity can best be illustrated by using clearing as an example. When a bank assumes the role of a clearing entity, the bank becomes an intermediary between two, separate, transacting parties. The bank acts as a buyer and seller for the respective parties, and takes on the associated risk, and confirms that the orders match. Thus, without exceptions for this buying and selling activity, banks would be unable to offer this service. This would negatively impact banks, but also many corporate and financial entities that rely on these services.

Permitted activities

The blanket prohibition above certainly has plenty of holes in it; a number of carve-outs were put in place to ensure that banks would continue to provide services necessary to a modern economy. These 'permitted activities' are exempt from the prohibition, with underwriting, market making, and risk-mitigating hedging activities being the most significant. Aside from traditional depository and lending services, banks provide liquidity to markets and the fuel (such as cash) that drives economic growth via market making and underwriting.[66] The Great Depression is a prime example, if one doubts such a necessity, of the chaos illiquidity wreaks on an economy.

Underwriting

The first permitted activity is underwriting. Traditional bank business loans (such as lending a specified amount of money in return for a promise to repay the principal plus fixed interest payments) are adequate for small- and medium-sized companies, but banks cannot provide the hundreds of millions of dollars that large corporations often need to finance new projects. Thus, corporations must issue bonds or stock to raise capital, which is not only slow, it may take over a year to sell such a large quantity of stock, but also expensive.

Table 11.3 Activities exempt from proprietary trading definition

Exempt activity	Rule
Repurchase or reverse repurchase agreements	§ 3(d)(1)
A purchase or sale of a security that arises under a written securities lending agreement as long as the lender (1) retains the economic interest in the security, and (2) has the right to terminate the transaction and recall the loaned security	§ 3(d)(2)
A purchase or sale of a security for the purpose of liquidity management (which must be in accordance with a liquidity management plan)	§ 3(d)(3)
A purchase or sale of a security by a derivatives clearing organization (or clearing agency) in connection with clearing activities	§ 3(d)(4)
Any excluded clearing activities as long as the banking entity is a member of a clearing agency, derivatives clearing organization, or a designated financial market utility	§ 3(d)(5)
Any purchase or sale of a financial instrument by a banking entity as long as (1) the transaction satisfies a pre-existing delivery obligation, or (2) the transaction satisfies an obligation arising from a judicial, administrative, self-regulatory organization, or arbitration proceeding	§ 3(d)(6)
Any purchase or sale of a financial instrument as long as the banking entity is acting solely as an agent, broker, or custodian	§ 3(d)(7)
Any purchase or sale of a financial instrument by a banking entity through a deferred compensation, stock bonus, profit-sharing, or pension plan	§ 3(d)(8)
Any purchase or sale of a financial instrument in the ordinary course of collecting a pre-existing debt, provided that the banking entity divest the instrument as soon as practicable	§ 3(d)(9)

The underwriting service provided by banks is the solution because it grants access to instant capital, and transfers risk onto banking entities that are better equipped to hedge that risk.[67] This underwriting activity is exempt as long as the banking entity is licensed as an underwriter, the underwriting position is designed not to exceed predicted near term demand, compensation for the services does not incentivize trading that would create a material conflict of interest, and an internal compliance programme is in place.[68]

Market making

The second permitted activity, market making, is important to the stability of securities markets. Market makers deal in OTC securities by holding securities in inventory, and standing ready to execute bid (buy) or ask (sell) orders from customers.[69] The prices are determined by the market maker, and the bid–ask spread, the difference between the two prices, provides profit for the market maker. Market making is essential to market stability because it provides the market with real-time information on the value of a given security, as well as providing liquidity by increasing investor's ability to buy or sell as needed.

On the one hand, without market makers, an investor seeking to sell a security must wait until a buyer is available. The investor may be stuck with a security, unable to unload it due to a lack of willing buyers, which is losing value, and the investor will assume the full loss of the stock's drop in value. On the other hand, in a market that has market makers available to buy or sell, the investor can minimize losses by dumping the stock. In addition to the same exemption requirements for underwriting activities, a bank engaging in market making constantly stands ready to buy or sell throughout market cycles and take prompt corrective action if any position limits, as designated in the internal compliance programme, are exceeded.[70]

Risk-mitigating hedging

The third permitted activity of significance is risk-mitigating hedging. This is arguably the most important of the three major permitted activities; without such risk-shifting abilities banks would not conduct underwriting or market making. It is also the most controversial. Hedging is a method of minimizing a position's risk to changes in price; for example, if the bank owns oil commodities, the risk the price of oil will rise or fall in the future. The bank can hedge the oil commodities' risk by purchasing an offsetting oil future (a contract in which the bank agrees to purchase or sell the oil at a specified price).[71]

The controversy surrounds the very nature of the activity; detractors see the exemption as a loophole for banks to engage in otherwise prohibited proprietary trading by claiming the transactions are solely meant to hedge risk.[72] Hedging certainly provides for an expansive grey area, undoubtedly many banks will use it to their advantage, but the potential for abuse does not diminish the need for the exemption.

Market making and underwriting would no longer be viable if banking entities were not permitted to hedge. If a bank engaged in market making is unable to offset the risks taken on by holding securities in inventory, then the bank assumes the full risk associated with a drop in the prices of all of the securities in inventory; this is often untenable. Because this exemption has the greatest potential for abuse, the rules governing the activity are stricter.

The purchase or sale of a financial instrument must be in connection with the hedging of a specified risk, and will significantly reduce that risk, in accordance with the internal compliance programme, and the hedging activity must be subject to continuous review.[73] Also, the hedging activity cannot create any new or additional risk, or provide compensation that incentivizes prohibited proprietary trading.[74]

Other permitted activities

Finally, in addition to the three major permitted activities, the Rule provides a carve-out for other permitted activities specifically listed therein.[75] A few examples of such permitted activities include purchases or sales of US government obligations (such as treasury or municipal bonds), and a banking entity's trading activities conducted, as a fiduciary, on a customer's behalf are exempt from the proprietary trading prohibition.[76] Two exemptions that are of particular importance, and thus worth greater discussion, are: purchases or sales of foreign government obligations, and foreign bank trading activities.

Purchases or sales of foreign government obligations are not prohibited, but the exemption is limited to two circumstances. First, transactions by US affiliates of foreign banking entities are permitted, but only if: (1) the foreign banking entity is organized under the laws of the government that issued the underlying obligation, and (2) the foreign banking entity is not owned or controlled by a US banking entity.[77] Second, activities by foreign affiliates of US banking entities are permitted, if: (1) the affiliate is a foreign bank or regulated securities dealer, (2) the affiliate is organized under the laws of the government that issued the underlying obligation, and (3) the affiliate owns the obligation, and did not receive any financing for the transaction from the US entity.[78]

This is important because the foreign sovereign bond market is enormous, and banking institutions have been short-trading these bonds for years. As written, the exemption is easier for foreign bank affiliates in the US as they do not have the same financing limitations that have been placed on US banks' foreign affiliates (such as money can flow from a foreign bank into its US affiliate for the purpose of purchasing foreign government obligations, but money cannot flow out to a US bank's foreign affiliate for that same purpose).

The other exemption is provided to foreign banks that own or control affiliates in the US.[79] Generally, all foreign bank trading activity is permitted, but there are restrictions placed on the location and parties involved in the transaction. The restrictions are: (1) the trading activity must be conducted outside the US, (2) financing for the transaction cannot be provided by a US affiliate of the banking entity, (3) a US banking entity does not own the foreign bank, and (4) a US entity's foreign operations cannot, with some exceptions, be involved in the transaction.[80]

Invalid permitted activities

As a final note, any exemption from, or exception to, either of Volcker's prohibitions will be invalid if the activity would: (1) create a material conflict of interest between the banking entity and clients or counterparties, (2) materially expose the banking entity to high-risk assets or trading strategies, or (3) threaten the entity's safety and soundness or the US's financial stability.[81]

Covered funds activities

The second activity addressed by Congress was affiliations between banking entities and investment funds; but where the proprietary trading prohibition was a bullet targeted at a bull's-eye, speculative high-risk trading, the prohibition on affiliations with covered funds is a shotgun blast trying to hit as much of the target as possible. The prohibition was included so as to limit banks' exposure to covered funds, prevent banks from bailing out covered fund investors, and stop banks from using covered funds as a proprietary trading vehicle.[82]

Under this prohibition, banking entities may not acquire or retain an ownership interest in a covered fund, nor can banking entities sponsor such a fund.[83] A banking entity is deemed to have sponsored a fund if it served as a general partner, controlled a majority of the fund's directors, or shared the same name with the fund for marketing or promotional purposes.[84]

Exempt activities

The prohibition does not apply to such activities by a banking entity, in relation to a covered fund, when the banking entity is acting solely as a broker on behalf of a customer and the entity does not retain beneficial ownership.[85] Also, activities are exempt when the bank is acting in a fiduciary status on a customer's behalf and does not retain a beneficial ownership interest as long as the customer is not a covered fund.[86]

Entities considered to be covered funds

Because funds can take on many forms, the Rule lists three types of entities that are to be considered covered funds: investment companies, commodity pools, and foreign investment companies. Most funds are considered an investment company, which is any issuer that is engaged primarily in investing, reinvesting, or trading securities.[87] As it pertains to foreign investment companies, the exemption applies only to funds owned or sponsored by the banking entity if the ownership interests in the fund are offered and sold solely outside of the US.

The classification of a fund as covered, or not covered, can be worth millions, or even billions, of dollars to a bank. If the fund is covered, the banking entity may not own more than 3 per cent of the outstanding ownership interests in that fund.[88] Also, the bank cannot commit more than 3 per cent of its tier-1 capital to investments in covered funds.[89]

Funds exempt from definition of covered fund

Certain funds are exempt from being classified as a covered fund, with foreign public funds and loan securitization exemptions being the most significant out of the 14 listed below:[90]

1. Foreign public funds
2. Wholly owned subsidiaries
3. Joint ventures
4. Acquisition vehicles
5. Foreign pension or retirement plans
6. Insurance company separate accounts
7. Bank-owned life insurance
8. Loan securitizations
9. Qualifying asset-backed commercial paper conduits
10. Qualifying covered bonds
11. Small business investment company (SBIC) and public welfare investment funds
12. Registered investment companies and excluded entities
13. Issuers in conjunction with the FDIC's receivership or conservatorship operations
14. Other excluded issuers.

Foreign public funds are issuers established outside the US that are authorized to sell ownership interests, and do conduct sales of such ownership interests via public offerings outside the US. However, the exemption from covered status is invalidated if the ownership interest is sold to the sponsoring US banking entity, the fund itself, affiliates of such entities, or the directors thereof.[91]

The exemption for loan securitizations, and what it does not cover, is the most vehemently criticized portion in the second prohibition. Loan securitization vehicles are funds created to purchase loan packages from banks, bundle the assets, and then issue asset-backed securities. Banks' overleveraging in, and overreliance on, these funds is seen as one of the causes for the 2008 crisis; when the underlying assets defaulted the funds quickly failed, and banks heavily invested in them experienced enormous losses.

Now, a banking entity may acquire ownership interest or sponsor a loan securitization fund only if the fund holds four specific underlying assets: (1) loans, (2) securities that guarantee payment rights to asset holders, (3) interest rate and foreign exchange rate derivatives that reduce the risk of a related underlying asset, and (4) special units of beneficial interest.[92]

The language within the statute makes clear the exemption applies only when a fund's underlying assets are comprised solely of these instruments, causing uproar from the banking industry. The fight centres on collateralized debt obligations (CDOs), and, specifically, collateralized loan obligations (CLOs). A CDO is one form of an asset-backed security, wherein cash-generating assets are pooled together. The assets within the pool are divided into 'tranches', and each tranche contains assets of the same riskiness.

For example, a fund will create a CDO to purchase bulk loans or other debt instruments from banks, which sell to the vehicle to shift risk from the banks' books and get immediate capital for the loans. The CDO then divides the loans into tranches depending on the risk of the underlying loan. Once the loans have been divided into tranches, the vehicle will sell the loans' interest payment rights on the OTC market.

CLOs are similar to the mortgage-backed securities that were at the heart of the 2008 crisis, but, instead of home mortgages, the assets held by CLOs are business loans. These loans may be classified as a loan or a bond. Bonds are not a permitted asset. This distinction is important; if the fund holds primarily loans, but holds any amount of bonds as well, then the fund falls under the covered prohibition. In such a case, a bank must comply with the 3 per cent ownership limit, and will be required to divest any such interest over the 3 per cent threshold. Obviously, the US's biggest banks are fighting to exempt these CLOs due to their high profitability and the fees received for sponsoring such funds.[93]

Permitted activities

In addition, the Rule permits banking entities to provide limited services for covered funds. Generally, banking entities may offer and organize a covered fund and issuers of asset-backed securities, as well as perform underwriting and market-making activities. As to organizing and offering activities, the banking entity may not retain more than 3 per cent ownership in the fund, guarantee the fund's performance, and share the same name as the fund.[94]

Underwriting and market-making activities are permitted as long as the banking entity complies with the permitted proprietary trading activities requirements.[95] Finally, risk-mitigating hedging activities and covered fund activities outside of the US are exempted as well. These exemptions share many of the same requirements placed on such activities regarding proprietary trading activities.[96]

Potential repercussions for banking entities

Before discussing the potential impact the Volcker Rule will have, it is important to differentiate between the (1) banking entities discussed above that are subject to Volcker, and (2) foreign banks that are organized, and located, abroad and are not owned by US banking entities (such as foreign banking entities that are not subject to Volcker.) Banking entities subject to Volcker and foreign banks considering entering into the US financial system must weigh the increased compliance and opportunity costs against the profits to be gained.

Documentation and compliance

Volcker requires that any banking entity engaged in the prohibited activities, via exemption or exception, must comply with extensive documentation and compliance standards.

All such banking entities must develop and implement an internal compliance programme that contains written policies and procedures to document, describe, and monitor the prohibited activities.[97] In addition, the programme must require: internal monitoring and compliance controls, independent testing and auditing of the compliance programme, management review of the programme, employee compliance training, and that records be kept for at least five years and be available upon a regulator's request.[98]

Also, Volcker includes additional reporting requirements depending on the size of the entity or the activity. US banking entities with consolidated assets of $50 billion or more must report the compliance programme documents every 30 days, and the threshold for reporting will drop to $10 billion in assets by 31 December 2016.[99] In the case of foreign banks with US operations, the requirement applies if the total assets minus liabilities of the US operation meets or exceeds the threshold.[100] Additionally, any entity engaged in covered funds activities (to be discussed below), with $10 billion in assets or more, must document the exemption for such activity.[101]

To illustrate this point, in 2014 the Office of the Comptroller estimated the aggregate compliance costs of the seven largest market making banks would surpass $4 billion over four years, with 88 per cent of the costs generated by market making and customer trading activities.[102] Remember, when conducting trades as a market maker the bank must ensure that the activity is designed so that it does not exceed the reasonably expected near term demand, and the bank must also maintain an internal compliance policy that sets trading limits and review procedures.[103]

The Volcker Rule's extraterritorial reach

Volcker's expansive extraterritorial reach will impact foreign banks with US operations, as well as those that do not. The impact will differ depending on this distinction, as the former will face higher regulatory costs than the latter. The following discussion will first consider the ramifications for foreign banks with US operations; then move on to highlight potential cost increases for all foreign banks, regardless of their presence in the US, who engage in proprietary trading and covered funds activities in non-US markets.

Foreign banks with US operations

As discussed above, the wide scope of the 'banking entity' definition covers all foreign banks owning a banking entity located in the US. Therefore, these banks will face the same documentation and compliance requirements, and the associated costs, as their US brethren.

As covered above, the compliance programme requires that all banking entities design and implement compliance and monitoring systems for every department involved in proprietary trading or covered funds activities.[104] Although many foreign banks' US affiliates do not hold $50 billion in net assets, by the end of 2016 the threshold will drop to $10 billion and many foreign banks will be subject to the additional reporting requirement.[105] The question remains whether foreign banks will be required to provide reports covering all non-US trading activity, but, if that is the case, the documentation cost will be enormous.

Additionally, it is important to remember that foreign banks without US affiliates will not experience these costs. Two interesting scenarios may occur because of this: (1) banks without US operations may be reticent to enter the US in the future, and (2) foreign banks with US operations may look to leave if costs make their ventures unprofitable.

Foreign banks solely outside the US

Generally, foreign banks located outside the US may conduct any activity without Volcker repercussions, but this generality has significant limitations.

Limited exemption for proprietary trading

The limitation that concerns foreign banks the most is the exemption from proprietary trading, and particularly with regard to transactions involving US banking entities. Strictly speaking, any proprietary trade conducted with or through a US banking entity, located in the US or abroad, would be subject to the prohibition unless one of three exceptions applies.

1. Proprietary trades made between a foreign bank and the foreign operations of a US entity – the proprietary trade is exempt if the personnel, of the US entity's foreign operations, involved in the transaction (such as individuals who arranged, negotiated, or executed the transaction) are not located in the US
2. The US entity, regardless of location, is an 'unaffiliated market intermediary' conducting the trade as the principal, and is promptly cleared.[106]
3. The US entity, regardless of location, is an unaffiliated market intermediary trading as an agent, and is conducted anonymously on an exchange then promptly cleared.[107]

Foreign banks may incur a heavy investigative burden in determining whether these exceptions apply. Remember, if a foreign bank inadvertently makes a proprietary trade with a US entity's foreign operation, that did not meet one of the above exceptions, then the foreign bank violated Volcker's first prohibition. Therefore, foreign banks need to conduct a multi-step investigation.

Step 1. The bank must determine whether the other party to the transaction is owned, controlled, or affiliated with a US banking entity.[108] If the trading partner is found to be a US entity's foreign operation, then further investigation is required to determine if an exception applies.

Presumably, banks engaged in such activity will incur this investigative cost for every new trading partner, and again, on occasion, to re-verify that ownership has not changed. This will become very expensive for banks engaged in high volumes of proprietary trading.

Step 2. If the US banking entity meets exception (2) or (3), then the inquiry is over. If that is not the case then the foreign bank must move on to Step 3.

Step 3. The foreign bank must determine whether the requirements for exception (1) are met (such as all of the personnel, of the US entity's foreign operation, involved in the transaction are located outside the US).[109]

This places an incredible burden on the foreign bank to know the operations of such trading partners. A single person located in the US would wipe out the exemption, and the bank may be required to divest the trade's underlying asset.[110] Researching a counter-party is a good business practice and a common occurrence; however, this requires that foreign banks know the location of every member on the counter-party's team.

378 *Legal issues in Asian investing*

This investigational imperative may lead to higher costs. For example, transaction costs will increase due to the human resources expended to perform investigations into each trading party. Furthermore, increased time spent on investigations may lead to decreased time trading, which is an opportunity cost. This opportunity cost, while difficult to measure, will particularly harm large, high-volume banks because more trades means more costs.

Limited exemption for covered funds activities

The covered fund exemption for foreign banks is straightforward. There is one problem, however, which is the requirement that any ownership interest in a covered fund must not be offered or sold to US residents.[111] The offering requirement is simple, but the 'sold to' language implies that foreign banks must investigate all potential purchasers of the offering. The cost of such an investigation will depend on the size of the offering, and the number of potential buyers.

Notes

1. This model is based in part on one developed by G. Dufey and T. Chung, "International Financial Markets: A Survey," R. Kuhn, ed., *International Finance and Investing* (1990): 6–8.
2. Dufey and Chung, 9.
3. "Fact Sheet," *International Organization of Securities Commissions*, accessed November 2013, www.iosco.org.
4. Ibid.
5. "About Us," *International Organization of Securities Commissions*, n.d., accessed 22 February 2014, http://www.iosco.org/about/.
6. Janet Austin, "IOSCO'S Multilateral Memorandum of Understanding Concerning Consultation, Cooperation and the Exchange of Information," *Criminal Law Forum* 23.4 (2012): 393–423.
7. Ibid.
8. "Fact Sheet."
9. IOSCO, "Multilateral Memorandum of Understanding Concerning Consultation and Cooperation and the Exchange of Information," May 2002, accessed http://www.iosco.org/library/pubdocs/pdf/IOSCOPD126.pdf. [hereinafter "MMoU"]
10. "MMoU," Paragraph 4.
11. "MMoU," Paragraph 4.
12. "Current Signatories and Members Listed," *International Organization of Securities Commissions*, accessed http://www.iosco.org/library/index.cfm?section=mou_siglist.
13. G. Palm and D. Walkovik, "United States – A Special Report," *Issuing Securities: A Guide to Securities Regulation Around the World, International Financial Law Review* 62 (July 1990, special supplement).
14. Palm and Walkovik, 63.
15. Palm and Walkovik, 63.
16. Palm and Walkovik, 65.
17. Palm and Walkovik, 65.
18. Palm and Walkovik, 77.
19. 4 Securities Act Rule 405; Exchange Act Rule 3b-4.
20. 17 C.F.R. § 249.220f (2003).
21. Howell E. Jackson and Eric J. Pan, "Regulatory Competition in International Securities Markets: Evidence from Europe in 1999 – Part I," *Business Lawyer* 56 (2001): 667.
22. Ibid., 666.
23. Palm and Walkovik, 70–1.
24. Palm and Walkovik, 71.
25. Ibid., 667.

26 Alternatively, the QIB can invest in securities of a company, which is owned entirely by one or more other QIBs.
27 Regulation S, 55 Fed. Reg. 18306, Executive Summary (2 May 1990), 17 C.F.R. Parts 200 and 230 (1993).
28 Ibid.
29 Regulation S, 55 Fed. Reg. 18306, (Background and Introduction) (2 May 1990), 17 C.F.R. Parts 200 and 230 (1993).
30 Regulation S, 55 Fed. Reg. 18306, (Background and Introduction) (2 May 1990), 17 C.F.R. Parts 200 and 230 (1993).
31 "Restatement of the Foreign Relations Law of the United States" (3rd ed. 1987).
32 "SEC v. Kasser," 548 F.2d 109, 114 (3rd Cir.), cert. denied, 431 U.S. 938 (1977); "ITT v. Vencap, Ltd.," 519 F.2d 1001 (2d Cir. 1975); "Leasco Data Processing Equipment Corp. v. Maxwell," 468 F.2d 1326 (2d Cir. 1972).
33 Consolidated Gold Fields Plc v. Minorco, S.A., 871 F.2d 252 (2d Cir. 19__), cert. dismissed, 110 S. Ct. 29 (1989); Des Brisay v. Goldfield Corp., 549 F.2d 133 (9th Cir. 1977); Schoenbaum v. Firstbrook, 405 F.2d 200, rev'd on other grounds, 405 F.2d 215 (2d Cir. 1968) (en banc), cert. denied, 395 U.S. 906 (1969).
34 Regulation S, 55 Fed. Reg. 18306, (Executive Summary) (May 2, 1990), 17 C.F.R. Parts 200 and 230 (1993). See also Preliminary Note 5 to Regulation S.
35 Regulation S, 55 Fed. Reg. 18306, (Executive Summary) (May 2, 1990), 17 C.F.R. Parts 200 and 230 (1993).
36 Regulation S, 55 Fed. Reg. 18306, (Executive Summary) (May 2, 1990), 17 C.F.R. Parts 200 and 230 (1993).
37 Regulation S, 55 Fed. Reg. 18306, (Executive Summary) (May 2, 1990), 17 C.F.R. Parts 200 and 230 (1993).
38 The issuer safe harbour also applies to affiliates of issuers and distributors, and persons acting on behalf of any of issuers and distributors.
39 Regulation S, 17 C.F.R. Section (1993).
40 It should be observed that once the initial offering of securities is completed, a distributor ceases to be a 'distributor' for purposes of Regulation S (except for any portion of the securities that is unsold in the primary market). At that juncture, the former distributor can rely on the resale safe harbour with respect to secondary market transactions.
41 In addition, to qualify under this safe harbour, officers and directors of the issuer or distributor must not receive a selling fee, other than a usual and customary brokerage commission.
42 SEC Internationalization Report, II-69.
43 C. Mooney, Jr., "Beyond Negotiability: A New Model for Transfer and Pledge of Interests in Securities Controlled by Intermediaries," *Cardozo Law Review* 12 (1990): 305, 316.
44 "Clearance and Settlement Reform: The Stock, Options, and Futures Markets Are Still At Risk," *U.S. General Accounting Office*, Publication GAO/GGD-90-33, 10 (April 1990).
45 Mooney, 317.
46 "Clearance and Settlement Reform."
47 Robert F. Weber, "New Governance, Financial Regulation, and Challenges to Legitimacy: The Example of the Internal Models Approach to Capital Adequacy Regulation," *Administrative Law Review* 62 (2010): 783–93.
48 Weber, 787.
49 Weber, 789.
50 'Shadow banking, as usually defined, comprises a diverse set of institutions and markets that, collectively, carry out traditional banking functions – but do so outside, or in ways only loosely linked to, the traditional system of regulated depository institutions. Examples of important components of the shadow banking system include securitization vehicles, asset-backed commercial paper (ABCP) conduits, money market mutual funds, markets for repurchase agreements (repos), investment banks, and mortgage companies. Before the crisis, the shadow banking system had come to play a major role in global finance.' Ben Bernanke, "Some Reflections on the Crisis and the Policy Response," 2012, accessed 17 April 2014, http://www.federalreserve.gov/newsevents/speech/bernanke20120413a.htm.

380 *Legal issues in Asian investing*

51 Basel III is a voluntary international agreement, among the Members of the Basel Committee on Banking Supervision, that set capital, liquidity, and leverage ratio requirements; Dodd–Frank Act, Pub.L. 111–203, July 21, 2010, 124 Stat. 1376.
52 'Systemic risks are developments that threaten the stability of the financial system as a whole and consequently the broader economy, not just that of one or two institutions.' Corey Boles, "Bernanke Offers Broad Definition of Systemic Risk," *Wall Street Journal, Real Time Economics blog* (2009), accessed 19 April 2014, http://blogs.wsj.com/economics/2009/11/18/bernanke-offers-broad-definition-of-systemic-risk/.
53 Final Rule Subparts B and C. Because changes to the Rule are ongoing, this paper analyses the Final Rule as adopted on 10 December, 2013.
54 Richard Scott Carnell, Jonathan R. Macey, and Geoffrey P. Miller, *The Law of Financial Institutions, Aspen Casebook Series*, 5th ed. (Netherlands: Wolters Kluwer Law and Business, 2013).
55 David H. Carpenter and M. Maureen Murphy, "Permissible Securities Activities of Commercial Banks Under the Glass–Steagall Act (GSA) and the Gramm–Leach–Bliley Act (GLBA)," *Congressional Research Service* (2010): 10, 11, accessed 16 April 2014, http://assets.opencrs.com/rpts/R41181_20100412.pdf.
  The Banking Act of 1933 also prohibited: (1) directors and officers of a depository bank from holding positions as directors or officers of investment banks, and (2) investment banks from accepting deposits. These two provisions, along with the two mentioned above, are typically the focus when "Glass–Steagall" is used.
56 Ibid., 25.
57 Whether the Rule will actually protect against systemic risk, or not, is hotly debated. For a summation of both sides' arguments please see: (1) Darrell Duffie, "Market Making Under the Proposed Volcker Rule," *Rock Center for Corporate Governance at Stanford University Working Paper No. 106*, (2012). [Arguing that cap. requirements and more intensive government oversight is sufficient]; and (2) Matthew Richardson, "Why the Volcker Rule Is a Useful Tool for Managing Systemic Risk," *NYU Stern School of Business*, accessed 10 April 2014, https://www.sec.gov/comments/s7-41-11/s74111-316.pdf (countering Duffie, and asserting that Volcker, in conjunction with cap. requirements, is needed).
58 12 U.S.C. 1851(b); the Volcker Rule regulations are in 12 CFR 44, 248, 351 and 17 CFR 255; Section 13 was added to the BHC Act by Section 619, an amendment to Dodd–Frank.
59 76 FR 68845, accessed 17 April 2014, http://www.gpo.gov/fdsys/pkg/FR-2011-11-07/pdf/2011-27184.pdf; Craig Torres and Cheyenne Hopkins, "Bernanke Says Dodd-Frank's Volcker Rule Won't Be Ready by July 21 Deadline," *Bloomberg*, 2012, accessed 17 April 2014, http://www.bloomberg.com/news/2012-02-29/bernanke-says-dodd-frank-s-volcker-rule-won-t-be-ready-by-july-21-deadline.html; "Joint press release, Agencies Issue Final Rules Implementing the Volcker Rule," accessed 10 April 2014, http://www.federalreserve.gov/newsevents/press/bcreg/20131210a.htm. [The Final Rule was jointly enacted by the Federal Reserve Board, CFTC, SEC, FDIC, and OCC].
60 Final Rule § 2(c).
61 12 U.S.C. 1813(c). An Affiliate is 'any company that controls, is controlled by, or is under common control with another company'. 12 U.S.C. 1841(k). Subsidiary is defined as any company in which: (1) 25 per cent or more ownership interest is owned or controlled by a BHC, (2) a majority of the directors may be elected by the BHC, or (3) its management policies are controlled or influenced by the BHC. 12 U.S.C. 1841(d).
62 Ibid. at 3 (a), (b), and (c). A financial instrument is a security, derivative or option on such; but does not include loans or commodities (if they are not prohibited under (c)(2)(ii)(A)-(D)). id. at (c). If the banking entity is a dealer, swap dealer, or security-based swap dealer, then trading account means: any account used to purchase or sale of financial instruments for any purpose in connection with the entity's activity as a dealer, etc. id. at (b)(1)(iii).
63 Paul Volcker, "Commentary on the Restrictions on Proprietary Trading by Insured Depository Institutions," 2012, accessed 4 April 2014, http://online.wsj.com/public/resources/documents/Volcker_Rule_Essay_2-13-12.pdf.
64 Charles K. Whitehead, "The Volcker Rule and Evolving Financial Markets," *Harvard Business Law Review* 1, No. 42 (2011), 39–73; Cornell Legal Studies Research Paper No. 11–9.

65 Julie A. D. Manasfi, "Systemic Risk and Dodd–Frank's Volcker Rule," *William and Mary Business Law Review* 4 (2013): 181, 195.
66 'In most contexts, "liquidity" is defined as financial instruments that are inherently safe, short-term, and readily turned into cash with little risk of loss (such as, Treasury Bills). "Market liquidity", defined as the ease of trading any financial (or even non-financial) instrument, is more intangible, and depends upon the particular circumstances'. Paul Volcker, "Commentary on the Restrictions on Proprietary Trading by Insured Depository Institutions," 2012, accessed 4 April 2014, http://online.wsj.com/public/resources/documents/Volcker_Rule_Essay_2-13-12.pdf.
67 Underwriting is the process wherein a bank syndicate bundles the collective funds of the member banks, purchases a full stock issuance from the corporation, breaks the bundle down into small packages that are easier to sell, and sells the individual packages of stock on the secondary market.
68 Final Rule § 4(a)(2). Position may be defined as: 'The amount of a security either owned (which constitutes a long position) or borrowed (which constitutes a short position) by an individual or by a dealer. In other words, it's a trade an investor currently holds open.' *Investopedia*, accessed 10 April 2014, http://www.investopedia.com/terms/p/position.asp.
69 Zvi Bodie, Alex Kane, and Alan J. Marcus, *Essentials of Investment*, 5th ed. (New York, NY: McGraw-Irwin/Hill, 2004), 68.
70 Final Rule § 4(b)(2).
71 Ibid.; Essentials of Investment, 51.
72 Lee Sheppard, "The Loopholes in the Volcker Rule," *Forbes*, 8 January 2014, accessed 29 March 2014, http://www.forbes.com/sites/leesheppard/2014/01/08/the-loopholes-in-the-volcker-rule/2/.
73 Final Rule § 5(b)(2).
74 Ibid., (b)(3).
75 Ibid., 6(a)-(e).
76 Ibid., (a), (c).
77 Ibid., (b)(1).
78 Ibid., (b)(2).
79 For this section, foreign bank means: (A) a qualifying banking organization under (12 CFR 211.23(a), (c) or (e)), or (B) a banking organization that meets one of the two following requirements: (1) total assets of the banking entity held outside of the United States exceed total assets of the banking entity held in the United States, (2) total revenues derived from the business of the banking entity outside of the United States exceed total revenues derived from the business of the banking entity in the United States; or (3) total net income derived from the business of the banking entity outside of the United States exceeds total net income derived from the business of the banking entity in the United States. id. at (e)(2)(A),(B).
80 Ibid., (e)(1)-(3); The exceptions: (A) all personnel of the US banking entity's foreign operation involved in the transaction must be located outside the US, (B) the purchase or sale is conducted with an unaffiliated market intermediary acting as principal, and is promptly cleared, or (C) the purchase or sale is conducted through an unaffiliated market intermediary acting as an agent, if done so anonymously on an exchange and promptly cleared. id. at (e)(3).
81 Ibid., 7, 15 [Pertaining to proprietary trading and covered fund activities, respectively].
82 Daniel K. Tarullo, "Testimony on Volcker Rule, Before the Committee on Financial Services," US House of Representatives, Washington, DC, 2014, accessed 10 March 2014, http://www.federalreserve.gov/newsevents/testimony/tarullo20140205a.htm; ". . . the Volcker rule's prohibition on hedge fund investments was never meant to bar the banking sector from investing in any type of fund. Rather, the Volcker rule's prohibition on banking entities investing in hedge funds was meant to be a prophylactic against evasion of the Volcker rule's prohibition on proprietary trading," Thomas Reuters Accelus, Regulators have several options in dealing with CLOs under Volcker rule – law firm analysis, (2014). Accessed 10 March 2014, http://blogs.reuters.com/financial-regulatory-forum/2014/02/20/regulators-have-several-options-in-dealing-with-clos-under-volcker-rule-law-firm-analysis/. (Article quoted Margaret Tayhar, Davis Polk, and Wardwell.)
83 Final Rule § 10(a).
84 Ibid., (d)(9).

85 Ibid., (a)(2)(i).
86 Ibid., (a)(2)(iv).
87 Ibid., (b)(1)(i); 15 U.S.C. 80a-3(a)(1)(A).
88 Ibid., 12(a)(2)(ii)(A).
89 Ibid., 12(a)(2)(ii)(B).
90 Ibid., 10(c)(1)-(14).
91 Ibid., (c)(1); As it pertains to foreign public funds: public offering means any distribution of securities outside of the United States to investors, provided that the distribution complies with the laws of the country in which the distribution occurred, the distribution does not have a minimum net worth restriction for investors, and the issuer has filed publicly available disclosure documents that comply with the laws of the country in which the issue was distributed. id. at (c)(iii).
92 Ibid., 10(c)(8).
93 Jesse Eisinger, "In Banking Overhaul Fight, a Ruckus Over an Obscure Product," *NY Times DealBook*, 2014, accessed 5 April 2014, at http://dealbook.nytimes.com/2014/03/05/a-banking-ruckus-not-many-follow-or-even-understand/?_php=true&_type=blogs&_r=0.; (71 percent of the CLO market is held by J.P. Morgan-Chase, Citigroup, and Wells Fargo). id.
94 Final Rule § 11(a), (b).
95 Ibid., (c).
96 Ibid., (a), (b).
97 Final Rule § 20(a).
98 Ibid., (b). Entities with less than ten billion in assets may satisfy the reporting requirements of § 20 by including references to requirements contained in section 13 of the BHC Act. id. (f)(2).
99 Ibid., (d)(1)(i).
100 Ibid., (d)(1)(ii).
101 Ibid., (e).
102 "Analysis of 12 CFR Part 44," OCC, 2014, accessed 5 April 2014, http://www.complinet.com/net_file_store/new_editorial/v/o/volcker-analysis.pdf.
103 Ibid., Footnotes, 29, 30.
104 Ibid.
105 Ibid.
106 Ibid., Footnote, 42.
107 Ibid.
108 Ibid.
109 Ibid.
110 Ibid.
111 Ibid., Footnotes, 14–19.

12 Overview of international banking law

12.1 Defining 'international banking' activities

How a foreign bank, in terms of its organizational form, enters a host-country market has significant implications. That form, or mode of entry, determines (*inter alia*) the activities in which it can engage, its capital requirements (if any), and the specific regulatory authorities to which it must answer. By using the US as a host market, this chapter identifies the features, benefits, shortcomings, and regulatory implications of each entry mode. This chapter lists each mode from least penetrative (correspondent relationships and representative offices) to most penetrative and concentrated (wholly owned subsidiaries and *Edge Act Corporations*).[1] Accordingly, each entry mode is outlined below. Regulatory details, such as the differences between home versus host regulation, activity regulation, safety and soundness, and capital adequacy, are discussed later in this chapter.

Mode 1: correspondent relationship

In a correspondent relationship, banks hold deposit accounts with one another. The accounts, otherwise known as *Nostro* and *Vostro* accounts, are 'owned' by a domestic bank, and held at a foreign bank. '*Nostro*' refers to 'our' account with 'you', while '*Vostro*' means 'your' account with 'us'. They are two sides of the same coin, as it were: from the perspective of the account holder, it has a *Nostro* account; from the perspective of the account-holding bank, it holds a *Vostro* account.[2]

Correspondent accounts are held by a foreign bank for the purpose of making payments to an inhabitant of the foreign country in the currency of that foreign country.[3] For example, Intrust Bank in Wichita, Kansas may hold a correspondent bank account with the Hong Kong Shanghai Banking Corporation (HSBC) in Hong Kong so that Intrust can make and receive payments in Hong Kong (as distinct from the US) dollars. In another illustration, Intrust might use the Agricultural Bank of China in Beijing as its correspondent for payments in Chinese Renminbi.

Generally speaking, one correspondent is not responsible for the actions of the other correspondent;[4] that is, the relationship is account-driven. So, the terms of the account, and the law of the country governing the account, which typically is the host country (such as the laws of the jurisdiction in which the foreign bank holds the account[5] – Hong Kong and China in the above illustrations), determine the rights and obligations of the correspondents.

384 *Legal issues in Asian investing*

Mode 2: representative office

A representative office is meant to 'drum up businesses' for foreign offices.[6] That is, the purpose of a representative office is to attract banking business to its parent bank from banks, non-banks, and individuals in the foreign jurisdiction in which the representative office is located. Representative offices of foreign banks do not take loans or deposits in the US. Indeed, they are not to do so under relevant banking law, because they are not chartered as a branch or agency.[7]

Generally, under US law, a representative office has a choice to become federally or state-chartered. A foreign institution may only operate a representative office in a state that allows them.[8] But, regardless of charter type, these offices are quite restricted in the range of permissible activities. One example of an activity in which they can engage is to be an international loan production office (LPO).[9] Essentially, an LPO is responsible for growing the business of the bank without taking deposits or loans. They accept loan applications and arrange financing agreements but they *never* approve loans. Loans are always approved at the foreign bank's main office or by an underwriter. The activities of the loan production office cannot be so broad as to constitute the normal business of banking.[10] Of course, US supervisors have jurisdiction over a representative office of a foreign bank in the US, but they have little jurisdiction over the general banking activities of the parent, or home entity of the representative office.

An example of a representative office, the International Bank of Azerbaijan from Baku, Azerbaijan, holds a representative office in New York. Under the 1991 *Foreign Bank Supervision Act* (as amended by the *International Banking Act*) the bank had to receive approval from both the Federal Reserve Board and the New York Department of Financial Services before operating the representative office. The International Bank of Azerbaijan cannot take deposits or make loans to US citizens using its representative office; their representatives may, however, direct them to the main office in Baku to complete these activities.

In 1984 Citibank opened a representative office in Beijing. That representative office eventually upgraded to full branch in 1995. The upgrade illustrates the typical foreign bank entry strategy.[11]

Mode 3: agencies

The 1978 *International Banking Act* (IBA), 12 U.S.C. § 3101, defines an agency as

> any office or any place of business of a foreign bank located in any state of the United States at which credit balances are maintained incidental to or arising out of the exercise of banking powers, checks are paid, or money is lent but at which deposits may not be accepted from citizens or residents of the United States.[12]

Federal- and state-chartered agencies may engage in many common banking powers, such as making loans, issuing letters of credit, exchanging foreign currency, and maintaining credit deposits.[13]

Agencies may not take *retail* deposits from domestic customers or the general public.[14] With no US retail account holders, the public is not at risk of problems, such as capital inadequacy, which might exist in the agency or its foreign bank parent. Likewise, the US taxpayer is not at risk for having to bail out a failed or failing agency, as no deposit insurance from the Federal Deposit Insurance Corporation (FDIC) protection is given to that agency.[15]

However, some states, such as New York, allow domestic deposits over US$100,000, meaning that large customers can deposit funds in the agency of a foreign bank. Federal supervisors treat such banks as branches.[16] That is because a purpose of an agency is to facilitate transfers of funds for business customers, making payments in the host country denominated in the currency of the host country. Note that such state rules help attract foreign banking business, which complements underlying international trade transactions. Simply put, then, the account holders at the US agency of a foreign bank often are business customers, typically foreign, engaged in import–export transactions. In that sense, it can be said that agencies are permitted to take deposits only from foreign account holders.

For example, suppose a US buyer of textile and apparel (T&A) items, such as Nordstrom Department Store, orders merchandise from a Vietnamese supplier. Nordstrom needs to pay the Vietnamese importer, which is located in Los Angeles, for those items. If this importer has an account with the agency of a Vietnamese bank, perhaps located in California, then Nordstrom may remit a dollar-denominated payment directly to that agency. Then, the agency can credit the account of the importer for the payment and, if necessary, record an in-house transfer of funds to the affiliate of the importer (e.g., its parent producer-exporter) in Vietnam.

Generally, an agency is not considered a separate entity from its home-country operator such as its parent. Usually, the agency must receive a license from its home country to operate in the host country, as well as get approval – such as receive a charter – from the relevant host-country supervisor.[17]

Mode 4: branches

The 1978 IBA, 12 U.S.C.A. § 3101, defines branch as any office or any place of business of a foreign bank located in any state of the US at which deposits are received.[18] A foreign bank establishes a branch in a host country when it seeks to practise a majority of 'normal' banking activities with domestic clients. 'Normal' banking activities include taking deposits and making loans in local (such as host-country) currency, and engaging in other activities permitted to a domestic bank, such as offering certain kinds of investment accounts and services, and security deposit boxes.[19] In the US, a branch may be chartered by the Board of Governors of the Federal Reserve System, Office of the Comptroller of Currency (OCC), which is the Department of the Treasury, or an individual state banking authority.

A branch is considered a 'part and parcel' of a foreign bank and is not a separate entity from that parent. So, the entire asset base of the foreign bank, whether located in the home country of the bank, the host country of the branch, or a third country, back up branch liabilities of that bank. Capital, equity, and financial soundness are also measured on an international, bank-wide basis, rather than through only its host-country operations.[20]

Of course, to speak of the 'liabilities' of the branch, when it has no assets separate from its parent, is rather artificial. Nevertheless, it is common, if technically misleading, parlance. Indeed, bank supervisors speak in these terms when they consider plans or rules to 'ring-fence' the 'assets' of a branch in a host country to ensure that there are some to cover the 'liabilities' of the branch. Indeed, host-country regulators are somewhat at the mercy of their counterparts in the home country, such as at the nature and quality of their supervision of the parent foreign bank and all its worldwide operations. A key issue in anticipation of problems at a foreign bank, or a banking crisis, concerns host country jurisdiction: to what extent is it limited to the activity regulation of a branch, and to what extent does it include isolating 'assets' of the branch to deal with the 'insolvency' of the branch? In other words, is the 'bankruptcy' of a branch a meaningful concept, and if so, what are the legal and policy implications?[21]

This type of problem arose with the 5 July 1991 closure of the Bank of Credit and Commerce International (BCCI).[22] Incorporated in Luxembourg, it had its corporate or operational nerve centre in London, and was active in around 72 countries through a network of branches, agencies, representative offices, and subsidiaries. Like the problem in any bankruptcy of creditors racing against one another to seize assets of a defaulting debtor as quickly as they can to realize the funds owed to them, national bank supervisors were sorely tempted to ring-fence assets of the BCCI in their jurisdictions. But, as with the creditor asset race problem, had they done so, the overall pool of BCCI assets available for payment to depositors and creditors worldwide would have been depleted quickly, with many left unpaid or reimbursed in unfairly low amounts. Fortunately, the BCCI closure was a coordinated regulatory action, with most bank supervisors acting in concert, and agreeing on a global consolidation of BCCI assets and payout scheme, administered by a major private accounting firm.[23]

An example of branching occurs when the Bank of China operates a branch out of New York City. In order to comply with capital adequacy and leverage standards set by US regulators, the bank's entire operation is reviewed and must comply with these standards. Furthermore, if that branch wishes to take retail deposits in the US, it must be FDIC insured. In order to be FDIC insured, the Bank of China must own a subsidiary in the US. If the Bank of China wishes to only branch in the US without owning a US subsidiary, it may still do so, but it may only participate in domestic 'wholesale' deposit taking.[24]

Mode 5: subsidiaries

A foreign bank or foreign bank holding company (BHC) may have a controlling interest or wholly own a subsidiary in a host country. These subsidiaries are subject to the same rules and regulations as domestic banks.[25] To use the International Trade Law term, they are accorded 'national treatment' by the host-country supervisor, meaning they are treated no less favourably than their domestic counterparts. Technically, under the World Trade Organization (WTO) *General Agreement on Trade in Services* (*GATS*) (discussed below), whether the host-country supervisor accords national treatment under Article XVI of that *Agreement* depends on whether that country has committed to doing so.[26]

A foreign bank subsidiary may be subject to additional safety and soundness rules, activity limitations, and capital adequacy standards, which the host country sets for and applies to foreign, but not domestic, institutions. Such differences would be listed in the WTO Schedule of Concessions of that country, pursuant to its GATS national treatment commitments.[27]

Like any responsible banking authority, US bank supervisors are concerned with the safety and soundness of the foreign bank parent of a subsidiary in the US. They care about the far-flung, non-US activities of the parent. Their concern is based on the Source of Strength Doctrine. This Doctrine holds that the strength of a parent determines whether it will be able to inject more capital and save a faulting subsidiary, or put differently, the key source of the strength of a subsidiary is its parent. Weakness in the parent may have

Overview of international banking law 387

a contagion effect on the subsidiary. Further, a weak foreign parent may try to 'loot' the capital of a local subsidiary. Despite this concern, the safety and soundness of a foreign parent is not within the direct regulatory control of the host country. The ultimate remedy of a host-country supervisor may be to disallow continued operations of the subsidiary, but that remedy may put it at odds with the home-country authority, and compel it to expend taxpayer-financed bailout funds.[28]

An example of such an arrangement occurs when the Sumitomo Mitsui Financial Group, one of Japan's largest financial institutions, purchased Manufacturers Bank, an insured California state, non-member bank located in Los Angeles, California. Not only is Manufacturers Bank subject to the full supervisory authority of state and federal supervisors, the Sumitomo Mitsui Financial Group, although incorporated in Japan, must still comply with requirements set by the Federal Reserve Board for foreign financial holding companies operating in the US or risk losing its ability to operate branches and subsidiaries in the US.[29]

Mode 6: Edge Act Corporations

Under Section 211.5 of Federal Reserve Regulation K, codified at 12 CFR 211, the Federal Reserve Board may approve and establish an Edge Act Corporation for the sole purpose of participating in international banking.[30] The Federal Reserve Board receives applications from both US banks and foreign banking organizations (often simply called 'FBOs'), and examines Edge Act Corporations and their subsidiaries. The Act itself is named after New Jersey Senator Walters Evans Edge, and was enacted by Congress in 1919. The basic purpose of the legislation is:

> [T]o afford to the United States exporter and importer in particular, and to United States commerce, industry, and agriculture in general, at all times a means of financing international trade, especially United States exports; to foster the participation by regional and smaller banks throughout the United States in the provision of international banking and financing services to all segments of United States agriculture, commerce, and industry, and, in particular small business and farming concerns; to stimulate competition in the provision of international banking and financing services throughout the United States; and, in conjunction with each of the preceding purposes, to facilitate and stimulate the export of United States goods, wares, merchandise, commodities, and services to achieve a sound United States international trade position.[31]

So, an Edge Act Corporation can accept deposits as well as make loans, but only if these functions are specifically related to international transactions.[32] In effect, they are rather narrow financial vehicles, in terms of the activities that they can or cannot undertake. The quintessential example of such transactions would be international trade in goods or services. Edge Act Corporations are not required to comply with state banking laws, a not insignificant alleviation of regulatory burden.[33] Furthermore, Section 632 provides federal court jurisdiction for suits involving Edge Act banks.[34]

An Edge Act Corporation may not participate in the trade of commodities or invest in Edge Corporations investing in foreign companies that engage in the general business of buying or selling goods, wares, merchandise, or commodities in the US. In addition, an Edge Corporation may not invest in foreign companies that transact any business in the

US that is not, in the Board's judgement, 'incidental' to its international or foreign business. The latter limitation also applies to investments by BHCs.[35]

A federally chartered bank is prohibited from investing more than 10 per cent of its surplus and capital in Edge Act Corporations, or 20 per cent with Federal Reserve Board approval.[36] The definitions of capital and surplus are discussed further in the capital adequacy section of this chapter.

12.2 International bank supervision and Basel Committee

The Basel Committee on Banking Supervision

The Basel Committee on Banking Supervision requires home and host-country governments to adopt standards to supervise and monitor the activities of international banks.[37] Bank supervisors are those in regulatory agencies charged under applicable domestic law responsible for the safety and soundness of their financial systems. Central to safety and soundness are monitoring and enforcement of prudential rules concerning capital adequacy, the nature of permissible activities, and the location of those activities.[38] That the focus of the Basel Committee is on international banks is sensible enough, as those banks by definition operate across borders, tend to be large, and frequently engage in high-value, high-volume transactions. So, because of them, or through them, systemic risks arise or are transmitted, threatening the safety and soundness of not only the financial systems in which they operate, but also other systems linked to their direct spheres of operation.

History

The Basel Committee works in conjunction with the Bank of International Settlements (BIS). The BIS has a long and intriguing history dating back to 1930. Initially, it was established to facilitate war reparation payments under the 1919 *Treaty of Versailles* by the Weimar Republic to the victorious Allied Powers.[39]

The Basel Committee was formed by the central bank governors of the G10 countries after the breakdown of the Bretton Woods systems of managed exchanged rates collapsed and the Franklin National Bank of New York failed in 1973.[40]

The Committee drafted the *Basel Concordat* in 1975. The committee 'sought to close gaps in international supervisory coverage so that (i) no foreign banking establishment would escape supervision; and (ii) that supervision would be adequate and consistent across member jurisdictions'. The Concordat created supervisory standards that supervisors and central banks may follow.[41]

The Committee meets about three to four times per year. Its decisions are not legally binding but are extremely persuasive. The Committee seeks to create a unified and common system by recommending supervisory right standards and best provinces and providing guidance to central banks and supervisors.[42] The Committee introduces new supervisory and capital frameworks in 'rounds' known as Basel I, Basel II, and Basel III. Each 'round' represents an evolving understanding of the relationship between supervisors, capital requirements, and banking risks.[43]

Basel I, known as the *Basel Capital Accord of 1988*, primarily focused on capital adequacy standards. The Committee used a *weighted risk* approach to measuring assets as well as including on-and off-balance sheet assets in its calculation of capital adequacy. The

Accord had several amendments from 1988 to 1997, which addressed measurements of loss reserves and focused on risks other than credit risk, such as market risk.[44]

Although groundbreaking, Basel I had its shortfalls. Basel I primarily and almost solely addresses credit risk (the risk of counter-party default) because it narrowly focuses on a static 8 per cent risk-based capital ratio. The framework does not address changing sources of risk such as systemic, market, or operational risks. Furthermore, it does not address who is the *lender of last resort* for failing banks, and it does not adequately address coordination of home-host regulators. Besides laying out the regulatory requirements and standards for capital adequacy, Basel I does little to account adequately for differing asset risks of institutional clients.[45]

Basel II began with a 1999 proposal for a new framework and concluded with a *Revised Capital Framework* in 2004. Basel II was finalized on 26 June 2004 and consisted of three pillars:

- *Pillar 1*: minimum capital requirements, which expands on the Basel I rules. The committee sought to define asset risks more specifically. Large banks have the ability to use their own *internal risk assessments* to calculate credit risk.
- *Pillar 2*: supervisory review of an institution's capital adequacy and internal assessment processes. These rules require a regulator to intervene when a financial institution does not meet minimum standards.
- *Pillar 3*: strengthening market discipline by increasing transparency. A bank must disclose its capital adequacy and a regulator must adequately disclose its requirements.[46]

The 2008 economic and liquidity crisis revealed several problems with the Basel II framework. Basel II requirements may have 'amplified the business cycle'. In other words, during the 2007–09 credit crisis, banks, unable to raise equity, were forced to lend less. Decreased lending contributed to stagnant economic growth. Central banks felt the internal risk models used by larger banks did not accurately measure their exposure to risk. Using their own internally based risk assessments, banks have the incentive to underestimate credit risk in order to avoid capital requirements and gain a competitive advantage.[47] Banks felt the framework was 'too complex', its capital requirements 'discourage lending during economic downturns', create competitive disadvantages and shift capital investments to non-banking institutions. Furthermore, many critics believe internal risk models of Basel II are too 'general' and do not adjust to the needs of differing member countries.[48]

Basel III came at the wake of the liquidity and leverage crisis of 2008. Basel III began with the Committee's issuance of the *international framework for liquidity risk measurement, standards and monitoring*, in December 2010. Basel III introduces new capital buffers, a countercyclical capital buffer that protects against losses that occur during economic downturns and a capital conservation buffer that prohibits pay outs of earnings to under-capitalized institutions. These buffers ensure that banks have enough capital to continue lending during an economic downturn. The Committee also introduced new liquidity requirements based on bank stress testing and an overall leverage ratio requirement. Finally, the committee deemphasized external ratings for investments and bolstered its standards for internal asset risk assessments.

Basel III is meant to supplement Basel II. Since their frameworks share many of the same components, they share many of the same criticisms. First, many believe the use of risk-weighted assets creates a race for banks to find high-return, low-risk measured assets. As risk weighting is backward-looking, regulators assume an asset that was less risky in the past will be less risky in the future. Using their internal, risk-measuring processes, banks may identify assets that have a low-risk *measure* but these assets may in fact be risky. An example of this was the increased use of high-rated mortgage-backed securities by banks in the years leading up to the 2008 financial crisis.[49] Many regulators feel Basel III does not adequately raise capital adequacy ratios and does not provide enough sanctions to deter banks from drawing capital lower than the capital conservation buffer range.[50] Despite these criticisms, many have praised the committee's quick reaction to the financial crisis of 2008 and consider the new countercyclical measures and liquidity requirements as much needed additions to the framework.[51]

Members

After starting as a G10 body, the Committee expanded its membership in 2009 to 27 members. Basel Committee members are Argentina, Australia, Belgium, Brazil, Canada, China, France, Germany, Hong Kong SAR, India, Indonesia, Italy, Japan, Korea, Luxembourg, Mexico, the Netherlands, Russia, Saudi Arabia, Singapore, South Africa, Spain, Sweden, Switzerland, Turkey, the United Kingdom, and the US.[52] Countries are represented by their central bank and 'by the authority with formal responsibility for the prudential supervision of banking business' if this is not already the responsibility for the central bank.[53]

Supervisory activities

There is no overarching international bank regulatory authority, or any genuinely multilateral entity akin to the WTO that serves as a negotiating forum, and drafts, implements, and enforces rules. International Banking Law is less institutionally well-developed than International Trade Law. Neither the International Monetary Fund (IMF) nor the World Bank, with their limited scope and dubious records, come close to a grand, universally acclaimed, cross-border authority.

However, in the 1970s, the Basel Committee came of age as an international bank 'supervisor'. 'The Basel Committee on Banking Supervision provides a forum for regular cooperation on banking supervisory matters. Its objective is to enhance understanding of key supervisory issues and improve the quality of banking supervision worldwide'.[54]

As a direct response to the BCCI scandal, international banking regulators became very concerned with the allocation of supervisory authority among jurisdictions of home/host countries. Basel I countries set the minimum components of an effective international banking supervisor in its *Core Principles of Effective Banking Supervision*. The conditions are:

1 a clear, achievable and consistent framework of responsibilities and objectives set by legislation for (each of) the supervisor(s) involved, but with operational independence to pursue them free from political pressure and with accountability for achieving them;
2 adequate resources (including staffing, funding and technology) to meet the objectives set, provided on terms that do not undermine the autonomy, integrity and independence of the supervisory agency;

3 a framework of banking law that sets out minimum standards that banks must meet; allows supervisors sufficient flexibility to set prudential rules administratively, where necessary, to achieve the objectives set as well as to utilize qualitative judgment; provides powers to gather and independently verify information; and, gives supervisors power to enforce a range of penalties that may be applied when prudential requirements are not being met (including powers to remove individuals, invoke sanctions and revoke licenses); protection (normally in law) from personal and institutional liability for supervisory actions taken in good faith in the course of performing supervisory duties; and,
4 a system of interagency cooperation and sharing of relevant information among the various official agencies, both domestic and foreign, responsible for the safety and soundness of the financial system; this cooperation should be supported by arrangements for protecting the confidentiality of supervisory information and ensuring that it is used only for purposes related to the effective supervision of the institutions concerned.[55]

The Basel Committee also legitimized the application of capital requirements by host countries on their branches. Basel recommendations heavily focus on the imposition of capital adequacy standards that are discussed further in this section. Liquidity has also become a noteworthy topic. Agreed-upon measures include requiring branches to hold local liquid assets and making home and host supervisors jointly responsible for ensuring adequate branch liquidity.[56]

Basel has yet to resolve a myriad of questions mainly addressing home/host and jurisdictional issues. It has yet to address who is the lender of last resort, a question that has picked up greater steam in the wake of recent financial crisis. Basel has also not addressed home-host issues for securities regulations.[57]

12.3 Inbound bank supervisors

Dual banking system

Given its federal system of government, the US is characterized by a dual banking system. That means that regulatory authority is at two levels: central (federal), and sub-central (state). For the most part, federal regulators are the most important in respect of international banking transactions. Indeed, the 1978 IBA, 12 U.S.C. 3101–11, pre-empts state law, with the practical result that its purview, and that of its implementing regulation – Federal Reserve Regulation K – pre-empt state law, and take priority over any inconsistent state law.[58]

Five key supervisors

At the federal level, the US has five principal supervisors of note in respect of international banking transaction:

1 Federal Reserve Board, which is an independent agency of the US government, and the 12 Federal Reserve banks, which are instrumentalities of that agency.
2 OCC, which is part of the Department of the Treasury.
3 FDIC, which is an independent agency of the government.

4 Commodity Futures Trading Commission (CFTC), which is also an independent agency of the government.
5 Consumer Financial Protection Bureau (CFPB), which is an externally funded wing of the Federal Reserve Board created by the *Dodd–Frank Act*.[59]

The Federal Reserve Board is charged with supervising all state-chartered foreign branches and agencies, BHCs, FHCs, and Edge Act Corporations. The fact that the Board has authority over a BHC, pursuant to the *Bank Holding Company Act of 1956*, 12 U.S.C. 1841–52, gives the nation's central bank a 'bird's-eye' view of an entire banking organization. While other regulators focus on subsidiaries of a BHC, it is the Federal Reserve that exercises ultimate supervisory authority if for no other reason than problems in one part of a BHC can undermine the safety and soundness of other parts, or indeed of the entire BHC.[60]

Of additional importance to Federal Reserve authority is the 1991 *Foreign Bank Supervision Enhancement Act* (FBSEA), 12 USC 3101, which prohibits a foreign bank from establishing a branch, agency, or subsidiary anywhere in the US without prior consent of the Federal Reserve Board. The 1978 IBA and its key amendments in the 1991 *Federal Deposit Insurance Corporation Improvement Act* (FDICIA), the *Interstate Banking and Branching Efficiency Act* (IBBEA), the *Bank Holding Company Act* (BHCA), and the *National Bank Act* (NBA) pre-empt and exclude many state banking laws. The general policy of the US has been to provide national treatment to foreign financial institutions doing business in the US. Title II of the FBSEA drastically strengthened federal oversight of foreign bank operations in the US as well as upgraded the transparency of international supervisors. The act requires consent from the Federal Reserve Board before any foreign bank can establish a branch, agency, or subsidiary, regardless if it was charted federally or through a state. The Federal Reserve Board typically examines the operations of member banks, BHCs, FHCs, or Edge Act Corporations from the bank's US head office; however, the Federal Reserve Board will send examiners to foreign operations of US banks when appropriate; such examinations will be made in cooperation with foreign supervisors.[61]

The OCC is charged with licensing and examining federal agencies, limited federal branches, or federal branches. The OCC has direct supervisory authority over all federally chartered banks, regardless if the bank is foreign. In other words, the Federal Reserve Board has supervisory authority over the parent holding company while the OCC has direct supervisory authority over its federally chartered subsidiaries. Only an authorized OCC rep (or CFPB rep) may enter a nationally chartered bank for supervisory purposes. State regulators may only enter a national bank when seeking information as a direct result of a court action or suit arising out of the enforcement of state law.[62] The OCC's International Bank Supervision group directly deploys examiners to examine the international activities of globally active banks. And the OCC actively cooperates with many foreign supervisors.[63]

The FDIC was created by the Banking Act of 1933 because of the slew of depression-era bank runs and failures. The FDIC insures banks. It supervises, examines, and regulates all insured, state-chartered, non-member (as in non-members of the Federal Reserve Board) banks. The FDIC provides up to $250,000 of coverage for all combined, single-held accounts and other deposit categories at an institution. Federal deposit insurance shifts failure risk to the federal government in order to enhance macroeconomic stability, prevent bank runs, and minimize excessive risk-taking. For international banking purposes, the FDIC generally does not regulate many branches or foreign institutions because there are not many state-chartered foreign banks that are not members of the Federal Reserve Board. Federal deposit insurance is only provided to 'citizens, or residents of the US' or 'other legally cognizable entity created under the laws of the US or any state and having its principal place of business within the US or any state'. In other words, FDIC does not cover foreign individuals or entities who do not reside or do business in the US.[64]

The CFTC regulates the futures and options markets. The mission of the CFTC is to 'protect market users and the public from fraud, manipulation, and abusive practices related to the sale of commodity and financial futures and options, and to foster open, competitive, and financially sound futures and option markets'. The CFTC is relevant to Edge Act Corporations, FHCs and some foreign-owned subsidiaries that may own entities that practise activities other than those normally reserved for banking.[65]

The CFPB was created by the Dodd–Frank Act as a result of the economic crisis of 2008. Its goal is to ensure that all consumers have access to financial products and all services are fair, transparent, and competitive. The bureau assumed all responsibilities for regulating consumer protection laws in the consumer banking industry.[66] The CFPB is housed in the Federal Reserve, but is an independent division with its own statutory source of funding. The CFPB has regulatory authority over all federally regulated depository institutions and FDIC-insured institutions. It has *direct* supervisory authority over all institutions with over $10 billion dollars in assets and *limited* supervisory authority over all other FDIC insured institutions.[67] There is a clear distinction between *supervisory* and *regulatory* activities. Supervision involves monitoring, inspecting, and examining banking organizations while regulating involves interpreting, passing regulations, and guidelines.

In summary, US banking law is complex with multiple regulators (Federal Reserve Board, OCC, FDIC, individual state banking law, Bureau of Consumer Financial Protection).

12.4 Inbound regulations

Federal reserve board approval

The 1991 FBSEA requires consent from the Federal Reserve Board before any foreign bank can establish a branch, agency, or subsidiary, regardless if a bank is federally chartered or state charted. When considering an application, the Federal Reserve Board reviews the 'managerial' and 'financial resources' of a foreign bank. The Federal Reserve Board may also consider several discretionary standards, such as the consent of home-country supervisors, nature of the relationship between the Federal Reserve Board and home country regulators, compliance with US laws, public need, size of the banks, and 'additional conditions as the Fed deems necessary'.[68]

Activities regulation (permissible activities)

The FBSEA gives the OCC general authority to examine all federal branches of a foreign bank. The FBSEA also attempts to eliminate possible competitive advantages available to state-chartered branches as opposed to federally chartered branches by pre-empting any state law favourable to state chartered banks.[69] The Act requires at least one onsite examination by either the Federal Reserve Board, OCC, FDIC, or state regulator in a 12-month period.[70]

The BHCA and section 8(a) of the International Banking Act list the permissible activities of a foreign branch, agency, or commercial lending company doing business in the US.[71] Foreign subsidiaries and branches, much like US depository institutions, are restricted to activities 'closely related to banking'.[72]

Under the BHCA a foreign holding company operating in the US may not hold:

1. shares of any company engaged or to be engaged solely in one or more of the following activities: (A) holding or operating properties used wholly or substantially by any banking subsidiary of such bank holding company in the operations of such banking subsidiary or acquired for such future use; or (B) conducting a safe deposit business; or (C) furnishing services to or performing services for such bank holding company or its banking subsidiaries; or (D) liquidating assets acquired from such bank holding company or its banking subsidiaries or acquired from any other source prior to 9 May 1956, or the date on which such company became a bank holding company, whichever is later;

   . . .

4. shares held or acquired by a bank in good faith in a fiduciary capacity;

   . . .

6. shares of any company which do not include more than 5 per centum of the outstanding voting shares of such company;

   . . .

7. shares of an investment company which is not a bank holding company and which is not engaged in any business other than investing in securities, which securities do not include more than 5 per centum of the outstanding voting shares of any company;

8. shares of any company the activities of which had been determined by the Board by regulation or order under this paragraph as of the day before 12 November 1999, to be so closely related to banking as to be a proper incident thereto (subject to such terms and conditions contained in such regulation or order, unless modified by the Board);

9. shares held or activities conducted by any company organized under the laws of a foreign country the greater part of whose business is conducted outside the United States, if the Board by regulation or order determines that, under the circumstances and subject to the conditions set forth in the regulation or order, the exemption would not be substantially at variance with the purposes of this chapter and would be in the public interest;

   . . .

13. shares of, or activities conducted by, any company which does no business in the United States except as an incident to its international or foreign business, if the Board by regulation or order determines that, under the circumstances and subject to the conditions set forth in the regulation or order, the exemption would not be substantially at variance with the purposes of this chapter and would be in the public interest; or

14. shares of any company which is an export trading company whose acquisition (including each acquisition of shares) or formation by a bank holding company has not been disapproved by the Board pursuant to this paragraph, except that such investments, whether direct or indirect, in such shares shall not exceed 5 per centum of the bank holding company's consolidated capital and surplus.[73]

The 'closely related to banking' rule applies to the foreign and domestic activities of banking and non-banking affiliates. Some notable exceptions to the 'closely related to banking' rule include a grandfather exception applied to foreign banks lawfully engaged in non-banking activities before 1978 and an exception for banks and BHCs that hold shares in companies that engage in non-banking activities before 10 August 1982. The Federal Reserve Board may exempt a foreign company if it determines it is in the public interest to permit its activities.[74]

Another exception for the foreign operations of a foreign bank arose out of Reg K through the classification of 'qualified foreign banking organizations' (QFBO). A QFBO must have more than half of its worldwide banking business in banking (its US operations are not used in this calculation). Most of a QFBO's assets and revenue stream must come from outside of the US. As a result of this qualification, a QFBO may engage in most other non-banking activities outside of the US. Those very same activities practised outside of the US may be practised within its borders with certain exceptions for insurance and securities.[75]

The 'closely related to banking rule' is further diluted by the *Gramm–Leach–Bliley Act* (*GLB*), otherwise known as the *Financial Services Modernization Act of 1999*, short title 12 U.S.C. 1811. Because of the Act, 'well-capitalized and well-managed' subsidiaries and branches of foreign banks may operate under a financial holding companies (FHCs). FHCs themselves must also be 'well capitalized and well managed'. FHC subsidiaries have a wider range of permissible activities. Not only can an FHC own bank subsidiaries, it may own subsidiaries that practise activities that are 'financial in nature'. Such activities include securities and merchant banking. Although an FHC may own a financial, non-bank subsidiary, its banking subsidiaries however are still restricted to activities 'closely related to banking'.[76] This creates a distinction between FHC subsidiaries that are bank entities and those that are financial, non-banking entities.

US supervisors require that all FHCs, their branches, and subsidiaries are 'well capitalized and well managed' regardless if the holding company is foreign or domestic.

In determining whether an activity is financial in nature or incidental to a financial activity, the Board considers:

1. the purposes of . . . the Gramm–Leach–Bliley Act;
2. changes or reasonably expected changes in the marketplace in which financial holding companies compete;
3. changes or reasonably expected changes in the technology for delivering financial services; and
4. whether such activity is necessary or appropriate to allow a financial holding company and the affiliates of a financial holding company to:
   a. compete effectively with any company seeking to provide financial services in the United States;
   b. efficiently deliver information and services that are financial in nature through the use of technological means, including any application necessary to protect the security or efficacy of systems for the transmission of data or financial transactions; and
   c. offer customers any available or emerging technological means for using financial services or for the document imaging of data.

Although a financial company may own a non-banking entity, bank subsidiaries must remain separate entities. The following are the statutorily permissible US activities for foreign banks.

1 Lending, exchanging, transferring, investing for others, or safeguarding money or securities.
2 Insuring, guaranteeing, or indemnifying against loss, harm, damage, illness, disability, or death, or providing and issuing annuities, and acting as principal, agent, or broker for purposes of the foregoing, in any state.
3 Providing financial, investment, or economic advisory services, including advising an investment company (as defined in section three of the Investment Company Act of 1940 [15 U.S.C.A. § 80a-3]).
4 Issuing or selling instruments representing interests in pools of assets permissible for a bank to hold directly.
5 Underwriting, dealing in, or making a market in securities.
6 Engaging in any activity that the Board has determined, by order or regulation that is in effect on 12 November 1999, to be so closely related to banking or managing or controlling banks as to be a proper incident thereto (subject to the same terms and conditions contained in such order or regulation, unless modified by the Board).
7 Engaging, in the United States, in any activity that

   a bank holding company may engage in outside of the United States; and
   b the Board has determined, under regulations prescribed or interpretations issued pursuant to subsection (c)(13) (as in effect on the day before 12 November 1999) to be usual in connection with the transaction of banking or other financial operations abroad.

. . .[77]

The 'well-capitalized' standard bases its measurement on *leverage capital*. Unlike the risk-weighted assessment of capital used in Basel III capital adequacy standards, leverage capital is simply the ratio of total capital to total assets (leverage capital = capital/total assets) and must be at least 5 per cent. These standards are 'substantially higher than Basel III international standards'.[78]

> The 'well managed' standard utilizes the CAMEL ratings system used by US regulators. It requires that a bank receive 'a CAMEL composite rating of 1 or 2 . . . and at least a satisfactory rating for management, if such rating is given; or . . . in the case of a company or depository institution that has not received an examination rating, the existence and use of managerial resources which the Board determines are satisfactory'. The CAMEL rating system will be further discussed in the Safety and Soundness section of this chapter.[79]

An FHC's depositary institution cannot directly participate in a non-banking activity; the activity must be done by a subsidiary. The GLB also permits an FHC to engage in merchant banking which allows for the ownership of purely commercial companies. A merchant banking investment is an investment in a non-financial company by a subsidiary security or insurance company. An investment by a merchant banking subsidiary must only be for the purposes of investment and resale, it must be relatively short term

Overview of international banking law 397

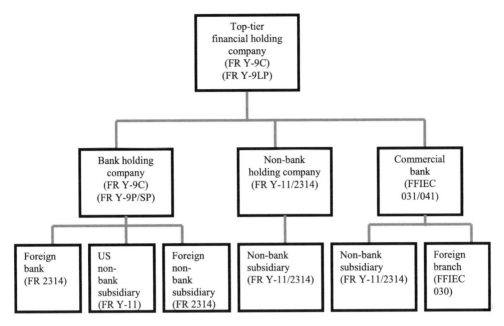

Figure 12.1 General organizational chart of financial holding company.[80]

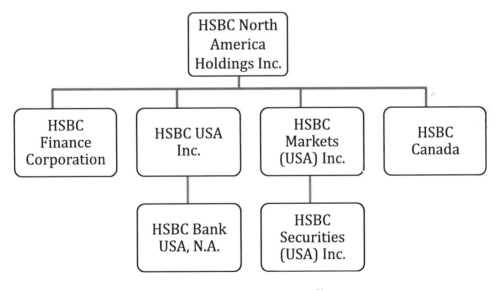

Figure 12.2 Organizational chart of HSBC North America.[81]

(10–15 years), and must not involve control over the company unless it is 'necessary to obtain a reasonable return on investment upon resale or deposition'. The common types of activity most commonly affiliated with merchant banking investments are portfolio investments, and private equity funds owned by FHC subsidiaries. FHCs may not cross-sell products between investment and depository banking companies and are subject to

398 *Legal issues in Asian investing*

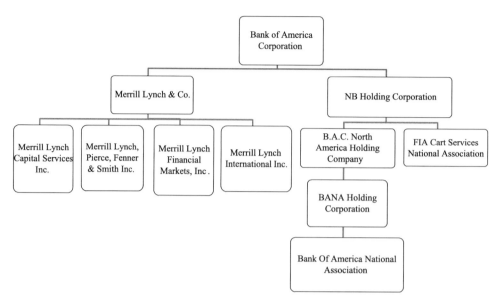

Figure 12.3 Basic organizational chart of Bank of America Corporation.[82]

higher capital charges as the level of equity in investment increases (this chapter addresses capital charges and its relation to capital adequacy in a later section).[83]

Consumer protection

Dodd–Frank created a new consumer protection watchdog called the Consumer Financial Protection Bureau (CFPB). The agency is charged with protecting consumers from complex financial products in order to 'ensur[e] that consumers have access to markets for consumer financial products and services and that markets for consumer financial products and services are fair, transparent, and competitive'. The CFPB regulates the areas of usury laws, equal credit opportunity, fair housing, fair credit reporting practices, truth in services, tying preventions, financial privacy, lender liability, truth in lending, real estate settlement procedures as well as many other consumer protection laws.[84] Consumer protection laws are the most complex and extensive of US financial laws.

Safety and soundness

The GLB act made the Federal Reserve Board the 'umbrella regulator' for the overall safety and soundness of BHCs and FHCs while the OCC is charged with regulating and supervising the safety and soundness of individual, federally chartered, subsidiary banks.[85] The *Collins Amendment* has established stricter, risk-based capital requirements, leverage limits, and liquidity requirements for large banks.[86]

US supervisors follow a supervisory rating system known as the CAMELS system that rates a bank's overall safety and soundness based on each of the following individual component categories on a scale from one to five (one being most sound, five the least sound): capital adequacy, asset quality, management, earnings, liquidity, and sensitivity to market risk. Supervisors also provide a composite rating of a bank's overall soundness. Individual component ratings are identified as: (1) strong, (2) satisfactory, (3) less than satisfactory, (4) deficient, and (5) critically deficient. A bank's overall composite rating may be identified as: (1) sound in every respect, (2) fundamentally sound, (3) some cause for concern, (4) unsafe and unsound, or (5) extremely unsafe and unsound. Regulators use the composite and component ratings in order to decide whether to take 'prompt corrective action' and whether to approve activities such as branching, mergers, acquisitions, or affiliate investments.[87]

Generally, many host-country supervisors are not interested in the soundness of a foreign parent holding company, which operates host-country subsidiaries. However, US supervisors are very concerned with the safety and soundness of foreign parents as they consider foreign parents as BHCs and FHCs and hold them under the same standards. This concern is based on the source of strength doctrine which states that the strength of a subsidiary is based upon its parent-company's strength. A strong foreign parent will be able to inject more capital and save a failing subsidiary while a weak foreign parent may try to 'loot' the capital of a local subsidiary.[88]

Risks

Banking regulations address several banking risk factors. Among them are credit, market, operational, liquidity, legal, and reputational risks. *Credit risk*, also known as *counter-party* or *default risk*, is the risk that a firm's trading partners will not meet their contractual obligations. For banks, credit risk is usually the risk of a client defaulting its loan. As this chapter later addresses, capital adequacy standards address credit risk by requiring a bank to hold certain capital reserves as a buffer in the event of an asset default. *Market risk* is the risk of an adverse change in the price or value of an asset. *Operational risk* is the risk of loss resulting from poor management, internal processes, systems, or external events. Such external risks may include *legal risk* which 'arises from the potential that unenforceable contracts, lawsuits, or adverse judgments can disrupt or otherwise negatively affect the operations or condition of a banking organization'. *Liquidity risk* is the risk that a bank cannot convert assets into cash fast enough to cover deposits (a bank's liabilities). Basel III has created new minimum liquidity requirements requiring a bank to carry a certain amount of 'highly liquid' assets in the event of a bank rush. *Reputational risk* 'is the potential that negative publicity regarding an institution's business practices, whether true or not, will cause a decline in the customer base, costly litigation, or revenue reductions'. *Systemic risk* affects all banks in a jurisdiction. It is the risk that an event will affect all banks in a jurisdiction and is present because of the linkages between institutions. It is also the risk that a failure of one firm can severely impair the entire financial system. Systemic risk is extremely difficult to mitigate because of the strong links between institutions in the financial system.[89]

Deposit insurance and bankruptcy

To reduce systemic risk to depositors, the FDIC issues deposit insurance for consumer deposit accounts. For foreign banks, the FDIC has created a system that emphasizes a bank's home-country deposit insurance system. Prior to the FDICIA, the 1978b allowed the FDIC to insure deposits held by branches of foreign banks if the foreign bank met certain criteria. Now, only branches of foreign banks with US subsidiaries may hold deposit insurance though the FDIC. Edge Act corporations may insure certain deposits, but are not required to hold federal deposit insurance. In other words, the FDIC does not insure deposits held in branches of foreign banks if the foreign bank does not own a US subsidiary. While limiting the competitiveness of foreign banks in the US market, the system ensures that banks lend under subsidiary capital rather than worldwide capital. Furthermore, the FDIC does not insure deposits from international organizations, non-US citizens and those who reside outside of the US.[90]

Issues arise in bankruptcy proceedings for failing branches and agencies of foreign banks. Subsidiary assets are available in the host country because subsidiaries are required to maintain a certain amount of capital in the host country. It is more difficult to access the assets of a failing branch or agency. To address this problem, regulators consider two approaches: (1) A 'quasi-capital requirement', and (2) a 'ring-fence' approach. As of now, assets of agencies or branches of foreign banks are not under the reach of the US bankruptcy court.[91]

'Quasi-capital' requirements require a bank to hold, pledge, or maintain a certain amount of assets in relation to liabilities. These assets must be held or made accessible to host-country bankruptcy courts or regulators.[92]

Home-country regulators apply the 'ring-fence' approach to preserve the assets of foreign operations through home-country insolvency proceedings. Assets are pooled to be distributed in host-country bankruptcy proceedings. Such an approach puts host-country depositors and creditors at the whim of home-country regulators.[93]

GATS and most favoured nation (MFN) treatment

By no means is the WTO an international bank supervisor. But, one of its important agreements covers cross-border trade in financial services, including commercial banking, securities activities, and insurance. That accord is the GATS, which stems from the Uruguay Round of multilateral trade negotiations (1986–94). GATS appears in Annex 1C of the *Agreement Establishing the World Trade Organization (WTO Agreement)*.[94]

Article I of GATS identifies the four ways, or 'Modes', by which financial (and all other) services are traded across international boundaries. They are:

   Mode I: Consumption Abroad
   Mode II: Cross-Border Supply
   Mode III: Foreign Direct Investment (FDI)
   Mode IV: Temporary Migration of Professionals.

Mode I: Consumption Abroad occurs when a consumer uses a service outside of her nation of origin. Typically the consumer moved abroad in order to use the service.[95] This typically occurs as a tourist, student, or the like. An example of this occurs when Person A, a foreign national and student from the US, travels to Taiwan as a foreign exchange student. Person A does not have a bank account with a Taiwanese bank, but visits the Bank of Taiwan, a Taiwanese Chartered bank, in order to purchase a cashier's cheque denominated in New Taiwan Dollars (TWD).

Mode II: Cross-Border Supply occurs when a citizen of an importing country uses a service originating from the importer's country. The service is predominately completed through a standard means of communication such as telephone, Internet, or a postal service.[96] An example of this occurs when Person A, a citizen of the US intends to transfer Japanese yen to his cousin, Person B, who lives in Tokyo, Japan. Person A holds an account with Chicago-based bank, Fidelity. Fidelity uses SWIFT, the predominant international bank communication service, to ask their Japanese correspondent bank, the Bank of Tokyo-Mitsubishi, to transfer funds to Person B's bank account at Sumitomo Mitsui Banking Corporation. The Bank of Tokyo-Mitsubishi then charges Fidelity a transfer fee that Fidelity passes along to Person A by debiting his account.

Mode III: Foreign Direct Investment (FDI) occurs when a foreign-owned company has a 'commercial presence' in the country whereby a service is being provided. The service is usually provided by a 'locally established affiliate, subsidiary, or representative office of a foreign-owned and controlled company'.[97] An example of this is the HSBC, a London and Hong Kong-based holding company that owns North American Holding Company HSBC North America, which owns the US chartered subsidiary bank HSBC USA NA.

Mode IV: Temporary Migration of Professionals occurs when a foreign national independently provides a service within a foreign country.[98] An example of this arrangement occurs when Person A, a US national and an international trade attorney specializing in GATS compliance in the banking sector, moves to Vietnam to help a local Vietnamese bank remain compliant in its global banking operations.

GATS sets rules for trade in services, and calls for dispute settlement under WTO procedures contained in a separate agreement (the dispute settlement understanding (DSU)).

Among other services, GATS focuses on the international activities of financial services. The unique provisions for financial services are known as the Understanding on Commitments in Financial Services and the Annex on Financial Services. GATS provides a schedule of each country's specific trade commitments. Absent specific exceptions, MFN applies to each country's specific commitments to one another. MFN requires a country to honour general obligations for all service sectors; however, it does not require specific commitments to be treated as an MFN obligation. Specific commitments include agreements on market access and national treatment, and are not applied across the board to all services; they are only applied to sectors listed on a country's schedule of commitments. Such sectors and subsectors are scheduled using a standard format that consists of eight entries. The entries indicate the presence or absence of market access or national treatment limitations with regard to each mode of supply. The first column contains the sector or subsector subject to the commitment; the second column indicates any limitation on market access; the third column contains limitations on national treatment, the fourth column shows any additional commitments that are not subject to scheduling under market access or national treatment.[99]

The Annex on Financial Services creates a prudential carve out for domestic regulation by allowing countries to take measures 'for protection of investors, depositors, policy holders, or persons to whom a fiduciary duty is owed' or 'to ensure the integrity and stability of the financial system'.[100]

12.5 Outbound regulation

Supervisory approval

Banks with capital over $1 million in capital or Edge Act Corporations are required to obtain approval from the Federal Reserve Board before entering a foreign market. A bank can enter a foreign market by establishing a branch or obtaining interest in a foreign institution. Federal Reserve approval is only needed when banks initially enter a market; established banks need not obtain approval for establishing another branch in the foreign market; they simply need to provide notice. Supervision by the OCC over this matter is limited to filing and notice requirements.[101]

Federal reserve board approval standards and foreign activities

A US bank's foreign activities are generally limited to those practices 'permissible for a national bank in the US' and 'usual in connection with the business of banking in the country where the bank transacts its business'. Only banks with capital over $1 million or Edge Act corporations may obtain approval from the Federal Reserve Board. Regulation K, codified at 12 C.F.R. § 211.10, provides an extensive list of permissible activities by US banks in foreign markets. The general policy is to confine permissible activities 'to activities of a banking or financial nature and those that are necessary to carry on such activities'.[102]

12 C.F.R. § 211.10 provides an extensive list of foreign activities considered 'usual in connection with banking' and permissible abroad. The list of activities is far more inclusive than permissible domestic activities and more directly reflects the permissible activities set by foreign supervisors. Activities include commercial banking, mortgaging, leasing real estate or acting as a broker, acting as a fiduciary, mutual fund management, and insurance. 'Well-capitalized and well-managed investors may participate in equity security activities outside of the US but are subject to additional notice and capital requirements'.[103]

Regulation K also restricts direct investment activities and sets investment limits on subsidiary and joint venture operations.[104] It limits direct investments to foreign banks, 'domestic or foreign organizations formed for the sole purpose of holding shares in a foreign bank', or organizations that assist in services 'incidental to the activities of a foreign ... affiliate of a member bank'. Regulation K also sets minimum capital adequacy standards for direct and indirect investors of foreign banks and states that a 'member bank shall be in compliance with applicable minimum standards for capital adequacy set out in the Capital Adequacy Guidelines'.[105] Member banks abroad and Edge Corporations engaged in banking shall have a minimum capital adequacy ratio (determined under the Capital Adequacy Guidelines) of 10 per cent. At least 50 per cent of this ratio shall consist of Tier 1 capital.[106]

Foreign branches and subsidiaries are to 'supervise and administer their foreign branches and subsidiaries in such a manner as to ensure that their operations conform to high standards of banking and financial prudence'. The Federal Reserve Board requires systems for effective record keeping that provide extensive information on risk, liquidity, and internal controls.[107]

These reports are necessary for the Federal Reserve Board to 'determine compliance with US banking law'. Edge Corporations and BHCs are required to file reports as required

Overview of international banking law 403

by the Federal Reserve Board. Edge Corporations may be required to provide 'reports of condition' to the Board as the Board deems fit. Members and Edge Act Corporations are also required to report any 'acquisition or disposition of shares' of foreign subsidiaries.[108]

12.6 Capital adequacy

Introduction

Capital ratio (the ratio of a bank's capital to its assets) has always been seen as a tool to measure a bank's safety and soundness. The regulatory purpose of capital adequacy standards is to ensure a bank is able to repay depositors and meet its other obligations in the event of an asset failure, bank run, or liquidity crisis. Banks hold capital (equity) for several reasons: (1) to deter risk-taking and gambling; (2) to create a buffer to absorb unexpected losses; (3) to protect depositors and other more senior creditors, in the event of a failure. The US began imposing capital adequacy standards in 1983 as a tool to mitigate credit risk.[109] The 1983 *International Lending Supervision Act (ILSA,* 12 U.S.C § 3907), requires undercapitalized banks to submit to a capital plan and gives regulators the authority to establish adequate capital levels. Because foreign supervisors were reluctant to issue capital adequacy standards of their own, the US feared its capital adequacy standards would place its banks at a competitive disadvantage.[110]

The BIS through the Basel Committee on Banking Regulations and Supervisory Practices enacted a multilateral framework for capital adequacy standards in 1988.[111] The focus of the framework was to 'asses[s] capital in relation to credit risk'. Using Basel II and Basel III, the committee adjusted its standards for capital requirements as well as adjusted its definition of 'capital' and 'assets'.[112]

Key terms

The generic term *capital* or *equity* is defined as a bank's assets minus its liabilities (capital = assets − liabilities). Generally, investors provide capital and a bank cannot directly or indirectly repurchase these instruments. Furthermore, a bank cannot guarantee the instrument, back it up with collateral, or improve the priority of repayment. The Federal Reserve Board's

> long-standing view is that common equity (that is, common stock and surplus and retained earnings) should be the dominant component of a banking organization's capital structure, and that organizations should avoid undue reliance on capital elements that do not form common equity'. The committee narrowly defines capital and divides it into two tiers so as to account for a bank's repayment obligations and differing levels of liquidity.[113]

Tier 1 'core' capital consists of two subgroups. (1) Common equity Tier 1 capital accounts for all capital stocks (common stock) issued with no obligations on account of the bank (no right to dividends and no maturity). All common shares are treated the same. These are the last shareholders reimbursed in the event of a failure. (2) Additional Tier 1 capital are shares that have no maturity date and no right to cumulative dividends. A bank only pays dividends on these shares from net income or retained earnings. Generally, a bank needs regulatory approval to repurchase or redeem these shares.[114]

Tier 2 'supplemental' capital includes cumulative preferred, intermediate and long-term preferred, and subordinated debt. To be considered Tier 2 capital, an ownership interest has to have an original maturity of at least five years. Dividends can be distributed or stock can be repurchased only after deposits and general claims have been reimbursed. As with Tier 1 capital, a bank needs regulatory approval to repurchase or redeem before maturity. No feature of the instrument can be linked to a bank's credit quality. For calculating capital adequacy, a bank's tier 2 capital can only be used in an amount up to a bank's Tier 1 capital while a bank's subordinated debt can only account for 50 per cent of its Tier 1 capital.[115]

Total assets are the sum of a bank's assets. A bank's total assets are used to measure its *leverage ratio* or *minimum Tier 1 leverage ratio*. US supervisors define leverage ratio as the ratio of Tier 1 capital to total assets (*Tier 1 capital/total assets*). To be considered adequately capitalized, FDIC-insured banks must generally maintain at least a 4 per cent ratio. This minimum ratio is a bank's leverage *limit*.[116]

Risk-weighted assets are a bank's assets measured by its risk of failure. A bank's assets are its primary source of revenue as well as its primary source of risk. The framework accounts for riskier assets in higher amounts than less risky assets. The higher the risk rating of the assets, the more capital will be needed to be considered adequately capitalized.[117]

US supervisors sort assets into five *risk-weight categories*. These categories are used to determine how much of these 'assets' need be backed up by capital. When calculating the denominator value for capital ratio for banks, each individual asset is multiplied by their equivalent category percentage before being added up together to determine total risk-weighted assets.[118]

1. 0 per cent category for the lowest risk assets that have 'little or no credit risk', such assets are cash, currency held in accounts, foreign currency, many federal government securities that are 'backed up with the full faith and credit of the US government or the central government of an OECD country', deposits or balances with the Federal Reserve Banks, and FDIC pre-paid insurance assessments.[119]

2. 20 per cent category for 'very high credit-quality' assets. These assets include securities issued or guaranteed by state government agencies such as those guaranteed by Fannie Mae or Freddie Mac. These also include assets collateralized by federal government securities, a portion of assets conditionally guaranteed by the US Government, general obligations of state and local governments, items collateralized by cash held in a segregated deposit account, balances on accounts held at domestic depository institutions, accounts held at depository institutions incorporated in an OECD country, all assets backed by the full faith and credit of depository institutions incorporated in an OECD country, asset-backed securities rated AAA or AA eligible, and certain claims on, or guaranteed by, qualifying securities.[120]

3. 50 per cent category for assets that are less risky than most credit held by private borrowers. The category includes some revenue bonds issued by state and local governments, qualifying 1–4 family mortgage loans defined at 12 CFR § 567.1, and mortgage- and asset-backed securities rated A1.[121]

4. 100 per cent 'standard risk weight category' for all other assets. These assets include loans to private borrowers, bank's premises and equipment, commercial loans, commercial real estate loans, consumer loans, construction loans, family housing loans that do not qualify for 50 per cent risk weighting, non-qualifying mortgage-backed securities rated BBB, corporate debt securities, repossessed assets, and past due loans.[122]

5   150 per cent category distressed assets such as loans that are 90 or more days past due or 'high volatility' commercial real estate loans.[123]

Off-balance sheet items are revenue-generating sources that are not accounted for on a bank's balance sheet. Such items include certain short-term loan commitments, standby letters of credit, and put back positions. These items are calculated as a part of a risk-weighted assets. They are converted to an equivalent asset-credit and then weighted by risk.[124]

Capital ratio and capital adequacy calculation

Risk-based capital standards were enacted to account for the shortfalls associated with using leverage ratio as the sole standard for capital adequacy. Basel II introduced more specific capital adequacy guidelines and ratios and introduced two approaches to measuring capital: a standardized approach, which was the method championed by Basel I, and an internal ratings-based approach (IRB).[125]

Core Tier 1 capital ratio measures a bank's *common equity* against its total risk-based assets. Basel III requires that a bank holds 4.5 per cent of *common equity*, otherwise known as common, non-preferred stock to its risk-based assets. Its formula is seen as:

$$\text{Core Tier 1 capital ratio per cent} = \left(\frac{\text{Common equity}}{\text{Sum of all risk-weighted assets}}\right) \times 100^{126}$$

Total Tier 1 capital ratio measures a bank's total Tier 1 capital against its total risk-based assets. Basel III requires that a bank holds 6 per cent of total Tier 1 capital to its risk-based assets. Its formula is seen as:

Total Tier 1 capital ratio per cent

$$\left(\frac{(\text{Common Tier 1 capital} + \text{all other Tier 1 capital})}{\text{Sum of all risk-weighted assets}}\right) \times 100^{127}$$

Total risk-based capital ratio measures a bank's total Tier 1 and Tier 2 capital (total capital) against its total risk-based assets. Basel III requires that a bank holds 8 per cent of total capital to its risk-based assets. Its formula is:

Total risk-based capital ratio per cent

$$\left(\frac{(\text{Tier 1 capital} + \text{Tier 2 capital})}{\text{Sum of all risk-weighted assets}}\right) \times 100^{128}$$

Leverage ratio does not account for asset risk weights. It simply measures a bank's total Tier 1 capital to its total assets. The ratio ignores off-balance sheet items and treats all assets similarly. Although rudimentary, the leverage ratio was seen as the original capital adequacy standard. Basel I and Basel II did not set leverage ratio standards. Basel III requires a bank to have a leverage ratio of at least 3 per cent. Its formal is seen as:

$$\text{Leverage ratio per cent} = \left(\frac{\text{Tier 1 capital}}{\text{Total assets}}\right) \times 100^{129}$$

Table 12.1 US capital standards Pre-31 December 2014[130]

Capital category	Leverage ratio	Tier 1 RBCR	Total RBCR
Well capitalized	≥5%	≥6%	≥10%
Adequately capitalized	≥4%	≥4%	≥8%
Undercapitalized	<4%	<4%	<8%
Significantly undercapitalized	<3%	<3%	<6%
Critically undercapitalized	<2%	N/A	N/A

Table 12.2 US capital standards post-31 December 2014[131]

Capital category	Leverage ratio	Common equity ratio	Tier 1 RBCR	Total RBCR
Well capitalized	≥5%	≥6.5%	≥8%	≥10%
Adequately capitalized	≥4%	≥4.5%	≥6%	≥8%
Undercapitalized	4%	4.5%	6%	8%
Significantly undercapitalized	3%	3%	4%	6%
Critically undercapitalized	2%	–	–	–

Table 12.3 Basel II and Basel III capital requirements[132]

	Basel II	Basel III			
		Minimum	Capital conservation buffer	Countercyclical buffer	Aggregate (difference between minimum ration and buffers)
Tier 1 common 'core' equity ratio	2%	4.5%	2.5%	0–2.5%	7–9.5%
Tier 1 capital ratio	4%	6%	2.5%	0–2.5%	8.5%
Total capital ratio	8%	8%	2.5%	0–2.5%	10.5%
Leverage ratio	NA			3%	

Basel I capital standards

The minimum capital adequacy standards set by Basel I are an 8 per cent minimum *total risk-based capital ratio (Tier 1 + Tier 2)/(Total risk-weighted assets)*, a 4 per cent minimum *Tier 1 risk-based capital ratio*, and no minimum leverage ratio.

Basel I risk-weighted categories differ from the Basel II and Basel III frameworks. The Basel I framework included 5 risk weights: 0 per cent, 10 per cent, 20 per cent, 50 per cent, and 100 per cent. The framework did not account for internal (operational) risks and was extremely rudimentary. The 'one-size-fits-all' framework did not account for the safety and soundness of individual banks. It did not differentiate between sound and unsound institutional clients. Furthermore, the framework was easily manipulated by larger banks.[133]

Basel II capital standards

Basel II requires banks hold at a 2 per cent *Core Tier 1 (common equity) risk-based capital ratio*, a 4 per cent total *Tier 1 risk-based capital ratio* (common equity + additional tier 1 capital), an 8 per cent *total capital ratio* (Tier 1 + Tier 2). Basel II does not require a bank hold a minimum leverage ratio.

Pillar 1 was hotly discussed and contested. The committee introduced two alternative ways to calculate asset risk in a capital adequacy determination, a *standardized approach*, and an *internal ratings based*, or *IRB, approach*. The standardized approach simply built on Basel I determinations of assets using more specific and transparent risk weights. The committee also requires international banks to account for the operation risks associated with overseas business.

Banks with the proper internal risk assessment methodology were able to use the IRB approach. The approach requires banks to use in-house analytical processes to determine asset risk. The processes are generally based on 'sophisticated computer modelling' and must estimate future losses on assets. Basel II provides several minimal standards for a bank to rely on its own system of risk analysis to set the appropriate level of capital: (1) an active independent risk control unit, (2) actively involved directors and senior managers, (3) a model closely integrated in daily risk management, (4) regular stress tests for exceptional plausible conditions, (5) thorough compliance procedures; and (6) regular internal review by the bank's internal audit unit.[134]

Basel III capital standards

Basel III set new capital adequacy standards that include a 4.5 per cent minimum *Core Tier 1 common equity risk-based capital ratio*, a 6 per cent minimum *Total Tier 1 risk-based capital ratio* (common equity + additional Tier 1) and an 8 per cent minimum *total capital ratio* (Tier 1 + Tier 2). Unlike Basel I and Basel II, Basel III has a *Leverage Ratio* requirement. A bank must hold at least a 3 per cent *leverage ratio* (Tier 1 capital/total assets).

Basel III introduces conservation and countercyclical buffers. These buffers require a bank to hold and build up additional capital in profitable times in order to draw down on such capital during times of a bank's loss or during an economic downturn.[135]

A bank's ability to distribute capital is hampered if a bank's common core Tier 1 capital falls under the *capital conservation buffer* range. By January 2019 a bank's common equity Tier 1 capital must be held at 2.5 per cent above the regulatory minimum. Banks may allow their capital levels to fall under the conservation range if it experiences losses; however, regulators will have the ability to determine whether a bank is drawing down on the buffer during a 'normal time' in order to simply gain market share. These distribution restrictions include restrictions on dividends, share buybacks, discretionary payments on other Tier 1 capital, and bonus payments to officers. The constraints imposed only relate to distributions, not the operation of the bank.[136]

The purpose of the *countercyclical capital buffer* is to protect the entire banking sector during a systemic credit crisis or during a time of sector-wide loss. It ensures capital and credit are available during a period of systemic stress. The buffer requires additional Tier 1 common capital during 'normal' periods. The requirement is released during times of systemic stress, allowing for a bank to draw down on its Tier 1 common capital. Individual regulatory authorities from each jurisdiction will have the discretion to set the countercyclical capital buffer based upon the extent of systemic risk in a given jurisdiction. The buffer adds an additional 0 per cent to 2.5 per cent to Tier 1 common capital requirement during 'normal' periods. Regulators will also have the discretion to define 'normal' periods and periods of systemic stress.

Because of the 2008 global liquidity crisis, Basel III requires banks to maintain enough highly liquid assets to cover deposits in the event of a crisis. A bank measures asset liquidity through stress testing. Banks are required to maintain a *liquidity coverage ratio* or *LCR* of 100 per cent by 2015. LCR measures a bank's proportion of high-quality liquid assets that could be converted into cash to meet liquidity needs for 30 days during a 'significantly severe stress test scenario'.[137] LCR's Formula is $Al/(Cash0-Cash1) = 100$ *per cent*. Al represents a bank's high-quality liquid assets and Cash0 and Cash1 represent a bank's cash outflows and cash inflows during liquidity stress tests.

High-quality assets have low-credit, low-market risk, are easily and accurately valued, are not dependent upon or correlated with risky assets, and are listed on a recognized exchange. There are two levels of eligible assets: level 1 assets can account for up to 100 per cent of A1 in the LCR formula. Example of level 1 assets are cash, central bank reserves, marketable securities guarantees by central banks, and international finance agencies that have a 0 per cent risk weight. Level 2 assets can only account for up to 40 per cent of A1.[138]

Notes

1 Hal S. Scott, *International Finance: Transactions, Policy and Regulation*, 8th ed. (St. Paul, MN: Foundation Press, 2010), 206–7.
2 Michael Malloy, *International Banking: Cases, Materials, and Problems*, 3rd ed. (Durham, NC: Carolina Academic Press, 2013), 143–4; Scott, 206.
3 Ibid.
4 Malloy, 143–4; Scott, 206.
5 Ibid.
6 Scott, 206–7.
7 12 C.F.R. § 211.24 (2014) (effective 1 October 1 2010); Supra, note 2, at 143–4; Supra, note 1, at 206–7
8 12 C.F.R. § 211.24 (2014) (effective October 1, 2010); 12 U.S.C. § 3107 (2014).
9 12 C.F.R. § 211.24 (2014) (effective October 1, 2010); CFR § 28.26 (2014).
10 St. Bnk. L. Rep. P 53-009 (CCH), (2009 WL 5303525).
11 "Our History: A Long Commitment to China," *Citi*, accessed http://www.citi.com.cn/html/en/about_us/Our_history.html.
12 12 U.S.C. § 3101 (2014).
13 12 C.F.R. § 211.24 (2014) (effective October 1, 2010); Supra, note 2, at 144; Scott, 206.
14 Supra, note 2, at 144.
15 FDIC Improvement Act of 1991 (FDICIA); codified at 12 U.S.C. § 3104(c) (2014); 12 U.S.C. § 1815 (2014).
16 Scott, 206–7; Malloy, 144.
17 12 C.F.R. § 211.24 (2014); Malloy, 144.
18 International Banking Act (IBA) 12 U.S.C. § 3101 (2014) (enacted 1978).
19 Maloy, 144; Scott, 206.
20 Scott, 206.
21 Raj Bhala, *Foreign Bank Regulation After BCCI* (Durham, NC: Carolina Academic Press, 1994).
22 Ibid.
23 Bhala Ibid.
24 12 U.S.C.. § 3104(c)(1) (2014).
25 Malloy, 144; Scott, 206.
26 "Marrakesh Agreement Establishing the World Trade Organization, Annex 1B, Article II," *GATS: General Agreement on Trade in Services*, 15 April 1994, accessed http://www.wto.org/english/docs_e/legal_e/26-gats.pdf (*hereinafter* GATS).
27 Ibid.

28 *Generally* Scott, 240.
29 "US Resolution Plan, FDIC," *Sumitomo Mitsui Financial Group*, accessed https://www.fdic.gov/regulations/reform/resplans/plans/smfg-165-1312.pdf.
30 12 C.F.R. § 211.5 (2014).
31 12 U.S.C. § 611a (2014).
32 12 U.S.C. § 601 (2014).
33 12 U.S.C. § 632 (2014); *Am. Int'l Grp., Inc. v. Bank of Am. Corp.*, 712 F.3d 775, 779 (2d Cir. 2013).
34 12 U.S.C. § 632 (2014); *Am. Int'l Grp., Inc. v. Bank of Am. Corp.*, 712 F.3d 775, 779 (2d Cir. 2013).
35 12 U.S.C. § 617 (2014); 12 U.S.C. § 601 (2014).
36 12 C.F.R. § 211.5(h)(1) (2014) (effective April 19, 2006); 12 U.S.C. § 601 (2014).
37 Scott, 413.
38 Scott, 413.
39 "History of the Basel Committee," *Bank of International Settlements*, last modified 28 October 2014, accessed http://www.bis.org/bcbs/history.htm; Charles Goodhart, *The Basel Committee on Banking Supervision: A History of the Early Years, 1974–1997* (Cambridge University Press, 2011), 3; Scott, 413.
40 "History of the Basel Committee"; Goodhart, 1.
41 "History of the Basel Committee"; Goodhart, 1–5.
42 "History of the Basel Committee."
43 Ibid.
44 "History of the Basel Committee"; Scott, 421–6.
45 Charles Goodhart, "Ratio Controls Need Reconsideration," *Journal of Financial Stability* 9, No. 2 (2013): 445–50; Scott, 226, 426–8.
46 Scott, 423–8.
47 Harald Benink and George Kaufman, "Turmoil Reveals the Inadequacy of Basel II," *The Financial Times* 11 (28 February 2008), Source folder; Scott, 423–28.
48 "Basel II Under Fire," *Financial Times*, 21 August 2003; Scott, 433, 444.
49 Felix Salmon, "The Biggest Weakness of Basel III," *Reuters*, (15 September 2010), accessed http://blogs.reuters.com/felix-salmon/2010/09/15/the-biggest-weakness-of-basel-iii/.
50 Goodhart, "Ration Controls," 445–50; Scott, 454–5.
51 Emily Lee, "Basel III and its New Capital Requirements, As Distinguished from Basel II," *The Banking Law Journal* 131, No. 1 (1 January 2014): 27–69; Sheila Blair, "The Road to Safer Banks Runs Through Basel," *The Financial Times* 9 (24 September 2010).
52 "Basel Committee Membership," *Bank of International Settlements*, accessed http://www.bis.org/bcbs/membership.htm.
53 Ibid.
54 "About the Basel Committee," *Bank of International Settlements*, accessed 20 June 2014, http://www.bis.org/bcbs/about.htm.
55 "Core Principles of Effective Banking Supervision," *Basel Committee on Banking Supervision*, September 1997, accessed http://www.bis.org/publ/bcbs30a.pdf.
56 "History of the Basel Committee."
57 Scott, 226.
58 12 U.S.C. § 3101–311; Scott, 211–13.
59 Scott, 209–16.
60 Scott, 213; 12 U.S.C. § 1841–52 (2014).
61 "Supervision and Regulation," *The Federal Reserve System: Purposes and Function*, accessed http://www.federalreserve.gov/pf/pdf/pf_5.pdf.
62 *Cuomo v. Clearing House Association, L.L.C.*, 557 U.S. 519, 535, 129 S. Ct. 2710, 2721, 174 L. Ed. 2d 464 (2009).
63 "International Banking Supervision," *Office of Comptroller of Currency*, accessed http://www.occ.gov/topics/international-banking/international-banking-supervision/index-international-banking-supervision.html.
64 12 U.S.C. 1811–1831 (2014).
65 "About The CFTC," *U.S. Commodity Futures Trading Commission*, accessed http://www.cftc.gov/about/index.htm.
66 12 U.S.C. § 5531 (2014).

67 12 U.S.C. § 5515 (2014).
68 12 U.S.C. § 3105(d) (2014).
69 12 U.S.C. § 3103 (2014); 12 U.S.C. § 3105 (2014); Scott, 228.
70 12 U.S.C. § 3108; 12 U.S.C. § 602; Scott, 229.
71 12 U.S.C. § 1843 (2014); 12 U.S.C. § 3106 (2014).
72 12 USC § 1843 (2014).
73 12 U.S.C. § 1843 (2014).
74 12 U.S.C. § 3106(b),(c) (2014).
75 12 C.F.R. § 211.23 (2014).
76 12 U.S.C. § 1843(k) (2014).
77 12 U.S.C. § 1843 (2014).
78 12 U.S.C. § 1843(l)(o)(9) (2014).
79 12 U.S.C. § 1841 (2014).
80 Dafna Avraham, Patricia Selvaggi, and James Vickery, "A Structural View of U.S. Bank Holding Companies," *Federal Reserve Bank of New York*, July 2012, accessed http://www.newyorkfed.org/research/epr/12v18n2/1207avra.pdf.
81 "HSBC: An Overview," *Securities and Exchange Commission*, 2012, accessed http://www.sec.gov/Archives/edgar/data/83246/000114420412052308/v744588-1_fwp.pdf.
82 "Bank of America," *Investor Hub*, 19 August 2006, accessed http://investorshub.advfn.com/Bank-of-America-Corp-BAC-6675/.
83 12 U.S.C. § 1843(k)(7) (2014).
84 12 U.S.C. § 5511 (2014).
85 12 U.S.C. § 1843 (2014); 12 U.S.C. § 161 (2014).
86 12 U.S.C. § 5371 (2014).
87 Fed. Banking L. Rep. P 37–437 (C.C.H.), 2009 WL 3686732.
88 Scott, 217.
89 Rating the Adequacy of Risk Management Processes and Internal Controls at State Member Banks and *Bank Holding Companies*, Board of Governors of the Federal Reserve System. SR 95-51 (SUP), 1995 WL 18021649.
90 12 U.S.C. § 3104(c) (2014); 12 U.S.C. § 1815 (2014).
91 Scott, 234–40.
92 Ibid.
93 Ibid.
94 Ibid., 250.
95 "GATS Training Model: Chapter 1 – Basic Purpose and Concepts," *World Trade Organization*, accessed http://www.wto.org/english/tratop_e/serv_e/cbt_course_e/c1s3p1_e.htm.
96 Ibid.
97 Ibid.
98 Ibid.
99 "Guide to Reading the GATS Schedules of Specific Commitments and the List of Article II (MFN) Exemptions," *World Trade Organization*, accessed http://www.wto.org/english/tratop_e/serv_e/guide1_e.htm.
100 Supra, note 26.
101 12 C.F.R. § 211.3 (2014).
102 12 C.F.R. § 2118 (2014).
103 12 C.F.R. § 211.8 (2014).
104 'Activities that are not otherwise permissible for a subsidiary may account for not more than 5 per cent of either the consolidated assets or consolidated revenues of the acquired organization'. 12 C.F.R. § 211.8 (2014).
105 'No member bank, under authority of this paragraph (a)(2), may hold, or be under commitment with respect to, such obligations for its own account in relation to any one country in an amount exceeding the greater of: (A) 10 percent of its tier 1 capital; or (B) 10 percent of the total deposits of the bank's branches in that country on the preceding year-end call report date (or the date of acquisition of the branch, in the case of a branch that has not been so reported).' 12 C.F.R. § 211.4 (2014). 'In the case of an Edge corporation engaged in banking, the minimum ratio of qualifying total capital to risk-weighted assets, as

determined under the Capital Adequacy Guidelines, shall not be less than 10 percent, of which at least 50 percent shall consist of tier 1 capital.' 12 C.F.R. § 211.12 (2014).
106 12 C.F.R. § 211.12 (2014).
107 12 C.F.R. § 211.12 (2014).
108 12 C.F.R. § 211.12 (2014).
109 Goodhart, "Ratio Controls."
110 Malloy, 123; 12 U.S.C. § 3907(a)(1) (2014).
111 Malloy, 124; Bank for International Settlements, Final Report on International Convergence of Capital Standards, *reprinted in* 4 Fed. Banking L. Rep. (OCH) (Mar. 15, 1996) (hereinafter Final Report).
112 Final Report at 51, 166.
113 *Consolidated Capital*, Fed. Banking L. Rep. (CCH) § 4060.7, 2014 WL 1611337.
114 *Risk-based Capital Guidelines*, Fed. Banking L. Rep. (CCH) Appendix A to Part 3, 2013 WL 5741455; Scott, 418.
115 *Risk-based Capital Guidelines*; Scott, 418.
116 OCC Bull. 2013–18, Regulatory Capital-Enhanced Supplementary Leverage Ratio, 2014 WL 1488300.
117 12 C.F.R. § 567.6; Scott, 421.
118 12 C.F.R. § 567.6; Scott, 421.
119 12 C.F.R. § 567.6; Scott, 421, 428.
120 12 C.F.R. § 567.6; Scott, 422, 428.
121 12 C.F.R. § 567.6; Scott, 422, 428.
122 Scott, 422, 429.
123 12 C.F.R. § 567.6; Scott, 422, 429.
124 Scott, 425.
125 Malloy, 128; Scott, 428–33.
126 *Generally* Scott, 412–17; Malloy, 128.
127 Ibid.
128 Ibid.
129 Ibid.
130 Richard Scott Carnell, Jonathan R. Macey, and Geoffrey P. Miller, *The Law of Financial Institutions: Aspen Casebook Series* 5th ed. (Netherlands: Wolters Kluwer, 2013).
131 Ibid.
132 Ibid.
133 Malloy, 122; Scott, 422.
134 Scott, 428–33; Malloy, 239; "A New Capital Adequacy Framework," *Basel Committee on Banking Supervision*, June 1999, accessed http://www.bis.org/publ/bcbs50.pdf.
135 "Basel III Phase In Arrangements," *Bank of International Settlements*, 2013, accessed, http://www.bis.org/bcbs/basel3/basel3_phase_in_arrangements.pdf; "Basel III: A Global Regulatory Framework for More Resilient Banks and Banking Systems," *Basel Committee on Banking Supervision*, December 2010 (1 June 2011 Revision), accessed http://www.bis.org/publ/bcbs189.htm.
136 "Basel III: A Global Regulatory Framework for More Resilient Banks and Banking Systems," *Basel Committee on Banking Supervision*, December 2010 (1 June 2011 Revision), accessed http://www.bis.org/publ/bcbs189.htm.
137 Malloy, 239; Scott, 453; "Basel III: A Global Regulatory Framework for More Resilient Banks and Banking Systems," *Basel Committee on Banking Supervision*, December 2010 (1 June 2011 Revision), accessed http://www.bis.org/publ/bcbs189.htm.
138 Malloy, 140; Scott, 453–4; "Basel III: A Global Regulatory Framework for More Resilient Banks and Banking Systems," *Basel Committee on Banking Supervision*, December 2010 (1 June 2011 Revision), accessed http://www.bis.org/publ/bcbs189.htm.

13 Investment, trade, and financial sanctions

Iran case study (1979–2012)

13.1 Why sanctions matter in international investment management

It is impossible to be an international investment manager and not have to deal with sanctions. Sanctions are an ever-present, and ever-changing, feature of the global economy. There are always efforts, in the form of restrictions on foreign direct investment (FDI), importation, exportation, and/or banking and securities transactions, to pressure a country – the target – to change its behaviour. Sometimes these efforts are multilateral sanctions, under United Nations (UN) auspices. Sometimes, sanctions are imposed unilaterally, by one country (often the US). Sometimes, they are cobbled together by a coalition of the willing.

Sanctions raise practical and ethical questions at two levels, macro and micro. At the macro level, practically speaking, are sanctions effective in achieving their goal? If so, then why do they work? If they do not work, then why not, and should they be amended, or dropped? The key ethical question is whether the imposition of sanctions is just. If imposition is just, then on what theory of justice, specifically? If they are unjust, then why not, and can they be amended to comport with an acceptable theory of justice?

At the micro level, practically speaking, what precisely is forbidden? The key ethical questions are whether, why, and how best to comply with sanctions rules. The micro-level questions demand considerable, careful attention to the details of sanctions legislation and implementing regulations. Those details can be enormously complex, requiring the international investment manager to consult closely with compliance officers, and internal and outside legal counsel.

International investment managers are involved at both macro and micro levels, and in both the ethical and practical senses. Overall, they shape the debate about whether to impose sanctions, and whether sanctions are working. Managers may be challenged to respond to actual and prospective shareholders, who seek to know what their portfolio positions are in respect of sanctions targets. On a day-to-day basis, managers must follow the sanctions rules, whether they like them or not. Penalties for violations are stiff, indeed, often criminal.

To examine all of the extant sanctions rules would consume a multi-volume treatise. (Indeed, there are such legal treatises.) There would be redundancies in that examination, because patterns cut across different sanctions regimes. It would be simplistic to assert that 'to know one sanctions regime is to know them all'. But, picking a case study, and analysing it carefully, can be both sufficient and efficient to develop sound familiarity with the practical and ethical challenges of sanctions regimes at the macro and micro levels. Iran is one such case study.

Sanctions against Iran provide a superb and enduring example of macro- and micro-level ethical and practical questions. History has known no more complex sanctions regime than that against Iran. Those sanctions, which date back to 1979, and evolved considerably in 1986 and the subsequent decades, raised difficult moral issues relating to nuclear energy, weapons proliferation, and (particularly given the status of Israel with regard to nuclear matters) hypocrisy. They also pointed to the dangers of committing a violation. Several international banks were fined billions of dollars for violating Iran sanctions rules. Thus, what follows in this and the next chapter is an in-depth case study of US-led sanctions against Iran.[1]

13.2 Four issues and responses

How do US trade sanctions against Iran work? Have they worked? Championed by 6 US Presidents and 16 sessions of Congress, these sanctions against Iran have spanned nearly 40 years. In that time, the bilateral relationship between the US and Iran has been dreadful, with each side fixated on monstrosities perpetrated by the other: the November 1979 seizure of the US Embassy in Tehran by Iranian militants and subsequent state-sponsored terrorist atrocities; the 1953 *coup d'état* orchestrated by the US of a democratically elected Iranian leader; and subsequent US support for human rights abuses by the Peacock Throne.

To Iran, the US became the 'Great Satan' to be confronted wherever and whenever possible. To the US, Iran perpetrated 'evil' and was to be targeted for sanctions. US trade sanctions against Iran thus became, and continue to be, an important part of international trade law. Around the globe, practise in this field is touched by the dysfunctional relationship between the 'Great Satan' and 'Evil *Āyatollāhs*'.[2]

The practical significance does not mean that the technical rules, or policy justifications for those rules are easily or well understood. The rules have become more intricate as they have evolved over nearly 40 years. The policies for them have been subject to polarizing debates. Accordingly, four issues are addressed herein:

1 What transactions with Iran are prohibited?
2 What are the penalties for violating those prohibitions?
3 What is the logic for the regime of prohibitions and sanctions?
4 Have the sanctions worked?

In addressing the first two issues, three points are clear.

First, as intimated, US trade rules against Iran are complex. Navigating them is not for the faint-hearted, but doing so is essential in the everyday practice of international trade law around the globe. The sanctions cover not only trade in goods and services, but also FDI, transportation, banking, securities, and insurance.

Second, aside from their relevance, they are a technically fascinating case study. They were imposed against a country that accounts for 1 per cent of the world's population.[3] Their imposition was despite the fact that Iran has no misunderstanding about the objective power asymmetry, for as its Foreign Minister, Mohammad Javad Zarif said in December 2013 to students at Tehran University: 'Do you think the US, which can destroy all our military systems with one bomb, is scared of our military system?'[4] They have had a considerable, but imperfect, extraterritorial reach, not only affecting third countries, but cajoling them (or trying to) into ostracizing

Iran. And, for critics and champions of the use of trade sanctions to effect political and national security goals in foreign countries, the case study of Iran gives both comfort and concern.

Third, Iran and third countries made clever adjustments to minimize, as best they could, adverse effects of the regime on them. Given those adjustments, the regime had to evolve. At inception, and for most of its life, it was not a comprehensive set of sanctions designed to put Iran, metaphorically speaking, in solitary confinement. Rather, the types of transactions barred grew, and so also did the penalties for violating those bars.

The third issue admits an unequivocal answer: the purpose of the regime always was two fold: deny Iran the ability to acquire a weapon of mass destruction (WMD), and stop it from supporting terrorist organizations. As a victim of chemical weapons in the 1980–88 Iran–Iraq War, Iran swore it had no interest in acquiring them. Accordingly, the key concern of the US was nuclear: Iran must not get a nuclear device, or the operational means to deliver that device. As for terrorist groups, the principal (but not only) one of interest was *Hezbollah*.

This answer begs two follow-on questions. First, given that the rules of the regime evolved, did the rationale for the regime ever change? While the US never waivered in its two purposes – deterrence in respect of WMDs and terrorism – it did add a third logic. Following the June 2009–February 2010 Green Revolution, the US viewed deterrence of human rights abuse as a third basis for the regime.

Second, why was acquisition by Iran of a nuclear weapon, or support for *Hezbollah*, the US's problem? Unlike North Korea, Iran did not threaten the US with a nuclear attack, and while *Hezbollah* inflicted deadly blows to Americans, it did not do so on US soil. The response – as politically incorrect as it may be to state – is the primary threat was to Israel and Gulf Arab countries. Reasonable minds can and do differ as to whether such a threat is a problem of such great moment to the US to justify not only the regime, but also a US military strike against Iran.

A single, clear response to the fourth issue is difficult, perhaps even imprudent. The fourth issue is one of efficacy, and should be dissected into three questions:

1 Were US trade sanctions against Iran necessary and sufficient to wreck the economy of Iran?
2 Were they necessary and sufficient to compel Iran to sign the November 2013 preliminary nuclear agreement?
3 Were they necessary and sufficient to achieve the three US policy goals for those sanctions, namely, deny Iran a nuclear weapon, convince Iran to cease support for international terrorism, and promote human rights in Iran?

Here the answers are, respectively, 'no', 'it depends', and 'uncertain'.

Until the November 2013 preliminary nuclear deal, sanctions looked set to be an epic failure. An ever-more expansive and detailed array of US measures met with more centrifuges spinning to enrich uranium in Iran. US rules failed to bring about their stated goals. The longer they dragged on, the more entrenched the two countries became. Between 1996 and 2012, the US increased the severity of its sanctions regime, widening the range of forbidden transactions and boosting the number of prohibited activities and penalties. Concomitantly, the number of centrifuges spinning in Iranian nuclear facilities, and stockpile of highly enriched uranium, grew, terrorist acts continued, and the human rights environment changed minimally.

But, thanks to the November 2013 deal, sanctions one day may be viewed retrospectively as efficacious. That is, on the first question, with the deal, it appeared sanctions were necessary, but not sufficient, to wreck the economy of Iran and bring it to sign the November 2013 agreement. Sanctions could not have been sufficient, because they were not systematic or seamless from inception. They were a confusing array of haphazard measures, mostly targeted on the Iranian energy sector, but with plenty of gaps that later needed plugging. Moreover, inefficient economic management, and corruption, in Iran were causal factors, without which the ever-more expansive and tighter regime might not have produced change.

On the second question, US and Iranian officials disagree on the role sanctions played in yielding the November 2013 accord. That 'it depends who is asked' is not surprising, as one side is eager to trumpet a foreign policy success, while the other seeks to show the world it was not cowed by foreign pressure.

As to the third question, whether the US measures were necessary and sufficient to achieve all three policy goals, is not certain. Time will tell whether the net result of the sanctions is one the US sought and with which Iran can live. Here, then, is a case study with lessons about the future to be revealed in the future.

13.3 Tragedy

On 4 November 1979, Iranian protestors stormed the US Embassy in Tehran, taking and holding hostage 52 US citizens for 444 days. Ten days after the Embassy seizure, President Jimmy Carter imposed trade sanctions against Iran. Except for a six-year respite in the 1980s, the US has had trade sanctions on Iran. That is true regardless of who was President, and which political party held power in Congress. Simply put, for nearly 40 years, the US has had a sanctions-based trade policy towards Iran. The template, conscious or not, for this policy, may well have been Cuba: since 1961,[5] US trade policy towards what President John F. Kennedy called 'that imprisoned island' has been nothing but sanctions.[6]

That policy looked unsuccessful, or (to use a contemporary youthful colloquialism) appeared to be an epic failure. US trade sanctions had not changed the behaviour of Iran.[7] Specifically, they had not achieved any of the goals embraced by six US Presidents, which were most clearly articulated by Bill Clinton (in 1996), and by every session of Congress from the 96th (1979–80) to the 112th (2011–12).[8] Declaring sanctions to be a policy of containment to isolate Iran, the Clinton Administration claimed they were justified because of Iran's (1) efforts to develop WMDs and (2) support for international terrorism. Additional rationales for isolating Iran were its (3) subversion of certain governments in the Middle East, (4) undermining of the Arab–Israeli peace process, and (5) poor human rights record.[9] Of them, the first two have loomed the largest for the US, though human rights concerns resurfaced in 2012 as a pertinent rationale for an explicit prohibition. In no way that is publicly observable or material have the sanctions caused Iran to alter the impression of the US on any of these five points.

The reasons for that failure laid partly in inconsistencies in the sanctions themselves. Through successive legislation, they generally tightened the noose around Iran, with ever tougher measures, but also with provisions allowing for flexibility or creating ambiguity. Taken individually, indubitably a cogent argument existed in defence of each twist or relaxation. Taken collectively, the pattern – especially from the Iranian perspective – was not a series of outright flip-flops, but somewhat 'on the one hand, ...

on the other hand, . . .', and thus intimated occasional legislative tentativeness masked by bellicose rhetoric. In other words, it was not that each particular prohibition, sanction, exception, or waiver, in isolation, was indefensible. Rather, it was that viewed across almost four decades, the overall impression was that the sanctions regime had become an evolving work in progress lacking from inception adamantine will and tenacious determination.

The reasons that the sanctions seemed unsuccessful were also in the limits of US sovereignty. Never has the long reach of US sanctions enforcement powers been endless, or the intelligence necessary to exercise that power flawless. The ability of third parties – whether allies, friends, or neutrals – to comply with US sanctions always has been limited. Wholly apart from their philosophical misgivings about those sanctions and the justification for them, they faced domestic and international political constraints they could not easily subordinate to US trade policy. In sum, external political and economic factors the US could not control, and internal legislative and regulatory factors that it could, were to blame for the four decades of failure.

Both factors are ones that the US could have, and should have, foreseen. In their official postures, rarely did US policy-makers respect Iran as an ancient and grand Persian civilization, understand the distinct nature of *Shī'īte* (much less Twelver *Shī'īsm*) and empathize with the historical *Shī'īte* sense of persecution by *Sunnites*, consider modern Iranian sensibilities about the 19 August 1953 *coup d'état* engineered by the US Central Intelligence Agency (CIA) and the British MI6 of democratically elected Prime Minister Mohammad Mosaddegh (1882–1967),[10] and subsequent human rights offences committed by the US-backed Shah, or address claims by Iran about its right under the 1968 *Nuclear Non-Proliferation Treaty* (*NPT*) to develop peaceful nuclear technologies, much less Iranian allegations of US violations of the *NPT*.[11] Instead, US officials tended to respond to the worst of Iranian rhetoric, especially hate speech by former President Mahmoud Ahmadinejad (1956–) against Israel and his monstrous denials of the Holocaust. Rather than rising above the ugliness emanating from some quarters in Tehran and Qom, the officials forged a trade sanctions policy in response to it.

To be sure, that ugliness is utterly indefensible. Nothing justifies Iranian threats to the Jewish State or Jews, nor human rights violations committed by the Islamic Republic against its own people. Nothing justifies the ruthless suppression of the Green Revolution of 13 June 2009–11 February 2010, or prior and subsequent democratic movements, and their champions.[12] Nothing justifies terrorism or support for Violent Extremist Organizations (VEOs). And, whether Iran has a right to peaceful nuclear technologies, or even nuclear weaponry, under the NPT, is debatable, albeit a debate for another time. Likewise, whether Iran was truthful in its consistent contention that its nuclear program has been for peaceful purposes to help it generate electricity, not for construction of an atomic weapon, is debatable.

What is certain, indeed palpable, are misunderstandings, ignorance, and hardheartedness on both sides. One side spoke of the leaders of the other as 'Evil *Āyatollāhs*'. Those leaders painted the other side as the 'Great Satan'. Their metaphors bespoke a tragic mutual hatred.

13.4 Metrics

Is it reasonable to consider US trade policy toward Iran as an 'epic failure'? The answer depends on the characterization of that trade policy and benchmark for its success. What has been and is US trade policy towards Iran, and has it worked? The answers, respectively, are 'sanctions' and 'no'. Of course, the work generated for lawyers has been outstanding. But, surely the enrichment of the class of juridical service providers cannot be the sole cause to sustain any legal regime.

Stephen Kinzer, a Visiting Fellow at Brown University, former *New York Times* correspondent who has covered over 50 countries on five continents, and author of *Overthrow: America's Century of Regime Change from Hawaii to Iraq*, summarized the reality: ' Years of sanctions and threats have produced only more spinning centrifuges in Iran. An earnest diplomatic effort to give Iran an honourable alternative is long overdue.'[13]

Indeed, Mr Kinzer argued that a different approach was the key not only to resolving America's nuclear dispute with Iran, but also Middle East regional conflicts:

> That refusal [of the United States to engage Iran diplomatically] is rooted largely in emotion stemming from the hostage crisis of 1979–80 and the following decades of semi-covert conflict between Washington and Tehran. Emotion has pushed Washington to adopt doctrine that posits Iran as a *strategic enemy*, meaning that any security gain for Iran implies an American loss. By that logic, allowing Iran a voice in shaping a peace settlement for Syria – or in any Middle East process – would enhance Iran's legitimacy and therefore undermine US interests.
>
> . . .
>
> This approach [of isolating Iran as an enemy] is misguided . . . . [T]he United States and Iran, though often rivals, have urgent security interests in common. Both want to calm Iraq and Afghanistan, deal with the Afghan drug trade and fight radical Sunni movements like the Taliban and al-Qaeda. Together they could do far more to achieve those goals than either can alone.
>
> . . .
>
> [N]o long-term stability in the Middle East is possible without the cooperation of Iran. *Look at a map of the region: Iran is the big country right in the middle.* Its cultural and political influence has been a dominant fact of regional life for thousands of years. Freezing it out of peace processes almost guarantees that those processes will fail.
>
> . . . [There is] the larger truth that negotiating with enemies and rivals is a way to promote national interest, not a concession or surrender. Hostility between powers – like the United States and Iran – should be an incentive to negotiate, not a barrier.[14]

America and American sanctions, it seemed, did not matter to the 'Evil *Āyatollāhs*' in Tehran and Qom, yet reinforcing the metaphor from the Iranian perspective that the 'Great Satan' clinged ever more tightly to his scepter.[15]

Indubitably, the sanctions do matter to everyday Iranians throughout their country – from Tabriz, near Armenia, in the north to the Persian Gulf port of Bandar-e Abbās in the south, and from the western boundaries with Turkey and Iraq to the eastern borders with Turkmenistan, Afghanistan, and Pakistan, Have they inflicted economic pain on Iran? Yes, though some of that pain has been self-inflicted (as discussed later). Have the sanctions hurt innocents in Iran? Almost certainly, yes. Commodities and services enjoyed by a healthy middle class are in short supply. Have these effects inspired greater affection on the Iranian street, and in towns and villages across the Persian landscape, for either the US or Iranian government? Probably, no. Have they at least provoked a 'rally around the flag' effect in Iran; that is, a sense of love of country if not of its politics? Probably, yes.

Have the sanctions helped the US understand Iran or its special position in Islamic history and religion any better?[16] No. Few Americans could identify the first three *Shī'īte* Imāms, or the Twelfth one, who has remained in occultation since about 940 AD. They would be shocked to learn orthodox Twelver *Shī'īte* belief holds that the Hidden Imām will come out of occultation and, with Jesus Christ, return to the world to restore peace and justice before a Day of Final Judgment. Have the sanctions altered the self-image of Iran? No. It is keenly aware it is the only *Shī'īte* nation in the world, and only the second one in history (the first being *Fatimid* Egypt). Its Constitution, written and approved after the 1979 Islamic Revolution, bespeaks its self-proclaimed role of guardian of *Shī'īsm* and exporter of its sense of socially just revolution on behalf of the poor and oppressed.

Misunderstanding turned to hardheartedness, hardheartedness to prejudice, and prejudice to hatred. Trade sanctions facilitated, if not contributed to, this tragic course. Of as yet unclear effect at their stated aim of compelling Iran to abandon its suspected clandestine nuclear weapons program, they manifested one obvious result: a fat set of laws. American sanctions on Iran span no less than 62 single-spaced pages (depending on page, font size, and minor exclusions). That figure, which grew over time with each new try, covered only the statutory regime specifically targeting Iran. It excluded dozens of pages of regulations.

Was there, then, a justification for this regime? The conventional wisdom was 'yes'. This wisdom said that without sanctions, Iran would have acquired nuclear weapons, and would have sponsored even more boldly terrorist organizations. The obvious rebuttal: that was not 'wisdom', but speculation about a historical counterfactual question: what would have happened had there been no sanctions regime?

A different kind of wisdom would have been to say that without the sanctions, Iran might not have been a pariah state, and might boast a burgeoning emerging market. It might have been more akin to Turkey than North Korea. It might even have become the first Islamic BRICS (Brazil, Russia, India, China, and South Africa) nation, and a new acronym – the I-BRICS – might be needed. After all, without sanctions, Iran could have earned and had full access to export revenues from oil, petrochemical products, and precious metals, invested them wisely in long-term infrastructure and human capital development projects, and diversified its economy so that it was less reliant on petroleum. After all, Iran incurred an opportunity cost if it could not exploit its energy and natural resources sectors via foreign market sales: it could not use foreign earnings from those sectors to fund development and gain an international competitive advantage in non-energy sectors. And, without sanctions on imports of refined gasoline and against access to world financial markets and payments systems, Iran might not have felt, or reacted with, hostility.

So, again, was there a justification – one that did not rely on counterfactual speculation – for the sanctions? The answer is 'yes'. The first lay in just war theory as developed (*inter alia*) by Catholic moral theologians. The use of force is unjust unless it comports with specific criteria, one of which is that it is truly the last resort to resolving a problem. All other efforts must be exhausted first. Such efforts may include sanctions. Accordingly, it may be argued that were armed conflict to occur between the US and Iran, it could be rationalized – if at all – as the last resort under just war theory, because sanctions were tried and failed. Of course, this rationalization would be parlous on either of two grounds:

the sanctions were merely a prelude to war; and another last resort – diplomacy – was tried in good faith and failed.

The second justification lay in deontology. Rather than utilitarianism, the better – perhaps only sure – argument for trade sanctions against Iran is that if, indeed, the behaviour of Iran is sinful, even evil, then the US ought not to sully itself dealing with that country. Whether sanctions effect a change in Iranian behaviour then becomes a secondary matter. Of primary importance is the effect on the American soul of dealing with a perpetrator of bad acts. Put in individual terms, the idea is that 'I do not want to damage my soul by selling to or buying from Iran because of what I understand to be official Iranian behaviour in respect of atomic weapons and terrorism'. However, a deontological justification never has been the official US one. Rather, consequentialism has been the cornerstone.

Even if in the unlikely event the rationale were to change, despite some evidence that utilitarian calculations across four decades appeared negative for the US, the sanctions regime would require modification. To focus on the effect of dealing with Iran on the American soul – that doing so is morally bad for Americans – is not a value judgement the US ought to impose on other countries or peoples. Thus, the secondary boycott features of US sanctions against Iran, which target foreign entities, would need to be dropped. It would be up to foreign parties, based on the free exercise of their conscience, to decide whether and to what extent they feel morally concerned about working with Iran.

13.5 First three of 10 phases to 1996

To ask whether US trade rules against Iran worked presumes an understanding of how they worked. That, in turn, requires appreciation of how and why they developed over time.

There have been 10 phases to US trade sanctions against Iran (outlined below).[17] Of course, it is possible to view them as a totality of rules as of the present day, but that static picture would veil an insight: since 1979, and especially since 1996, the US has tightened sanctions progressively on Iran, but until the November 2013 interim nuclear deal, Iranian behaviour changed little, if at all, towards the outcomes the US sought from the sanctions.

The US applied sanctions to a broader range of commercial and financial transactions, identifying an ever-larger number of prohibited forms of business conduct. The US insisted on an extraterritorial scope to these prohibitions. It mandated an ever-increasing number of penalties for violating the prohibitions. Still, Iran does what it does. Metaphorically, the 'Evil Āyatollāhs' did what they did in their neighbourhood playground, the Near East, to the irritation of the 'Great Satan'. The more they did in disregard of the 'Great Satan', the hotter the 'Great Satan' got, but each new flame it sent up (or over) only emboldened them.

The first three phases of US sanctions against Iran were:

Phase 1: Carter era (14 November 1979–19 January 1981)
Phase 2: Respite era (19 January 1981–29 October 1987)
Phase 3: Reagan–Clinton era (29 October 1987–5 August 1996).

The first three phases are discussed elsewhere.[18]

The focus here is on the subsequent evolution of the sanctions. In reviewing them, it is important to note as a practical matter that the sanctions all apply. That is, the evolution is cumulative: one set of sanctions does not substitute for another, but rather supplements all previous sanctions. Each of the 10 phases, perhaps especially the last seven, might be described tellingly as a 'try', an effort to knock out the spectre of Iran obtaining a WMD, particularly a nuclear weapon, along with deterring it from sponsoring terrorism and abusing the human rights of its citizens.[19]

13.6 Phase 4: 1996 *ILSA* emphasis on petroleum

ILSA, subsequent strengthening, and five practical questions

President Clinton signed the *Iran and Libya Sanctions Act* (*ILSA*) on 5 August 1996.[20] ILSA – which in 2006 under the *Iran Freedom Support Act* was renamed the *Iran Sanctions Act* (*ISA*) – became the most significant statutory enactment against Iran. It remained so until 2010, when Congress passed, and President Barack H. Obama signed, another key bill. Overall, Congress strengthened the baseline 1996 statute no fewer than six times via:

1. *ILSA Extension Act of 2001*[21]
2. *Iran Freedom Support Act of 2006*[22]
3. *Comprehensive Iran Sanctions, Accountability, and Divestment Act of 2010 (CISADA)*[23]
4. *National Defense Authorization Act of 2012*[24]
5. *Iran Threat Reduction and Syria Human Rights Act of 2012*[25]
6. *Iran Freedom and Counter-Proliferation Act of 2012 (Sub-Title D of the National Defense Authorization Act for Fiscal Year 2013).*[26]

Not only did these six Acts amend ILSA, but also the fourth and fifth Acts changed the 2010 Act, which with ILSA had become the second of the two most important statues targeting Iran. In turn, the 2010 Act also altered the first one, ILSA.[27]

Not surprisingly, for the practitioner and scholar alike, and *a fortiori* for a domestic or foreign commercial or financial enterprise seeking in good faith to stay on the right side of US justice, the accretion of legislative enactments is dizzying. It is necessary to study ILSA and CISADA, plus sections of those enactments codified in other Titles, especially 22, and thereafter consult pertinent provisions of the Code of Federal Regulations (CFR).[28]

Perhaps the easiest path through the legal thicket is to keep five practical questions in mind:

1. *Prohibitions*: What transactions are prohibited?
2. *Penalties*: What are the possible sanctions for engaging in a prohibited transaction?
3. *Scope*: To what, or to whom, are the prohibitions and sanctions applicable?
4. *Exceptions*: What limitations on, or outright exemptions to, the prohibitions and sanctions exist?
5. *End game*: What (if any) criteria exist for removing the prohibitions and terminating the sanctions?

The first two questions highlight the fact that a punishment is imposed for committing a transgression. The third question identifies the breadth of application of the rules. The fourth and fifth questions search for flexibility in the rules.

Crossing the rubicon with ILSA

(5 August 1996–30 September 2006)

ILSA, which dates from the 104th Congress,[29] marked a significant legal and political shift in US sanctions policy against Iran.[30] Until ILSA, the *International Emergency Economic Powers Act (IEEPA)* and Presidential Executive Orders were the legal mechanisms to implement that policy.[31] Using the broad discretion delegated by the Legislative to the Executive branch, the President, not Congress, principally determined what sanctions to put on Iran, and how. Yet, inside and outside the Senate and House, doubts arose as to whether this approach was effective in coaxing other countries to punish Iran. To shift international attitudes, in third countries as well as Iran, Congress passed ILSA.

Congress stated (in findings contained in ILSA) Iran behaved in two ways adverse to US national security: it sought to acquire WMDs; and it supported international terrorism.[32] To further these pursuits, Iran used its governmental and quasi-governmental facilities outside of its territory.[33] Then extant bilateral and multilateral efforts to deter it were ineffective. Sanctions with real 'bite' – ones that cut into Iranian revenues – were needed.[34] Iranian behaviour threatened the national security (and foreign policy) interests of the US and its allies and friends, hence Congress:

> declare[d] that it is the policy of the United States to deny Iran the ability to support acts of international terrorism and to fund the development and acquisition of weapons of mass destruction and the means to deliver them by limiting the development of Iran's ability to explore for, extract, refine, or transport by pipeline petroleum resources of Iran.[35]

So, in ILSA, Congress mandated sanctions against two types of transactions: (1) foreign investment in the development of the petroleum sector of Iran; and (2) exportation of sensitive weaponry, both WMDs and advanced conventional ordnance, to Iran.[36]

With its legal and political shift via ILSA, and its findings in ILSA, Congress crossed the Rubicon. Was there to be any more debate about whether Iran had the legal right under the NPT to develop peaceful atomic energy, or even perhaps acquire nuclear weapons? No. Was there to be any more debate about why Iran might be supporting terrorism, and what other measures might deter it from doing so? No. In 1996, six years before President George W. Bush declared in his 2002 State of the Union Address that Iran is part of an 'axis of evil' (along with Cuba and North Korea), Congress declared Iran so.[37]

To be sure, Congress still encouraged the President to pursue multilateral channels. Indeed, ILSA obliged the President to report on his efforts 'to mount a multilateral campaign to persuade all countries to pressure Iran to cease its nuclear, chemical, biological, and missile weapons programs and its support of acts of international terrorism . . .[38]'.

The President also had to report on his efforts to get other countries to reduce their diplomatic ties with Iran, and expel any Iranian representatives who participated in the

4 November 1979 takeover of the US Embassy in Tehran or holding of hostages during the 444 days thereafter,[39] the use by Iran of diplomats to acquire WMDs or promote terrorism,[40] and the inspection activities of the International Atomic Energy Agency (IAEA) of nuclear facilities (actual or under construction) in Iran.[41]

But, the purpose of pursuing multilateral efforts is manifest from the nature of the reporting obligation about them: Congress did not seek to talk with Iran; rather, it wanted stringent sanctions on Iran to 'limit[] the development of [Iran's] petroleum resources . . . [so as to] inhibit Iran's efforts to acquire WMDs or support terrorism'.[42]

Two sanctions for petroleum resource development and sensitive

Weaponry export prohibitions

With ILSA, Congress aimed to strike Iran at its most significant revenue-generating sector: energy. Perhaps Iranian support for the likes of *Hezbollah* and its efforts to acquire nuclear arms technology would be thwarted if Iran did not have funds to cover those expenses. Where else did the bulk of that funding come from but oil exports? And, what else made oil exportation possible but foreign investment in exploration, drilling, and transportation of oil in Iran for onward shipment abroad?

Moreover, via the ILSA Congress specifically targeted any 'foreign person'. Therein lay a key shift in US strategy, and another feature of the Rubicon crossing. Sanctions were no longer just a primary boycott, barring Americans from dealing with Iran. With ILSA, they became a secondary boycott: no one else was supposed to deal with Iran, at least not in the petroleum sector, either. The definition of 'foreign person' was broad, covering (1) an individual (regardless of citizenship), (2) a firm, be it a partnership, corporation, or other form of business association, and (3) government enterprise, thereby including a wholly or partly state-owned enterprise (SOE) or state-trading enterprise (STE). The trigger for sanctions under ILSA (later revised, as discussed below) was US$40 million.

So, as to the first transaction ILSA forbade, the *actus reus* (culpable act) was any 'investment that directly and significantly contributes to the enhancement of Iran's ability to develop petroleum resources'.[43] 'Petroleum resources' was defined broadly: it refers not only to 'petroleum' (such as crude oil), 'refined petroleum products', 'oil or liquefied natural gas' (LNG), and 'natural gas resources', but also to tankers and products used to build or maintain pipelines for transporting oil or natural gas.[44] In turn, 'refined petroleum products' covers gasoline, diesel, and jet fuel.[45] So, the term 'petroleum resources' covered the entire sector pertaining to this form of energy.

Without clarification, the key terms 'directly and significantly' could be read to ensnare virtually any economic transaction connected to that sector: providing buttons for uniforms of Iranian petroleum workers, and shoelaces for their shoes, distributing bottled water to them, or selling them goods such as prescription eyeglasses or pharmaceuticals like aspirin could be considered an 'investment'. After all, clothes, shoes, water, glasses, and aspirin all are used by those workers, without which they could not easily perform their duties. Unfortunately, ILSA provided no guidance as to the meaning of 'directly and significantly'.

What the statute did define was 'investment' and 'develop and development'. An 'investment' was any agreement with the government or Iran, or a non-governmental entity in Iran, involving (1) a contract that includes responsibility for 'the development of petroleum resources' in Iran (including supervising or guaranteeing that another person will perform such a contract), (2) taking a share ownership (such as an equity interest) in 'that development', or (3) a contract for participating in any form in the 'royalties, earnings, or profits of that development'.[46] To 'develop' those Iranian petroleum resources was to explore for them, extract or refine them, or transport them by pipeline.[47] Query, however, whether these definitions suggested a contract to provide Iranian workers with clothes, shoes, water, glasses, and aspirin was covered, if those workers engaged in petroleum exploration, extraction, refining, or pipeline transportation, and that work was judged direct and significant?

Not under prongs (2) or (3), because no share ownership or profit sharing redounds to the suppliers of clothes, shoes, water, glasses, or aspirin. But, perhaps under prong (1), insofar as these items help guarantee the workers can develop Iranian petroleum resources. Admittedly, that would be a strained interpretation, but not one denied by the definitions if an aggressive approach is preferred.

ILSA did not establish a strict liability offence. Rather, it contained a *mens rea* (culpable intent) requirement: 'knowingly'. ILSA defined the term broadly to include actual or constructive knowledge: if a foreign person actually knew, or should have known, of the conduct, circumstance, or result in respect of an investment in the Iranian petroleum resources sector, then that sufficed.[48]

As to the second prohibited transaction, ILSA took aim at helping Iran develop WMDs or certain other military capabilities.[49] It was illegal for any foreign person to export, transfer, or otherwise provide to Iran:

> any goods, services, technology, or other items *knowing* that the provision of such goods, services, technologies, or other items *would contribute materially* to the ability of Iran to –
>
> (A) acquire or develop chemical, biological, or nuclear weapons or related technologies; or
> (B) acquire or develop *destabilizing* numbers and types of *advanced* conventional weapons.[50]

The statute did not define 'chemical' or 'biological' weapons, nor identify what conventional weapons are 'advanced', or how many of them would be 'destabilizing'. It offered precision only in respect of 'nuclear' weapons, saying a 'nuclear explosive device' was any item (assembled or disassembled) 'designed to produce an instantaneous release of ... nuclear energy from special nuclear material ... greater than the ... energy ... from' detonating one pound of trinitrotoluene.[51]

Like the first offence, this offence was not a strict liability one: the foreign person had to know the items shipped to Iran would help Iran in its weapons program. Moreover, as the italicized terms indicate, the contribution had to be 'material', and as to conventional weapons, they had to be both 'advanced' and in 'destabilizing numbers'. Assuredly, a missile designed to carry a conventional weapon would qualify, all the more so if the item transferred to Iran would help it modify the missile to carry a nuclear payload.[52] But, as to WMDs, 'related technologies' were enough, and as to both categories of ordinance, the items shipped need not be weapons. Any item that helped Iran 'develop' the forbidden weapons could not be sent to Iran. So, for example, information from research conducted in a laboratory at the University of Kansas School of Engineering was within the scope of banned material. That meant faculty had to take special care in sharing information with research assistants, particularly ones from overseas.

In sum, ILSA, as originally conceived, targeted the development of Iranian petroleum resources[53] (as explained below, later changes to ILSA added several more sectoral targets, plus individual ones, such as the production of refined petroleum products in Iran, and exportation of refined petroleum products to Iran). Any foreign person investing more than $40 million in any one year in the petroleum sector was liable.[54] The period of measurement was one year, and multiple investments that summed to or exceeded the threshold were illegal. Thus, a foreign person could not lawfully structure a transaction into a series of smaller ones, and expect they would be treated in isolation.

ILSA required the President to impose two of six sanctions on a foreign person that transgressed its prohibitions, referred to as the 'sanctioned person' or 'sanctioned entity':[55]

(1) Export Financing Sanction[56]

The US Export–Import Bank (Ex-Im Bank) had to refuse to grant any loan to finance exports of goods or services to a sanctioned person. Such financing otherwise included Ex-Im Bank issuance of a guarantee, insurance, extension of credit, or participation by the Bank in a credit syndicate.

(2) Export License Sanction[57]

A sanctioned person was prohibited from obtaining a specific license for exports of controlled items. Such items were controlled under the *Export Administration Act of 1979*, *Arms Export Control Act of 1976*, *Atomic Energy Act of 1954*, or any other legislation mandating prior review and approval as a condition for export or re-export of goods or services.

Note ILSA contained a second kind of export license sanction, which applied specifically in instances in which the prohibition against exportation of sensitive weaponry is violated.[58] No license for the export, transfer, or re-transfer, direct or indirect, of nuclear material, facilities, components, or related goods, services, or technology, could be issued to the government of any country with primary jurisdiction over a person who violates that prohibition. This additional species of Export License Sanction was designed to coax foreign governments to police their citizens and residents against shipping WMDs or destabilizing numbers and types of advanced conventional weapons to Iran.

This second species was a qualified one. The President need not impose the sanction if (1) the government of the pertinent country neither knew nor had reason to know about a person violating the prohibition, (2) that government had taken 'all reasonable steps necessary' to prevent a recurrence of the violation and penalize the person, or (3) approving, on a case-by-case basis, an export license was 'vital to the national security interests of the United States'.[59]

(3) US Bank Loans Sanction[60]

Any US bank was obliged to deny to a sanctioned person any loan over $10 million in one year. Any 'US financial institution' defined the scope, and meant any depository institution, credit union, securities firm (e.g., broker or dealer), insurance company, or other financial services provider in the US, including a branch or agency in the US of a foreign bank.[61] The financial institution was barred from providing loans or credits totalling annually $10 million to a sanctioned person, unless that person helped 'relieve human suffering',[62] and the financing was for that purpose.

(4) Primary Dealer And Repository Sanctions[63]

Any sanctioned person that was a US or foreign 'financial institution' had to be disallowed from serving as a primary dealer of, or repository for, US government funds. 'Financial institution' meant any depository institution, credit union, securities firm (e.g., broker or dealer), insurance company, or other financial services provider based or operating anywhere in the world. So, the sanctioned financial institution had to be barred from serving as a primary dealer in the US government Treasury securities for the Federal Reserve Bank of New York, or a repository for US government funds as agent for the US government.[64] Note that primary dealer status was (and is) considered on Wall Street to be both prestigious and potentially lucrative.

(5) Government Procurement Sanction[65]

A sanctioned entity had to be excluded from any US government procurement contracts; that is, the US government had to refuse to procure goods or services from that entity. Though not expressly mentioned, presumably coverage extended to intangible merchandise, such as software or databases, and to intellectual property (IP).

(6) Additional Sanctions[66]

Import sanctions declared by the President under the IEEPA had to be applied to imports from a sanctioned person.[67] The point of such additional IEEPA sanctions was to prevent importation of goods (and, presumably, services) from the sanctioned entity into the US.

Sanctions (unless waived, as discussed below) had to remain in place for at least two years from the date of imposition, or until such time (not less than one year) the President receives 'reliable assurances' the sanctioned person has ceased engagement in any prohibited activity, and will not do so knowingly again.[68]

Sanctions decisions were not subject to judicial review.[69] Presumably a court might decline jurisdiction under the political question doctrine, but the statue avoided that matter by making clear a Presidential decision to impose sanctions is not reviewable by any court.

Waiver of sanctions was possible as a general matter, and via delay. ILSA authorized the President to waive imposition of any otherwise mandatory sanction if the decides 'it is necessary to the national interest' of the US to do so.[70] Obviously, the criterion is open-ended: any interest, be it national security or otherwise, may be a justification, and the President decides what is 'necessary'. The President could delay for up to 90 days (renewable for a second 90-day period) imposition of sanctions if Congress urged him to do so, and in lieu of imposing a punishment, pursue a diplomatic course.[71] Specifically, Congress could call upon the President, and the President might determine, that consultations with the government of the country that has primary jurisdiction over the sanctioned person 'has taken specific and effective actions, including, as appropriate, the imposition of appropriate penalties' to end the illegal conduct with Iran.[72]

So, for example, suppose the Malaysian energy company, Petronas, invests in the petroleum sector of Iran in an amount above the trigger threshold. The President could waive sanctions, if imposing them on Petronas would damage the US's national interests. Perhaps many US companies have energy contracts with Petronas, and an interest in bidding on energy projects in Malaysia. Petronas and the Malaysian government might retaliate against them if the President imposes sanctions. Or, at least, the President might turn to the Malaysian government for satisfaction that it is disciplining Petronas in some way. Here, then, would be grounds for waiver or delay, respectively.

Relatedly, ILSA created two incentives to join a multilateral sanctions regime led by the US against Iran.[73] As a positive incentive, the President could waive sanctions against any foreign person from a country that joined such a regime. As a negative incentive, ILSA dropped the trigger permissible investment threshold from $40 to $20 million for any person from a country that did not join.

All such sanctions, of course, fell into the category of 'on the one hand . . .'; that is, disciplines to enforce compliance. The legislation contained '. . . on the other hand'; that is, provisions, ones designed to balance disciplines with flexibilities. The President did not have to impose a sanction if:

1 Doing so would inhibit procurement of defense articles or services under existing contracts or subcontracts (including option contracts 'to satisfy requirements essential to the national security of the US', or co-production agreements for goods or services 'essential to the national security').[74]
2 The person to be sanctioned was 'a sole source supplier' of those articles, and those articles were 'essential' and no substitute was 'readily or reasonably available'.[75]
3 At issue were eligible countries and merchandise under the World Trade Organization (WTO) *Agreement on Government Procurement (GPA)* or a pertinent free trade agreement (FTA);[76]
4 The items involved were (i) pipeline goods, services, or technology (such as items contracted for before the identity of the sanctioned person appeared in the Federal Register),[77] (ii) spare parts, components, or information technology 'essential' to US production or products, or routine servicing and maintenance of products where no alternative arrangements were 'readily or reasonably available',[78] or (iii) medicines, medical supplies, or other 'humanitarian items'.[79]

The first two exceptions manifestly were self-interested – for defense items essential to national security and other items essential to US manufacturing. The third exception, for humanitarian reasons, comported with principles of human dignity and minimizing harm to innocent life.

How might Iran have escaped from ILSA sanctions? The 1996 legislation contained two termination criteria.[80] They matched the purposes of the statute: Iran had to drop its WMD ambitions and stop supporting terrorism. Never mind the possibility that Iran might have to prove the negative (e.g., that it did not actually pursue a WMD). The termination criteria were linked to US suspicions about Iranian behaviour, and those suspicions underpinned the prohibitions and sanctions.

The first criterion was that Iran 'has ceased its efforts to design, develop, manufacture, or acquire' a nuclear bomb, chemical or biological weapons, or ballistic missiles or ballistic missile launch technology.[81] The second criterion was Iran 'has been removed' from the list of countries that (under Section 6(j) of the 1979 *Export Administration Act*) 'have been determined . . . to have repeatedly provided support for acts of international terrorism'.[82] Both criteria required Presidential certification to the appropriate Congressional committees, and both had to be met for termination.

13.7 Phases 5 and 6: 2001 ILSA extension, 2006 IFSA, and extraterritoriality

Phase 5: ILSA extension

(29 September 2006–1 July 2010)

ILSA contained a five-year Sunset Rule, meaning that but for renewal, it would have lapsed on 5 August 2001. It did not, because the 107th Congress produced the ILSA Extension Act of 2001.[83] Aside from extending ILSA until 29 September 2006, the Extension Act both strengthened the sanctions and Congressional oversight.

First, the 2006 legislation lowered from $40 to $20 million the threshold for investment in Iranian petroleum resources that triggered mandatory sanctions against any foreign person.[84] So, the disincentive of a differential trigger, designed under ILSA to discourage deviant behaviour from a multilateral sanctions regime, was dropped. There never was such a regime, so why not tighten the noose around the Iran's most strategic economic sector?

Second, via the Extension Act Congress took another significant step in managing closely US trade policy towards Iran. Congress required the President to report to it on three questions:

1   Were the sanctions achieving their national security objectives?[85]
2   What effect did the sanctions have on humanitarian interests in Iran, a country in which a sanctioned person is located, or other countries?[86]
3   What impact did the sanctions have on other US security and economic interests, 'including relations with countries friendly to the United States', and on the US economy?[87]

Each such matter was a sensible enough topic for which the President ought to report, but two points were critical.

First, the third matter easily allowed for sanctions to be evaluated according to Israeli and Gulf Arab interests. They are countries 'friendly' to the US. If these friends thought the sanctions useful – as they tended to – then so, too, would many in Congress. Second, predictably, the report largely supported the sanctions regime, with one branch of government (the Executive) echoing what the other (the Legislature) wanted to hear.[88] Yet, arguably a robust response to these questions would have been (1) 'no, or at least, not clear', (2) 'possibly hurting innocents', and (3) 'annoying, if not alienating, certain friends and allies, including India and Japan'. Consider each suggestion in turn.

First, during that period, Iran had not abandoned its nuclear energy program, or forsworn WMDs. Second, in contrast to Burmese opposition leader Aung San Suu Kyi (1945–), who called upon the world to boycott the regime of General Than Shwe

(1933–), Iranian opposition figures had not clearly done so.[89] In other words, Mrs Suu Kyi and her National League for Democracy (NLD) were willing to accept the pain of sanctions. The situation in Iran was different: continued sanctions risked giving the Āyatollāh's regime an argument to galvanize people against foreign interference, in effect, to rally around the flag. Third, the likes of India and Japan could not easily and quickly substitute Iran for other sources of energy. US sanctions inflicted difficulties on them, at a time when their support, respectively, for fighting Islamist extremism and ensuring the rise of China was peaceful was critical.

India is an important case in point of limits of US sanctioning power set by factors beyond US control. To meet its growing energy needs as an emerging country and member of the BRICS, India must import up to 80 per cent of its energy. Iran is a historical trading partner for India: Mughal emperors like Shah Jahan (1592–1666) brought architects from Persia to design grand buildings, including the Taj Mahal. Manifestly, with some of the largest oil and natural gas reserves of any country in the world,[90] Iran has a comparative advantage over India in energy production, while India has a comparative advantage over Iran in agricultural goods like rice (a staple in Persian cuisine) and industrial products like generic pharmaceuticals.

As the value of the *rupee* depreciates against hard currencies like the US dollar, energy prices in India rise, causing import-driven inflation. Poor people are particularly hard hit, and government funding to subsidize fuel for them is stretched. If India ceases all imports of Iranian energy, without adequate substitutes, then fuel prices rise. (In effect, the supply curve of energy available in the Indian domestic market shifts in, and if demand is steady or increases, then prices rise.)

Indeed, US sanctions themselves may contribute to higher fuel prices, insofar as they keep off of the world market Iranian oil, thus artificially constricting supply (again, in effect, causing an inward shift in the supply curve). In India and many other developing countries, fuel price hikes are a well-known cause of social and political unrest, and many of India's poor also happen to be Muslim. Surely these factors weigh heavily in the calculations in South Block (the office of the Indian Prime Minister in New Delhi) when considering whether and how to accommodate pressure from the White House to 'toe the line' on Iran.

Phase 6: IFSA

(29 September 2006–1 July 2010)

But for the IFSA, US trade sanctions against Iran dating from 1996 under ILSA and renewed under the Extension Act until 2006 would have lapsed on 29 September of that year. Via IFSA, the 109th Congress extended the regime for another five years, specifically until 31 December 2011.[91] Cancelling sanctions against Libya, IFSA also changed the rubric from 'ILSA' to, or 'ISA'. IFSA loosened sanctions in one respect, and tightened them in three others.

As for relaxation, IFSA empowered the President to waive application of sanctions on the national of any country, for up to six months, 'on a case by case basis', which otherwise would be imposed on that person for investing in the development of Iranian petroleum resources.[92] To exercise this authority, called a 'General Waiver', the President needed to certify to the appropriate Congressional Committees that waiver was 'vital to the national security interests of the United States'.[93] The President could renew the waiver, if 'appropriate', for periods not to exceed six months.[94]

Similarly, IFSA allowed for a 'Waiver with respect to Persons in Countries that Cooperate in Multilateral Efforts with Respect to Iran'.[95] In particular, on a case-by-case basis for up to 12 months, the President could waive imposition of sanctions on a person, if the government with primary jurisdiction over that person 'is closely cooperating' with the US in its efforts to keep Iran from acquiring WMDs or destabilizing numbers and types of advanced conventional weaponry, and such a waiver is 'vital to the national security interests' of the US. The President could renew this waiver, if 'appropriate', for periods not to exceed 12 months.[96]

As for strengthening, first, IFSA created the possibility that the President would launch an investigation into imposing sanctions against a person involved in petroleum investment activity in Iran. If he did so, which he would upon receipt of 'credible information indicating' the person is engaged in a sanctionable activity, then the results of the investigation would be due in 180 days.[97]

Second, IFSA made termination of sanctions more difficult: it added as a third criterion for termination of trade sanctions that (based on Presidential certification to the appropriate Congressional committees) Iran posed 'no significant threat' to the national security or interests of the US or its allies.[98] Israel – though it is the only country in the Middle East not to be a signatory to the NPT, and reputed to be the only nuclear-armed power in that region – could claim both an alliance with the US and a threat to its security or interests.

Indeed, it did so again after President Obama spoke by telephone with Iranian President Hassan Rouhani (1948–). Their 15-minute discussion on 27 September 2013 was the first direct communication between the leaders of the two countries since before the fall of the Shah of Iran.[99] Fearing a possible *rapprochement* between Washington and Tehran on issues of WMDs and terrorism that could involve loosening or eliminating sanctions, Israeli President Benjamin Netanyahu (1949–) flew to the US capital, meeting with President Obama just three days after his historic phone call with President Rouhani. That the Iranian President had the backing of the Iranian Supreme Leader, *Āyatollāh* Ali Khamenei, who authorized his team to show 'heroic flexibility', surely worried the Prime Minister.[100] The Israeli leader dubbed stopping the Iranian nuclear program the 'defining issue of his premiership', and demanded Iran 'stop all uranium enrichment, close the enrichment facility at Qom, remove all enriched uranium, and halt its development of plutonium'.[101]

True enough, by the account of President Rouhani in his September 2013 address to the UN General Assembly, Iranian 'nuclear technology has already reached industrial scale'.[102] Its program included about 18,000 centrifuges across multiple uranium enrichment sites, and stockpiles of enriched uranium to various degrees.[103] But, Israeli demands set a considerably higher threshold for termination of sanctions: without enriching uranium at all, Iran could not have even a peaceful nuclear energy program, but denying Iran such a program never was the aim of the US sanctions.

Prime Minister Netanyahu continued his counter-offensive against what he sarcastically called 'sweet talk and the onslaught of smiles' from Iran surrounding the September 2013 UN General Assembly meeting.[104] The Israeli delegation at the UN walked out of President Rouhani's September 2013 speech, making Israel – in the words of Yair Lapid (1963–), the Israeli Finance Minister – look like a 'serial objector to negotiations'. And, so it was. The Israeli Prime Minister used his time at the General Assembly podium to launch an *ad hominem* attack on the Iranian President, calling him a 'wolf in sheep's clothing'.[105] Surely, the charm offensive from Tehran was a devilishly clever plot to buy Iran time to enrich more plutonium over the 85 per cent threshold needed for a nuclear device. In sum, the third criterion for termination of sanctions added by IFSA nearly subcontracted the US policy on Iran to Israel. As a practical matter, given the overwhelming influence of Israel through the American Israel Political Action Committee (AIPAC) in Congress, it would be difficult to get sanctions lifted without Israeli support – and that support looked well nigh impossible.[106]

Third, and most importantly in respect of strengthening, IFSA clarified the sanctions regime applies to any 'person', not just 'foreign person'. By 'person', the legislation means:

(i) a natural person;
(ii) a corporation, business association, partnership, society, trust, financial institution, insurer, underwriter, guarantor, and any other business organization, any other non-governmental entity, organization, or group, and any governmental entity operating as a business enterprise; and
(iii) any successor to any entity described in clause (ii).[107]

Crucially, the term included any kind of financial institution or provider of financial services. This inclusion facilitated yet tighter prohibitions and tougher sanctions ushered in 2010, 2012, and 2013 (discussed below).

The only explicit exclusion from the term 'person' was a government or governmental entity that did not operate as a business enterprise.[108] So, to the extent the Iranian Revolutionary Guard Corps ran a business, they are within the scope of the sanctions – an understandable inclusion. So, too, was a Chinese SOE, or an Australian STE, or for that matter – and arguably less understandably – the Canadian Wheat Board, or the Indian Coffee Marketing Board.

So, IFSA expanded the universe of potential sanctions targets, and this expansion applied to both prohibitions. No longer were foreign persons investing in the Iranian petroleum sector the only targets. Now, any person materially contributing to the ability of Iran to develop a WMD, or even 'advanced conventional weapons in destabilizing numbers and types', was a target.[109] Indeed, sanctions were mandatory against such a person.

As for the terms 'United States person' and 'foreign person', they remained in the sanctions statute.[110] This distinction was drawn in terms of nationality of an individual or place of organization of a business. A 'United States person' was a (1) natural person who is a US citizen, or who owed 'permanent allegiance to the United States' (presumably, a holder of a permanent residency (green) card, or (2) a legal person, that is, a corporation or other legal entity organized under federal or state law, if over 50 per cent of the capital stock or beneficial interest in the capital stock was owned (directly or indirectly) by a US citizen or green card holder.[111] A 'foreign person' was a foreign citizen who does not hold a US green (that is, permanent residency) card, or a corporation, partnership, or non-governmental organization (NGO) that is not a 'United States person'.[112] So, for example, a subsidiary corporation incorporated in Kansas the majority of the shares of which were held by one or more foreign persons (such as an Indian parent company) was a foreign, not United States, person.

But, was there much practical difference in this distinction? No, because the sanctions apply equally to both types of person. Simply put, by switching to the term 'person', the US made clear that anyone anywhere was a potential target. Once sanctions were imposed, the person on whom or which they were imposed was dubbed – as before – a 'sanctioned person' (sometimes called a 'sanctioned entity').[113] The punishments applied to (1) any successor entity, (2) any person owning or controlling the sanctioned entity with 'actual knowledge or [that] should have known' of the illegal activities of the sanctioned person, and (3) any person owned or controlled by, or under common control with, the sanctioned person, if that person 'knowingly engaged' in the illegal activities.[114]

What principles of Public International Law jurisdiction justified the switch from 'foreign person' to 'person'? While the question is beyond the present scope, a brief digression is worthwhile. Manifestly, neither the nationality nor territoriality principles did: the sanctions did not apply only to 'United States persons' or acts on US soil.

The rationale would have to lay in the 'acts outside, effects inside' standard, whereby an action in support of Iran occurring outside US territory had effects inside the US. What might those effects be? If Iran acquired a WMD, then it could threaten the national security of the US, or even launch an attack on it or its overseas posts (such as embassies and military bases) and nationals (both civilian and military).

13.8 Phase 7: 2010 CISADA emphases on trade embargo, refined gasoline, asset freezes, and human rights

Getting tougher with eight new measures

(1 July 2010–31 December 2016)

The 111th Congress enacted the CISADA.[115] The legislation extended sanctions to 31 December 2016.[116] This six-year extension of the ISA contrasted with the five-year extension by the Extension Act (2001–06), and the five-year extension by the IFSA (2006–11). CISADA 'expanded significantly' the original ILSA sanctions.[117] Having crossed the Rubicon with ILSA in 1996, the US in 2010 with CISADA pushed more aggressively than ever before, broadening and deepening its unilateral prohibitions and punishments.

By no means did the US abandon multilateral efforts. Indeed, CISADA expressed a preference for multilateral over unilateral measures to compel behavioural change in Iran.[118] The problem was multilateral sanctions were not causing that change. So, the US had to lead a 'get tougher' approach. Eight new measures defined its push, as follows.

Notably, the US reaffirmed its justifications for its rules against Iran through the termination criteria, or Sunset Rule, in CISADA. This Rule stated:

> The provisions of this Act (other than sections 105 and 305 [22 U.S.C. §§ 8514 and 8544, concerning the human rights abuse prohibition, discussed below, and enforcement authority, respectively] and the amendments made by sections 102, 107, 109, and 205 [concerning expansion of *ISA* sanctions, harmonization of criminal penalties, capacity to combat terrorist financing, and technical corrections to sanctions rules against Sudan]) shall terminate, and section 80a-13(c)(1)(B) of title 15 [concerning changes in investment policy by registered investment companies], as added by section 203(a), shall cease to be effective, on the date that is 30 days after the date on which the President certifies to Congress that
>
> 1. the Government of Iran has *ceased providing support for acts of international terrorism* and no longer satisfies the requirements for designation as a state sponsor of terrorism (as defined in section 301 [22 U.S.C. Section 8541] . . .

432 *Legal issues in Asian investing*

2. Iran has ceased the pursuit, acquisition, and development of, and verifiably dismantled its, nuclear, biological, and chemical weapons and ballistic missiles and ballistic missile launch technology.[119]

Succinctly put, CISADA terminated when the long-standing goals of the US to change Iranian behaviour on WMDs and terrorism nuclear weaponry were met.

Measures 1 and 2: import and export prohibitions

The first two measures constituted a total trade embargo on Iran. First, the US banned importation from Iran.[120] That ban covered direct or indirect importation of goods or services.[121] Consequently, buying saffron harvested in Iran, but sold in a market in Sharjah, and bringing it into the US, was illegal. There were precious few exceptions, namely, those allowed under the IEEPA, and for information or informational materials.[122]

Note the import ban applied to products of 'Iranian origin'. CISADA did not specify what rules of origin (ROO) should be used to determine whether a product indeed came from Iran. The example of saffron is an easy case of the well-known grown and harvested ROO: a product grown and harvested in a particular country is the product of that country, even if the seeds planted or fertilizer used came from another country, or the water for the crop was irrigated from another country. A harder case could be woven from the famed Iranian carpet industry. Suppose silk for a carpet comes from India, the design is the lovely Qom style, weaving occurs in Iran, and brushing, cleaning, and finishing occurs in Turkey. Is the carpet 'Iranian' based on the place in which it is woven?

The question may be even trickier with regard to services, for which there are no clear ROOs. Imagine a film crew consisting of Iranian and non-Iranian nationals, based in Tehran, seeking to make a movie about a family that migrated from Shiraz to Kansas City just before the fall of the Shah in 1979. The movie is a co-production with a Hollywood studio. Services are provided through various modes: via the Internet (cross-border supply; that is, Mode I), travel by Iranian–American actors portraying the family members from the US to Iran (consumption abroad; that is, Mode II), the joint venture (JV) with the Hollywood studio (FDI; that is, Mode III). Are these services 'from' Iran, and thus barred?

Relatedly, CISADA required the President to report annually to the appropriate Congressional committees on global trade relating to Iran.[123] In particular, he was supposed to identify the dollar value amount of trade between Iran and each country holding membership in the Group of 20 (G-20) Finance Ministers and Central Bank Governors. Plainly, the requirement was designed to give the US data to use to pressure its G-20 partners not to export to or import from Iran. Such data, for instance, not only could identify the 'outlaw' G-20 countries, but also highlight the relevant merchandise, for which (presumably) the US could assist in finding alternative markets or sources. In turn, G-20 Finance Ministers and Central Bank officials could work to block trade financing and payments transactions.

Second, by closing various loopholes, CISADA barred essentially all exports from the US to Iran. All exports from the US, whether goods, services, or technology, including those of or containing Iranian-originating merchandise, and including luxury items (e.g., Persian carpets, or processed pistachios), were illegal.[124] Notably, the ban applied to exports from the US, or from a 'United States person, wherever located'.[125] In other words, a foreign citizen shipping to Iran from Kansas City, or a Kansas citizen residing in Dubai shipping to Iran, would run afoul of the ban.

The only exceptions to the export ban were for (1) personal communications, (2) informational material, (3) transactions incident to travel (4) services for internet communications, (5) agricultural commodities (such as food), (6) medicine or medical devices, (7) humanitarian assistance and/or articles to relieve human suffering, (8) goods, services, or technology necessary to ensure the safe operation of commercial aircraft made in the US (e.g., components for Boeing aircraft used by Iran Air), with the approval of the Treasury Secretary in consultation with the Commerce Secretary, (9) goods, services, or technology to support the IAEA for its work in Iran or international organizations (IOs) or NGOs in their efforts to build democracy in Iran, and (10) exports in the national interest of the US.[126]

As the tenth category intimated, the exceptions advanced the goals underlying the sanctions by facilitating political change in Iran. Leaflets, Twitter, and Facebook accounts, and NGOs all could help in this regard. So, for example, under exceptions (1) and (2), a law professor at the University of Kansas could respond to an email from a prospective law student in Iran about degree programmes at the University, and also honour a request from that student, or a researcher, to email a PDF copy of a previously published, publicly available, law journal article. Arguably, educating Iranians in the US legal system is also in the national interest of the US (item (10)).

Measures 3, 4, and 5: refined gasoline prohibitions

The third, fourth, and fifth measures were mutually reinforcing, and reflected a broadening of the type of sanctionable activity. No longer was investment in the Iranian petroleum sector the only forbidden activity. With CISADA, the refined gasoline sector also was off limits. The US sought to deny not only Iran the ability to find and extract crude oil, but also to refine that oil into gasoline, or import gasoline.

So, the third new measure made illegal any 'knowing' transaction by any 'person' that would assist Iran in producing refined petroleum products.[127] Supplying equipment to, or helping to construct, oil refineries in Iran became forbidden. The sale, lease, or provision to Iran of 'goods, services, technology, information, or support' that 'could directly and significantly facilitate the maintenance or expansion of Iran's domestic production of refined petroleum products, including any direct and significance assistance . . . [for] the construction, modernization, or repair of petroleum refineries. . .' was illegal.[128] By barring Iran from expanding its refining capacity, another potential source of export revenues – and thus of funds for WMDs or terrorist activities – would be closed off.

Like the original 1996 ILSA bar on investment in the Iranian petroleum sector, which had a $40 million threshold that the 2001 Extension Act reduced to $20 million, the CISADA measure had a threshold of $1 million. Any sale, lease, or provision of a good, service, technology, information, or support with a fair market value (FMV) of $1 million or more (or, to prevent structuring, multiple items aggregating to a FMV of $5 million or more in one year) was illegal.[129] The market in which 'fair value' was to be tested was unclear: Iran? The US? A third country? The world market?

Interestingly, the problem of the relevant market is one that occurs in WTO subsidies jurisprudence, when a Panel or the Appellate Body needs to decide whether a challenged measure confers a benefit on a recipient. The test typically is to measure the support against a market-based benchmark, but deciding on the correct market can be controversial – as the arguments between the US and Brazil in the famous 2005 *Cotton* case bespeak.

This CISADA change bore the same ambiguity as did the initial ILSA legislation in 1996 forbidding 'direct and significant' investments to help Iran with its petroleum resources: what kind of transaction 'could directly and significantly' help it with gasoline refining? But, the change introduced a new strategic ambiguity by virtue of one word: 'could'. The pertinent verb in the initial legislation was 'directly and significantly contributes', which demands proof an investment does, in fact, achieve the end of assisting Iran. In CISADA, the relevant verb was 'could directly and significantly facilitate'. No proof was required; speculation as to what Iran might be able to do with the goods, services, technology, information, or support is enough.

That ambiguity surely allowed for aggressive US enforcement. Recall the above hypothetical about supplying Iran with buttons, shoelaces, bottled water, prescription eyeglasses, and aspirin. It remains apposite, indeed, even more so than before CISADA. That is because selling $20 million worth of such merchandise is a high-value threshold to meet, but selling $1 million is not. It is also because any such items 'could' constitute direct, significant, facilitation.

Foreseeably, if the third measure worked and Iran could not refine crude oil into gasoline, then it would look for a substitute: importation. The fourth new measure anticipated and sought to block this move: CISADA barred sale of refined gasoline to Iran. With a view to constricting export revenues that Iran could use to acquire WMDs or support terrorism, ILSA had long made it illegal to buy petroleum from Iran. Now, it also was forbidden to sell gas to it. Iran (redolent of Nigeria) has substantial petroleum reserves, but with little refining capacity, it must import gas for domestic consumption. CISADA would choke off those imports, forcing up gas prices in Iran. In turn, Iranians might pressure their government to comply with US demands for international inspections of nuclear facilities, and abjuring WMDs and terrorists. It might even lead to a change in the government of Iran.

So, in legal terms, CISADA forbade exportation of refined petroleum products to Iran. No person could sell or otherwise provide Iran with them.[130] Likewise, helping Iran upgrade its capacity to import these products was illegal: no person could 'sell[ ], lease[ ], or provide[ ] to Iran goods, services, technology, information, or support . . . that could directly and significantly contribute to the enhancement of Iran's ability to import refined petroleum products'.[131] Again, the valuation thresholds were $1 million in FMV terms (or $5 million in annual aggregate FMV), with no guidance on where or how to calculate FMV.[132] Again, speculation was enough – what 'could' happen is what mattered. And, again, the *mens rea* requirement, 'knowingly', could be met with actual or constructive knowledge. In brief, by expanding prohibited engagement from the export to the import sector, the rule deliberately sought to weaken, if not wreck, the Iranian economy.

As for the fifth measure, consider again the hypothetical example concerning buttons, shoelaces, bottled water, prescription eyeglasses, and aspirin, consider insurance, financial, and shipping services. Suppose a Russian trading house in Vladivostok brokers a transaction, denominated in Indian rupees, between a supplier and an importer in Iran. The deal is a contract for refined petroleum (or, alternatively, for the sale, lease, or provision of goods, services, technology, information, or support that could substantially help

Iran import gasoline). Siam Bank in Bangkok issues a commercial letter of credit (L/C) on behalf of the importer. The importer pays the supplier via the L/C when appropriate and conforming documents, as called for under the terms of the L/C, are presented to its bank, the Bank of Baroda, in Bombay. The documents are couriered between the banks, from Bombay to Bangkok, by DHL. Lloyd's of London underwrites an insurance or reinsurance contract for this transaction. Finally, suppose the Danish freight company, Maersk, provides a Liberian-flagged tanker to carry the refined oil from Pusan, Korea, via Singapore, to Bandar Abbas, Iran.

What parties in the above hypothetical transaction are potentially liable for violating the ban on exporting refined petroleum products to Iran? The answer is 'everybody'. Brokering and financing a deal is a sanctionable act, rendering the Russian trading house and Siam Bank liable.[133] Providing ships and shipping services are forbidden, rendering Maersk liable, and possibly also DHL, if 'shipping services' includes air courier (thus making DHL, a 'courier', a 'shipper'), and 'support' covers transmission of L/C documents.[134] Underwriting insurance or reinsurance contracts is forbidden, putting Lloyd's in legal peril.[135] Simply put, the fifth CISADA measure created a new sanctionable prohibition: shipping and insurance services.

Consider an alteration to the hypothetical: instead of using the formal banking and payments system, the Russian trading house arranges a barter trade. Indian Oil will import crude oil from Iran, and pay Iran for it with Basmati rice. Refined petroleum is not involved in the transaction, nor is any merchandise, or any services, used to build a refinery. There is no liability under the original ILSA sanctionable act of investing $20 million in the Iranian petroleum sector. Indian Oil made no such investment, and the barter deal was not worth such a high figure. Is there liability under the CISADA measures – helping produce, or exporting to, Iran refined petroleum products?

Arguably, yes. Iranian workers whose job it is to build a refinery or upgrade seaport facilities might eat the Indian rice and thereby ingest the carbohydrates they need to work. Moreover, by paying for the rice with crude oil, Iran does not incur the opportunity cost of using precious hard currency. That saving 'could directly and significantly contribute' to Iran's ability to import gasoline.[136] Iran could use that hard currency to import materials to build a new or repair an existing refinery, or for gasoline, which in both cases would be overt sanctions violations.

The hypothetical and its alteration manifest how broad ILSA became thanks to the fifth CISADA measure. CISADA barred shipping, insurance, and related services that might help Iran import gasoline: not only was it illegal to sell gasoline to Iran, but it was also unlawful to facilitate gasoline importation to Iran by insuring vessels or other transport modes for that gasoline.

'Ubiquitous' might be an overstatement, as the amended sanctions did not invariably apply to every transaction involving Iran. For example, CISADA offered a safe harbour for underwriters and insurers. If they:

> exercise[] due diligence in establishing and enforcing official policies, procedures, and controls to ensure that the person does not underwrite or enter into a contract to provide insurance or reinsurance for the sale, lease, or provision of goods, services, technology, or information [that could help Iran improve its ability to import refined petroleum products,

436   *Legal issues in Asian investing*

then they were exempt from sanctions.[137] Still, with CISADA, US trade sanctions against Iran rightly could be characterized as a 'brooding global omnipresence', casting a shadow of caution, if not doubt, on nearly all dealings with Iran.

In brief, by supplementing the trade embargo of the first two measures, the third, fourth, and fifth measures suggest 'CISADA' might have been more succinctly and accurately labelled the '*Trade Embargo and No Gasoline for Iran Act*' (*TENGIA*). US rules denied it the ability to refine crude oil into petroleum products, or to import those products.

From a US perspective, a TENGIA seemed logical: Iran had plenty of petroleum (albeit unrefined), so why should it need nuclear power as an energy source? If Iran insisted on developing nuclear power, and concomitantly nuclear weapons, then surely the US was right to choke off a potential source of support funds for that development, namely, refined gasoline. But, from an Iranian perspective, opportunity cost was the rationale for developing its petroleum and refined gasoline sectors, plus peaceful nuclear energy.

Suppose Iran consumed all its petroleum domestically, and shipped any surplus overseas. By the time it exhausts this natural resource, would it have diversified its economic and export base? Or, would peaceful nuclear energy have allowed allow Iran to stretch out the period before it exhausts its precious natural resource, and in that extra time allowed it to nurture broad-based industrial and service sector development? Put differently, might energy diversification help Iran avoid the resource curse afflicting so many other countries in the Organization of Petroleum Exporting Countries (OPEC)?

Such questions suggest the opportunity cost for Iran of not developing a nuclear energy program was time for prudent diversification beyond oil dependency. Pursuing that alternative energy source could avoid the opportunity cost of a faster run-down of its petroleum reserves, giving it more time for a major, successful structural adjustment. All that could occur, of course, without pursuing a WMD or supporting terrorism. Indeed, diverting funds for those activities would inhibit Iran from avoiding this opportunity cost.

Measure 6: Asset Freeze Prohibition

The sixth measure took the form of another prohibition, namely, violation of an asset freeze.[138] Any funds or other assets belonging to a person in Iran that satisfied the criteria for sanctions under the IEEPA were blocked via Presidential order. Those persons included governmental and quasi-governmental officials, and individuals connected with the Iranian military, Revolutionary Guard Corps, or their affiliates. Transfers of funds or assets to their family members were forbidden. Any US financial institution holding such funds or assets was required to report those holdings to the Office of Foreign Assets Control (OFAC) of the Department of the Treasury, and the President was obliged to report to appropriate Congressional committees on the persons subject to freeze orders.[139] Penalties for violation of any asset freeze order were the same as those for all the others.[140]

Why did the statute expressly mention the Revolutionary Guards? Congress explained that the US should 'persistently target' economic sanctions against the Guards because of 'its support for terrorism, its role in proliferation, and its oppressive activities against the people of Iran'.[141] That was because, said Congress, the Guards were the locus among hardliners pursuing the most vehemently anti-US policies, and the principal instrument for crushing the Green Revolution (as discussed below). Hence, Congress sought to force the hand of the President: he was to impose sanctions on individual Guard officials, such as travel restrictions or other punishments available to him via the 1996 Iran Sanctions Act, as amended in 2010 CISADA, and under the IEEPA.[142]

Most obviously, then, the asset freeze prevented Iranian officials from taking money out of US banks and to assist their country in obtaining a WMD or supporting terrorism. A less obvious consequence was they could not as easily shop for designer brand items at luxury stores like Harrods in London or Chanel in Paris. That consequence may seem insignificant. Yet, as the examples of some North Korean and Syrian government officials indicate, elites enjoy shopping regardless of the plight of their country or fellow nationals. Circumscribing what they regard as a personal entitlement potentially 'hits' them in a poignant manner.

Measure 7: Human Rights Prohibition

The seventh measure represented a policy addition to the US sanctions regime: two more types of behaviour became illegal, but they did not involve the energy sector of Iran. For the first time, the US took aim at human rights abuses and press censorship in Iran, declaring them to be punishable under the regime. The goal of the regime thereby expanded from preventing Iran from acquiring WMDs and disrupting its support for terrorism to deterring it from committing human rights abuses or censorship.

Why bother to seek even more behavioural modification in Iran? The repression of pro-democracy by Iranian authorities and their thuggish proxies in the Green Revolution certainly was one reason. That violence, splashed across the world's media, was too monstrous to ignore: if the Āyatollāhs and their minions were 'evil' for pursuing nuclear weapons and supporting terrorists, then surely they were condemnable for crushing street protests.

So, the President was obliged to identify, and keep updated, for the appropriate Congressional committees officials of the Iranian government, or their agents, including *Hezbollah* and the *Basij-e* militia, which were responsible for, or complicit in, 'serious human rights abuses' against Iranians, wherever located.[143] (That Congress thought the US should strike hard at these officials for their support of *Hezbollah*, which posed an overt threat to Israel, as well as Lebanon and the US, was clear from its declared sense.[144]) 'Credible evidence', which could include announcements or information about the activities of a person by a 'reputable' public or private sector entity, or by a foreign government (e.g., Israeli intelligence services) or NGO (e.g., Amnesty International), was needed to support this blacklisting.[145]

Because this prohibition targeted individuals, the sanctions the President was required to impose differed from the normal menu. They were targeted at the individuals, namely, denial of a visa to enter the US (save for appearance at the UN Headquarters in New York), blocking personal property or its importation or exportation (assuming it was within reach of the US authorities), and barring financial transactions (assuming the US authorities could identify and stop them). Such punishments could be lifted only when Iran (1) unconditionally released 'all political prisoners', (2) ceased 'violence, unlawful detention, torture, and abuse' of Iranians engaged in 'peaceful political activity', (3) did a 'transparent investigation' of the repression of political activists following the Green

Revolution, and (4) made 'demonstrable progress' towards an 'independent judiciary' and implementing the *Universal Declaration of Human Rights*.[146]

Measure 8: expanded and increased sanctions

As for the eighth measure, the 2010 legislation expanded the ILSA list of sanctions from six to nine, and increased the number of sanctions the President had to impose from at least two to three.[147] The new sanctions on the President's menu, all prohibitions, were (numbering consecutively from ILSA):

(7) Foreign Exchange Sanction[148]

Any foreign exchange (FX) transaction with a sanctioned person was forbidden. That party could be barred from any FX transactions over which the US claims jurisdiction and in which that entity has an interest.

That might mean the US did not claim jurisdiction over all dollar transactions under a *lex monetaire* (such as a theory of the law of the currency), so the sanctioned entity might be able to enter into certain FX deals in offshore dollars not involving US financial institutions. But, if the transaction cleared or settled through the US payments system, such as Fedwire or CHIPS (the New York Clearing House Interbank Payments System), or involved a US financial institution, then it could be blocked.[149]

An obvious example, coupled with the Property Transaction sanction (below) would be where a sanctioned entity from Yemen sought to sell financial assets or real property in the US, convert the proceeds from dollars to Yemeni *rial*, and repatriate those funds to Yemen. Both the sale and the FX conversion could be blocked.

(8) Inter-bank Transactions Sanction[150]

Any transfer of credit to, or payment transaction, with a sanctioned entity, by, through, or between any 'financial institutions' was barred.[151] That is, to the extent a transfer or payment was subject to the jurisdiction of the US and involves any interest of a sanctioned person, it may be blocked.

As with the FX Sanction, the Inter-Bank Transactions Sanction could be interpreted broadly to cover any electronic funds transfer through Fedwire or CHIPS, insofar as movements of funds through these systems involve electronic debit and credit entries on banks located in or subject to the jurisdiction of the US, including, of course, the Federal Reserve Bank of New York. Unlike the FX Sanction, however, the Inter-Bank Transactions Sanction covered any 'financial institution'; that is, both American and foreign. Thus, for example, a foreign bank branch or agency in the US was covered (because it operates on US territory), as well as a US bank overseas (because it is subject to supervision by US bank regulators).

Arguably, so, too, was a foreign bank branch or agency located overseas, though exactly how far the reach could extend as a practical matter was unclear. It was not easy for US authorities to block dollar transfers through every office of every offshore foreign bank, and *a fortiori* for them to do so with regard to transfers in other currencies.

Not surprisingly, that is why Iran had little choice but to substitute out of dollars, and into other currencies, for payments purposes. This response, whereby Iranians reduced their legal risk of losing funds denominated in dollars, raised a general policy problem created by the purported long-arm reach of the Sanction: it injected legal risk into operating in US dollars.

Parties, both Iranian and non-Iranian, preferred to transact in other currencies, to argue that those transactions were not subject to the jurisdiction of the US. The dollar, then, became a less desirable currency to hold, because of the greater legal risk associated with it, than did (for instance) Japan's yen or even India's rupee. Similarly, this Sanction also created an incentive for barter trade (discussed below), which occurred between Iran and India in respect of petroleum products (from Iran to India) and rice (vice versa).

(9) Property Transaction Sanction[152]

Any transaction involving property of a sanctioned entity subject to the jurisdiction of the US was prohibited. In effect, this Sanction tied up assets of the sanctioned person. Accordingly, the sanctioned person could be barred from 'acquiring, holding, withholding, using, transferring, withdrawing, transporting, importing, or exporting any property', or 'conducting any transaction involving such property', in or otherwise within the reach of the US in which that person had an interest.[153]

For instance, a sanctioned entity owning an apartment on the Kansas City Country Club Plaza could be barred from staying in it, or selling it to a non-sanctioned party. The Property Transaction Sanction extended to 'dealing in or exercising any right, power, or privilege with respect to such property'.[154] Thus, for example, a sanctioned entity could be prohibited from exercising voting rights associated with stock, or exercising rights on a call or put option on a financial instrument. The term 'property' was not restricted to tangible items, so the stock or other financial instrument could be uncertificated (electronic book entry) securities.

To continue the hypothetical illustration with Lloyd's, suppose it underwrites an insurance policy for a vessel owned by Maersk that shipped gasoline to Iran.

Suppose further the President chooses as the three sanctions on Lloyd's (7), (8), and (9). It would be illegal to enter into a FX transaction, such as exchanging Iranian rial for Indian rupees, or to lend funds to Lloyd's. If Lloyd's held property in Kansas City, then it would be unlawful to buy that property, or (interpreting 'any transaction' broadly) provide services (such as air conditioning or gardening) to that property. Furthermore, CISADA mandated sanctions for any financial institution that helped a sanctioned entity. So, if Bangkok Bank assists Lloyd's by acting as a correspondent bank (e.g., holding an account of Lloyd's through which Lloyd's made or received payments to or from Maersk), then those banks would be sanctioned.

Two final aspects of CISADA buttressed its aggressive stance: any firm seeking a US government contract had to certify it was in compliance with ILSA;[155] and any country that the parent country of an entity sanctioned for providing Iran with WMD technology had to be refused a license of nuclear materials, facilities, or technology.[156]

To be sure, CISADA was not all 'on the one hand . . .'; that is, not entirely aggressive. Its '. . . on the other hand, . . .' measures were a waiver from any sanctions on 'vital national security interest grounds',[157] and a waiver from the government contract certification obligation on the basis of 'the national interest of the United States'.[158] Note the ambiguity created by the lack of a uniform waiver standard: only the first waiver had the adjective 'vital'.

Moreover, while CISADA amended IFSA to make mandatory a Presidential investigation, to be completed within 180 days total, of potentially sanctionable activity, it also contained a 'Special Rule'.[159] So, on the one hand, the President had to initiate an

440 *Legal issues in Asian investing*

investigation with a view to imposing sanctions against any person, if the US received 'credible information' that the person had engaged in sanctionable activity. Such activity (as noted earlier), concerns the (1) development of petroleum resources in Iran, (2) production of refined petroleum products in Iran, or (3) exportation of refined petroleum to Iran.[160]

On the other hand, there was a Special Rule – literally dubbed that.[161] If a person ceased, or had taken 'significant verifiable steps' to cease, activity that was sanctionable, and if that person provided 'reliable assurances' to the President that it 'will not knowingly engage' in any such activity in the future, then no investigation ensued (or one that has commenced was terminated).[162]

There remained textual ambiguities. What information was 'credible'? What steps were 'significant'? How was verification to occur? What assurances are 'reliable'? There also remained interpretative problems relating to the scope of application of the sanctions. For example, suppose an air courier company, such as FedEx, transported a package from an exporter in North Korea to Iran. Did it have the same liability as the exporter, or was it an innocent transporter?

Notes

1 This case study is drawn from Raj Bhala, "Fighting Iran with Trade Sanctions," *Arizona Journal of International and Comparative Law* 31, No. 2 (Spring 2014): 251–356.
2 Both extreme metaphors, 'Great Satan' and 'Evil *Āyatollāhs*', are used only to reflect what many in each country think of the other, but otherwise rejected. Accordingly, the metaphors are put in quotations throughout.
3 The population of Iran is nearly 80 million (as of July 2013). "Middle East: Iran," *United States Central Intelligence Agency World Fact Book*, https://www.cia.gov/library/publications/the-world-factbook/geos/ir.html. The world population is 7.1 billion. "World Population," *United States Central Intelligence Agency World Fact Book*, https://www.cia.gov/library/publications/the-world-factbook/geos/xx.html.
4 Quoted in Najmeh Bozorgmehr, "Zarif Pressed by Iran Hardliners," *Financial Times* (10 December 2013): 2.
5 Committee On Ways And Means, US House Of Representatives, *Overview And Compilation Of Us Trade Statutes*, 111th Congress, 2nd Session, Committee Print (December 2010), Part I of II. [Hereinafter, Overview, Part I.] America's trade embargo dates from the Foreign Assistance Act of 1961, Public Law 87–195, 22 U.S.C. § 2370(a)(1), and is explained in Overview, Part I, at 267–70.
6 John F. Kennedy, "Radio and Television Report to the American People on the Soviet Arms Buildup in Cuba." (Presidential address, The White House, Washington, DC, 22 October 1962), http://microsites.jfklibrary.org/cmc/oct22/doc5.html.
7 Hope springs eternal. The election in June 2013 of a relatively pragmatic, reform-minded President, Hassan Rohani, offers the possibility that Iran may be more transparent with the US about the operation of its nuclear program. It was Mr. Rouhani, a former nuclear negotiator, who convinced his government to suspend uranium enrichment between 2003 and 2005. (He served as National Security Adviser to President Akbar Hashemi Rafsanjani, a pragmatist, and also to President Mohammad Khatami, a reformist. It was the latter capacity in which he agreed to suspend enrichment.)

President Rohani is well aware of the economic damage US sanctions have inflicted on Iran, and the desire of many Iranians to reintegrate into the global economy. But, surely President Rohani appreciates America would ease those sanctions only if what he seeks – constructive engagement and reconciliation – with other countries includes stringent limits on Iran's nuclear program. Yet, his room for maneuvre is limited, given the consistent hard line stance of *Āyatollāhs* Ali Khamenei, the Supreme Leader of Iran. Akbar Ganji, "Who Is Khamenei? The Mind of Iran's Supreme Leader," *Foreign Affairs* 92 (September–October

2013): 24–48 (arguing Khamenei 'is not a crazy, irrational, or reckless zealot searching for opportunities for aggression, but his intransigence is bound to make any negotiations with the West difficult').

The Supreme Leader did not support the efforts of President Khatami to engage President Bill Clinton, and the next President Mahmoud Ahmedinejad spouted fiery, defiant, and sometimes objectionable rhetoric against the US and her allies.

In effect, whether President Rohani can satisfy the US by submitting to its demands to drop its alleged nuclear weapons ambitions, without losing the support of the Supreme Leader and the Revolutionary Guard Corps that backs the $\bar{A}yatoll\bar{a}hs$ is dubious. Najmeh Bozorgmehr and Monavar Khalaj, "Rohani Raises Hopes for Change with Pledges on Iran's Nuclear Programme," *Financial Times* (18 June 2013): 1; Najmeh Bozorgmehr, "Tehran Crowds Take to Streets to Cheer Reformist's Triumph," *Financial Times* (17 June 2013): 2; James Blitz, "West Cautious as Cleric Unlikely to Soften Nuclear Stance Swiftly," *Financial Times* (17 June 2013): 2; Martin Indyk, "The West Must Temper Its Enthusiasm for Iran's New President," *Financial Times* (17 June 2013): 9.

8 For a Chart of the Sessions of Congress, *see* "Guide: Congressional Session Chart," *Indiana University Bloomington Library*, https://libraries.indiana.edu/guide-congressional-session-chart.
9 Overview, Part I, 273.
10 "CIA Documents Acknowledge Its Role in Iran's 1953 Coup," *BBC News*, 20 August 2013, http://www.bbc.co.uk/news/world-middle-east-23762970. The United States and Britain were angered at the Prime Minister's nationalization of Iran's oil industry, which Britain effectively had controlled since 1913 through the Anglo-Persian Oil Company (APOC, sometimes called the Anglo-Iranian Oil Company, or AIOC). APOC later was renamed 'British Petroleum' (BP). "Mohammad Mosaddegh," *Wikipedia*, http://en.wikipedia.org/wiki/Mohammad_Mosaddegh.
11 The NPT was concluded in 1968 and entered into force in 1970. There are 190 Parties, including Iran. Three nuclear nations, India, Pakistan, and North Korea (which withdrew in 2003), are not Parties. "Treaty on the Non-Proliferation of Nuclear Weapons," *Wikipedia*, en.wikipedia.org/wiki/Treaty_on_the_Non-Proliferation_of_Nuclear_Weapons.
12 The dates of the Green Revolution are indicated at "2009–10 Iranian Election Protests," *Wikipedia*, http://en.wikipedia.org/wiki/2009–10_Iranian_election_protests.

US sanctions legislation does not list an end date, but does indicate a start date one day earlier; namely, 12 July 2009. Comprehensive Iran Sanctions Accountability and Divestment Act of 2010, Section 105B(b)(1), Public Law 111–195 (1 July 2010), as amended by Public Law 112–58 (Iran Threat Reduction and Syria Human Rights Act of 2012) and Public Law 112–239 (Iran Freedom and Counter-Proliferation Act of 2012, Sub-Title D of the National Defense Authorization Act for Fiscal Year 2013), codified at 22 U.S.C. §§ 8512, 8513a, 8514, 8514a, 8514b, *reprinted in Committee on Ways and Means*, US House of Representatives, Compilation of US Trade Statutes, 113th Congress, 1st Session, Committee Print (January 2013): 715 (concerning censorship as a sanctionable offense, discussed below). [Hereinafter, 2013 Compilation.]
13 Stephen Kinzer, "To Resolve the Syrian Crisis, the US Must Negotiate with Iran," *Al Jazeera America*, 4 September 2013, http://america.aljazeera.com/articles/2013/9/4/to-resolve-the-syriacrisistheusmustnegotiatewithiran.html (emphasis added).

In this regard, the news that President Barack H. Obama and President Hassan Rouhani exchanged letters concerning Syria, and later spoke briefly by telephone, was welcome. Roula Khalaf, Lionel Barber, and Najmeh Bozorgmehr, "Rouhani's 100-Day Revolution," *Financial Times* (30 November–1 December 2013): 6; "Syria Hails US-Russia Deal on Chemical Weapons," *BBC News*, 15 September 2013, http://www.bbc.co.uk/news/world-middle-east-24100296.
14 Stephen Kinzer, "To Resolve the Syrian Crisis, the US Must Negotiate with Iran," *Al Jazeera America*, 4 September 2013, http://america.aljazeera.com/articles/2013/9/4/to-resolve-the-syriacrisistheusmustnegotiatewithiran.html (emphasis added).
15 Notably, in November 2013, the Foreign Minister of Iran, Mohammad Javad Zarif (1960–), said to the BBC 'we need to come to understand that a sectarian divide on the Islamic world is a threat to all of us.' Quoted in David Gardner, "Iran Can Be Made a Force for Middle East Peace," *Financial Times* (23–24 November 2013): 23–4.

16 Raj Bhala, *Understanding Islamic Law (Sharī'a)* (New Providence, NJ: LexisNexis, 2011): ch. 8–9. (concerning the points about *Shī'ism* made herein). [Hereinafter, *Understanding Islamic Law.*]
17 To be sure, this figure depends on how the legal history of the sanctions is organized.
18 Raj Bhala, *International Trade Law: Interdisciplinary Theory and Practice* 3rd ed. (Newark, NJ: LexisNexis, 2008): ch. 19; Raj Bhala, "Fighting Bad Guys with International Trade Law," *University of California at Davis Law Review* 31 (Fall 1997): 1–121. [Hereinafter, *International Trade Law*, and "Fighting Bad Guys", respectively.]
19 Starting in 2006, Iran was the target of four rounds of United Nations Security Council sanctions. "Iran Says Geneva Nuclear Deal Possible on Friday," BBC News, 7 November 2013, www.bbc.co.uk/news/world-middle-east-24857981. Both the US and the EU have implemented their own sanctions regime, to reinforce that of the UN. GATT Article XXI(c) justifies the US and European sanctions: they concern atomic weapons proliferation (covered by Article XXI(b)(i)), and are taken pursuant to UN Security Council Resolutions (encompassed by Article XXI(c)). While not discussed herein, United Nations sanctions are less comprehensive and aggressive than US trade sanctions.

This discussion focuses on the US sanctions regime. For a brief summary of them, followed by an overview of European, Canadian, and Korean trade measures against Iran, see Edward J. Krauland and Anthony Rapa, "Between Scylla and Charybdis: Identifying and Managing Secondary Sanctions Risks Arising from Commercial Relationships with Iran," *Business Law International* 15 (January 2014): 3–17. Appendix A of that article provides a synopsis of non-United States persons on which sanctions were imposed between October 2010 and May 2013.
20 Public Law 104–72, 110 Stat. 1541–51, as amended, codified at 50 U.S.C. § 1701 note *et seq.* Overview, Part I, at 273–4. The effective date for ILSA was the date of enactment, 5 August 1996. Iran Sanctions Act of 1996, as amended, Section 13(a), *reprinted in* Committee on Ways and Means, US House of Representatives, Overview and Compilation of US Trade Statutes, 111th Congress, 2nd Session, Committee Print (December 2010), Part II of II, at 1147. [Hereinafter, Overview, Part II.]
21 Public Law 107–24, 115 Stat. 199–200, enacted 3 August 2001, amending 50 U.S.C. § 1701 note.
22 Public Law 109–293, 120 Stat. 344–50, enacted 30 September 2006, amending Iran Sanctions Act of 1996, 50 U.S.C. § 1701 note.

The features of this and successor legislation dealing with Libya are not discussed herein. "Fighting Bad Guys," 1–121 (assessing sanctions on both Iran and Libya). Likewise, aspects of the sanctions regime touching on Iraq – for example, the ILSA Extension Act mandate that the President report to Congress on the effect of sanctions on humanitarian interests in Iraq – are not discussed herein.

Herein, statutory references are to ILSA including amendments to it through successive legislation. The amendments, and when and why they occurred, are explained below, with appropriate citations to Overview, Part I, at 273–5.
23 Public Law 111–95, 124 Stat. 1312–51 (1 July 2010), codified at 22 U.S.C. § 8501 note *et seq.* and 50 U.S.C. § 1701 note *et seq.*, enacted 1 July 2010, amending Iran Sanctions Act of 1996, 50 U.S.C. § 1701 note.
24 Public Law 112–81, 125 Stat. 1298, 1647–50, Section 1245, as amended by Public Law 112–58 (Iran Threat Reduction and Syria Human Rights Act of 2012) and Public Law 112–239 (Iran Freedom and Counter-Proliferation Act of 2012, Sub-Title D of the National Defense Authorization Act for Fiscal Year 2013), codified at 22 U.S.C. § 8513a. This Act did not amend either the 1996 or 2010 legislation, but rather supplemented them with an additional prohibition concerning Iranian financial institutions, including the Central Bank of Iran.
25 Public Law 112–58, 126 Stat. 1214–69, enacted 10 August 2012, codified at 22 U.S.C. §§ 8711, 8721–24, 8741–44, 8781, amending Iran Sanctions Act of 1996, 50 U.S.C. § 1701 note, and also amending the 2010 Comprehensive Iran Sanctions, Accountability, and Divestment Act.

The 2012 legislation also supplemented Section 1245 of the *National Defense Authorization Act of 2012*, Public Law 112–81, 22 U.S.C. § 8513a, in respect of financial sanctions against Iran and the third country short supply exception. (These points are discussed below.) The National Defense Authorization Act was amended further by the Iran Freedom and Counter-

Proliferation Act of 2012 (Sub-Title D of the National Defense Authorization Act for Fiscal Year 2013), Public Law 112–239.

26 Public Law 112–239, 126 Stat. 1632, 2004–18, enacted 2 January 2013, codified at 22 U.S.C. §§ 8801–11.

27 Comprehensive Iran Sanctions Accountability and Divestment Act of 2010, parenthetical note (concerning 2012 amendments to 2010 law), and Iran Sanctions Act of 1996, parenthetical note (concerning 2010 amendments to 1996 law) *reprinted in* Committee on Ways and Means, US House of Representatives, Compilation of US Trade Statutes, 113th Congress, 1st Session 685, 708 (Committee Print, January 2013). [Hereinafter, 2013 Compilation.]

28 Additionally, recourse to legislative history and various issuances from pertinent US authorities is helpful, and in specific client matters, likely to be essential. Research into these sources was beyond the present scope.

29 "Guide: Congressional Session Chart," *Indiana University Bloomington Library*, https://libraries.indiana.edu/guide-congressional-session-chart.

30 The statute defines 'Iran' as 'any agency or instrumentality of Iran.' Iran Sanctions Act of 1996, as amended, Section 14(10), *reprinted in* Overview, Part II, at 1148. Albeit circular, this definition suggests a distinction between the government and people.

31 Public Law 95–223, Title II, 28 December 1977, 91 Stat. 1626, *codified at* 50 U.S.C. §§ 1701 *et seq.*

32 Iran Sanctions Act of 1996, as amended, Section 2(1)–(3), *reprinted in* Overview, Part II, at 1133.

33 The statute speaks of 'Iranian diplomats and representatives of other government and military or quasi-military institutions of Iran,' and lists such entities. They include the Foreign, Intelligence and Security, and Interior Ministries, Revolutionary Guards, and several Foundations. Iran Sanctions Act of 1996, as amended, Section 14(11), *reprinted in* Overview, Part II, at 1148.

34 Iran Sanctions Act of 1996, as amended, Section 2(2)–(3), *reprinted in* Overview, Part II, at 1133.

35 Iran Sanctions Act of 1996, as amended, Section 3, *reprinted in* Overview, Part II, at 1133. The statutory definition of 'act of international terrorism' is discussed in a later footnote.

36 Iran Sanctions Act of 1996, as amended, Section 5(a)(1) and 5(b), respectively, *reprinted in* Overview, Part II, at 1136, 1138.

37 The pertinent excerpt from the 29 January 2002 speech may be viewed at "President Bush Axis of Evil Speech," *YouTube*, 2 April 2013, http://www.youtube.com/watch?v=btkJhAM7hZw.

38 Iran Sanctions Act of 1996, as amended, Section 10(a)(1), *reprinted in* Overview, Part II, at 1145.

39 Iran Sanctions Act of 1996, as amended, Section 10(a)(2), *reprinted in* Overview, Part II, at 1145.

40 Iran Sanctions Act of 1996, as amended, Section 10(a)(4), *reprinted in* Overview, Part II, at 1145.

41 Iran Sanctions Act of 1996, as amended, Section 10(a)(3), *reprinted in* Overview, Part II, at 1146.

42 Iran Sanctions Act of 1996, as amended, Section 4(a), *reprinted in* Overview, Part II, at 1133. Section 4(b) mandated Presidential reports to the 'appropriate Congressional committees' on countries that have, and have not, agreed to support the US in its policy towards Iran. Those Committees were the Senate Committees on Banking, Housing, and Urban Affairs, and on Foreign Relations, and the House Committees on Foreign Affairs, Financial Services, and Ways and Means. Ibid., Section 14(2), at 1147 (defining 'appropriate Congressional committees'). The same Committees are referred to throughout the legislation as 'appropriate Congressional committees'; e.g., ibid., Section 4(d) at 1135 (concerning interim reports on multilateral sanctions and monitoring).

43 Iran Sanctions Act of 1996, as amended, Section 5(a)(1)(B), *reprinted in* Overview, Part II, at 1136.

44 Iran Sanctions Act of 1996, as amended, Section 14(15), *reprinted in* Overview, Part II, at 1149.

45 Iran Sanctions Act of 1996, as amended, Section 14(16), *reprinted in* Overview, Part II, at 1149.

46 Iran Sanctions Act of 1996, as amended, Section 14(9), *reprinted in* Overview, Part II, at 1148. The pertinent date at which such contracts became illegal was the date of enactment

of ILSA, which was its effective date. Ibid., Section 13(a), at 1147. Any amendment to a contract made on or after 13 June 2001 (a few weeks before the entry into force of the ILSA Extension Act) to a pre-existing contract is considered entry into a contract, and thus forbidden. Ibid.

47 Iran Sanctions Act of 1996, as amended, Section 14(4), *reprinted in* Overview, Part II, at 1147. Likewise, such activities would constitute 'development.'
48 Iran Sanctions Act of 1996, as amended, Section 14(12), *reprinted in* Overview, Part II, at 1149.
49 Iran Sanctions Act of 1996, as amended, Section 5(b), *reprinted in* Overview, Part II, at 1138.
50 Iran Sanctions Act of 1996, as amended, Section 5(b)(1), *reprinted in* Overview, Part II, at 1138.

'Goods and technology' are defined in Section 14(8) in the same manner as in Section 16 of the 1979 Export Administration Act (50 U.S.C. App. § 2415), but 'services' is not expressly defined. Ibid., Section 14(8), at 1148.

51 Iran Sanctions Act of 1996, as amended, Section 14(13), *reprinted in* Overview, Part II, at 1149.
52 Iran Sanctions Act of 1996, as amended, Section 5(b)(2)(A), *reprinted in* Overview, Part II, at 1138 (mentioning 'missiles or advanced conventional weapons that are designed or modified to deliver a nuclear weapon').
53 Iran Sanctions Act of 1996, as amended, Section 5(a), *reprinted in* Overview, Part II, at 1135–1136.
54 Iran Sanctions Act of 1996, as amended, Section 5(a)(1)(A), *reprinted in* Overview, Part II, at 1136. As explained below, the ILSA Extension Act of 2001 reduced the permissible investment threshold to $20 million. Overview, Part I, at 274.
55 Iran Sanctions Act of 1996, as amended, Section 5(c), *reprinted in* Overview, Part II, at 1139.
56 Iran Sanctions Act of 1996, as amended, Section 6(a)(1), *reprinted in* Overview, Part II, at 1141.
57 Iran Sanctions Act of 1996, as amended, Section 6(a)(2), *reprinted in* Overview, Part II, at 1141.
58 Iran Sanctions Act of 1996, as amended, Section 5(b)(2), *reprinted in* Overview, Part II, at 1138.
59 Iran Sanctions Act of 1996, as amended, Section 5(b)(2)(B)-(C), *reprinted in* Overview, Part II, at 1138–9. As to the first two grounds for exception for imposing the Sanction, the President had to give notification to the appropriate Congressional committees. Ibid., Section 5(b)(2)(B)(i)-(ii). As to the third ground, which resulted in issuance of a license despite a violation, the President had to justify doing so to the Senate Committee on Foreign Affairs and House Committee on Foreign Relations. Ibid., Section 5(b)(2)(C)(ii).
60 Iran Sanctions Act of 1996, as amended, Section 6(a)(3), *reprinted in* Overview, Part II, at 1141.
61 Iran Sanctions Act of 1996, as amended, Section 14(5), *reprinted in* Overview, Part II, at 1147. ILSA incorporates by reference the definition of 'financial institution' from Section 3(c)(1) of the Federal Deposit Insurance Act of 1950, and the definition of a foreign bank 'branch' or 'agency' from Section 1(b)(7) of the International Banking Act of 1978. Ibid.
62 Iran Sanctions Act of 1996, as amended, Section 6(a)(3), *reprinted in* Overview, Part II, at 1141.
63 Iran Sanctions Act of 1996, as amended, Section 6(a)(4)(A)–(B), *reprinted in* Overview, Part II, at 1141.
64 This sanction is potentially two separate sanctions. If a financial institution is denied primary dealer status, or its status as such is revoked, then that action is considered one sanction. If it also is barred from serving as a repository, or its ability to serve as such is revoked, that action is considered a second sanction. Iran Sanctions Act of 1996, as amended, Section 6(a)(4), *reprinted in* Overview, Part II, at 1141.
65 Iran Sanctions Act of 1996, as amended, Section 6(a)(5), *reprinted in* Overview, Part II, at 1141.
66 Iran Sanctions Act of 1996, as amended, Section 6(a)(9), *reprinted in* Overview, Part II, at 1142.
67 50 U.S.C. § 1701 et seq.
68 Iran Sanctions Act of 1996, as amended, Section 9(b), *reprinted in* Overview, Part II, at 1144.

69 Iran Sanctions Act of 1996, as amended, Section 11, *reprinted in* Overview, Part II, at 1146–1147. The President must report to the appropriate Congressional committee his rationale for the waiver. His report must discuss the nature and significance for Iran's acquisition of WMDs or destabilizing numbers and types of advanced conventional weapons of the prohibited conduct in which the sanctioned person engaged, the actions of the government holding primary jurisdiction over the person to end or penalize that conduct, and possible US responses if the person resumes the conduct. Ibid., Section 9(c)(2).
70 Iran Sanctions Act of 1996, as amended, Section 9(c)(1), *reprinted in* Overview, Part II, at 1145.
71 Iran Sanctions Act of 1996, as amended, Section 9(a)(1), (3), *reprinted in* Overview, Part II, at 1145. The President must report to Congress about the consultations and his decision in favour of delay. Ibid. at Section 9(4).
72 Iran Sanctions Act of 1996, as amended, Section 9(a)(2), *reprinted in* Overview, Part II, at 1144.
73 Iran Sanctions Act of 1996, as amended, Section 4(d), *reprinted in* Overview, Part II, at 1135 (calling for an interim report from the President to the appropriate congressional committees on multilateral sanctions as to (1) whether Australia, European Union, Israel, or Japan have trade sanctions on persons or their affiliates from doing business with or investing in Iran, and if so, their duration and effect, and (2) any decisions under the General Agreement on Tariffs and Trade (GATT) or World Trade Organization (WTO) on sanctions against Iran).
74 Iran Sanctions Act of 1996, as amended, Section 5(f)(1)(A), (C), *reprinted in* Overview, Part II, at 1140.
75 Iran Sanctions Act of 1996, as amended, Section 5(f)(1)(B), *reprinted in* Overview, Part II, at 1140.
76 Iran Sanctions Act of 1996, as amended, Section 5(f)(2), *reprinted in* Overview, Part II, at 1140.
77 Iran Sanctions Act of 1996, as amended, Section 5(f)(3), *reprinted in* Overview, Part II, at 1140.
78 Iran Sanctions Act of 1996, as amended, Section 5(f)(4), (6), *reprinted in* Overview, Part II, at 1140.
79 Iran Sanctions Act of 1996, as amended, Section 5(f)(7), *reprinted in* Overview, Part II, at 1140.
80 Iran Sanctions Act of 1996, as amended, Section 8(1)–(2), *reprinted in* Overview, Part II, at 1143–1144.
81 Iran Sanctions Act of 1996, as amended, Section 8(1)(A)–(C), *reprinted in* Overview, Part II, at 1143.
82 Iran Sanctions Act of 1996, as amended, Section 8(2), *reprinted in* Overview, Part II, at 1144. The statute defined an 'act of international terrorism' as any act that is (1) 'violent or dangerous to human life,' (2) violates federal or state criminal law (or would do so if committed in the US or a state), and (3) 'appears . . . intended' to 'intimidate or coerce a civilian population or influence government policy by intimidation or coercion, or affect government conduct by assassination or kidnapping.' Note there was no link between the act and ideology; that is, there is no requirement the act be done in pursuit of a religious or political agenda. That absence distinguished this definition from others used in the United States. *Understanding Islamic Law* § 50.01[A]. Moreover, there was no requirement in the Iran Sanctions Act definition that the civilian or government target should be American. Overview, Part II, Section 14(1), at 1147.
83 Public Law 107–24, 115 Stat. 199–200 (3 August 2001), *codified at* 50 U.S.C. § 1701 note. Overview, Part I, at 274; "Guide: Congressional Session Chart," *Indiana University Bloomington Library*, https://libraries.indiana.edu/guide-congressional-session-chart. To extend ILSA, Section 4 of the Extension Act amended Section 13(b) of ILSA. The renewals and extensions of ILSA are summarized in Iran and Libya Sanctions Act, Wikipedia, *posted at* en.wikipedia.org/wiki/Iran_and_Libya_Sanctions_Act.
84 Iran Sanctions Act of 1996, as amended, Section 5(a)(1)(A), *reprinted in* Overview, Part II, at 1136; Overview, Part I, at 274.
85 Iran Sanctions Act of 1996, as amended, Section 10(b)(1)(A), *reprinted in* Overview, Part II, at 1146.
86 Iran Sanctions Act of 1996, as amended, Section 10(b)(1)(B), *reprinted in* Overview, Part II, at 1146.
87 Iran Sanctions Act of 1996, as amended, Section 10(b)(2), *reprinted in* Overview, Part II, at 1146.

88 The report was due between 24 and 30 months after the date of enactment of the Extension Act; that is, 24–30 months from 30 September 2006. Iran Sanctions Act of 1996, as amended, Section 10(b), *reprinted in* Overview, Part II, at 1146.

89 Generally Connie Ng, "Comment, Burma and the Road Forward: Lessons from Next Door and Possible Avenues Towards Constitutional and Democratic Development," Santa Clara Law Review 53 (2013): 267–99. (discussing the transition to democracy in Burma).

90 Yeganeh Torbati & Lesley Wroughton, "Kerry Meets Iran Foreign Minister to Close Gaps in Iran Nuclear Talks," Reuters, 8 November 2013, http://mobile.reuters.com/article/topNews/idUSBRE9A709G20131108?irpc=932.

91 Public Law 109–293, 120 Stat. 344–350 (30 September 2006), codified at 50 U.S.C. § 1701 note. Overview, Part I, at 274. Section 204 contained the extended sunset date.

On 23 April 2004, President George W. Bush waived application of sanctions on Libya because of the agreement of that country to abandon pursuit of WMDs and cooperate with the US on counterterrorism. 69 Fed. Reg. 24,907 (5 May 2004); Overview, Part I, at 274. Pursuant to the Iran Freedom Support Act, enacted 30 September 2006, Libya no longer was subject to ILSA sanctions. Overview, Part I, at 274. The ISA initially was known as the Iran and Libya Sanctions Act, under the 1996 legislation, and under the ILSA Extension Act of 2001. But, when sanctions were removed on Libya under the 2006 Iran Freedom Support Act, the nomenclature of 'Iran Sanctions Act,' or 'ISA,' was used. Iran Sanctions Act of 1996, as amended, Section 1, *reprinted in* Overview, Part II, at 1133.

92 Iran Sanctions Act of 1996, as amended, Section 4(c)(1)(A), *reprinted in* Overview, Part II, at 1134.

93 Iran Sanctions Act of 1996, as amended, Section 4(c)(1)(A), *reprinted in* Overview, Part II, at 1134. The President must make this certification at least 30 days before the waiver takes effect. Ibid.

94 Iran Sanctions Act of 1996, as amended, Section 4(c)(2)(A), *reprinted in* Overview, Part II, at 1134–5.

95 Iran Sanctions Act of 1996, as amended, Section 4(c)(1)(B), *reprinted in* Overview, Part II, at 1134. As with the General Waiver, with the Waiver for a person from a cooperating country, the President must make this certification at least 30 days before the waiver takes effect. Ibid.

96 Iran Sanctions Act of 1996, as amended, Section 4(c)(2)(A), *reprinted in* Overview, Part II, at 1134–5.

97 Overview, Part I, at 275; Iran Sanctions Act of 1996, as amended, Section 4(e)(2), *reprinted in* Overview, Part II, at 1135.

98 Overview, Part I, at 275; Iran Sanctions Act of 1996, as amended, Section 8(3), *reprinted in* Overview, Part II, at 1144.

99 Saeed Kamali Dehghan, "Obama and Rouhani's Telephone Call of Huge Significance, Says Iranian Deputy," *The Guardian*, 2 October 2013, http://www.theguardian.com/world/2013/oct/02/obama-rouhani-phone-call-us-iran.

100 *Quoted in* Najmeh Bozorgmehr, "Rouhani Lifts Hope for Solutions," *Financial Times* (30 September 2013): 4.

101 John Reed and Geoff Dyer, "Netanyahu to Talk Tough on Iran to Obama", *Financial Times* (30 September 2013): 4. [Hereinafter, Netanyahu to Talk Tough.]

102 *Quoted in* Richard Haas, "A Diplomatic Dance Will Be No Waltz For Either Iran or America" *Financial Times* (30 September 2013): 11. [Hereinafter, A Diplomatic Dance.]

103 *A Diplomatic Dance*. In December 2013, Iran was estimated to have 19,000 centrifuges. Geoff Dyer and John Reed, "Israel Opts to Shift Tactics on Iran Talks," *Financial Times*, (7–8 December 2013): 4.

104 Netanyahu to Talk Tough.

105 *Quoted in* Geoff Dyer, "Iran's 'Good Cop, Bad Cop' Breeds Divided Feelings in Washington," *Financial Times* (12 December 2013): 12.

106 Netanyahu to Talk Tough.

107 Iran Sanctions Act of 1996, as amended, Section 14(4)(A), *reprinted in* Overview, Part II, at 1149.

108 Iran Sanctions Act of 1996, as amended, Section 14(4)(B), *reprinted in* Overview, Part II, at 1149.

109 Overview, Part I, at 275.
110 Iran Sanctions Act of 1996, as amended, Section 14(7), (18), *reprinted in* Overview, Part II, at 1148–9 (defining 'foreign person' and 'United States person,' respectively).
111 Iran Sanctions Act of 1996, as amended, Section 14(18), *reprinted in* Overview, Part II, at 1149 (defining 'United States person').
112 Iran Sanctions Act of 1996, as amended, Section 14(7), (18), *reprinted in* Overview, Part II, at 1148 (defining 'foreign person').
113 Iran Sanctions Act of 1996, as amended, Section 5(c), *reprinted in* Overview, Part II, at 1135. Such persons are identified in the Federal Register, as is a list of all significant oil and gas projects that Iran has put for public tender. Ibid., Section 5(d)-(e), at 1139–40.
114 Iran Sanctions Act of 1996, as amended, Section 5(c)(2), *reprinted in* Overview, Part II, at 1139 (defining 'foreign person').
115 Comprehensive Iran Sanctions Accountability and Divestment Act of 2010, Public Law 111–95, 124 Stat. 1312–51 (1 July 2010), *codified at* 22 U.S.C. § 8501 note *et seq.* and 50 U.S.C. § 1701 note *et seq.*, as amended by Public Law 112–158 (Iran Threat Reduction and Syria Human Rights Act of 2012) and Public Law 112–239 (Iran Freedom and Counter-Proliferation Act of 2012, Sub-Title D of the National Defense Authorization Act for Fiscal Year 2013), *codified at* 22 U.S.C. §§ 8512, 8513a, 8514, 8514a, 8514b, *reprinted in* 2013 Compilation, at 708–21.
116 Iran Sanctions Act of 1996, as amended, Section 13(b), *reprinted in* Overview, Part II, at 1147.
117 Overview, Part I, at 275.
118 Comprehensive Iran Sanctions Accountability and Divestment Act of 2010, Section 114(1), Public Law 111–195 (1 July 2010), as amended by Public Law 112–58 (Iran Threat Reduction and Syria Human Rights Act of 2012) and Public Law 112–239 (Iran Freedom and Counter-Proliferation Act of 2012, Sub-Title D of the National Defense Authorization Act for Fiscal Year 2013), codified at 22 U.S.C. §§ 8512, 8513a, 8514, 8514a, 8514b, *reprinted in* 2013 Compilation, at 717.
119 CISADA, Section 401(a), *codified at* 22 U.S.C. § 8551(a) (emphasis added).
120 CISADA, Section 103(a), (b)(1)(A), *reprinted in* 2013 Compilation, at 708–9.
121 It appeared the addition of services to the import ban was the result of an amendment by the Iran Threat Reduction and Syria Human Rights Act of 2012, Public Law 112–81, as amended by Public Law 112–158 (Iran Threat Reduction and Syria Human Rights Act of 2012) and Public Law 112–239 (Iran Freedom and Counter-Proliferation Act of 2012, Sub-Title D of the National Defense Authorization Act for Fiscal Year 2013), *codified at* 22 U.S.C. § 8513a, *reprinted in* 2013 Compilation, at 721–736. Note that unlike the export ban (discussed below), the import ban did not apply to technology; that is, Iranian technology could be imported into the US, but US technology could not be exported to Iran.
122 CISADA, Section 103(b)(1)(B), *reprinted in* 2013 Compilation, at 708–09; Overview, Part I, at 275. The *IEEPA* exceptions are set out at 50 U.S.C. Section 1702(b).
123 Iran Sanctions Act of 1996, as amended, Section 10(d), *reprinted in* Overview, Part II, at 1146.
124 CISADA, Section 103(a), (b)(2), *reprinted in* 2013 Compilation, at 708–09.
Note there had been a ban on exports, and CISADA introduced the exemption for internet communications, or exports of goods or services, to help support democracy in Iran. Overview, Part I, at 275. It appeared the addition of services to the import ban was the result of an amendment by the Iran Threat Reduction and Syria Human Rights Act of 2012, Public Law 112–81, as amended by Public Law 112–58 (Iran Threat Reduction and Syria Human Rights Act of 2012) and Public Law 112–239 (Iran Freedom and Counter-Proliferation Act of 2012, Sub-Title D of the National Defense Authorization Act for Fiscal Year 2013), *codified at* 22 U.S.C. § 8513a, *reprinted in* 2013 Compilation, at 721–36.
125 CISADA, Section 103(b)(2)(A), *reprinted in* 2013 Compilation, at 709; Iran Sanctions Act of 1996, as amended, Section 14(18), *reprinted in* Overview, Part II, at 1149–1150.
126 CISADA, Section 103(b)(2)(B)(i)–(vi), *reprinted in* 2013 Compilation, at 709; Overview, Part I, at 275.
127 Iran Sanctions Act of 1996, as amended, Section 5(a)(2), *reprinted in* Overview, Part II, at 1136.

128 Iran Sanctions Act of 1996, as amended, Section 5(a)(2)(A)–(B), *reprinted in* Overview, Part II, at 1136.
129 Iran Sanctions Act of 1996, as amended, Section 5(a)(2)(A)(i)–(ii), *reprinted in* Overview, Part II, at 1136.
130 Iran Sanctions Act of 1996, as amended, Section 5(a)(3)(A)(i), *reprinted in* Overview, Part II, at 1137.
131 Iran Sanctions Act of 1996, as amended, Section 5(a)(3)(A)(ii)–(B), *reprinted in* Overview, Part II, at 1137.
132 Iran Sanctions Act of 1996, as amended, Section 5(a)(3)(A)(i)–(ii), *reprinted in* Overview, Part II, at 1137.
133 Iran Sanctions Act of 1996, as amended, Section 5(a)(3)(B)(ii), *reprinted in* Overview, Part II, at 1137.
134 Iran Sanctions Act of 1996, as amended, Section 5(a)(3)(B)(ii), *reprinted in* Overview, Part II, at 1137.
135 Iran Sanctions Act of 1996, as amended, Section 5(a)(3)(B)(i), *reprinted in* Overview, Part II, at 1137.
136 Iran Sanctions Act of 1996, as amended, Section 5(a)(3)(B), *reprinted in* Overview, Part II, at 1137.
137 Iran Sanctions Act of 1996, as amended, Section 5(a)(3)(C), reprinted in Overview, Part II, at 1137.
138 Comprehensive Iran Sanctions Accountability and Divestment Act of 2010, Section 103(b)(3)(A), (D), Public Law 111–95 (1 July 2010), as amended by Public Law 112–58 (Iran Threat Reduction and Syria Human Rights Act of 2012) and Public Law 112–239 (Iran Freedom and Counter-Proliferation Act of 2012, Sub-Title D of the National Defense Authorization Act for Fiscal Year 2013), codified at 22 U.S.C. §§ 8512, 8513a, 8514, 8514a, 8514b, *reprinted in* 2013 Compilation, at 710–11.
139 Comprehensive Iran Sanctions Accountability and Divestment Act of 2010, Section 103(b)(3)(B)–(C), Public Law 111–95 (1 July 2010), as amended by Public Law 112–58 (Iran Threat Reduction and Syria Human Rights Act of 2012) and Public Law 112–239 (Iran Freedom and Counter-Proliferation Act of 2012, Sub-Title D of the National Defense Authorization Act for Fiscal Year 2013), codified at 22 U.S.C. §§ 8512, 8513a, 8514, 8514a, 8514b, *reprinted in* 2013 Compilation, at 710–11.
140 Comprehensive Iran Sanctions Accountability and Divestment Act of 2010, Section 103(c), Public Law 111–195 (1 July 2010), as amended by Public Law 112–158 (Iran Threat Reduction and Syria Human Rights Act of 2012) and Public Law 112–239 (Iran Freedom and Counter-Proliferation Act of 2012, Sub-Title D of the National Defense Authorization Act for Fiscal Year 2013), codified at 22 U.S.C. §§ 8512, 8513a, 8514, 8514a, 8514b, *reprinted in* 2013 Compilation, at 711.
141 Comprehensive Iran Sanctions Accountability and Divestment Act of 2010, Section 112(1), Public Law 111–95 (1 July 2010), as amended by Public Law 112–158 (Iran Threat Reduction and Syria Human Rights Act of 2012) and Public Law 112–239 (Iran Freedom and Counter-Proliferation Act of 2012, Sub-Title D of the National Defense Authorization Act for Fiscal Year 2013), codified at 22 U.S.C. §§ 8512, 8513a, 8514, 8514a, 8514b, *reprinted in* 2013 Compilation, at 716.
142 Comprehensive Iran Sanctions Accountability and Divestment Act of 2010, Section 112(3), Public Law 111–95 (1 July 2010), as amended by Public Law 112–58 (Iran Threat Reduction and Syria Human Rights Act of 2012) and Public Law 112–239 (Iran Freedom and Counter-Proliferation Act of 2012, Sub-Title D of the National Defense Authorization Act for Fiscal Year 2013), codified at 22 U.S.C. §§ 8512, 8513a, 8514, 8514a, 8514b, *reprinted in* 2013 Compilation, at 716.
143 Comprehensive Iran Sanctions Accountability and Divestment Act of 2010, Section 105(a)–(b), Public Law 111–95 (1 July 2010), as amended by Public Law 112–58 (Iran Threat Reduction and Syria Human Rights Act of 2012) and Public Law 112–239 (Iran Freedom and Counter-Proliferation Act of 2012, Sub-Title D of the National Defense Authorization Act for Fiscal Year 2013), *codified at* 22 U.S.C. §§ 8512, 8513a, 8514, 8514a, 8514b, *reprinted in* 2013 Compilation, at 711–12.

144 Comprehensive Iran Sanctions Accountability and Divestment Act of 2010, Section 113(1)–(2), Public Law 111–95 (1 July 2010), as amended by Public Law 112–158 (Iran Threat Reduction and Syria Human Rights Act of 2012) and Public Law 112–239 (Iran Freedom and Counter-Proliferation Act of 2012, Sub-Title D of the National Defense Authorization Act for Fiscal Year 2013), *codified at* 22 U.S.C. §§ 8512, 8513a, 8514, 8514a, 8514b, *reprinted in* 2013 Compilation, at 716.

145 Comprehensive Iran Sanctions Accountability and Divestment Act of 2010, Section 105(b), Public Law 111–95 (1 July 2010), as amended by Public Law 112–58 (Iran Threat Reduction and Syria Human Rights Act of 2012) and Public Law 112–239 (Iran Freedom and Counter-Proliferation Act of 2012, Sub-Title D of the National Defense Authorization Act for Fiscal Year 2013), *codified at* 22 U.S.C. §§ 8512, 8513a, 8514, 8514a, 8514b, *reprinted in* 2013 Compilation, at 711; Iran Sanctions Act of 1996, as amended, Section 14(4), *reprinted in* 2013 Overview, Part II, at 705 (defining 'credible information').

146 Comprehensive Iran Sanctions Accountability and Divestment Act of 2010, Section 105(c)–(d), Public Law 111–95 (1 July 2010), as amended by Public Law 112–58 (Iran Threat Reduction and Syria Human Rights Act of 2012) and Public Law 112–239 (Iran Freedom and Counter-Proliferation Act of 2012, Sub-Title D of the National Defense Authorization Act for Fiscal Year 2013), *codified at* 22 U.S.C. §§ 8512, 8513a, 8514, 8514a, 8514b, *reprinted in* 2013 Compilation, at 712–3.

147 Iran Sanctions Act of 1996, as amended, Sections 5(a)(1)(A) (mandating the President impose three or more sanctions for a violation of the Petroleum Resource Development Prohibition), 5(a)(2)(A) (mandating the President impose three or more sanctions for violation of the Refined Petroleum Production Prohibition), 5(a)(3)(A) (mandating three or more sanctions for violations of the Refined Petroleum Export Sanction), 5(a)(b) (mandating the President impose three or more sanctions for the Sensitive Weapons Export Prohibition), *reprinted in* Overview, Part II, at 1135–8.

148 Iran Sanctions Act of 1996, as amended, Section 6(a)(6), *reprinted in* Overview, Part II, at 1141.

149 Delphine Strauss, "America's 'Exorbitant Privilege' Is Ebbing," *Financial Times* (27 January 2014): 8 (correctly stating 'because payment in dollars ultimately involves a transfer on the books of the Federal Reserve, the US can enforce a financial blockade') (reviewing Alan Wheatly, ed., *The Power of Currencies and Currencies of Power* (New York, NY: Routledge, 2013)).

150 Iran Sanctions Act of 1996, as amended, Section 6(a)(7), *reprinted in* Overview, Part II, at 1141.

151 Iran Sanctions Act of 1996, as amended, Section 14(5), *reprinted in* Overview, Part II, at 1147. Again, the statute incorporates by reference the definition of 'financial institution' from Section 3(c)(1) of the Federal Deposit Insurance Act of 1950, and the definition of a foreign bank 'branch' or 'agency' from Section 1(b)(7) of the International Banking Act of 1978. Ibid.

152 Iran Sanctions Act of 1996, as amended, Section 6(a)(8), *reprinted in* Overview, Part II, at 1141.

153 Iran Sanctions Act of 1996, as amended, Section 6(a)(8)(A), (C), *reprinted in* Overview, Part II, at 1142.

154 Iran Sanctions Act of 1996, as amended, Section 6(a)(8)(B), *reprinted in* Overview, Part II, at 1142.

155 Iran Sanctions Act of 1996, as amended, Section 6(b)(1), *reprinted in* Overview, Part II, at 1142. Parties excluded from federal procurement are listed in the Federal Acquisitions Register. Ibid. at Section 6(b)(2)(B).

'Eligible products' from designated 'eligible countries' are exempt from the certification requirement. Ibid., Section 6(b)(2)(B), Section 308(4) of the Trade Agreements Act of 1979, 19 U.S.C. § 2518(4) (defining 'eligible products'), and Section 301(b) of the Trade Agreements Act of 1979, 19 U.S.C. § 2511(b) (defining 'eligible countries'). Essentially, they are products originating in a country in the WTO Agreement on Government Procurement (GPA) (or willing to assume *GPA* obligations) or North American Free Trade Agreement (NAFTA), a least developed country, a country that will provide reciprocal procurement opportunities for US suppliers, or a country where the US has a free trade agreement (FTA) that took effect after 31 December 2003 and before 2 January 2005; that is, Australia (effective 1 January 2005), Chile (effective 1 January 2004), and Singapore (also effective 1 January 2004).

156 Iran Sanctions Act of 1996, as amended, Section 5(b)(2)(A), *reprinted in* Overview, Part II, at 1138.
157 Overview, Part I, at 275.
158 Iran Sanctions Act of 1996, as amended, Section 6(b)(5), *reprinted in* Overview, Part II, at 1143.
159 Iran Sanctions Act of 1996, as amended, Section 4(e), *reprinted in* Overview, Part II, at 1135; Overview, Part I, at 275.
160 Iran Sanctions Act of 1996, as amended, Section 4(e)(1) and 5(a), *reprinted in* Overview, Part II, at 1135–7.
161 Iran Sanctions Act of 1996, as amended, Section 4(e)(3) and 5(a), *reprinted in* Overview, Part II, at 1135–7. The President invoked the Special Rule by written certification to the appropriate Congressional committees.
162 Iran Sanctions Act of 1996, as amended, Section 4(e)(3), *reprinted in* Overview, Part II, at 1135.

14 More investment, trade, and financial sanctions

Iran case study, continued (2012–16)

14.1 Phase 8: 2012 Defense Act tightening financial sanctions

Targeting Iranian financial sector (1 January 2012–1 December 2016)[1]

The 1996 and 2010 legislation (discussed in Chapter 13) did not establish a comprehensive set of prohibitions and sanctions in respect of the Iranian financial sector. The 2010 changes included new measures against foreign exchange or inter-bank transactions involving a sanctioned person or entity, or dealings in property in the US of a sanctioned person. But, they did not target the Central Bank of Iran (CBI), nor did they address specific concerns of Iranian banks in money laundering or financing weapon of mass destruction (WMD) proliferation or terrorism.[2] And, they did nothing to help third countries eschew purchases of Iranian crude oil to cut their dependence on it, and constrict sale proceeds flowing to Iran that it would use to fund WMD acquisitions or terrorist causes.

After the 2010 legislation, in November 2011, the Financial Crimes Enforcement Network (FINCEN) of the US Department of the Treasury found that the CBI transferred billions of dollars to the Export Development Bank of Iran (EDBI),[3] Bank Mellat ('Bank of the Nation'),[4] Bank Melli ('National Bank of Iran'),[5] Bank Sadrat Iran (the Export Bank of Iran),[6] and other Iranian banks that the CBI is supposed to regulate.[7] Doing so facilitated evasion of sanctions by reducing the involvement of US and other non-Iranian banks, which were trying to comply with the prohibitions set out in the 1996 and 2010 legislation with the CBI and Iranian banks. In effect, via schemes to funnel payments to Iranian banks, the CBI covered for the loss of banking relationships they incurred thanks to the pressure of sanctions on US and other international banks to eschew dealings with them.

Thus, in the defence budget bill for fiscal year (FY) 2012; namely, Section 1245 of the *National Defense Authorization Act of 2012* (*Defense Act*), Congress took aim at the financial sector of Iran.[8] This new legislation contained the following three key measures.

Measure 1: primary money laundering concern designation

First, Congress expressly designated the entire Iranian financial sector, including the CBI, to be of 'primary money laundering concern'.[9] This sector posed a threat to UK government and banks because it laundered proceeds from illicit activities in pursuit of

WMDs and terrorist causes, evaded sanctions, and deceived the government and banks about its operations. Such designations are made pursuant to Section 311 of the *USA PATRIOT Act*, which Congress passed in 2001, and which is codified at 31 U.S.C. § 5318A. That Act has 10 Titles, the third of which is called the *International Money Laundering Abatement and Financial Anti-Terrorism Act*. This name bespeaks the purpose of Title III: to bolster the ability of US authorities to detect, deter, and prosecute money laundering and terrorist financing.

Under Section 5318A, the Secretary of the Treasury could order, on a temporary basis, that financial institutions implement special measures for any transaction outside the US in an area of primary money laundering concern. Those measures pertained to detailed record keeping, for example, the identities, addresses, and roles of all participants in a transaction, including a wire transfer, and the identity of any foreigner authorized to use or route a transaction through a payable-through account (PTA) (discussed below). In short, designation as a primary money laundering concern opened the possibility of obtaining more and better information about proliferation and terrorist financing.[10]

Measure 2: Iranian bank asset freeze

Second, Section 1245 of the 2012 *Defense Act* established a freeze on all assets of Iranian financial institutions within reach of US authorities.[11] In particular, Congress ordered the President to block all transactions in any property or property interests of any Iranian financial institution, if that property or interests were in, or came within, the US, or within the possession of a US person.[12] Here, then, was an extension of the Property Transaction Sanction from the 1996 and 2010 from dealings in assets of a sanctioned entity to those of Iranian banks, including Iran's Central Bank. Likewise, the new measure went beyond the 2010 Comprehensive Iran Sanctions, Accountability, and Investment Act (*CISADA*) freeze of assets belonging to individual Iranian government officials.

For example, suppose the CBI held funds in the Kansas City, Missouri branch of a foreign bank. Those funds would be frozen in that branch. Notwithstanding the fact the branch was of a non-US bank, it was located in the US, and hence subject to the freeze order.

Likewise, consider a wire transfer of US dollars from the account of an Iranian bank held at an Australian bank in Singapore to a Korean bank in Seoul. Insofar as the wire transfer is routed through the US, via Fedwire, or clears and settles on the books of an institution in the US, such as the Federal Reserve Bank of New York, it comes within the US, and thus could be frozen – even though the originator, originator's bank, beneficiary's bank, and beneficiary are all non-US persons. Still another example, hypothetically, would be bonds owned by an Iranian bank for investment purposes, and held at the New Delhi branch of Citibank. The Iranian investor could not move them. While the investment account was in an overseas branch, the branch was that of a United States person, namely, a US bank.[13]

Curiously, the asset freeze did not specify a punishment. In one sense, the prohibition was its own punishment: Iranian banks could not get their property if US officials got to it first, which was likely assuming that holders of the property alerted the officials to what was in their possession. But, what if a foreign bank in the US, or a US person abroad, violated the asset freeze by relinquishing funds or other property or property interests to their Iranian orders? Possibly, the **International Emergency Economic Powers Act** (*IEEPA*) sanctions would apply, because the basic statutory authority for the asset freeze was the IEEPA.[14]

A dramatic instance of the effect of the prohibition on transactions involving Iranian bank assets came on 18 September 2013. The case involved Bank Melli.[15] US District Judge Katherine Forrest approved the seizure by federal law enforcement authorities of the entire office block building at 650 Fifth Avenue in Manhattan. Led by the US Attorney for the Southern District of New York, Preet Bharara, prosecutors explained a non-profit organization operated by the Shah of Iran built the 36-storey structure in the 1970s. A loan from Bank Melli funded the construction.

Following the Islamic Revolution, the new government expropriated the building in 1979, and renamed the non-profit organization (NPO) the 'Alavi Foundation'. Alavi then co-owned the building with Assa Corporation, and the owners transferred rental income to Bank Melli. Those co-owners acted as 'fronts' for Bank Melli, and their transfers to it violated both the US sanctions prohibition and money laundering laws. The forfeiture of the building was the largest ever related to terrorism, and Mr Bharara said proceeds from its sale would be used to compensate victims of terrorism sponsored by Iran.

Measure 3: payments system prohibition

To be engaged in international banking is to work with foreign banks. Even the largest of multinational banking organizations do not have subsidiaries, branches, agencies, or representative offices in all the countries of the world. Only in the minority of cases can they make and receive payments, and move assets, from one owner to another, and from one jurisdiction to another, as an 'in house transfer'. Frequently, they must work with one or more other banks where they hold an account, and which the ultimate transferee, or beneficiary, also has an account.

Technically, those 'accounts' are known as a 'correspondent' ones; that is,, as defined in Section 311(e)(1)(B) of the *USA PATRIOT Act*, a 'correspondent account' is 'an account established to receive deposits from, make payments on behalf of a foreign financial institution, or handle other financial transactions related to such institution'.[16] Logically, a bank holding a 'correspondent account' is called a 'correspondent bank'.

For example, consider a transfer of funds from the Indonesian *rupiah*-denominated account of a Jakarta-based importer of Persian carpets held at Hong Kong Shanghai Banking Corporation (HSBC) in Jakarta. The transfer is to pay for carpets shipped by an Iranian exporter in Tabriz, but the exporter seeks payment in Indian *rupees*, not Indonesian *rupiah*. (The payment could be pursuant to a commercial letter of credit issued by HSBC for the benefit of the Tabriz exporter.) Could the rupee transfer be in-house? That could happen only if HSBC holds a rupee-denominated account for both the importer-originator-payor and exporter-beneficiary-payee.

Assume HSBC does not hold both accounts. But, suppose the exporter has a rupee-denominated account at an account of Bank Melli that is held at Karnataka Bank (KB), which is a private sector entity, in Bangalore.[17] (That is, KB holds a rupee account for Bank Melli, which in turn holds a rupee account for the exporter.) Also assume HSBC also has *a rupee* account at KB.[18] Then, HSBC in Jakarta can (1) debit the rupiah account of the importer for the rupee-equivalent of the price of the carpets, (2) transfer electronically the rupees to its account at KB, and (3) instruct KB to debit its account with KB and credit the account of Bank Melli at KB for onward payment to the exporter at KB.

In this instance, KB serves as a correspondent bank, with the HSBC account at KB being the correspondent account. KB links the Jakarta importer with the Tabriz exporter because it (KB) holds the accounts of both the importer's bank and the exporter. As this hypothetical example suggests, correspondent banking is essential to the smooth flow of international trade transactions. The example also intimates there are foreign banks, like KB, that maintain correspondent accounts and that conduct financial transactions with Iranian banks, like Melli.

Accordingly, via the third key measure in the 2012 Defense Act, Congress sought to cut off Iranian financial institutions from correspondent banking, with limited exceptions. Congress prohibited the opening or maintaining of a correspondent account (or the imposition of strict conditions on any extant such account) by a 'foreign financial institution' that the President decides 'has knowingly conducted or facilitated any significant financial transaction' with the CBI or any Iranian bank that the Secretary of the Treasury designated for imposition of IEEPA sanctions.

The same ban applied to payable-through accounts at a foreign financial institution: they were forbidden (or strictures could be imposed on them) if that institution knowingly did big business with the CBI or sanctioned Iranian banks. Under Section 311(e)(1)(C) of the *USA PATRIOT Act*, a:

> 'payable-through account' means an account, including a transaction account (as defined in section 19(b)(1)(C) of the Federal Reserve Act), opened at a depository institution [in the United States] by a foreign financial institution by means of which the foreign financial institution permits its customers to engage, either directly or through a subaccount, in banking activities usual in connection with the business of banking in the United States.[19]

Essentially, a 'PTA' is a demand deposit (that is checking) account at a United States bank whereby a customer of a foreign bank can write cheques. Such a customer – the end user – may not be subject to the same scrutiny by the American bank as is a regular customer of that bank, meaning an Iranian customer could use the account to launder funds from, or make payments for, unlawful purposes.

Accordingly, to alter the above hypothetical, suppose KB holds a rupee-denominated PTA for HSBC. That would mean customers of HSBC, such as the Jakarta importer, could make payments via cheques, money orders, and other instruments from that PTA. The Jakarta exporter then could draw such an instrument, in rupees, on that PTA for the order of the Tabriz exporter.

So, in the original and modified version of the above hypothetical, suppose the President determines KB has knowingly engaged in significant financial dealings with the CBI or an Iranian bank to which US sanctions apply. Then, the President could forbid the KB from maintaining the correspondent account or the PTA of HSBC (or impose strict conditions on either).

As with the Iranian bank asset freeze, with the payments system prohibition, Congress did not mandate a sanction. That is, Congress authorized (but did not require) the President to impose IEEPA sanctions on the CBI.[20] As for other Iranian banks, there was no need for Congress to specify a penalty: the Treasury Secretary already had designated them for IEEPA sanctions under the existing 1996 and 2010 Act regime, or did so contemporaneously with application of the prohibition.[21]

Manifestly, the prohibition was designed to ostracize Iranian banks from the international banking network, making payments to or for them all but impossible. Of significance was the prohibition that vastly expanded the architecture of measures against Iran from the energy sector to all sectors. Whether payments were made in connection with petroleum or petroleum products did not matter: Iran was to be denied the use of correspondent banking facilities and PTAs for all purposes. So, even if (as in the hypothetical) Iran could sell Persian carpets (or for that matter, pistachios) to a non-US buyer, it could not get paid for them – and, therefore, would have to resort to barter trade, if not subterfuge.

Payments system prohibition definitional issues

Taking specific aim at Iran's Central Bank was a key to ostracizing the entire Iranian financial sector. As in any country, Iranian banks rely on their Central Bank for a variety of foreign exchange, clearing and settlement, and payments functions in transactions with the rest of the world. Yet, as its language and the hypothetical suggest, that objective was not easy to enforce.

There were definitional issues. First, a 'foreign financial institution' under Section 104(i) of the CISADA actually was not defined at all: it depended on what the Treasury Secretary thought.[22] Though not a major difficulty, recourse to Treasury regulations was necessary.

Second, exactly what did Congress mean by 'significant' financial transactions between a foreign financial institution and the CBI or a sanctioned Iranian bank? Was the President to look at the volume or value of transactions, or both? How would a single $100 million dollar event occurring six years ago rate in comparison to three $25 million events occurring three years ago? Similarly, how would the President determine the foreign financial institution intentionally engaged in the deal, thus meeting the 'knowingly' requirement? Third, precisely how was the President to go about convincing a foreign financial institution like the State Bank of India (SBI) to close a correspondent account in furtherance of the US's sanctions policy goal of ostracizing Iran from the world of international banking?

Third country central bank exception to payments system prohibition

More serious than definitional issues surrounding enforcement of the payments system prohibition was navigating its exceptions. The 2012 Defense Act contained an obvious exception for sales of food and medicine to Iran.[23] A person supplying agricultural commodities, medicines, or medical devices could do so under the 1996 and 2010 sanctions rules, so it would be illogical to forbid a foreign financial institution from opening or maintaining a correspondent account or PTA used by or for the benefit of the CBI for these essentially humanitarian transactions.

A greater controversy concerned potential application of the prohibition and sanctions to a foreign central bank other than the CBI. In the above hypothetical, could the RBI, or a state-owned bank like the Punjab National Bank, be in trouble? Surely Congress did not mean to threaten the RBI – or, for that matter, the likes of the Bank of England and Bank of Japan – and all nationalized, public sector banks in India? Indeed, to avoid ensnaring all non-Iranian foreign central banks, Congress deemed that sanctions would apply to them only if they engaged in a financial transaction for the sale or purchase of petroleum or petroleum products to or from Iran.[24] In doing so, Congress both created the necessary exemption and tightened the prohibitions on Iran's energy sector.

To illustrate, suppose Iran sold crude oil to, or purchased refined gasoline from, the Indian Oil Corporation, the state-owned oil and gas firm headquartered in New Delhi, and India's largest commercial enterprise.[25] Indian Oil seeks to pay for the crude, or receive payment for the gasoline, via its account held with the SBI, which in turn holds an account at the RBI. If the RBI conducts the payment transaction for Indian Oil, then the President must apply sanctions to the RBI. Obviously, then, Congress sought to knock out any central bank from assisting Iran in receiving or transferring funds in connection with its energy resources.

It is difficult, if not impossible, to find a precedent for this kind of measure. It is unilateral, undertaken by the US, against sovereign foreign central banks of third countries not accused directly of wrongdoing. Denying access to the payments system itself was an aggressive move against foreign financial institutions. Threatening foreign central banks, too, albeit in respect of energy dealings with Iran, was all the more dramatic. Traditionally, the world of central banks is a collegial, if not clubby, one. For the US to take a potentially adversarial approach to foreign central banks, essentially declaring it would not tolerate them as accomplices of Iran, was incongruous with the trusting, diplomatic culture central banks enjoyed.

Third country short supply exception to payments system prohibition

Still another exception to imposition of sanctions was for short supplies of crude oil to third countries.[26] Congress mandated bi-monthly reporting on non-Iranian petroleum and petroleum product prices and availability.[27] It did so in connection with a mandate to the President that he determine whether non-Iranian crude oil sources were sufficient to allow buyers in third countries around the world to 'reduce significantly' the volume of their purchases from Iran.[28] By that Congress meant cutting dependence (as shown by paying lower prices or buying less quantities) on Iranian energy, specifically crude oil, with a view towards complete cessation of dependence on Iran.[29]

The link to sanctions was this: suppose a foreign financial institution, such as the KB in the above hypothetical, engaged in a financial transaction via a correspondent account or a PTA, where the underlying commercial deal involved Iranian petroleum or petroleum products and a third country. For instance, assume that deal entailed an Indian oil importer, like Indian Oil Corporation, buying Iranian crude. Suppose Iran is paid via funds credited to the correspondent account or the PTA held by the KB.

Without the third country short supply exception, a foreign bank like the KB was vulnerable to sanctions, because of the correspondent account or PTA used to conduct payment from the third country, India, to Iran for the oil. With this exception, however, sanctions would apply only if the supply of crude oil from non-Iranian sources was sufficient to permit a significant reduction in sourcing crude oil from Iran. After all, it would be unfair to India or other third countries to penalize their banks if they had no choice but to buy oil from Iran to meet their energy needs.

Yet, administering the third country short supply exception was fraught with economic and political difficulties. The President had to ascertain the energy demand and supply situation in every country, and compare and contrast Iranian and non-Iranian sources. In evaluating what third countries could or should have done, the President risked looking like he was dictating to them what their energy policies ought to be. India, China, and other energy-hungry emerging countries were hardly happy with that scenario, one in which they might wind up dependent on sources controlled, directly or indirectly, by the US.

In fact, third countries persisted in buying Iranian crude, evidenced by Iranian oil revenues: 'Astonishingly, Iran earned $600 bn [billion] in oil revenues over the past eight years [2006–2013] in oil revenues over the past eight years, more than its total accumulation since oil was discovered more than a century ago.'[30]

Of course, owing to US financial sanctions, between $50 and $100 billion of Iran's holdings of foreign exchange were in frozen bank accounts.[31] Thus, '[o]ne of Mr [Hassan] Rouhani's most troubling discoveries upon taking office [as President in August 2013] was to find the treasury empty'.[32]

Moreover, pressure from the US on India (or other third countries) created an internal political dynamic within India. Sanctions relief would be for a foreign financial institution (e.g., an Indian bank like the KB) based on the country with primary jurisdiction (India) over that institution cutting its dependence on Iranian oil.[33] A foreign bank then had the choice of pleasing the United States by lobbying its government to push its oil importers to eschew Iranian crude, or pleasing its government by rejecting the role of a US agent. Being in this position hardly would endear the foreign bank, its government, or its oil importers to the US sanctions regime.

Perhaps in anticipation of this dynamic, Congress obligated the President to 'carry out an initiative of multilateral diplomacy to persuade [third] countries purchasing oil from Iran . . .' that they should limit the use by Iran of revenues Iran earned from oil sales to those third countries to buy non-luxury consumer goods from those countries.[34] For example, if India buys oil from Iran, then it should try to cut sales of consumer items to Iran. In effect, the initiative was designed to weaken bilateral trade ties between Iran and third countries. (It also aimed to prohibit Iran from buying military or dual use items, or any other material that could enhance its WMD capabilities.[35])

That this initiative was multilateral hardly changed the optics of the sanctions regime. From the perspective of third countries like India, the initiative was impelled by a US statute, led by a US President, and designed to suit US foreign policy and national security goals. Indeed, the unilateralism-cloaked-in-multilateralism affected not only third country oil consumers like India, but also non-Iranian oil sources, like Iran's partners in the Organization for Petroleum Exporting Countries (OPEC). Congress instructed the President to 'conduct outreach' to the likes of Saudi Arabia and Indonesia to encourage them

> to increase their output of crude oil to ensure there is a sufficient supply of crude oil from countries other than Iran, and to minimize any impact on the [world market] price of oil resulting from the imposition of [the asset freeze and payments system] sanctions under this section [1245 of the 2012 *Defense Act*].[36]

Simply put, the US was to lead a multi-country charge at third country suppliers to cajole them into boosting production to fill the diminution in Iranian oil caused by third country purchasers, under pressure, looking elsewhere than Iran.[37]

It must be underscored that the overall goal of these provisions was breathtaking: the US aimed to change the pattern of world trade in crude oil by knocking Iran out of that pattern. That is why the President had to monitor the supply–demand picture in third countries, and sign on as many countries as possible to a coalition of the willing.

That the US was one potential supplier also cannot go unmentioned.[38] Thanks to new drilling technologies (including the controversial hydraulic fracturing, or 'fracking') the Energy Information Administration forecast that the US by 2016 would produce more crude oil than at any time since the banner year of 1970 (9.6 millions barrels per day). Yet, because of an export ban on oil implemented in 1975, following the 1973 Arab oil embargo, the US could not ship crude abroad. Why not remove the statutory ban and thereby not only help third countries forego Iranian oil, but also hand over to US producers the market share in those countries held by Iran?[39]

The third country short supply exception also was problematic from a practical legal perspective. The kind of financial transaction for which a foreign bank could be penalized had to be one involving (1) 'trade in goods or services between the country with primary jurisdiction [e.g., India] over the foreign financial institution [e.g., KB] and Iran' and (2) 'any funds owned to Iran as a result of such trade are credited to an account located in the country with primary jurisdiction over the foreign financial institution'.[40] The above hypothetical easily meets both prongs. But, what if Indian Oil Corporation was a middle party, brokering an oil sale by Iran to Bhutan? Would a payment routed from the Bhutanese capital, Thimpu, to Tehran via KB render KB liable? Or, what if the underlying transaction was not for 'goods'; that is, crude oil, but for consulting provided by Iranian petroleum engineers to the Bhutanese government? Would KB be liable on the rationale that consulting is a 'service' within the first prong?

Sanctions waiver criteria ambiguities

Congress granted the President discretion to waive sanctions on a foreign financial institution for violations of the payments system prohibition. To qualify, the President had to apply four criteria. First, it had to be in the 'national security interest of the United States' not to impose on that institution.[41] Second, the President had to justify the waiver to Congress.[42] Third, there had to be 'exceptional circumstances' preventing the country with primary jurisdiction over the foreign financial institution from reducing significantly its purchases of Iranian petroleum and petroleum products.[43] Fourth, the President had to explain the 'concrete cooperation' he received, or would receive, thanks to the waiver.[44] Even if all four criteria were met, the President could waive sanctions for only up to 120 days, with additional 120 day renewals possible under those same criteria.

The language of the first criterion was commonplace among sanctions waiver provisions, and the second criterion was unsurprising. The third and fourth were ambiguous. 'Exceptional circumstances' were undefined, as was 'concrete cooperation'. Suppose in the above hypothetical India argued to the President that a surge in energy consumption in India, thanks to strong growth in the manufacturing sector, caused India to import more oil than expected from Iran. Was this scenario exceptional, or one to be expected given India's efforts at industrialization? To take another example, suppose China outmanoeuvred India in trying to obtain sources of oil in Africa to substitute for Iran. That is, China was able to secure foreign direct investment (FDI) and energy supply contracts in Sub-Saharan Africa for which India had also competed, but lost. In consequence, India could not lessen its dependence on Iranian crude oil. Would these circumstances be 'exceptional'? Even what might be traditionally thought of as 'exceptional' – war or other violent conflict – arguably could be regarded as expected. For example, if India urged that it could not lessen its dependence on oil from Iran because of unrest in three substitute countries – Iraq, Nigeria, and Venezuela – would that be 'exceptional'?

Likewise, hypothetical illustrations point out the difficulty in ascertaining what kind of cooperation from India would be 'concrete'. Would the cooperation need to be related directly to Iran? Or, would help on other matters – such as stepped-up patrols against piracy in the Straits of Malacca by Indian Naval vessels, or increased FDI in Afghanistan to help it repair its infrastructure – suffice?

14.2 Phase 9: 2012 *Iran–Syria Act* new expansive constrictions

10 Further Measures (10 August 2012–31 December 2016)

With the *Iran Threat Reduction and Syria Human Rights Act of 2012* (Iran–Syria Act), the United States continued its traverse far across the Rubicon, as it were, tightening the 1996 *Iran Sanctions Act*, as amended in 2010 by CISADA, and tightening CISADA, yet again.[45] It did so in 10 principal manners: six concerning illegal business conduct with Iran; one dealing with human rights; one pertaining to punishments for engaging in prohibited conduct; and one affecting criteria for waiving those punishments.[46] Succinctly put, the US dubbed more activities with Iran illegal, closed loopholes to behaviour it previously identified as unlawful, set additional sanctions for transgressions, and increased the difficulty of obtaining a waiver of penalties.[47] All in all, the new constrictions were expansive.

As with the *Iran and Libya Sanctions Act* (*ILSA*) in 1996 and CISADA in 2010, with the Iran–Syria Act in 2012, the 112th Congress professed not to abandon multilateralism.[48] The problem with a team approach, however, was that even after – or maybe because of – decades of sanctions, not everyone was playing on the US team against Iran by the rules the US set.

So, Congress called for 'prompt enforcement of the current multilateral sanctions regime with respect to Iran' and 'expanded cooperation with international sanctions enforcement' thereby intimating its displeasure that third countries were not adhering to United Nations (UN) or US rules.[49] Congress indicated its view sanctions imposed by the Security Council and allies did not go far enough by urging the President to 'intensify diplomatic efforts' at the UN and with individual allies to expand prohibitions and penalties sanctions to include a bar on (1) issuing visas to Iranian officials involved in WMD development, terrorist support, or human rights abuses and (2) landing at seaports by vessels of the Islamic Republic of Iran Shipping Lines and at airports of cargo flights of Iran Air, because of their 'role . . . in proliferation and illegal arms sales' and (3) to limit the development of petroleum resources in Iran, and (4) importation of refined petroleum by Iran.[50]

In keeping with the 2012 *Budget Act*, Congress instructed the President to coax out increased crude oil production in third country suppliers to help third country buyers wean themselves off of Iranian energy, and thereby reduce to zero revenues Iran could generate from sales to those buyers.[51] To be sure, the rest of the world was clear about what Congress wanted, and perhaps to jawbone compliance, Congress told the President he had to report biannually on third countries that were not imposing measures against Iran.[52] Interestingly, Congress had a word about the World Trade Organization (WTO), and its predecessor, the General Agreement on Tariffs and Trade (GATT). If either body adjudicated a decision about sanctions on Iran, then Congress wanted to know, perhaps as an *a priori* admonition against an adverse outcome or notification it would take countermeasures against such an outcome.[53]

First: expanded prohibitions against Iranian energy sector

The 2012 Iran–Syria Act clarified – in effect, expanded – the list of prohibited transactions. The two broad sanctionable behaviours remained the same: (1) economic transactions in the energy (meaning petroleum or refined gasoline) sector of Iran, and (2) dealings relating to WMDs or advanced conventional weaponry. But, comparing the lists of prohibited transactions under the (1) 1996 Iran Sanctions Act, as amended in 2010 by CISADA, and (2) 2012 legislation showed how Congress plugged gaps, sometimes with expansive language, and other times with precise terms.

Its main target again was the sector in which Iran traditionally held an international comparative advantage: energy. In both the 1996–2010 and 2012 iterations of the legislation, the prohibition against investing more than $20 million in a 12-month period in the petroleum sector of Iran remained the same.[54] But, the new legislation effectively lowered the threshold to $1 million per transaction, or $5 million annually. That was because it barred provision of goods, services, technology, or support to Iran that 'could' help it develop its petroleum resources.[55] In other words, not only was FDI in that sector illegal, but so, too, was nearly any transaction.

Moreover, the 2012 Iran–Syria Act tightened other economic prohibitions against dealing with Iran's most important sector, energy, as follows:

1 Prohibition against helping Iran produce refined petroleum products:[56]

   a In the 2012 legislation, Congress clarified this prohibition applied not just to providing Iran with goods, services, technology, information, or support for it to construct, modernize, or repair petroleum refineries (as under the 1996 and 2010 legislation). It also covered any 'direct and significant assistance . . . *directly associated* with *infrastructure*, including construction of port facilities, railways, and roads, the *primary use* of which is to support the delivery of refined petroleum products'.[57] This expansive language essentially barred any trade or investment in the infrastructure of Iran, as long as such transactions were entered into 'knowingly' (meaning actual or constructive knowledge),[58] exceeded a US$1 million threshold (or $5 million in 12 months), and 'could' possibly help Iran.

   b Exactly how the US would determine whether a particular Iranian port, railway, or road was 'primarily used' by petroleum refiners was unclear. Did 'primary use' mean 51 per cent of the traffic? Over what period? By what measure (value or volume)? Who would obtain the data and check the figures? Would a telecommunications facility, or a petroleum engineering school, be considered 'infrastructure' (given that the new language was non-exclusive by virtue of the preposition 'including'). Perhaps these questions were what Congress intended, namely, to deter traders and investors by injecting uncertainty into their dealings with Iran.

2 Prohibition against exportation of refined petroleum products to Iran:[59]

   a It remained illegal to sell refined petroleum to Iran, and to provide it with goods, services, technology, information, or support that might help it import refined petroleum. But, the 2012 language closed a loophole and broadened the meaning of what 'could directly and significantly contribute' to Iran's ability to import gasoline. The loophole concerned barter trade.

   b Suppose a country, such as China or India, shipped gasoline it refined (possibly from Iranian crude oil) to Iran, in exchange for pistachios. Such bartering, and any insurance for it, was illegal under the new language.[60] After all, barter trade easily 'could' be a 'significant contribution' to Iran's ability to import refined petroleum – indeed, it was.

3 Prohibition against joint ventures (JVs) for Iranian petroleum resource development:[61]

   a   American sanctions under the 1996 legislation, as amended in 2010, barred investments above $20 million in petroleum resource development in Iran. They did not expressly forbid investments in petroleum resources outside of Iran that may redound to the benefit of Iran. For instance, a person could enter into a JV agreement in petroleum resources in Venezuela, and that deal might help Iran develop its petroleum resources within Iran. It could do so if Iran was a JV partner, or otherwise obtained goods, services, or know-how from the Venezuelan project that Iran could transfer and apply to its own sector.

   b   Once again, Congress moved to close the loophole and, in so doing, unilaterally expanded the extraterritorial reach of the sanctions. Via the 2012 amendments, Congress forbade any JV in petroleum resources anywhere in the world outside of Iran if the Iranian government was a '*substantial* partner or investor' or Iran '*could*, through a direct *operational* role ... or by *other means*, receive technological knowledge or equipment not previously available to Iran that *could* directly and significantly contribute to the enhancement of Iran's ability to develop petroleum resources in Iran'.[62] The italicized terms gave wide latitude for interpretation. In turn, prospective JV partners would be uncertain as to whether a project might run afoul of the prohibition, and likely eschew the project – an effect Congress no doubt sought.

   c   Two points about this amendment were remarkable. First, the fact the JV might help a developing or least developed country, such as in West Africa, was irrelevant. If a deal had the potential to help Iran, then never mind it might also help a poor country seeking to grow, alleviate internal poverty, or combat Islamist extremism.

   d   Second, the amendment applied retroactively to all JVs on or after 1 January 2002 through enactment of the 2012 Iran–Syria Act.[63] That is, any JVs in the last decade were sanctionable. The only way to avoid sanctions was to terminate the JV within 180 days of enactment of the 2012 Act.[64] Bluntly put, this sanction barred not only future investments in all third countries, but also demanded disinvestment around the world. That such retroactivity might be an unconstitutional taking, or at least an unfair one, seemed not to matter.

4 Prohibition against buying Iranian petrochemical products:[65]

   a   So eager was Congress in 2012 to impede Iran from developing its petroleum resources that it expanded the sanctions regime to cover 'petrochemical products'. These downstream articles included 'any aromatic, olefin, or synthesis gas, and any derivative of such a gas, including ethylene, propylene, butadiene, benzene, toluene, xylene, ammonia, methanol, and urea'.[66]

   b   Suppose Iran produced ammonia for use in household cleaning solutions, or urea as a component in agricultural fertilizer. Suppose, further, a British firm making such solutions, or a Swiss company producing fertilizer, bought the component petrochemicals from Iran. If the fair market value of their purchases exceeded US$250,000 (or $1 million annually), then Congress forbade them.[67]

   c   As this hypothetical example illustrates, this prohibition meant persons in third countries could not source petrochemical inputs – sometimes called

462 *Legal issues in Asian investing*

'feedstock' – from Iran. In turn, Iran, even if it could develop the feedstock, would have a difficult time finding foreign markets for it if persons in those markets complied with the sanctions.

5   Prohibition against transporting crude oil from Iran:[68]

   a   Shipping crude oil out of Iran certainly could help Iran develop both its petroleum resources and ability to obtain gasoline. Presumably, Congress meant to bar such shipments under its 1996 and 2010 legislation, but with major oil importers like China, India, and Japan dependent on foreign – including Iranian – crude, ferrying oil out of Iran persisted. With its 2012 changes, Congress made clear it wanted them to cease by targeting not just persons in the importing countries, but also the shippers themselves.

   b   Carriage companies thus found themselves in the sight line of Congress: anyone who was a 'controlling beneficial owner' or who otherwise owned, operated, controlled, or insured a vessel used to transport crude oil from Iran to any other country in the world, was liable.[69] Congress allowed a small safe harbour for underwriters or insurers that 'exercised due diligence' to ensure the persons for which they were providing protective policies were not shipping from Iran.[70]

   c   Interestingly, for this particular prohibition, Congress limited in three ways the circumstances in which sanctions could be imposed. First, Congress bifurcated the *mens rea* requirement: a 'controlling beneficial owner' had to have 'actual knowledge' of the use of their vessel, whereas for all other owners, operators, controllers, or insurers, actual or constructive knowledge ('knew or should have known') was sufficient.[71] This adjustment made it more difficult to impose sanctions on controlling beneficial owners, but easier on all others involved in shipping crude oil from Iran. Why Congress chose to do so is unclear, if its goal was to tighten sanctions unreservedly.

   d   Second, sanctions were inapplicable if the President determined that a third country to which Iranian crude oil was shipped had a 'sufficient supply or petroleum and petroleum products' of non-Iranian origin.[72] Congress apparently appreciated that some third countries could not easily or swiftly substitute their supply sources away from Iran, so it did not want to impose sanctions on transporting Iranian crude to them unless they could 'reduce significantly their purchases from Iran'.[73]

   e   Third, sanctions also were inapplicable to a foreign financial institution from a country that 'has significantly reduced its volume of crude oil purchases from Iran'.[74] This limitation, linked to the 2012 *National Defense Authorization Act* (discussed below), referred to successive 180-day periods in which the President must report on the extent to which third countries are complying with sanctions against transactions with the CBI and Iranian financial institutions. Essentially, a country had six months to reduce its dependence on Iranian crude, otherwise its banks could be targeted for sanctions.

6   Prohibition against concealing Iranian origin of crude oil or refined petroleum products:[75]

   a   Smuggling was an obvious, albeit wicked, response of a person determined to ship crude oil, or refined petroleum products, from Iran to a third country to skirt the US prohibition against doing so. Setting moral or reputational concerns aside, a prospective smuggler might balance reward against risk to calculate whether concealing the true origin of energy resources it transports is worthwhile. As sanctions tightened around Iran, the price of those resources would rise. Depending on how high the price rose, the potential reward from shipping Iranian crude oil or refined petroleum products, disguised as originating elsewhere, could offset the expected value (that is the probability of imposition multiplied by dollar value of penalty) of any sanction.

b   To deter smuggling, Congress made concealment itself a sanctionable offence.[76] In doing so, it was not breaking new legal ground in that accurate country of origin reporting is required under US customs law. But, what was novel was – again – the extraterritorial reach of the sanction. It now was illegal to report falsely the true Iranian origin of crude oil or refined petroleum products, regardless of the recipient of the report. Whether US or foreign was irrelevant; it was the act of concealment that mattered.

c   Congress applied the prohibition against concealing Iran as the country of origin of crude oil or refined petroleum products coextensively with the prohibition against transporting crude oil: any person that was 'a controlling beneficial owner' of, or that 'otherwise owns, operates, or controls' a vessel used to transport Iranian energy resources.[77] It used the same bifurcated *mens rea* requirement – 'actual knowledge' to the first group, and 'knowingly' (that is actual or constructive knowledge) for the second group – as before. And, as before, it granted a small safe harbour to underwriters or insurers if they 'exercised due diligence' to ensure the persons for which they were providing protective policies were transporting energy products out of Iran.[78]

d   Two points are noteworthy. First, lest prospective smugglers have any doubt whether US legislators were aware of how they might conceal what they were transporting, Congress listed two non-exclusive examples of sanctionable behaviour: allowing the vessel operator to disenable the satellite tracking device on the vessel, or obscuring the fact the vessel is owned, operated, or controlled by the Iranian government, National Iranian Tanker Company (NITC), or Islamic Republic of Iran Shipping Lines (IRISL) (or by entities controlled by them).[79] Moreover, a prospective smuggler was deemed to have 'actual knowledge' that Iran, the NITC, or IRISL had an interest in a vessel if the Office of Foreign Assets Control (OFAC) listed the International Maritime Organization (IMO) of that vessel.[80] In effect, if OFAC published the IMO number of the vessel, then every person regardless of where located was deemed to know that the vessel was Iranian, and use of it to ship crude oil or petroleum products out of Iran was barred.

e   Second, lest prospective smugglers have any doubt as to how serious Congress was in its intention to ensure countries of origin of crude oil and refined petroleum products were reported accurately and transparently, it empowered the President to impose a supplemental sanction on them.[81] In addition to choosing and applying five of nine sanctions from the standard menu, the President could impose a sixth punishment, namely, on the vessel used to ship Iranian energy resources a ban. The President could bar that vessel from landing at any US port for up to two years.

f   The prohibition against smuggling adduced two other dimensions of the sanctions amendments wrought by the 2012 Iran–Syria Act. First, Congress effectively widened the ban on FDI in the Iranian energy sector and trade in Iranian energy products to a ban on cargo ships in which Iran had an interest. Doing so was consistent with the 2010 CISADA expansion of sanctions from the petroleum sector *per se* to downstream products; namely, refined petroleum. (That same kind of expansion is seen below with regard to allied services such as financing and insurance.)

g Second, Congress anticipated how particular prohibitions might be violated, and tried to block such moves. Doing so was consistent with the 2010 CISADA expansion of sanctions from FDI to exportation and importation, and with the 2012 Iran–Syria Act further expansion to JVs. In brief, the unmistakable trend was one from an initial narrow definition, targeting one product category and behaviour, to downstream products, supporting services, and anticipated reactions by would-be wrongdoers.

In sum, the 2012 Iran–Syria Act amendments to the 1996 sanctions regime, as amended by the 2010 legislation, were breathtaking. The US closed loopholes quite literally to strangle the Iranian energy sector, and did so in the most extraterritorial of manners.

Second: barring transshipment of military items

The 2012 Iran–Syria Act rewrote the prohibition in the 1996 Iran Sanctions Act aimed at preventing Iran from obtaining a WMD. The 1996 Act, coupled with the 2010 CISADA amendments, barred knowing exportation of goods, services, or technology that would contribute materially to the ability of Iran to obtain a WMD or destabilizing numbers of advanced conventional weaponry. That prohibition left open three loopholes: transshipment, constructive knowledge, and JVs in uranium mining. Congress closed them with the 2012 Act.[82]

First, any 'person' that 'exported or transferred, or *permitted or otherwise facilitated the transshipment* of, any goods, services, technology, or other items to *any other person*' now was liable.[83] Second, actual knowledge was not necessary; constructive knowledge – that a person 'should have known' – was enough.[84] Of what did a person need actual or constructive knowledge? Two points: first, that the export, transfer, or transshipment to another person 'would likely result' in that other person exporting, transferring, or transshipping prohibited items to Iran, and second, that the result 'would contribute materially to the ability of Iran' to develop WMDs or destabilizing numbers of advanced conventional weapons.

To be clear, closing the first two loopholes meant:

1 A person need not ship forbidden items directly to Iran. Shipping them through one or more intermediaries was enough. For example, a person in Belarus could export such items to another person in Singapore. If that other person in Singapore subsequently transferred the items to Iran, directly or through another stage of transshipment, for example, through Yemen, then liability could attach to the first person, and indeed every person in the transactional chain.

2 The first person in the chain need not know for sure that the second or a subsequent person is sending the forbidden items onward to Iran. If that person ought to have known the next or a follow-on person likely would send the items to Iran, then that rather speculative anticipation was enough. Presumably, constructive know-

ledge would exist if the first person should have known the goods, services, technology, or other items at issue were headed to Dubai, and that Dubai was a prominent location for smuggling items in small vessels across the Gulf to Iran.

3   As for the second of the two *mens rea* elements – actual or constructive knowledge that the items 'would contribute materially' to Iran's weapons programs, there was no need for a person to have detailed knowledge of those programs. Rather, that knowledge presumably could be inferred from the nature of the goods, services, technology, or items that were exported, transferred, or transshipped. For example, if the goods were centrifuges for enriching uranium, or the technology was used for drones, then could there be doubt that the contribution would be material?

Yet, even with these changes, arguably a rather large and threatening loophole remained: a person might not ship or transship anything to Iran, but might engage in a JV that involves mining, producing, or transporting uranium. Would that participation be sanctionable?

Even reading the amended statutory language broadly, with the closure of the first two loopholes, the answer was 'no'. Uranium is a 'good' but helping to mine or produce it is not the same as 'exporting', 'transferring', or 'transshipping it'. For example, a person could simply assist in the removal of uranium from Russia, even in partnership with an Iranian government entity or person connected to that entity. If the first person did no more, then it did not engage in a prohibited transaction. (Note the person did not invest in Iran, much less in the petroleum resources sector of Iran.) Yet, if the uranium mined in Russia found its way to Iran, then surely Iran's ability to construct a nuclear weapon would be enhanced.

So, with the 2012 *Iran–Syria Act*, Congress closed this loophole. Any person, anywhere in the world, was barred from participating in a JV 'that involves *any activity* relating to the mining, production, or transportation of uranium' with (1) the government of Iran', (2) an entity incorporated in or subject to the jurisdiction of Iran, or (3) a person acting on behalf, at the direction of, or owned or controlled by that government or such an entity.[85] The *mens rea* requirement, 'knowingly', covered actual or constructive knowledge.[86] So, for example, Rio Tinto Zinc, the Australian mining multinational corporation, could not participate in a JV with Tata Mining, the Indian natural resources company, if Tata had an understanding with a business association located in Tehran, if that JV engaged in manufacturing apparel to protect mining workers against radiation. After all, tracking the statutory language, making such apparel is an 'activity' that 'relat[es] to' uranium mining.

Here again, it is worth reminding that in closing all three loopholes, Congress again asserted its extraterritorial reach. None of the persons in the transactional chain, or a JV, needed to be American or anywhere close to the homeland.

Third: government procurement certification against revolutionary guards

Government contracting certifications were another notable change ushered by the 2012 Iran–Syria Act.[87] Any prospective contractor for the US government was obligated not only to certify it was not engaging in a prohibited activity (as before), but also it was not 'knowingly' involved in a 'significant transaction' with Iran's Revolutionary Guard Corps.[88] This certification extended to any officials, agents, or affiliates of the Guard, the property or interest in property of which were blocked by the US under the IEEPA. False certification was punishable by exclusion from the list of approved government contractors (again, as before) for at least two years (a curious decrease from three years).[89]

The additional certification rule, while seemingly minor, reflected a continuation of the earlier shift in US sanctions policy. Up until the 2010 CISADA, and aside from IEEPA asset freezes, the US had not focused on targeting the Guards. Prohibited transactions took aim at economic sectors of Iran, especially petroleum and refined gasoline, not necessarily at economic agents within Iran. From a US perspective, the problem with looking at transactions, not transactors, was that the Guard actually controlled (directly or indirectly) businesses in Iran. Moreover, the Guards were politically powerful, and close to the Supreme Leader. So, the 2012 *Iran-Syria Act* certification requirement was a step towards weakening the Guards as an anti-US economic and political force.

Fourth: diversion prohibition

Pursuant to CISADA, the US had a trade embargo against Iran, and a humanitarian exception thereto.[90] Unscrupulous individuals, in public and private areas, sometimes exploited such an exception for their own benefit. They diverted goods, such as food and medicine, or they misappropriated the proceeds from the sale or resale of the excepted goods. The embargo did not expressly prohibit these corrupt behaviours. The 2012 Iran–Syria Act closed this loophole.

The Act directed the President to submit to the appropriate Congressional committees a list of persons he determined had channelled goods (be they food, medicine, or other humanitarian items) intended for the Iranian people away from them, or made off with funds from their sale or resale.[91] Here, too, there was no intent requirement – the offence was a strict liability one. He then was required to impose sanctions targeted against those persons, namely, the same punishments as applicable to human rights abusers (except, logically, for the sanction of forbidding importation of goods, as that would be counterproductive to the aim of humanitarian goods reaching needy Iranians).[92] That it was a strict liability offence made sense, because at issue was corruption interfering with aid reaching the Iranian people, and thus undermining any pretence that the punishments targeted bad actors, not innocent civilians.

Fifth: shipping and insurance prohibition

None of the aforementioned constrictions affected carriage of goods to or from Iran if those goods were unrelated to the energy sector. But, what if a shipping company provided a vessel on which goods Iran could use to acquire WMDs or support terrorists were transported to Iran? Centrifuges and rocket-propelled grenades (RPGs) would be quintessential examples, and perhaps a state-owned Chinese freight company, such as the Chinese Ocean Shipping Company (COSCO) or China Shipping Container Lines (CSCL), might carry them from their port of origin to Bandar Abbas.[93] Similarly, suppose P&I Clubs or Munich Re provided marine cargo insurance or reinsurance for the transportation of these items.[94]

To discourage the likes of COSCO and CSCL, and non-state owned enterprise (SOE) carriage companies, from shipping goods to Iran, the 2012 Iran–Syria Act rendered them liable for any 'knowing' (that is, actual or constructive knowledge of a) sale, lease, or provision of a vessel used to carry 'to or from Iran . . . goods that could materially contribute to' the WMD or terrorist activities of Iran.[95] Likewise, the Act sought to bar financial institutions, indeed, any person, from providing marine cargo insurance for Iranian transport of the forbidden merchandise.[96] So expansive was the prohibition that it covered 'any other shipping service'.[97] Hence, supplying merchant marine crews, catering, or sanitation, or possibly even tugboat assistance, was barred. Ironically, pre-shipment inspection (PSI) services might even be ensnared in this phraseology.

Any 'person', American or otherwise, legal or natural, was potentially liable, as was any person in a position of ownership, control, or common ownership control.[98] The sanction was a blocking one: the US would forbid any transaction in the property or interests of that person on which it could lay hands. So, for instance, a COSCO or CSCL vessel in the port of Baltimore might be seized, or accounts of P&I Clubs or Munich Re in New York might be frozen. Even the assets of companies that hired workers from impoverished towns and villages in developing countries, such as Magsaysay, a Philippine provider of (*inter alia*) shipping personnel from captains to bakers, were at risk.[99] A Presidential waiver was possible, but only if it was 'vital to the national interests' of the US, and the President explained his decision to Congress.[100]

Notably, however, the sanction was different if the National Iranian Oil Company (NOIC) or National Iranian Tanker Company (NITC) were involved. Suppose P&I Clubs or Munich Re underwrote insurance (or reinsurance) for the NIOC or NITC. Then, the insurer would be subject to five of the nine sanctions (discussed below).[101] The tough insured parties apparently were premised on the view that the NIOC and NITC were directly engaged in helping Iran obtain revenues for its petroleum and petroleum resources that Iran funnelled to WMD and terrorist activities. Only if P&I Clubs or Munich Re exercised due diligence to avoid underwriting policies for NIOC or NITC, or if their policies were for shipments of food, medicine, or humanitarian assistance, could they escape sanctions.[102]

To be sure, it remained lawful to carry or insure goods, or give shipping services for, transportation between Iran and third countries not related to these activities. But, doing so meant freight companies had to ascertain what truly was inside the containers on vessels they provided. That meant more rigorous inspections, which drove up shipping costs to Iran. The possibility of mishaps, coupled with the threat of US penalties, pressed up insurance premiums. Why bother with the headaches, transactions costs, and risks associated with compliance? Perhaps it was better not to carry or insure, or give attendant shipping services for, goods to or from Iran. That would be an outcome Congress would approve, as it would turn the *de jure* US trade embargo against Iran into a *de facto* global trade ban.

Sixth: sovereign debt prohibition

Continuing its efforts to ostracize Iran from the world of international finance, Congress moved to deny Iran access to sovereign debt markets. Congress identified sovereign debt as potential assistance to the energy sector of Iran. Central and sub-central governments around the world issue debt to finance infrastructure development projects. In the case of Iran, FDI projects, valued above a defined threshold, in that sector had been illegal since 1996, but Iran could finance them by tapping financial markets outside of the US. Simply put, Iran could substitute portfolio for direct investment. To the extent Iran did so, it could funnel the consequent revenues from successful energy projects toward production of a nuclear bomb or support for *Hezbollah*.

Congress endeavoured to choke off this source of funds by making it illegal to buy, subscribe to, or otherwise facilitate in the issuance of bonds or other debt instruments by the Iranian government.[103] This move was a bold extraterritorial one over world financial markets: no person, wherever located, could purchase, or even clear or settle trades, in Iranian sovereign debt. Where that potential investor was located, the financial market or markets on which Iran attempted to float its bonds, or the place at which its debt instruments were cleared and settled, did not matter. Of significance was whether the person acted 'knowingly'; that is, with active or constructive knowledge that the debt was that of the Iranian government or any entity, such as an SOE, owned or controlled by it.[104] If the President found a person to have violated this prohibition, then he had to impose five of ten sanctions (discussed below) on that violator.

So, for instance, suppose a prominent hedge fund, such as Apollo Management Asia Pacific Limited, based in Hong Kong,[105] invested in an over-the-counter (OTC) issuance or private placement of convertible bonds by the NIOC. The bonds are denominated in the *euro*. The Spanish bank, Santander, underwrites the offering.[106] Would the fact Apollo and Santander are not US persons immunize them from liability? Would the fact the bonds are not denominated in dollars, or that they may be converted to equity, matter? Would the fact the transaction is not conducted on an organized exchange, and performed entirely overseas, matter?

The answer to these questions is 'no:' nothing on the face of the pertinent statute circumscribed the prohibition and attendant sanctions in accordance with these facts.

Similarly, whether the investors in Apollo were high net worth Americans or not would be immaterial. To the contrary, the reality that Apollo and Santander have offices in New York, and Apollo surely has US investors, renders them and their assets vulnerable.

Seventh: affiliates prohibition

Thanks to CISADA, assets of Iran's Revolutionary Guard Corps on which the United States could obtain jurisdiction were frozen. But, what about foreigners, especially non-Iranians, who operated as agents for the Corps? What if they entered into energy or financial transactions with the Corp, or bartered deals for the Corps that did not involve a monetary payment? CISADA did not directly target these aiders and abettors, nor put their assets at risk, and did not cover counter-trade. The 2012 Iran–Syria Act addressed these questions, while maintaining the extant primary sanctions on the Corps.[107]

First, the Act closed the loophole by which a foreigner could help the Corps with impunity.[108] Congress directed the President to identify and designate for sanctions any foreign person who was an 'official[], agent[], or affiliate[]' of the Corps, and to 'block and prohibit all transactions in all property and interests in property of that foreign person' that were in the US or in the possession or control of a US person.[109] Likewise, the President was to deny entry to the US of a Corps agent (unless that agent was coming to speak at the UN, or it was 'vital to . . . [American] national security interests' to permit him entry).[110]

Read literally, this language could apply to a salesperson for Nestlé who sold baby formula to the spouse of an official in the Corps. To screen out inconsequential agency relationships, Congress conveyed to the President the agents in which it had special interest: the President was to give priority in investigation those persons who conducted, or tried to conduct, a 'sensitive transaction' with the Corps.[111] 'Sensitive transactions' meant (exclusively) any (1) financial deal involving a non-Iranian bank in excess of US$1 million (or summing above that threshold in a 12-month period), (2) manufacture, importation, or exportation of items Iran needed to develop a WMD, (3) production, purchase, or sale of any goods, services, or technology relating to the Iranian energy or petrochemical sector, or (4) procurement of restricted technology that would aid Iran in restricting the flow of news or expression of free speech.[112] Thus, respectively, a bank account manager in a Malaysian bank who provided investment advice, a mine director in Russia who supervised the extraction of uranium, a port official in Rotterdam who oversaw shipments of crude oil, or an engineering professor at the University of Kansas who conducted research into plastics – all were potentially liable for violations of the agency prohibition if their dealings involved the Corps and the President identifies them as 'officials, agents, or affiliates' of the Corps.[113]

Significantly, Congress wrote the prohibition expansively to include another step downstream in the chain of a financial or commercial transaction. Suppose a foreign person 'knowingly materially assist[s]' the Corps, or an agent or affiliate thereof who has been sanctioned, by providing funds, goods, services, or technology to Corps officials or agents.[114] For example, suppose a Dutch commodities trader at ABN AMRO in Amsterdam brokers a sale of liquefied petroleum gas (LPG) by NatGaz, which is headquartered in Beirut, to the Bangkok office of the UK-based ITS Trading Company.[115] If the President has sanctioned ITS Bangkok as a Corps agent, then the broker potentially is liable for having materially assisted the agent by arranging the sale of goods (LPG) and concomitant payment of funds.[116]

Likewise, suppose a foreign person enters into a 'significant transaction' with the Corps or one of its affiliates.[117] For instance, suppose a Singaporean businessman brokers an exchange of basmati rice from India for Iranian crude oil. The businessman is potentially liable, because 'significant transaction' includes barter trade involving the Corps or its network, assuming the President designated and sanctioned him as an affiliate.[118]

In sum, the affiliate prohibition was up to two steps removed from the Corps: it extended not only to (1) the agent, but also (2) any foreign person who supports that agent. In both hypothetical transactions, the statutory language did not require that the Corps itself bought the LPG or sold the crude oil. And, in both cases, the mandatory penalty was an imposition of five from the standard menu of nine sanctions (discussed below).[119] Sanctions on the foreign person-supporter could not be waived unless that person had ceased the forbidden behaviour, or a waiver was 'essential' to US national security interests, and would not terminate until the person stopped the behaviour and gave assurances against re-engagement.[120]

In this two-step chain, foreign agents or supporters of the Corps the President had to identify and punish were not limited to private natural or legal persons. Public sector bodies were included, too. Congress made sure in the 2012 Iran–Syria Act to forbid any foreign government agency of any country in the world aside from transacting with the Corps or its agents. That is, suppose the President determined a third-country government entity 'knowingly and materially assisted, sponsored, or provided financial, material, or technological support for, or goods or services in support of, or knowingly and materially engaged in a significant financial transaction with'[121] a foreign person, and that this person was an 'official, agent, or affiliate' of the Corps. Then, the entity was potentially liable.

To illustrate via modest modifications to the above hypotheticals, suppose the Dutch Ministry of Finance renders advisory services to the ABN AMRO trader on the application of bank secrecy laws to commodity brokerage, or the Ministry of Commerce in India lends support in the form of material and technology on the proper conduct of barter trade to the Singaporean businessman broker. Assuming the trader or broker qualify as Corps agents or affiliates, then the Dutch and Indian government bodies could be held to account.[122]

Sanctions on those sovereign bodies were not mandatory, but Congress clearly nudged the President to do so by listing the possible punishments: denial of foreign aid, defence assistance, and financial or credit support; rejection of export licences for controlled (in particular, weapons) items; opposition to official international financial institution lending and technical assistance; and IEEPA penalties.[123] Once imposed, sanctions could be terminated only if doing so was 'essential' to US national security, the foreign government entity ceased its behaviour, or the foreign person with whom or which it dealt no longer acted for Iran's Revolutionary Guards.[124] Congress further indicated its preference for sanctions against foreign government agencies that transacted with the Corps or its supporters by obliging the President to explain to it why he opted (if he did) for clemency.[125] Manifestly, then, Congress sought to isolate as far as possible the Corps by telling the private and public sectors around the world not to deal with them or their affiliates.

Eighth: tightening human rights and censorship prohibitions

The 2012 Iran–Syria Act amended the 2010 CISADA rules on human rights abuses. Those rules directed sanctions against individual Iranian officials for disrespecting the human rights of Iranians during and after the Green Revolution. But, specifically who were those officials? Moreover, should not the supply to Iran of the physical instruments of torture and devices for censorship be forbidden? Finally, ought not the faceless transferors, sometimes white-collar professionals, who gave torturers and censors their tools, be held accountable?

CISADA did not answer these three questions. The Act did, essentially close the loopholes by naming names and establishing as prohibited behaviours the shipment of those heinous tools.[126] First, Congress stated its sense that:

> the Supreme Leader of Iran, the President of Iran, senior members of the Intelligence Ministry of Iran, senior members of Iran's Revolutionary Guard Corps, Ansar-e-Hezbollah and Basij-e-Mostaz'afin, and the Ministries of Defense, Interior, Justice, and Telecommunications are ultimately responsible for ordering, controlling, or otherwise directing a pattern and practice of serious human rights abuses against the Iranian people . . .[127]

Thus, the President 'should' include those people on the CISADA list of human rights violators.[128] To be sure the President understood what 'should' meant, Congress ordered a 'detailed report' to the appropriate committees on whether each named person was on the blacklist, and if not, why not.[129]

Second, the amended statute directed the President to name to (and regularly update) the appropriate Congressional committees any person the President thinks 'knowingly engaged' in transferring (or facilitating the transfer) to Iran, or any Iranian, of 'goods or technologies he decides are likely to be used by Iran to commit serious human rights abuses against the people of Iran'.[130] Whether it was 'likely' an item would be put to abusive use, or whether an abuse was 'serious', might be unclear.

But, lest the President doubt what Congress intended in respect of 'goods or technologies', the legislature gave him with a non-exclusive list of examples: ammunition, batons, electroshock weapons, firearms, rubber bullets, spray (chemical or pepper), stun grenades, surveillance technology, tear gas, water cannons.[131] So, for instance, dual use items such as pepper spray, which some US runners carry while training for protection, was off limits. The list was non-exclusive, as it had to be: an evil mind can turn everyday items like cigarettes or pliers into an instrument of repression, so better to be potentially over- than under-inclusive, if the human rights facilitation prohibition is not to be easily circumvented. The prohibition applied regardless of whether the engagement involved a formal contract, and its scope included services (e.g., consulting, engineering, hardware, or software) to support forbidden goods or technologies.[132]

Third, the amended statute directed the President to provide the appropriate Congressional committees with a list (and updates to it) of persons he thinks 'engaged in censorship'.[133] By that Congress meant they barred, restricted, or punished the freedom of expression, or limited access to the media (including, for instance, by jamming or manipulating international frequency signals).[134] Note Congress did not preface the forbidden behaviour with the adverb 'knowingly'. But, that preface was implicit. Censors surely know what they are doing; that is, why interfere with freedom of expression unless suppression of thought, word, and picture is the intended consequence?

The 2012 Act relied on the same individually-targeted sanctions CISADA specified for human rights abusers, with one exception.[135] Hence, officials transferring goods, services, or technologies used for serious human rights abusers, or censoring the press, were subject to restrictions on their bank accounts and other property. The exception concerned a particularly infamous recipient of torture instruments: Iran's Revolutionary Guard Corps. If it was the transferee of a banned item, then any other sanction from the standard 12-item menu (discussed below) under the 1996 Iran Sanctions Act (that is ILSA, as amended) as supplemented in 2010 by CISADA, also could be imposed on the transferor.[136]

Ninth: five of twelve sanctions

The aforementioned amendments to the 1996 Iran Sanctions Act and 2010 CISADA concerned forbidden transactions with Iran. Beyond tightening the sanctions regime by making more transactions unlawful, the 2012 Iran–Syria Act heightened penalties for illegal conduct. Instead of requiring the President to impose just three of nine sanctions on any person that knowingly engaged in a prohibited transaction, the 2012 Iran–Syria Act mandated imposition of 5 of 12 punishments.[137] In upping the penalties, Congress also restricted further the discretion of the President, thereby asserting more control over US trade policy towards Iran.

That is, Congress compelled the President to impose five, not just three, sanctions. But, it gave the President three more sanctions options overall from which to choose. Accordingly, the sanctions menu under the 2012 Iran–Syria Act contained the same nine items as those under the 1996 ILSA and 2010 CISADA scheme:

1 Export Financing Sanction[138]
2 Export License Sanction[139]
3 American Bank Loans Sanction[140]
4 Primary Dealer and Repository Sanctions[141]

472 *Legal issues in Asian investing*

5   Government Procurement Sanction,[142]
6   Foreign Exchange Sanction,[143]
7   Inter-bank Transactions Sanction,[144]
8   Property Transaction Sanction, and[145]
9   Additional Sanctions.[146]

In addition, the 2012 legislation added the following three new punishment choices. The three new options were as follows:

10 Equity or Debt Investment Sanction:[147]

   a   First, the President could bar any United States person (natural or legal) from buying 'significant amounts' of the equity or debt of a sanctioned person. So, hypothetically, if the Japanese multinational electronics corporation, Panasonic, were a sanctioned person, then the President could prohibit American individuals or firms from investing in Panasonic stock or bonds. (Whether he could compel divestment was uncertain, but not an option expressly listed in the menu.)

11 Corporate Officer Exclusion Sanction:[148]

   b   Second, the President could exclude corporate officers. In particular, he could order the Department of Homeland Security to deny issuance of a visa to visit the United States to any officer, principal, or shareholder with a controlling interest in a sanctioned person.
   c   To illustrate, consider a modified version of the facts in *US v. Kaiga*, a 2013 criminal case involving export control violations.[149] Suppose the allegations in the *Kaiga* criminal complaint by the United States Attorney's Office for the Northern District of Illinois are true: a Belgian businessman living in Brussels and affiliated with the Belgian company Industrial Metal and Commodities (IMC) shipped 7075 T6 aluminium tubes with an outside diameter of 4.125 inches and an ultimate tensile strength of 572 megapascals.[150] These tubes are used in aerospace products, and are controlled items for nuclear non-proliferation purposes under the *Export Administration Act* and *International Emergency Economic Powers Act*. The Belgian businessman did not obtain an export license as the shipment was from the tube supplier in Schaumburg, Illinois, to IMC in Brussels. None was needed for shipments to Brussels. In fact, the tubes were shipped from Schaumburg to a front company in Malaysia that was operated by a party with ties to Iran. This shipment violated American export control regulations, because a license is needed for shipments to Malaysia.
   d   Suppose the party with ties to Iran arranged for the tubes to be sent from Malaysia to Iran. In consequence, the Belgian businessman also violated American trade prohibitions against Iran. Assume IMC and the Malaysian intermediary also are found liable. Under the corporate officer exclusion sanction, any officer, principal, or controlling shareholder in IMC or the Malaysian intermediary – the sanctioned persons – could be barred from obtaining a visa to the United States. Note the 2012 legislation did not define 'controlling' in a rigid fashion. So, a 51 per cent shareholding might be required to control IMC, but – given a more diffuse pattern of shareholding in the intermediary – perhaps a 15 per cent stake would suffice.

12 Principal Executive Officer Sanction:[151]

    e   Third, the President could impose any of the aforementioned 11 sanctions on high-ranking officials working for a sanctioned person. Such officials included 'the principal executive officer or officer, or ... persons performing similar functions and with similar authorities as such officer or officer'. This sanction was not tied to formal business titles, but rather targeted individuals with decision-making authority. The idea was that none of them should feel safe with the thought that they, personally, did not engage in prohibited conduct with Iran. All that mattered is they held an important post with an entity that did.

    f   So, for example, in the above hypothetical based on the *Kaiga* case, consider the predicament of colleagues of the Belgian businessman working for IMC. They could be sanctioned, as could senior officers in the Malaysian intermediary.

Collectively, then, the three new sanctions pertained to corporate finance and officials. Their thrust was to strangle the Iranian economy by scaring individuals who might invest in or work for companies that did business with Iran. Put differently, they were an extension of the American strategy of imposing a secondary boycott on Iran, with this extension addressing private parties.

Tenth: arguably tougher waiver criteria

The 2012 Act altered the criteria under which the President could waive imposition sanctions. Up to that Act, the President could do so for any illegal transaction with Iran if he determined it was 'necessary to the national interest' to do so.[152] Prior law did not clarify how long the waiver would last, and did not have explicit authority to renew the waiver. The 2012 Act explicitly limited any waiver to one-year waiver, and concomitantly allowed for renewals of up to one year on a case-by-case basis.[153]

The Act also bifurcated the substantive waiver criteria according to the type of prohibited conduct that occurred. Suppose that conduct concerned the energy sector of Iran. Then, the President could waive sanctions if it was 'essential to the national security interests of the United States' to do so.[154] But, suppose the transgression was helping Iran develop WMDs or advanced military capabilities by Iran. Then, the President could waive sanctions if it was 'vital to the national security interests' of the US.[155]

What is the difference between 'essential' and 'vital'? The Act did not answer that question. Arguably, helping Iran acquire a WMD was an even more serious violation than investing in its energy sector, or trading in its energy products, making 'vital' a higher standard than 'essential' to meet for a waiver.

14.3 Phase 10: 2013 Defense Act tightening energy, shipping, and financial sanctions, plus shipbuilding, port, and precious metal sanctions

Novel link between Iranian human rights abuses and American national security (2 January 2013–31 December 2016)

The *Iran Freedom and Counter-Proliferation Act of 2012* was the final legislation against Iran before the November 2013–January 2014 preliminary nuclear agreement Congress passed and the President signed. This legislation was Sub-Title D of the *National Defense Authorization Act for Fiscal Year 2013* (2013 *Budget Act*).[156] Thus, like the 2012 Budget Act, it tacked on sanctions against Iran to a defense appropriation bill, as doing so minimizes difficulties with Congressional passage vis-à-vis a stand-along measure concerning Iran.[157] In the 2013 Act, the 113th Congress stressed the newest and third of its three rationales for the sanctions regime: fighting human rights abuses.[158]

Congress expressly linked 'the interests of the United States and international peace' to the 'threat[]' of 'ongoing and destabilizing actions of the Government of Iran, including its massive, systematic, and extraordinary violations of the human rights of its own citizens'.[159] That linkage was novel: Congress had not tied those violations to US national security in prior sanctions legislation. Why exactly those violations might undermine that security any more than, say, human rights abuses in China, was not entirely certain. But, constructing a cogent argument was not difficult. Assume Iranian liberals and reformists are less interested in developing a WMD or sponsoring terrorists than their opponents, yet suppose the opponents crush their democratic movement. The victorious hardliners may have free rein to threaten the US and its allies with a nuclear weapon or by funding terrorist causes.

Thus, via 2013 *Budget Act*, Congress sought to impede the ability of the Iranian government to 'oppress the people of Iran and to use violence and executions against pro-democracy protestors and regime opponents' and 'jam or otherwise obstruct international satellite broadcast signals', and bolster the ability of those people to secure 'basic freedoms that build the foundation for the emergence of a freely elected, open, and democratic political system'.[160]

Energy, shipping, shipbuilding, and port prohibition

Congress ordered the President to block all transactions in property or property interests located in, or coming into, the US, or under the control of a US person, of any person connected to the Iranian energy, shipping, or shipbuilding sectors, or to any Iranian port, or of any Iranian or sanctioned person knowingly helping such a person.[161] Further, the President had to impose five sanctions from the standard menu (discussed above) on such a person.[162] Congress also designated any entity that operated a port in Iran, including the NIOC, NITC, and Islamic Republic of Iran Shipping Lines (IRISL), as 'entities of proliferation concern'.[163] Finally, Congress instructed the President to bar (or impose strict conditions on) any correspondent account or PTA in the US of any foreign financial institution that conducts 'significant financial transaction' for the sale, supply, or transfer of energy, shipping, or shipbuilding goods or services in Iran, including for ultimate use by the NIOC, NITC, and IRISL. Congress allowed a limited exception to the prohibition for humanitarian aid (food, pharmaceuticals, or medical devices) to Iran,[164] and a waiver of sanctions if 'vital to . . . [American] national security' and justified in a report to the appropriate Congressional committees.[165]

Simply put, Congress yet again tightened the noose around Iranian energy, shipping, and banking, and created a new noose around Iranian shipbuilding and ports. Why did it do so? The answer is that notwithstanding its aforementioned reaffirmation of support for human rights causes in Iran, Congress stuck to its two long-standing policy justifications for the sanctions: deterrence with respect to a WMD and terrorism. In the 2013 Act, Congress explicitly found:

1   Iran's energy, shipping, and shipbuilding sectors and Iran's ports are facilitating the Government of Iran's nuclear proliferation activities by providing revenue to support proliferation activities.

    . . .

5   United Nations Security Council Resolution 1929 (2010) recognizes the 'potential connection between Iran's revenues derived from its energy sector and the funding of Iran's proliferation sensitive nuclear activities'.

6   The National Iranian Tanker Company is the main carrier for the Iranian Revolutionary Guard Corps-designated National Iranian Oil Company and a key element in the petroleum supply chain responsible for generating energy revenues that support the illicit nuclear proliferation activities of the Government of Iran.[166]

These findings helped shape the new prohibitions and attendant penalties it established.

Despite sanctions from the 1996 ILSA, 2010 CISADA, and amendments wrought by the 2012 Iran–Syria Act and 2012 Defense Act, support for the energy and shipping sectors was getting through to Iran. Some of that assistance came from Iran's own shipbuilding and port facilities, which thanks to repairs and upgrades could be used by the likes of the NITC to transport NIOC crude oil, the sale proceeds could be used for a nuclear bomb or diverted to *Hezbollah*? Put simply, Congress moved to plug holes in the vertical supply chain, which started with its ban on FDI in energy exploration in 1996, expanded to downstream petroleum products in 2010, and to financing and insurance for energy transactions in 2012.

Precious metals prohibition

Energy, shipping, and shipbuilding, were not the only sectors, nor were ports the routes, though which Iran and its Revolutionary Guard Corps obtained funds, goods, or services for possible use to acquire a WMD, sponsor terrorists, abuse human rights, or censor the press. Global commodities markets (other than energy) afforded another opportunity. Iran or the Corps could barter or swap gold, silver, or other precious metals for such purposes. For instance, it could exchange aluminium with a dealer in Johannesburg, South Africa, to acquire gold, which it then could list as an asset in its national balance sheet,[167] and possibly use that gold as payment for guidance systems for ballistic missiles.

Indeed, holding 7 per cent of total global mineral reserves,[168] Iran had an incentive to do so: skirt the US sanctions against the Iranian financial sector, which made electronic transfers of funds illegal. That Iran did so may be inferred from Congress opting to identify in the 2013 Defense Act a new kind of forbidden transaction with Iran: selling, supplying, or transferring, directly or indirectly, a commodity in any one of three broad categories:

1   Any 'precious metal'.[169]
2   Certain raw or semi-finished metals, specifically, 'graphite, raw, or semi-finished metals such as aluminium and steel, coal (including coking, fuel, or metallurgical coal),[170] and software for integrating industrial processes',[171]
3   'Any other material' in the second category that Iran uses for its energy, shipping, or shipbuilding sectors, for any economic sector controlled by the Corps, or for its 'nuclear, military, or ballistic missile programs'.[172]

Any person that knowingly (that is knew or should have known about their conduct)[173] transacted in these commodities with Iran was subject to five sanctions from the standard menu.[174]

Likewise, Congress forbade any foreign financial institution from opening a correspondent account or PTA that the institution knew was used to facilitate a 'significant financial transaction' associated with a sanctionable sale, supply, or transfer of precious metals or other listed commodities.[175] In other words, what Congress barred was both an underlying transactions in those items, and payments for such deals. Only if a person or financial institution 'exercised due diligence' to eschew commodity transactions and payments therefore could the President except them from otherwise mandatory penalties.[176] And, only if it were 'vital' to US national security could the President waive these prohibitions.[177]

Three reinforcements of existing prohibitions

In the 2013 Defense Act, Congress buttressed three existing prohibitions and attendant sanctions. First, to strengthen the precious metals prohibition, and the prohibition concerning the Iranian energy, shipping, shipbuilding sectors, and its ports, Congress supplemented rules from the 2012 Iran–Syria Act against providing underwriting, insurance, or reinsurance services to Iran. Congress expressly banned provision of those services in any way that might benefit those sectors or ports, or help Iran transact in precious metals. Any person knowingly doing so was liable for five or more penalties from the sanctions menu.[178] This expanded denial of access for Iran to shipping insurance posed yet another challenge for the Islamic Republic to arrange for carriage of goods to its shores.

Second, to ostracize Iran further from global financial services, Congress clarified that it was illegal for a foreign financial institution to open a correspondent account or PTA in the US, if that institution 'knowingly facilitated a significant financial transaction' for any proscribed Iranian person or sanctioned entity.[179] The mandatory penalty for running afoul of this bar was the familiar five-of-nine punishments selected by the President.[180] Here again, along with a humanitarian assistance exception, a third country short supply exception existed for financial transactions associated with petroleum or petroleum products, if the President determined the price and supply conditions did not allow for such countries to eschew significant sourcing from Iran.[181]

Though technically convoluted, a noteworthy exception existed for a foreign financial institution that facilitated:

1   financial transactions pertaining to goods and services,[182] or natural gas exports to or imports from Iran, which were
2   not subject to US sanctions, and were
3   conducted directly between Iran and a third country with primary regulatory authority over the foreign financial institution, as long as
4   that institution credited any funds owed to Iran to an account in the third country.[183]

This intriguing exception presumably preserved both a modicum of bilateral trade between third countries and Iran, and denial of access by Iran to any cash from such trade.

For instance, the San Francisco, California branch of Hanmi Bank (HB) could open or maintain a correspondent account or PTA for the benefit of Iran, under the aforementioned conditions.[184] But, to avoid US sanctions, HB would have to credit funds to the Iranian beneficiary to an account in Korea, because Korea is the country holding primary regulatory authority over HB. In effect, the exception forces a change in the location of the beneficiary's bank from any country in the world to the foreign bank primary regulatory jurisdiction.

Third, Congress reinforced sanctions motivated by its human rights concerns. It ordered the President to penalize the Islamic Republic of Iran Broadcasting, including specifically its President, Ezzatollah Zargami. It did so because IRIB and its President had 'contributed to the infringement of individuals' human rights by broadcasting forced television confession and show trials', thus 'clear[ly] violate[ing] ... international law with respect to the right to a fair trial and due process'.[185] The mandatory penalties were those set forth in CISADA for human rights abuses, including IEEPA penalties, visa denials, and asset freezes, as well as OFAC blacklisting.[186]

14.4 Necessary, but not sufficient?

November 2013 Joint Plan of Action

Six US Presidents and 16 sessions of Congress, spanning nearly 40 years, have pursued a sanctions-based policy towards Iran. For most of that period, the results were plain enough: no change in behaviour, and deepened distrust, even hatred. The 'Great Satan' piled on sanctions. The 'Evil *Āyatollāhs*' kept the centrifuges spinning, and even managed to procure more of them.

Then, on 24 November 2013, in Geneva, Switzerland, Iran agreed to a historic preliminary accord with the US and five other signatories (collectively called the 'P – 5 + 1'), the five permanent UN Security Council members (China, France, Russia, UK, and US), plus an additional European country (Germany).[187] Israel dubbed the accord a 'historic mistake'.[188] Nonetheless, subsequently, these countries elaborated on this '*Joint Plan of Action*', which also is called the '*Geneva Interim Agreement*', or simply the '*Iran Nuclear Deal*', and began its implementation on 20 January 2014.[189]

The Deal had an initial lifespan of six months. It was extended on 18 July 2014 for another six months, until 24 November 2014, as negotiations towards a permanent solution continued. That meant the bulk of US sanctions stayed on. To the irritation and sometimes outrage of the Iranians, President Barack H. Obama designated via Executive Orders in the summer and fall 2014 new individuals, companies, and shipping vessels as subject to sanctions.

Table 14.1 summarizes the key points of the Plan, listing what Iran 'gave' and what it 'got'. Can it be inferred from the agreement that the sanctions worked? Was it both necessary and sufficient, first, in wrecking the economy of Iran, and second, in leaving Iran no choice but to agree to the Plan?

If statements of the players are to be believed, then the answer is 'it depends who is asked'. The US President said 'unprecedented sanctions and tough diplomacy helped to bring Iran to the negotiating table'.[190] The Iranian narrative was different: diplomacy mattered more than sanctions.[191] Both sides can point to facts supporting their opposing views that sanctions were necessary and sufficient, or not, to pressure Iran economically so as to force it to bargain. A fair assessment is the midpoint between the two perspectives: sanctions were a necessary, but not sufficient, cause to pressure Iran economically to sign a nuclear accord.

Table 14.1 Synopsis of November 2013 *Joint Plan of Action*[192]

What Iran 'gave' (Conversely, what the US 'got')	What Iran 'got' (Conversely, what the US 'gave')
Conversion of existing stockpile of highly enriched uranium[193]	
From its existing uranium enriched to 20 per cent (that is, 20 per cent uranium hexafluoride, UF_6), Iran dilutes (blends down) half to no more than 5 per cent purity.[194] There is no line for reconversion.	From its existing uranium enriched to 20 per cent, Iran retains the other half as working stock of 20 per cent oxide for fabrication of fuel for the Tehran Research Reactor (TRR).
Once the line for conversion of UF_6 enriched up to 5 per cent purity to uranium dioxide (UO_2) is ready, Iran converts to oxide UF_6 newly enriched up to 5 per cent, in accordance with a schedule of the conversion plant declared to the International Atomic Energy Agency (IAEA).	
Further enrichment[195]	
Iran does not enrich uranium over 5 per cent purity.	Iran continues its safeguarded research and development (R&D), including enrichment R&D practices that are not designed to accumulate enriched uranium.
Iran also does not add any uranium at the 3.5 per cent enrichment level or higher to its current stock.[196]	
Enrichment capacity[197]	
Iran does not make any further advances of activities at its:	Iran may manufacture items for its nuclear facilities off of the premises of those facilities, but it may not install any such items into the facilities.
(1) Natanz Fuel Enrichment Plant,	
(2) Fordow Enrichment Facility, or	
(3) Arak reactor (which the IAEA designated as IR-40).[198]	At Natanz and Fordow, Iran may replace existing centrifuges with centrifuges of the same type.[201]
In particular, with respect to Natanz and Fordow, Iran:	
(1) Leaves inoperable 50 per cent of the centrifuges at Natanz,	
(2) Does not install, or prepare for installation, any new centrifuges for uranium enrichment at Natanz.[199]	
(3) Leaves inoperable 75 per cent of the centrifuges at Fordow,[200] and	
(4) Does not use its more sophisticated IR-2 centrifuges for uranium enrichment.	
With respect to Arak, Iran does not:	
(1) Commission this reactor.	
(2) Make or transfer fuel or heavy water to the site of the reactor.	
(3) Test additional fuel, or produce more fuel, for the reactor.	

(4) Install remaining components in the reactor.

Iran does add any new facilities for enrichment.

Iran does not reprocess uranium, or construct a facility capable of reprocessing.

Enhanced monitoring (International Inspections)[202]

Iran provides (within three months of the January 2014 implementation) specific information to the IAEA, including:

(1) its plans for nuclear facilities,

(2) descriptions of each building on each nuclear site, including the design details of the Arak reactor, and of the scale of operations for each location engaged in specified nuclear activities, and

(3) data on uranium mines and mills, and source material.

Iran submits to the IAEA an updated DIQ for the Arak reactor.

Iran agrees with the IAEA on steps on a 'Safeguards Approach' for the Arak reactor.

At Natanz and Fordow, Iran grants daily access to IAEA inspectors when inspectors are not present for the purpose of design information verification, interim inventory verification, physical inventory verification, or unannounced inspections, so that inspectors may obtain offline surveillance records.

Also at certain sites at Natanz and Fordow, Iran permits 24 hour surveillance cameras.

Iran grants managed access to IAEA inspectors to:

(1) centrifuge assembly workshops,

(2) centrifuge rotor production workshops and storage facilities, and,

(3) uranium mines and mills.

Iran responds to IAEA questions about possible military aspects of its nuclear program, and gives the IAEA data as part of the *Additional Protocol* (the model for which the IAEA established in 1997) that Iran is expected to sign with the IAEA. (Under an *Additional Protocol* to the *Treaty on the Non-Proliferation of Nuclear Weapons* (*Non-Proliferation Treaty*, or *NPT*), the IAEA receives more information from the signatory

Consistent with Iran's plans, it may produce centrifuges for the purpose of replacing damaged machines.[203]

(continued overleaf)

Table 14.1 Continued

What Iran 'gave' (Conversely, what the US 'got')	What Iran 'got' (Conversely, what the US 'gave')
country about its nuclear activities, including imports and exports, has enhanced inspection access rights including to suspected locations on short notice, and greater administrative flexibilities, including automatic visa renewals for its inspectors.)	
Sanctions relief: crude oil and related insurance and shipping[204]	
Overall, all forms of sanctions relief amount to roughly $7 billion.	The US (and EU) pauses efforts to cajole third countries to significantly reduce, and ultimately cease, buying crude oil from Iran, and agrees those countries may maintain their current average amounts of Iranian oil. In essence, the US suspends its third country short supply measures.
Of that, $4.2 billion are revenues from crude oil sales that are transferred to Iran in instalments as Iran complies with its obligations under the Plan.[205]	
Iran could revive its sagging crude oil industry. As of January 2014, Chinese state oil companies dominated the Iranian crude oil industry, and President Hassan Rouhani sought to attract large Western energy multinationals to revive that industry, starting with a major address at the World Economic Forum in Davos, the first there by an Iranian President in 10 years.[206]	To facilitate third country oil sales, the US (and EU) also suspends sanctions on insurance and transportation for crude oil shipments. The US (and EU) also permits repatriation of an agreed amount of crude oil revenue of Iran frozen in bank accounts overseas.
Sanctions relief: petrochemical products and related insurance and shipping[207]	
	The US (and EU) suspends sanctions against exports from Iran of petrochemical products, and on services related to those exports, namely, financial, insurance, and transportation sanctions.[208]
Sanctions relief: precious metals[209]	
Iran has access to $1.5 billion of revenues from gold and precious metal trade.[210]	The US (and EU) suspends sanctions on precious metals (including gold), and on services related to transactions in precious metals involving Iran, namely, financial, insurance, and transportation sanctions.
Sanctions relief: autos and aircraft[211]	
	The US suspends sanctions against Iran with respect to auto and auto parts, and related financial, insurance, and transportation sanctions. The US permits licensing for (1) export licensing of spare parts for safety of flight of Iranian civil aircraft (including, but not

	limited to, Iran Air),[212] (2) installation services for these parts, and (3) repair and safety inspections services for those aircraft, and (4) suspends related financial, insurance, and transportation sanctions.
Possible new sanctions[213]	The American President will not impose any new nuclear-related sanctions, and will discourage Congress from imposing any such sanctions.[214]
	The EU and UN Security Council also will refrain from imposing any new nuclear-related sanctions.
Humanitarian issues[215]	
Via the humanitarian financial channel, Iran can use its oil revenues frozen in overseas to acquire food and other agricultural products, medicine, medical devices, and to pay for medical expenses incurred outside Iran, and thereby fulfil some of its domestic needs.	The US establishes a financial channel to facilitate trade with Iran for humanitarian purposes. Only designated foreign banks, or non-sanctioned Iranian banks, may participate in the channel.
Also via this channel, Iran may make payments (1) for UN obligations, (2) to overseas universities hosting Iranian students for their tuition expenses (up to a defined threshold).	(Similarly, the EU increases its thresholds to an agreed level for which it authorizes non-sanctioned trade with Iran (so called 'authorization thresholds')).

For the US, it is true sanctions helped wreck the Iranian economy. The ever-growing number of transactions it forbade, and the ever-larger number of attendant sanctions it created, hurt Iran. Before the tightening of sanctions in 2012, the Iranian economy was 'fragile'.[216] Following their tightening, the challenges worsened. Numerous realities evinced the parlous state of Iran's economy, including:

1 The GDP of Iran shrank by 6 per cent in 2012, and another 5 per cent in 2013.[217] In the year up to October 2013, GDP declined by 6 per cent.[218]
2 The value of the Iranian rial relative to the dollar tumbled by over 50 per cent between January 2012 and October 2013.[219]
3 In October 2013, Iran's unemployment and inflation rates, respectively, were 30 and 40 per cent, respectively[220] – in effect, a monstrous combination of joblessness and price hikes called 'stagflation'. In January 2014, inflation had eased only to 36 per cent,[221] but as of September 2014 it was over 50 per cent.[222]
4 In 2011 and 2012, Iran's revenues from daily crude oil sales fell 60 per cent.[223]
5 In 2011, Iran produced 3.5 million barrels of oil per day.[224] In September 2013, that figure fell to the lowest level since 1989, just after the September 1980-August 1988 Iran–Iraq War: 2.58 million barrels per day. In 2012 alone, and through January 2014, Iran's production of crude oil dropped from 3.7 to 2.7 million barrels per day.[225] These drops were harbingers of a further fall in sales receipts.

6   Between 2011 and 2013, Iranian oil export sales revenues tumbled from $100 to $35 billion. That was because its oil exports dropped 60 per cent, from 2.5 to 1 million barrels per day. The fall in revenues hurt government expenditures, because they finance about half of Iran's public spending.[226]
7   For decades, roughly US$50 billion in Iranian funds have been frozen outside of Iran as a result of sanctions; that is, Iran has not had access to a large sum of funds.[227]
8   The Iranian travel and tourism market was 'stagnant' between 2006 and 2013, despite the country being 'home to a treasure trove of antiquities and world class archaeological sites'.[228]

Still, in evaluating whether sanctions truly caused the damage, it is important not to confuse correlation and causation, or over-attribute causation to one independent variable amid others.

On the one hand, other intervening domestic and foreign variables may have contributed to Iran's woes. For example, there was likely self-inflicted damage caused by internal political upheaval and mass street protests (or the prospects thereof), which exacerbated an unpredictable, uncertain climate for business. Assuredly, the global economic recession commencing in 2008 dampened demand for Iran's energy products and interest in investing in its energy sector. On the other hand, the vicissitudes appear to follow the tightening of sanctions, and tend to mount with the 2012 legislative changes. It strains credibility to assert that the long, strong arm of US justice had no effect in deterring prospective investors and traders from dealing with Iran. Surely among the many that dearly wanted to, at least some calculated that the risk of detection and punishment offset any anticipated returns.

Conversely, for Iran, internal economic mismanagement and corruption also helped wreck the economy, along with a 'suffocating security atmosphere'.[229] That is, the sanctions hardly were the sole cause of Iranian woes. Even climate change played a role. Global warming (along with neglectful government) helped diminish water supplies from *qanats* – trenches created 3,000 years ago to irrigate Ancient Persia whereby water from aquifers beneath mountains flows across hundreds of miles.[230] So, Iranian pistachio output has fallen.

Amid self-inflicted wounds and shifts in Mother Nature was prideful determination:

> Contrary to the claims of some US lawmakers and Israeli officials, sanctions only caused a dramatic rise in nuclear capability, as Tehran sought to show it would not respond to pressure. Before, Iran was enriching uranium to below 5 per cent at one site with 3,000 centrifuges and possessed a minute stockpile of enriched uranium. Today [*i.e.*, four days before signing the *Joint Action Plan*], it is enriching to 20 per cent at two sites with 19,000 centrifuges. It has a stockpile of 8,000 kg of enriched uranium and more sophisticated centrifuges.[231]

Moreover, of enormous significance to Iran's participation in the *Joint Action Plan* were two points.

First, the US 'red line . . . changed from "no enrichment of uranium" to "no nuclear bomb" '.[232] That is, the US ceased to insist Iran could not enrich uranium at all, which it had done up through 2005, when negotiations with Iran failed:

In past negotiations, the US demanded that some Iranian nuclear facilities should be closed in exchange for a modest reversal of sanctions. But, this dialogue failed, partly because it was never made clear to Iran what kind of nuclear program it would retain in the long run.[233]

The Joint Action Plan does commit the US to recognize the right of Iran to enrich uranium for peaceful purposes. Whether such a 'right' exists in International Law itself may be a question. Still, the accord 'gave Iran *de facto*, if not explicit, recognition' to do so.[234] So, in signing the deal, the US pivoted to the narrower goal of denying Iran a nuclear weapon. To be sure, the latter goal was the explicit one in US sanctions rules, so whether there was a change in substance or rhetoric is unclear. But, at least from the perspective of Iran, there was a meaningful shift whereby it could enrich uranium for peaceful nuclear energy purposes and maintain its long-standing disinterest in a nuclear weapon.

Second, the election of Hassan Rouhani as President of Iran mattered. He sought 'rapprochement' with the US, Europe, and other countries.[235] Generally, perhaps the new President, like an earlier predecessor, Mohamed Khatami (1943–, who was President from 1997 to 2005), understood the importance of Iran not being a pariah state in a globalized world, and sought to avoid a clash of civilizations. Specifically, perhaps he embodied changes in style and substance in part to help bring about relief from the suffering inflicted on his people by the sanctions. Softening Iran's position in nuclear negotiations was necessary if the US was to loosen the sanctions, which in turn was needed if the people who voted him to office in a 'landslide' were not to be disappointed.[236] That is, the causal chain may have been from (1) sanctions to (2) economic pressure to (3) the election of a moderate to (4) agreement from Iran's Supreme Leader, *Āyatollāh* Ali Khamenei to sign a deal.[237] But, that chain was by no means assured, and the 2005 election of a hardliner before Mr Rouhani, that is, of Mahmoud Ahmedinejad, who was President until 2013, suggests a 'rally around the flag' effect may have occurred amid sanctions.

In sum, have US sanctions against Iran worked? Have they caused economic pain to Iran that, in turn, caused a change in the behaviour of the Iranian government in respect of its nuclear ambitions? A resolute 'no' is implausible. Iranians suffered economically. But, an unqualified 'yes' gives the Americans more credit than they deserve. The sanction regime was a work in progress, evolving into a tight noose, not a carefully designed and comprehensive regime from inception.

If the question of efficacy is about achieving policy goals, then the sure answer is indeterminate. Whether the deal becomes a permanent one, and sees Iran without WMDs in the long run, is uncertain. Moreover, nothing in the terms of the agreement address two of the three US justifications for sanctions: deterring Iran from sponsoring cross-border terrorism, and promoting human rights, including press freedom, in Iran. In the context of entry into this agreement, the US made a strategic decision to champion one policy goal, and set aside two others – at least for an indeterminate period.

Time will tell whether a sanctions regime that the most powerful nation in human history designed, and that evolved into the most comprehensive set of economic strictures on a foreign country in human history, was necessary and sufficient to achieve all of its purposes. Until then, what is certain for as long as the prohibitions and penalties remain in place is that their sheer technical intricacy creates plenty of work for international trade lawyers.

As for the US and Iran, if the two countries were individuals, then a psychologist surely would label their relationship dysfunctional, and recommend therapy. Perhaps the sanctions-induced Joint Action Plan is the start of that therapy towards a modality other than confrontation.

April 2015 **Framework Agreement**

In April 2015 in Lausanne, Switzerland, the P5+1 issued a four-page joint statement, commonly known as the '*Framework Agreement*' or '*Lausanne Accord*'.[238] It was the product of negotiations that carried over under the November 2013 *Joint Plan of Action*, which after its extension until 24 November 2014 was extended again until 30 June 2015. The June deadline passed, but the P5+1 and Iran sensed they were sufficiently close to reaching a final accord that they extended the deadline once again, until 7 July 2015. During the protracted negotiations, in May 2015, the 114th Congress passed the *Iran Nuclear Agreement Review Act of 2015* (Senate Bill 615, House Resolution 1191, Public Law 114–17, 22 May 2015, amending the *Atomic Energy Act of 1954*, 42 U.S.C. Sections 2011 *et seq*.), which mandated it review any final deal before President Barack H. Obama signed it. Under the Act, Congress had 30 days for review of a deal completed by 10 July, but 60 days for a deal thereafter. Fearing a deal would be picked apart by legislators ideologically intransigent in their approach to Iran, and thus unravel, the P5+1 and Iran endeavoured to finish the deal in the first week of July.

The April 2015 *Framework Agreement* provided broad outlines of a final deal, leaving the parties until the end of June to agree on key technical details. This Agreement created no binding obligations; the legal status quo remained that under the *Joint Plan of Action*. In effect, the *Agreement* laid out a path forward for a final agreement by highlighting the remaining details in need of resolution, and thus was a face-saving way for all parties to keep talking.

The April 2015 *Framework Agreement* addressed four major issues in broad terms:

1. *Enrichment*: Iran would limit its capacity for uranium enrichment, the levels of that enrichment, and the stockpiles of enriched uranium, for periods of time to be agreed on. Iran could have no enrichment facility other than Natanz, and it would convert its underground enrichment centre at Fordow to a 'nuclear physics and technology centre'. Iran could continue it program of R&D on centrifuges, with a scope and schedule to be agreed on. But, it could have.
2. *Reprocessing*: With international assistance, Iran would redesign its heavy water facility at Arak to a 'heavy water research reactor' that would not yield any weapons-grade plutonium byproducts. Iran would not reprocess any spent fuel, but instead would export it.
3. *Monitoring*: Iran would implement the *Additional Protocol*, and thus follow IAEA procedures concerning enhanced access to its modern technologies so the IAEA could ascertain Iran's prior and current activities.
4. *Sanctions*: Once the IAEA verified Iran had implemented its key obligations, then the US would drop all nuclear-related secondary economic and financial sanctions. The EU would end all nuclear-related economic sanctions, and the UN Security Council would pass a resolution terminating all of its previous nuclear sanctions.

Yet, disputes broke out immediately after *the Lausanne Accord*. The US, EU, and Iran issued statements about what they thought they had agreed to.[239] For example, the P5+1 said Iran had promised to accept the Additional Protocol of *the NPT* to allow for IAEA inspectors to access military as well as civilian installations. Iran said the P5+1 had pledged to eliminate all economic sanctions. Thus, the narratives about the Accord conflicted on key points of verification and sanctions relief. That is why negotiations dragged on past their 30 June 2015 deadline.

Table 14.2 summarizes the points of the *Framework Agreement*, including the perspectives from the narratives in the US, European, and Iranian statements.

Despite optimism on both sides following that Agreement, they failed to meet the June deadline, for which each blamed the other. The P5+1 accused Iran of backsliding on its *Framework Agreement* pledge to allow inspectors access to all its nuclear sites, civilian and military, to ensure any final deal was verifiable. Iran accused the P5+1 of backsliding on its position that the P5+1 did not need Iran to produce a comprehensive historical account of its civilian or military nuclear activities, because Western intelligence agencies already knew what had happened. Iran also called for sanctions relief before implementing any final deal. The P5+1 retorted that demand was wrongly sequenced, and sought a procedural mechanism to bypass the Security Council so that sanctions could be reimposed without the threat of a Chinese or Russian veto, if the P5+1 thought Iran breached a final agreement.

Historic July 2015 Joint Comprehensive Plan of Action (JCPOA)

In retrospect, sanctions were necessary to persuade Iran to sign the November 2013 *Joint Plan of Action* and April 2015 *Framework Agreement*. However, they were not sufficient to compel Iran to sign a final nuclear agreement, at least not quickly thereafter. After all, Iran stayed at the negotiating table, but resolutely defended what it perceived to be its interests, for nearly two years after November 2013. It might even be vouched that obstinacy by the P5+1 about sanctions relief served only to harden Iran in its positions. Why compromise further if the nature and timing of that relief is a promise that cannot be trusted? For both sides, no deal was better than a bad deal.

What else was needed to move from 'necessary' to 'sufficient'? First, and foremost, diplomacy. Negotiators from the P5+1 and Iran laboured long and hard across 20 months to strike a final deal, which they announced on 14 July 2015. All parties wanted a deal, and had the political will to reach one. In respect of the necessity versus sufficiency of sanctions, Iranian President Hassan Rouhani said it best in announcing the deal to his people in a televised address: 'The sanctions regime was never successful, but at the same time it affected people's lives'.[240] Put differently, the regime on its own was unsuccessful in bringing about the final deal, but its adverse effects on everyday people were enough to cause negotiations.

A second reason moving the parties from 'necessary' to 'sufficiency' surely was Islamic State in the Levant (ISIL, also known as Islamic State in Shams (ISIS), or simply Islamic State). Its horrific methods and monstrous goals were anything but authentically 'Islamic', and the P5+1 and Iran had a shared goal of defeating it before it created yet more chaos and inflicted more human suffering and cultural damage in the Middle East and beyond. Solving the nuclear problem and moving on to the immediate and potentially existential threat was essential.

Table 14.2 Synopsis of April 2015 *Framework Agreement* (Lausanne Accord)[241]

What Iran 'gave' (conversely, what the US 'got')	*What Iran 'got'* (conversely, what the US 'gave')
Enrichment generally	
Under the Agreement, Iran committed to:[242] (1) Reduce by about two-thirds the total number of its installed centrifuges, namely, from about 19,000 to 6,104. (2) Restrict all 6,104 centrifuges to Iran's first generation centrifuges, IR-1. (3) Of the remaining 6,104 installed centrifuges, to use no more than 5,060 for enriching uranium for 10 years. (4) Restrict for at least 15 years uranium enrichment at 3.67 per cent or less. (5) Reduce its current stockpile of low enriched uranium (LEU) from 10,000 to no more than 300 kg (all at 3.67 per cent) for 15 years. (6) Place all excess centrifuges and enrichment infrastructure in storage monitored by the IAEA, and use that surplus only to replace operating centrifuges and equipment. (7) For 15 years, build no new facilities for uranium enrichment and limit its stockpile of enriched uranium. (8) For 10 years, extend its 'break out time' (that is the time Iran needs to obtain enough fissile material to make one nuclear weapon) from two–three months to at least one year, by limiting its domestic enrichment capacity and R&D, and after 10 years complying with a plan on enrichment and enrichment R&D shared with the P5+1. In addition, the US narrative stressed that Iran agreed: (1) Not to build any new enrichment facility. (2) Reduce its current stockpile of enriched uranium to 300 kg of 3.67 per cent low-enriched uranium across 15 years. (3) Limit its enriched uranium to 3.67 per cent for at least those 15 years, a threshold sufficient for peaceful civilian energy uses, but insufficient for a nuclear weapon. (4) Cap the total number of installed centrifuges at 6,104. (5) Restrict the number of those 6,104 installed centrifuges uses to enrich uranium to 5,060 for 10 years.	Under the Agreement, the P5+1 pledged: (1) Iran may continue to enrich uranium within Iran, and to produce nuclear fuel for the purpose of providing nuclear energy. (2) Iran may use its current stockpile of enriched uranium to produce nuclear fuel, or may trade it for uranium on international markets.

Fordow Underground Enrichment Facility

According to the Agreement, Iran committed to:[243]

(1) Enrich no uranium at Fordow for at least 15 years.
(2) Convert the Fordow facility for use for peaceful purposes only, namely, into a centre for research on nuclear science and physics.
(3) Conduct no R&D on uranium enrichment at Fordow for 15 years.
(4) Have no fissile material at Fordow for 15 years.
(5) Of the 6,104 centrifuges it kept (reduced from the total of 19,000), 1,044 would be at Fordow and 5,060 would be at Natanz, all of which would be IR-1 models for 10 years.
(6) Remove almost two-thirds of the centrifuges and infrastructure at Fordow, and place them under IAEA monitoring.
(7) Using the remaining roughly 13,000 centrifuges (the difference between about 19,000 and the 1,044 at Fordow and 5,060 at Natanz) only for spare, as needed.

In addition, the US narrative stressed that Iran agreed to:

(1) Convert the Fordow facility into a centre for nuclear physics and technology research, and not engage in any uranium enrichment R&D at Fordow for 15 years.

Natanz Enrichment Facility

Under the Agreement, Iran committed to:[244]

(1) Enrich uranium with only 5,060 IR-1 model centrifuges for 10 years.
(2) Remove more advanced centrifuges (e.g., IR-2, IR-4, IR-5, IR-6, and IR-8 models), and not use those centrifuges for at least 10 years to enrich uranium.
(3) Remove the 1,000 IR-2M centrifuges currently installed at the Natanz facility and place them in storage monitored by the IAEA for 10 years.
(4) For 10 years, limit uranium enrichment, and R&D relating to that enrichment, to ensure a break out time of at least 1 year.
(5) After 10 years, follow a plan for enrichment and enrichment R&D submitted to the IAEA, complying with limitations in the Additional Protocol on enrichment capacity.

According to the Iranian (and European) narrative, Iran could:

(1) Dedicate roughly half of the Fordow facility to advanced nuclear research and the production of stable isotopes for application in agriculture, industry, and medicine.
(2) Keep over 1,000 centrifuges for the purpose in item (1).

(continued overleaf)

Table 14.2 Continued

What Iran 'gave' (conversely, what the US 'got')	What Iran 'got' (conversely, what the US 'gave')
Reactors, reprocessing, and Arak Heavy Water Facility	
Under the Agreement, Iran committed to:[245] (1) Redesign and rebuild its Arak heavy water research reactor according to plans the P5+1 approves to ensure no weapons-grade plutonium is produced. (2) Destroy or remove from Iran the original core of the Arak reactor (because it would allow for production of significant quantities of weapons-grade plutonium). (3) Ship out of Iran all of the spent fuel from the reactor. (4) For an indefinite period, engage in no reprocessing or R&D on spent nuclear fuel. (5) For 15 years, accumulate no heavy water beyond the needs of the Arak facility, and sell any excess amounts on the international market. (6) For 15 years, not build any additional heavy water reactor.	Under the Agreement, the P5+1 committed to:[246] (1) Allow Arak to remain a heavy water reactor to produce a minimal amount of non-weapons grade plutonium. (2) Permit Iran to engage in peaceful nuclear research and radioisotope production in the redesigned, rebuilt Arak facility.
Inspections and transparency (Monitoring)	
According to the *Agreement*, Iran committed to:[247] (1) Grant the IAEA access to all of its nuclear facilities, including Natanz and Fordow, and allow the IAEA to use its most up-to-date monitoring technologies. (2) Allow the IAEA to inspect the supply chain that supports Iran's nuclear program, and ensure materials and components are not diverted to a secret program. (3) For 25 years, permit IAEA inspectors to visit Uranium mines, and put under continuous surveillance uranium mills (where Iran produces 'yellowcake'). (4) For 20 years, permit IAEA inspectors to put under continuous surveillance centrifuge rotors and bellows production and storage facilities, thus freezing Iran's centrifuge manufacturing base. (5) Place under continuous IAEA monitoring all centrifuges and enrichment infrastructure removed from Fordow and Natanz. (6) Grant the IAEA access anywhere in Iran to investigate any suspicious site or allegation of a covert facility for enrichment, conversion, yellowcake, or centrifuge production.	According to the Iranian narrative, Iran: (1) Did not agree to allow for IAEA inspection of military sites. (2) Agreed to implement the Additional Protocol only on a temporary and voluntary basis, as a confidence building measures. (3) After the temporary period referred to in (2), agreed its Parliament (*Majlis*) would ratify the Additional Protocol in a time frame it sets.

(7) Implement the Additional Protocol of the IAEA to give the IAEA greater access to declared and undeclared facilities, and to provide early notification of construction of any new facility under Modified Code 3:1.
(8) Follow an agreed-upon mechanism for monitoring and approval of procurement (that is, the supply, sale, or transfer to Iran) of nuclear-related and dual-use materials and technology.
(9) Follow an agreed-upon set of procedures to address IAEA concerns about the Possible Military Dimensions (PMD) of its nuclear program.
(10) For 25 years, permit inspections of its uranium supply chain, and adhere to the Additional Protocol of the IAEA permanently.
(11) Remain a party to the NPT, even after the end of the 'most stringent limitation on Iran's nuclear program'.

Sanctions relief

According to the Agreement:

(1) Iran must follow its commitments in a verifiable manner to receive relief from sanctions.
(2) Sanctions will snap back in place if, at any time, Iran fails to fulfil its commitments.
(3) Likewise, the 'architecture' of US nuclear-related sanctions will remain in place for 'much of the duration' of a final deal and snap back in place 'in the event of significant non-performance'.
(4) A dispute settlement process will be created and open to all parties to resolve issues of 'non-performance', and if that process does not achieve a resolution, then all UN sanctions can be reimposed.
(5) The UN Security Council will enact a new resolution concerning the channel by which Iran procures nuclear-related and dual use materials and technology, incorporating restrictions on ballistic missiles and conventional arms, and allowing for cargo inspections and asset freezes.
(6) US sanctions on Iran concerning ballistic missiles (which can be used to deliver WMDs), terrorism, or human rights abuses will remain in place under a final deal.

According to the Agreement:[248]

(1) Iran will receive sanctions relief from the P5+1, if it follows its commitments in a verifiable manner.
(2) The US and EU will suspend their nuclear-related sanctions 'after the IAEA has verified that Iran has taken all of its key nuclear-related steps', meaning (*inter alia*) the US will remove sanctions against foreign and domestic companies that do business with Iran, and the EU will remove energy and banking sanctions against Iran.
(3) The UN Council will remove all of its resolutions concerning the Iran nuclear issue 'simultaneously with the completion by Iran of' its obligations on 'all key concerns (enrichment, Fordow, PMDs, and transparency').

(*continued overleaf*)

Table 14.2 Continued

What Iran 'gave' (conversely, what the US 'got')	What Iran 'got' (conversely, what the US 'gave')
In addition, the US stressed: (1) American and European nuclear-related sanctions will be suspended only after the IAEA verified implementation of the key nuclear-related steps by Iran. (2) A mechanism to restore the sanctions if Iran failed to comply with IAEA reports and inspections was essential.	In addition, according to the Iranian narrative, Iran emphasized: (1) Sanctions would be lifted in respect of all sanctions under UN Security Council resolutions. (2) Sanctions also would be lifted with respect to the economic and financial embargoes by the US and EU against Iran's banks, insurance, investment, and all other related services in different fields, including petrochemical, oil, gas and automobile industries. (3) The sanctions measured referred to in items (1) and (2) will be lifted immediately, all at once.

The July 2014 *JCPOA* spans roughly 100 pages, with five technical annexes. It draws heavily on the 2013 *Joint Plan Of Action* and April 2015 *Framework Agreement*. That makes sense, because there was no need to revisit points settled from those accords. Table 14.3 summarizes the key points of the JCPOA. Arguably the most notable ones – which took the greatest time and effort to resolve – concern access of IAEA inspectors to military sites, and phased removal of sanctions.

Reflections

For international investment management professionals, whatever the ultimate outcome of the nuclear agreement between the P5+1 and Iran, the Iran case study is an enduring one. The macro and micro practical and ethical questions in this case are sure to manifest in future geopolitical disputes that trigger sanctions. Portfolio managers and their teams will be at the 'front lines' of policy debates shaping sanctions regimes, and 'in the trenches' implementing financial facets of those regimes. The inextricable links between geopolitics and global finance are forged swiftly, and once operative, are a transmission mechanism for 'good', 'evil', or both. Those links, and the ends to which they are used, simply cannot be avoided. Nor should they be. Investment professionals, while often pre-occupied with Excel spread sheets, are part of a bigger picture of war and peace. Put differently, and to apply President Theodore Roosevelt's insight, investment professionals are moral as well as financial agents 'in the arena' in pursuit of 'a worthy cause:'

> It is not the critic who counts; not the man who points out how the strong man stumbles, or where the doer of deeds could have done them better. *The credit belongs to the man who is actually in the arena*, whose face is marred by dust and sweat and blood; who strives valiantly; who errs, who comes short again and again, because there is no effort without error and shortcoming; but who does actually strive to do the deeds; who knows great enthusiasms, the great devotions; *who spends himself in a worthy cause*; who at the best knows in the end the triumph of high achievement, and who at the worst, if he fails, at least fails while daring greatly, so that his place shall never be with those cold and timid souls who neither know victory nor defeat.[249]

Table 14.3 Key details of July 2015 *Joint Comprehensive Plan of Action*[250]

What Iran 'gave' (conversely, what the US 'got')	What Iran 'got' (conversely, what the US 'gave')

Uranium enrichment, Natanz, and Fordow[251]

(1) Iran must reduce its uranium stockpile of about 10,000 kg of low-enriched UF_6 by 98 per cent, to 300 kg (660 lbs.), of up to 3.67 per cent enriched UF_6, and respect those thresholds for 15 years. Note the 3.67 per cent limit is a decrease from the November 2013 *Joint Plan of Action*, under which Iran enriched uranium to nearly 20 per cent.	(1) Iran may conduct limited, specific R&D activities in respect of uranium enrichment during the first eight years of the JCPOA.
(2) Iran cannot install more than 5,060 centrifuges at Natanz for 10 years.	(2) After the first eight years of the JCPOA, Iran's uranium enrichment activities may evolve gradually, at a reasonable pace, solely for peaceful purposes.
(3) Those centrifuges must be the oldest and least efficient models; that is, IR-1 centrifuges.	(3) At Fordow, Iran will be permitted to keep 1,044 IR-1 centrifuges in six cascades, on one wing of the Fordow facility, and employ them to produce radioisotopes for use in medicine, agriculture, industry, and science.
(4) Because Iran has roughly 19,000 IR-1 and IR-2M centrifuges installed at Natanz, it must remove the excess centrifuges and enrichment-related infrastructure, and put these items in storage under continuous IAEA monitoring.	(4) In respect of point (3), of the 6 cascades, Iran can use two for spinning without uranium to produce stable isotopes, but must keep the remaining four idle.
(5) Any R&D activities Iran conducts must be done at Natanz.	
(6) Iran is not permitted to conduct any uranium enrichment, or uranium enrichment R&D, at Fordow for 15 years.	
(7) Iran must convert Fordow to a nuclear, physics, and technology centre, which means Iran must dismantle some of the 2,700 IR-1 centrifuges installed at Fordow (of which 700 are enriching uranium). (As per the next column, Iran is permitted to keep 1,044 centrifuges, and thus must dismantle 1,656 of them.)	

Plutonium and Arak Facility[252]

(1) With an international partnership that will certify the final design, Iran will redesign and re-build its heavy water reprocessing facility at Arak to ensure the new facility cannot produce any weapons-grade plutonium.	(1) Iran may use its redesigned Arak facility for peaceful nuclear research and radioisotope production for medical and teaching purposes.
(2) Iran may not use its Arak facility to produce weapons-grade plutonium.	(2) Iran may keep pace with international technological advancements in using light water for research and power, in cooperation with international partners.
(3) Iran will build no new heavy water reactors, or accumulate heavy water, for 15 years.	(3) Those partners will assure Iran a supply of necessary fuel.
(4) Iran will export all of its spent fuel from its present and future research and power nuclear reactors.	

Transparency and inspections[253]

(1) Iran will allow the IAEA to continuously monitor its declared nuclear sites.
(2) Iran will provisionally adhere to the Additional Protocol to its IAEA Comprehensive Safeguards Agreement (as per Article 17(b) of the Additional Protocol). Under this Additional Protocol, Iran must allow IAEA inspectors to access any site they deem suspicious.
(3) With respect to possible military dimensions (PMDs) of Iran's nuclear program, Iran will allow the IAEA to prevent it from developing a nuclear program in secret by verifying that Iran has not covertly moved fissile material to a secret location to build a bomb.
(4) Also with respect to PMDs, Iran will allow IAEA inspectors to request visits to military sites.
(5) Iran will implement fully its agreement with the IAEA to resolve all past and present issues in respect of its nuclear program.
(6) Iran will allow the IAEA a long-term presence in Iran.
(7) For 25 years, Iran will allow the IAEA to monitor its production of uranium ore concentrate.
(8) For 20 years, Iran will allow the IAEA to contain and monitor centrifuge rotors and bellows.
(9) Iran will use only IAEA approved technologies, including online enrichment measures and electronic seals.
(10) For 15 years, Iran will follow a reliable mechanism to ensure speedy resolution of concerns about IAEA access.

Break out time[254]

(1) By implementing the JCPOA, Iran will remove the dimensions of its nuclear program it would need to create a nuclear weapon, and increase its break out time to at least 1 year.
(2) Iran will not engage in any activities, including R&D, uranium, or plutonium metallurgy activities, which could contribute to building a nuclear weapon.
(3) Iran will adhere to a procurement channel (set out in Annex IV of the JCPOA) endorsed by the UN Security Council.

(1) IAEA access to military sites is not guaranteed, and could be delayed, by Iran.
(2) Iran has the right to challenge an IAEA request to inspect a military site.
(3) In the event of such a challenge, an arbitration panel will decide the issue.

(continued overleaf)

Table 14.3 Continued

What Iran 'gave' (conversely, what the US 'got')	What Iran 'got' (conversely, what the US 'gave')
Sanctions removal[255]	
(1) Under a UN Security Council resolution, all previous Security Council resolutions on the Iranian nuclear issue will be terminated. (2) The termination in point (1) will be simultaneous with IAEA verification that Iran is implementing the terms of the JCPOA, specifically the items in Annex V. That is, sanctions are lifted only upon IAE confirmation that Iran has complied with its obligations under the JCPOA. (3) The US will cease application of all sanctions listed in Annex II of the JCPOA, simultaneously with the IAEA certification in point (2). (4) The American sanctions to be lifted are those relating to Iran's nuclear program. However, US sanctions targeting Iran's support for terrorism, missile activities, and human rights abuses will remain in effect. (5) Eight years after the JCPOA has entered into force, or when the IAE concludes all nuclear material in Iran is for peaceful purposes, whichever is earlier, the US will repeal its Iran nuclear sanctions statutes. (6) The EU will terminate all of its nuclear-related economic and financial sanctions, simultaneously with the IAEA certification in point (2). (7) If Iran violates the JCPOA, then sanctions will snap back automatically for 10 years, with the possibility of a further five-year extension.	(1) Iran will obtain sanctions relief at the same time as the IAEA certifies its compliance with the JCPOA, specifically the items in Annex V. (2) Following point (1), Iran stands to receive more than $100 billion in assets frozen overseas; may resume selling oil on international markets; and (3) use the international banking system for trade purposes.
Arms embargo and ballistic missile sanctions removal[256]	
(1) The UN arms embargo on Iran will continue for up to five years, but could end earlier if the IAEA certifies that Iran's nuclear program is entirely peaceful. (2) The UN ban on Iran importing ballistic missile technology will remain in place for up to eight years.	(1) The UN arms embargo and ballistic missile import ban against Iran will be lifted within five and eight years, respectively.

Dispute resolution[257]

(1) An 8-member Joint Commission is established consisting of representatives from each P5+1 country, the EU, and Iran.
(2) The P5+1 may refer to the Joint Commission any claim against Iran that Iran is failing to meet a commitment under the JCPOA.
(3) The Joint Commission must resolve the claim within 15 days, unless a longer period is agreed by consensus.
(4) If the claim remains unresolved after the period in point (2), and if the P5+1 deems the claim involves significant non-performance by Iran, then the P5+1 may treat the unresolved claim as grounds for it to cease performing all or some of its obligations under the JCPOA, and/or notify the UN Security Council of its view of significant non-performance by Iran.

(1) Iran is formally represented on the Joint Commission.
(2) Iran may refer to the Joint Commission any claim against the P5+1 that the P5+1 is failing to meet a commitment under the *JCPOA*.
(3) The Joint Commission must resolve the claim within 15 days, unless a longer period is agreed by consensus.
(4) If the claim remains unresolved after the period in point (2), and if Iran deems the claim involves significant non-performance by the P5+1, then Iran may treat the unresolved claim as grounds for it to cease performing all or some of its obligations under the JCPOA, and/or notify the UN Security Council of its view of significant non-performance by the P5+1.

Notes

1 The implementation dates of certain provisions discussed below varied. For example, the payments system prohibition took effect 60 days after the legislation entered into force; that is, 29 February 2012, while the provision on applicability of sanctions to foreign central banks other than that of Iran took effect 180 days thereafter, *i.e.*, 28 June 2012. *See* National Defense Authorization Act of 2012, Section 1245(d)(1), (3), Public Law 112–81, 125 Stat. 1298, 1647–1650, Section 1245, codified at 22 U.S.C. § 8513a(d)(1), (3), as amended by Iran Threat Reduction and Syria Human Rights Act of 2012, Public Law 112–58, codified at 22 U.S.C. §§ 8711, 8721–8724, 8741–8744, 8781, and by Iran Freedom and Counter-Proliferation Act of 2012 (Sub-Title D of the National Defense Authorization Act for Fiscal Year 2013), Public Law 112–239, *reprinted in Committee on Ways and Means, U.S. House of Representatives, Compilation of U.S. Trade Statutes*, 113th Congress, 1st Session, Committee Print (January 2013), at 718. [Hereinafter, 2013 Compilation.]
2 National Defense Authorization Act of 2012, Section 1245(a)(1), (3), Public Law 112–81, Section 1245, codified at 22 U.S.C. § 8513a(a)(1), (3), as amended by Iran Threat Reduction and Syria Human Rights Act of 2012, Public Law 112–158, codified at 22 U.S.C. §§ 8711, 8721–8724, 8741–8744, 8781, and by Iran Freedom and Counter-Proliferation Act of 2012 (Sub-Title D of the National Defense Authorization Act for Fiscal Year 2013), Public Law 112–239, *reprinted in* 2013 Compilation, at 717–721.
3 "Export Development Bank of Iran," *Wikipedia*, http://en.wikipedia.org/wiki/Export_Development_Bank_of_Iran.
4 "Bank Mellat," *Wikipedia*, http://en.wikipedia.org/wiki/Bank_Mellat.
5 "Bank Melli Iran," *Wikipedia*, http://en.wikipedia.org/wiki/Bank_Melli_Iran.
6 "Bank Saderat Iran," *Wikipedia*, http://en.wikipedia.org/wiki/Bank_Saderat_Iran.
7 National Defense Authorization Act of 2012, Section 1245(a)(2), Public Law 112–81, codified at 22 U.S.C. § 8513a(a)(2), as amended by Iran Threat Reduction and Syria Human Rights Act of 2012, Public Law 112–158, codified at 22 U.S.C. §§ 8711, 8721–8724, 8741–8744, 8781, and by Iran Freedom and Counter-Proliferation Act of 2012 (Sub-Title D of the National Defense Authorization Act for Fiscal Year 2013), Public Law 112–239, *reprinted in* 2013 Compilation, at 717–721.
8 National Defense Authorization Act of 2012, Public Law 112–81, Section 1245, codified at 22 U.S.C. § 8513a, as amended by Iran Threat Reduction and Syria Human Rights Act of 2012, Public Law 112–158, codified at 22 U.S.C. §§ 8711, 8721–8724, 8741–8744, 8781, and by Iran Freedom and Counter-Proliferation Act of 2012 (Sub-Title D of the National Defense Authorization Act for Fiscal Year 2013), Public Law 112–239, *reprinted in* 2013 Compilation, at 717–721.
9 National Defense Authorization Act of 2012, Public Law 112–81, Section 1245(b), as amended by Public Law 112–158 (Iran Threat Reduction and Syria Human Rights Act of 2012) and Public Law 112–239 (Iran Freedom and Counter-Proliferation Act of 2012, Sub-Title D of the National Defense Authorization Act for Fiscal Year 2013), codified at 22 U.S.C. § 8513a(b), *reprinted in* 2013 Compilation, at 717.
10 Section 5318A also contained the criteria by which a jurisdiction is designated to be of 'primary money laundering concern'. Those criteria included evidence of organized crime, terrorism or corruption, pervasive bank secrecy, and a high ratio of the volume of financial transactions to the size of the economy of the jurisdiction.
11 National Defense Authorization Act of 2012, Public Law 112–81, Section 1245(c), as amended by Public Law 112–158 (Iran Threat Reduction and Syria Human Rights Act of 2012) and Public Law 112–239 (Iran Freedom and Counter-Proliferation Act of 2012, Sub-Title D of the National Defense Authorization Act for Fiscal Year *2013*), codified at 22 U.S.C. § 8513a(c), *reprinted in* 2013 Compilation, at 717.
12 On 6 February 2012, President Barack H. Obama signed Executive Order 13599 implementing the financial sanctions in the 2012 Defense Act, particularly the freezing of assets and other property held by Iranian banks, including the CBI, in the US or by US persons. *See* Executive Order 13599 – Blocking Property of the Government of Iran and Iranian Financial Institutions, 77 Federal Register 66599 (8 February 2012). The 2012 Iran Threat Reduction and Syria Human Rights Act of 2012 (discussed below) answered a question

the Defense Act failed to address: under what conditions would the assets be unfrozen? The second Act said the blocking would continue until the President certified to the appropriate Congressional committees in a written report (which could contain classified Annex) that the CBI no longer provided financial services to help Iran acquire a WMD, or help or facilitate transactions for the Revolutionary Guard Corps. See Iran Threat Reduction and Syria Human Rights Act of 2012, Section 217(a), (c)–(d)(1)–(2), codified at 22 U.S.C. §§ 8711, 8721–8724, 8741–8744, 8781, *reprinted in* 2013 Compilation, at 727–728.

13 National Defense Authorization Act of 2012, Public Law 112–81, Section 1245(h)(4), as amended by Public Law 112–158 (Iran Threat Reduction and Syria Human Rights Act of 2012) and Public Law 112–239 (Iran Freedom and Counter-Proliferation Act of 2012, Sub-Title D of the National Defense Authorization Act for Fiscal Year 2013), codified at 22 U.S.C. § 8513a(h)(4), *reprinted in* 2013 Compilation, at 721 (defining 'United States person' to mean a natural person who is a citizen or resident of the US, or an entity organized under US or state law).

14 National Defense Authorization Act of 2012, Public Law 112–81, Section 1245(c), as amended by Public Law 112–158 (Iran Threat Reduction and Syria Human Rights Act of 2012) and Public Law 112–239 (Iran Freedom and Counter-Proliferation Act of 2012, Sub-Title D of the National Defense Authorization Act for Fiscal Year *2013*), codified at 22 U.S.C. § 8513a(c), *reprinted in* 2013 Compilation, at 717. The basic statutory authority for the asset freeze was the IEEPA, 50 U.S.C. § 1701 *et seq.*

Note the expansion of the menu of mandatory sanctions from three to five out of nine occurred via the other bill Congress passed against Iran in 2012, the Iran Threat Reduction and Syria Human Rights Act of 2012 (discussed below).

15 *New York Office Tower Seized Over Payments to Iran*, BBC News, 18 September 2013, *posted at* http://www.bbc.co.uk/news/world-us-canada-24146454.

16 31 U.S.C. § 5318A(e)(1)(B). *See also* National Defense Authorization Act of 2012, Public Law 112–81, Section 1245(h)(1), as amended by Public Law 112–158 (Iran Threat Reduction and Syria Human Rights Act of 2012) and Public Law 112–239 (Iran Freedom and Counter-Proliferation Act of 2012, Sub-Title D of the National Defense Authorization Act for Fiscal Year 2013), codified at 22 U.S.C. § 8513a(h)(1), *reprinted in* 2013 Compilation, at 721 (defining 'correspondent account' by reference to Section 5318A).

17 "List of Banks in India," *Wikipedia*, http://en.wikipedia.org/wiki/List_of_banks_in_India

18 A correspondent account may be classified as 'nostro' or vostro.' from the perspective of HSBC, its account with SBI is a 'nostro' account, meaning 'our account with you'. Conversely, from the perspective of SBI, the account is a 'vostro' one – 'your account with us.'

19 31 U.S.C. § 5318A(e)(1)(C). *See also* National Defense Authorization Act of 2012, Public Law 112–81, Section 1245(h)(1), as amended by Public Law 112–158 (Iran Threat Reduction and Syria Human Rights Act of 2012) and Public Law 112–239 (Iran Freedom and Counter-Proliferation Act of 2012, Sub-Title D of the National Defense Authorization Act for Fiscal Year 2013), codified at 22 U.S.C. § 8513a(h)(1), *reprinted in* 2013 Compilation, at 721 (defining 'payable through account' by reference to Section 5318A).

20 National Defense Authorization Act of 2012, Public Law 112–81, Section 1245(d)(1)(B), as amended by Public Law 112–158 (Iran Threat Reduction and Syria Human Rights Act of 2012) and Public Law 112–239 (Iran Freedom and Counter-Proliferation Act of 2012, Sub-Title D of the National Defense Authorization Act for Fiscal Year 2013), codified at 22 U.S.C. § 8513a(d)(1)(B), *reprinted in* 2013 Compilation, at 718 (stating the President 'may' impose *IEEPA* sanctions on the CBI).

The sanctions potentially applied to an individual, as well as the CBI, who violated, attempted to violate, conspired to violate, or caused a violation of the payments system prohibition. *See* id., Section 1245(g)(2), 22 U.S.C. § 8513(g)(2).

21 National Defense Authorization Act of 2012, Public Law 112–81, Section 1245(d)(1)(A), as amended by Public Law 112–158 (Iran Threat Reduction and Syria Human Rights Act of 2012) and Public Law 112–239 (Iran Freedom and Counter-Proliferation Act of 2012, Sub-Title D of the National Defense Authorization Act for Fiscal Year 2013), codified at 22 U.S.C. § 8513a(d)(1)(A), *reprinted in* 2013 Compilation, at 718 (referring to 'another Iranian financial institution designated by the Secretary of the Treasury for the imposition of sanctions. . . .').

498 *Legal issues in Asian investing*

The sanctions potentially applied to an individual, as well as a foreign financial institution, who violated, attempted to violate, conspired to violate, or caused a violation of the payments system prohibition. *See* id., Section 1245(g)(2), 22 U.S.C. § 8513a(g)(2).
22 National Defense Authorization Act of 2012, Public Law 112–81, Section 1245(h)(2), as amended by Public Law 112–158 (Iran Threat Reduction and Syria Human Rights Act of 2012) and Public Law 112–239 (Iran Freedom and Counter-Proliferation Act of 2012, Sub-Title D of the National Defense Authorization Act for Fiscal Year 2013), codified at 22 U.S.C. § 8513a(h)(2), reprinted in 2013 Compilation, at 721, referring to CISADA, Section 104(i), codified at 22 U.S.C. § 8513(i), *reprinted in* Overview, Part II, at 721 (referencing Section 8513(i), but Sub-Section (1)(D) thereof leaves to the discretion of the Treasury Secretary the delineation of 'foreign' from 'domestic' financial institutions).
23 National Defense Authorization Act of 2012, Public Law 112–81, Section 1245(d)(2), as amended by Public Law 112–158 (Iran Threat Reduction and Syria Human Rights Act of 2012) and Public Law 112–239 (Iran Freedom and Counter-Proliferation Act of 2012, Sub-Title D of the National Defense Authorization Act for Fiscal Year 2013), codified at 22 U.S.C. § 8513a(d)(2), reprinted in 2013 Compilation, at 721, referring to *CISADA*, Section 104(i), codified at 22 U.S.C. § 8513(i), *reprinted in* Committee on Ways and Means, U.S. House of Representatives, Overview and Compilation of U.S. Trade Statutes, 111th Congress, 2nd Session, Committee Print (December 2010), Part II of II, at 718. [Hereinafter, Overview, Part II.]
24 National Defense Authorization Act of 2012, Public Law 112–81, Section 1245(d)(3), as amended by Public Law 112–158 (Iran Threat Reduction and Syria Human Rights Act of 2012) and Public Law 112–239 (Iran Freedom and Counter-Proliferation Act of 2012, Sub-Title D of the National Defense Authorization Act for Fiscal Year 2013), codified at 22 U.S.C. § 8513a(d)(3), reprinted in 2013 Compilation, at 721, referring to CISADA, Section 104(i), codified at 22 U.S.C. § 8513(i), *reprinted in* Overview, Part II, at 718.
25 "About Us," *Indian Oil Corporation*, https://www.iocl.com/aboutus.aspx.
26 National Defense Authorization Act of 2012, Public Law 112–81, Section 1245(d)(4)(C), as amended by Public Law 112–158 (Iran Threat Reduction and Syria Human Rights Act of 2012) and Public Law 112–239 (Iran Freedom and Counter-Proliferation Act of 2012, Sub-Title D of the National Defense Authorization Act for Fiscal Year 2013), codified at 22 U.S.C. § 8513a(D)(4)(C), *reprinted in* 2013 Compilation, at 721, referring to CISADA, Section 104(i), codified at 22 U.S.C. § 8513(i), *reprinted in* Overview, Part II, at 719.
27 National Defense Authorization Act of 2012, Public Law 112–81, Section 1245(d)(4)(A), as amended by Public Law 112–158 (Iran Threat Reduction and Syria Human Rights Act of 2012) and Public Law 112–239 (Iran Freedom and Counter-Proliferation Act of 2012, Sub-Title D of the National Defense Authorization Act for Fiscal Year 2013), codified at 22 U.S.C. § 8513a(d)(4)(A), *reprinted in* 2013 Compilation, at 718. The Energy Information Administration prepares the reports, in consultation with the State and Treasury Departments, and Central Intelligence Agency (CIA). *See* id.
28 National Defense Authorization Act of 2012, Public Law 112–81, Section 1245(d)(4)(B), as amended by Public Law 112–158 (Iran Threat Reduction and Syria Human Rights Act of 2012) and Public Law 112–239 (Iran Freedom and Counter-Proliferation Act of 2012, Sub-Title D of the National Defense Authorization Act for Fiscal Year 2013), codified at 22 U.S.C. § 8513a(D)(4)(B), *reprinted in* 2013 Compilation, at 718–719.
29 National Defense Authorization Act of 2012, Public Law 112–81, Section 1245(d)(4)(C)–(D)(i)(I)–(II), as amended by Public Law 112–158 (Iran Threat Reduction and Syria Human Rights Act of 2012) and Public Law 112–239 (Iran Freedom and Counter-Proliferation Act of 2012, Sub-Title D of the National Defense Authorization Act for Fiscal Year 2013), codified at 22 U.S.C. § 8513a(d)(4)(C)–(D)(i)(I)–(II), *reprinted in* 2013 Compilation, at 719. Note Section 1245(d)(4)(C) called for reporting on 'petroleum and petroleum products,' whereas the sanctions exception in Section 1245(d)(4)(D)(i)(I)–(II) focused on crude oil; that is, third countries had to cut their dependence on unrefined Iranian oil to avoid imposition of sanctions on their financial institutions.
30 Roula Khalaf, Lionel Barber, and Najmeh Bozorgmehr, "Rouhani's 100-Day Revolution," *Financial Times* (30 November-1 December 2013): 6. [Hereinafter, Rouhani's 100-Day Revolution.]

31 Rouhani's 100-Day Revolution. As to where some oil revenues not in frozen accounts may have gone, the *Financial Times* reported the previous Administration of President Mahmoud Ahmedinejad 'used Iran's central bank as a piggy bank, ordering it to dole out loans [*e.g.*, on politically favorable projects that were not economically viable] that had little chance of being repaid.' Id.
32 Rouhani's 100-Day Revolution.
33 National Defense Authorization Act of 2012, Public Law 112–81, Section 1245(d)(4)(B), as amended by Public Law 112–158 (Iran Threat Reduction and Syria Human Rights Act of 2012) and Public Law 112–239 (Iran Freedom and Counter-Proliferation Act of 2012, Sub-Title D of the National Defense Authorization Act for Fiscal Year 2013), codified at 22 U.S.C. § 8513a(d)(4)(B), *reprinted in* 2013 Compilation, at 718–719.
34 National Defense Authorization Act of 2012, Public Law 112–81, Section 1245(e)(1)(A)(i), as amended by Public Law 112–158 (Iran Threat Reduction and Syria Human Rights Act of 2012) and Public Law 112–239 (Iran Freedom and Counter-Proliferation Act of 2012, Sub-Title D of the National Defense Authorization Act for Fiscal Year 2013), codified at 22 U.S.C. § 8513a(e)(1)(A)(i), *reprinted in* 2013 Compilation, at 720.
35 National Defense Authorization Act of 2012, Public Law 112–81, Section 1245(e)(1)(A)(ii), as amended by Public Law 112–158 (Iran Threat Reduction and Syria Human Rights Act of 2012) and Public Law 112–239 (Iran Freedom and Counter-Proliferation Act of 2012, Sub-Title D of the National Defense Authorization Act for Fiscal Year 2013), codified at 22 U.S.C. § 8513a(e)(1)(A)(ii), *reprinted in* 2013 Compilation, at 720.
36 National Defense Authorization Act of 2012, Public Law 112–81, Section 1245(e)(1)(A)(ii), as amended by Public Law 112–158 (Iran Threat Reduction and Syria Human Rights Act of 2012) and Public Law 112–239 (Iran Freedom and Counter-Proliferation Act of 2012, Sub-Title D of the National Defense Authorization Act for Fiscal Year 2013), codified at 22 U.S.C. § 8513a(e)(1)(A)(ii), *reprinted in* 2013 Compilation, at 720.
37 The President was obliged to report to congress biannually on these efforts, and the reports could have a classified Annex. *See* National Defense Authorization Act of 2012, Public Law 112–81, Section 1245(e)(2), as amended by Public Law 112–158 (Iran Threat Reduction and Syria Human Rights Act of 2012) and Public Law 112–239 (Iran Freedom and Counter-Proliferation Act of 2012, Sub-Title D of the National Defense Authorization Act for Fiscal Year 2013), codified at 22 U.S.C. § 8513a(e)(2), *reprinted in* 2013 Compilation, at 720.
38 Ari Natter, "Wyden 'Hopes' to Hold Hearing on Crude Oil Exports Soon; Spokesman Cites Concerns," *International Trade Reporter (BNA)* 31 (16 January 2014): 103.; Ari Natter, "Chamber of Commerce President Predicts End of 40-Year Ban on Crude Oil Exports," *International Trade Reporter (BNA)* 31 (16 January 2014): 103.
39 *Generally* Ajay Makan and Neil Hume, "The Cartel's Challenge," *Financial Times*, (2 December 2013): 10. (discussing the shale gas revolution and prospects for the United States to become the largest oil producer in the world); Ed Crooks and Geoff Dyer, "Strength in Reserve," *Financial Times* (6 September 2013): 5 (discussing how the shale boom, while not likely to allow the United States to disengage from the Middle East, will enhance its international diplomatic authority).
40 National Defense Authorization Act of 2012, Public Law 112–81, Section 1245(d)(4)(D)(ii)(I)–(II), as amended by Public Law 112–158 (Iran Threat Reduction and Syria Human Rights Act of 2012) and Public Law 112–239 (Iran Freedom and Counter-Proliferation Act of 2012, Sub-Title D of the National Defense Authorization Act for Fiscal Year 2013), codified at 22 U.S.C. § 8513a(d)(4)(D)(ii)(I)–(II), *reprinted in* 2013 Compilation, at 719.
41 National Defense Authorization Act of 2012, Public Law 112–81, Section 1245(e)(1)(B), as amended by Public Law 112–158 (Iran Threat Reduction and Syria Human Rights Act of 2012) and Public Law 112–239 (Iran Freedom and Counter-Proliferation Act of 2012, Sub-Title D of the National Defense Authorization Act for Fiscal Year 2013), codified at 22 U.S.C. § 8513a(e)(1)(B), *reprinted in* 2013 Compilation, at 721, referring to CISADA, Section 104(i), codified at 22 U.S.C. § 8513(i), reprinted in Overview, Part II, at 720.
42 National Defense Authorization Act of 2012, Public Law 112–81, Section 1245(d)(5)(B)(i), as amended by Public Law 112–158 (Iran Threat Reduction and Syria Human Rights Act of 2012) and Public Law 112–239 (Iran Freedom and Counter-Proliferation Act of 2012,

500 *Legal issues in Asian investing*

Sub-Title D of the National Defense Authorization Act for Fiscal Year 2013), codified at 22 U.S.C. § 8513a(d)(5)(B)(i), reprinted in 2013 Compilation, at 721, referring to CISADA, Section 104(i), codified at 22 U.S.C. § 8513(i), *reprinted in* Overview, Part II, at 719.

43 National Defense Authorization Act of 2012, Public Law 112–81, Section 1245(d)(5)(B)(ii), as amended by Public Law 112–158 (Iran Threat Reduction and Syria Human Rights Act of 2012) and Public Law 112–239 (Iran Freedom and Counter-Proliferation Act of 2012, Sub-Title D of the National Defense Authorization Act for Fiscal Year 2013), codified at 22 U.S.C. § 8513a(d)(5)(B)(ii), *reprinted in* 2013 Compilation, at 721, referring to *CISADA*, Section 104(i), codified at 22 U.S.C. § 8513(i), *reprinted in* Overview, Part II, at 720.

44 National Defense Authorization Act of 2012, Public Law 112–81, Section 1245(d)(5)(B)(iii), as amended by Public Law 112–158 (Iran Threat Reduction and Syria Human Rights Act of 2012) and Public Law 112–239 (Iran Freedom and Counter-Proliferation Act of 2012, Sub-Title D of the National Defense Authorization Act for Fiscal Year 2013), codified at 22 U.S.C. § 8513a(d)(5)(B)(iii), *reprinted in* 2013 Compilation, at 721, referring to CISADA, Section 104(i), codified at 22 U.S.C. § 8513(i), *reprinted in* Overview, Part II, at 720.

45 Iran Threat Reduction and Syria Human Rights Act of 2012, Public Law 112–158, 126 Stat. 1214–1269, enacted 10 August 2012, codified at 22 U.S.C. §§ 8711, 8721–8724, 8741–8744, 8781, *reprinted in* 2013 Compilation, at 721–736.

To be clear, some of the changes ushered by the Iran–Syria Act were to the 1996 *Iran Sanctions Act* (as amended in 2010 by *CISADA*), while other changes made by the *Iran-Syria Act* were to the 2010 *CISADA*. That is evident from the 2013 Compilation, at 685, 708, which indicates the 1996 and 2010 legislation were amended by Public Law 112–158 (Iran Threat Reduction and Syria Human Rights Act of 2012), which is, of course, the 2012 Act. It also is clear simply by comparing the Overview, which includes the 1996 and 2010 Acts before the 2012 Act, with the 2013 Compilation, which includes the 2012 Act amendments.

Also, the changes discussed above occurred via the 2012 *Iran-Syria Act*, as well as via Sub Title D of the 2012 Iran Freedom and Counter-Proliferation Act (Sub Title D of the National Defense Authorization Act for Fiscal Year 2013), Public Law 112–239, *reprinted in* 2013 Compilation, at 736–748. But, they applied retroactively to 90 days after enactment of the original CISADA. *See*, e.g., Section 103(a), 105(b)(1).

46 Various features of the sanctions regime did not need amendment, and thus remained unchanged. These included provisions on publication in the Federal Register and publication of projects. Compare Iran Sanctions Act of 1996, as amended by *CISADA*, Section 5(d)–(e), *reprinted in* Overview, Part II, at 1139–1140 with Iran Sanctions Act of 1996, as further amended by Iran Threat Reduction and Syria Human Rights Act of 2012, Section 5(d)–(e), *reprinted in* 2013 Compilation, at 696.

No substantive changes (only minor renumbering) were made under the 2012 *Act* to the list of exceptions under which the President was not mandated to apply sanctions. Compare Iran Sanctions Act of 1996, as amended by CISADA, Section 5(f), reprinted in Overview, Part II, at 1140 with Iran Sanctions Act of 1996, as further amended by Iran Threat Reduction and Syria Human Rights Act of 2012, Section 5(f), *reprinted in* 2013 Compilation, at 696–697. That is, the key exceptions remained for (1) procurement of defense goods and services 'essential to the national security of the United States,' defense goods or services supplied by a 'sole source supplier' with no 'readily or reasonably available' alternative, or defense goods or services 'essential to the national Security' under coproduction agreements, (2) spare parts or components (but not finished goods) 'essential' to American manufacturing,' (3) service and maintenance of products where there is no 'readily or reasonably available' alternative, (4) information and technology 'essential' to American products or production, or (5) humanitarian items, such as medicines. See Iran Sanctions Act of 1996, as amended by Iran Threat Reduction and Syria Human Rights Act of 2012, Section 5(f) (1)–(6), *reprinted in* 2013 Compilation, at 696–697.

Likewise, the 2012 *Act* did not change (aside from minor cross-referencing updates) the statutory provisions on advisory opinions, the termination, delay, or duration of sanctions, the contents of any report in support of a Presidential waiver of sanctions, required reports to the appropriate Congressional committees, the non-reviewability of sanctions, exclusion of certain activities, or the 31 December 2016 sunset date. Compare *Iran Sanctions Act of*

1996, as amended by *CISADA*, Section 7–8, 9(a)–(b), 9(c)(2), 10–13, *reprinted in* Overview, Part II, at 1143–1147 with Iran Sanctions Act of 1996, as further amended by Iran Threat Reduction and Syria Human Rights Act of 2012, Sections 7–8, 9(a)–(b), 9(c)(2), 10–13, *reprinted in* 2013 Compilation, at 700–704.

Definitions of key terms – namely, 'act of international terrorism,' 'appropriate congressional committees,' 'component part,' 'develop and development,' 'financial institution,' 'finished product,' 'foreign person,' 'goods and technology,' 'investment,' 'Iran,' 'Iranian diplomats and representatives of other government and military or quasi-governmental institutions of Iran,' 'knowingly,' 'nuclear explosive device,' 'person,' 'petroleum resources,' 'refined petroleum products,' 'services,' 'United States or State,' and 'United States Person' – also remained the same. Compare Iran Sanctions Act of 1996, as amended by CISADA, Section 14(a)(1)–(18), reprinted in Overview, Part II, at 1147–1150 with Iran Sanctions Act of 1996, as further amended by Iran Threat Reduction and Syria Human Rights Act of 2012, Section 14(1)–(3), (5)–(15), (17)–(21), *reprinted in* 2013 Compilation, at 704–707. But, the 2012 *Act* added three new terms: 'credible information,' 'petrochemical product,' and 'services.' *See* Iran Sanctions Act of 1996, as further amended by Iran Threat Reduction and Syria Human Rights Act of 2012, Section 14(4), (16) and (19), *reprinted in* 2013 Compilation, at 705, 707. As explained above, all three terms helped delineate an enlarged scope of behavior prohibited under Section 5.

47 Among the loopholes closed was clarification sanctions could be imposed on foreign persons who assisted in the evasion of US sanctions. The clarification came, however, not via the 2012 Iran–Syria Act statutory language, but via Executive Order Number 13608. President Barack H. Obama signed this Order on 1 May 2012, invoking the authority (*inter alia*) of the *IEEPA*. See Executive Order – Prohibiting Certain Transactions with and Suspending Entry into the United States of Foreign Sanctions Evaders with Respect to Iran and Syria, 77 Federal Register 26409, *posted at* http://www.whitehouse.gov/the-press-office/2012/05/01/executive-order-prohibiting-certain-transactions-and-suspending-entry-un. Sanctions on evaders could be lifted only if the criteria for the *CISADA* Sunset Rule (discussed earlier) were met, namely, Iran changed its behavior with respect to WMDs and terrorism. *See* Iran Threat Reduction and Syria Human Rights Act of 2012, Section 217(b), codified at 22 U.S.C. §§ 8711, 8721–8724, 8741–8744, 8781, *reprinted in* 2013 Compilation, at 727; CISADA, Section 401(a), 22 U.S.C. § 8551(a).

48 For a Chart of the Sessions of Congress, *see* "Guide: Congressional Session Chart," *Indiana University Bloomington Library* https://libraries.indiana.edu/guide-congressional-session-chart.

49 Iran Threat Reduction and Syria Human Rights Act of 2012, Section 101(b)(1), (2)(D), codified at 22 U.S.C. §§ 8711, 8721–8724, 8741–8744, 8781, *reprinted in* 2013 Compilation, at 722.

50 Iran Threat Reduction and Syria Human Rights Act of 2012, Section 102(a)(1)(A)–(B), (2)–(3), codified at 22 U.S.C. §§ 8711, 8721–8724, 8741–8744, 8781, *reprinted in* 2013 Compilation, at 723.

51 Iran Threat Reduction and Syria Human Rights Act of 2012, Section 102(b)(4)–(5), codified at 22 U.S.C. §§ 8711, 8721–8724, 8741–8744, 8781, *reprinted in* 2013 Compilation, at 723.

52 Iran Threat Reduction and Syria Human Rights Act of 2012, Section 102(b)(1)–(2), (4), codified at 22 U.S.C. §§ 8711, 8721–8724, 8741–8744, 8781, *reprinted in* 2013 Compilation, at 723–724.

53 Iran Threat Reduction and Syria Human Rights Act of 2012, Section 102(b)(6), codified at 22 U.S.C. §§ 8711, 8721–8724, 8741–8744, 8781, *reprinted in* 2013 Compilation, at 724.

54 Compare Iran Sanctions Act of 1996, as amended by CISADA, Section 5(a)(1), *reprinted in* Overview, Part II, at 1135–1136 with Iran Sanctions Act of 1996, as further amended by Iran Threat Reduction and Syria Human Rights Act of 2012, Section 5(a)(1), *reprinted in* 2013 Compilation, at 688.

55 Compare Iran Sanctions Act of 1996, as amended by CISADA, Section 5(a)(1), *reprinted in* Overview, Part II, at 1135–1136 with Iran Sanctions Act of 1996, as further amended by Iran Threat Reduction and Syria Human Rights Act of 2012, Section 5(a)(5(A), (B)(i), *reprinted in* 2013 Compilation, at 690.

56 Compare Iran Sanctions Act of 1996, as amended by CISADA, Section 5(a)(2)(B), *reprinted in* Overview, Part II, at 1135–1136 with Iran Sanctions Act of 1996, as further amended by

Iran Threat Reduction and Syria Human Rights Act of 2012, Section 5(a)(2)(B), *reprinted in* 2013 Compilation, at 688.
57 Iran Sanctions Act of 1996, as further amended by Iran Threat Reduction and Syria Human Rights Act of 2012, Sections 5(a)(2)(A)–(B), (5)(A), (B)(ii), *reprinted in* 2013 Compilation, at 688, 690.
58 Iran Sanctions Act of 1996, as further amended by Iran Threat Reduction and Syria Human Rights Act of 2012, Section 14(13), *reprinted in* 2013 Compilation, at 706.
59 Compare Iran Sanctions Act of 1996, as amended by CISADA, Section 5(a)(3)(B)(i)–(iii), *reprinted in* Overview, Part II, at 1137 with Iran Sanctions Act of 1996, as further amended by Iran Threat Reduction and Syria Human Rights Act of 2012, Section 5(a)(3)(B)(i)–(v), *reprinted in* 2013 Compilation, at 689.
60 Iran Sanctions Act of 1996, as further amended by Iran Threat Reduction and Syria Human Rights Act of 2012, Section 5(a)(3)(B)(iv), *reprinted in* 2013 Compilation, at 689.
61 Compare Iran Sanctions Act of 1996, as amended by CISADA, Section 5(a), reprinted in Overview, Part II, at 1135–1137 with Iran Sanctions Act of 1996, as further amended by Iran Threat Reduction and Syria Human Rights Act of 2012, Section 5(a)(4), *reprinted in* 2013 Compilation, at 689–690.
62 *Iran Sanctions Act of 1996*, as further amended *by Iran Threat Reduction and Syria Human Rights Act of 2012*, Section 5(a)(4)(A)(ii), *reprinted in* 2013 Compilation, at 690. The *mens rea* requirement again was 'knowingly.' *See* id., Section 14(13), at 706.
63 Iran Sanctions Act of 1996, as further amended by Iran Threat Reduction and Syria Human Rights Act of 2012, Section 5(a)(4)(A)(i), *reprinted in* 2013 Compilation, at 690.
64 Iran Sanctions Act of 1996, as further amended by Iran Threat Reduction and Syria Human Rights Act of 2012, Section 5(a)(4)(B), reprinted in 2013 Compilation, at 690.
65 Compare Iran Sanctions Act of 1996, as amended by CISADA, Section 5(a), *reprinted in* Overview, Part II, at 1135–1137 with Iran Sanctions Act of 1996, as further amended by Iran Threat Reduction and Syria Human Rights Act of 2012, Section 5(a)(6), *reprinted in* 2013 Compilation, at 691.
66 Iran Sanctions Act of 1996, as further amended by Iran Threat Reduction and Syria Human Rights Act of 2012, Section 14(16), *reprinted in* 2013 Compilation, at 707.
67 Iran Sanctions Act of 1996, as further amended by Iran Threat Reduction and Syria Human Rights Act of 2012, Section 5(a)(6)(A)(i)–(ii), reprinted in 2013 Compilation, at 691.
68 Compare Iran Sanctions Act of 1996, as amended by CISADA, Section 5(a), reprinted in Overview, Part II, at 1135–1137 with Iran Sanctions Act of 1996, as further amended by Iran Threat Reduction and Syria Human Rights Act of 2012, Section 5(a)(7), *reprinted in* 2013 Compilation, at 691–692.
69 Iran Sanctions Act of 1996, as further amended by Iran Threat Reduction and Syria Human Rights Act of 2012, Section 5(a)(7)(A)(i), *reprinted in* 2013 Compilation, at 691.
70 Iran Sanctions Act of 1996, as further amended by Iran Threat Reduction and Syria Human Rights Act of 2012, Section 5(a)(9), *reprinted in* 2013 Compilation, at 693.
71 Iran Sanctions Act of 1996, as further amended by Iran Threat Reduction and Syria Human Rights Act of 2012, Section 5(a)(7)(A)(ii)(I)–(II), *reprinted in* 2013 Compilation, at 691.
72 Iran Sanctions Act of 1996, as further amended by Iran Threat Reduction and Syria Human Rights Act of 2012, Section 5(a)(7)(B)(i), *reprinted in* 2013 Compilation, at 691.
73 Iran Sanctions Act of 1996, as further amended by Iran Threat Reduction and Syria Human Rights Act of 2012, Section 5(a)(7)(B)(i), *reprinted in* 2013 Compilation, at 691.
74 Section 1245(d)(4)(D) of the National Defense Authorization Act for Fiscal Year 2012, 22 U.S.C. § 8513a(d)(4)(D); Iran Sanctions Act of 1996, as further amended by Iran Threat Reduction and Syria Human Rights Act of 2012, Section 5(a)(7)(B)(ii), *reprinted in* 2013 Compilation, at 691–692.
75 Compare Iran Sanctions Act of 1996, as amended by CISADA, Section 5(a), *reprinted in* Overview, Part II, at 1135–1137 with Iran Sanctions Act of 1996, as further amended by Iran Threat Reduction and Syria Human Rights Act of 2012, Section 5(a)(8), *reprinted in* 2013 Compilation, at 692–693.
76 Iran Sanctions Act of 1996, as further amended by Iran Threat Reduction and Syria Human Rights Act of 2012, Section 5(a)(8), *reprinted in* 2013 Compilation, at 692.

77 Iran Sanctions Act of 1996, as further amended by Iran Threat Reduction and Syria Human Rights Act of 2012, Section 5(a)(8)(A), *reprinted in* 2013 Compilation, at 692.
78 Iran Sanctions Act of 1996, as further amended by Iran Threat Reduction and Syria Human Rights Act of 2012, Section 5(a)(9), *reprinted in* 2013 Compilation, at 693.
79 Iran Sanctions Act of 1996, as further amended by Iran Threat Reduction and Syria Human Rights Act of 2012, Section 5(a)(8)(A)(i)–(ii), *reprinted in* 2013 Compilation, at 692.
80 Iran Sanctions Act of 1996, as further amended by Iran Threat Reduction and Syria Human Rights Act of 2012, Section 5(a)(8)(C)(i)–(ii), *reprinted in* 2013 Compilation, at 692–693.
81 Iran Sanctions Act of 1996, as further amended by Iran Threat Reduction and Syria Human Rights Act of 2012, Section 5(a)(8)(B), *reprinted in* 2013 Compilation, at 692.
82 Compare Iran Sanctions Act of 1996, as amended by CISADA, Section 5(b), reprinted in Overview, Part II, at 1138–1139 with Iran Sanctions Act of 1996, as further amended by Iran Threat Reduction and Syria Human Rights Act of 2012, Section 5(b), *reprinted in* 2013 Compilation, at 693–695.
83 Iran Sanctions Act of 1996, as further amended by Iran Threat Reduction and Syria Human Rights Act of 2012, Section 5(b)(1)(A), *reprinted in* 2013 Compilation, at 693.
84 Iran Sanctions Act of 1996, as further amended by Iran Threat Reduction and Syria Human Rights Act of 2012, Section 5(b)(1)(B), *reprinted in* 2013 Compilation, at 693.
85 Iran Sanctions Act of 1996, as further amended by Iran Threat Reduction and Syria Human Rights Act of 2012, Section 5(b)(2)(A)(i), *reprinted in* 2013 Compilation, at 693–694.
  Note this proscription applied on or after 2 February 2012. Before that date, an additional set of criteria applied: the uranium had to be transferred directly or indirectly to Iran, the Iranian government had to receive 'significant revenue,' or Iran could have obtained technology or equipment it did not previously have that could have contributed materially to it developing nuclear weapons. See id., Section 5(b)(2)(A)(ii). This prohibition and attendant sanctions thus applied retroactively, unless a person agreed to terminate its JV participation within 180 days of enactment of the *Iran-Syria Act. See id.*, Section 5(b)(2)(B).
  The other aspects of the prohibition against helping Iran obtain WMDs or destabilizing numbers of advanced conventional weapons remained the same, namely, the statutory provisions concerning the additional mandatory sanction, and the exception thereto, about export licensing. Compare *Iran Sanctions Act of 1996*, as amended by CISADA, Section 5(b)(2), *reprinted in* Overview, Part II, at 1138–1139 with Iran Sanctions Act of 1996, as further amended by Iran Threat Reduction and Syria Human Rights Act of 2012, Section 5(b)(3) *reprinted in* 2013 Compilation, at 694–695.
86 *Iran Sanctions Act of 1996, as further amended by Iran Threat Reduction and Syria Human Rights Act of 2012, Sections 5(b)(2)(A) and 14(13), reprinted in* 2013 Compilation, at 693.
87 Compare Iran Sanctions Act of 1996, as amended by CISADA, Section 6(b), *reprinted in* Overview, Part II, at 1142–1143 with Iran Sanctions Act of 1996, as further amended by Iran Threat Reduction and Syria Human Rights Act of 2012, Section 6(b), *reprinted in* 2013 Compilation, at 698–700.
  The basic requirement concerning Iran certifications relating to Section 5 prohibitions remained the same, but with minor renumbering. Compare Iran Sanctions Act of 1996, as amended by CISADA, Section 6(b)(1), *reprinted in* Overview, Part II, at 1142 with Iran Sanctions Act of 1996, as further amended by Iran Threat Reduction and Syria Human Rights Act of 2012, Section 6(b)(1)(A), *reprinted in* 2013 Compilation, at 698–699.
  Likewise, clarifications regarding certain products, the rule of construction, and waivers were unchanged. Compare Iran Sanctions Act of 1996, as amended by CISADA, Section 6(b)(3)–(5), *reprinted in* Overview, Part II, at 1143 with Iran Sanctions Act of 1996, as further amended by Iran Threat Reduction and Syria Human Rights Act of 2012, Section 6(b)(3)–(5), *reprinted in* 2013 Compilation, at 699–700.
  The definition of 'executive agency' stayed the same, and to it the *2012 Act* added a definition of 'federal acquisition regulation.' Compare *Iran Sanctions Act of 1996*, as amended by CISADA, Section 6(b)(6), *reprinted in* Overview, Part II, at 1143 with Iran Sanctions Act of 1996, as further amended by Iran Threat Reduction and Syria Human Rights Act of 2012, Section 6(b)(6)(A)–(B), *reprinted in* 2013 Compilation, at 699–700. The *2012 Act* amended the provisions on applicability to reflect its certification requirement against

dealing with the Guards. Compare *Iran Sanctions Act of 1996*, as amended by *CISADA*, Section 6(b)(7), *reprinted in* Overview, Part II, at 1143 with Iran Sanctions Act of 1996, as further amended by Iran Threat Reduction and Syria Human Rights Act of 2012, Section 6(b)(7)(A)–(B), r*eprinted in* 2013 Compilation, at 699–700.

88 Iran Sanctions Act of 1996, as further amended by Iran Threat Reduction and Syria Human Rights Act of 2012, Section 6(b)(1)(B), *reprinted in* 2013 Compilation, at 699.

89 Compare Iran Sanctions Act of 1996, as amended by CISADA, Section 6(b)(2)(A)–(B), *reprinted in* Overview, Part II, at 1142–1143 with Iran Sanctions Act of 1996, as further amended by Iran Threat Reduction and Syria Human Rights Act of 2012, Section 6(b)(2)(A)–(B), *reprinted in* 2013 Compilation, at 699–700.

90 CISADA, Section 103(a), (b)(1)(A), (b)(2), *reprinted in* 2013 Compilation, at 708–709.

91 Comprehensive Iran Sanctions Accountability and Divestment Act of 2010, Section 105C(b)(1), Public Law 111–195 (1 July 2010), as amended by Public Law 112–158 (Iran Threat Reduction and Syria Human Rights Act of 2012) and Section 1249 of Public Law 112–239 (Iran Freedom and Counter-Proliferation Act of 2012, Sub-Title D of the National Defense Authorization Act for Fiscal Year 2013), codified at 22 U.S.C. §§ 8512, 8513a, 8514, 8514a, 8514b, *reprinted in* 2013 Compilation, at 715, 748.

92 Comprehensive Iran Sanctions Accountability and Divestment Act of 2010, Section 105C(a)(1), Public Law 111–195 (1 July 2010), as amended by Public Law 112–158 (Iran Threat Reduction and Syria Human Rights Act of 2012) and Section 1249 of Public Law 112–239 (Iran Freedom and Counter-Proliferation Act of 2012, Sub-Title D of the National Defense Authorization Act for Fiscal Year 2013), codified at 22 U.S.C. §§ 8512, 8513a, 8514, 8514a, 8514b, *reprinted in* 2013 Compilation, at 715, 748.

93 "List of Freight Ship Companies," *Wikipedia,* http://en.wikipedia.org/wiki/List_of_freight_ship_companies.

94 These companies are among the top insurers in the world. See "Top ten Insurance Personalities," *Lloyd's List,* http://www.lloydslist.com/ll/news/top100/insurance/.

95 Iran Threat Reduction and Syria Human Rights Act of 2012, Section 211(a), codified at 22 U.S.C. §§ 8711, 8721–8724, 8741–8744, 8781, *reprinted in* 2013 Compilation, at 724. In respect of the definition of 'knowing,' see Iran Sanctions Act of 1996, as further amended by Iran Threat Reduction and Syria Human Rights Act of 2012, Sections 5(b)(2)(A) and 14(13), *reprinted in* 2013 Compilation, at 693.

96 Iran Threat Reduction and Syria Human Rights Act of 2012, Section 211(a), codified at 22 U.S.C. §§ 8711, 8721–8724, 8741–8744, 8781, *reprinted in* 2013 Compilation, at 724.

97 Iran Threat Reduction and Syria Human Rights Act of 2012, Section 211(a), codified at 22 U.S.C. §§ 8711, 8721–8724, 8741–8744, 8781, *reprinted in* 2013 Compilation, at 724.

98 Iran Threat Reduction and Syria Human Rights Act of 2012, Section 211(b)(1), (2)(B)–(C), codified at 22 U.S.C. §§ 8711, 8721–8724, 8741–8744, 8781, *reprinted in* 2013 Compilation, at 724. *See also* Section 211(e) (containing a rule of construction to ensure Section 211 does not restrict the authority of the President under the IEEPA to sanction a person).

The *mens rea* requirement for owners or controllers was 'actual knowledge or should have known,' and for a one owned, controlled by, or under common ownership of the primary person was 'knowing[] engage[ment]' in the provision of a vessel, marine insurance, or other shipping service. Ibid.

99 "Magsaysay Home Page," *Magsaysay,* www.magsaysay.com.ph.; "Magsaysay Maritime Corporation Job Postings," *WorkAbroad,* www.workabroad.ph/list_specific_jobs.php?by_what=agency&id=2459.

100 Iran Threat Reduction and Syria Human Rights Act of 2012, Section 211(c)(1)–(2), codified at 22 U.S.C. §§ 8711, 8721–8724, 8741–8744, 8781, *reprinted in* 2013 Compilation, at 724.

Also subject to reporting, in this instance every 90 days, were vessel operators or others conducting or facilitating 'significant financial transactions with persons managing ports in Iran.' Ibid., Section 211(d)(1). Such reports could contain a classified Annex. *See* ibid., Section 211(d)(2).

101 *Iran threat reduction and syria human rights act of 2012*, Section 212(a), codified at 22 U.S.C. §§ 8711, 8721–8724, 8741–8744, 8781, *reprinted in* 2013 Compilation, at 725.

102 Iran Threat Reduction and Syria Human Rights Act of 2012, Section 212(b)(1)–(2), codified at 22 U.S.C. §§ 8711, 8721–8724, 8741–8744, 8781, *reprinted in* 2013 Compilation, at

725. If an insurer (or reinsurer) already had been underwriting policies for the NIOC or NITC, then it could escape sanctions by terminating its provision of those services to them. *See* id., Section 212(b)(3). *See also* Section 212(e) (containing a rule of construction to ensure Section 211 does not restrict the authority of the President under the *IEEPA* to sanction a person).

103 Iran Sanctions Act of 1996, as further amended by Iran Threat Reduction and Syria Human Rights Act of 2012, Section 5(a)(3)(B)(v), *reprinted in* 2013 Compilation, at 689.
104 Iran Threat Reduction and Syria Human Rights Act of 2012, Section 213(a)(1)–(2), codified at 22 U.S.C. §§ 8711, 8721–8724, 8741–8744, 8781, *reprinted in* 2013 Compilation, at 727.
105 *Generally* "Apollo Home,"*Apollo Global Management*, www.agm.com/Home.aspx. (discussing the activities and locations of the hedge fund).
106 *Generally* "Santander Bank Home," *Santander Bank*, www.santanderbank.com. (discussing the activities and locations of the bank).
107 *Iran Threat Reduction and Syria Human Rights Act of 2012*, Section 301(d)–(f), codified at 22 U.S.C. §§ 8711, 8721–8724, 8741–8744, 8781, *reprinted in* 2013 Compilation, at 729.
108 Iran Threat Reduction and Syria Human Rights Act of 2012, Section 301, codified at 22 U.S.C. §§ 8711, 8721–8724, 8741–8744, 8781, *reprinted in* 2013 Compilation, at 728–729.
109 Iran Threat Reduction and Syria Human Rights Act of 2012, Section 301(a)(1)–(2), codified at 22 U.S.C. §§ 8711, 8721–8724, 8741–8744, 8781, *reprinted in* 2013 Compilation, at 729.
110 Iran Threat Reduction and Syria Human Rights Act of 2012, Section 301(d)–(e), codified at 22 U.S.C. §§ 8711, 8721–8724, 8741–8744, 8781, *reprinted in* 2013 Compilation, at 728–729. The first exception was needed if the United States was to comply with its United National treaty obligation, namely, the 26 June 1947 *Agreement Between the United Nations and the United States of America Regarding the Headquarters of the United Nations*, which entered into force on 21 November 1947. *See* id., Section 301(d)(2). Invocation of the second exception required a Presidential report to the appropriate Congressional committees, which could contain a classified Annex. *See* id., Section 301(e)(1)–(2).
111 *Iran Threat Reduction and Syria Human Rights Act of 2012*, Section 301(b)(2), codified at 22 U.S.C. §§ 8711, 8721–8724, 8741–8744, 8781, *reprinted in* 2013 Compilation, at 729.
112 Iran Threat Reduction and Syria Human Rights Act of 2012, Section 301(c)(1)–(5), codified at 22 U.S.C. §§ 8711, 8721–8724, 8741–8744, 8781, *reprinted in* 2013 Compilation, at 729. *See also* CISADA Section 106(c), codified at 22 U.S.C. § 8515(c), concerning the last defined type of 'sensitive transaction.'
113 Iran Threat Reduction and Syria Human Rights Act of 2012, Section 301(a)(1), codified at 22 U.S.C. §§ 8711, 8721–8724, 8741–8744, 8781, *reprinted in* 2013 Compilation, at 729.
114 Iran Threat Reduction and Syria Human Rights Act of 2012, Section 302(a)(1)(A), codified at 22 U.S.C. §§ 8711, 8721–8724, 8741–8744, 8781, *reprinted in* 2013 Compilation, at 730.
115 "Home," *ABN Amro Group*, http://www.abnamro.com/en/index.html; "About Us," NatGaz, http://www.natgaz.com.lb/aboutus.aspx?aspxerrorpath=/default.aspx; "Home," *ITS Trading Company Ltd.*, http://www.itstradingcompany.com.
116 Iran Threat Reduction and Syria Human Rights Act of 2012, Section 302(b), codified at 22 U.S.C. §§ 8711, 8721–8724, 8741–8744, 8781, *reprinted in* 2013 Compilation, at 731.
117 Iran Threat Reduction and Syria Human Rights Act of 2012, Section 302(a)(1)(B), codified at 22 U.S.C. §§ 8711, 8721–8724, 8741–8744, 8781, *reprinted in* 2013 Compilation, at 730.
118 Iran Threat Reduction and Syria Human Rights Act of 2012, Section 302(a)(1)(B), (a)(3), (b), codified at 22 U.S.C. §§ 8711, 8721–8724, 8741–8744, 8781, *reprinted in* 2013 Compilation, at 731.
119 Iran Threat Reduction and Syria Human Rights Act of 2012, Section 302(b)(1), codified at 22 U.S.C. §§ 8711, 8721–8724, 8741–8744, 8781, *reprinted in* 2013 Compilation, at 731.
120 Iran Threat Reduction and Syria Human Rights Act of 2012, Section 302(b)–(c), codified at 22 U.S.C. §§ 8711, 8721–8724, 8741–8744, 8781, *reprinted in* 2013 Compilation, at 731. *See also* id., Section 302(e), at 732 (concerning waiver of Presidential identifications and designations of foreign person-supporters on the ground of 'damage' to national security).
121 Iran Threat Reduction and Syria Human Rights Act of 2012, Section 303(a)(1), codified at 22 U.S.C. §§ 8711, 8721–8724, 8741–8744, 8781, *reprinted in* 2013 Compilation, at 732.

506   *Legal issues in Asian investing*

Culpability also could arise if the foreign person was subject to financial sanctions under pertinent United Nations Security Council Resolutions. *See* id., Section 303(a)(2)(B), at 732–733.

122 Iran Threat Reduction and Syria Human Rights Act of 2012, Section 303(a)(1), codified at 22 U.S.C. §§ 8711, 8721–8724, 8741–8744, 8781, *reprinted in* 2013 Compilation, at 733.
123 Iran Threat Reduction and Syria Human Rights Act of 2012, Section 303(b)(1)(A)–(G), codified at 22 U.S.C. §§ 8711, 8721–8724, 8741–8744, 8781, *reprinted in* 2013 Compilation, at 733–734. *See also* Section 304 (containing a rule of construction against limiting Presidential authority to impose sanctions under the IEEPA).
124 Iran Threat Reduction and Syria Human Rights Act of 2012, Section 303(c)(1)–(3), codified at 22 U.S.C. §§ 8711, 8721–8724, 8741–8744, 8781, *reprinted in* 2013 Compilation, at 734.
125 Iran Threat Reduction and Syria Human Rights Act of 2012, Section 303(d), codified at 22 U.S.C. §§ 8711, 8721–8724, 8741–8744, 8781, *reprinted in* 2013 Compilation, at 734. Reporting was to be to all House and Senate Committees with jurisdiction over foreign relations, appropriations, financial institutions, armed services, and intelligence. *See* id., Section 303(e)(1)–(2), at 734–735.
126 Comprehensive Iran Sanctions Accountability and Divestment Act of 2010, Section 105A(a)–(b), 105B(a)–(b), Public Law 111–195 (1 July 2010), as amended by Public Law 112–158 (Iran Threat Reduction and Syria Human Rights Act of 2012) and Public Law 112–239 (*Iran Freedom and Counter-Proliferation Act of 2012*, Sub-Title D of the National Defense Authorization Act for Fiscal Year 2013), codified at 22 U.S.C. §§ 8512, 8513a, 8514, 8514a, 8514b, *reprinted in* 2013 Compilation, at 713–715.
127 Iran Threat Reduction and Syria Human Rights Act of 2012, Section 401(a), codified at 22 U.S.C. §§ 8711, 8721–8724, 8741–8744, 8781, *reprinted in* 2013 Compilation, at 735.
128 Iran Threat Reduction and Syria Human Rights Act of 2012, Section 401(a), codified at 22 U.S.C. §§ 8711, 8721–8724, 8741–8744, 8781, *reprinted in* 2013 Compilation, at 735.
129 Iran Threat Reduction and Syria Human Rights Act of 2012, Section 401(b)(1), codified at 22 U.S.C. §§ 8711, 8721–8724, 8741–8744, 8781, *reprinted in* 2013 Compilation, at 735. Those committees were the Senate Foreign Relations and Banking, and House Foreign Affairs and Financial Services, Committees. *See* id., Section 401(b)(3)(A)–(B), at 735–736.
130 Comprehensive Iran Sanctions Accountability and Divestment Act of 2010, Section 105A(b)(1), (2)(A)(i), (2)(B), (4), Public Law 111–195 (1 July 2010), as amended by Public Law 112–158 (Iran Threat Reduction and Syria Human Rights Act of 2012) and Public Law 112–239 (Iran Freedom and Counter-Proliferation Act of 2012, Sub-Title D of the National Defense Authorization Act for Fiscal Year 2013), codified at 22 U.S.C. §§ 8512, 8513a, 8514, 8514a, 8514b, *reprinted in* 2013 Compilation, at 713.
131 Comprehensive Iran Sanctions Accountability and Divestment Act of 2010, Section 105A(b)(C), Public Law 111–195 (1 July 2010), as amended by Public Law 112–158 (Iran Threat Reduction and Syria Human Rights Act of 2012) and Public Law 112–239 (Iran Freedom and Counter-Proliferation Act of 2012, Sub-Title D of the National Defense Authorization Act for Fiscal Year 2013), codified at 22 U.S.C. §§ 8512, 8513a, 8514, 8514a, 8514b, *reprinted in* 2013 Compilation, at 713.
132 Comprehensive Iran Sanctions Accountability and Divestment Act of 2010, Section 105A(b)(2)(A)(ii), (C), Public Law 111–195 (1 July 2010), as amended by Public Law 112–158 (Iran Threat Reduction and Syria Human Rights Act of 2012) and Public Law 112–239 (Iran Freedom and Counter-Proliferation Act of 2012, Sub-Title D of the National Defense Authorization Act for Fiscal Year 2013), codified at 22 U.S.C. §§ 8512, 8513a, 8514, 8514a, 8514b, *reprinted in* 2013 Compilation, at 713.
133 Comprehensive Iran Sanctions Accountability and Divestment Act of 2010, Section 105B(b)(1)–(2), Public Law 111–195 (1 July 2010), as amended by Public Law 112–158 (Iran Threat Reduction and Syria Human Rights Act of 2012) and Public Law 112–239 (Iran Freedom and Counter-Proliferation Act of 2012, Sub-Title D of the National Defense Authorization Act for Fiscal Year 2013), codified at 22 U.S.C. §§ 8512, 8513a, 8514, 8514a, 8514b, *reprinted in* 2013 Compilation, at 714–715.
134 Comprehensive Iran Sanctions Accountability and Divestment Act of 2010, Section 105B(b)(1)(A)–(B), Public Law 111–195 (1 July 2010), as amended by Public Law 112–158 (Iran

Threat Reduction and Syria Human Rights Act of 2012) and Public Law 112–239 (Iran Freedom and Counter-Proliferation Act of 2012, Sub-Title D of the National Defense Authorization Act for Fiscal Year 2013), codified at 22 U.S.C. §§ 8512, 8513a, 8514, 8514a, 8514b, *reprinted in* 2013 Compilation, at 715.

135 Comprehensive Iran Sanctions Accountability and Divestment Act of 2010, Section 105A(c), 105B(a), Public Law 111–195 (1 July 2010), as amended by Public Law 112–158 (Iran Threat Reduction and Syria Human Rights Act of 2012) and Public Law 112–239 (Iran Freedom and Counter-Proliferation Act of 2012, Sub-Title D of the National Defense Authorization Act for Fiscal Year 2013), codified at 22 U.S.C. §§ 8512, 8513a, 8514, 8514a, 8514b, *reprinted in* 2013 Compilation, at 713–715. *See also* Iran Threat Reduction and Syria Human Rights Act of 2012, Section 601(a)(3), (b)(1), (b)(2)(B), codified at 22 U.S.C. §§ 8711, 8721–8724, 8741–8744, 8781, *reprinted in* 2013 Compilation, at 736 (authorizing the President to use his IEEPA authority to implement penalties under Sections 105A and 105B of CISADA as amended by the 2012 *Act*.

136 Comprehensive Iran Sanctions Accountability and Divestment Act of 2010, Section 105A(c)(2)(B), Public Law 111–195 (1 July 2010), as amended by Public Law 112–158 (Iran Threat Reduction and Syria Human Rights Act of 2012) and Public Law 112–239 (Iran Freedom and Counter-Proliferation Act of 2012, Sub-Title D of the National Defense Authorization Act for Fiscal Year 2013), codified at 22 U.S.C. §§ 8512, 8513a, 8514, 8514a, 8514b, *reprinted in* 2013 Compilation, at 713–5.

137 Iran Sanctions Act of 1996, sanctions relating to the energy sector of Iran set out in Sections 5(a)(1)(A) (concerning development of petroleum resources), 5(a)(2)(A) (concerning production of refined petroleum products), 5(a)(3)(A) (concerning exportation of refined petroleum products to Iran), 5(a)(4)(A) (concerning joint ventures with Iran relating to developing petroleum resources), 5(a)(5)(A) (concerning support for the development of petroleum resources and petroleum products in Iran), 5(a)(6)(A) (concerning development of petrochemical products from Iran), 5(a)(7)(A) (concerning transportation of crude oil from Iran), 5(a)(8)(A) (concerning concealment of Iranian origin of crude oil and refined petroleum products), and sanctions relating to the development of WMDs or other military capabilities by Iran as set out in Section 5(b)(1) (concerning exports, transfers, or transshipments of goods, services, or technology relating to WMD or advanced conventional weapons), 5(b)(2)(A) (concerning joint ventures relating to mining, production, or transportation of uranium), as amended by *Iran Threat Reduction and Syria Human Rights Act of 2012*, *reprinted in* 2013 Compilation, at 688–694.

That the changes discussed were made by the 2012 *Iran-Syria Act* may be inferred from the facts that mandating imposition of five of nine sanctions was not in the 2010 *CISADA*, and such a mandate would have been unlikely to be included in Section 1245 or Sub-Title D, as those 2012 laws both were simply National Defense Authorizations.

138 Compare Iran Sanctions Act of 1996, as amended by CISADA, Section 6(a)(1), *reprinted in* Overview, Part II, at 1141 with Iran Sanctions Act of 1996, as further amended by Iran Threat Reduction and Syria Human Rights Act of 2012, Section 6(a)(1), *reprinted in* 2013 Compilation, at 697.

139 Compare Iran Sanctions Act of 1996, as amended by CISADA, Section 6(a)(2), *reprinted in* Overview, Part II, at 1141 with Iran Sanctions Act of 1996, as further amended by Iran Threat Reduction and Syria Human Rights Act of 2012, Section 6(a)(2), *reprinted in* 2013 Compilation, at 697.

140 Compare Iran Sanctions Act of 1996, as amended by *CISADA*, Section 6(a)(3), *reprinted in* Overview, Part II, at 1141 with Iran Sanctions Act of 1996, as further amended by Iran Threat Reduction and Syria Human Rights Act of 2012, Section 6(a)(3), *reprinted in* 2013 Compilation, at 697.

141 Compare Iran Sanctions Act of 1996, as amended by CISADA, Section 6(a)(4)(A)–(B), *reprinted in* Overview, Part II, at 1141 with *Iran Sanctions Act of 1996*, as further amended by Iran Threat Reduction and Syria Human Rights Act of 2012, Section 6(a)(4)(A)–(B), *reprinted in* 2013 Compilation, at 697.

142 *Compare Iran Sanctions Act of 1996, as amended by CISADA*, Section 6(a)(5), *reprinted in* Overview, Part II, at 1141 with Iran Sanctions Act of 1996, as further amended by Iran

Threat Reduction and Syria Human Rights Act of 2012, Section 6(a)(5), *reprinted in* 2013 Compilation, at 698.
143 Compare Iran Sanctions Act of 1996, as amended by CISADA, Section 6(a)(6), *reprinted in* Overview, Part II, at 1141 with Iran Sanctions Act of 1996, as further amended by Iran Threat Reduction and Syria Human Rights Act of 2012, Section 6(a)(6), *reprinted in* 2013 Compilation, at 698.
144 Compare Iran Sanctions Act of 1996, as amended by *CISADA*, Section 6(a)(7), *reprinted in* Overview, Part II, at 1141 with Iran Sanctions Act of 1996, as further amended by Iran Threat Reduction and Syria Human Rights Act of 2012, Section 6(a)(7), *reprinted in* 2013 Compilation, at 698.
145 Compare Iran Sanctions Act of 1996, as amended by CISADA, Section 6(a)(8), *reprinted in* Overview, Part II, at 1141 with Iran Sanctions Act of 1996, as further amended by Iran Threat Reduction and Syria Human Rights Act of 2012, Section 6(a)(8), *reprinted in* 2013 Compilation, at 698.
146 Compare Iran Sanctions Act of 1996, as amended by CISADA, Section 6(a)(9), *reprinted in* Overview, Part II, at 1141 with Iran Sanctions Act of 1996, as further amended by Iran Threat Reduction and Syria Human Rights Act of 2012, Section 6(a)(12), *reprinted in* 2013 Compilation, at 698.
147 Iran Sanctions Act of 1996, as further amended by Iran Threat Reduction and Syria Human Rights Act of 2012, Section 6(a)(9), *reprinted in* 2013 Compilation, at 698.
148 Iran Sanctions Act of 1996, as further amended by Iran Threat Reduction and Syria Human Rights Act of 2012, Section 6(a)(10), *reprinted in* 2013 Compilation, at 698.
149 United States District Court for the Northern District of Illinois, Number 13 CR 00531, plea, 31 October 2013.
150 Michael Bologna, "Importer Charged in Scheme to Ship Controlled Aluminum Sources to Iran," *International Trade Reporter (BNA)* 30 (7 November 2013): 1731.
151 Iran Sanctions Act of 1996, as further amended by Iran Threat Reduction and Syria Human Rights Act of 2012, Section 6(a)(11), *reprinted in* 2013 Compilation, at 698.
152 *Iran Sanctions Act of 1996*, as amended by CISADA, Section 9(c)(1), *reprinted in* Overview, Part II, at 1145.
153 Iran Sanctions Act of 1996, as amended by *CISADA*, Section 9(c)(1)(C), *reprinted in* Overview, Part II, at 1145.
154 Iran Sanctions Act of 1996, as further amended *by Iran Threat Reduction and Syria Human Rights Act of 2012*, Section 9(c)(1)(A), *reprinted in* 2013 Compilation, at 702.
155 Iran Sanctions Act of 1996, as further amended *by Iran Threat Reduction and Syria Human Rights Act of 2012*, Section 9(c)(1)(B), *reprinted in* 2013 Compilation, at 702.
156 Iran Freedom and Counter-Proliferation Act of 2012, Sub-Title D of the National Defense Authorization Act for Fiscal Year 2013, Sections 1241–1255, Public Law 112–239, 126 Stat. 1632, 2004–2018, enacted 2 January 2013, codified at 22 U.S.C. § 8801–8811, *reprinted in* 2013 Compilation, at 736–748. Section 1241, 22 U.S.C. § 8801, sets out the Short Title.
157 *IEEPA* penalties applied to actual or attempted conspiracies to violate the 2013 *Defense Act*, and the *Act* did not limit the authority of the President to apply yet more sanctions on Iran. *See* Iran Freedom and Counter-Proliferation Act of 2012, Sub-Title D of the National Defense Authorization Act for Fiscal Year 2013, Sections 1253(a)–(b), 1255, codified at 22 U.S.C. §§ 8809(a)–(b), 8811 *reprinted in* 2013 Compilation, at 748. But, sanctions under Section 1254 of the 2013 *Act*, 22 U.S.C. § 8810, do not apply to:
(i) the Shah Deniz natural gas field in Azerbaijan's sector of the Caspian Sea and related pipeline projects, (ii) projects that provide Turkey and European countries energy security and independence from Russia and Iran, or (iii) projects initiated before August 10, 2012, pursuant to a production-sharing agreement entered into with, or a license granted by, a government other than Iran's before August 10, 2012. This is the same exception for natural gas projects found in ITRA [the 2012 *Iran-Syria Act*] Section 603(a).
Baker & McKenzie, "U.S. Congress Enacts Additional Sanctions Against Iran," *Lexology*, 31 January 2013, http://www.lexology.com/library/detail.aspx?g=1dbeb762–9695–4817–88a8–f0130cf20844.
158 For a Chart of the Sessions of Congress, *see* "Guide: Congressional Session Chart," *Indiana University Bloomington Library* https://libraries.indiana.edu/guide-congressional-session-chart.

159 Iran Freedom and Counter-Proliferation Act of 2012, Sub-Title D of the National Defense Authorization Act for Fiscal Year 2013, Section 1243(a), codified at 22 U.S.C. 22 U.S.C. § 8802(a).
160 Iran Freedom and Counter-Proliferation Act of 2012, Sub-Title D of the National Defense Authorization Act for Fiscal Year 2013, Section 1243(b), codified at 22 U.S.C. 22 U.S.C. § 8802(b).
161 Iran Freedom and Counter-Proliferation Act of 2012, Sub-Title D of the National Defense Authorization Act for Fiscal Year 2013, Section 1244(c)(1)(A), (c)(2)(A)–(B), codified at 22 U.S.C. § 8803(c)(1)(A), (c)(2)(A)–(B), *reprinted in* 2013 Compilation, at 738–739. Such 'help' could take the form of material, financial, technological, or other goods, services, or support to such a person. *See* id. Iranian or other blocked persons did not include Iranian banks that had not already been designated for the imposition of sanctions. *See* id., Section 1244(c)(2)(iii)–(3), 22 U.S.C. § 8803(c)(2)(iii)–(3), at 739. Importation of goods was not sanctionable under this measure. *See id.*, Section 1244(c)(1)(B), 22 U.S.C. § 8803(c)(1)(B), at 739.
162 Iran Freedom and Counter-Proliferation Act of 2012, Sub-Title D of the National Defense Authorization Act for Fiscal Year 2013, Section 1244(d)(1)(A), codified at 22 U.S.C. § 8803(d)(1)(A), *reprinted in* 2013 Compilation, at 738–739. Importation of goods was not sanctionable under this measure. *See* id., Section 1244(d)(1)(B), 22 U.S.C. § 8803(d)(1)(B), at 739.
163 Iran Freedom and Counter-Proliferation Act of 2012, Sub-Title D of the National Defense Authorization Act for Fiscal Year 2013, Section 1244(b), codified at 22 U.S.C. § 8803(b), *reprinted in* 2013 Compilation, at 738.
164 Iran Freedom and Counter-Proliferation Act of 2012, Sub-Title D of the National Defense Authorization Act for Fiscal Year 2013, Section 1244(e), codified at 22 U.S.C. § 8803(e), *reprinted in* 2013 Compilation, at 740.

The 2013 *Defense Act* also provided an exception linked to Section 1245 of the 2013 *Defense Act*, namely, the new prohibition and attendant penalties applied to buying petroleum and petroleum products from Iran if the President determined that third country sources of these items were in sufficient quantities at reasonable prices so as to permit third country buyers to 'reduce significantly' sourcing them from Iran. *Id.*, Section 1244(g)(1), codified at 22 U.S.C. § 8803(g)(1), *reprinted in* 2013 Compilation, at 740. This exception meant the President had to monitor global petroleum and petroleum product market conditions, in addition to global crude oil supply and demand conditions thanks to the 2012 Defense Act.

165 Iran Freedom and Counter-Proliferation Act of 2012, Sub-Title D of the National Defense Authorization Act for Fiscal Year 2013, Section 1244(i)(1), codified at 22 U.S.C. § 8803(i)(1), *reprinted in* 2013 Compilation, at 741.
166 Iran Freedom and Counter-Proliferation Act of 2012, Sub-Title D of the National Defense Authorization Act for Fiscal Year 2013, Section 1244(a)(1), (5)–(6), codified at 22 U.S.C. § 8803(a)(1), (5)–(6), *reprinted in* 2013 Compilation, at 738.
167 Iran Freedom and Counter-Proliferation Act of 2012, Sub-Title D of the National Defense Authorization Act for Fiscal Year 2013, Section 1245(e)(1)(B), (h), codified at 22 U.S.C. § 8804(e)(1)(B), (h), *reprinted in* 2013 Compilation, at 743 (concerning the definition of 'national balance sheet of Iran' as the ratio of government assets to liabilities, and its listing of precious metals and other minerals as assets).
168 "Mining in Iran," *Wikipedia*, https://en.wikipedia.org/wiki/Mining_in_Iran. (providing statistics for several precious metals and commodities); Glenn E. Curtis and Eric Hooglund, *Iran: A Country Study*, 5th ed. (Washington, DC: Library of Congress, Federal Research Division, 2008), xxvii, 178–80 (concerning the Iranian mining industry, including aluminum).
169 Iran Freedom and Counter-Proliferation Act of 2012, Sub-Title D of the National Defense Authorization Act for Fiscal Year 2013, Section 1245(a)(1)(A), codified at 22 U.S.C. § 8804(a)(1)(A), *reprinted in* 2013 Compilation, at 741–742. This term is undefined. *See* id., Section 1242(a), codified at 22 U.S.C. § 8801(a), *reprinted in* 2013 Compilation, at 736–7.
170 Iran Freedom and Counter-Proliferation Act of 2012, Sub-Title D of the National Defense Authorization Act for Fiscal Year 2013, Section 1242(a)(3), codified at 22 U.S.C. § 8804(a)(3), *reprinted in* 2013 Compilation, at 737.

171 Iran Freedom and Counter-Proliferation Act of 2012, Sub-Title D of the National Defense Authorization Act for Fiscal Year 2013, Section 1245(a)(1)(B), (d), codified at 22 U.S.C. § 8804(a)(1)(B), (d), *reprinted in* 2013 Compilation, at 742–3.

172 Iran Freedom and Counter-Proliferation Act of 2012, Sub-Title D of the National Defense Authorization Act for Fiscal Year 2013, Section 1245(a)(1)(C)(i)(I)-(III), codified at 22 U.S.C. § 8804(a)(1)(C)(I)-(III), *reprinted in* 2013 Compilation, at 742.

173 Iran Freedom and Counter-Proliferation Act of 2012, Sub-Title D of the National Defense Authorization Act for Fiscal Year 2013, Section 1242(a)(9), codified at 22 U.S.C. § 8801(a)(1)(A), *reprinted in* 2013 Compilation, at 737.

174 Iran Freedom and Counter-Proliferation Act of 2012, Sub-Title D of the National Defense Authorization Act for Fiscal Year 2013, Section 1245(a), codified at 22 U.S.C. § 8804(a)(1), *reprinted in* 2013 Compilation, at 741–742. The prohibited conduct covered re-sales, re-supplies, or re-transfers, for example, through an intermediary that is a sanctioned person to an end user in Iran, like the Corps. *See id.*, Section 1245(a)(1)(C)(ii), codified at 22 U.S.C. § 8804(a)(1)(C)(ii), *reprinted in* 2013 Compilation, at 742.

175 Iran Freedom and Counter-Proliferation Act of 2012, Sub-Title D of the National Defense Authorization Act for Fiscal Year 2013, Section 1245(c), codified at 22 U.S.C. § 8804(c), *reprinted in* 2013 Compilation, at 742.

176 Iran Freedom and Counter-Proliferation Act of 2012, Sub-Title D of the National Defense Authorization Act for Fiscal Year 2013, Section 1245(f), codified at 22 U.S.C. § 8804(f), *reprinted in* 2013 Compilation, at 743.

177 Iran Freedom and Counter-Proliferation Act of 2012, Sub-Title D of the National Defense Authorization Act for Fiscal Year 2013, Section 1245(g)(1)(A), codified at 22 U.S.C. § 8804(g)(1)(A), *reprinted in* 2013 Compilation, at 743. If the President chose to exercise this waive discretion, then – as with other provisions in the sanctions regime – he was obliged to provide a written justification to the appropriate Congressional committees, possibly with a classified Annex. *See id.*, Section 1245(g)(1)(B), codified at 22 U.S.C. § 8804(g)(1)(B), *reprinted in* 2013 Compilation, at 743.

178 Iran Freedom and Counter-Proliferation Act of 2012, Sub-Title D of the National Defense Authorization Act for Fiscal Year 2013, Section 1246(a)(1)(A)-(B)(i)-(ii), codified at 22 U.S.C. § 8805(a)(1), *reprinted in* 2013 Compilation, at 743–744. The prohibition also applied to underwriting or reinsurance services for any person sanctioned under the IEEPA that helped Iran acquire WMDs or support terrorism, or any other Iranian or blocked person listed by OFAC (excluding Iranian financial institutions not sanctioned). *See id.*, Section 1246(a)(1)(B)(iii)-(C), (a)(2), (b), codified at 22 U.S.C. § 8805(a)(1)(B)(iii)-(C), (a)(2), (b).

Here, too, exceptions existed for (1) humanitarian exports to Iran, and (2) any person exercising due diligence to avoid the forbidden behaviour, and there was Presidential waiver authority on the ground of 'vital ... national security' interest if justified to appropriate Congressional committees. *See id.* Section 1246(c)-(e), codified at 22 U.S.C. § 8805(c)-(d), *reprinted in* 2013 Compilation, at 744. An exception also existed with respect to the bar, under Section 6(a)(8) of the 1996 *ISA*, against any person from importing property within the jurisdiction of the US in which a sanctioned person had an interest: such importation was not subject to the revised underwriting and insurance measure. *See* ibid., Section 1246(a)(2), codified at 22 U.S.C. § 8805(a)(2).

179 Iran Freedom and Counter-Proliferation Act of 2012, Sub-Title D of the National Defense Authorization Act for Fiscal Year 2013, Section 1247(a)-(b), codified at 22 U.S.C. § 8806(a)-(b), *reprinted in* 2013 Compilation, at 745. OFAC maintained the list of proscribed persons, which as per the Section title were called 'Specially Designated Nationals,' or 'SDNs.' *See* ibid.

180 Iran Freedom and Counter-Proliferation Act of 2012, Sub-Title D of the National Defense Authorization Act for Fiscal Year 2013, Section 1247(a), codified at 22 U.S.C. § 8806(a), *reprinted in* 2013 Compilation, at 745. Congress provided the President with the familiar waiver authority on the basis of 'vital ... national security' interests, with a justification to appropriate Congressional committees. Ibid. Section 1247(f)(1)(2), codified at 22 U.S.C. § 8806(f)(1)–(2).

181 Iran Freedom and Counter-Proliferation Act of 2012, Sub-Title D of the National Defense Authorization Act for Fiscal Year 2013, Section 1247(c)-(d)(1), codified at 22 U.S.C. § 8806(c)-(d)(1), *reprinted in* 2013 Compilation, at 746.

182 If the underlying commercial transaction involved goods or services other than natural gas, then to qualify for the exception, a foreign financial institution also had to be from a country holding primary regulatory authority over it that the President had certified, under the 2012 Defense Act, had significantly reduced or stopped crude oil purchases from Iran. *See* Iran Freedom and Counter-Proliferation Act of 2012, Sub-Title D of the National Defense Authorization Act for Fiscal Year 2013, Section 1247(d)(2)(A), codified at 22 U.S.C. § 8806(d)(2)(A), *reprinted in* 2013 Compilation, at 746 (containing the additional qualification); National Defense Authorization Act of 2012, Public Law 112–81, Section 1245(d)(4)(D)(i), as amended by Public Law 112–158 (Iran Threat Reduction and Syria Human Rights Act of 2012) and Public Law 112–239 (Iran Freedom and Counter-Proliferation Act of 2012, Sub-Title D of the National Defense Authorization Act for Fiscal Year 2013), codified at 22 U.S.C. § 8513a(d)(4)(D)(i), *reprinted in* 2013 Compilation, at 719. In other words, to avoid sanctions on their banks, third countries had to prove to the US President they tried to, or did, get oil from anywhere but Iran.

183 *Iran Freedom and Counter-Proliferation Act of 2012, Sub-Title D of the National Defense Authorization Act for Fiscal Year 2013*, Section 1247(d)(2)(B)(i)-(ii), (e)(1)–(2), codified at 22 U.S.C. § 8806(d)(2)(B)(i)-(ii), (e)(1)–(2), *reprinted in* 2013 Compilation, at 746.

184 "Home," *Hanmi Bank*, https://www.hanmi.com/.; "Hanmi Bank Branches," *Hanmi Bank*, https://www.hanmi.com/about/branches/northern-california/san-francisco.

185 Iran Freedom and Counter-Proliferation Act of 2012, Sub-Title D of the National Defense Authorization Act for Fiscal Year 2013, Section 1248(a)(1), codified at 22 U.S.C. § 8807(a)(1), *reprinted in* 2013 Compilation, at 747.

186 Iran Freedom and Counter-Proliferation Act of 2012, Sub-Title D of the National Defense Authorization Act for Fiscal Year 2013, Section 1248(b)(1)(A)-(B), codified at 22 U.S.C. § 8807(b)(1)(A)-(B), *reprinted in* 2013 Compilation, at 747. An exception to the requirement to impose sanctions existed for importation of goods. *See id.*, Section 1248(b)(1)(A)-(B), codified at 22 U.S.C. § 8807(b)(1)(A)-(B), *reprinted in* 2013 Compilation, at 747.

187 "Iran Nuclear Deal: Joint Plan of Action – Full Text," *The Guardian*, 24 November 2013, http://www.theguardian.com/world/interactive/2013/nov/24/iran-nuclear-deal-joint-plan-action.; "The Iran Nuclear Deal: Full Text," 24 November 2013, *CNN*, www.cnn.com/2013/11/24/world/meast/iran-deal-text/. [Hereinafter, *Joint Plan of Action*.]

Given that there are 3 EU countries (France, Germany, and the UK Kingdom), the P5+1 sometimes is referred to as the 'E3+3' or E3/EU +3.' *See* ibid.; P5+1, *Wikipedia*, https://en.wikipedia.org/wiki/P5%2B1.

188 "Iran Nuclear Deal Makes Mid-East Peace Safer Place – Kerry," *BBC News*, 24 November 2013, http://www.bbc.co.uk/news/world-middle-east-25078961.

189 The timetable for implementation was set in a January 2014 accord, which was not been publicly released, and reportedly contains an informal addendum that is secret. *See* Paul Richter, "New Iran Agreement Includes Secret Side Deal, Tehran Official Says," *Los Angeles Times*, 13 January 2014, www.latimes.com/world/worldnow/la-fg-wn-iran-nuclear-side-deal-20140113,0,4116168.story#axzz2rLwaPbUK.

190 *Quoted in* Richard McGregor and Geoff Dyer, "U.S. and Iran Start Sanctions Countdown," *Financial Times* (13 January 2013): 3.

191 For examples of this narrative, *see, e.g.*, "Diplomacy, Not Sanctions Key to Securing Iran Nuclear Deal," *RT*, 25 November 2013, http://rt.com/op-edge/role-of-diplomacy-iran-deal-263/.

192 The *Joint Plan of Action* is rather sketchy, and credible published analyses of its details are limited. Hence, the Table draws on following additional sources to fill in certain details about provisions of the Plan: "Geneva Interim Agreement on Iran Nuclear Program," *Wikipedia*, http://en.wikipedia.org/wiki/Geneva_interim_agreement_on_Iranian_nuclear_program.; "Uranium Oxide," *Wikipedia*, http://en.wikipedia.org/wiki/Uranium_oxide.; "Nuclear Fuel Cycle," *Wikipedia*, http://en.wikipedia.org/wiki/Nuclear_fuel_cycle.; "Additional Protocol," *Wikipedia*, http://en.wikipedia.org/wiki/Additional_Protocol.; "Treaty on the Non-Proliferation of Nuclear Weapons," *Wikipedia*, http://en.wikipedia.org/wiki/Nuclear_Nonproliferation_Treaty.

193 *Joint Plan of Action*, bullet point 1 at 1, bullet point 4 at 2.

512 *Legal issues in Asian investing*

194 At the 5 per cent purity level, uranium can be enriched for nuclear fuel, but not weapons, purposes. *See* Hossein Mousavian, *It Was Not Sanctions that Brought Tehran to the Table*, *Financial Times*, 20 November 2013, at 11. The concentration of 5 per cent is suitable for operating a nuclear power station. At higher degrees of refinement, uranium serves in the core of a nuclear warhead. *See* Parisa Hafezi and Justyna Pawlak, "Breakthrough Deal Curbs Iran's Nuclear Activity," *Reuters*, 24 November 2013, http://www.reuters.com/article/2013/11/24/us-iran-nuclear-idUSBRE9AI0CV20131124.
195 *Joint Plan of Action*, bullet point 2 at 1.
196 Uranium purified to 3.5 per cent or below is considered low enriched. "There's a Chink of Hope," *The Economist* (19 October 2013): 51–2.
197 *Joint Plan of Action*, bullet point 3 at 2, bullet points 5, 7 at 2.
198 Natanz and Fordow are underground uranium enrichment facilities, with Fordow beneath a mountain. Geoff Dyer and John Reed, "Iran's Arak Plant Reveals Depth of Distrust," *Financial Times* (13 November 2013): 6; Roula Khalaf, Lionel Barber, Najmeh Bozorgmehr, and Geoff Dyer, "Rouhani Takes Tough Nuclear Line," *Financial Times* (30 November–1 December 2013): 1. Natanz and Fordow are Iran's two uranium enrichment facilities. In them, 'uranium hexafluoride [UF_6] gas is fed into centrifuges to separate out the most fissile isotope U-235. Low-enriched uranium, which has a 3 per cent–4 per cent concentration of U-235, can be used to produce fuel for nuclear power plants. But it can also be enriched to the 90 per cent needed to produce nuclear weapons.' *See* "Iran Nuclear Deal: Key Deals," *BBC News*, 14 July 2015, http://www.bbc.com/news/world-middle-east-33521655. [Hereinafter, *Iran Nuclear Deal: Key Details*.]

Spent fuel from a heavy water nuclear reactor has plutonium, and that plutonium may be used for a nuclear weapon. *See Iran Nuclear Deal: Key Deals*. The heavy water reactor at Arak has been called 'the second string of Iran's [nuclear] program,' because it 'has the potential to produce plutonium for a bomb' – possibly 5–10 kg 'of weapons-grade plutonium, enough for a nuclear weapon every year.' Geoff Dyer and John Reed, "Iran's Arak Plant Reveals Depth of Distrust," *Financial Times*, 13 November 2013): 6. If that were to occur, then it would be 'invulnerable' to the kind of military attack the Israelis successfully conducted against the Iraqi nuclear reactor at Osirak in 1981, and a facility in Syria in 2007. Ibid. That is because, even though Arak is above ground, once it is loaded with nuclear fuel, it cannot be destroyed without causing tremendous damage to surrounding areas, as occurred with respect to Chernobyl in 1986. In sum, the Arak facility, which had been projected to be operational in late 2014, was 'an alternative, plutonium, path to creating the fissile material for a nuclear bomb.' "There's a Chink of Hope," *The Economist* (19 October 2013): 51–2.

At least as early as 2002, Iranian exiles identified undeclared nuclear facilities in Iran. Subsequently, the IAEA confirmed those facilities were a uranium enrichment plant at Natanz, and a heavy water production facility at Arak. That was one reason why 'Western intelligence agencies are convinced Iran had a nuclear arms program that went dormant, possibly as far back as 2003.' Louis Charbonneau, "Factbox: A Guide to Nuclear Talks between Iran and Six Major Powers," *Reuters*, 28 June 2015, http://mobile.reuters.com/article/topNews/idUSKCN0P80JF20150628?irpc=932.
199 *Joint Plan of Action*, fn. 1 at 2.
200 This provision is set out in the *Joint Plan of Action*, fn. 2 at 2, which states that at Fordow, Iran will not further enrich over 5 per cent at 4 cascades currently enriching uranium, but not increase their enrichment capacity, and not feed UF_6 into the other 12 cascades, which are to remain non-operative.
201 *Joint Plan of Action*, fns. 1–2 at 4.
202 *Joint Plan of Action*, bullet points 6, 8 at 2.
203 *Joint Plan of Action*, fn. 4 at 2.
204 *Joint Plan of Action*, bullet point 1 at 3.
205 Parisa Hafezi and Justyna Pawlak, "Breakthrough Deal Curbs Iran's Nuclear Activity," *Reuters*, 24 November 2013, http://www.reuters.com/article/2013/11/24/us-iran-nuclear-idUSBRE9AI0CV20131124.
206 Gideon Rachman and Ajay Makan, "Rouhani Tries to Lure Western Oil Majors to Iran," *Financial Times* (24 January 2014): 3.
207 *Joint Plan of Action*, bullet point 2 at 3.

208 These 'associated services' are identified in a non-exclusive manner in the *Joint Plan of Action*, fn. 5 at 3.
209 *Joint Plan of Action*, bullet point 2 at 3.
210 Parisa Hafezi and Justyna Pawlak, "Breakthrough Deal Curbs Iran's Nuclear Activity," *Reuters*, 24 November 2013, http://www.reuters.com/article/2013/11/24/us-iran-nuclear-idUSBRE9AI0CV20131124.
211 *Joint Plan of Action*, bullet points 3–4 at 3.
212 *Joint Plan of Action*, fn. 6 at 3.
  Implementing this part of the *Deal*, in April 2014, the US Department of the Treasury licensed Boeing to sell certain commercial aircraft spare parts to Iran – the first dealing Boeing had with Iran since 1979. Iran Air still flew aircraft sold to it by Boeing from that era. General Electric received a similar license. The BBC reported '[t]here have been more than 200 accidents involving Iranian planes in the past 25 years, leading to more than 2,000 deaths.' "U.S. Allows Boeing Air Component Sales to Iran," *BBC News*, 4 April 2014, www.bbc.com/news/world-us-canada-26896983.
213 *Joint Plan of Action*, bullet points 5–7 at 3.
214 That there was considerable pressure from Congress for new sanctions legislation, and pushback from the Administration of President Barack H. Obama, in the weeks and months following the Iran Nuclear Deal was clear. The legislation was 'pushed strongly' (*inter alia*) by 'pro-Israel lobby groups such as the America Israel Public Affairs Committee . . .' Geoff Dyer and Najmeh Bozorgmehr, "Obama Lobbies Senate Democrats to Drop Plan for More Iran Sanctions," *Financial Times* (15 January 2014): 4.
215 *Joint Plan of Action*, bullet points 8–9 at 3.
216 "The Best v. The Not-Too-Bad," *The Economist* (19 October 2013): 16. [Hereinafter, *The Best*.]
217 Gideon Rachman and Ajay Makan, "Rouhani Tries to Lure Western Oil Majors to Iran," *Financial Times* (24 January 2014): 3; *The Best*.
218 *The Best*.
219 *The Best*.
220 *The Best*.
221 "Nothing Idyllic," *The Economist* (11 January 2013): 42.
222 Kenneth Katzman, "Iran Sanctions, Congressional Research Service Report 7–5700, RS 20871," *US Department of State*, 19 August 2014, http://fpc.state.gov/documents/organization/138727.pdf.; Stephanie Cohen, "Sanctions Against Iran Cut Oil Exports by More Than Half, CRS Reports," *International Trade Reporter (BNA)* 31 (4 September 2014): 1590.
223 Yeganeh Torbati and Lesley Wroughton, "Kerry Meets Iran Foreign Minister to Close Gaps in Iran Nuclear Talks," *Reuters*, 8 November 2013, http://mobile.reuters.com/article/topNews/idUSBRE9A709G20131108?irpc=932. [Hereinafter, *Kerry Meets Iran Foreign Minister*.]
224 Najmeh Bozorgmehr, "Iran Poised to Offer Lucrative Oil Deals," *Financial Times* (29 October 2013): 1.
225 Gideon Rachman and Ajay Makan, "Rouhani Tries to Lure Western Oil Majors to Iran," *Financial Times* (24 January 2014): 3.
226 Kenneth Katzman, "Iran Sanctions, Congressional Research Service Report 7–5700, RS 20871," *US Department of State*, 19 August 2014, http://fpc.state.gov/documents/organization/138727.pdf; Stephanie Cohen, "Sanctions Against Iran Cut Oil Exports by More Than Half, CRS Reports," *International Trade Reporter (BNA)* 31 (4 September 2014): 1590.
227 *Kerry Meets Iran Foreign Minister*.
228 Monavar Khalaj, "Hope glimmers for Iran's Tourism Industry," *Financial Times*, 15 November 2013, http://www.ft.com/intl/cms/s/0/7be25910-40a4-11e3-8775-00144feabdc0.html~ide0.
229 "Nothing Idyllic," *The Economist* (11 January 2013): 42. [Hereinafter, *Nothing Idyllic*.]
230 *Nothing Idyllic*.
231 Hossein Mousavian, "It Was Not Sanctions that Brought Tehran to the Table," *Financial Times* (20 November 2013): 11. [Hereinafter, *It Was Not Sanctions*.]

232 *It Was Not Sanctions*.
233 "Give Iran a Limited Right to Enrich," *Financial Times* (21 October 2013): 12.
234 Roula Khalaf, Lionel Barber, and Najmeh Bozorgmehr, "Rouhani Celebrates Triumph of His First 100 Days,", *Financial Times* (25 November 2013): 2.
235 *It Was Not Sanctions*.
236 *The Best*.
237 *The Best*.
238 "Parameters for a Joint Comprehensive Plan of Action Regarding the Islamic Republic of Iran's Nuclear Program," *US Department of State*, 2 April 2015, http://www.state.gov/r/pa/prs/ps/2015/04/240170.htm.
239 For the American narrative, *see* "Fact Sheet: Parameters for a Joint Comprehensive Plan of Action regarding the Islamic Republic of Iran's Nuclear Program," *US Department of State*, 2 April 2015, http://www.state.gov/e/eb/tfs/spi/iran/fs/240539.htm.

   The European view was conveyed in "Joint Statement by EU High Representative Federica Mogherini and Iranian Foreign Minister Javad Zarif Switzerland," *European External Action Service*, 2 April 2015, http://www.eeas.europa.eu/statements-eeas/2015/150402_03_en.htm.

   For the Iranian narrative, *see* "Iran DM [Defense Minister] Rejects Report on Inspection of Military Centers Based on Lausanne Understanding," *FARS News Agency*, 8 April 2015, http://english.farsnews.com/newstext.aspx?nn=13940119001411. The Iranian perspective also was conveyed by Twitter feed from the Supreme Leader, *Āyatollāh* Ali Khamenei, which is referenced in the Wikipedia entry below.
240 "Iran Nuclear Deal Framework," *Wikipedia*, https://en.wikipedia.org/wiki/Iran_nuclear_deal_framework.
241 *Framework Agreement*, pp. 1, 4 (six bullet points concerning 'Enrichment,' 4 bullet points concerning 'Phasing').
242 *Framework Agreement*, pp. 1–2 (five bullet points concerning Fordow).
243 *Framework Agreement*, pp. 2–3 (four bullet points concerning Natanz).
244 *Framework Agreement*, pp. 3–4 (six bullet points concerning 'Reactors and Reprocessing,' and 4 bullet points concerning 'Phasing').
245 *Framework Agreement*, p. 3 (six bullet points concerning 'Reactors and Reprocessing').
246 *Framework Agreement*, pp. 2–4 (ten bullet points concerning 'Inspections and Transparency,' and four bullet points concerning 'Phasing').
247 *Framework Agreement*, pp. 3–4 (eight bullet points concerning 'Sanctions').
248 *Quoted in* "Iran Nuclear Talks: 'Historic' Agreement Struck," *BBC News*, 14 July 2015, http://www.bbc.com/news/world-middle-east-33518524.
249 *Quote from* from Theodore Roosevelt, "Citizenship in a Republic" (speech, Sorbonne, Paris, 23 April 1910). The full text of the speech is available at http://design.caltech.edu/erik/Misc/Citizenship_in_a_Republic.pdf.
250 "Key Excerpts of the Joint Comprehensive Plan of Action (JCPOA)," *Document Cloud*, 14 July 2015, https://www.documentcloud.org/documents/2165489-key-excerpts.html [hereinafter, JCPOA]; "Iran Nuclear Deal: Key Details," *BBC News*, 14 July 2015, http://www.bbc.com/news/world-middle-east-33521655.
251 *JCPOA*, pp. 1–2 (eight bullet points concerning 'Enrichment, Enrichment R&D, Stockpiles').
252 *JCPOA*, p. 2 (three bullet points concerning 'Arak, Heavy Water, Reprocessing').
253 *JCPOA*, pp. 2–3 (five bullet points concerning 'Transparency and Confidence Building Measures').
254 *JCPOA*, pp. 1–4 (generally, last two bullet points concerning 'Transparency and Confidence Building Measures,' 4 bullet points concerning 'Sanctions').
255 *JCPOA*, pp. 2–3 (last two bullet points concerning 'Transparency and Confidence Building Measures,' four bullet points concerning 'Sanctions').
256 *JCPOA*, p. 3 (four bullet points concerning 'Sanctions').
257 *JCPOA*, p. 4 (three bullet points concerning 'Dispute Resolution Mechanism')

Part V
Case studies in Asian financial markets

15 Disclosure and market manipulation

The case of CITIC Pacific

15.1 CITIC Pacific

CITIC Pacific (中信泰富; 'CITIC') is a conglomerate holding company headquartered in Hong Kong. It is 58 per cent owned by the state-owned CITIC Group in Beijing and has shareholders around the world. CITIC listed on the Stock Exchange of Hong Kong (HKEX) on 26 February 1986. CITIC is the parent company of a number of subsidiaries, including Sino Iron Pty Limited (SIPL), CITIC Pacific Mining Management Pty Limited (CITIC Mining), and Dah Chong Hong Holdings Limited (DCH). CITIC conducts a range of businesses, including special steel manufacturing, iron ore mining, and property development.

Table 15.1 lists the parties involved ('specified persons'), and they are all high-ranking members of CITIC's board.

On 12 September 2008, CITIC Hong Kong ('Holdings') Limited ('CITIC Holdings') held 29 per cent of CITIC's shares, and Yung, CITIC's Chairman, held 19 per cent of its issued share capital.[1]

Legal framework

Hong Kong's Securities and Futures Ordinance (SFO), chapter 571 section 277(1), prohibits the disclosure of false or misleading information inducing transactions. The disclosure occurs when 'a person discloses, circulates or disseminates, or authorizes or is concerned with the disclosure, circulation or dissemination of, information that is likely' to induce another person to subscribe for securities, or deal in futures contracts, in Hong Kong; to induce another person to sell or purchase securities; or to maintain, increase, reduce, or stabilize the price of securities for dealings in futures contracts.[2]

Table 15.1 Specified persons

Name	Role	Appointment date	Resignation date
Li Hsien Leslie Chang	Deputy Managing Director	1 April 2005	20 October 2008
Larry Chi-kin Yung	Chairman	1990	8 April 2009
Hung Ling Fan	Managing Director	1990	8 April 2009
Chung Hing Peter Lee	Deputy Managing Director	1990	1 April 2010
Chi Yin Chau	Executive Director	1 April 2006	20 October 2008

The information concerned must be false or misleading as to a material fact, or is false or misleading through the omission of a material fact.[3] Furthermore, the SFO stipulates that the person disseminating the false or misleading information must do so recklessly or negligently.[4]

Forex controversy

On 12 September 2008, the specified persons 'disclosed, circulated and/or disseminated, or alternatively authorized or were concerned in the disclosure, circulation and/or dissemination of a circular' on the HKEX website ('the Circular').[5] The Circular contained information about a disclosable and connected transaction in respect of the acquisition by DCH of a 49 per cent interest in FAW Toyota 4S company and a 50 per cent interest in Lexus 4S Company and related shareholders' loans. The Consideration is in the amount of HK$143,716,000. In the Circular, CITIC stated that 'the Directors [of CITIC] are not aware of any material adverse change in the financial or trading position of the Group since 31 December 2007, the date to which the latest published audited accounts of the Company were made up'.[6]

On 20 October 2008, CITIC issued a Profit Warning Announcement ('the Announcement') on losses linked to the Target Redemption Forward Contracts ('TRF Contracts') that CITIC entered into, to manage and hedge against the fluctuation against the US dollar (USD) of the Australian dollar (AUD), Euro (EUR), and the Renminbi (RMB). The Announcement identified a potential loss of HK$14.7 billion, primarily in connection with the TRF Contracts, and stated that CITIC 'becam[e] aware of the exposure arising from [primarily the TRF Contracts] on 7 September 2008'.[7] The date identified on the Statement notably precedes the publication date of the Circular (12 September 2008), as well as the 'Latest Practicable Date' identified within the Circular (9 September 2008).

In fact, a material adverse change arose in CITIC's financial position, originating from the various TRF Contracts that CITIC had entered into. This rendered the Statement false and misleading; as of 9 September 2008, the specified persons were aware of the material adverse change. This is clear from the Announcement, which provided that CITIC 'became aware of the exposure arising from [primarily the TRF Contracts] on 7 September 2008', which is prior to the publication of the Circular and the 'Latest Practicable Date' identified in the Circular.

The material adverse change in CITIC's financial position manifested in the estimated mark-to-market losses on the TRF Contracts, supplemented by the fact that CITIC had substantially overhedged its AUD exposure under the TRF Contract. Both the estimated mark-to-market losses and the amount of AUD deliverable under the TRF Contracts are identified in a Scenario Analysis prepared by CITIC's Finance Department on 4 September 2008 ('the Scenario Analysis'), which determined the mark-to-market loss and deliverable AUD under the TRF Contracts.

Table 15.2 Mark-to-market loss

AUD/USD spot rate[8]	*EUR/USD spot rate*	*Mark-to-market loss*
0.85	1.45	HK$4.6 billion
0.82	1.43	HK$6.6 billion
0.80	1.40	HK$8.6 billion

Table 15.3 Amount of deliverable AUD

AUD/USD spot rate	Deliverable AUD
0.85	AUD$6.7 billion
0.82	AUD$7.7 billion
0.80	AUD$8.6 billion

On 4 September 2008, the spot rates of the AUD and EUR were 0.83 and 1.45, respectively. Based on the Scenario Analysis, the estimated mark-to-market loss would therefore be between HK$4.6 billion and HK$6.6 billion. Put in perspective, this represented 105 per cent to 152 per cent of CITIC's net profit for the first six months of 2008; 42 per cent to 61 per cent of CITIC's net profit for the whole year of 2007; and 7.5 per cent to 10.9 per cent of CITIC's net asset value as of 30 June 2008. That same day, the estimated amount of deliverable AUD under the TRF Contracts were between AUD$6.7 billion (HK$43.6 million) and AUD$7.7 billion (HK$50.2 billion). This is substantially higher than the AUD$500 million exposure that the TRF Contracts were intended to hedge.

On 7 September 2008, the specified persons conducted another scenario analysis, which determined that, on 29 August 2008, the AUD/USD spot rate was 0.86 and the mark-to-market loss for CITIC arising from the AUD TRF Contracts was approximately HK$3.12 billion. This scenario analysis also determined the updated mark-to-market loss and deliverable AUD numbers (see Table 15.4 and 15.5).

On 9 September 2008 – the 'Latest Practicable Date' identified in the Circular – the AUD/USD and EUR/USD spot rates remained at a low level, around 0.81 and 1.42 respectively. Each and any estimated mark-to-market loss and the substantial overhedging of CITIC's AUD exposure therefore had a high material impact on CITIC's 2008 financial results and constituted a material adverse change in CITIC's financial position. The unauthorized trades were a gross exaggeration of hedging – AUD$9 billion was taken out to cover against an AUD$1.6 billion prospective acquisition and capital expenditure. The subsequent currency decline, from 98.5 per cent against the USD to less than 10 per cent, all constituted losses against CITIC.[9] The Statement was likely

Table 15.4 Mark-to-market loss

AUD/USD spot rate	EUR/USD spot rate	Mark-to-market loss
0.82	1.43	HK$6.6 billion
0.80	1.40	HK$8.6 billion

Table 15.5 Amount of deliverable AUD

AUD/USD spot rate	Deliverable AUD
0.82	AUD$7.7 billion
0.80	AUD$8.6 billion

made to maintain the price of CITIC's securities in Hong Kong despite the risky actions taken.

On 20 October 2008, Yung disclosed that CITIC suffered HK$15 billion in losses to 'unauthorized trades'.[10] CITIC subsequently faced questioning from the Hong Kong Securities and Futures Commission and judgment from the Market Misconduct Tribunal, both about the severe delays in their disclosure. The situation was especially exacerbated because 'the Directors [were] not aware of any material adverse change in the financial or trading position of the Group since 31 December 2007'.[11] The MMT ultimately determined that the Specified Persons engaged in market misconduct in contravention of section 277(1) of the SFO. When the shares of CITIC resumed trading, the share price had fallen by some 75 per cent since the previous close.[12]

15.2 Ethical analysis

The Hong Kong SFO rule against a company giving false and misleading information to the market with the intent to manipulate the price of the company's shares is clearly based on ethical principles. Indeed, ultimately, ethics is the grounding for almost all legal and regulatory statutes. For example, it is obvious the law against stealing (almost universal in its existence) is based on the ethical principle that stealing is wrong. As we saw in Chapter 8 stealing is immoral when evaluated under all moral theories, from utilitarianism and deontology to virtue ethics. In this case study, and the ones in Chapters 14–18, we discover why a particular act proscribed by regulators is not only illegal but also unethical. The aim is to use the tools that moral theories provide to help evaluate whether an act in an area of finance is right or wrong.

To tease out the ethical infringements of an act, first state the act as clearly, concisely, and objectively as possible. In the case of CITIC, the company acted as follows (the Act):

> CITIC did not disclose the loss from its hedging activities, which were substantial, to shareholders and the market in its Circular, disseminated for the main purpose to inform about the purchase of a 49 per cent interest in FAW Toyota 4S company and a 50 per cent interest in Lexus 4S Company. From the facts available, CITIC knew about the losses. On the contrary, the Circular stated that the Directors were not aware of any material adverse change in the financial or trading position of the Group.

Applying deontological theory

The basic tenet of deontology or duty-based ethics is that the agent has a moral duty to follow accepted ethical principles. There are two principles relevant in the CITIC case. The first is the principle of full disclosure (truth telling). The management of a company is obliged to make full disclosure of relevant and material information to shareholders and the market so the latter two can make financial decisions with full knowledge. The second relevant ethical principle is the principle of fiduciary duty. Fiduciary agents, in this case the directors and senior management of CITIC, have a duty to put the interest of their clients, or those who entrust them with the fiduciary responsibilities, first. These principles are fully accepted by the financial community pretty much around the world.

The directors and senior management of CITIC violated both the principles when they failed to disclose the forex hedging losses to the market and shareholders. CITIC management had prior knowledge of these losses, but they did not tell the public about the losses. To put it simply, management and the board of CITIC lied in the Circular. The Act was, therefore, wrong.

Applying justice theory

The form of justice theory most relevant to finance and business is commutative justice. It is the form of justice relevant to transactions or exchanges. Commutative justice demands fair prices for both the buyer and seller. The determination of fair prices requires information for both parties. Therefore, one crucial criterion for an exchange to be fair to both parties is that the parties have access to pertinent information about the transaction.

There are at least two transactions taking place in this CITIC case. First, there is the transaction between the company and the shareholders and potential shareholders. Announcing a purchase of assets may have the effect of making the acquirer seem more attractive, depending on the asset acquired and the price of acquisition. By not informing the public of adverse losses, the share price did not fall. Investors who bought CITIC shares at the manipulated price, therefore, were harmed because the price was not a fair one.

The second transaction is the one between the seller or sellers of the assets, FAW Toyota 4S and Lexus 4S. If the transaction was done through a share swap, then the inflated price of CITIC stock, due to the price manipulation, was not a fair price for the seller or sellers.

In sum, CITIC directors and senior management acted unjustly when they did not disclose information about the forex losses and lied about the absence of any material change in the financial condition of the company.

Applying virtue ethics

According to virtue ethics, the character of the moral agent is determinative of the ethical valuation of an act. A virtuous character possesses the virtues. One undisputed virtue is the virtue of honesty. In the CITIC case, the senior management and directors of the company did not exhibit honesty when they published the Circular. The question in evaluating an act under the virtue ethics framework is whether an ideal virtuous character who possesses the virtues would have acted in the same way. In the CITIC case, the answer is that an ideal virtuous character would not have lied and withheld pertinent information to shareholders and the market. Therefore, the Act in question was wrong.

Applying utilitarianism

Finally, we can evaluate the act in question in the CITIC case using a utilitarian framework. As you recall from Chapter 8, utilitarianism is a form of consequentialism. According to consequentialist theories, the rightness or wrongness of an act depends on the consequences of that act. In Chapter 8, we performed a utilitarian calculation of an act, weighing the good consequences against the bad consequences. If the good consequences outweigh the bad, then the act is ethical. If the bad outweigh the good, then the act is unethical. Utilitarianism is generally stated as the measure of the greatest good for the greatest number.

In the CITIC case, the good consequences were:

1 Management and directors could make the purchase of the assets FAW Toyota 4S and Lexus 4S with the use of an inflated and manipulated share price.
2 The management and directors received some good press and perhaps elevated their status as good custodians of the company.

These consequences were short term in nature and limited in the number of people affected.

The bad consequences were:

1 Investors who bought the shares at the time the Circular went public paid inflated prices that were manipulated using false and precluded information.
2 The sellers of the assets FAW Toyota 4S and Lexus 4S were given the wrong impression of the share price of CITIC. Consequently, they may have been paid less than the assets were worth.
3 The public was not given relevant information and was, in fact, lied to about the financial position of the company. This lack of disclosure and misinformation adds to the loss of trust in the market by the investors and the public in general.

The bad consequences of the act affected more people and ranged over a greater length of time than the good consequences. Weighing the two up, we conclude the bad consequences were greater than the good. Thus, the Act was unethical.

In all the evaluations of the act done above, the results were the same. The ethical analyses under different frameworks determine that the act done by senior management and directors of CITIC was unethical.

Notes

1 CITIC Group is the direct holding company of CITIC Holdings.
2 "Hong Kong's Securities and Futures Ordinance ('SFO') Chapter 571 Section 270(1)(a)," *Department of Justice of the Hong Kong Special Administrative Region*, accessed 27 July 2015, http://www.legislation.gov.hk/blis_pdf.nsf/6799165D2FEE3FA94825755E0033E532/5167961DDC96C3B7482575EF001C7C2D/$FILE/CAP_571_e_b5.pdf.
3 Ibid.
4 Ibid.
5 "In the Matter of the Listed Securities of CITIC Limited (Formerly Known as CITIC Pacific Limited) and Others: Notice to the Market Misconduct Tribunal Pursuant to Section 252(2) and Schedule 9 of the Securities and Futures Ordinance, CAP. 571," *Market Misconduct Tribunal*, 11 September 2014, accessed 28 July 2015, http://www.mmt.gov.hk/eng/rulings/CITIC.11092014_e.pdf.
6 "CITIC Pacific Limited Discloseable and Connected Transaction: Acquisition of a 49% Interest in FAW Toyota 4S Company and a 50% Interest in Lexus 4S Company and the Related Shareholders' Loans," *Hong Kong Stock Exchange*, 16 September 2008, 43, accessed 27 July 2015, http://www.hkexnews.hk/listedco/listconews/sehk/2008/0912/LTN20080912310.pdf.
7 Ibid., 5.
8 Spot rate: "The price quoted for immediate settlement on a commodity, a security or a currency. In currency transactions, the spot rate is influenced by the demands of individuals and businesses wishing to transact in a foreign currency, as well as by forex traders."
9 Maria Chan, "Company Exposed Itself to High Levels of Risk," *South China Morning Post* 22 (October 2008): A3.

10 Carol Chan, "Daughter Demoted," *South China Morning Post* 22 (October 2008): A1.
11 Dennis Eng and Fanny Fung, "SFC Urged to Launch CITIC Pacific Probe," *South China Morning Post* 22 (October 2008): A3.
12 Jonathan Cheng and Carlos Tejada, "CITIC Pacific Raided Over Currency Bets," *Wall Street Journal* 6, April 2009, accessed 3 August 2015, http://online.wsj.com/article/SB123880204272688577.html.

16 Insider trading

The case of Huiyuan Juice

16.1 Huiyuan Juice Group

China Huiyuan Juice Group Limited (中国汇源果汁集团有限公司; 'Huiyuan Juice') is a leading fruit and vegetable juice company in China.[1] It manufactures and sells juice and other beverage products, including fruit juice, vegetable juice, nectars, bottled water, tea, and dairy drinks.[2] Huiyuan Juice was established in 1992 and is currently the largest privately owned juice producer in China.[3] On 23 February 2007, Huiyuan Juice listed on the Hong Kong Stock Exchange (HKEX), opening shares at HK$6.00.

Legal framework

Hong Kong's Securities and Futures Ordinance (SFO), chapter 571 section 270(1)(f)(i),[4] defines insider dealing as:

> When a person having received, directly or indirectly, from a person whom he knows or has reasonable cause to believe is contemplating or is no longer contemplating making a take-over offer for the corporation, information to that effect which he knows is inside information in relation to the corporation deals in the listed securities of the corporation or their derivatives, or in the listed securities of a related corporation of the corporation or their derivatives.

To constitute market misconduct, 'inside information' must be received from a person 'connected with the corporation'. For the purposes of the Market Misconduct Tribunal's (MMT) proceedings, a 'connected' person is broadly defined in section 247 of the SFO to include all those persons who may receive confidential, price-sensitive information by reason of their relationship with a company.

The key elements to consider when deciding whether an act constitutes insider trading are:

1 The information must both be material and non-public.
2 The trader has violated a fiduciary and/or legal duty to corporation and its shareholders.
3 The source of the information has a fiduciary and/or legal duty and the one who trades on this information knows the source is violating that duty.

Coca-Cola buy-out

On 29 August 2008, Huiyuan Juice shares closed at HK$4.14 per share. On 3 September 2008, ABN AMRO Asia Corporate Finance Limited announced, on behalf of Atlantic Industries – a wholly owned subsidiary of The Coca-Cola Company ('Coca-Cola') – three proposed voluntary conditional cash offers to acquire all of Huiyuan Juice's issued shares.[5] The primary share offer included HK$12.20 for each issued share listed on the HKEX, totalling HK$17.90 billion. Following the announcement, Huiyuan shares increased from HK$4.14 per share to HK$10.94 per share—a 164 per cent increase from its pre-offer price.[6]

Sun Min ('Min') and her husband, Peter Mo Fung ('Fung'), were both directors and shareholders of Transfield Resources Limited, a company involved in the shipping and trading business.[7] In July 2008, Sun Qiang Chang, a director at Huiyuan Juice,[8] approached Goldman Sachs inviting the investment bank to run an auction for shares held by major shareholders of Huiyuan Juice. Min and Fung submitted non-binding indicative bids later that month. Prior to Coca-Cola's buy-out announcement on 3 September 2008, there was no publicly available information regarding these bids or voluntary conditional cash offers.

From 30 July 2008 to 29 August 2008 – months ahead of the Cola-Cola buy-out announcement – Min bought 8,613,500 Huiyuan Juice shares on six separate occasions, at HK$3.78 and HK$4.66 (US$0.48–$0.60) per share. Min used three separate brokerage firms and four separate companies that she co-owned with Fung:

1 Perth Asset Management Limited using DBS Vickers (Hong Kong) Limited;
2 Bombetta Development Limited using BOCI Securities Limited;
3 Bartlock Investment Limited using Citi Private Bank; and
4 Transfield Asset Management Limited using Goldman Sachs (Asia) Securities Limited.

From 3 September 2008 to 4 September 2008 – within 48 hours of the buy-out offer being made public – Min sold all of their Huiyuan Juice shares at prices between HK$10.24 and HK$11.12, netting over HK$55.1 million (US$7.09 million) in profits.[9]

The proposed takeover was subject to an anti-monopoly review by the Chinese Ministry of Commerce, which was scheduled to finish on 20 March 2009.[10] On 17 March, it was reported that Coca-Cola was considering abandoning the deal, as Chinese authorities insisted on relinquishing the Huiyuan Juice brand name after acquisition.[11] On 18 March, the Ministry of Commerce disallowed the bid, citing market competition concerns.[12] The Ministry of Commerce rejected the acquisition on the grounds that the US soft drink giant would dominate the mainland market.[13]

Min denied having any knowledge about the take-over offer, whether through rumour or otherwise, and insisted the decision to purchase was part of a 'bottom feeding' trading strategy. Although she had close connections within the management of Huiyuan, there was no direct evidence that she had received price-sensitive information about the take-over from any insider. Rather, the case hinged on circumstantial and inferential evidence from Tera Cheung's ('Cheung') – Sun Min's secretary – diary. Min had asked Cheung to trade Huiyuan Juice's shares on her behalf. Entries dated 30 July 2008 and 1 August 2008 indicate references to Huiyuan Juice and notes about China's antitrust laws.[14] The phrase in the diary entries which the MMT viewed as the most discriminating evidence against Min was, '(1) someone is discussing about general offer, largest shareholder has agreed but the terms haven't [illegible], price too high; (2) Anti-trust Law in PRC, the State might not agree to sell. There are risk(s)'.[15] The MMT determined that although Min's diary did not identify the bidding company in the negotiations, it would nonetheless constitute insider information if the information came from any of the following classes of 'connected' persons:

1 A director, employee or officer of Huiyuan;
2 An officer of any subsidiary or related company;
3 A substantial shareholder of Huiyuan or a related company; or
4 A person occupying a position which may reasonably be expected to give him access to confidential price-sensitive information by virtue of a professional or business relationship with Huiyuan or any of its related companies. In respect of the takeover negotiations, this last category would include a member of the professional parties advising Huiyuan; namely, its investment bankers, bankers, business advisers, solicitors, and accountants.

According to the MMT, the diary entries show that Min (and possibly Peter) had knowledge of a potential take-over of Huiyuan. In particular, the phrase concerning the anti-trust law of China and the possibility the deal would be derailed by that law was a powerful determining factor for the MMT. Based on the diary entries of Tera Cheung, the MMT convicted Min for having dealt in 3.13 million Huiyuan shares in August 2008[16] and fined her HK$20 million (US$2.56 million).[17]

16.2 Ethical analysis

A detailed analysis of the ethics of insider trading was given in Chapter 10. There, we gave the arguments for viewing insider trading as unethical. We also discussed the arguments provided by proponents of legalizing insider trading. The arguments for the latter are based on market efficiency, which is an economic reason, not an ethical one. Moreover, the empirical evidence that insider trading increases market efficiency is still debatable. Market efficiency is, perhaps, one positive outcome of insider trading based on a neoliberal economic perspective. As the first section of this book shows, however, there are three paradigms of finance: (1) modern finance theory, (2) behavioural finance, and (3) Islamic finance. Viewed from the perspective of behavioural finance, the negative outcomes of insider trading are a loss of trust in the market and the damaging belief that markets are rigged. These beliefs may be even more significant and consequential than the market efficiency outcomes.

In the Huiyuan case, was Min right to trade on insider information she was judged to have received? There are two main reasons why her insider trading was unethical. First, there is the fairness issue. Second, there is the utilitarian argument that the negative outcomes of pervasive insider trading outweigh the positive outcome of efficient price recovery.

Fairness argument

As mentioned in Chapter 10, fairness does not require that all parties in the market possess the same information. Some players have superior information due to in-depth research, intellectual perspicacity, or years of market experience. Fairness is, therefore, not an issue when investors gain supernormal profits due to skill, hard work, and just pure luck. However, fairness does require all market players to have access to the same information. The fact that insider information is not available to everyone makes the practice unfair. Why should insiders be able to profit from information they obtained by dint of their privileged positions? Insider trading is like playing poker with a marked deck. In the end, the game is so corrupted, nobody plays anymore and the game is over – permanently.

Deontological argument: violating an ethical principle

Min received the information about the Coca Cola takeover of Huiyuan from an insider. Min was the tippee, while the person who gave her the information was the tipper. As we mentioned in Chapter 10, both the tipper and the tippee are guilty of insider trading even if the tippee has nothing to do with the companies involved. The MMT did not discover who the tipper was and Min did not reveal the name of the person. Most likely, the tipper was employed by Atlantic Industries, Coca-Cola, ABN AMRO, or the law firm working on the takeover. In any case, the tipper broke her fiduciary duty to the client, the corporation, or the shareholders. This violation of fiduciary duty is unethical because it is the breaking of a key principle in finance. While the tipper broke a major rule, the tippee, Min, did not have a fiduciary duty because she was not employed or had any financial involvement with Huiyuan, Atlantic Industries or Coca-Cola. However, she was trading on stolen goods because insider information is, after all, stolen. There is no doubt Min knew of the nature of the information as it had not gone public yet. Despite this knowledge, she deliberately profited from stolen information by buying large amounts of shares of Huiyuan and selling them within 48 hours of the takeover announcement. She was, therefore, party to theft.

Consequentialism: loss of trust in markets

When Min traded on insider information, she was adding to a systemic problem of damaged trust in the markets. Trust is a virtue that underlies financial markets. We cannot always and solely rely on laws to ensure players are true to their word and do not cheat. There is an implicit agreement in all markets that players will be honest. As the ultimatum game described in Chapter 5 demonstrates, people are not just self-interested profit maximizers. People are also motivated by the principle of fairness. When players realize that the markets are rigged, some will stay out of the market while some will also indulge in rigging the market. Ultimately, the markets become dysfunctional and fail in their roles as efficient allocators of capital. This consequence must be weighed against the arguable positive outcome of efficient price discovery.

The MMT was likely cognizant of the systemic negative consequence of pervasive insider trading. The regulator, like most regulators, is concerned with maintaining the integrity of the financial markets. It therefore pursued the Huiyuan case because it wanted to make sure the market got the message that insider trading is not tolerated.

Notes

1 "China Huiyuan Juice Group: 1886 Stock Exchange of Hong Kong Limited," *Bloomberg Business*, accessed 4 August 2015, http://www.bloomberg.com/research/stocks/snapshot/snapshot.asp?capId=32444159.

2 Ibid.
3 "Huiyuan Juice Set for HK Listing," *People's Daily*, 10 February 2007, accessed 28 July 2015, http://english.people.com.cn/200702/10/eng20070210_349100.html.
4 "Hong Kong's Securities and Futures Ordinance ('SFO') Chapter 571 Section 270(1)(a)," *Department of Justice of the Hong Kong Special Administrative Region*, 1 January 2013, accessed 27 July 2015, http://www.legislation.gov.hk/blis_ind.nsf/d2769881999f47b3482564840019d2f9/51eccb21e85422ae48257ae50024874b?OpenDocument.
5 "In the Matter of the Listed Securities of China Huiyuan Juice Group Limited: Notice to the Market Misconduct Tribunal Pursuant to Section 252(2) and Schedule 9 of the Securities and Futures Ordinance, CAP. 571," *Webb-Site Reports*, 13 March 2012, accessed 2 August 2015, http://webb-site.com/codocs/MMT120313.pdf.
6 Stephanie Wong, "Coca-Cola to Buy China's Huiyuan for $2.3 Billion (Update 4)," *Bloomberg Business*, 3 September 2008, accessed 4 August 2015, http://www.bloomberg.com/apps/news?pid=20601087&sid=aI9_PX_Btrqs&refer=home.
7 "In the Matter of the Listed Securities of China Huiyuan Juice Group Limited: Notice to the Market Misconduct Tribunal Pursuant to Section 252(2) and Schedule 9 of the Securities and Futures Ordinance, CAP. 571," *Webb-Site Reports*, 13 March 2012, accessed 2 August 2015, http://webb-site.com/codocs/MMT120313.pdf.
8 Sun Qiang Chang was also a non-executive director at Gourmet Grace International Limited, a major shareholder of Huiyuan.
9 "In the Matter of the Listed Securities of China Huiyuan Juice Group Limited: Notice to the Market Misconduct Tribunal Pursuant to Section 252(2) and Schedule 9 of the Securities and Futures Ordinance, CAP. 571," *Webb-Site Reports*, 13 March 2012, accessed 2 August 2015, http://webb-site.com/codocs/MMT120313.pdf.
10 Xinhua, "Coca-Cola Purchase of Huiyuan 'Still Under Antimonopoly Review'," *China Daily*, 16 March 2009, accessed 7 June 2015, http://www.chinadaily.com.cn/china/2009-03/16/content_7584295.htm.
11 Sundeep Tucker, "Coca-Cola's $2.4bn China deal at risk," *Financial Times*, 17 March, 2009, accessed 5 August 2015, http://www.ft.com/cms/s/0/daf851e8-1327-11de-a170-0000779fd2ac.html.
12 Ibid.
13 Peter Wang, Mark Allen Cohen, and Stephen G. Harris, "Coca-Cola/Huiyuan Deal Is First Acquisition Blocked By China Antitrust Review," *Mondaq*, 25 March 2009, accessed 2 August 2015, http://www.mondaq.com/article.asp?articleid=76710.
14 Wang Duan and Dai Tian, "Tribunal to Hold Last Hearing into Huiyuan Insider Trading Case," *Caixin Online*, 23 October 2012, accessed 4 August 2015, http://english.caixin.com/2012-10-23/100451000.html.
15 "In the Matter of the Listed Securities of China Huiyuan Juice Group Limited: Notice to the Market Misconduct Tribunal Pursuant to Section 252(2) and Schedule 9 of the Securities and Futures Ordinance, CAP. 571 Amended Pursuant to Section 15 of Schedule 9 of the Ordinance by Order of the Market Misconduct Tribunal," *Market Misconduct Tribunal*, 14 September 2012, accessed 2 August 2015, http://www.mmt.gov.hk/eng/rulings/Amended.FS.Notice.Huiyuan.14.9.2012_e.pdf.
16 "Case of Insider Trade Settled," *Flanders-China Chamber of Commerce*, 11 March 2013, accessed 4 August 2015, http://news.flanders-china.be/case-of-insider-trade-settled.
17 "The Report of the Market Misconduct Tribunal into Dealings in the Shares of China Huiyuan Juice Group Limited on and between 30 July 2008 to 4 September 2008," *Market Misconduct Tribunal*, 10 May 2013, http://www.mmt.gov.hk/eng/reports/Huiyuan.Report.Part.II_e.pdf.

17 Market manipulation, price rigging, and false trading
The case of Sino Katalytics

17.1 Sino Katalytics

Sino Katalytics Investment Corporation ('Sino Katalytics'), who has since changed its name to Capital VC Limited, is an investment holding company in Hong Kong and the People's Republic of China.[1] Sino Katalytics's shares were listed on the Stock Exchange of Hong Kong on 23 October 2003, when 50 million shares were made available to professional investors.

Legal framework

False trading

Hong Kong's Securities and Futures Ordinance (SFO), chapter 571 section 274(1), provides that false trading takes place when 'a person does anything or causes anything to be done, with the intention that, or being reckless as to whether, it has, or is likely to have, the effect of creating a false or misleading appearance of active trading in securities'. Additionally, section 274(3) further defines false trading as '[carrying] out, directly or indirectly, one or more transactions, with the intention that, or being reckless as to whether . . . [it is likely to have] the effect of creating an artificial price'. Section 274(5) recognizes – and prohibits – offers to purchase or sell securities 'at a price that is substantially the same as the price at which he . . . knows that an associate of his has made or proposes to make'.[2]

Price rigging

Section 275 defines price rigging as

> [entering] into or [carrying] out, directly or indirectly any fictitious or artificial transaction or device, with the intention that, or being reckless as to whether, it has the effect of maintaining, increasing, reducing, stabilising or causing fluctuations in the price of securities, or the price for dealings in futures contracts.

Stock market manipulation

Section 278 defines stock market manipulation as

530 *Case studies in Asian financial markets*

[entering] into or [carrying] out, directly or indirectly, two or more transactions in securities of a corporation that by themselves or in conjunction with any other transaction increase, or are likely to increase, the price of any securities traded on a relevant recognised market.

Market misconduct

Mr Peter Yau Chung Hong ('Mr Yau') and Mr Duncan Chui Tak Keung ('Mr Chui') were Executive Directors at Sino Katalytics. From November 2005 to December 2005, Mr Chui began purchasing Sino Katalytics shares, becoming its single largest shareholder, controlling 26.25 per cent of its issued shares. On 2 July 2008, Mr Yau began purchasing Sino Katalytics shares under his own name and his wholly owned company, Sellwell International Enterprises Limited. By August 2008, Mr Yau controlled about 18.5 per cent of Sino Katalytics's issued shares, while Mr Chui controlled about 11.3 per cent. On 28 August 2008, Mr Yau and Mr Chui engaged in an off-market trade whereby Mr Chui acquired 55 million shares from Mr Yau. Consequently, Mr Yau's shares amounted to 12.6 per cent and Mr Chui's shares amounted to 23 per cent of issued shares.

Sino Katalytics was a thinly traded stock.[3] Between July 2007 and December 2008, Sino Katalytics raised HK$121 million in capital through two rights issues and two placements. On 16 December 2008, Sino Katalytics issued bonds in the principal amount of HK$8.1 million convertible into new shares, representing approximately 19.48 per cent of the issued share capital. From 2–9 January 2009 (the 'specified period'), Mr Yau and Mr Chui heavily transacted in Sino Katalytics's shares:

Table 17.1 Purchases by Mr Yau (volume and price per share)

Date	Shares purchased (shares)	Price (cents)
2 January 2009	2,000,000	4.2
5 January 2009	50,000	3.8
	50,000	3.7
	2,000,000	4.1
6 January 2009	2,050,000	4.1
	700,000	4.2

Table 17.2 Purchases by Mr Chui (volume and price per share)

Date	Shares purchased (shares)	Price (cents)
7 January 2009	400,000	4.2
	1,950,000	4.1
8 January 2009	250,000	4.1
	2,200,000	4.2
9 January 2009	850,000	5.5
	100,000	5.4
	1,300,000	5.1
	2,200,000	5.0
	1,000,000	4.9

Table 17.3 Sales by Mr Yau (volume and price per share)

Date	Shares sold (shares)	Price (cents)	
9 January 2009	2,000,000	5.0	Via Quam
	1,000,000	5.1	Via Quam
	900,000	5.5	Via Quam
	1,000,000	4.9	Via Barclays/UOB
	2,000,000	5.0	Via Barclays/UOB
	1,000,000	5.1	Via Barclays/UOB

Table 17.4 Percentage of sales and purchases of total trade in shares

Date	Sales via Mr Yau	Purchases via Mr Chui
2 January 2009	100%	
5 January 2009	86%	
6 January 2009	90%	
7 January 2009		92%
8 January 2009		85%
9 January 2009	89%	62%

During the specified period, Mr Yau and Mr Chui were responsible for the bulk of Sino Katalytics's purchases and sales, repeatedly transacting between one another to artificially pad Sino Katalytics's stock. For example, on 9 January 2009, over 97.2 per cent of Mr Chui's acquired shares were purchased from Mr Yau within 20 minutes of the market close.[4] The market price of the shares at the close was HK$0.055, a rise of 31 per cent over the previous day's close. By the end of the specified period, Sino Katalytics's shares appeared drastically more valuable (see Table 17.5).

By 12 January 2009, Mr Yau and Mr Chui had ceased transacting Sino Katalytics's shares. On 7 January 2009, Mr Yau proposed a placement of Sino Katalytics's shares to Guoyuan Securities Brokerage (Hong Kong) Limited. Those discussions continued until 12 January 2009, when Sino Katalytics's board elected to proceed with the placement, to raise another HK$8.31 million by allotting new shares equivalent to 20 per cent of Sino Katalytics's issued share capital. The placement was undersubscribed by 19 per cent and raised HK$6.76 million.

Table 17.5 Price and turnover of Sino Katalytic shares

Date	Average turnover (shares)	Price (cents)
5 January 2009	2,600,000	4.1
6 January 2009	2,600,000	4.2
7 January 2009	2,600,000	4.2
8 January 2009	2,600,000	4.2
9 January 2009	8,850,000	5.5
12 January 2009	650,000	5.4

In interviews with the Securities and Futures Commission of Hong Kong, both Mr Yau and Mr Chui denied collaborating on 9 January 2009 to inflate Sino Katalytics's share price, despite evidence of frequent telephone contact and the scale of the transaction 20 minutes prior to the market close. The Market Misconduct Tribunal (MMT) determined that the 9 January 2009 transactions between Mr Yau and Mr Chui constituted market misconduct undertaken in a manner designed to manipulate the market in Sino Katalytics's shares ahead of the placement, in violation of sections 274, 275, and 278 of the SFO. The MMT also found Mr Yau and Mr Chui culpable of false trading and price rigging.

17.2 Ethical analysis

Market manipulation is the practice of buying or selling securities with the aim of creating a false or misleading impression about the price. Manipulators want to induce other investors to buy or sell securities at false prices. In this case, Mr Yau and Mr Chui employed the manipulation methods of price rigging and false trading to achieve the goal of increasing the share price of Sino Katalytics prior to a share placement to obtain a falsely high placement price.

Ethics of market manipulation

Chapter 10 (section 10.3) gave a detailed discussion of the ethics of market manipulation. There is general agreement that market manipulation is bad for markets. Harm is done to the integrity of the market and to players in the market who are either underpaid for the securities they sell or overpay for securities they buy. In the case of Sino Katalytics, subscribers to the share placement were harmed because they paid a price inflated by the false trading of Mr Chui and Mr Yau. In contrast, little good results from market manipulation. Good consequences flow largely to the manipulators. Both the manipulators in this case profited because they received a higher price for their shares than the fair market value. In manipulating the share price, market efficiency was hampered because the price was pushed away from its fundamental value. This result leads to increasing the level of distrust in capital markets.

Consequently, the greatest harm caused by market manipulation is to the integrity of the capital markets. People trade in a market if they believe it is fair and free. Markets function efficiently when they are fair and transparent. It follows that if the integrity of markets is harmed, then their efficiency is also impaired. This consequence is neither good nor desirable. As the CFA Code of Ethics and Standards of Professional Conduct states:

> If investors believe that capital market participants – investment professionals and firms – cannot be trusted with their financial assets or that the capital markets are unfair such that only insiders can be successful, they will be unlikely to invest or, at the very least, will require a higher risk premium. Decreased investment capital can reduce innovation and job creation and hurt the economy and society as a whole. Reduced trust in capital markets can also result in a less vibrant, if not smaller, investment industry.[5]

From a utilitarian perspective, therefore, market manipulation is unethical because the practice results in more bad outcomes than good ones. Thus, Mr Chui and Mr Yau engaged in unethical behaviour in manipulating the price of Sino Katalytics.

Price rigging

According to the categorization of market manipulation given in Chapter 10 (section 10.3), the type of market manipulation in which Mr Chui and Mr Yau engaged is a form of trade-based runs. This style of manipulation involves the manipulator taking either a long or short position in a stock. In the Sino Katalytics case, the manipulators took long positions. They pumped up the share price by buying and selling to each other. The manipulator then inflates or deflates the price of the stock, while increasing the liquidity of the stock. Mr Chui and Mr Yau manipulated the price by trading the stock, hence the name 'trade-based run'. This manipulation method leads to a steep price increase as desired by the manipulators. In sum, the price of Sino Katalytics was rigged.

Commutative justice demands transparency and fair pricing in the exchange of goods and in business transactions. Each person is entitled to be given that to which he is due in exchange transactions. Accordingly, in financial trades, sellers give the buyers a fair price for securities sold, according to the rule of the price system, which in this case is the free market system. In other words, in capital markets, the price is determined by fair market demand and supply. Everyone who trades in the markets understands and agrees to this pricing mechanism. In commutative justice, the principle is 'Exchange genuine equivalents'.[6] Equality is expected between market value and the monetary price of the security. This equivalence makes the exchange just because each party receives what is hers and neither party to the exchange gives too much to the other.

The price of Sino Katalytics's shares at the time of placement was not discovered through market efficiency. Instead, the price emerged out of a rigged system of false trading. From a justice and fairness perspective we conclude that price rigging is unethical.

False trading

Mr Chui and Mr Yau were Executive Directors at Sino Katalytics. As Executive Directors they are ethically obligated to perform their fiduciary duty. This duty is fourfold. First, Executive Directors should act in the best interest of the shareholders and the company. Second, Executive Directors are obliged to exercise their powers for a proper purpose. Third, Executive Directors are to avoid conflicts between personal interests and the interests of the company. Fourth, Executive Directors should not make secret profits.

According to the CFA Code of Ethics and Standards of Professional Conduct, 'The duty required in fiduciary relationships exceeds what is acceptable in many other business relationships because a fiduciary is in an enhanced position of trust'.[7] Both legal and ethical standards expect a high level of loyalty, prudence, and care from fiduciaries in the performance of their duties.

Both Mr Chui and Mr Yau failed to uphold their duty as Executive Directors and therefore violated the principle of fiduciary. In deontological terms, the two manipulators broke an ethical principle essential in finance. The two acted unethically when they engaged in false trading of Sino Katalytics's shares.

Notes

1 "About Us," *Capital* VC *Limited*, accessed 27 July 2015, http://www.capital-vc.com.
2 Section 245(1) defines an associate as 'any employee or partner of the person' or 'any corporation of which the person is a director'.

3 See Exhibit 1 (Stock Historical Data records for the period 1 December 2008 to 13 February 2009).
4 "In the Matter of the Listed Securities of Sino Katalytics Investment Corporation: Notice to the Market Misconduct Tribunal Pursuant to Section 252(2) and Schedule 9 of the Securities and Futures Ordinance, CAP. 571," *Market Misconduct Tribunal*, 12 April 2011, accessed 28 July 2015, http://www.mmt.gov.hk/eng/rulings/SKIC.Ruling.12042011.pdf.
5 CFA Institute, *Standards of Practice Handbook*, 11th ed. (Charlottesville, VA: CFA Institute, 2014), 2.
6 Peter Koslowski, *Principles of Ethical Economy* 17 (Netherlands: Springer Science & Business Media, 2001), 185.
7 CFA Institute, *Standards of Practice Handbook*, 82.

18 Insider dealing

The case of Water Oasis

18.1 Water Oasis Group

Water Oasis Group Limited (奧思集團; 'Water Oasis') is an investment holding company that distributes skincare and beauty products. Water Oasis is also involved in the distribution of beauty service equipment and products: retail sale of skincare and cosmetic products, property holding business, and operation of a florist shop in Hong Kong. It has operations in Hong Kong, Macau, Taiwan, Singapore, and the People's Republic of China. Water Oasis was listed on the Stock Exchange of Hong Kong (HKEX) in March 2002.

Prior to 6 July 2012, Salina Lai Si Yu ('Ms Yu') was an Executive Director, the Chief Executive Officer, and a substantial shareholder of Water Oasis. As of 19 January 2012, Ms Yu held 167,683,760 shares in Water Oasis, representing 21.94 per cent of the issued share capital. Of those shares, 1.57 million shares were held in her security account at Hang Seng Bank Limited; 4.78 million shares were held in her securities account at Tung Shing Securities (Brokers) Limited; and the remaining shares were held in physical share certificates.[1]

Legal framework

Hong Kong's Securities and Futures Ordinance (SFO), chapter 571 section 270(1)(a) provides that insider dealings have taken place

> when a person connected with the corporation and having information which he knows is inside information to the corporation deals in the listed securities of the corporation or their derivatives . . . [or] counsels or procures another person to deal in such listed securities or derivatives, knowing or having reasonable cause to believe that the other person will deal in them.[2]

H_2O Plus termination

As of 30 November 2008, Water Oasis was the exclusive distributor of H_2O Plus LLC's (H_2O) skincare products in Mainland China and Taiwan. Water Oasis was also an exclusive distributor of the same products in Hong Kong, Macau, and Singapore. As of 30 September 2011, Water Oasis operated 307 H_2O retail outlets comprising 17 in Hong Kong, 1 in Macau, 274 in Mainland China, 14 in Taiwan, and 1 in Singapore. The H_2O business was a main contributor to Water Oasis's turnover. On 30 September 2011,

H_2O's net profits in Mainland China and Taiwan amounted to HK$17.7 million, approximately 21.82 per cent of Water Oasis's total net profit of HK$81.1 million.

On 20 January 2012, Bob Seidl ('Mr Seidl'), H_2O's President and Chief Executive Officer, conducted a telephone conference with Water Oasis's senior management, namely Ms Yu, Mr Henry Au (Water Oasis's Chief Financial Officer) ('Mr Au'), and Mr Kam Shui 'Erastus' Yu (Water Oasis's Executive Director) ('Mr Yu'). During the telephone conference, Mr Seidl informed Ms Yu that H_2O would terminate Water Oasis's exclusive distributorship in H_2O's products in Mainland China and Taiwan with immediate effect due to Water Oasis's breaches of the Mainland China and Taiwan distributorship agreements.[3] Later that day, Mr Seidl emailed a cover letter and two termination notices to Ms Yu. The two notices terminated the exclusive distributorship in Mainland China and Taiwan immediately.

Before making the announcement public, the general public was unaware of H_2O's specific contributions to Water Oasis's net profits. However, Water Oasis's Board, including Ms Yu, knew of it. Furthermore, people who were likely to deal in the shares of Water Oasis and recognize the significance of H_2O's termination of distributorship to the share price did not have knowledge of the termination.

Approximately 20 minutes after the telephone conference with Mr Seidl, Ms Yu instructed Ms Lucinda Cheung ('Ms Cheung'), her relationship manager at Hang Seng Private Banking, to sell all of the 1.57 million shares in Water Oasis held in her account at Hang Seng Bank. In the recording of the telephone conversation between Ms Yu and Ms Cheung, Ms Yu denied having any special news and stated that 'we abide by the rules'.[4] Ms Cheung reminded Ms Yu that her average price of acquisition for her Water Oasis shares at Hang Seng Bank was HK$0.83 and the shares were trading around HK$1.44 to HK$1.45. Ms Cheung also told Ms Yu that trading in shares of Water Oasis was thin, especially compared with the quantity of shares Ms Yu was selling. Ms Yu instructed Ms Cheung to sell all of her shares anyway, as long as there was a profit. Ms Yu provided a specific minimum price of HK$1.00 per share and instructed Ms Cheung to sell immediately. Later that day, all of Ms Yu's 1.57 million shares were sold at an average price of HK$1.40.

On the same day that Ms Yu sold her shares held at Hang Seng Bank (20 January 2012), Water Oasis publicly announced the termination of the exclusive distributorship of H_2O's products in Mainland China and Taiwan. The announcement stated that H_2O's operation in Mainland China and Taiwan contributed to approximately 21.8 per cent of Water Oasis's audited consolidated net profits for the year. On 26 January 2012, the first trading day after the announcement, Water Oasis's shares dropped 14.08 per cent to close at HK$1.22. On the same day, the Hang Seng Index rose 329 points, or 1.64 per cent, to 20,439.[5]

Ms Yu was determined to be a person connected with Water Oasis having information about the termination and contribution of H_2O's operations in Mainland China and Taiwan to Water Oasis's net profits. Ms Yu knew the information significantly impacted profits and was, therefore, material information in relation to Water Oasis. Despite this knowledge Ms Yu traded in the shares of Water Oasis by selling them prior to the announcement.

The Market Misconduct Tribunal (MMT) of Hong Kong charged Ms Yu with insider dealing in shares of Water Oasis. The MMT determined Ms Yu to have engaged in market misconduct contrary to rules on insider dealing. Based on this finding, the MMT disqualified Ms Yu from being a director or being involved in the management of any listed corporation, without leave of the court, for a period of two years effective

15 February 2015. The MMT also ordered Ms Yu to disgorge HK$281,346, the profits she made from her insider dealing trade in Water Oasis.[6]

18.2 Ethical analysis

In the case study of Huiyuan Juice in Chapter 16, we argued insider trading is unethical using the support of ethical theories on justice, deontology, and consequentialism. Applying the three major ethical frameworks on the Huiyuan case study, we concluded insider trading is unethical.

The same arguments and methods apply to this case of insider dealing in Water Oasis shares by Ms Yu. In sum, there are four most common arguments against insider trading. First, the information used for insider trading is stolen. The information belongs to the corporation and not to the inside trader.

Second, the information advantage is unfair. Both parties in a stock transaction do not have equal knowledge because of differences in research or analysis. However, inside information is fundamentally different. The party without inside information is unable to obtain that information regardless of the extent and depth of research or analysis.

Third, insider trading reduces the size of the market because people are hesitant to participate in a market with significant insider trading. Experiments in behavioural finance show economic actors do not appreciate unequal and unfair behaviour. When participants in an experiment see others benefitting because of unfair behaviour, these participants forsake profits to punish the other participant who behaves unfairly. According to the current rational model of economics, this result cannot occur because economic agents maximize profits and do not give any consideration to values such as unfairness. However, in reality, people are offended by unfairness and prefer to opt out of a game or punish those who acted unfairly.[7] Hence, investors may stay out of the market if they observe significant insider trading. Fewer investors in a market results in a market that is less efficient, less liquid, and more variable.[8]

Fourth, and most appropriately for the Water Oasis case, there is the fiduciary duty argument. The underlying premise of this argument is that officers and directors have a fiduciary duty to their shareholders, which requires them to fully disclose any and all significant information that shareholders can benefit from knowing. Insider trading puts at risk the fiduciary relationships that are central to business. Officers and directors of companies should not participate in activities that constitute a conflict of interest to their duties. If interests of officers and directors are not aligned with the interests of shareholders, then people are much less likely to be willing to invest in companies. The fiduciary duty argument applies particularly to Ms Yu because she was both an Executive Board Director and the Chief Executive Officer (CEO) of Water Oasis.

Notes

1 "Notice to the Market Misconduct Pursuant to Section 252(2) and Schedule 9 of the Securities and Futures Ordinance CAP.571, In the Matter of the Listed Securities of Water Oasis Group Limited," *Market Misconduct Tribunal*, 2 August 2014, accessed 28 July 2015, http://www.mmt.gov.hk/eng/rulings/Water.Oasis.08082014_e.pdf.
2 "Hong Kong's Securities and Futures Ordinance ('SFO') Chapter 571 Section 270(1)(a)," *Department of Justice of the Hong Kong Special Administrative Region*, accessed 27 July 2015, http://www.legislation.gov.hk/blis_pdf.nsf/6799165D2FEE3FA94825755E0033E532/5167961DDC96C3B7482575EF001C7C2D/$FILE/CAP_571_e_b5.pdf.

3 Those breaches were financially irrelevant to the case at hand.
4 "Hong Kong's Securities and Futures Ordinance ('SFO') Chapter 571 Section 270(1)(a)," *Department of Justice of the Hong Kong Special Administrative Region*, accessed 27 July 2015, http://www.legislation.gov.hk/blis_pdf.nsf/6799165D2FEE3FA94825755E0033E532/5167961DDC96C3B7482575EF001C7C2D/$FILE/CAP_571_e_b5.pdf.
5 "SFC commences Market Misconduct Tribunal proceedings against former CEO of Water Oasis Group Limited," *Hong Kong Securities and Futures Commission*: Enforcement News, 14 August 2014, accessed 3 August 2015, http://www.sfc.hk/edistributionWeb/gateway/EN/news-and-announcements/news/enforcement-news/doc?refNo=14PR100.
6 "Market Misconduct Tribunal disqualifies Water Oasis's former CEO and orders disgorgement for insider dealing," *Hong Kong Securities and Futures Commission*: All News, 5 February 2015, accessed 3 August 2015, http://www.sfc.hk/edistributionWeb/gateway/EN/news-and-announcements/news/doc?refNo=15PR11.
7 Samuel Clowes Huneke, "Raj Rajaratnam and Insider Trading," *Seven Pillars Institute for Global Finance and Ethics: Case Studies*, accessed 27 July 2015, http://sevenpillarsinstitute.org/case-studies/raj-rajaratnam-and-insider-trading-2.
8 Larry Sayler, "Ethical Analysis of Insider Trading," *Christian Business Faculty Association*, accessed 27 July 2015, http://www.cbfa.org/Sayler_Paper.pdf.

Bibliography

Online sources

"A New Capital Adequacy Framework," *Basel Committee on Banking Supervision*, June 1999, accessed http://www.bis.org/publ/bcbs50.pdf.

"About BIS," *Bank for International Settlements*, accessed 18 November 2014, http://www.bis.org/about/index.htm?l=2.

"About ETFs," *Bloomberg*, accessed 14 May 2014, http://www.bloomberg.com/markets/etfs/etf_about.html.

"About the Basel Committee," *Bank of International Settlements*, accessed 20 June 2014, http://www.bis.org/bcbs/about.htm.

"About the CFTC," *U.S. Commodity Futures Trading Commission*, http://www.cftc.gov/about/index.htm.

"About the IMF," *International Monetary Fund*, accessed 7 June 2013, http://www.imf.org/external/about.htm.

"About Us," *Capital VC Limited*, accessed 27 July 2015, http://www.capital-vc.com.

"About Us," *Indian Oil Corporation*, https://www.iocl.com/aboutus.aspx.

"About Us," *International Organization of Securities Commissions*, accessed 22 February 2014, http://www.iosco.org/about/.

"About Us," *NatGaz*, http://www.natgaz.com.lb/aboutus.aspx?aspxerrorpath=/default.aspx.

"Analysis of 12 CFR Part 44," *OCC*, 2014, accessed 5 April 2014, http://www.complinet.com/net_file_store/new_editorial/v/o/volcker-analysis.pdf.

"Apollo Home," *Apollo Global Management*, www.agm.com/Home.aspx.

"Applying Virtue Ethics: The Rajat Gupta Case," *Seven Pillars Institute for Global Finance and Ethics*, 11 February 2013, accessed 19 June 2014, http://sevenpillarsinstitute.org/morality-101/applying-virtue-ethics-the-rajat-gupta-case.

"Bank of America," *Investor Hub*, 19 August 2006, accessed http://investorshub.advfn.com/Bank-of-America-Corp-BAC-6675/.

"Bank Profits Head East," *The Economist*, 3 July 2012, accessed 21 April 2013, http://www.economist.com/comment/1505488.

"Basel Committee Membership," *Bank of International Settlements*, accessed http://www.bis.org/bcbs/membership.htm.

"Basel II: Under Fire," *Financial Times*, 21 August 2003.

"Basel III: A Global Regulatory Framework for More Resilient Banks and Banking Systems," *Basel Committee on Banking Supervision*, December 2010, revised 1 June 2011, accessed http://www.bis.org/publ/bcbs189.htm.

"Basel III: Phase In Arrangements," *Bank of International Settlements*, 2013, accessed, http://www.bis.org/bcbs/basel3/basel3_phase_in_arrangements.pdf.

"Basic Structure of Clearing and Settlement," *Japan Securities Clearing Corporation*, accessed 26 August 2014, http://www.jscc.co.jp/en/cash.html.

"Beginner's Guide to Financial Statements," *US Securities and Exchange Commission*, accessed 28 January 2015, www.sec.gov/pubs/begfinstmtguide.htm.

"BIS Quarterly Review, June 2013," *Bank of International Settlements*, accessed 25 June 2013, http://www.bis.org/publ/qtrpdf/r_qa1306.pdf.

"Bunching Definition," *Investopedia*, accessed 10 September 2014, http://www.investopedia.com/terms/b/bunching.asp.

"Case of Insider Trade Settled," *Flanders-China Chamber of Commerce*, 11 March 2013, accessed 4 August 2015, http://news.flanders-china.be/case-of-insider-trade-settled.

"China Huiyuan Juice Group: 1886 Stock Exchange of Hong Kong Limited," *Bloomberg Business*, accessed 4 August 2015, http://www.bloomberg.com/research/stocks/snapshot/snapshot.asp?capId=32444159.

"China," *Asia eTrading*, 15 October 2009, accessed 27 August 2014, http://asiaetrading.com/industry/clearing/china/.

"CIA Documents Acknowledge Its Role in Iran's 1953 Coup," *BBC News*, 20 August 2013, http://www.bbc.co.uk/news/world-middle-east-23762970.

"CITIC Pacific Limited Discloseable and Connected Transaction: Acquisition of a 49% Interest in FAW Toyota 4S Company and a 50% Interest in Lexus 4S Company and the Related Shareholders' Loans," *Hong Kong Stock Exchange*, 16 September 2008, 43, accessed 27 July 2015, http://www.hkexnews.hk/listedco/listconews/sehk/2008/0912/LTN20080912310.pdf

"Clearing," *ASX*, accessed 27 August 2014, http://www.asx.com.au/services/clearing.htm.

"Clearing and Settlement," *BM & FBOVESPA*, accessed 28 August 2014, http://www.bmfbovespa.com.br/en-us/services/post-trade-services/clearing-and-settlement/clearing-and-settlement.aspx?idioma=en-us.

"Clearing and Settlement," *CDS*, accessed 28 August 2014, http://www.cds.ca/cdsclearinghome.nsf/Pages/-EN-Clearingandsettlement?Open.

"Clearing and Settlement," *Credit Financial Risk*, www.credfinrisk.com/clearing.html.

"Clearing House Activities," *BOI Shareholding Ltd.*, 2007, accessed 27 August 2014, http://boislindia.com/Clearinghouse.html.

"Clearing Organizations," *U.S. Commodity Futures Trading Commission*, accessed 28 August 2014, http://www.cftc.gov/IndustryOversight/ClearingOrganizations/index.htm.

"Clearing Services," *DTCC*, accessed 28 August 2014, http://www.dtcc.com/clearing-services.aspx.

"Clearing Services," *HKEx*, accessed 27 August 2014, https://www.hkex.com.hk/eng/prod/clr/ClearingService.htm.

"Company Info," *EuroCCP*, accessed 28 August 2014, http://euroccp.com/content/company-info.

"Company Overview," *NYSE Euronext*, accessed 26 August 2014, http://www.nyx.com/who-we-are/company-overview. (The NYSE lists around 8,000 companies, representing over 55 different countries.)

"Complete Guide to Corporate Finance: Introduction – Types of Financial Institutions and Their Roles," *Investopedia*, accessed 4 April 2013, http://www.investopedia.com/walkthrough/corporate-finance/1/financial-institutions.aspx.

"Convertibles," *Investopedia*, accessed 13 May 2014, http://www.investopedia.com/terms/c/convertibles.asp.

"Core Principles of Effective Banking Supervision," *Basel Committee on Banking Supervision*, September 1997, accessed http://www.bis.org/publ/bcbs30a.pdf.

"Credit and Liquidity Programs and the Balance Sheet," *Board of Governors of the Federal Reserve System*, 7 January 2013, accessed 27 March 2014, http://www.federalreserve.gov/monetarypolicy/bst.htm.

"Current Signatories and Members Listed," *International Organization of Securities Commissions*, accessed http://www.iosco.org/library/index.cfm?section=mou_siglist.

"Declining US High Frequency-Trading," *The New York Times*, 15 October 2012, http://www.nytimes.com/interactive/2012/10/15/business/Declining-US-High-Frequency-Trading.html.

"Definition of Global Financial System," *Financial Times Lexicon*, accessed 27 March 2014, http://lexicon.ft.com/Term?term=global-financial-system.

"Derivatives," *Office of the Comptroller of the Currency*, accessed 25 August 2014, http://www.occ.gov/topics/capital-markets/financial-markets/trading/derivatives/index-derivatives.html.

"Differences Between Stockbrokers, Investment Advisors, and Financial Planners," *Forbes*, 20 March 2013, accessed 20 April 2013, http://www.forbes.com/sites/investopedia/2013/03/20/differences-between-stockbrokers-investment-advisors-and-financial-planners/.

"Diplomacy, Not Sanctions Key to Securing Iran Nuclear Deal," *RT*, 25 November 2013, http://rt.com/op-edge/role-of-diplomacy-iran-deal-263/.

"Dodd-Frank Act," *CFTC*, accessed 18 November 2014, http://www.cftc.gov/lawregulation/doddfrankact/index.htm.

"European Market Infrastructure Regulation (EMIR)," *Market Structure Partners*, accessed 18 November 2014, http://www.marketstructure.co.uk/european-legislation/european-market-infrastructure-regulation/#2014.

"Fact Sheet," *International Organization of Securities Commissions*, accessed November 2013, www.iosco.org.

"Fact Sheet: Parameters for a Joint Comprehensive Plan of Action regarding the Islamic Republic of Iran's Nuclear Program," *US Department of State*, 2 April 2015, http://www.state.gov/e/eb/tfs/spi/iran/fs/240539.htm.

"Federal Funds Rate," *Investopedia*, accessed 27 August 2013, http://www.investopedia.com/terms/f/federalfundsrate.asp.

"Field Listing: GDP (official exchange rate)," *Central Intelligence Agency: The World Fact Book*, accessed 15 April 2013, https://www.cia.gov/library/publications/the-world-factbook/fields/2195.html.

"Frequently Asked Questions About Checks and the Check Payments System," *Check Payment Systems Association*, accessed 12 June 2013, http://www.cpsa-checks.org/i4a/pages/index.cfm?pageid=1.

"Futures Sale Spurred May 6 Panic as Traders Lost Faith in Data," *Bloomberg*, 1 October 2010, www.bloomberg.com/news/2010-10-01/automatic-trade-of-futures-drove-may-6-stock-crash-report-says.html.

"GATS Training Model: Chapter 1 – Basic Purpose and Concepts," *World Trade Organization*, accessed http://www.wto.org/english/tratop_e/serv_e/cbt_course_e/c1s3p1_e.htm.

"GDP (current US$)," *The World Bank*, accessed 15 April 2013, http://data.worldbank.org/indicator/NY.GDP.MKTP.CD.

"General Information on the Regulation of Investment Advisers," *Securities Exchange Commission*, accessed 10 September 2014, http://www.sec.gov/divisions/investment/iaregulation/memoia.htm.

"Germany's new High-Frequency Trading Act," *Baker & McKenzie*, accessed 19 May 2013, http://www.bakermckenzie.com/files/Publication/837d847c-b132-40d7-b638-fecb6b858cb9/Presentation/PublicationAttachment/155464bb-d225-4498-a4b3-03971b885f33/AL_GermanyHighFrequencyTradingAct.pdf.

"Give Iran a Limited Right to Enrich," *Financial Times* (21 October 2013): 12.

"Glass–Steagall Act (1933)," *The New York Times*, accessed 20 March 2013, http://topics.nytimes.com/top/reference/timestopics/subjects/g/glass_steagall_act_1933/index.html.

"Glass–Steagall and the Volcker Rule," *American Enterprise Institute*, 10 December 2012, accessed 22 March 2013, https://www.aei.org/publication/glass-steagall-and-the-volcker-rule/.

"Guide to Reading the GATS Schedules of Specific Commitments and the List of Article II (MFN) Exemptions," *World Trade Organization*, accessed http://www.wto.org/english/tratop_e/serv_e/guide1_e.htm.

"Guide: Congressional Session Chart," *Indiana University Bloomington Library*, https://libraries.indiana.edu/guide-congressional-session-chart.

"Hanmi Bank Branches," *Hanmi Bank*, https://www.hanmi.com/about/branches/northern-california/san-francisco.

"Historical Growth of Asian LCY Bond Market," *Asian Bonds Online*, accessed 15 July 2013, http://asianbondsonline.adb.org/regional/data/bondmarket.php?code=LCY_in_USD_Local_Total, visited July 15, 2013.

"History of OTC Markets Group Inc," OTC Markets, accessed 10 August 2014, http://www.otcmarkets.com/history-pink-otc.

"History of the Basel Committee," *Bank of International Settlements*, last modified 28 October 2014, accessed http://www.bis.org/bcbs/history.htm.

"Home," *ABN Amro Group*, http://www.abnamro.com/en/index.html.

"Home," *Hanmi Bank*, https://www.hanmi.com/.

"Home," *ITS Trading Company Ltd.*, http://www.itstradingcompany.com.

"Hong Kong Exchanges and Clearing," *World Federation of Exchanges*, 19 November 2013, accessed 26 August 2014, www.world-exchanges.org/member-exchanges/key-information-/hong-kong-exchanges-and-clearing.

"Hong Kong's Securities and Futures Ordinance ('SFO') Chapter 571 Section 270(1)(a)," *Department of Justice of the Hong Kong Special Administrative Region*, 1 January 2013, accessed 27 July 2015, http://www.legislation.gov.hk/blis_pdf.nsf/6799165D2FEE3FA94825755E0033E532/5167961DDC96C3B7482575EF001C7C2D?OpenDocument&bt=0.

"How We Classify Countries," *The World Bank*, accessed 15 April 2013, http://data.worldbank.org/about/country-classifications.

"HSBC: An Overview," *Securities and Exchange Commission*, 2012, accessed http://www.sec.gov/Archives/edgar/data/83246/000114420412052308/v744588-1_fwp.pdf.

"Huiyuan Juice Set for HK Listing," *People's Daily*, 10 February 2007, accessed 28 July 2015, http://english.people.com.cn/200702/10/eng20070210_349100.html.

"ICE at a Glance," *InterContinental Exchange*, accessed 26 August 2014, https://www.theice.com/publicdocs/ICE_at_a_glance.pdf.

"In the Matter of the Listed Securities of China Huiyuan Juice Group Limited: Notice to the Market Misconduct Tribunal Pursuant to Section 252(2) and Schedule 9 of the Securities and Futures Ordinance, CAP. 571 Amended Pursuant to Section 15 of Schedule 9 of the Ordinance by Order of the Market Misconduct Tribunal," *Market Misconduct Tribunal*, 14 September 2012, accessed 2 August 2015, http://www.mmt.gov.hk/eng/rulings/Amended.FS.Notice.Huiyuan.14.9.2012_e.pdf.

"In the Matter of the Listed Securities of Sino Katalytics Investment Corporation: Notice to the Market Misconduct Tribunal Pursuant to Section 252(2) and Schedule 9 of the Securities and Futures Ordinance, CAP. 571," *Market Misconduct Tribunal*, 12 April 2011, accessed 28 July 2015, http://www.mmt.gov.hk/eng/rulings/SKIC.Ruling.12042011.pdf.

"International Banking Supervision," *Office of Comptroller of Currency*, accessed http://www.occ.gov/topics/international-banking/international-banking-supervision/index-international-banking-supervision.html.

"Investment Banking Scorecard," *The Wall Street Journal*, accessed 20 April 2013, http://graphics.wsj.com/investment-banking-scorecard/.

"Investment Banking," *Investopedia*, accessed 3 April 2013, http://www.investopedia.com/terms/i/investment-banking.asp.

"Iran DM [Defense Minister] Rejects Report on Inspection of Military Centers Based on Lausanne Understanding," *FARS News Agency*, 8 April 2015, http://english.farsnews.com/newstext.aspx?nn=13940119001411.

"Iran Nuclear Deal Makes Mid-East Peace Safer Place – Kerry," *BBC News*, 24 November 2013, http://www.bbc.co.uk/news/world-middle-east-25078961.

"Iran Nuclear Deal: Joint Plan of Action – Full Text," *The Guardian*, 24 November 2013, http://www.theguardian.com/world/interactive/2013/nov/24/iran-nuclear-deal-joint-plan-action.;

"The Iran Nuclear Deal: Full Text," 24 November 2013, CNN, www.cnn.com/2013/11/24/world/meast/iran-deal-text/.
"Iran Nuclear Deal: Key Details," *BBC News*, 14 July 2015, http://www.bbc.com/news/world-middle-east-33521655.
"Iran Nuclear Talks: 'Historic' Agreement Struck," *BBC News*, 14 July 2015, http://www.bbc.com/news/world-middle-east-33518524.
"Iran Says Geneva Nuclear Deal Possible on Friday," *BBC News*, 7 November 2013, www.bbc.co.uk/news/world-middle-east-24857981.
"ISDA," *International Swaps and Derivatives Association*, accessed 13 May 2014, www.ISDA.org.
"Joint Press Release, Agencies Issue Final Rules Implementing the Volcker Rule," *Federal Reserve*, accessed 10 April 2014, http://www.federalreserve.gov/newsevents/press/bcreg/20131210a.htm.
"Joint Statement by EU High Representative Federica Mogherini and Iranian Foreign Minister Javad Zarif Switzerland," *European External Action Service*, 2 April 2015, http://www.eeas.europa.eu/statements-eeas/2015/150402_03_en.htm.
"Key Excerpts of the Joint Comprehensive Plan of Action (JCPOA)," *Document Cloud*, 14 July 2015, https://www.documentcloud.org/documents/2165489-key-excerpts.html.
"List of Members," *International Monetary Fund*, 13 June 2012, accessed 27 March 2014, https://www.imf.org/external/np/sec/memdir/memdate.htm.
"Listing Standards – US Standards," *NYSE Euronext*, accessed 15 April 2013, http://usequities.nyx.com/regulation/listed-companies-compliance/listings-standards/us.
"Magsaysay Home Page," *Magsaysay*, www.magsaysay.com.ph.
"Magsaysay Maritime Corporation Job Postings," *WorkAbroad*, www.workabroad.ph/list_specific_jobs.php?by_what=agency&id=2459.
"Maimonides' Eight Levels of Charity," *Chabad*, accessed 20 November 2013, http://www.chabad.org/library/article_cdo/aid/45907/jewish/Eight-Levels-of-Charity.htm.
"Market Capitalization of Listed Companies (Current US$)," *The World Bank*, accessed 15 April 2013, http://data.worldbank.org/indicator/CM.MKT.LCAP.CD/countries?display=default.
"Market Misconduct Tribunal Disqualifies Water Oasis's Former CEO and Orders Disgorgement for Insider Dealing," *Hong Kong Securities and Futures Commission: All News*, 5 February 2015, accessed 3 August 2015, http://www.sfc.hk/edistributionWeb/gateway/EN/news-and-announcements/news/doc?refNo=15PR11.
"Market," *Investopedia*, accessed 28 August 2014, http://www.investopedia.com/terms/m/market.asp.
"Marrakesh Agreement Establishing the World Trade Organization, Annex 1B, Article II," *GATS: General Agreement on Trade in Services*, 15 April 1994, accessed http://www.wto.org/english/docs_e/legal_e/26-gats.pdf (hereinafter GATS).
"Middle East: Iran," *United States Central Intelligence Agency World Fact Book*, https://www.cia.gov/library/publications/the-world-factbook/geos/ir.html.
"Monetary Policy," *Federal Reserve Bank of Richmond*, accessed 27 March 2014, https://www.richmondfed.org/faqs/monetary_policy.
"Multilateral Memorandum of Understanding Concerning Consultation and Cooperation and the Exchange of Information," *IOSCO*, May 2002, accessed http://www.iosco.org/library/pubdocs/pdf/IOSCOPD126.pdf.
"National Securities Clearing Corporation," *DTCC*, accessed 27 August 2014, http://www.dtcc.com/about/businesses-and-subsidiaries/nscc.aspx.
"New York Office Tower Seized Over Payments to Iran," *BBC News*, 18 September 2013, posted at http://www.bbc.co.uk/news/world-us-canada-24146454.
"Nothing Idyllic," *The Economist* (11 January 2013): 42.
"Notice to the Market Misconduct Pursuant to Section 252(2) and Schedule 9 of the Securities and Futures Ordinance CAP.571, In the Matter of the Listed Securities of Water Oasis Group Limited," *Market Misconduct Tribunal*, 2 August 2014, accessed 28 July 2015, http://www.mmt.gov.hk/eng/rulings/Water.Oasis.08082014_e.pdf.

"Odd Lot Definition," *Investopedia*, accessed 10 September 2014, http://www.investopedia.com/terms/o/oddlot.asp.

"Open Market Operations," *Board of Governors of the Federal Reserve System*, 6 February 2013, accessed 27 March 2014, http://www.federalreserve.gov/monetarypolicy/openmarket.htm.

"Our History: A Long Commitment to China," *Citi*, accessed http://www.citi.com.cn/html/en/about_us/Our_history.html.

"Parameters for a Joint Comprehensive Plan of Action Regarding the Islamic Republic of Iran's Nuclear Program," *US Department of State*, 2 April 2015, http://www.state.gov/r/pa/prs/ps/2015/04/240170.htm.

"Payment System Risk," *Federal Reserve*, accessed 27 August 2014, http://www.federalreserve.gov/paymentsystems/psr_overview.htm#tocI.

"Payment Systems: Central Bank Roles Vary, but Goals Are the Same," *US General Accounting Office: Report Number GAO-02-303*, 25 February 2002, accessed 26 March 2014, http://www.gao.gov/assets/240/233724.pdf.

"Penny Stock," *Investopedia*, accessed 27 August 2014 http://www.investopedia.com/terms/p/pennystock.asp.

"Position," *Investopedia*, accessed 10 April 2014, http://www.investopedia.com/terms/p/position.asp.

"Principles for Financial Market Infrastructures," *Bank for International Settlements and International Organization of Securities Commissions* (April 2012): 8, accessed 18 November 2014, http://www.bis.org/publ/cpss101a.pdf.

"Proposal for Resolution of Mini-Bond Issue," *Hong Kong Democratic Foundation*, November 2008, accessed 24 March 2013, http://www.hkdf.org/pr.asp?func=show&pr=178.

"Regulators have Several Options in Dealing with CLOs under Volcker Rule – Law Firm Analysis," *Reuters*, 20 February 2014, accessed 10 March 2014, http://blogs.reuters.com/financial-regulatory-forum/2014/02/20/regulators-have-several-options-in-dealing-with-clos-under-volcker-rule-law-firm-analysis/.

"Santander Bank Home," *Santander Bank*, www.santanderbank.com. (discussing the activities and locations of the bank).

"Saudi Stock Exchange (Tadawul) Annual Review – 2006," *Market Information Department: Tadawul*, accessed 26 August 2014, http://www.tadawul.com.sa/static/pages/en/Publication/PDF/Annual_Report_2006_English.pdf.

"Saudi Stock Exchange (Tadawul) Annual Review – 2008," *Market Information Department: Tadawul*, accessed 26 August 2014, http://www.tadawul.com.sa/static/pages/en/Publication/PDF/Annual_Report_2008_English.pdf.

"SEC Approves Rules Expanding Stock-by-Stock Circuit Breakers and Clarifying Process for Breaking Erroneous Trades," *United States Securities and Exchange Commission*, 2010, accessed 25 August 2014, www.sec.gov/news/press/2010/2010-167.htm.

"Services," *CCV Grupo BMV*, accessed 28 August 2014, http://www.contraparte-central.com.mx/.

"Settlement," *Korea Securities Depository*, accessed 27 August 2014, https://www.ksd.or.kr/eng/static/EB0102010000.home?menuNo=93.

"SFC Commences Market Misconduct Tribunal Proceedings against Former CEO of Water Oasis Group Limited," *Hong Kong Securities and Futures Commission: Enforcement News*, 14 August 2014, accessed 3 August 2015, http://www.sfc.hk/edistributionWeb/gateway/EN/news-and-announcements/news/enforcement-news/doc?refNo=14PR100.

"SOES (Small Order Execution System)," *FinancialWeb*, accessed 26 August 2014, http://www.finweb.com/investing/soes-small-order-execution-system.html.

"Supervision and Regulation," *The Federal Reserve System: Purposes and Function*, accessed http://www.federalreserve.gov/pf/pdf/pf_5.pdf.

"Surge in Sukuk Demand Outpaces the Issuance," *Financial Times*, 5 November 2012.

"Syria Hails US–Russia Deal on Chemical Weapons," *BBC News*, 15 September 2013, http://www.bbc.co.uk/news/world-middle-east-24100296.

"Technical Assistance," *International Monetary Fund*, accessed 7 June 2013, http://www.imf.org/external/about/techasst.htm.

"The Bank Holding Company Act of 1956," *Duke Law Journal* 7.1 (Durham, NC: Duke Law, 1956): 1–24, accessed 21 March 2013, http://scholarship.law.duke.edu/cgi/viewcontent.cgi?article=1637&context=dlj.

"The Best v. The Not-Too-Bad," *The Economist* (19 October 2013): 16.

"The Global Finance Regime," *Council on Foreign Relations*, 25 June 2013, accessed 10 June 2014, http://www.cfr.org/financial-regulation/global-finance-regime/p20177.

"The Investment Act of 1940," *Columbia Law Review* 41 (1941): 269, 286.

"The Long Demise of Glass–Steagall," *Frontline*, 8 May 2003, accessed 21 March 2013, http://www.pbs.org/wgbh/pages/frontline/shows/wallstreet/weill/demise.html.

"The Report of the Market Misconduct Tribunal into Dealings in the Shares of China Huiyuan Juice Group Limited on and between 30 July 2008 to 4 September 2008," *Market Misconduct Tribunal*, 10 May 2013, http://www.mmt.gov.hk/eng/reports/Huiyuan.Report.Part.II_e.pdf.

"There's a Chink of Hope," *The Economist* (19 October 2013): 51–2.

"Top 10 largest stock exchanges," *China Daily*, accessed 27 August 2014, http://www.chinadaily.com.cn/business/2014-04/29/content_17472002_4.htm.

"Top Ten Insurance Personalities," *Lloyd's List*, http://www.lloydslist.com/ll/news/top100/insurance/.

"Triennial Central Bank Survey of Foreign Exchange and Derivatives Market Activity in 2010," *Bank for International Settlements*, 17 September 2011, accessed, www.bis.org/publ/rpfxf10t.pdf.

"Two-Speed Future for High-Frequency Algorithmic Trading," *EuroMoney*, accessed 19 May 2013,http://www.euromoney.com/Article/3204810/Two-speed-future-for-high-frequency-algorithmic-trading.html.

"U.S. Allows Boeing Air Component Sales to Iran," *BBC News*, 4 April 2014, www.bbc.com/news/world-us-canada-26896983.

"Underwriter," *Investing Answers*, accessed 4 April 2013, http://www.investinganswers.com/financial-dictionary/insurance/underwriter-873.

"Universal Banking Together, Forever?" *The Economist*, 18 August 2012, accessed 22 March 2013, http://www.economist.com/node/21560577.

"US Bond Market Issuance and Outstanding: Quarterly Data to Q1 2013," *The Securities Industry and Financial Markets Association (SIFMA)*, accessed 25 June 2013, http://www.sifma.org/research/statistics.aspx.

"US Resolution Plan, FDIC," *Sumitomo Mitsui Financial Group*, accessed https://www.fdic.gov/regulations/reform/resplans/plans/smfg-165-1312.pdf.

"Volcker Rule," *Investopedia*, accessed 22 March 2013, http://www.investopedia.com/terms/v/volcker-rule.asp.

"What is Clearing?" *EuroCCP*, accessed 18 November 2014, http://euroccp.com/qa/clearing-ccp%E2%80%99s/what-clearing.

"What is IDA?" *The World Bank*, accessed 8 June 2013, http://www.worldbank.org/ida/what-is-ida.html.

"What Makes an M&A Deal Work?" *Investopedia*, 17 June 2008, accessed 20 April 2013, http://www.investopedia.com/articles/financial-theory/08/ma-deal.asp.

"Who We Are: Overview," *Multilateral Investment Guarantee Agency*, accessed 8 June 2013, https://www.miga.org/who-we-are.

"Wonders of Convertible Bonds," *Yahoo! Finance*, accessed 12 May 2014, http://finance.yahoo.com/news/wonders-convertible-bonds-160000020.html.

"World Bank Atlas Method," *The World Bank*, accessed 15 April 2013, http://data.worldbank.org/about/country-classifications/world-bank-atlas-method.

"World Exchanges Monthly Report for 2014," *World Federation of Exchanges*, accessed 25 August 2014, http://www.world-exchanges.org/statistics/monthly-reports.

"World Population," *United States Central Intelligence Agency World Fact Book*, https://www.cia.gov/library/publications/the-world-factbook/geos/xx.html.

"World's Best Investment Banks 2012," *Global Finance*, 17 February 2012, accessed 20 April 2013,https://www.gfmag.com/awards-rankings/best-banks-and-financial-rankings/worlds-best-investment-banks-2012.

Author sources

Aggarwal, R. K. and G. Wu, "Stock Market Manipulations," *Journal of Business* 79, No. 4 (2006): 1915–53.

Alexander, Philip, "Top 1000 World Banks 2011," *The Banker*, 30 June 2011, accessed 21 April 2013, http://www.thebanker.com/Top-1000-World-Banks/Top-1000-World-Banks-2011.

Alexander, Sidney S., "Price Movements in Speculative Markets: Trends or Random Walks," *Industrial Management Review* (May 1961): 26.

Allen, F. and D. Gale, "Stock Price Manipulation," *Review of Financial Studies* 5 (1992): 503–29.

Altman, Edward, B. Jacquillat, and M. Levasseur, "Comparative Analysis of Risk Measures: France and the United States," *Journal of Finance* 29, No. 5 (December 1974): 1495–511.

Altman, Morris, "Prospect Theory and Behavioral Finance," *Behavioral Finance: Investors, Corporations, and Markets*, eds. H. Kent Baker and John R. Nofsinger, (Hoboken, NJ: John Wiley & Sons, 2010).

Anderson, S. C., "Closed-End Funds, Exchange-Traded Funds, and Hedge Funds," *Innovations in Financial Markets and Institutions* 18, Springer Science+Business Media (2010): 89.

Aquil, Bilal, and Imran Mufti, "Innovation in the Global Sukuk Market and Legal Restructuring Considerations," *Islamic Finance*, ed. Rahali Ali (London, UK: Globe Business Publishing, 2008).

Avraham, Dafna, Patricia Selvaggi, and James Vickery, "A Structural View of U.S. Bank Holding Companies," *Federal Reserve Bank of New York*, July 2012, accessed http://www.newyorkfed.org/research/epr/12v18n2/1207avra.pdf.

Ayub, Muhammad, *Understanding Islamic Finance* (Chichester: John Wiley & Sons, 2007).

Baker and McKenzie, "U.S. Congress Enacts Additional Sanctions Against Iran," *Lexology*, 31 January 2013, http://www.lexology.com/library/detail.aspx?g=1dbeb762-9695-4817-88a8-f0130cf20844.

Banz, Rolf, "The Relationship between Return and Market Value of Common Stocks," *Journal of Financial Economics* 9 (March 1981): 3–18.

Barbash, Barry P. and Jai Massari, "The Investment Advisers Act of 1940: Regulation by Accretion," *Rutgers Law Journal* 39.3 (2008): 627, accessed http://org.law.rutgers.edu/publications/lawjournal/issues/39_3/03BarbashVol.39.3.r_1.pdf.

Barberis, Nicolas C. and Richard H. Thaler, "A Survey of Behavioral Finance," *Handbook of the Economics of Finance*, eds. George Constantinides, Milton Harris, and Rene Stulz (Amsterdam: North-Holland, 2003).

Basu, Sanjoy, "The Investment Performance of Common Stocks in Relation to Their Price Earnings Rations: A Test of the Efficient Market Hypothesis," *Journal of Finance* 32 (June 1977): 663–82

Basu, Sanjoy, "The Relationship between Earnings Yield, Market Value, and Return for NYSE Common Stocks: Further Evidence," *Journal of Financial Economics* 12 (June 1983): 129–56.

Benink, Harald and George Kaufman, "Turmoil Reveals the Inadequacy of Basel II," *Financial Times* 11 (28 February 2008)

Berg, Joyce, John Dickhaut, and Kevin McCabe, "Trust, Reciprocity, and Social History," *Games and Economic Behavior* 10, No. 1 (1995): 122–42.

Bernanke, Ben, "Some Reflections on the Crisis and the Policy Response," *Federal Reserve*, 2012, accessed 17 April 2014, http://www.federalreserve.gov/newsevents/speech/bernanke 20120413a.htm.

Bernard, Victor L. and Jacob K. Thomas, "Post-Earnings-Announcement Drift: Delayed Price Response or Risk Premium?" *Journal of Accounting Research* 27 (1989): 1–36.

Bazinga, "What is High Frequency Trading?" *Nasdaq*, 9 April 2013, accessed 18 November 2014, http://www.nasdaq.com/article/what-is-high-frequency-trading-cm235032#.UXVg_yv70Vl.

Bhala, Raj, *Foreign Bank Regulation After BCCI* (Durham, NC: Carolina Academic Press, 1994).

Bhala, Raj, "Fighting Bad Guys with International Trade Law," *University of California at Davis Law Review* 31 (Fall 1997): 1–121.

Bhala, Raj, *International Trade Law: Interdisciplinary Theory and Practice*, 3rd ed. (Newark, NJ: LexisNexis, 2008): ch. 19.

Bhala, Raj, *Islamic Law (Shari'a)* (New Providence, NJ: LexisNexis, 2011).

Bhala, Raj, *Modern GATT Law, Volume I, Chapter VI, Section VII* (London: Thomson Sweet & Maxwell, 2013).

Bhala, Raj, "Fighting Iran with Trade Sanctions," *Arizona Journal of International and Comparative Law* 31, No. 2 (Spring 2014): 251–56.

Bilimoria, Purusottama, "Indian Ethics," *A Companion to Ethics*, ed. Peter Singer, (Oxford, UK: Blackwell Publishing, 1993), 49.

Black, Fischer and Myron Scholes, "The Pricing of Options and Corporate Liabilities," *Journal of Political Economy* 81 (1973): 637–54.

Black, Fischer, Michael C. Jensen, and Myron Scholes, "The Capital Asset Pricing Model: Some Empirical Tests," *Studies in the Theory of Capital Markets*, ed. Michael C. Jensen (New York, NY: Praeger, 1972).

Blair, Sheila, "The Road to Safer Banks Runs Through Basel," *Financial Times* (24 September 2010): 9.

Blitz, James, "West Cautious as Cleric Unlikely to Soften Nuclear Stance Swiftly," *Financial Times* (17 June 2013): 2.

Bloomfield, Robert, "Traditional Versus Behavioral Finance," *Behavioral Finance: Investors, Corporations, and Markets*, eds. H. Kent Baker and John R. Nofsinger (Hoboken, NJ: John Wiley & Sons, 2010), 29.

Blume, Marshall E. and Robert F. Stambaugh, "Biases in Computed Returns: An Application to the Size Effect," *Journal of Finance Economics* (1983): 387–404.

Boatright, John, *Ethics in Finance*, 3rd ed. (Malden, MA: John Wiley & Sons, 2014), 188.

Bodie, Zvi, Alex Kane, and Alan Marcus, *Essentials of Investments*, 5th ed. (New York: McGraw-Hill/Irwin, 2003).

Bogle, John C., "The Mutual Fund Industry 60 years Later: For Better or Worse?" *Financial Analysts Journal* (January–February 2005): 15–24.

Boles, Corey, "Bernanke Offers Broad Definition of Systemic Risk," *Wall Street Journal Real Time Economics*, 2009, accessed 19 April 2014, http://blogs.wsj.com/economics/2009/11/18/bernanke-offers-broad-definition-of-systemic-risk/.

Bologna, Michael, "Importer Charged in Scheme to Ship Controlled Aluminum Sources to Iran," *International Trade Reporter (BNA)* 30 (7 November 2013): 1731.

Bozorgmehr, Najmeh, "Tehran Crowds Take to Streets to Cheer Reformist's Triumph," *Financial Times* (17 June 2013): 2.

Bozorgmehr, Najmeh, "Rouhani Lifts Hope for Solutions," *Financial Times* (30 September 2013): 4.

Bozorgmehr, Najmeh, "Iran Poised to Offer Lucrative Oil Deals," *Financial Times* (29 October 2013): 1.

Bozorgmehr, Najmeh, "Zarif Pressed by Iran Hardliners," *Financial Times* (10 December 2013): 2.

Bozorgmehr, Najmeh and Monavar Khalaj, "Rohani Raises Hopes for Change with Pledges on Iran's Nuclear Programme," *Financial Times* (18 June 2013): 1.

Brown, Montague, *The Quest for Moral Foundations: An Introduction to Ethics* (Washington DC: Georgetown University Press, 1996).

Carhart, M., R. Kaniel, D. Musto, and A. Reed, "Leaning for the Tape: Evidence of Gaming Behavior in Equity Mutual Funds," *Journal of Finance* 57 (2002): 661–93.

Carnell, Richard Scott, Jonathan R. Macey and Geoffrey P. Miller, *The Law of Financial Institutions, Aspen Casebook Series*, 5th ed. (Netherlands: Wolters Kluwer Law and Business, 2013).

Carpenter, David H. and M. Maureen Murphy, "Permissible Securities Activities of Commercial Banks Under the Glass–Steagall Act (GSA) and the Gramm-Leach-Bliley Act (GLBA)," *Congressional Research Service* (2010): 10, 11, accessed 16 April 2014, http://assets.opencrs.com/rpts/R41181_20100412.pdf.

CFA Institute, *Standards of Practice Handbook*, 11th ed. (Charlottesville, VA: CFA Institute, 2014), 2.

Champ, Norm, "Current SEC Priorities Regarding Hedge Fund Matters," *The Securities and Exchange Commission*, 12 September 2013, accessed 22 September 2014, http://www.sec.gov/News/Speech/Detail/Speech/1370539802997#.VCG-gku4nHg.

Chan, Carol, "Daughter Demoted," *South China Morning Post* 22 (October 2008): A1.

Chan, Maria, "Company Exposed Itself to High Levels of Risk," *South China Morning Post* 22 (October 2008): A3.

Chapman, Gretchen B. and Eric J. Johnson, "Incorporating the Irrelevant: Anchors in Judgment of Belief and Values," *Heuristics and Biases: The Psychology of Intuitive Judgment*, eds. Thomas Gilovich, Dale Griffin, and Daniel Kahneman, (Cambridge, UK: Cambridge University Press, 2002).

Charbonneau, Louis, "Factbox: A Guide to Nuclear Talks between Iran and Six Major Powers," *Reuters*, 28 June 2015, http://mobile.reuters.com/article/topNews/idUSKCN0P80JF20150628?irpc=932.

Chen, Nai-fu, "Some Empirical Tests of the Theory of Arbitrage Pricing," *Journal of Finance* 38 (December 1983): 1393–410.

Cheng, Jonathan and Carlos Tejada, "CITIC Pacific Raided Over Currency Bets," *Wall Street Journal* 6, April 2009, accessed 3 August 2015, http://online.wsj.com/article/SB123880204272688577.html.

Choi, Stephen and A. C. Pritchard, *Securities Regulation: Cases and Analysis*, 3rd ed. (New York: Foundation Press, 2012), 3.

Chopra, Navin, Joseph Lakonishok, and Jay R. Ritter, "Measuring Abnormal Performance: Do Stocks Overreact?" *Journal of Financial Economics* 31 (1992): 235–68.

Coase, R., "The Problem of Social Cost," *Journal of Law and Economics* 3 (1960): 1–44.

Cohen, Stephanie, "Sanctions Against Iran Cut Oil Exports by More Than Half, CRS Reports," *International Trade Reporter (BNA)* 31 (4 September 2014): 1590.

Comstock, Courtney, "Huge: First High Frequency Trading Firm is Fined For Quote Stuffing and Manipulation," *Business Insider*, 13 September 2010, accessed 31 March 2015, www.businessinsider.com/.

Cornell, B. and E. Sirri, "The Reaction of Investors and Stock Prices to Insider Trading," *Journal of Finance* 47 (1992): 1031–59.

Corrigan, E. Gerald, "Are Banks Special?" *Federal Reserve Bank of Minneapolis: Annual Report Summary*, 1 January 1983, accessed 27 March 2014, https://www.minneapolisfed.org/publications/annual-reports/are-banks-special.

Crespo, R. M., "Spanish Mutual Fund Fees and Less Sophisticated Investors: Examination and Ethical Implications," *Business Ethics: A European Review* 18, No. 3 (July 2009): 224–40.

Crooks, Ed and Geoff Dyer, "Strength in Reserve," *Financial Times* (6 September 2013): 5.

Curtis, Glenn E. and Eric Hooglund, *Iran: A Country Study*, 5th ed. (Washington, DC: Library of Congress, Federal Research Division, 2008), xxvii, 178–80.

Dalai Lama, *A Simple Path* (New York, NY: Harper Collins Publishers, 2009), 89.

Davies, Paul J. and Jeremy Grant, "OTC Trading Reform Threatens Asian Markets," *Financial Times*, accessed 17 September 2014, http://www.ft.com/cms/s/0/6b6d30b8-b0a9-11e2-9f24-00144feabdc0.html.

Davilas, Christina, "New Dark Pool Regulation On the Horizon," *Law360*, 14 June 2013, accessed 17 September 2014, http://www.law360.com/articles/450159/new-dark-pool-regulation-on-the-horizon.

Davis, Gregory S., "Has Anyone Seen Glass or Steagall?" *Investopedia*, 18 September 2008, accessed 22 March 2013.

De Bondt, W. F. M. and R. H. Thaler, "Does the Stock Market Overreact?" *Journal of Finance* 40 (1985): 793–805

De Bondt, W. F. M. and R. H. Thaler, "Further Evidence of Investor Overreaction and Stock Market Seasonality," *Journal of Finance* 42 (1987): 557–81

De George, Richard T., *Business Ethics*, 6th ed. (Upper Saddle River, NJ: Pearson Prentice Hall, 2006).

De Silva, Padmasiri, "Buddhist Ethics," *A Companion to Ethics*, ed. Peter Singer (Oxford, UK: Blackwell Publishing, 1993), 64.

Dehghan, Saeed Kamali, "Obama and Rouhani's Telephone Call of Huge Significance, Says Iranian Deputy," *The Guardian*, 2 October 2013, http://www.theguardian.com/world/2013/oct/02/obama-rouhani-phone-call-us-iran.

Denning, Steve, "Big Banks and Derivatives: Why Another Financial Crisis Is Inevitable," *Forbes* (8 January 2013), accessed 15 April 2013, http://www.forbes.com/sites/stevedenning/2013/01/08/five-years-after-the-financial-meltdown-the-water-is-still-full-of-big-sharks/.

Derman, Emanuel, *Models.Behaving.Badly.: Why Confusing Illusion with Reality can Lead to Disaster, on Wall Street and in Life* (New York, NY: Free Press, 2011).

Douglas, G. W. "Risk in the Equity Markets: An Empirical Appraisal of Market Efficiency," *Yale Economic Essays* 9, No. 1 (1969): 3–48.

Duan, Wang and Dai Tian, "Tribunal to Hold Last Hearing into Huiyuan Insider Trading Case," *Caixin Online*, 23 October 2012, accessed 4 August 2015, http://english.caixin.com/2012-10-23/100451000.html.

Dufey, G. and T. Chung, "International Financial Markets: A Survey," R. Kuhn, ed., *International Finance and Investing* (1990): 6–8.

Duhigg, Charles, "Stock Traders Find Speed Pays, in Milliseconds," *The New York Times*, 24 July 2009, accessed 18 November 2014, http://www.nytimes.com/2009/07/24/business/24trading.html?ref=highfrequencyalgorithmictrading.

Dusuki, A. W., "Do Equity-based Sukuk Structures in Islamic Capital Markets Manifest the Objectives of Shari'a?" *Journal of Financial Services Marketing* 15, No. 3 (2010): 203–14.

Dyer, Geoff, "Iran's 'Good Cop, Bad Cop' Breeds Divided Feelings in Washington," *Financial Times* (12 December 2013): 12.

Dyer, Geoff and John Reed, "Iran's Arak Plant Reveals Depth of Distrust," *Financial Times* (13 November 2013): 6.

Dyer, Geoff and John Reed, "Israel Opts to Shift Tactics on Iran Talks," *Financial Times*, (7–8 December 2013): 4.

Dyer, Geoff and Najmeh Bozorgmehr, "Obama Lobbies Senate Democrats to Drop Plan for More Iran Sanctions," *Financial Times* (15 January 2014): 4.

Ellis, Charles D., "The Rise and Fall of Performance Investing," *Financial Analysts Journal* 70, No. 4 (July–August 2014): 14–23.

Eng, Dennis and Fanny Fung, "SFC Urged to Launch CITIC Pacific Probe," *South China Morning Post* (22 October 2008): A3.

Engelen, P. J. and L. V. Liedekerke, "Insider Trading," *Finance Ethics: Critical Issues in Theory and Practice*, ed. John R. Boatright (Hoboken, NJ: Wiley and Sons, 2010), 201.

Fama, Eugene F., "The Behavior of Stock Market Prices," *Journal of Business* 38, No. 1 (January 1965): 34–105.

Fama, Eugene F., "Efficient Capital Markets: A Review of Theory and Empirical Work," *Journal of Finance* 25 (1970): 383–417.

Fama, Eugene F. and James MacBeth, "Risk, Return and Equilibrium: Empirical Tests," *Journal of Political Economy* 81 (March 1973): 607–36.

Fama, Eugene F. and Kenneth R. French, "Permanent and Temporary Components of Stock Prices," *Journal of Political Economy* 96 (April 1988): 246–73.

Fama, Eugene F. and Kenneth R. French, "Dividend Yields and Expected Stock Returns," *Journal of Financial Economics* 22 (October 1988): 3–25.

Fama, Eugene F. and Kenneth R. French, "The Cross Section of Expected Stock Returns," *Journal of Finance* 47 (June 1992): 427–65.

Fama, Eugene F. and Kenneth R. French, "The Capital Asset Pricing Model: Theory and Evidence," *Journal of Economic Perspective* 18, No. 3 (Summer 2004): 25–46.

Fama, Eugene F. and Robert Litterman, "An Experienced View on Markets and Investing," *Financial Analysts Journal* 68, No. 6 (November–December 2012): 15–19.

Findlay, M. C. and E. E. Williams, "Financial Economics at 50: An Oxymoronic Tautology," *Journal of Post Keynesian Economics* 31, No. 2 (Winter 2008–09): 213–26.

Findlay, M. C., E. E. Williams, and J. R. Thompson, "Why We All Held Our Breath When the Market Reopened," *Journal of Portfolio Management* (Spring 2003): 91–100.

Foley, Stephen, "High-Frequency Traders Face Speed Limits," *CNBC*, 29 April 2013, accessed 23 August 2014, www.cnbc.com/id/100682552.

Foster, George, Chris Olsen, and Terry Shevlin, "Earnings Releases, Anomalies, and the Behavior of Security Returns," *The Accounting Review* 59, No. 4 (October 1984): 574–603.

Gabrielcik, Adele and Russell H. Fazio, "Priming and Frequency Estimation: A Strict Test of the Availability Heuristic," *Personality and Social Psychology Bulletin* 10, No. 1 (1984): 85–9.

Gallagher, D. R., P. Gardener, and P. L. Swan, "Portfolio Pumping: An Examination of Investment Manager Quarter-End Trading and Impact on Performance," *Pacific-Basin Finance Journal* 17 (2009): 1–27.

Ganji, Akbar, "Who Is Khamenei? The Mind of Iran's Supreme Leader," *Foreign Affairs* 92 (September-October 2013): 24–48.

Gardner, David, "Iran Can Be Made a Force for Middle East Peace," *Financial Times* (November 2013): 23–4.

Giarraputo, Chris, "World's Best Investment Banks 2013," *Global Finance*, 22 February 2013, accessed 20 April 2013, https://www.gfmag.com/awards-rankings/best-banks-and-financial-rankings/worlds-best-investment-banks-2013.

Gilovich, Thomas and Dale Griffin, "Introduction—Heuristics and Biases: Then and Now," *Heuristics and Biases: The Psychology of Intuitive Judgment*, eds. Thomas Gilovich, Dale Griffin, and Daniel Kahneman (Cambridge, UK: Cambridge University Press, 2002), 1–18.

Goldberg, Linda, Cindy E. Hull, and Sarah Stein, "Do Industrialized Countries Hold the Right Foreign Exchange Reserves?" *Current Issues in Economics and Finance* 19, 1 (2013), accessed 11 June 2013, http://www.newyorkfed.org/research/current_issues/ci19-1.pdf.

Goodhart, Charles, *The Basel Committee on Banking Supervision: A History of the Early Years, 1974–1997* (Cambridge, UK: Cambridge University Press, 2011), 3.

Goodhart, Charles, "Ratio Controls Need Reconsideration," *Journal of Financial Stability* 9, No. 2 (2013): 445–50.

Goyal, Amit and Sunil Wahal, "The Selection and Termination of Investment Management Firms by Plan Sponsors," *Journal of Finance* 3, No. 4 (2008): 1805–47.

Green, Ronald M., "Foundations of Jewish Ethics," *The Blackwell Companion to Religious Ethics*, ed. William Schweiker (Oxford, UK: Blackwell Publishing, 2003), 169.

Greenspan, Alan, "Mea Culpa," *Financial Times* (7 January 2009): 1.

Haas, Richard, "A Diplomatic Dance Will Be No Waltz For Either Iran or America," *Financial Times* (30 September 2013): 11.

Hafezi, Parisa and Justyna Pawlak, "Breakthrough Deal Curbs Iran's Nuclear Activity," *Reuters*, 24 November 2013, http://www.reuters.com/article/2013/11/24/us-iran-nuclear-idUSBRE9AI0CV20131124.

Harper, Christine, "Breaking up Banks Won't Make Them Safer, Ex-Senator Says," *Bloomberg Business*, 26 July 2012, accessed 22 March 2013, http://www.bloomberg.com/news/articles/2012-07-26/breaking-up-banks-won-t-make-them-safer-ex-senator-says.

Harvey, Peter, *An Introduction to Buddhist Ethics* (Cambridge, UK: Cambridge University Press, 2000), 198.

Heakal, Reem, "What Was the Glass–Steagall Act?" *Investopedia*, 26 February 2009, accessed 20 March 2013, http://www.investopedia.com/articles/03/071603.asp.

Hirt, Geoffrey and Stanley B. Block. *Fundamentals of Investment Management*, 10th ed. (New York: McGraw-Hill, 2012).

Hourani, Husam, "Three Principles of Islamic Finance Explained," *International Financial Law Review* (May 2005): 1.

Huneke, Samuel Clowes, "Raj Rajaratnam and Insider Trading," *Seven Pillars Institute for Global Finance and Ethics: Case Studies*, accessed 27 July 2015, http://sevenpillarsinstitute.org/case-studies/raj-rajaratnam-and-insider-trading-2.

Hursthouse, Rosalind, *On Virtue Ethics* (Oxford, UK: Oxford University Press, 1999), 11.

Hussain, Mustafa, "A General Introduction to Islamic Finance," *Islamic Finance*, ed. Rahali Ali (London: Globe Business Publishing, 2008).

Indyk, Martin, "The West Must Temper Its Enthusiasm for Iran's New President," *Financial Times* (17 June 2013): 9.

Iosebashvili, Ira, "EBS to Rein in High Frequency Traders," *The Wall Street Journal*, 29 April 2013, accessed 15 August 2014, http://online.wsj.com/article/SB10001424127887323528404578453183303289790.html.

Jackson, Howell E. and Eric J. Pan, "Regulatory Competition in International Securities Markets: Evidence from Europe in 1999 – Part I," *Business Lawyer* 56 (2001): 667.

Jarrow, R. A., "Market Manipulation, Bubbles, Corners, and Short Squeezes," *Journal of Financial and Quantitative Analysis*, 27 (1992): 311–36.

Johnson, Noel D. and Alexandra Mislin, *Cultures of Kindness: A Meta-Analysis of Trust Game Experiments* (2008), accessed August 27, 2015, http://extranet.isnie.org/uploads/isnie2009/johnson_mislin.pdf.

Jones, Charles, "The Reality of High-Frequency Trading," *Politico*, March 2013, accessed 20 March 2013, http://www.politico.com/story/2013/03/correcting-the-record-on-high-frequency-trading-89082.html.

Jung-a, Song, "Seoul Takes Kimchi Bonds off the Menu," *Financial Times*, 19 July 2011, accessed 18 November 2014, http://www.ft.com/cms/s/0/b7153548-b1e0-11e0-a06c-00144feabdc0.html#axzz3jlqF55xj.

Kahneman, Daniel, Jack L. Knetsch, and Richard H. Thaler, "Fairness and the Assumptions of Economics," *Journal of Business* 59 (1986): 285–300.

Kahneman, Daniel and Amos Tversky, "On the study of statistical intuition," *Judgement Under Uncertainty: Heuristics and Biases*, eds. Daniel Kahneman, Paul Slovic, and Amos Tversky (Cambridge, UK: Cambridge University Press, 1982), 498–508.

Kahneman, Daniel and Amos Tversky, "Prospect Theory: An Analysis of Decision under Risk," *Econometrica* 47, No. 2 (March 1979): 263–92.

Kant, Immanuel, *Lectures on Ethics*, trans. Louis Infield (New York, NY: Hackett Publishing, 1981), 193–4.

Katzman, Kenneth, "Iran Sanctions, Congressional Research Service Report 7-5700, RS 20871," *US Department of State*, 19 August 2014, http://fpc.state.gov/documents/organization/138727.pdf.

Keim, Donald B. and Robert F. Stambaugh, "Predicting Returns in the Stock and Bond Markets," *Journal of Financial Economics* 17 (1986): 357–90.

Keim, Donald B., "Size Related Anomalies and Stock Return Seasonality: Further Empirical Evidence," *Journal of Financial Economics* 12 (June 1983): 13–32.

Keller, Menachem, "Jewish Ethics," *A Companion to Ethics*, ed. Peter Singer (Oxford, UK: Blackwell Publishing, 1993), 84.

Kennedy, President John F., "Radio and Television Report to the American People on the Soviet Arms Buildup in Cuba," Washington, DC, The White House, Television and Radio Address, 22 October 1962, http://microsites.jfklibrary.org/cmc/oct22/doc5.html.

Kenny, Thomas, "Introduction to Emerging Market Bonds," *About.com*, accessed 18 November 2014, http://bonds.about.com/od/bondinvestingstrategies/a/Introduction-To-Emerging-Markets-Bonds.htm.

Kentz, Mike, "Corrected–Refile–US Regulator Nears New FX Clearing Guidelines," *Reuters*, 13 March 2014, accessed 27 August 2014, http://www.reuters.com/article/2014/03/13/derivatives-cftc-fx-idUSL2N0MA1R220140313.

Kettell, Brian, *Introduction to Islamic Banking and Finance* (Chichester: John Wiley & Sons, 2011).

Khalaf, Roula, et al., "Rouhani Takes Tough Nuclear Line," *Financial Times* (30 November–1 December 2013): 1.

Khalaf, Roula, Lionel Barber, and Najmeh Bozorgmehr, "Rouhani Celebrates Triumph of His First 100 Days," *Financial Times* (25 November 2013): 2.

Khalaf, Roula, Lionel Barber, and Najmeh Bozorgmehr, "Rouhani's 100-Day Revolution," *Financial Times* (30 November–1 December 2013): 6.

Khalaj, Monavar, "Hope glimmers for Iran's Tourism Industry," *Financial Times*, 15 November 2013, http://www.ft.com/intl/cms/s/0/7be25910-40a4-11e3-8775-00144feabdc0.html#slide0.

Khan, Muhammad Akram, *An Introduction to Islamic Economics* (Islamabad: International Institute of Islamic Thought and Institute of Policy Studies, 1994).

Khwaja, A. and A. Mian, "Unchecked Intermediaries: Price Manipulation in an Emerging Stock Market," *Journal of Financial Economics* 78 (2005): 203–41.

Kidney, Sean, "9 Useful Facts about the Global Bond Market," *Climate Bonds*, 27 February 2013, accessed 20 May 2013, http://www.climatebonds.net/2014/05/9-useful-facts-about-global-bond-market.

Kinzer, Stephen, "To Resolve the Syrian Crisis, the US Must Negotiate with Iran," *Al Jazeera America*, 4 September 2013, http://america.aljazeera.com/articles/2013/9/4/to-resolve-the-syriacrisistheusmustnegotiatewithiran.html.

Knight, F., *Risk, Uncertainty and Profit* (New York: Harper & Row, 1921).

Koh, Peter, "Islamic Finance Moves on with Debut Eurobond," *Euromoney* (September 2003): 1.

Kolb, Robert, "Ethical Implications of Finance," *Finance Ethics*, ed. John R. Boatright (Hoboken, NJ: John Wiley & Sons, 2010).

Kolb, Robert W., "Risk Management and Risk Transfer: Distributive Justice in Finance," *Journal of Alternative Investments* (Spring 2011): 90–8.

Konczal, Mike, "What Are You Worth to Your Bank?" *The Washington Post*, 6 April 2010, accessed 20 March 2013, http://voices.washingtonpost.com/ezra-klein/2010/04/what_are_you_worth_to_your_ban.html.

Kong, Teresa, "Why Invest in Asia Bonds?" *Matthews Asia*, March 2012, accessed 18 November 2014, http://matthewsasia.com/perspectives-on-asia/asia-insight/article-497/default.fs.

Koslowski, Peter, *Principles of Ethical Economy* 17 (Netherlands: Springer Science & Business Media, 2001): 185.

Kothari, S. P., Jay Shanken, and Richard G. Sloan, "Another Look at the Cross Section of Expected Stock Returns," *Journal of Finance* 50, No. 2 (March 1995): 185–224

Krauland, Edward J. and Anthony Rapa, "Between Scylla and Charybdis: Identifying and Managing Secondary Sanctions Risks Arising from Commercial Relationships with Iran," *Business Law International* 15 (January 2014): 3–17.

Lee, Emily, "Basel III and its New Capital Requirements, as Distinguished from Basel II," *The Banking Law Journal* 131, No. 1 (1 January 2014): 27–69.

Lee, Justin, "High-frequency Trading No Threat to Financial Markets, Regulators Find," *Risk*, 22 April 2013, accessed 27 August 2014, www.risk.net/asia-risk/feature/2263010/highfrequency-trading-no-threat-to-financial-markets-regulators-find.

Levy, Robert A., "On the Short-Term-Stationarity of Beta Coefficients," *Financial Analysts Journal* 27, No. 6 (November–December 1971): 55–62.

Light, John, "What's Going on with the Volcker Rule," *Moyers & Company*, 7 December 2012, accessed 22 March 2013, http://billmoyers.com/2012/12/07/whats-going-on-with-the-volcker-rule/.

Lo, Andrew W. and Crais MacKinlay, "Stock Market Prices Do Not Follow Random Walks: Evidence from a Simple Specification Test," *Review of Financial Studies* 1 (Spring 1988): 41–66.

Lopez, Linette, "GASPARINO: Mysterious Dark Pools Are Seeing More Trading Action Than The NYSE For The First Time Ever," *Business Insider*, March 2013, accessed 19 May 2013, http://www.businessinsider.com/more-trading-in-dark-pools-than-nyse-2013-3.

Lopez, Linette, "What The Heck Is A Dark Pool And Why Are People Trading In Them?" *Business Insider*, October 2012, accessed 17 October 2013, http://www.businessinsider.com/what-is-a-dark-pool-2012-10.

Lyster, Lauren, "Dark Pools: What Are They And Should You Be Concerned?" *Yahoo! Finance*, 19 April 2013, accessed 19 May, 2013, http://finance.yahoo.com/blogs/daily-ticker/dark-pools-concerned-164905843.html.

Makan, Ajay and Neil Hume, "The Cartel's Challenge," *Financial Times* (2 December 2013): 10.

Malloy, Michael, *International Banking: Cases, Materials, and Problems*, 3rd ed. (Durham, NC: Carolina Academic Press, 2013), 143–4.

Manasfi, Julie A. D., "Systemic Risk and Dodd–Frank's Volcker Rule," *William and Mary Business Law Review* 4 (2013): 181, 195.

Markowitz, Harry, "Portfolio Selection," *Journal of Finance* 7 (1952): 77–91.

Markowitz, Harry M., "Market Efficiency: A Theoretical Distinction and So What?" *Financial Analysts Journal* (September–October 2005): 17–30.

McCosh, Andrew M., *Financial Ethics* (Scotland, UK: Kluwer Academic Publishers, 1999).

McCrum, Dan, "The Obscene Cost of Hedge Funds," *FT Alphaville: Financial Times*, 17 September 2014, http://ftalphaville.ft.com/2014/09/17/1974492/the-obscene-cost-of-hedge-funds/.

McGregor, Richard and Geoff Dyer, "U.S. and Iran Start Sanctions Countdown," *Financial Times* (13 January 2013): 3.

Menski, Werner, "Hinduism," *Ethical Issues in Six Religious Traditions*, eds. Peggy Morgan and Clive A. Lawton (Edinburgh, UK: Edinburgh University Press, 2010), 27.

Mercurio, Christopher, "Dark Pool Regulation," *Review of Banking and Financial Law* 33 (2013): 69–77.

Meulbroek, L., "An Empirical Analysis of Illegal Insider Trading," *Journal of Finance* 47 (1992): 1661–99.

Mews, Constant J. and Ibrahim Abraham, "Usury and Just Compensation: Religious and Financial Ethics in Historical Perspective," *Journal of Business Ethics* 72 (2007): 1–15.

Monaco, Stephanie M. and Lawrence P. Stadulis, "Current Issues Relating to Investment Adviser Trade Aggregation and Allocation," *Morgan, Lewis & Bockius LLP*, 2000, 2, accessed 10 September 2014, http://www.morganlewis.com/pubs/ebe9da6b-370d-4853-9e8f23899f3b6f48_publication.pdf.

Mooney Jr., C., "Beyond Negotiability: A New Model for Transfer and Pledge of Interests in Securities Controlled by Intermediaries," *Cardozo Law Review* 12 (1990): 305, 316.

Morgan, Peggy, "Buddhism," *Ethical Issues in Six Religious Traditions*, eds. Peggy Morgan and Clive A. Lawton (Edinburgh, UK: Edinburgh University Press, 2007), 80.

Morgan, Thomas J., "Raising Capital – What You Don't Know Could Hurt You," *The National Law Review*, 6 March 2013, accessed 5 April 2013, http://www.natlawreview.com/article/raising-capital-what-you-don-t-know-could-hurt-you.

Mossin, J., "Equilibrium in a Capital Asset Market," *Econometrica* 34, No. 4 (October 1966): 768–83.

Mousavian, Hossein, "It Was Not Sanctions that Brought Tehran to the Table," *Financial Times* (20 November 2013): 11.

Natter, Ari, "Chamber of Commerce President Predicts End of 40-Year Ban on Crude Oil Exports," *International Trade Reporter (BNA)* 31 (16 January 2014): 103.

Natter, Ari, "Wyden 'Hopes' to Hold Hearing on Crude Oil Exports Soon; Spokesman Cites Concerns," *International Trade Reporter (BNA)* 31 (16 January 2014): 103.

Naylor, Bartlett "Here's the Real Deal on the Volcker Rule," *Huffington Post*, 18 December 2012, accessed 21 March 2013, http://www.huffingtonpost.com/bartlett-naylor/volcker-rule_b_2317541.html.

Ng, Connie, "Comment, Burma and the Road Forward: Lessons from Next Door and Possible Avenues Towards Constitutional and Democratic Development," *Santa Clara Law Review* 53 (2013): 267–99.

Nozick, Robert, *Anarchy, State, and Utopia* (New York, NY: Basic Books, 1974).

O'Malley, Terrance, "The Consequences of Investment Adviser Registration with the SEC," *Journal of Investment Compliance* 1 Issue 1 (2000): 47–54.

Odean, Terence, "Are Investors Reluctant to Realize Their Losses?" *Journal of Finance* 53 (1998): 1775–98.

Olsen, R. A., "Investment Risk: The Experts' Perspective," *Financial Analysts Journal* 53 (1997): 62–6.

Osborn, Tom, "Clearing Houses Move Their FX Pieces Into Place," *Financial News*, 29 November 2012, accessed 27 August 2014, www.efinancialnews.com/story/2012-05-14/clearing-houses-move-their-fx-pieces-into-position.

Pacheco, Barbara S., "The U.S. Retail Payments System in Transition: Federal Reserve Iniatives," *Federal Reserve Bank of Kansas City*, August 2006, accessed 11 June 2013, https://www.kansascityfed.org/publicat/psr/Briefings/PSR-BriefingAug06.pdf.

Palm, G. and D. Walkovik, "Issuing Securities: A Guide to Securities Regulation Around the World," *International Financial Law Review* 62 (July 1990, special supplement).

Patrikis, Ernest T., Thomas C. Baxter, Jr., and Raj Bhala, *Wire Transfers* (Chicago, IL: Irwin/Probus, 1993).

Patterson, Scott and Andrew R. Johnson, "New York Attorney General Sues Barclays Over Stock-Trading Business," *The Wall Street Journal*, 25 June 2014, accessed 17 September 2014, http://online.wsj.com/articles/new-york-attorney-general-plans-lawsuit-against-barclays-1403723283.

Patterson, Scott and Jean Eaglesham, " 'Dark Pools' Face New SEC Probe," *The Wall Street Journal*, 9 June 2014, accessed 17 September 2014, http://online.wsj.com/articles/dark-pools-face-new-sec-probe-1402356915.

Pennacchi, George, "Narrow Banking," *Annual Review of Financial Economics* 4 (2012), accessed 3 April 2013, https://business.illinois.edu/gpennacc/GPNarrowBankARFE.pdf.

Permjit, Singh, "The Ins and Outs of Corporate Eurobonds," *Investopedia*, 2009, accessed 23 September 2013, http://www.investopedia.com/articles/bonds/09/issuing-a-corporate-eurobond.asp.

Perret, Roy W., "Hindu Ethics?" *The Blackwell Companion to Religious Ethics*, ed. William Schweiker (Oxford, UK: Blackwell Publishing, 2003).

Persky, Joseph, "From Usury to Interest," *Journal of Economic Perspectives* 21 (Winter 2007): 227–36.

Pettengill, Glenn, Sridhar Dundaram, and Ike Matthur, "The Conditional Relation between Beta and Returns," *Journal of Financial and Quantitative Analysis* 30, No. 1 (March 1995): 101–15.

Pope Benedict XVI, *Caritas in Veritate* (San Francisco, CA: Ignatius Press, 2009).

Pope Francis, "Pope: Financial Reform Along Ethical Lines," *The Vatican Today*, 16 May 2013, accessed 24 March 2015, http://www.news.va/en/news/pope-financial-reform-along-ethical-lines.

Popper, Nathaniel, "As Market Heats Up, Trading Slips Into Shadows," *The New York Times* (2013), 31 March 2013, accessed 19 May 2013, http://www.nytimes.com/2013/04/01/business/as-market-heats-up-trading-slips-into-shadows.html?pagewanted=all&_r=0.

Poterba, James and Lawrence Summers, "Mean Reversion in Stock Prices: Evidence and Implications," *Journal of Financial Economics* 22 (October 1988): 22–59.

Preston, Ronald, "Christian Ethics," *A Companion to Ethics*, ed. Peter Singer (Oxford, UK: Blackwell Publishing, 1993), 95.

Putnins, Talis J., "Market Manipulation: A Survey," *Journal of Economic Surveys* 26, No. 5 (2011): 952–67.

Rachels, James and Stuart Rachels, *The Elements of Moral Philosophy*, 6th ed. (New York, NY: McGraw Hill, 2010).

Rachman, Gideon and Ajay Makan, "Rouhani Tries to Lure Western Oil Majors to Iran," *Financial Times* (24 January 2014): 3.

Radcliffe, Brent, "Should You Be Afraid Of Dark Pool Liquidity?" *Investopedia*, 6 October 2009, accessed 19 May 2013, http://www.investopedia.com/articles/trading/09/dark-pool-liquidity.asp.

Reilly, Frank K. and David J. Wright, "A Comparison of Published Betas," *Journal of Portfolio Management* 14, No. 3 (Spring 1988): 64–9.

Reilly, Frank K. and Keith C. Brown, *Investment Analysis and Portfolio Management*, 7th ed. (Mason, OH: Thomson South-Western, 2003).

Reilly, Frank K. and Rashid A. Akhtar, "The Benchmark Error Problem with Global Capital Markets," *Journal of Portfolio Management* 22, No. 1 (Fall 1995): 33–52.

Reinganum, Marc R., "The Anomalous Stock Market Behavior of Small Firms in January: Empirical Tests for Tax-Loss Effects," *Journal of Financial Economics* 12 (June 1983): 89–104.

Reinganum, Marc R., "The Anatomy of a Stock Market Winner," *Financial Analysts Journal* (March–April 1988): 272–84.

Rich, Georg and Christian Walter, "The Future of Universal Banking," *CATO Journal* 13, No. 2 (Fall 1993): 310–11, accessed 11 June 2013, http://object.cato.org/sites/cato.org/files/serials/files/cato-journal/1993/11/cj13n2-8.pdf.

Richardson, Matthew, "Why the Volcker Rule Is a Useful Tool for Managing Systemic Risk," *NYU Stern School of Business*, accessed 10 April 2014, https://www.sec.gov/comments/s7-41-11/s74111-316.pdf.

Richter, Paul, "New Iran Agreement Includes Secret Side Deal, Tehran Official Says," *Los Angeles Times*, 13 January 2014, www.latimes.com/world/worldnow/la-fg-wn-iran-nuclear-side-deal-20140113,0,4116168.story#axzz2rLwaPbUK.

Roberts, Harry, "Stock Market 'Patterns' and Financial Analysis: Methodological Suggestions," *Journal of Finance* 1 (March 1959): 11–25.

Roll, Richard, "A Critique of the Capital Asset Theory Tests: Part I: On Past and Potential Testability of the Theory," *Journal of Financial Economics* 4 (1977): 129–76.

Roll, Richard and Stephen A. Ross, "An Empirical Investigation of the Arbitrage Pricing Theory," *Journal of Finance* 35 (December 1980): 1073–1103.

Roosevelt, Theodore, "Citizenship in a Republic" (speech, Sorbonne, Paris, 23 April 1910), http://design.caltech.edu/erik/Misc/Citizenship_in_a_Republic.pdf.

Ross, Stephen A., "Return, Risk and Arbitrage," *Risk and Return in Finance*, eds. I. Friend and J. Bicksler (Cambridge, MA: Ballinger, 1976).

Rozeff, Michael S. and Mir A. Zaman, "Market Efficiency and Insider Trading: New Evidence," *Journal of Business* (January 1988): 24–5.

Russell-Kraft, Stephanie, "NY AG Sues Barclays Over Dark Pool Fraud," *Law360*, 25 June 2014, accessed 17 September 2014, http://www.law360.com/articles/551825/ny-ag-sues-barclays-over-dark-pool-fraud.

Salmon, Felix, "The Biggest Weakness of Basel III," *Reuters*, 15 September 2010, accessed http://blogs.reuters.com/felix-salmon/2010/09/15/the-biggest-weakness-of-basel-iii/.

Sayler, Larry, "Ethical Analysis of Insider Trading," *Christian Business Faculty Association*, accessed 27 July 2015, http://www.cbfa.org/Sayler_Paper.pdf.

Schwartz, Hugh, "Heuristics or Rules of Thumb," *Behavioral Finance: Investors, Corporations, and Markets*, eds. H. Kent Baker and John R. Nofsinger (Hoboken, NJ: John Wiley & Sons, 2010).

Schwarz, Norbert and Leigh Ann Vaughn, "The Availability Heuristic Revisited: Ease of Recall and Content of Recall as Distinct Sources of Information," *Heuristics and Biases: The Psychology of Intuitive Judgment*, eds. Thomas Gilovich, Dale Griffin, and Daniel Kahneman (Cambridge, UK: Cambridge University Press, 2002).

Scott, Hal S., *International Finance: Transactions, Policy and Regulation*, 8th ed. (St. Paul, MN: Foundation Press, 2010), 206–7.

Scott, Hal S., *International Finance: Law and Regulation*, 3rd ed. (London, UK: Sweet & Maxwell, 2012).

Seyhun, H. Nejat, "Insiders' Profits, Costs of Trading and Market Efficiency," *Journal of Financial Economics* 16 (1986): 189–212.

Shari, Michael, "Investment Banking in Asia," *Global Finance*, 6 February 2012, accessed 21 April 2013, https://www.gfmag.com/magazine/february-2012/investment-banking-in-asia.

Sharpe, William F., "Capital Asset Prices: A Theory of Market Equilibrium Under Conditions of Risk," *Journal of Finance* 19 (1964): 425–42.

Sharpe, William F. and Guy M. Cooper, "Risk-Return Classes of New York Stock Exchange Common Stocks 1931–1967," *Financial Analysis Journal* 28, No. 2 (March–April 1972): 46–54.

Shefrin, Hersh and Meir Statman, "The Disposition to Sell Winners too Early and Ride Losers too Long," *Journal of Finance* 40, No. 3 (1985): 777–92.

Shefrin, Hersh and Meir Statman, "Ethics, Fairness and Efficiency in Financial Markets," *Financial Analysts Journal* 49, No. 6 (November–December 1993): 21–9.

Shefrin, Hersh and Meir Statman, "The Contributions of Daniel Kahneman and Amos Tversky," *The Journal of Behavioral Finance* 4, No. 2 (2003): 54–8.

Sheppard, Lee, "The Loopholes in the Volcker Rule," *Forbes*, 8 January 2014, accessed 29 March 2014, http://www.forbes.com/sites/leesheppard/2014/01/08/the-loopholes-in-the-volcker-rule/2/.

Shiller, Robert, "Do Stock Prices Move too Much to be Justified by Subsequent Changes in Dividends?" *The American Economic Review* 71, No. 3 (1981): 421–36.

Shleifer, Andrei, *Inefficient Markets: An Introduction to Behavioral Finance* (Oxford, UK: Oxford University Press, 2000).

Simpson, Stephen D, "The Banking System: Commercial Banking – How Banks Are Regulated." *Investopedia*, accessed 14 April 2013, http://www.investopedia.com/university/banking-system/banking-system6.asp.

Slovic, Paul, et al., "The Affect Heuristic," *Heuristics and Biases: The Psychology of Intuitive Judgment*, eds. Thomas Gilovich, Dale Griffin, and Daniel Kahneman, (Cambridge, UK: Cambridge University Press, 2002).

Smith, Jeffrey W., James P. Selway, and D. Timothy McCormick, "The Nasdaq Stock Market: Historical Background and Current Operation, NASD Working Paper 98–01," *NASD Economic Research Department* (1998), 8, accessed 26 August 2014, https://cobweb.business.nd.edu/Portals/0/MendozaIT/Research/Shared%20Documents/Nastraq/Nasdaq%20Stock%20Market%20Historical%20Background%20and%20Current%20Operation.pdf.

Solomon, Robert C., "Business Ethics and Virtue," *A Companion to Business Ethics*, ed. Robert E. Frederick (Oxford, UK: Blackwell Publishing, 2003).

Stackhouse, Max L., "Economics," *The Blackwell Companion to Religious Ethics*, ed. William Schweiker (Oxford, UK: Blackwell Publishing, 2003), 455.

Statman, Meir, "Betas Compared: Merrill Lynch vs. Value Line," *Journal of Portfolio Management* 7, No. 2 (Winter 1981): 41–4.

Statman, Meir, "The Cultures of Insider Trading," *Journal of Business Ethics* 89 (May 2009): 51–8.

Stevenson, Alexandra, "With Ban on Ads Removed, Hedge Funds Test Waters," *DealBook: The New York Times*, 20 February 2014, accessed 22 September 2014, http://dealbook.nytimes.com/2014/02/20/with-ban-on-ads-lifted-hedge-funds-test-waters/?_php=true&_type=blogs&_r=0.

Steyer, Roy H., "The Investment Company Act of 1940," *Yale Law Journal* 50 (1941): 440.

Stout, Lynn A., "Trust Behavior: The Essential Foundation of Securities Markets," *Behavioral Finance: Investors, Corporations, and Markets*, eds. H. Kent Baker and John R. Nofsinger (Hoboken, NJ: John Wiley & Sons, 2010), 513–22.

Strauss, Delphine, "America's 'Exorbitant Privilege' is Ebbing," *Financial Times* (27 January 2014): 8.

Taffler, Richard J., "The Representative Heuristic," *Behavioral Finance: Investors, Corporations, and Markets*, eds. H. Kent Baker and John R. Nofsinger (Hoboken, NJ: John Wiley & Sons, 2010).

Tarullo, Daniel K., "Testimony on Volcker Rule, Before the Committee on Financial Services," (testimony, US House of Representatives, Washington, DC, 2014), accessed 10 March 2014, http://www.federalreserve.gov/newsevents/testimony/tarullo20140205a.htm.

Thel, S., "$850,000 in Six Minutes – The Mechanics of Securities Manipulation," *Cornell Law Review* 79 (2004): 219–98.

Thompson, Mel, *Ethical Theory* (Abingdon, Oxford: Hoddington & Stoughton, 1999).

Tole, Thomas M., "How to Maximize Stationarity of Beta," *Journal of Portfolio Management* 7, No. 2 (Winter 1980): 45–9.

Torbati, Yeganeh and Lesley Wroughton, "Kerry Meets Iran Foreign Minister to Close Gaps in Iran Nuclear Talks," *Reuters*, 8 November 2013, http://mobile.reuters.com/article/topNews/idUSBRE9A709G20131108?irpc=932.

Torres, Craig and Cheyenne Hopkins, "Bernanke Says Dodd–Frank's Volcker Rule Won't Be Ready by July 21 Deadline," *Bloomberg*, 2012, accessed 17 April 2014, http://www.bloomberg.com/news/2012-02-29/bernanke-says-dodd-frank-s-volcker-rule-won-t-be-ready-by-july-21-deadline.html.

Touryalai, Halah, "Can Knight Capital Be Saved?" *Forbes*, 2 August 2012, accessed 7 May 2013, http://www.forbes.com/sites/halahtouryalai/2012/08/02/can-knight-capital-be-saved/.

Tucker, Sundeep, "Coca-Cola's $2.4bn China deal at risk," *Financial Times*, 17 March, 2009, accessed 5 August 2015, http://www.ft.com/cms/s/0/daf851e8-1327-11de-a170-0000779fd2ac.html.

Tversky, Amos and Daniel Kahneman, "Availability: A Heuristic for Judging Frequency and Probability," *Cognitive Psychology* 5, Issue 2 (1973): 677–95.

Tversky, Amos and Daniel Kahneman, "Judgment Under Uncertainty: Heuristics and Biases," *Science* 185, 4157 (1974): 1124–31.

Tversky, Amos and Daniel Kahneman, "Rational Choice and the Framing of Decisions," *Choices, Values, and Frames*, eds. Daniel Kahneman and Amos Tversky (Cambridge, UK: Cambridge University Press, 2000).

Van Hooft, Stan, *Understanding Virtue Ethics* (Chesham, UK: Acumen Publishing, 2006), 11.

Volcker, Paul, "Commentary on the Restrictions on Proprietary Trading by Insured Depository Institutions," *Wall Street Journal*, 2012, accessed 4 April 2014, http://online.wsj.com/public/resources/documents/Volcker_Rule_Essay_2-13-12.pdf.

Wang, Peter, Mark Allen Cohen, and Stephen G. Harris, "Coca-Cola/Huiyuan Deal Is First Acquisition Blocked By China Antitrust Review," *Mondaq*, 25 March 2009, accessed 2 August 2015, http://www.mondaq.com/article.asp?articleid=76710.

Warde, Ibrahim, *Islamic Finance in the Global Economy* (Edinburgh: Edinburgh University Press, 2000).

Weber, Max, *The Religion of India* (New York, NY: Free Press, 1958).

Weber, Robert F., "New Governance, Financial Regulation, and Challenges to Legitimacy: The Example of the Internal Models Approach to Capital Adequacy Regulation," *Administrative Law Review* 62 (2010): 783–93.

Weithers, Tim, *Foreign Exchange: A Practical Guide to the FX Markets* (Hoboken, New Jersey: John Wiley & Sons, Inc., 2006), 129–32.

Werhane, P. H., "The Indefensibility of Insider Trading," *Journal of Business Ethics* 10 (1991): 729–31.

Wheatly, Alan ed., *The Power of Currencies and Currencies of Power* (New York, NY: Routledge, 2013).

Whitehead, Charles K., "The Volcker Rule and Evolving Financial Markets," *Harvard Business Law Review* 1, No. 42 (2011): 39–73.

Wilson, T. D., et al., "A New Look at Anchoring Effects: Basic Anchoring and its Antecedents," *Journal of Experimental Psychology: General* 4 (1996): 387–402.

Wisley, H. Lawrence, "The Investment Advisers Act of 1940," *Journal of Finance* 4, No. 4, (1949): 289.

Wojciechowski, W. C. and J. R. Thompson, "Market Truths: Theory Versus Empirical Simulations," *Journal of Statistical Computing and Simulations* 76, No. 5 (2006): 385–95.

Wong, Stephanie, "Coca-Cola to Buy China's Huiyuan for $2.3 Billion (Update 4)," *Bloomberg Business*, 3 September 2008, accessed 4 August 2015, http://www.bloomberg.com/apps/news?pid=20601087&sid=aI9_PX_Btrqs&refer=home.

Xinhua, "Coca-Cola Purchase of Huiyuan 'Still Under Antimonopoly Review,' " *China Daily*, 16 March 2009, accessed 7 June 2015, http://www.chinadaily.com.cn/china/2009-03/16/content_7584295.htm.

Zhou, Wanfeng and Nick Olivari, "Exclusive: EBS take new step to rein in high-frequency traders," *Reuters*, 23 August 2013, accessed 27 August 2014, http://www.reuters.com/article/2013/08/23/us-markets-forex-hft-idUSBRE97M0YJ20130823.

Index

References in *italics* indicate a figure and tables are shown in **bold**.

Accounting and Auditing Organization for Islamic Financial Institutions (AAOIFI), Shari'a Board of 344
accredited investors 336–7
Agarwal, V. 65
Aggarwal, R.K. 331–2
Akhtar, A. 46
Al Baraka Bank in Bahrain 100
Allen, F. 330
alternative trading systems (ATS) 155
analogical reasoning 42
analysts: availability heuristic and 61; representativeness heuristic and 65
arbitrage pricing theory (APT): assumptions of 31; beta (sensitivity measure) 32; calculation 31–3; error term 32; research on 33
Aristotle 284, 292
Asia: asset management 200; bond markets in 158; corporate bond market in 159; derivatives market regulation 146; high-frequency trading (HFT) 151; local currency bonds 158–9, *160*; OTC markets in 145–6
Asian investment banks 192–4
asset managers 197, 198, 199–200
asset weighting, portfolios 20, *20*
asset-backed securities (ABS) 145
assets under management (AUM) 199–200, 339
Association of South East Asian Nations (ASEAN) 165
Australia 151

balance sheets 216
bank certificates of deposit (CDs) 12
Bank for International Settlements (BIS) 168
bank holding companies (BHCs) 180–1, 182, 186, 395
Bank Holding Company Act of 1956 (BHCA) (USA) 180–1, 392, 394–5

Bank Islam Malaysia 99
Bank of America Corporation *398*
Bank of Credit and Commerce International (BCCI) 386, 390
Bank of International Settlements (BIS) 388
Bank Simpanan, Shari'a Board members 88–9
banks: capital adequacy 403–12; pre-tax profits of 1,000 largest banks in the world *193*; *see also* central banks; commercial banks; correspondent banks; foreign banks; Islamic banks
Basel Committee on Banking Supervision: Basel I capital standards 388–9, 406; Basel II and Basel III capital requirements **406**; Basel II capital standards 368, 389–90, 396, 407; Basel III capital standards 407–8; capital adequacy standards 403; history of 388–90; members 390; supervisory activities 390–1
Bayes' rule 60, 65
behavioural finance: analyst stock recommendations 65; disposition effect 62–3; equity premiums 63; future research areas 69–70; herding and bubbles 63–4; history of 52–3; insider trading and 328–9; overview of 51–2; portfolio construction 63; rationality in 51; stock selection, winners and losers 64–5; *see also* prospect theory
Benartzi, S. 63
Bentham, Jeremy 272
Berg, J. 68
beta: beta coefficient calculation 44; defined 25, 44; and expected return equation 44–5; and the market portfolio 25–6, 44, 46–7, **46**; published data of 47; research on 47; as systemic risk (CAPM) 25–6, 44, 399
biases: availability heuristic and 60–1; representativeness heuristic and 59–60

560 Index

Black Scholes options pricing model 48
Boatright, R. 329
bond markets: in Asia 158; in developing economies 165–6; Eurobonds 161–4; foreign bonds 160–1, 162; globalization of 157–8; government (treasury) bonds 118, 158–9; investors and offshore markets 164–6; limits of local currency bonds 159–60; local currency bonds (Asia) 158–9, *160*; offshore bonds **163**; offshore markets 160, 161–4; overview of 156–7; size of 157–8
bonds: bond yield calculations 164; clearing and settlement 168–9; corporate bonds 118–19; defined 349; government (treasury) bonds 118, 158–9; mortgage-backed securities 119; municipal bonds 118; overview of 117–18; sukuk (Shari'a compliant investment certificates) 105–8
Brazil *see* BRICS
BRICS (Brazil, Russia, India, China and South Africa): cumulative stock market capitalization 138, **139–40**; domestic equity market capitalization for domestic exchanges **141**
broker-dealers: defined 194; discount 136, 195; discretionary accounts 194–5; full service 136, 194–5; licensing 196; online brokerage 195; pricing brokerage deals 195–6
Buddhism: central authority 299; charity and 303–4; conduct of business 304–5; and debt 304; economic ethics 304; emptiness 302; enlightenment/awakening 301–2; ethics and finance 303–5, **319**; fundamental precepts 299–301; karma 302; moral precepts 302–3; non-attachment principle 303; wealth and 303

CAMEL rating system 396, 398–9
Canary Capital 333–4
capital adequacy: Basel 1 capital standards 406; Basel II and Basel III capital requirements **406**; Basel II capital standards 407; Basel III capital standards 407–8; capital, term 403; capital ratio and capital adequacy calculation 405; off-balance sheet items 405; overview of 403; risk-weighted assets 404–5; Tier 2 supplemental capital 404; Tier I core capital 403; total assets 404; US Capital standards post-2014 **406**; US Capital standards pre-2014 **406**
capital allocation lines (CAL): under the CAPM 23–5, *24*; portfolios risk assessment and 14–15, *15*

capital asset pricing model (CAPM): assumptions of 30; capital allocation lines (CAL) 23–5, *24*; capital market lines (CML) 24, *24*; efficient frontiers 23–5, *24*; equilibrium pricing model 49; internal rate of return (IRR) 26; lending and borrowing 28–9, *29*, 48; market portfolio definition and 46; passive strategy using CML 29–30; portfolio theory and 23; within real-world data 30–1; reliability of risk/return relationship 44–5; returns of individual securities 26; risk of individual stock vs. the market 25–6; security market line (SML) 26, 27, *27*, *28*; studies on 48, 51; systemic risk (beta) 25, 26, 44; theory 23–5, *24*; undervalued/overvalued asset identification 27, *28*; use by asset managers 199
capital market lines (CML): under the CAPM 24, *24*; lending and borrowing at risk-free rate *29*; overview of 15–16, *16*; passive strategies and 29–30
cash 203–4
cash flow statements 216–18
central banks: clearing and settlement 168; currency management 203–4; discount rates 204, 207; foreign currency reserves 207–8; foreign exchange (FX) policy implementation 207–8; monetary policy implementation 206–7; open market operations (OMOs) 207; overview of 200; payment system supervision 202; reserve requirements 204, 206–7; role in financial crisis 200
Chartered Financial Analysts (CFA) *Standards of Practice Handbook* 67, 68
cheques 202–3
Cherian, J. A. 329
China: foreign corporate bond issuance 163–4; investment banks 192; *see also* BRICS; Hong Kong
Christianity: central authority 305; charity and 308; Christian economics 309–10; Christian ethics 306–7; conduct of business 309; debt and 308–9; ethics and finance 307–10, **319**; metaphysics 306; traditions of 305; wealth and 307–8
churning 195
CITIC Pacific (case study): background 517; deontological theory applied to 520–1; ethical analysis 520–2; forex controversy 518–20, **518**, **519**; justice theories applied to 521; specified persons **517**; utilitarianism applied to 521–2; virtue ethics applied to 521
Citigroup, formation 181

clearing and settlement (C&S): of derivatives 169–71; DvD systems 169; DvP systems 169; Federal Reserve payment system 167, *167*; for foreign exchange (FX) 171–2; investment manager duties and 198–9; major regional clearing houses **170**; OTC markets 146, 169–71; for outbound international transactions 367; overview of 166–8; risk 168; of stocks and bonds 168–9

clearing houses 168

closed-end investment companies (CEFs) 120

collateralized debt obligations (CDOs) 145

commercial banks: Bank Holding Company Act,1956 180–1, 392, 394–5; defined 179; Glass–Steagall Act *180–1*, 182, 183, 184, 200, 369; Gramm-Leach-Bliley Act *180–1*, 182, 183, 184, 200, 369, 395; income sources 179; intermediary banks, use of 167; narrow banking 185, *185*; primary regulators 200; separation from investment banks 180–1, 182, 369; size of financial institutions and 182–3; universal banking 184–5, *185*; Volcker Rule 182–3, *184*; wire transfers 204

commercial papers 12

Commodity Exchange Act (CEA) 171

Commodity Futures Trading Commission (CFTC) 169–71, 186, 393

compensation schemes, insider trading and 326, 327

compliance, Volcker Rule 375–6

compound interest 4–6

Confucius 292

Consumer Financial Protection Bureau (CFPB) 392, 393, 398

Consumer Price Index (CPI) 9

Cooper, M. 45

corporate bonds 118–19, 159, 163–4; *see also* bonds

corporate entity interests: convertible securities 117; ordinary stock 115, 117; preferred stock 115, 135; warrants 116–17

correlation coefficients 17–18

correspondent banks: for international banking activities 202, 383–4; and sanctions against Iran 453–4, 476–7

covariance formula 18

Crespo, M. 342

Daiwa Securities 192

dark pools: compared to OTC markets 151–2; development of 152–3; ethical issues 154–5; high-frequency trading (HFT) and 149; increased trading in 154; indications of interest 154; internalization 154; and Regulation ATS (alternative trading system) 155; and Regulation NMS (National Market System) 153–4, 155; regulatory reform of 155–6

DeBondt, W. 64

decision-making: framing effects 57–8; use of expected utility theory 53; *see also* heuristic behaviour

deontological theory *see* duty-based (deontological) theories

depository institutions (DI) 207

Depository Trust and Clearing Corporation (DTCC) 168–9

derivatives: and the 2007 financial crisis 145; clearing and settlement of 169–71; defined 144–5; second-order derivatives 145

Derman, E. 38, 42, 43

developed economies: payment systems 202; World Bank definition 137

developing economies: bond markets 165–6; market capitalization and 137–8; payment systems 202; stock market performances **141**; World Bank definition 137; *see also* BRICS

Dickhaut, J. 68

disclosure: Hong Kong SFO regulation 517–18, 520; initial public offering (IPO) 186–7; investment banks 186–7; US securities markets 365–6

disposition effect 62–3

dividends: ordinary stock 115; preferred stock 116; tax on 197

Dobson, J. 66

Dodd–Frank Wall Street Reform and Consumer Protection Act 145, 169, 183, 368, 398

dollar-weighted average return 9

domestic transactions 350

Dopuch, N. 52, 53

Douglas, G. W. 45

Dow Jones Industrial Average **46**

duty-based (deontological) theories: application framework 281–2; categorical imperatives 279–81, 286; CITIC Pacific case study 520–1; criticisms of 283–4; fiduciary duty and 282; Huiyuan Juice Group case study 527; hypothetical imperatives 279; Iran trade sanctions and 419; principles of 278; the will 278–9

Dworkin, Ronald 288

economic analysis 265–8

efficient frontiers: under the CAPM 23–5, *24*; for portfolios 20, *21*; and utility curves 21, *23*

efficient market hypothesis (EMH): arguments against 68; assumed market behaviour 33–4, 42–3; equilibrium pricing model 49; impact of high-frequency trading on 148; and legalization of insider trading 325; overview of 33–4, 51; random walk/diffusion 34, 43; risk assumptions 43; risk measures 43; semi-strong form of 34–5, 36–7; strong form of 35–6, 37; studies on 36, 37–8, 49, 51; volatility measurements 43; weak form of 34, 36
Efficient Market Model (EMM) 43
Electronic Booking Service (EBS) 151
Ellis, C. 341, 342–3
emerging economies *see* developing economies
emerging markets: efficiency of 34; market manipulation in 331; *see also* developing economies
equity, term 403; *see also* capital adequacy
equity risk premium 12
ethics: in Buddhism 303–5; in Christianity 306–10; for dark pools 154–5; fairness 66–7; in Hinduism 312–14, **319**; insider trading as unethical 323–5; in Islamic finance 74, 79, 86; in Judaism 316–18; of major religions 318, **319**; market manipulation, ethical evaluation of 331–2, 532–3; market timing and 334–5; mutual fund fees 341–3; profit maximization ethic, MFT 50–1, 66, 67–8, 79, 328; and sanctions 412; trust 67–9; *see also* duty-based (deontological) theories; justice theories; utilitarianism; virtue ethics
Eurobonds 367
Euromarket instruments 350
Euronext 138, 140, 142, **142**
European Infrastructure Regulation (EMIR) 169, 171
European Union (EU): European Infrastructure Regulation (EMIR) 169, 171; Market Abuse Directive (MAD) (insider trading) 323, 329; Markets in Financial Instruments Directive II (MiFID II) 150; regulation of high-frequency trading 150
exchange traded funds (ETFs) 119–20
exchanges: in BRICS 138; defined 134–5; developed countries 138–43; developing economies 137–8; electronic communication networks (ECNs) 136; fixed commissions on trades (historical) 143; internet trading 136; mergers between 138, 140–2, **142**; National Association of Securities Dealers Automated Quotations (NASDAQ) 136, 138, 142, **142**; Small Orders Execution System (SOES) 136; traditional exchanges 135
expected utility theory (EUT) 53, 55, *56*
expected value 10–11, **11**

fair market value (FMV) 189
fairness principle: ethics of 66–7; fees for performance, mutual funds 342–3; Huiyuan Juice Group case study 526–7; insider trading and 324; market manipulation and 332; and the ultimatum game 66–7, 328
false trading, case study 529–33
Fama, E. 30–1, 36–7, 45, 340–1
Federal Deposit Insurance Corporation (FDIC) 180, 201, 385, 386, 391, 392–3, 399–400, 404
Federal Reserve Board: approval, Capital Edge Corporations 387–8; capital adequacy standards 403–5; regulation of outbound transactions 402–3; supervisory role, foreign bank branches and agencies 384, 387–8, 391, 392–3, 395
Federal Reserve Reform Act 200
Federal Reserve Regulation J 205–6
Federal Reserve System (Fed): creation of 200; Fedwire (transfers) 201, 204, 205; monetary policy implementation 206; money supply control 203–4; open market operations (OMOs) 207; payment systems 167, *167*; reserve requirements 204; state-chartered bank membership of 201; supervisors, international banking transactions 391–2
fees: hedge funds 337–9; mutual funds 339–43; sales loads (mutual funds) 339, 340
fiduciary duty: CITIC Pacific case study 520; deontological theory applied to 282; insider trading and 290, 322–3, 324–5; market timing and 335; Sino Katalytics case study 533; Water Oasis Group Limited 537
financial crisis *see* 2007–08 Financial crisis
financial holding companies (FHC) 392, 393, 395–8, *397*
Financial Industry Regulatory Authority (FINRA) 155–6, 186
financial intermediaries 349
financial markets: defined 134; role of trust in 68–9; virtue ethics and 294–5
financial ratios: comparative ratio analysis 221–2; leverage ratios 221, 396; liquidity ratios 219; operating

performance ratios 220; price earnings ratio (P/E ratios) 218
Financial Services Modernization Act of 1999 see Gramm-Leach-Bliley Act
financial statements: balance sheets 216, 241–51; cash flow statements 216–18, 252–9; income statements 216, 233–40; types of 215
Findlay, M. C. 49
foreign banks: financial holding companies (FHC) 392, 393, 395–8, *397*; statutorily permissible US activities 396; *see also* inbound transactions to the US; international banking activities; outbound transactions
foreign direct investment (FDI) 401
foreign exchange (FX): clearing and settlement for 171–2; currency swaps 130–2, *131*; foreign exchange controls, outbound transactions 367; forex controversy, CITIC Pacific 518–20; forwards transactions 123–8; futures 128–9; impact of high-frequency trading on 151; par value system (historical) 208–9; policy implementation, central banks 207–8; put and call options 129–30; spot transactions 121–2, *123*
French, K. R. 30–1, 36–7, 45
front running 149, 153, 155
fund management companies 330, 340, 341–2
fund managers: availability heuristic and 61; marking the close manipulation (window dressing) 331; selection of and the representativeness heuristic 65
fundamental analysis, stocks 34–5
future value of interest factors 6
future value of money 4–6
FX (foreign exchange) *see* foreign exchange (FX)

Gale, D. 330
General Agreement on Trade in Services (GATS) 386, 400–1
Glass–Steagall Act 180–1, 182, 183, *184*, 200, 369
global financial system (GFS) 178–9
globalization 349
Gonedes, N. 52, 53
government (treasury) bonds 158; *see also* bond markets
Goyal, A. 65
Gramm-Leach-Bliley Act 180–1, 182, 183, *184*, 200, 369, 395
Greenspan, Alan 66
Gross Domestic Product (GDP): and economic categorization of countries 137; and stock market capitalization, BRICS **139–40**
Gupta, Rajat 295–6

hedge funds: fee structure 337–9; financial crisis impact on 336; history of 336; lock-up of investor funds 337; market manipulation and 330; regulation 336–7; sales to accredited investors 336–7; use of leverage 337
hedonism 273
Herstatt risk 122, 123, 172
heuristic behaviour: anchoring and adjustment heuristic 61–2; availability heuristic 60–1; for decision-making 58–9; representativeness heuristic 59–60, 65
high-frequency trading (HFT): asset mispricing and 31; circuit breakers 149–50; dark pools and 149; impact of 146–8; impact on efficient market hypothesis 148–9; impact on foreign exchange markets 151; liquidity issues 149; market declines and 147, 149; market manipulation and 330; origins 143, 146; regulatory reform of 150–1
Hinduism: caste system 310, 311, 312, 313; central authority 310; and charity 313; ethics 312–14, **319**; karma 313; metaphysics 311–12; and wealth 313–14; and work 313
historical data 43
honesty 294
Hong Kong: disclosure regulation, SFO 517–18, 520; false trading regulation, SFO 529; high-frequency trading (HFT) 151; insider trading regulation, SFO 524, 535; price rigging regulation, SFO 529; stock market manipulation regulation, SFO 529–30; universal banking 184–5
Hong Kong Stock Exchange (HKSE) 193–4
HSBC North America *397*
Huiyuan Juice Group: background 524; Coca-Cola buy out 525; consequentialism and 527; deontological theory applied to 527; ethical analysis 526–7; fairness principle and 526–7; insider trading regulation, SFO 524
human psyche: in modern finance theory 50, 66; opportunism 66; perception of in Islamic finance 110–11; self-interested economic actors 66
Hume, David 50, 66, 272, 292, 293
Hursthouse, R. 293
hybrid securities 349

iceberg orders 153
inbound transactions to the US: activities regulation (permissible activities) 393–8; Bank Holding Company Act,1956 180–1, 394–5; bankruptcy proceedings 400; CAMEL rating system 396, 398–9; closely related to banking rule 394–5; consumer protection 398; deposit insurance 399–400; disclosure requirements 365–6; exempt offerings 359–65; Federal Reserve Board approval 393; financial activities, determining 395–6; foreign private issuers 359; GATS accord and 400–1; issuing companies, types of **366**; qualified foreign banking organization (QFBO) 395; registration process 355–6; registration statements 356–9; regulations 393–401; risk 399; safety and soundness 398–9; supervision of 391–3; US securities laws 355; *see also* foreign banks
income statements 216
India 428; *see also* BRICS
Indonesia, cumulative stock market capitalization 138, **139–40**
industry analysis: competitors 264–5; market for product/service 264; purpose of 263; suppliers and inputs 265
inflation, returns 9–10
initial public offering (IPO): disclosure 186–7; traditional exchanges 135; underwriting 187–9
insider trading: abnormal returns of 323; behavioural finance applied to 328–9; as a compensation scheme 326, 327; and dark pools 155; defined 322–3; and efficient price discovery 324, 326, 327; empirical studies 326; fairness argument and 324; fiduciary duty and 290, 322–3, 324–5; Hong Kong SFO regulation 524, 535; Huiyuan Juice Group case study 524–7; justice theories, application of 289–90; legal form of 322; managerial incentive argument 326; market efficiency argument and 325, 526; negative consequences of 327; Rajat Gupta case 295–6, 323; theory of legalization of 289–90, 324, 325–6; ultimatum game applied to 328–9; as unethical practice 323–5; US Securities Exchange Act, 1934 35–6, 186, 323, 329; utilitarian evaluation of 327–8; Water Oasis Group case study 535–7
institutional fund managers 198
insured depository institutions (IDI) 369
Intercontinental Exchange, Inc. (ICE) 142, **142**

interest: and commercial banks revenue generation 179; compound interest 4–6; discount rates 204, 207; in forwards FX transactions 123–8; history of 80–1; interest rates and the Federal Reserve 204; interest rates as benchmarks, Islamic finance 109; nominal interest rates 9; prohibition against, Islamic finance 80, 81–3; real interest rates 9–10
intergovernmental organizations (IGOs) 208
internal rate of return (IRR) 9, 26
International Association of Islamic Banks (IAIB) 87
International Bank for Reconstruction and Development (IBRD) 210
International Banking Act (IBA), 1978 384, 385
international banking activities: agencies 384–5; branches 385–6; correspondent relationships 202, 383–4; Edge Act Corporations 387–8, 400; GATS accord 400–1; most favoured nation (MFN) treatment 401; representative offices 384; Source of Strength Doctrine 386–7, 399; subsidiaries 386–7; *see also* foreign banks; inbound transactions to the US; outbound transactions
International Centre for Settlement of Investment Disputes (ICSID) 210
International Development Association (IDA) 210
International Emergency Economic Powers Act (IEEPA) 421, 425, 436, 452, 454
International Finance Corporation (IFC) 210
International Monetary Fund (IMF) 208–9
international non-governmental organizations (INGOs) 208
International Organization of Securities Commissioners (IOSCO): committees of 351; membership categories 351–2; Multilateral Memorandum of Understanding (MMoU) Concerning Consultation and Cooperation and the Exchange of Information 352–3; objectives 351; principles of 353–5
international organizations 208
international securities transactions: destination of 350; inbound transactions to the US 355–66; means of transfer 349–50; outbound transactions 367–8
International Swaps and Derivatives Association (ISDA) 132
internet trading 136, 195; *see also* high-frequency trading (HFT)
Investment Advisers Act, 1940 120–1

investment banks: Asian investment banks 192–4; best effort sales 189; defined 186; direct sales 189–90; disclosure 186–7; as merger and acquisitions (M&A) advisers 191; private placements 190; separation from commercial banks 180–1, 182, 369; shelf registration 190; syndicates 190; underwriting 187–9

Investment Company Act of 1940 121, 335, 336

investment grade ratings 358

investment management firms 197

investment managers: clearing and settlement monitoring 198–9; compensation 199–200; defined 196–7; loss prevention strategies 199; portfolio management 198, 199; selection of and the representativeness heuristic 65; tax considerations 197

investors: passive investors 29–30; utility/indifference curves 21–2, *22–3*

Iran, sanctions case study: affiliates prohibition 468–70; asset freeze prohibition 436–7; background issues around sanctions 413–15; Comprehensive Iran Sanctions, Accountability, and Divestment Act of 2010 (CISADA) 420, 431–2; diversion prohibition (humanitarian goods) 466; economic impact 481–2; efficacy of 483–4; energy, shipping, shipbuilding, and port prohibition 474–5, 476; energy sector prohibitions 421, 422–3, 424, 427, 433–6, 459–64, 474–5; evaluation of 415–19, 491; financial sector sanctions 451–9; first three phases of 419; Framework Agreement (Lausanne Accord), 2015 484–5, **486–90**; human rights prohibitions 437–8, 470–1; import/export prohibitions, CISADA 432–3; incentives for multilateral sanctions 426, 427, 431; Iran and Libya Sanctions Act (ILSA) 420–2, 427–8; Iran Freedom and Counter-Proliferation Act of 2012 473–4; Iran Freedom Support Act (IFSA) 420, 428; Iran Threat Reduction and Syria Human Rights Act of 2012 (Iran–Syria Act) 459; Iranian bank asset freeze 452–3; Joint Comprehensive Plan of Action, 2015 485, 491, **492–5**; Joint Plan of Action, 2013 477, **478–81**, 482–3; payments system prohibition 453–8, 476–7; precious metals prohibition 475–6; primary money laundering concern designation 451–2; Revolutionary Guard Corps prohibition 436–7, 465–6, 468–9; sanctions against a transgressor (sanctioned person) 424–7, 429–31, 438–40, 471–3; shipping and insurance prohibition 466–7; sovereign debt prohibition 467–8; termination criteria, ILSA 426–7; third country short supply exception 456–8, 476; trade with India 428; uranium enrichment 429, 465, **478–9**, 482–3, 484, **486–9**, **492–3**; US-Israeli relations and 429; waiver criteria 425–6, 428–9, 458, 473; weaponry transactions 421, 423–4, 464–5

Islam: ethics **319**; four schools of jurisprudence 79; history of 74–5; Muslim beliefs 75–6; role of money 81–3; *see also* Shari'a

Islamic banks: banking model *92*; financing structure 91–2; istisna'a (contracts) 99–100; Mudaraba mode of financing *92*; Murabaha contract (cost-plus contract) 95–7; salam contracts 100–1; structure of 90–1; *see also* Shari'a Supervisory Boards (SSB)

Islamic Development Bank 110

Islamic finance: contracts 86; credit enhancement mechanisms 344; defaults 96–7; defined 74; equity-based sukuk 343–4; ethical principles 79, 86; excessive risk (Gharar) prohibition 83–4; forms of, summary table **102**; the free market in 86; ijara (leasing) 98–9, **102**; interest (riba) prohibition 80, 81–3; interest rates as benchmarks 109; istisna'a (contracts) 99–100, **102**; LIBOR benchmarking 109; liquidity issues 110; loan decisions 82; Mudaraba mode of financing 90–2, **102**; Murabaha contract (cost-plus contract) 95–7, **102**, 109–10; Musharaka mode of financing 93–5, **102**; non-profit and loss-sharing-based transactions 95–101, *97*; profit- and loss-sharing-based transactions 90–5, *97*; relationship with conventional finance 110–11; salam contracts 100–1, **102**; securitization 105–8; Shari'a compliance and 343–4; Shari'a compliant asset management 343–4; Shari'a compliant products 85–6; short selling and Gharar 84–5; speculation/gambling prohibition 85; sukuk (Shari'a compliant investment certificates) 104–5; sukuk, secondary trading in 107–8; sukuk al-ijara 105–6; sukuk al-istisna'a 107; sukuk al-mudarabah 106, 343–4; sukuk al-musharaka 106–7, 343–4; sukuk al-salam 107; sukuk in international markets 108; zakat (charity) principle 76; *see also* Shari'a; Shari'a Supervisory Boards (SSB)

Islamic Financial Services Board (IFSB) 89–90
Islamic insurance (takaful): retakaful (reinsurance) 103, *104*; takaful 101–3
Israel 429, 477

Japan: Daiwa Securities 192; high-frequency trading (HFT) 151; yen bonds 158
Jarrow, R. A. 329
joint hypothesis 49
Judaism: central authority 314–15; charity and wealth 316–17; ethics 316–18, **319**; laws 315–16; social justice 316; and work 317–18
justice theories: application framework, insider trading 289–90; CITIC Pacific case study 520–1; commutative justice 284–5, 521, 533; compensatory justice 284, 285; distributive justice 284, 285–6, 290; equality of opportunity principle 287–8; forms of justice 284–5; notion of rights within 288–9; principle of equal liberty 286–7, 288; procedural justice 284; retributive justice 284, 285; Sino Katalytics case study 533; the veil of ignorance 286

Kahneman, Daniel 51, 52, 53–61, 63
Kant, Immanuel 50, 278–9, 286, 288
Keynes, John 49
Kinzer, Stephen 417
Knight, Frank 49
Kolb, R. 290

leverage ratios 221, 396
Levy, R. A. 47
LIBOR (London Interbank Offered Rate) 109, 285, 330
liquidity risk 399
loan production offices (LPO) 384
London Stock Exchange (LSE) 142, **142**

MacBeth, J. 30
McCabe, K. 68
Malaysia: Bank Simpanan 88–9; global sukuk market 104; Islamic Financial Services Board (IFSB) 89–90
market capitalization 137–8
market indexes 199
market makers 143, 144, 371–2
market manipulation: action-based manipulation 331; aim of 329; contract-based manipulation 329–30; in emerging markets 331; ethical evaluation of 331–2, 532–3; fairness principle and 332; forms of 329–30, *332*; Hong Kong SFO regulation 529–30; information-based manipulation 330, 331–2; LIBOR manipulation 285, 330; market power techniques 330; negative consequences of 329, 533; runs (pump-and-dump) 329; Sino Katalytics case study 529–33; trade-based manipulation 330, 533; US Securities Exchange Act, 1934 186; utilitarianism and 533; window dressing (marking the close) 331
market portfolios: ascertaining true market portfolio 30, 45–6; beta measurements and 25–6, 44, 46–7, **46**; lending and borrowing and 28, 48; as mean-variance efficient portfolio 48; passive strategies and 29, 47–8; risk diversification in 25; *see also* portfolios
market timing: Canary Capital case 333–4; ethics of 334–5; late trading 333; practice overview 333
markets, defined 134–5
Markowitz, Harry 3, 20, 23, 47–8
Marx, Karl 298
mean-variance theory 54, 62, 63
Mercurio, C. 155
merger and acquisitions (M&A): of exchanges 140–2, **142**; investment bank advisers 191
Meulbroek, L. 326
Mexico 138, **139–40**
Mill, John Stuart 272–3
modern finance theory: assumptions of 42; definitional critique of 41–2; insider trading as violation of justice 290; lack of human psychology in 50; neoclassical assumptions 50; profit maximization ethic 50–1, 66, 67–8, 79, 328; rationality in 50, 51; research critiques of 47–8; risk assumptions 49; self-interested economic actors 66; as a social science 41–2; theoretical assumptions 3; *see also* arbitrage pricing theory (APT); capital asset pricing model (CAPM); efficient market hypothesis (EMH)
Mokoaleli-Mokoteli, T. 65
mortgage-backed securities 119, 144–5
most favoured nation (MFN) treatment 401
Multilateral Investment Guarantee Agency (MIGA) 210
mutual funds: fees 339–43; growth in 339; investment returns vs. fees 340–1; overview of 120; percentage that outperform their indices *340*; sales loads (mutual funds) 339, 340

NASDAQ (National Association of Securities Dealers Automated Quotations) 136, 138, 142, **142**

National Association of Securities Dealers (NASD) 136
national banks 201
National Quotation Bureau (NQB) 143
neoclassical economics 50, 110
New York Stock Exchange (NYSE): electronic communication networks (ECNs) 136; market share of 143; merger with Euronext 138, 140; as secondary market 189; subsidiaries 138
1997–99 Asian financial crisis 159
Nozick, Robert 289

Office of the Comptroller of the Currency (OCC or Comptroller): activities regulation (permissible activities) 393–4; functions of/remit of 200–1, 385, 392
offshore bond markets: Eurobonds 161–4; for investors 164–6; need for 160; types of offshore bonds **163**
open market operations (OMOs) 207
OTC (over-the-counter) markets: in Asia 145–6; bid-offer/bid-ask spread 144; clearing and settlement 146, 169–71; compared to dark pools 151–2; contrasted with exchanges 143; defined 135, 350; derivatives market regulation 146; derivatives markets 132, 144–5; history of 143–4; market makers 144; and NASDAQ 136; Pink Sheets 143, 144; spot FX transactions 122
OTC Bulletin Board (OTCBB) 143–4
outbound transactions: capital adequacy 367–8; defined 367; limitations to outbound stock 367; regulations 402–3

payment systems: cash 203–4; cheques 202–3; overview of 201–2; prohibition against, Iran sanctions 453–8; wire transfers 202, 204–6, *205*
portfolio theory 3, 20
portfolios: asset weighting 20, *20*; benchmarks (market indexes) 199; capital allocation lines 14–15, *15*; capital market lines (CML) 15–16, *16*; construction of, behavioural finance 63; correlation coefficient 17–18, 20; covariance formula 18, **19**, 20; diversification and foreign bonds 166; efficient frontiers 20, *21*; investment managers and 197; management of 198, 199; multiple asset portfolio 19, **19**; risk diversification 20, 197; standard deviation, two-asset portfolios 17–18, 20; two-asset portfolios 17–19, **17**, 20, **20**; *see also* market portfolios
present value of money 4, 6–7
price bubble model 69

price rigging, case study 529–33
primary markets: defined 135; legal framework 186; securities offerings 189
private trading 154
privileged information 35–6
probability distributions 10–11, **11**
proprietary trading (Volcker Rule): exempt activities 370, **371**; limited exceptions 377–8; prohibition on 369–70
prospect theory: assumptions of 54; decision weights 55–7; disposition effect 62–3; equity premiums 63; framing effects 57–8; gains and losses 54–5, 63; Kahneman–Tversky value function 55, *56*; overview of 53; probability weighting function 56–7, *58*, 63
Putnins, T. J. 329

Qatar International Islamic Bank (International Islamic) 97
Qatar International Islamic Bank (QIIB) 108
Qatar Islamic Bank (QIB) 97
qualified foreign banking organization (QFBO) 395
Qualified Institutional Buyers (QIBs) 361
Qur'an 76–7, 78, 80, 81–2, 83, 85

rational expectations theory 67–8
rationality: in behavioural finance 51; in expected utility theory 53; fairness (ultimatum game) 66–7, 328; profit maximization ethic and 50–1, 66, 67–8, 79, 328
Rawls, John 286–8
real rates of return 9–11
regulations: Bank Holding Company Act,1956 180–1, 392, 394–5; Dodd–Frank Wall Street Reform and Consumer Protection Act 145, 169, 183, 368, 398; Glass–Steagall Act 180–1, 182, 183, *184*, 200, 369; Gramm-Leach-Bliley Act 180–1, 182, 183, *184*, 200, 369, 395; inbound transactions to the US 393–401; insider trading regulations 35–6, 186, 323, 329; international regulation of securities 350–5; outbound transactions from the US 402–3; US Investment Company Act Rule 121, 333; US Securities Act of 1933 (Securities Act) 186, 187, 355; US Securities Exchange Act of 1934 (Exchange Act) 35–6, 120, 186, 196, 323, 329, 355; *see also* International Organization of Securities Commissioners (IOSCO); Volcker Rule
regulatory capture 179

Reilly, F. K. 46, 47
relativism 294–6
religion 298; *see also* individual religions
reserve bank *see* central banks
reserve requirements 204, 206–7
returns: alpha (excess return) 27; arbitrage pricing theory (APT) 31; arithmetic average return 8; beta of a security 25–6; dollar-weighted average return 9; efficient frontier 20, *21*, *23*; expected value 10–11, **11**; gains and losses (prospect theory) 54–5, 63; geometric average return 8; inflation 9–10; internal rate of return (IRR) 9; investor utility/indifference curves 21–2, *22–3*; multi-period rate of return 8; multiple asset portfolio 19; nominal interest rates 9–10; probability distributions 10–11, **11**; real rates of return 9–11; risk-free assets 12; risk-return trade-off *13*; standard deviation 11–12; time-weighted average return 8; two-asset portfolio 19; variances 11–12
risk: assumptions in modern finance theory 49; beta of a security 25–6, 44, 399; capital asset pricing model (CAPM) and 25–6, 44–5; and clearing houses 168; credit risk (counter-party/default risk) 399; decision-making under risk 53; defined 7; and distributive justice theories 290; diversifiable 166; diversification, portfolios 20, 197; in efficient market hypothesis 43; equity risk premium 12; forwards FX transactions 123–4; gains and losses (prospect theory) 54–5, 63; *Herstatt* risk 122, 123, 172; investor utility/indifference curves 21–2, *22–3*; in Islamic finance (Gharar) 74, 80, 83–4; legal risk 399; liquidity risk 399; market risk 399; measurement of risk 7–8; of Mudaraba mode of financing 92; Murabaha contract (cost-plus contract) 96; non-diversifiable 166; operational risk 399; rates of return 7–8; reputational risk 399; risk premiums 12, 25–6; risk-free assets 12, 23; risk-free profits 31; risk-mitigating hedging (Volcker Rule) 372; risk-return trade-off 7, *13*; risk-weighted assets 404–5; risky assets 12; short selling and Gharar 84–5; spot FX transactions 122; standard deviation 7, 14, 23; stocks 44; systemic risk (beta) 25, 26, 44, 399; uncertainty 49; unsystematic risk 25, 44; *see also* beta
Ross, Stephen 31
Russia *see* BRICS

sanctions 412; *see also* Iran, sanctions case study
Scott Baggett, L. 47, 48
secondary markets: bond trading 156–7; bonds 117; defined 135, 189; for Islamic financial products 110; legal framework 186; overview of 135; securities offerings 189; for sukuks 107–8; for warrants 116; *see also* bond markets; exchanges; OTC (over-the-counter) markets
Securities Act of 1933 (Securities Act) 186, 187, 355
Securities Exchange Act of 1934 (Exchange Act) 35–6, 120, 186, 196, 323, 329, 355
Securities Exchange Commission (SEC): investment advisor registration with 120–1; Regulation ATS (alternative trading system) 155; Regulation NMS (National Market System) 153–4; regulatory reform of dark pools 156
securities markets 349–50; *see also* US securities markets
securitization: Islamic finance 105–8; mortgage-backed securities 119; under the Volcker Rule 374–5
security analysis: aim of 215; economic analysis 265–8; financial ratios 218–22; financial statements 215–18; industry analysis 263–5; stock analysis 232; top-down and bottom up investment analysis *267*, *268*; valuations 222–31
security market line (SML) 26, 27, *27*, *28*
semi-international transactions 350
shareholders 115
shares: creation units (ETFs) 119–20; market capitalization and 137–8; *see also* stocks
Shari'a: and ethics of Islamic finance 79; ijma (consensus) 77–8; ijtihad (individual reasoning) 78; prohibition of interest (riba) 80, 81–3; qiyas (analogical reasoning) 78; the Qur'an 76–7; the Sunnah 77; *see also* Islam; Islamic finance
Shari'a compliance: Shari'a compliant asset management 343–4; stock indices 85–6
Shari'a Supervisory Boards (SSB): advisory role 88, 110; duties 87; panel expertise 87, 88–90; supervisory role 87
Sharpe, W. J. 23, 45
Sharpe–Lintner–Mossin (SLM) CAPM 23; *see also* capital asset pricing model (CAPM)
Shefrin, H. 289
Shleifer, A. 69
short selling 84–5
Singapore 146

Sino Katalytics: background 529; commutative justice applied to 533; ethical analysis 532–3; false trading regulation, SFO 529; market misconduct 530–2, **530**, **531**; price rigging regulation, SFO 529; stock market manipulation regulation, SFO 529–30; utilitarianism applied to 533
Small Orders Execution System (SOES) 136
Smith, Adam 66, 81, 292
social contract theory 286
Source of Strength Doctrine 386–7, 399
South Africa *see* BRICS
special purpose vehicles (SPV) 145
Standard & Poor (S&P) 26, 46, 331, 358
standard deviation: calculation 11–12; and the capital allocation line 14–16; defined 7; multiple asset portfolio 19, **19**; of risk-free assets 7, 14, 23; two-asset portfolios 17–19, **17**, 20, **20**
Standards of Practice Handbook (CFA Institute) 67, 68
state-chartered banks 201
statistics: anchoring and adjustment heuristic and 61–2; probability and availability heuristic 60–1; representativeness heuristic and 59–60
Statman, M. 47, 289
stock analysis 231–2; *see also* Tencent Holdings, stock analysis
stock price drift 43
stock valuation *see* security analysis
stocks: capital gains taxes 197; clearing and settlement 168–9; contrasted with bonds 117; defined 349; equity risk premium 12; fundamental analysis 34–5; head and shoulder formation 34, *35*; initial public offering (IPO) 135; risk 44; stock selection, winners and losers 64–5; technical analysis 34; value of 35; *see also* shares
systemic risk (beta) 25, 26, 44, 399
systemically important financial institutions' (SIFIs) 182

Taffler, R. 65
Tejoori Musharaka Deal 94
Tencent Holdings, stock analysis: balance sheets 241–51; cash flow statements 252–9; company background 233; economic analysis 266–8; income statements 233–40; industry analysis 263–5; P/E ratios 260–2, **260**, **261**; peer group valuation comparison 265, **265**; sum of parts valuation 262–3, **263**
Thaler, R. H. 63, 64

Thel, S. 329
Thompson, J. R. 47, 48, 49
time value of money: calculation 3–4; compound interest 4–6; discounting calculations 6–7; interest and 80–1
transparency principle 335
Trillium Capital 330
trust 67–9, 328
trust experiments 68
Tversky, Amos 51, 52, 53–61, 63
2007–08 financial crisis: bank holding companies during 182; ethics, discussions on 67; impact on hedge funds 336; legislation, post 146; OTC derivatives markets and 144–5, 169; role of central banks 200

ultimatum game 66–7, 328
uncertainty 49
underwriting: investment banks 187; overview of 156–7; Volcker Rule 370–1
unit investment trusts (UITs) 119
United Kingdom 108
United States of America (USA): bond market 157; Commodity Futures Trading Commission (CFTC) 169–71; Consumer Price Index (CPI) 9; Depository Trust and Clearing Corporation (DTCC) 168–9; Dodd–Frank Wall Street Reform and Consumer Protection Act 145, 169, 183, 368, 398; Glass–Steagall Act 180–1, 182, 183, *184*, 200, 369; Gramm-Leach-Bliley Act 180–1, 182, 183, *184*, 200, 369, 395; insider trading and fiduciary duty 325; payment systems 202; private placements 190; time-weighted average return, mutual funds 8; Treasury bonds 117; use of cheques 203; Wall Street cash 180, *184*; *see also* Federal Reserve Board; Federal Reserve System (Fed); inbound transactions to the US; Iran, sanctions case study; Securities Exchange Commission (SEC); Volcker Rule
unsystematic risk 25, 44
US Investment Company Act 121, 333
US securities markets: disclosure requirements 365; exempt offerings 359–65; exempt securities 359; From F-2 357–8; From F-3 358–9; foreign private issuers 359; Form 8-K 365; Form 10-K 365; Form 10-Q 365–6; Form F-1 356–7; investment grade ratings 358; private placement exemption (Section 4(2) Exemption) 360; Qualified Institutional Buyers (QIBs) 361; registration process

355–6; registration statements 356–9; Regulation D 361–2, **363**; Regulation S 362–5; Rule 144A 360–1; types of issuing companies *366*
US Treasury 186
US Treasury Bills 12, 158
US Treasury Bonds 157, 158
US Treasury securities 350
utilitarianism: act utilitarianism 273; case study, bank bailouts 275, *276*; CITIC Pacific case study 521–2; consequentialism and 271, 419, 521–2, 527; criticisms of 275–8; framework analysis 274–5, *276*; happiness/pleasure measures 272–3; Huiyuan Juice Group case study 527; insider trading, applied to 327–8; market manipulation and 533; principles of 271–2; rights' approaches and 288–9; rule utilitarianism 273–4; Sino Katalytics case study 533

valuations: discounted cash flow (DCF) methods 223–7; dividend discount model (DDM) 224–6; enterprise value to EBITDA 231; overview of 222–3; present value of free cash flows (PVFCF) 226–7; present value of operating cash flows (PVOFCF) 226; price to book value (P/BV) ratio 230–1; price to cash flow (PCF) ratio 229–30; price to earnings growth ratio (PEG) 229; price/earnings ratio (P/E) 227–9; relative valuation methods 227–31; sum of parts valuation, Tencent Holdings 262–3, **263**
variances 11–12
Vietnam 158–9
virtue ethics: CITIC Pacific case study 521; criticisms of 294; financial markets and 294–5; flourishing/happiness (eudaimonia) 293; overview of 290–2; virtues 291, 292–3
volatility measurements 43
Volcker Rule: background 368–9; banking entities, definition 369, 375; commercial banks 182–3, *184*; covered fund permitted activities 375; covered funds activities 373–5; documentation and compliance standards 375–6; entities considered as covered funds 373–4; exempt activities, proprietary trading 370, **371**; extraterritorial reach 376–8; foreign banks solely outside the US 377–8; foreign banks with US operations 376–7; funds exempt from covered fund definition 374–5; invalid permitted activities 373; loan securitization under 374–5; market making 371–2; permitted activities 370–3; proprietary trading and 369–70, **371**, 377–8; risk-mitigating hedging 372; underwriting 370–1

Wahal, S. 65
Wall Street crash 180, *184*
Water Oasis Group Limited: background 535; ethical analysis 536–7; H2O plus termination 535–7
Weber, Max 298
Williams, E. E. 47, 48, 49
wire transfers 202, 204–6, *205*
Wojciechowski, W. C, 47, 48
World Bank (WB) 137, 210–11
World Trade Organization (WTO): GATS accord 386, 400–1; most favoured nation (MFN) treatment 401
Wright, D. J. 47
Wu, G. 331–2

zakat (charity) principle 76